P9-DNU-428

THE COMPLETE DOG BREED BOOK

THE COMPLETE DOG BREED BOOK

Consultant Editor
DR. KIM DENNIS-BRYAN

Commissioned photography by
TRACY MORGAN

LONDON, NEW YORK, MELBOURNE,
MUNICH, AND DELHI

DORLING KINDERSLEY

Senior Editor Kathryn Hennessy
Design Manager Amanda Lunn
Editors Cressida Tuson, Nicola Hodgson, Jemima Dunne
US Editor Rebecca Warren
Designer Steve Woosnam Savage
Design Assistant Kirsty Tizzard
Art Worker Philip Fitzgerald
Picture Researcher Kate Lockley
DK Picture Library Claire Bowers, Emma Shepherd
Database Peter Cook, David Roberts
Deputy Production Editorial Manager Luca Frassinetti
Senior Production Controller Angela Graef
Managing Editor Esther Ripley
Managing Art Editor Karen Self
Publisher Laura Buller
Art Director Phil Ormerod
Associate Publishing Director Liz Wheeler
Publishing Director Jonathan Metcalf

Consultant Editor Kim Dennis-Bryan
Contributors Ann Baggaley, Adam Beral,
Candida Frith-Macdonald, James Harrison

DK INDIA

Deputy Managing Editor Pakshalika Jayaprakash
Senior Editor Garima Sharma
Editor Antara Moitra
Assistant Editor Archana Ramachandran
Managing Art Editor Arunesh Talapatra
Deputy Managing Art Editor Priyabrata Roy Chowdhury
Senior Art Editor Chhaya Sajwan
Project Art Editor Anjana Nair
Art Editors Shruti Soharia Singh, Priyanka Singh
Assistant Art Editors Nidhi Mehra, Vidit Vashisht,
Payal Rosalind Malik, Aastha Tiwari, Mansi Nagdev
DTP Manager Balwant Singh
Senior DTP Designer Dheeraj Arora, Jagtar Singh
DTP Designer Bimlesh Tiwari, Nand Kishor Acharya, Mohammad
Usman, Arjinder Singh, Tanveer Abbas
Production Manager Pankaj Sharma

First published in the United States as *Top Dog* in 2012
This paperback edition first published in 2014
by DK Publishing, 345 Hudson Street,
New York, New York 10014
14 15 16 17 18 19 10 9 8 7 6 5 4 3 2 1
001–276460–12/14

Published in Great Britain by Dorling Kindersley Limited.
A catalog record for this book is available from the Library of Congress.

ISBN: 978-1-4654-2976-6

Printed and bound in China by Leo Paper Products Ltd

Discover more at
www.dk.com

CONTENTS

2 GUIDE TO BREEDS

3 CARE AND TRAINING

INTRODUCTION TO DOGS

WHAT IS A DOG?

The evolution of the dog from wild predator to domestic companion has been greatly influenced by human intervention. It has taken just a few hundred years to produce seemingly endless variations on the canine theme—but planned breeding has not removed the basic characteristics of the dog's ancestor, the wolf.

Dogs are social animals

Evolution of the dog

All dogs share a common ancestor: the gray wolf. While this relationship is fairly apparent in breeds such as the German Shepherd or Spitz-type dogs, with their wolflike heads and pricked ears, it is hard to see the connection between wolves and toy Poodles or Saint Bernards. Genetically, however, any dog of any breed is virtually identical to the wolf. The transition from wolf to the huge diversity of domestic dogs known today happened relatively quickly. The process began gradually, with random changes in size and shape, but accelerated when humans began to selectively breed those dogs that exhibited characteristics they desired.

In from the wild

Dogs were the first animals to be domesticated, but exactly when and where wolves came in from the wild to take their place at human hearths is still under debate. Archaeological investigations have helped to narrow down the possibilities. The earliest findings of human skeletons buried with their dogs are in the Middle East, suggesting that this is the most likely region for the beginnings of the dog's development from wild wolf to domestic animal, which is thought to have taken place around 15,000 years ago.

It is probable that wolves crept up to tribal camps, attracted by food and waste scattered around the perimeters. At first these opportunist wolves may have been killed for their skins and meat. Over time humans started to tame and hand-rear orphaned wolf cubs, which as social animals took readily to adoption by the human "pack." Once their potential was recognized—as hunters and natural guardians that raised the alarm when intruders approached—the wolves were put to work by the tribe, and the domestication of the dog was under way. It is surmised that in an early form of deliberate selection, human-reared

RELATIONSHIPS OF THE DOG FAMILY

This diagram shows the relationship between the dog and some of the other canids (members of the dog family), based on genetic evidence. The dog and the gray wolf are more closely related to one another than to any other canids.

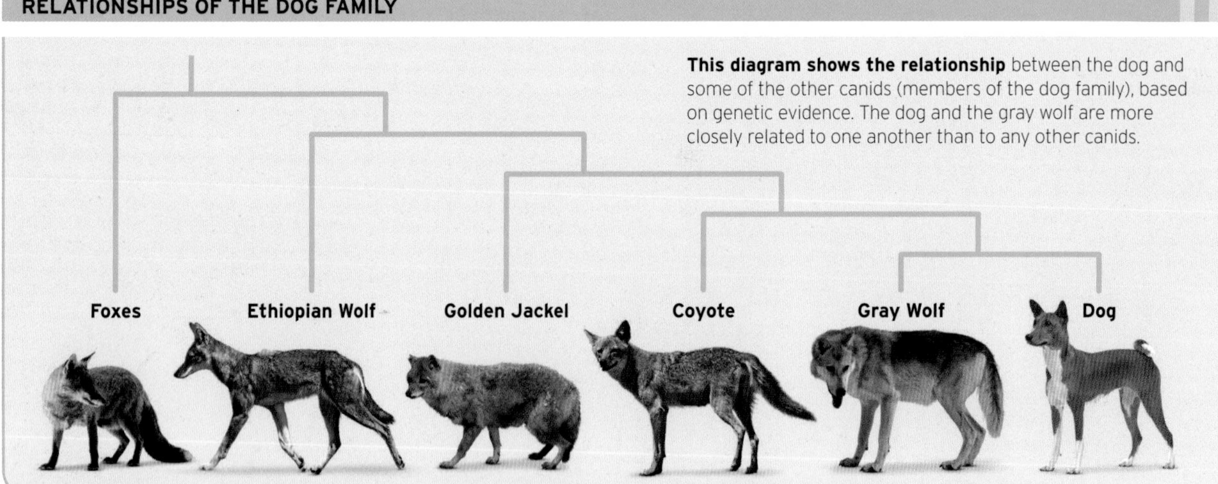
Foxes
Ethiopian Wolf
Golden Jackel
Coyote
Gray Wolf
Dog

THE SHAPE OF A PREDATOR
The canid family are shaped to be efficient hunters. This Weimaraner remains true to his ancestral body plan and can move with speed and grace.

wolves with particular promise—perhaps being stronger or easier to tame than others, or possessing an exceptional nose for game—were used for breeding. Many hundreds of years passed before deliberate breeding became more sophisticated, selecting for refinements of coat types and colors, temperament, and specialized skills, and eventually creating hundreds of different types of dog in a multitude of shapes and sizes. The selection processes used by breeders to introduce desirable traits have altered over the years, and while certain characteristics fall out of favor others become embedded in the breed standard. Many new breeds have been introduced in the last 150 years.

Dog DNA

In the past the history of a dog breed was pieced together from written records, pictures, and information handed down from past breeders and owners. Today the analysis of DNA (the hereditary template found in body cells) has made it possible to track the inheritance of features such as size and coat color, and to look at the differences and similarities between one breed and another. Most importantly, looking at DNA has made it possible to identify which breeds are at risk of specific genetic diseases and conditions (see pp.338–39). Scientists sequenced the first complete dog genome (the complete set of genetic information possessed by an organism) in 2005 using the DNA of a Boxer.

Even with the use of genetic analysis, unraveling the history of a particular breed is not easy. Some breeds are commonly said to be very ancient, but genetic evidence suggests that the majority are, in fact, modern recreations. With few exceptions, most breeds known today were developed no earlier than the 19th century.

Dog anatomy

The physical characteristics of a dog are typical of a predator whose survival relies on efficiency in locating and catching prey. Humans have done much to adapt canine design, but the basic anatomy of all breeds of dog is the same.

The skeleton of the dog evolved to provide speed, strength, and maneuverability. A highly flexible spine and freely moving forelimbs allow a dog to move with a long, swinging stride. The most important characteristics of a dog's skeleton are seen in the legs. The two large forearm bones, the radius and the ulna, are locked together in such a way that a dog can make rapid changes of direction without the bones rotating and breaking. In a further adaptation, two of the wrist bones are fused together—unlike the separate bones seen in humans—to give a dog strength and stability when moving in a straight line. Combined with long, powerful toes, with claws like spikes on running shoes, this limb arrangement gives a dog a high degree of control whether it is running, jumping, or turning.

Classified as carnivores, dogs are anatomically adapted to eat primarily meat, although, given the opportunity, domestic dogs will eat almost anything. A dog's teeth are designed to deal with tough foods such as hide, flesh, and

PACK MENTALITY
Doing things cooperatively is an inbuilt canine characteristic. Most domestic dogs look to humans as their pack leaders.

bone. Four large canine teeth at the front of a dog's mouth are used for grabbing and biting prey, while the sides of the jaw include specially modified teeth, the carnassials, which the dog uses for shearing off meat. Dogs have a capacious stomach for the storage of large quantities of food and, since meat can be digested rapidly, a short intestinal tract.

Dogs have a wide-angled field of vision that functions best at long distance and they are extremely sensitive to movement. Out of the corner of an eye, a dog can pick up the flicker of a rabbit a hundred feet away, but at close range, canine vision is less efficient, which is why a dog may fail to spot a toy on the ground in front of his nose. Dogs have little use for sophisticated color vision and their eyes have far fewer color-receptive cells than those of humans.

Sharp hearing and the ability to pinpoint the direction of sounds is essential to wild hunting dogs. Breeds with erect ears shaped like those of the wolf are likely to have more acute hearing than breeds with drop ears, which rely more on sight or scent when hunting. A dog's highly sensitive ears allow it to pick up sounds at a far higher frequency than can be heard by humans. Smell is the most important of all canine senses. Sniffing is the way a dog reads its surroundings and the area of the brain that interprets smells is around 40 times larger than the corresponding area in a human brain. Dogs' noses are packed with far more scent receptive cells than humans: while a person has an estimated 5 million scent receptors, a small dog may have closer to 130 million. In breeds renowned for their scenting ability, such as hounds, the number of scent receptors may be as many as 200–300 million.

TALL AND SHORT
The extreme diversity of dog breeds is illustrated by the differences in leg length between an Irish Wolfhound and a Wire-haired Dachshund.

Unlike humans, dogs do not have sweat glands in their skin, except on the bottoms of their paws. To cool down dogs must pant, tongue hanging out. The tongue produces copious saliva, some of which evaporates and so helps to reduce body temperature.

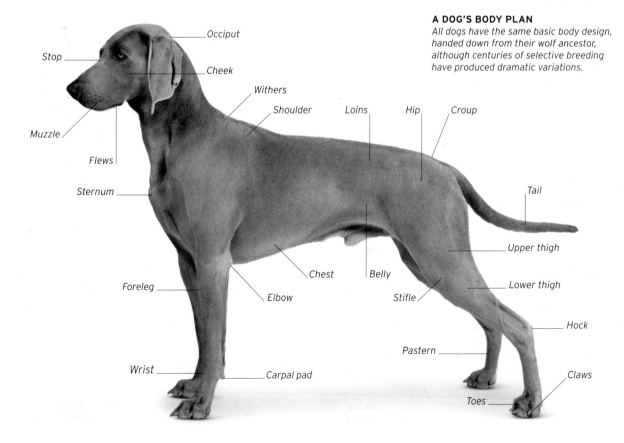

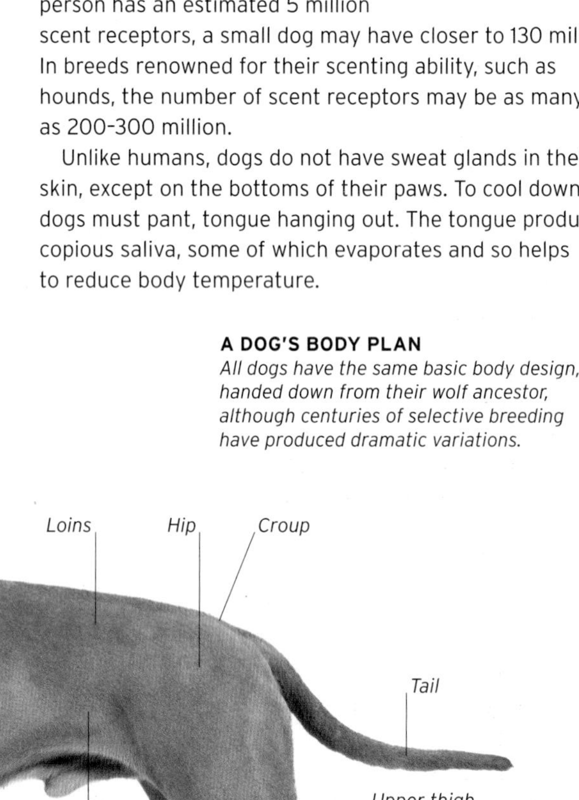
Occiput
Stop
Cheek
Withers
Shoulder
Loins
Hip
Croup
Muzzle
Flews
Sternum
Tail
Upper thigh
Chest
Belly
Foreleg
Lower thigh
Elbow
Stifle
Hock
Pastern
Wrist
Carpal pad
Claws
Toes

A DOG'S BODY PLAN
All dogs have the same basic body design, handed down from their wolf ancestor, although centuries of selective breeding have produced dramatic variations.

Head shapes

Canine heads are all variations on three basic shapes. The majority of dogs have a mesaticephalic head, in which length and width are of medium proportions. A dolichocephalic head is long and narrow, with a barely noticeable stop. Brachycephalic heads are broad based and short in length.

Dolichocephalic head (Saluki)

Mesaticephalic head (German Pointer)

Brachycephalic head (Bulldog)

Ear types

Pricked, sensitive wolflike ears—the original canine shape—occur in many breeds of dog, but centuries of planned selection have created a large variety of other ear shapes. There are three main types: erect, semierect, and drop. Within these categories are many variations, such as the type of erect ear known as candle flame. Ear types are often the defining characteristic of a dog group; for example, scent hounds usually have long, pendant ears. Ears strongly influence a dog's overall appearance. The correct set, shape, and carriage of the ears are considered very important in recognized breeds, and are described precisely in official breed standards.

Erect (Alaskan Malamute)

Candle flame (Russian Toy)

Button (Pug)

Drop (Broholmer)

Rose (Greyhound)

Pendant (Bloodhound)

Coat varieties

The majority of dog breeds have a double coat like their wolf ancestor. This usually consists of an insulating layer of soft, dense hair covered by a harsher outer coat of varying length and texture. A few thinner-coated breeds, such as greyhounds, have just a single layer of hair (no undercoat). In some breeds, chance genetic mutation has produced dogs that are either completely hairless or have just a few strands of hair on the head and legs.

Hairless (Chinese Crested)

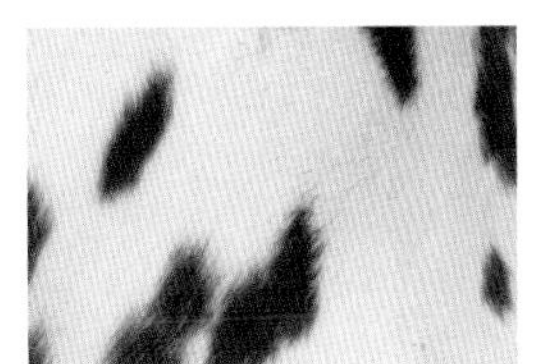

Short (Dalmatian)

Curly (Poodle)

Corded (Komondor)

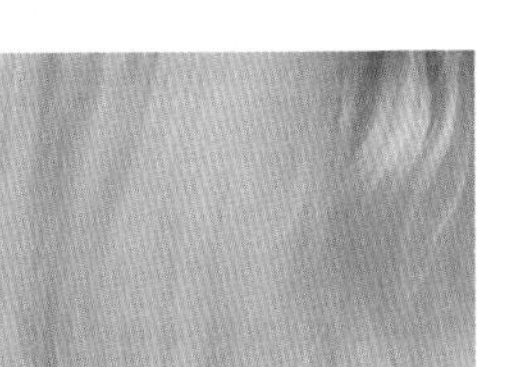

Long, straight (Maltese)

Long, fluffy (Pekingese)

Breeds and breed groups

Although many distinct varieties of dog were recognized earlier, until the early 20th century their breeding was not necessarily strictly controlled. When dog breeders started to cooperate with one another and form clubs they were able to produce dogs of consistent type. This led to the writing of breed standards that describe the ideal appearance (with permissible variations) and temperament of a breed, and its suitability for function. Dogs were also registered in stud books to enable their pedigrees to be reviewed for future breeding.

Despite the detailed dog breed standards that exist, there are as yet no universally recognized criteria for classifying dog breeds in groups. The main regulatory bodies are the Kennel Club (KC) in the UK; the Fédération Cynologique Internationale (FCI)—the World Canine Organization, which includes 86 member countries; and the American Kennel Club (AKC). These all group breeds together based loosely on function, but no two systems are exactly the same. Both the UK and American Kennel Clubs recognize seven groups, while the FCI has ten. The number of individual breeds recognized by these organizations also varies.

This book places breeds together in eight major groups: primitive dogs; working dogs; spitz-type dogs; sight hounds; scent hounds; terriers; gundogs; and companion dogs; plus a section on crossbreeds and random bred dogs. The groupings of the so-called primitive dogs, sight hounds, and the spitz-type dogs in this book have been made on the basis of well-established genetic relationships. In some cases, this results in a breed appearing in a different group from the one that might be expected. The Basenji, for example, is often grouped functionally with hounds but genetic evidence places it among the primitive breeds, which is where this book, and the FCI, place it. For the remainder of the groups, more traditional, functional groupings are used.

HOW DOGS ARE GROUPED IN THIS BOOK

The dog groupings used in this book are illustrated below with an example of a dog that appears in each category.

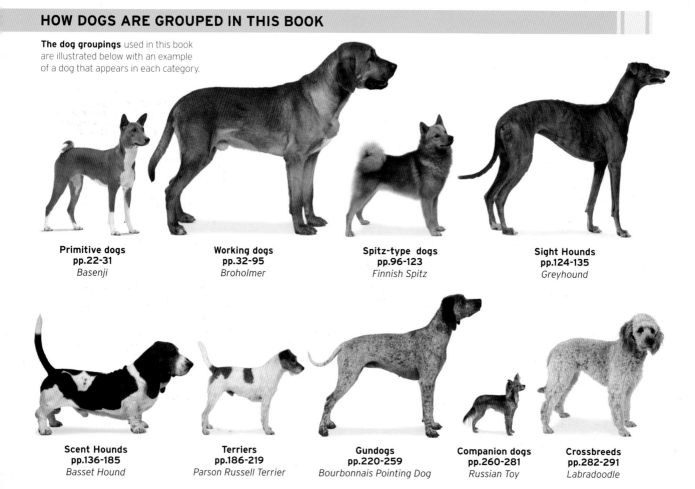

Primitive dogs
pp.22-31
Basenji

Working dogs
pp.32-95
Broholmer

Spitz-type dogs
pp.96-123
Finnish Spitz

Sight Hounds
pp.124-135
Greyhound

Scent Hounds
pp.136-185
Basset Hound

Terriers
pp.186-219
Parson Russell Terrier

Gundogs
pp.220-259
Bourbonnais Pointing Dog

Companion dogs
pp.260-281
Russian Toy

Crossbreeds
pp.282-291
Labradoodle

HOW TO USE THE BREED CATALOG

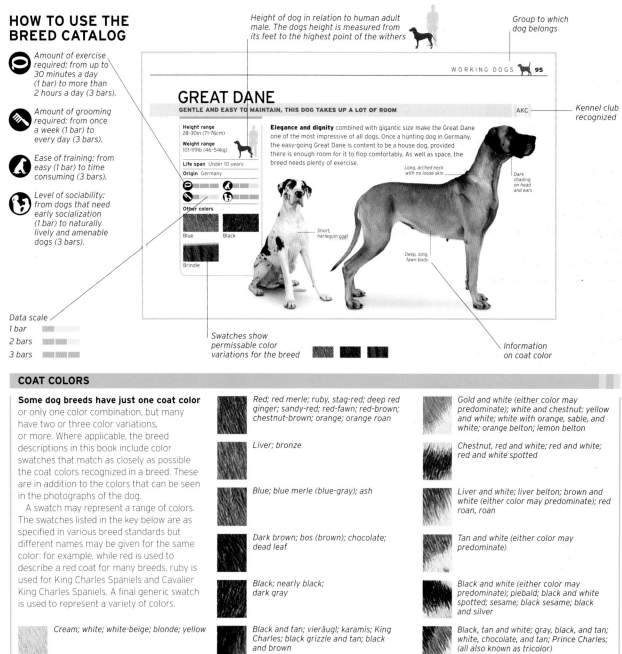

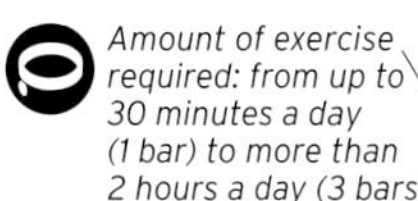

Amount of exercise required: from up to 30 minutes a day (1 bar) to more than 2 hours a day (3 bars).

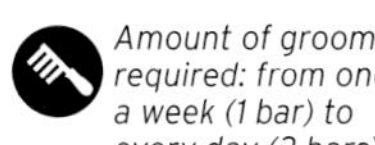

Amount of grooming required: from once a week (1 bar) to every day (3 bars).

Ease of training: from easy (1 bar) to time consuming (3 bars).

Level of sociability: from dogs that need early socialization (1 bar) to naturally lively and amenable dogs (3 bars).

Height of dog in relation to human adult male. The dogs height is measured from its feet to the highest point of the withers

Group to which dog belongs

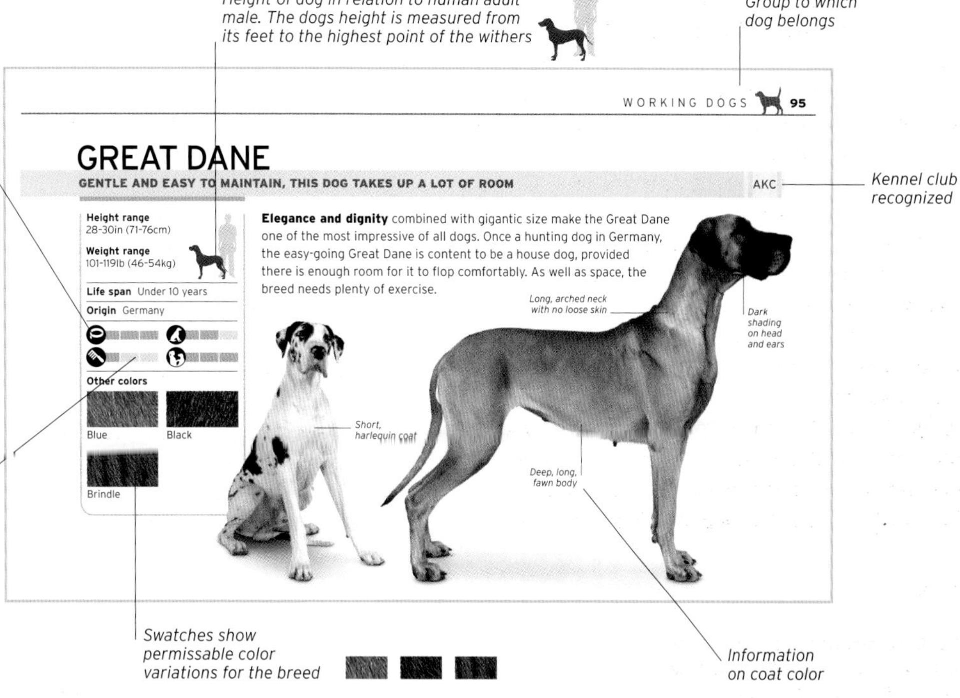
WORKING DOGS 95
GREAT DANE
GENTLE AND EASY TO MAINTAIN, THIS DOG TAKES UP A LOT OF ROOM
AKC
Height range 28-30in (71-76cm)
Weight range 101-119lb (46-54kg)
Life span Under 10 years
Origin Germany
Other colors
Blue
Black
Brindle
Elegance and dignity combined with gigantic size make the Great Dane one of the most impressive of all dogs. Once a hunting dog in Germany, the easy-going Great Dane is content to be a house dog, provided there is enough room for it to flop comfortably. As well as space, the breed needs plenty of exercise.
Long, arched neck with no loose skin
Dark shading on head and ears
Short, harlequin coat
Deep, long, fawn body

Kennel club recognized

Data scale
1 bar
2 bars
3 bars

Swatches show permissable color variations for the breed

Information on coat color

COAT COLORS

Some dog breeds have just one coat color or only one color combination, but many have two or three color variations, or more. Where applicable, the breed descriptions in this book include color swatches that match as closely as possible the coat colors recognized in a breed. These are in addition to the colors that can be seen in the photographs of the dog.

A swatch may represent a range of colors. The swatches listed in the key below are as specified in various breed standards but different names may be given for the same color: for example, while red is used to describe a red coat for many breeds, ruby is used for King Charles Spaniels and Cavalier King Charles Spaniels. A final generic swatch is used to represent a variety of colors.

Cream; white; white-beige; blonde; yellow

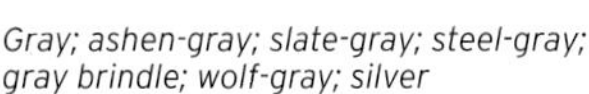

Gray; ashen-gray; slate-gray; steel-gray; gray brindle; wolf-gray; silver

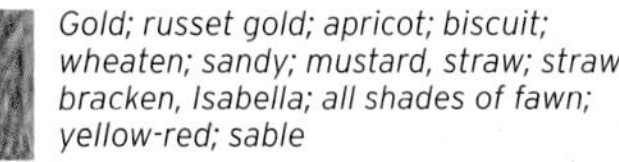

Gold; russet gold; apricot; biscuit; wheaten; sandy; mustard, straw; straw bracken, Isabella; all shades of fawn; yellow-red; sable

Red; red merle; ruby, stag-red; deep red ginger; sandy-red; red-fawn; red-brown; chestnut-brown; orange; orange roan

Liver; bronze

Blue; blue merle (blue-gray); ash

Dark brown; bos (brown); chocolate; dead leaf

Black; nearly black; dark gray

Black and tan; vieräugl; karamis; King Charles; black grizzle and tan; black and brown

Blue, mottled with tan; blue and tan

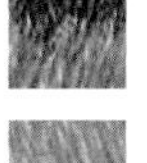

Liver and tan

Gold and white (either color may predominate); white and chestnut; yellow and white; white with orange, sable, and white; orange belton; lemon belton

Chestnut, red and white; red and white; red and white spotted

Liver and white; liver belton; brown and white (either color may predominate); red roan, roan

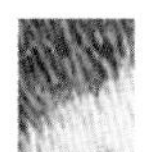

Tan and white (either color may predominate)

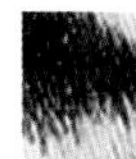

Black and white (either color may predominate); piebald; black and white spotted; sesame; black sesame; black and silver

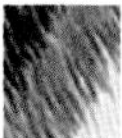

Black, tan and white; gray, black, and tan; white, chocolate, and tan; Prince Charles; (all also known as tricolor)

Brindle; black brindle; dark brindle; fawn brindle; pepper and salt; range of red brindles

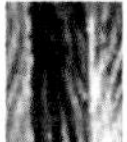

Variety of colors or any color

CHOOSING THE RIGHT DOG

A puppy can grow into a big dog, so know what you are buying

The dog you choose will probably be your companion for the next ten or twelve years, so making the right decision is important. Being faced with more than 400 different breeds with a variety of exercise, training, and grooming needs can be bewildering. This section provides advice and flowcharts to help you narrow down your choice.

The perfect match

You may be attracted to a particular breed because of its looks, or have fallen in love with a beguiling puppy, but before going any further consider carefully whether you and the dog are a good match. To avoid difficulties and disappointments later on, take a look at your lifestyle and ask yourself the following questions.

What type of home do you live in, and are you a town or country dweller? A small apartment is obviously no place for a very large breed if both owner and dog are to cohabit comfortably. Remember, though, that a small dog with exceptionally high energy levels can also seem to take up a lot of room. Whether or not you have a yard, you will need access to open spaces where your dog can safely let off steam and meet other dogs. How house proud are you? Can you tolerate loose hairs, slobber, and muddy pawprints? Keeping the place tidy can be harder with a dog around.

Can you give a dog the exercise he needs to stay physically and mentally fit? Some owners want an undemanding companion who is content with a short daily walk followed by a long snooze. If you enjoy an active lifestyle yourself you may want a lively running mate to help set the pace for jogging or on long hikes. Large dogs do not necessarily need more exercise than small ones. Some of the bigger breeds have a very laid-back attitude to life, while many small dogs, such as terriers, have boundless energy.

How much effort are you willing to put into grooming your dog? Long-coated breeds look beautiful but they are high maintenance and may need daily brushing and detangling. You should also consider the likely cost of professional grooming: some dogs have coats that are easy to care for in day-to-day terms but may need regular trimming.

Is your dog to be part of a family that includes children or other pets? Be wary of picking a breed that is large or exuberant enough to knock over a small child or an older person, or a dog with a natural chasing instinct that might put a beloved cat or guinea pig at risk.

Do you have enough room in your life for a dog? Exercise will take up time every day, but what dogs need as much as walks is company; any dog left alone for too long is likely to become bored, morose, and destructive. If you work away from the house all week, then unless you can make adequate care arrangements, a dog may not be a suitable pet for you.

Owning a dog is a long-term commitment in financial and practical terms. Make it a joy by choosing the breed that is as near as possible the perfect one for you.

HOW TO USE THE FLOWCHARTS

The following flowcharts will help you to choose a dog. They are based on three criteria: exercise, grooming, and training. Decide if you want a dog with high, medium, or low exercise requirements, and follow the paths to find suggestions for suitable breeds. Also look at the breed catalog data to find further dogs not listed here.

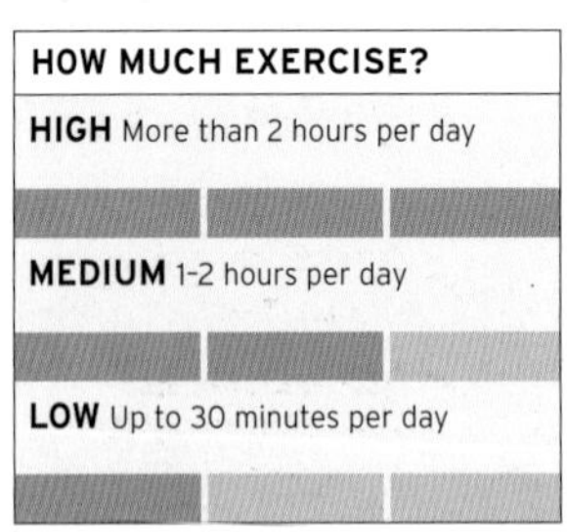
HOW MUCH EXERCISE?
HIGH More than 2 hours per day
MEDIUM 1-2 hours per day
LOW Up to 30 minutes per day

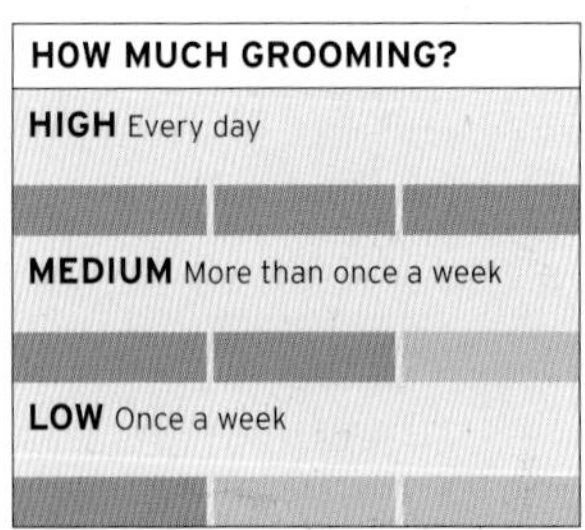
HOW MUCH GROOMING?
HIGH Every day
MEDIUM More than once a week
LOW Once a week

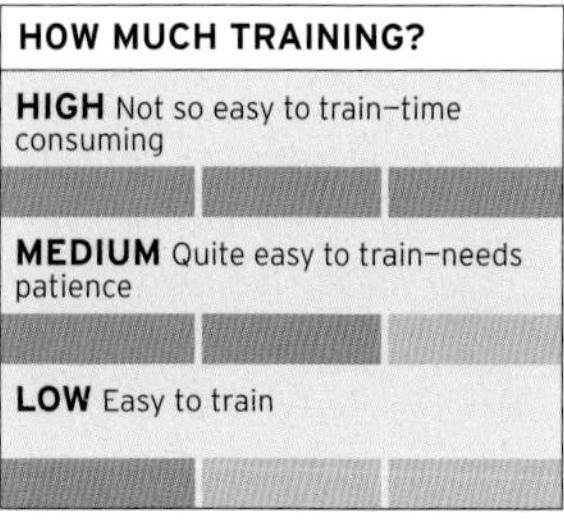
HOW MUCH TRAINING?
HIGH Not so easy to train–time consuming
MEDIUM Quite easy to train–needs patience
LOW Easy to train

HIGH EXERCISE DOGS

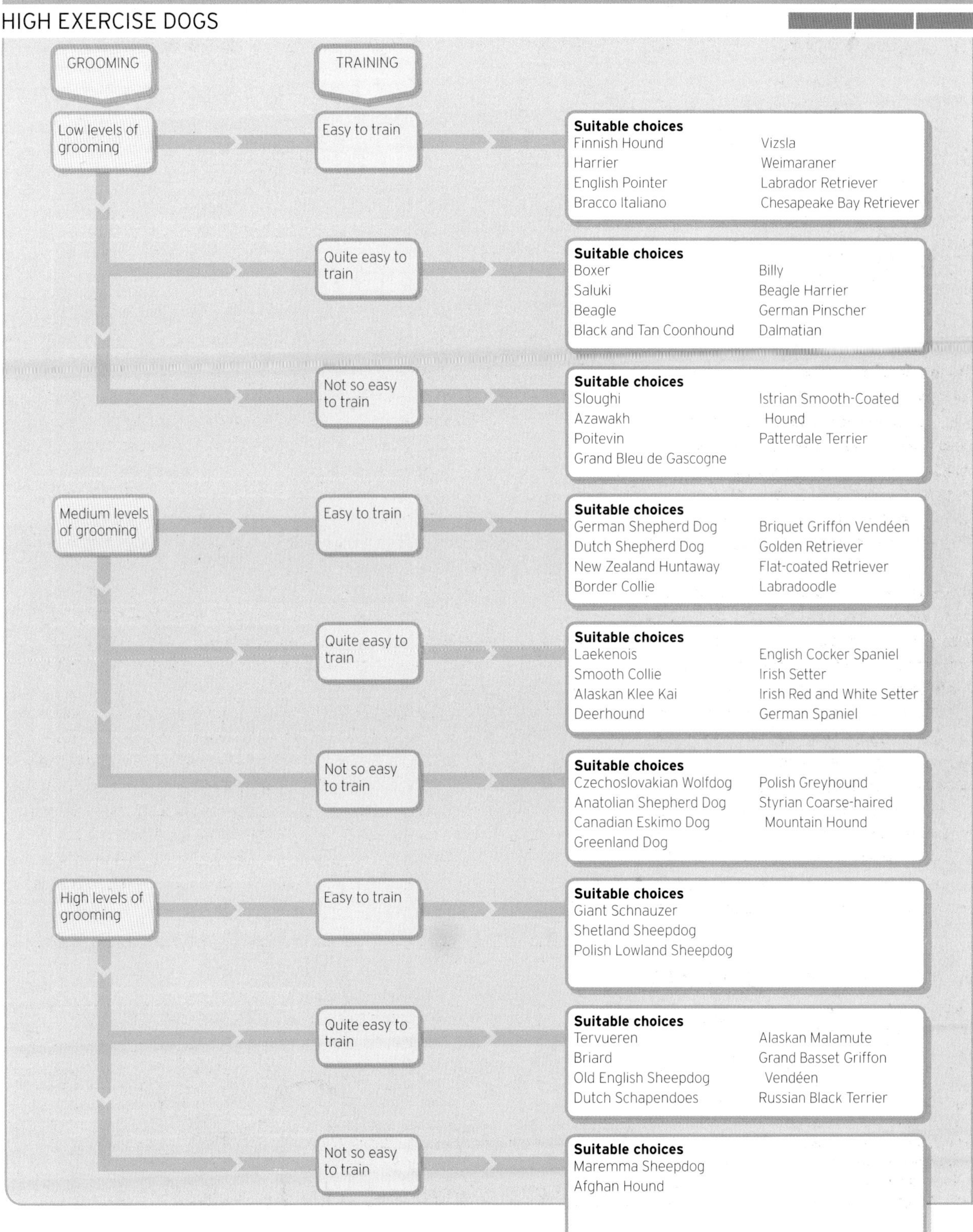
GROOMING
TRAINING
Low levels of grooming
Easy to train
Suitable choices
Finnish Hound
Harrier
English Pointer
Bracco Italiano
Vizsla
Weimaraner
Labrador Retriever
Chesapeake Bay Retriever
Quite easy to train
Suitable choices
Boxer
Saluki
Beagle
Black and Tan Coonhound
Billy
Beagle Harrier
German Pinscher
Dalmatian
Not so easy to train
Suitable choices
Sloughi
Azawakh
Poitevin
Grand Bleu de Gascogne
Istrian Smooth-Coated Hound
Patterdale Terrier
Medium levels of grooming
Easy to train
Suitable choices
German Shepherd Dog
Dutch Shepherd Dog
New Zealand Huntaway
Border Collie
Briquet Griffon Vendéen
Golden Retriever
Flat-coated Retriever
Labradoodle
Quite easy to train
Suitable choices
Laekenois
Smooth Collie
Alaskan Klee Kai
Deerhound
English Cocker Spaniel
Irish Setter
Irish Red and White Setter
German Spaniel
Not so easy to train
Suitable choices
Czechoslovakian Wolfdog
Anatolian Shepherd Dog
Canadian Eskimo Dog
Greenland Dog
Polish Greyhound
Styrian Coarse-haired Mountain Hound
High levels of grooming
Easy to train
Suitable choices
Giant Schnauzer
Shetland Sheepdog
Polish Lowland Sheepdog
Quite easy to train
Suitable choices
Tervueren
Briard
Old English Sheepdog
Dutch Schapendoes
Alaskan Malamute
Grand Basset Griffon Vendéen
Russian Black Terrier
Not so easy to train
Suitable choices
Maremma Sheepdog
Afghan Hound

MEDIUM EXERCISE DOGS

GROOMING	TRAINING	Suitable choices
Low levels of grooming	Easy to train	Swedish Vallhund, Alapaha Blue Blood Bulldog, Greyhound, Blue Gascony Griffon, Rat Terrier, Drentsche Partridge Dog, Australian Terrier
	Quite easy to train	Basenji, Canaan Dog, Pembroke Welsh Corgi, Bulldog, Nordic Spitz, Whippet, Drever, Bull Terrier
	Not so easy to train	Boerboel, Spanish Mastiff, Neapolitan Mastiff, Tosa, Dogo Canario, Basset Hound, Griffon Nivernais
Medium levels of grooming	Easy to train	Bernese Mountain Dog, Keeshond, West Highland White Terrier, Small Munsterlander, Picardy Spaniel, English Setter, Tibetan Spaniel
	Quite easy to train	Pyrenean Mountain Dog, Finnish Spitz, Italian Greyhound, Dachshund (long-haired), Norfolk Terrier, Airedale Terrier, Cavalier King Charles Spaniel
	Not so easy to train	Aïdi, Kuvasz, Borzoi, Cesky Terrier, Wire Fox Terrier, Lakeland Terrier
High levels of grooming	Easy to train	Rough Collie, Puli, Newfoundland, Miniature Schnauzer, Portuguese Water Dog, Standard Poodle, Shih Tzu
	Quite easy to train	Bouvier des Flandres, Bearded Collie, Saint Bernard, Chow Chow, Eurasier, American Eskimo Dog, Scottish Terrier, Tibetan Terrier
	Not so easy to train	Komondor, Bergamasco, Tibetan Mastiff, Sealyham Terrier

LOW EXERCISE DOGS

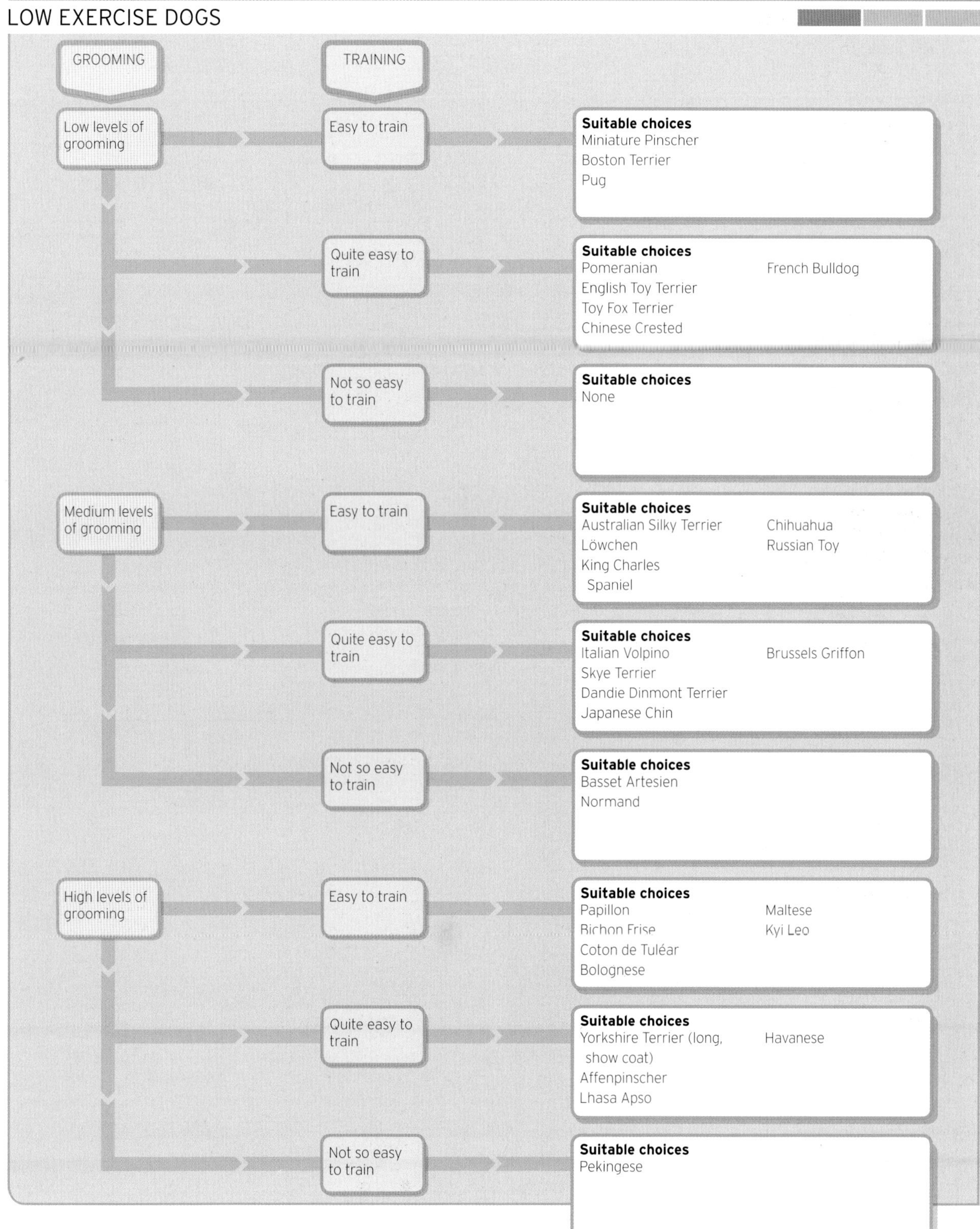
GROOMING
TRAINING
Low levels of grooming
Easy to train
Suitable choices
Miniature Pinscher
Boston Terrier
Pug
Quite easy to train
Suitable choices
Pomeranian
English Toy Terrier
Toy Fox Terrier
Chinese Crested
French Bulldog
Not so easy to train
Suitable choices
None
Medium levels of grooming
Easy to train
Suitable choices
Australian Silky Terrier
Löwchen
King Charles Spaniel
Chihuahua
Russian Toy
Quite easy to train
Suitable choices
Italian Volpino
Skye Terrier
Dandie Dinmont Terrier
Japanese Chin
Brussels Griffon
Not so easy to train
Suitable choices
Basset Artesien Normand
High levels of grooming
Easy to train
Suitable choices
Papillon
Bichon Frise
Coton de Tuléar
Bolognese
Maltese
Kyi Leo
Quite easy to train
Suitable choices
Yorkshire Terrier (long, show coat)
Affenpinscher
Lhasa Apso
Havanese
Not so easy to train
Suitable choices
Pekingese

Finding a breeder

If you decide to buy a pedigree dog, you need to find a reputable breeder. A recommendation from your vet or a friend is ideal, and some kennel clubs provide lists of breeders; otherwise, the best way to choose a breeder is to visit several armed with a list of questions (see box opposite for the most important ones to ask).

Good breeders will be happy to give you plenty of time to observe the litter. It is particularly important to see puppies with their litter mates and their mother. Young puppies should never be kept in isolation, and if this is the case at any kennels you visit, then do not consider buying from them. The sire may not be at the same breeders, but if he is, ask if you can see him too. The appearance, behavior, and temperament of the adult dogs will enable you to make a judgement on the likely future development of your puppy.

Watch how the puppies interact with each other and with people. Some puppies are boisterous and outgoing from the start, showing no reservations about approaching strangers, while others hang back from rough play and are nervous or shy. A confident puppy is usually a good choice, but a quieter dog may appeal to you more. However, check that a seemingly subdued puppy does not have health problems and is failing to thrive.

Expect breeders to ask you some questions too. They will want to know what sort of home and lifestyle you are offering, whether you are an experienced or a first-time owner, and if you are fully aware of the time and cost that keeping a dog entails. Do some homework before you pay your visit, and be honest with your answers.

FAMILY GROUP
Never consider buying a puppy unless you can see the litter with their mother. No reputable breeder will keep young puppies in separate accommodation.

PICK OF THE LITTER
Even very young puppies have distinct personalities. Whether you favor a shy one or the boss of the litter, make sure that he has bright eyes, a clean coat, and appears used to a home environment.

A breeder should be able to supply vet's references and provide other credentials such as membership of a breed association. Also find out if your chosen breeder offers "after-sales" service, such as advice on feeding or health. Once you have come to an agreement, expect to collect your new puppy when he is about eight weeks of age.

Puppy farms

Never buy a dog from one of the many so-called "puppy farms." Such establishments are usually little more than canine battery farms, where dogs are kept in inhumane conditions, bred to exhaustion, and given little or nothing in the way of health care. Avoid buying from pet shops too, as the puppies they sell do not usually have a history and may come from puppy farms. Also beware of advertisements offering a selection of different breeds, because these are often placed by dealers who trade in farmed puppies.

Buying a rescue dog

Unless you are set on buying a young puppy from a recognized breeder, you may find just what you want at a dog rescue center. These centers occasionally have litters of puppies but in most cases their dogs are either fully mature or at least a few months old. Many rescue dogs are of mixed breeding, although some purebreds do turn up. If you prefer a pedigree dog, you could also try one of the numerous rescue organizations that specialize in rehousing particular breeds, such as greyhounds.

Not all rescue dogs come from a background of neglect or cruelty. Some need rehousing because of an owner's death or change in family circumstances. However, many have an unknown or traumatic history, and may display behaviorial problems and anxieties that can be difficult to overcome. Think carefully before being tempted to take on such a dog in the hope of rehabilitating him, because you could end up with more than you bargained for. A good, loving home goes a long way, but traumatized dogs need experienced handling, an above-average amount of patience, and possibly professional retraining. Most rescue centers will offer you back-up advice and support.

When buying a dog from a rescue home, use the same approach as you would if buying from a breeder. Observe the dogs closely and ask, and expect to be asked, questions. Rescue homes screen prospective owners very carefully and will probably want to visit your home.

MAKING A GOOD MATCH

Adopting a rescue dog is a two way process. While you are deciding which dog you want, a good rescue center will assess your suitability as an owner. It will want to know as much as possible about you, your home, and your family.

10 IMPORTANT QUESTIONS TO ASK A BREEDER

- Will the puppy have received his first vaccinations and been wormed before I collect him?
- Are your dogs screened for inherited diseases, and may I take a look at the screening certificates?
- Can you provide a written guarantee of the puppy's health?
- Will you provide a written contract of sale and does it specify what I should do if I can no longer care for my puppy?
- Can you provide references from, for example, a vet or previous customers?
- Have you registered the puppy with a kennel club?
- Can you provide a printed pedigree for the puppy?
- What do you consider the most important characteristics of this breed?
- How long have you been working with this breed?
- Have your puppies been well socialized in your home as well as in the outside environment?

GUIDE TO BREED

AFRICAN HUNTER
Elegant and immaculate, the Basenji makes the most civilized of pets, but this African breed worked as a hunting dog for thousands of years.

PRIMITIVE DOGS

Many modern dog breeds are the result of hundreds of years of breeding for particular characteristics, but a few, commonly regarded as primitive dogs, have remained close to the original "blueprint" of their wolf ancestors. As a group, primitive dogs are not clearly defined, and not all authorities agree that such a category should be recognized.

Hairless dogs are depicted in ancient Pre-Incan artifacts

As variously listed, primitive dogs are a diverse group but many of them share typically wolflife characteristics. These include erect ears, a wedge-shaped head with a pointed muzzle, and a tendency to howl rather than bark. Their coats are usually short but vary in color and density according to the region from which the dog originates. Most primitive dogs come into season only once a year, unlike other domestic dogs, which have two cycles of estrus a year.

Canine specialists are now taking an interest in dogs that have had little to do with humans and nothing to do with breed development programs. These primitive dogs, which come from various parts of the world, include the Carolina Dog of North America and the rare New Guinea Singing Dog, which is genetically very close to the dingo of Australia. Such dogs have evolved naturally rather than through breeding for temperament or appearance and cannot be considered completely domesticated. The New Guinea Singing Dog, which is on the verge of extinction, is more likely to be seen in zoos than in homes.

Several dogs are included in the primitive group because they are believed to to be uninfluenced by any other types over thousands of years. Among them is the Basenji from Africa, long used for hunting in its native country before becoming a popular pet. Other examples are hairless dogs from Mexico and South America, genetic mutations of coated breeds, which resemble dogs depicted in the art and artifacts of ancient civilizations.

Recent genetic investigations suggest that two dogs included in this section—the Pharaoh Hound and the Ibizan Hound—should no longer be considered primitive. These breeds are popularly supposed to be the direct descendants of big-eared Egyptian hounds pictured in drawings dating back 5,000 years. However, there is genetic evidence that the line of descent may not have remained unbroken down the centuries. It is probable that the Pharaoh and Ibizan Hounds are in fact modern recreations of an ancient breeds.

STILL WILD
The dingo-like New Guinea Singing Dog does not adapt well to domestic life. It may have inhabited New Guinea from prehistoric times.

MAGICAL DOG
The Aztecs believed that hairless dogs were sent by the gods and had magical properties.

NEW GUINEA SINGING DOG

IN TOUCH WITH ITS WILD SIDE, THIS DOG HAS A UNIQUE VOCAL RANGE

Height range
16–18in (40–45cm)

Weight range
18–31lb (8–14kg)

Life span 15–20 years

Origin New Guinea

Other colors

Sable

Black and tan

White markings are common with all color types.

This rare dingo-like breed is a native of New Guinea, where it lives feral or in semidomestication. The Singing Dog is kept as a curiosity in zoos worldwide but has become a challenging pet for a few dedicated owners. It has the extraordinary ability to vary the notes of its howl, hence the name.

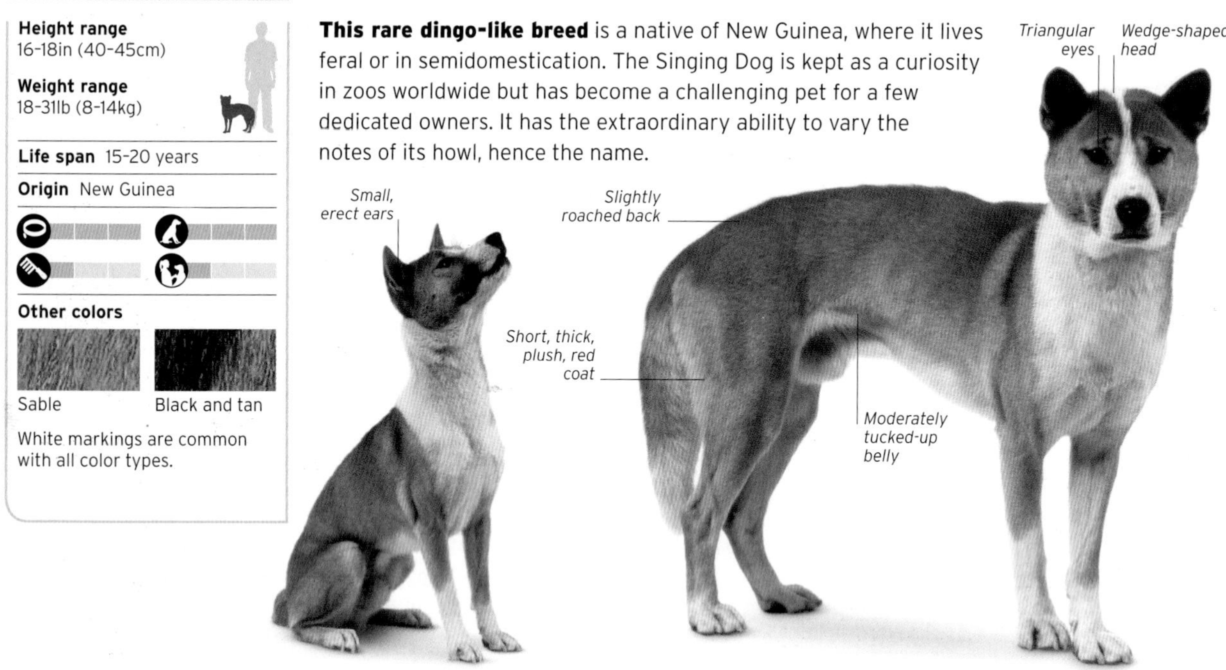
Triangular eyes
Wedge-shaped head
Small, erect ears
Slightly roached back
Short, thick, plush, red coat
Moderately tucked-up belly

BASENJI

THIS NEAT AND GRACEFUL DOG IS SOMETIMES SHY WITH STRANGERS, BUT DOES NOT BARK AKC

Height range
16–17in (40–43cm)

Weight range
22–24lb (10–11kg)

Life span Over 10 years

Origin Central Africa

Other colors

Variety of colors

White markings may appear on chest, feet, and tail tip.

A hunting dog from Africa, the Basenji was used for driving big game, locating its prey by both sight and scent. Sleek and beautifully built with an immaculate appearance, the Basenji is affectionate and fun-loving, and is a popular house dog. Unable to bark, it can, however, make yodelling noises.

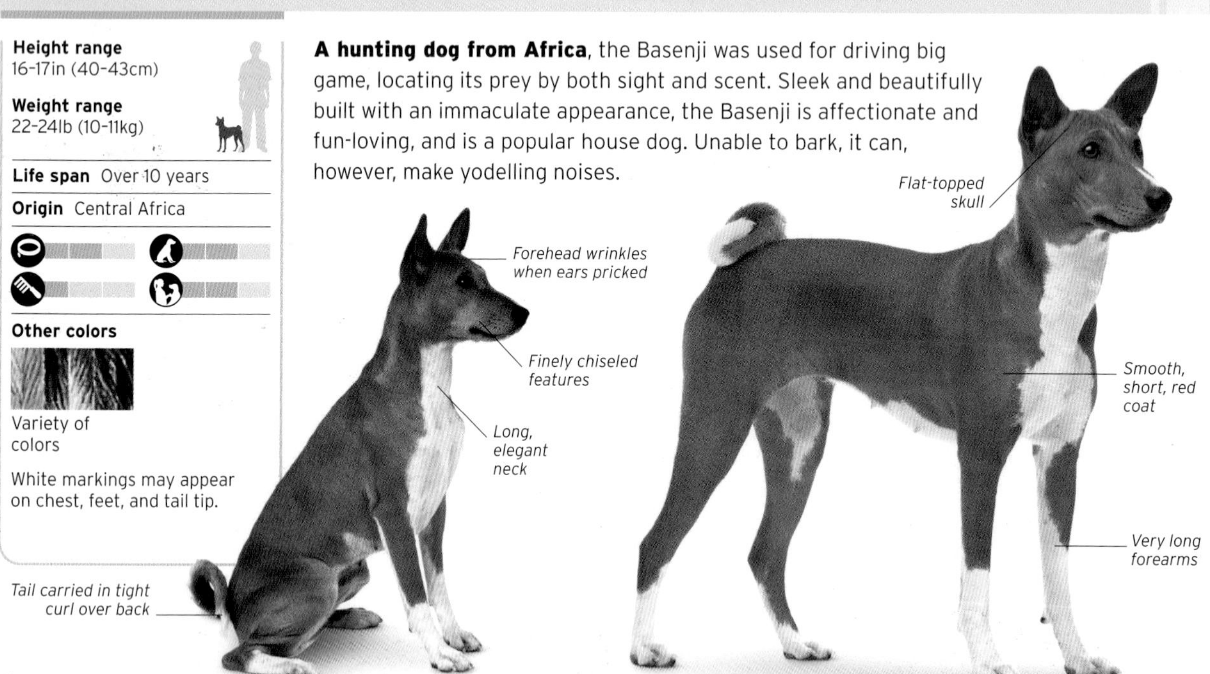
Flat-topped skull
Forehead wrinkles when ears pricked
Finely chiseled features
Long, elegant neck
Smooth, short, red coat
Very long forearms
Tail carried in tight curl over back

CANAAN DOG

THIS STURDY AND STEADFAST DOG IS ALWAYS ON THE ALERT AND READY TO PROTECT AKC

Height range
20–24in (50–60cm)

Weight range
40–55lb (18–25kg)

Life span Over 10 years

Origin Israel

Other colors

White

Black

Red and white spotted

Black and white spotted

Gray, brindle, black and tan, or tricolor undesirable.

Bred in Israel as a watchdog and herder, the Canaan Dog has strong protective instincts that do not usually turn into aggression. It is highly intelligent, and with steady training makes a reliable and affectionate companion. Not a common breed, it has yet to achieve widespread popularity.

Dark, slightly slanting, eyes
Brush-like, thick tail, carried high and curled
Low-set, broad ears
White chest marking
Tucked-up belly
Dense, harsh, sandy coat

PHARAOH HOUND

THIS STREAMLINED, ELEGANT DOG IS GOOD IN THE HOUSE BUT WILL CHASE ANYTHING SMALL OUTDOORS AKC

Height range
21–25in (53–63cm)

Weight range
44–55lb (20–25kg)

Life span Over 10 years

Origin Malta

Although the modern Pharaoh Hound was developed in Malta, this graceful breed bears a strong resemblance to the prick-eared hunting dogs illustrated in the art and artifacts of ancient Egypt. The Pharaoh Hound is calm tempered but needs a lot of exercise and, unless restrained outdoors, will fly off in pursuit of small animals, including other pets.

Large, erect ears
Amber-colored eyes
Well-arched, long neck
White marks on chest common
Whippy tail, carried in a high curve when active
Short, glossy, slightly harsh, rich tan coat
Slender, elegant body
Toes often marked white

CANARIAN WARREN HOUND

HIGHLY STRUNG DOG THAT IS BRED TO HUNT, AND NEEDS AN OUTDOOR LIFE

FCI

Height range
21-25in (53-64cm)

Weight range
35-49lb (16-22kg)

Life span 12-13 years

Origin Spain

Also known as the Podenco Canario, this hound—found on all the Canary Islands—has Egyptian roots dating back thousands of years. The breed has long been used as a rabbit-hunter and is highly valued for its speed, keen sight, and excellent nose. Sensitive and restless, the Canarian Warren Hound is unable to adapt to a quiet life indoors.

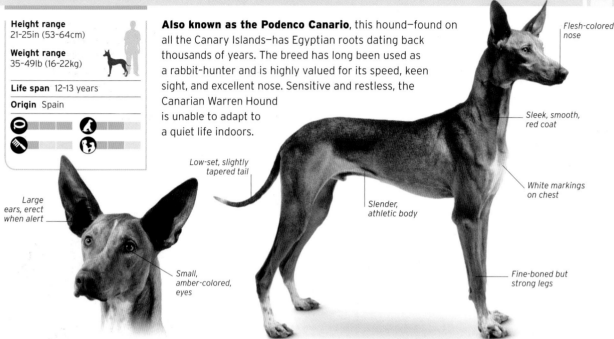

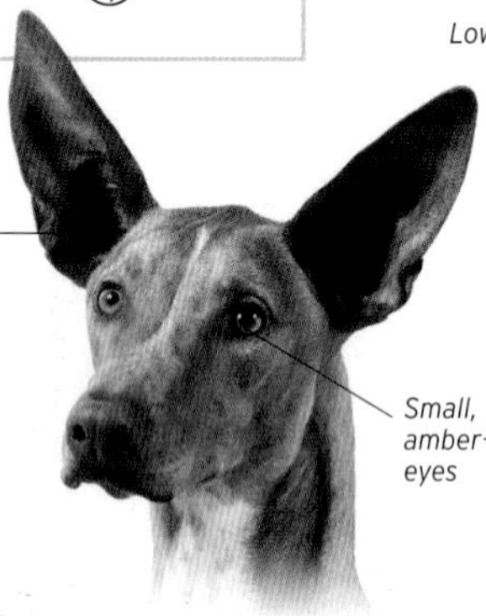

Flesh-colored nose

Sleek, smooth, red coat

Low-set, slightly tapered tail

White markings on chest

Large ears, erect when alert

Slender, athletic body

Small, amber-colored, eyes

Fine-boned but strong legs

CIRNECO DELL'ETNA

GENTLE BUT LIVELY, THIS IS A HUNTER RATHER THAN A HOUSE DOG

KC

Height range
17-20in (42-52cm)

Weight range
18-26lb (8-12kg)

Life span 12-14 years

Origin Italy

Other colors

White

White with orange

This Sicilian breed, which may well have originated in the area immediately around Mount Etna, is rare outside its native country. Lithe and strong, the Cirneco dell'Etna is built to run and hunt. Although good-natured, this dog is not an ideal option for owners who want a placid house pet.

Narrow, almost flat, skull

Short, glossy, fawn coat

Erect, rigid ears set high on head

Strong, arched neck

White markings on chest

Low-set tail

Powerful, muscular hind quarters

IBIZAN HOUND

THIS FAST RUNNER WITH AN OUTSTANDING ABILITY TO JUMP NEEDS SPACE AND EXERCISE AKC

Height range
22-29in (56-74cm)

Weight range
45-50lb (20-23kg)

Life span 10-12 years

Origin Spain

Other colors

Red

Used in Spain as a pack dog for hunting rabbits, the Ibizan Hound can cover the roughest ground at a "raking trot" characteristic of the breed. This dog also has an enormous jump and can easily leap over a garden fence. As long as an owner bears security in mind, the Ibizan Hound is not difficult to keep, but it is an all-action dog that needs relentless exercise. The breed has a charming temperament and fits in well with family life. There are two coat types, smooth and rough, both of which are easy to maintain.

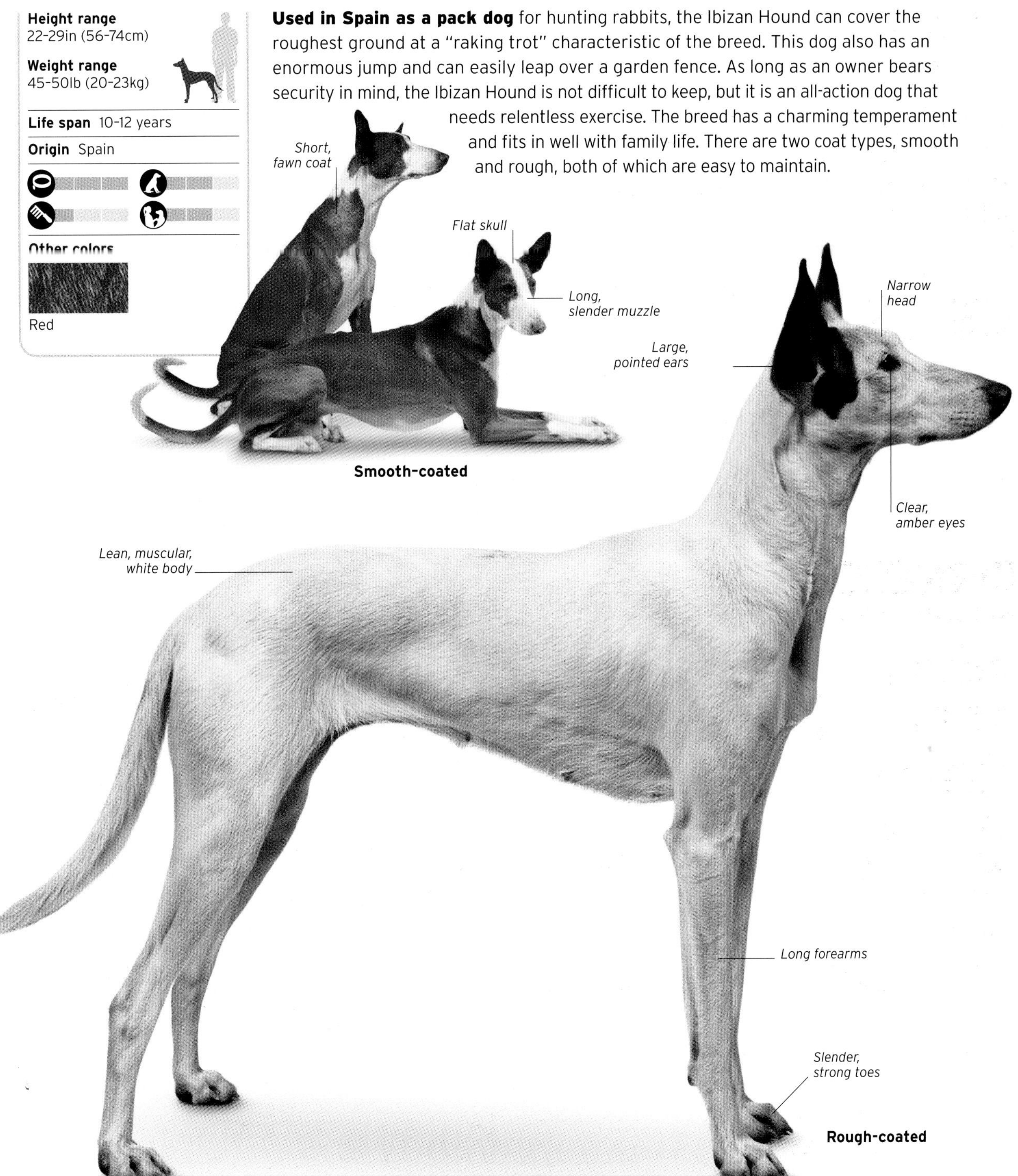
Short, fawn coat
Flat skull
Long, slender muzzle
Narrow head
Large, pointed ears
Clear, amber eyes
Lean, muscular, white body
Long forearms
Slender, strong toes

Smooth-coated

Rough-coated

PORTUGUESE PODENGO

AN ALERT WATCHDOG THAT MAKES A GOOD COMPANION

KC

Height range
Pequeno:
8–12in (20–30cm)
Medio:
16–21in (40–54cm)
Grande:
22–28in (55–70cm)

Weight range
Pequeno:
9–11lb (4–5kg)
Medio:
35–44lb (16–20kg)
Grande:
44–66lb (20–30kg)

Life span Over 12 years

Origin Portugal

Other colors

White, yellow | Black

White dogs have patches of yellow, black, or fawn. Pequeno dogs may be brown.

Commonly known as the Portuguese Warren Hound, this breed has developed into several varieties with distinct differences in size and coat. Today's dogs may be small (pequeno), medium (medio), or large (grande), and some are smooth-haired while others have moderately long, wiry coats. All were traditionally used for hunting, and in Portugal some are still kept for that purpose, working either in a pack or alone. Regardless of size, their intelligence and alertness make them excellent watchdogs.

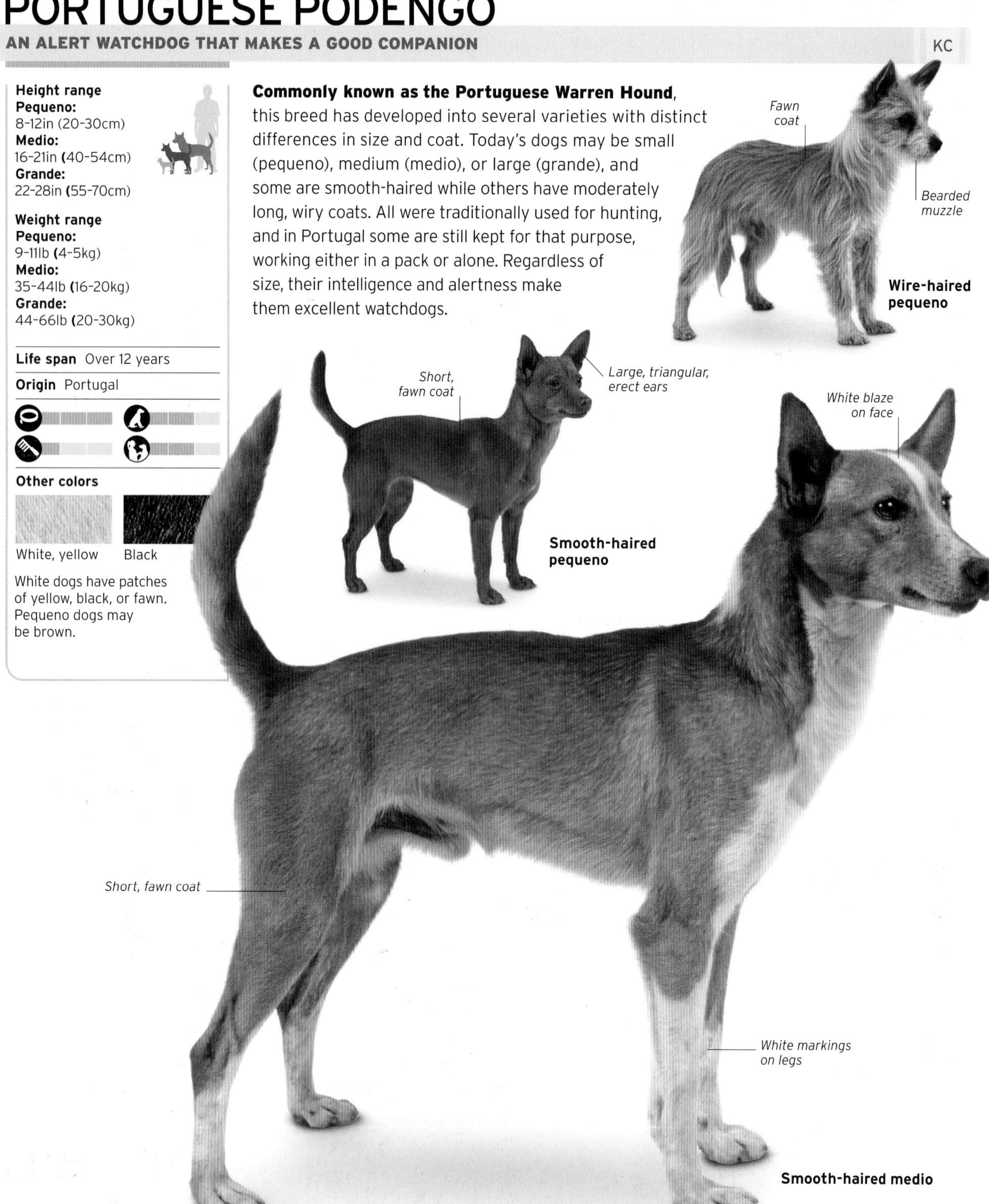
Fawn coat
Bearded muzzle
Short, fawn coat
Large, triangular, erect ears
White blaze on face
Short, fawn coat
White markings on legs

Wire-haired pequeno

Smooth-haired pequeno

Smooth-haired medio

CAROLINA DOG

THIS DOG RESPONDS TO TRAINING BUT CAN BE SHY

Height range
18-20in (45-50cm)

Weight range
33-44lb 15-20kg

Life span 12-14 years

Origin USA

Other colors

Deep red-ginger

Black and tan

Also known as the "American Dingo," this dog's ancestors are thought to have been domesticated and brought into North America by early settlers from Asia. In America's southeastern states, some still live semi-wild. Naturally wary, this dog needs early socializing to make it an acceptable pet.

Triangular, erect ears
Longer hairs on neck
Lighter-colored chest
Short, dense, wheaten coat
Tail carried in distinctive hook when alert

PERUVIAN INCA ORCHID

A HAIRLESS, STRIKINGLY PATTERNED DOG WHOSE SKIN NEEDS PROTECTION FROM THE ELEMENTS

Height range
20-26in (50-65cm)

Weight range
26-51lb (12-23kg)

Life span 11-12 years

Origin Peru

Other colors

Any color

Hairless dogs always have pink skin but the color of mottling can vary.

The true origins of the Peruvian Inca Orchid are lost in time, but dogs of this type are known to have been important in Inca civilizations. There are two varieties of this breed: hairless and coated. The hairless Inca Orchid is better suited to indoor rather than outdoor life because of its delicate skin.

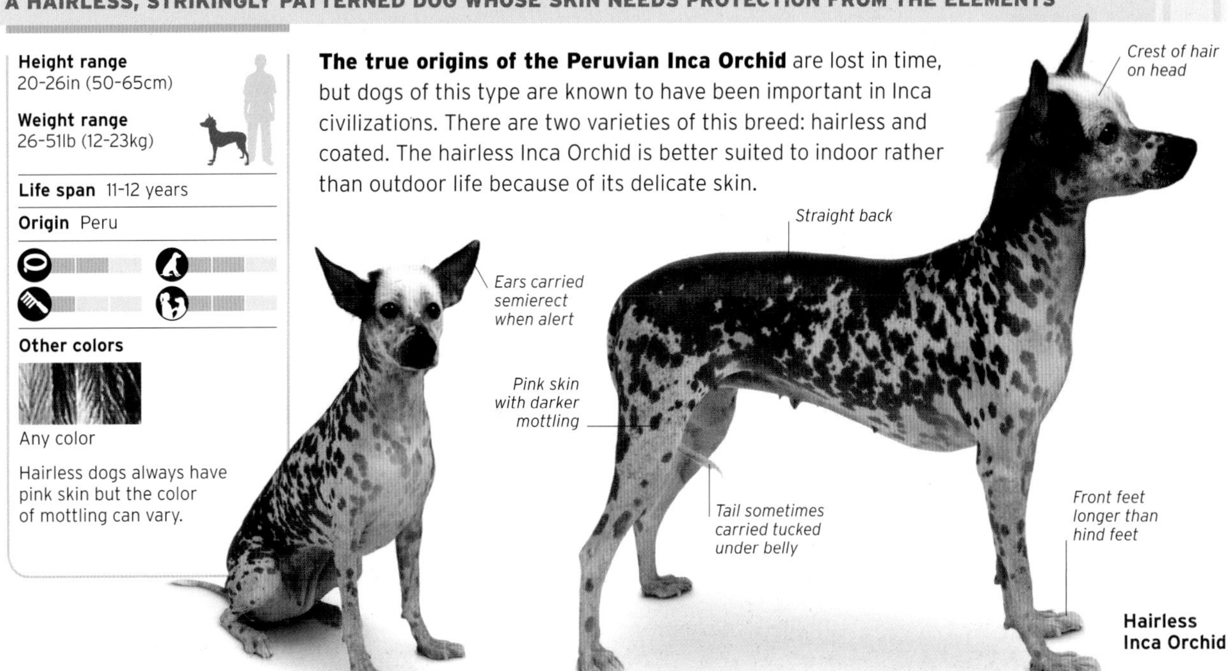
Crest of hair on head
Straight back
Ears carried semierect when alert
Pink skin with darker mottling
Tail sometimes carried tucked under belly
Front feet longer than hind feet

Hairless Inca Orchid

PERUVIAN HAIRLESS

THIS BRIGHT AND AGILE DOG IS AFFECTIONATE WITH OWNERS BUT SHY WITH STRANGERS

FCI

Height range
Miniature:
10-16in (25-40cm)
Medio:
16-20in (40-50cm)
Grande:
20-26in (50-65cm)

Weight range
Miniature:
9-18lb (4-8kg)
Medio:
18-26lb (8-12kg)
Grande:
26-55lb (12-25kg)

Life span 11-12 years

Origin Peru

Other colors

Blonde

Dark brown

Black

Records of hairless dogs in South America date back to pre-Inca times. It has been suggested that this lively and graceful breed may have originated in China or Africa before it was introduced in Peru. Hairlessness, often accompanied by the absence of certain teeth, is produced by a particular recessive gene, but occasionally, coated dogs do occur in litters. The Peruvian Hairless breeds come in three sizes—miniature, medio, and grande. The fine skin needs some protection because these dogs are susceptible to the cold and easily sunburned.

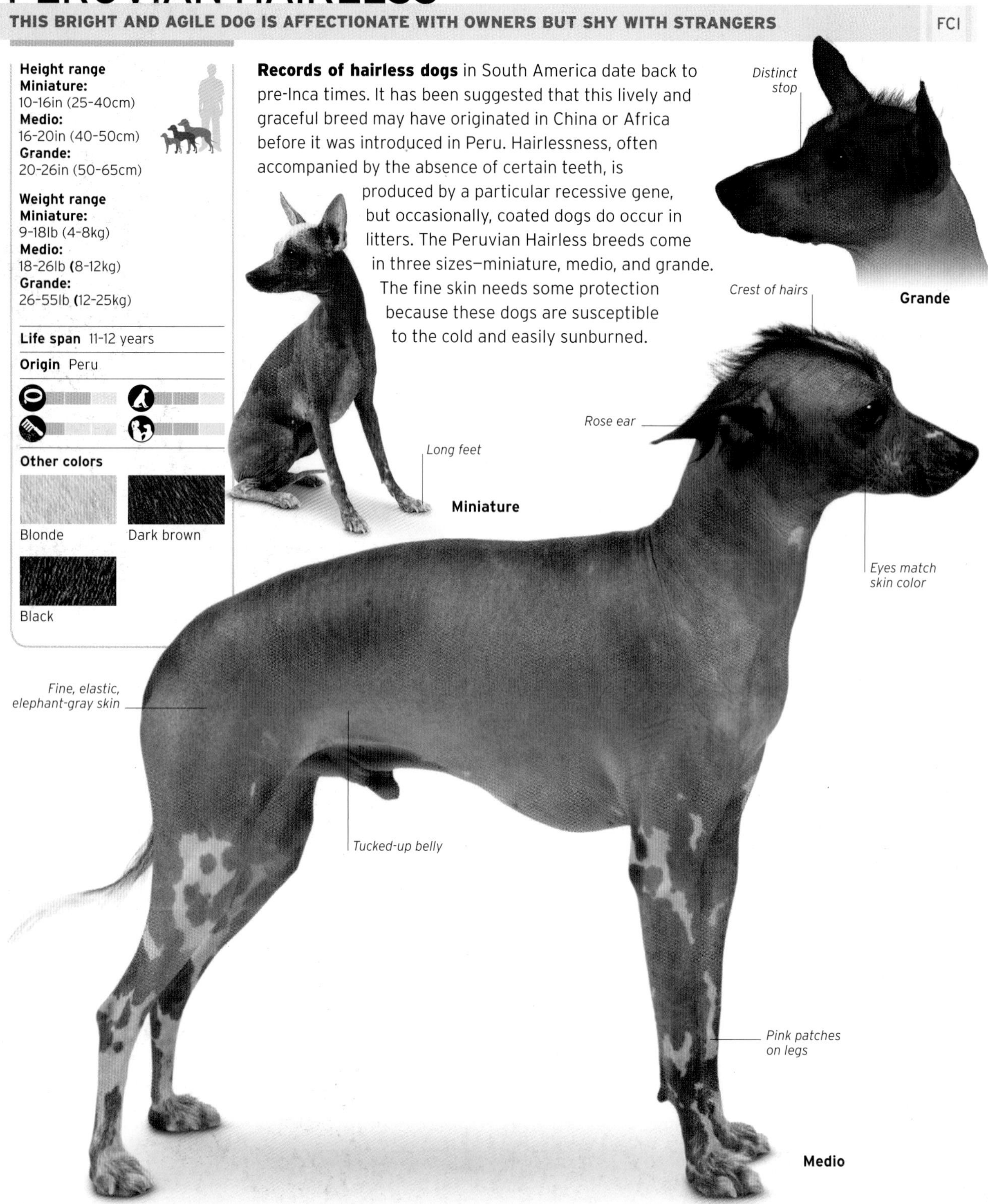
Distinct stop
Grande
Crest of hairs
Rose ear
Long feet
Miniature
Eyes match skin color
Fine, elastic, elephant-gray skin
Tucked-up belly
Pink patches on legs
Medio

XOLOITZCUINTLI

THIS CALM-NATURED, ALERT DOG IS EASY TO CARE FOR AND MAKES A DELIGHTFUL COMPANION

AKC

Height range
Miniature:
10-14in (25-35cm)
Intermediate:
14-18in (36-45cm)
Standard:
18-24in (46-60cm)

Weight range
Miniature:
5-15lb (2-7kg)
Intermediate:
15-31lb (7-14kg)
Standard:
24-40lb (11-18kg)

Life span Over 10 years

Origin Mexico

Other colors
Red
Liver

In pre-Conquest Mexico hairless dogs were believed to have sacred significance and were often used as a sacrifice or ritually eaten in religious ceremonies. Because of these practices, the Mexican Hairless barely escaped extinction and it was not until the mid-20th century that breeders began to work toward its recovery. Three different sizes are now recognized. Like all hairless dogs, this breed has limited general appeal and remains something of a rarity. Nonetheless, the Xoloitzcuintli, also known as the Mexican Hairless, is charming, good-tempered, and intelligent, and is likely to reward its owner with loyalty and affection.

Black skin
Standard
Tufts of hair on forehead
Large, long ears, erect when alert
Bronze skin
Miniature (puppy)
Head has slight stop and tapering muzzle
Traces of dark hair on tail
Firm, slender neck
Dark gray skin
Intermediate

RESCUE WORK
A German Shepherd Dog working for a search-and-rescue team hunts for survivors in a collapsed building following an earthquake.

WORKING DOGS

The list of jobs that humans ask dogs to perform is almost endless. In the thousands of years since dogs were domesticated, canine helpers have guarded homes, rescued people in danger, gone to war, and looked after the sick and disabled—to give only a few examples. In this book the working group is represented by breeds traditionally developed for pastoral work and guard duties.

Shepherd dogs work as herders and guardians

In general, the dogs in this highly diverse group tend to be large, though there are a few small but nonetheless robust exceptions. Working dogs are bred for strength and stamina, and many of them are capable of living outdoors in all weathers.

A collie rounding up its flock is for most people the archetypal shepherd dog, but many other types of dog are used to work with livestock. These pastoral breeds, as they are known, are used for both herding and guarding. Herding dogs have a natural instinct for driving stock, though not all of them work in the same way. Border Collies, for example, keep their sheep in order by stalking and staring, while the traditional cattle-herders such as Welsh Corgis and the Australian Cattle Dog nip at heels, and some herders bark as they work. Guardian sheepdogs, which include mountain breeds such as the Maremma and Pyrenean Mountain Dog, are designed to protect their flocks from predators such as wolves. Usually very large, many of these dogs are white and heavy coated, scarcely distinguishable from the sheep they spend their lives guarding.

Guard duties of another kind are often carried out by dogs of the mastiff type, recognizable as descendants of the enormous Molossus dogs seen in friezes and artifacts from the ancient world. Such breeds as the Bullmastiff, the Dogue de Bordeaux, and the Neapolitan Mastiff are used worldwide by security forces and for guarding property. Typically, these dogs are massively built and powerful, with small ears (often cropped in countries where the practice is still legal) and pendulous lips.

Many working breeds are excellent as companion dogs. Pastoral herders are extremely intelligent and generally easy to train, and often enjoy using their skills in agility trials and other canine competitions. Livestock guardian dogs, because of their sheer size and protective nature, are less likely to be suited to family life. In recent decades a number of the mastiff-type breeds have achieved great popularity as companions. Although some were produced originally for fighting, if reared in the home and socialized early they can adapt to life as a pet.

AGILITY TRIALS
Border Collies are often seen displaying their agility and intelligence at working dog trials.

LIVESTOCK GUARDIANS
The guarding instincts of breeds such as the Kuvasz make these dogs unsuitable for the inexperienced owner.

SAARLOOS WOLFDOG

THIS SELF-WILLED DOG IS RESERVED WITH STRANGERS BUT MAKES A LOYAL COMPANION FCI

Height range
24-30in (60-75cm)

Weight range
77-88lb (35-40kg)

Life span Over 10 years

Origin The Netherlands

Other colors

Cream

Bos (brown)

The Saarloos Wolfdog is the result of selective crossbreeding to produce a German Shepherd-type dog with natural traits closer to those of its wolf ancestors. Although it was suggested that this new breed could be useful as a guide dog, the Saarloos Wolfdog has proved better suited to life as a pet and companion. However, it needs sensitive handling.

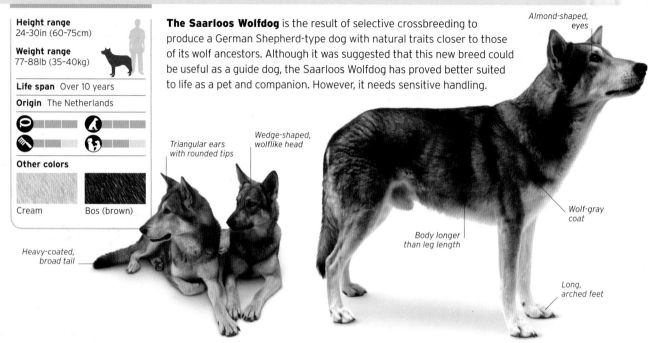

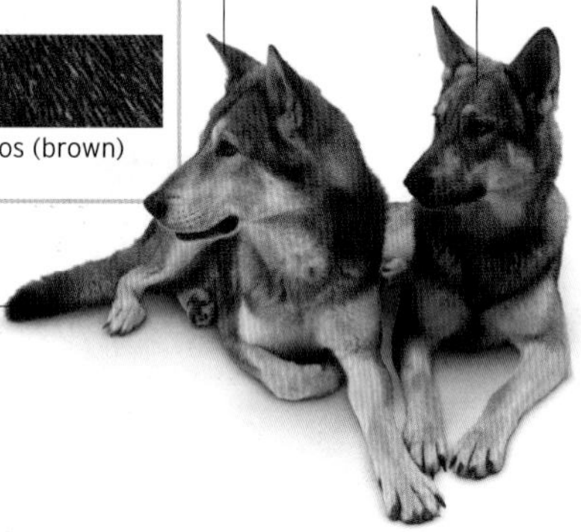

Almond-shaped, eyes

Triangular ears with rounded tips

Wedge-shaped, wolflike head

Heavy-coated, broad tail

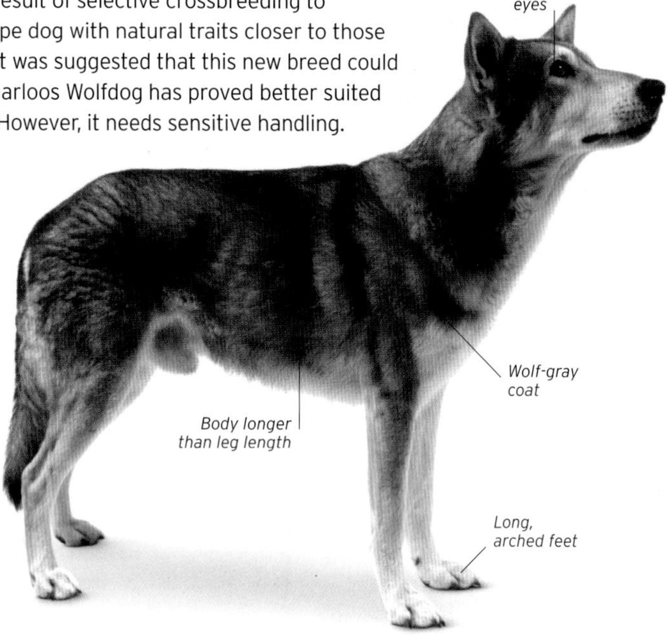

Wolf-gray coat

Body longer than leg length

Long, arched feet

CZECHOSLOVAKIAN WOLFDOG

A WOLFLIKE DOG WITH A DOCILE TEMPERAMENT FCI

Height range
24-26in (60-65cm)

Weight range
44-57lb (20-26kg)

Life span 12-16 years

Origin Czech Republic

Created through breeding programs that initially crossed German Shepherd Dogs with wolves, the Czechoslovakian Wolfdog has inherited many of the traits of its wild ancestors. This breed is quick, fearless, resilient, and wary of strangers. It is also faithful and obedient with familiar handlers, qualities that make it an excellent house dog.

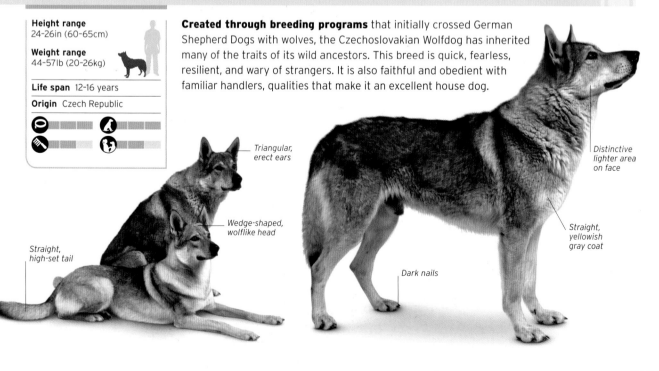

Triangular, erect ears

Wedge-shaped, wolflike head

Straight, high-set tail

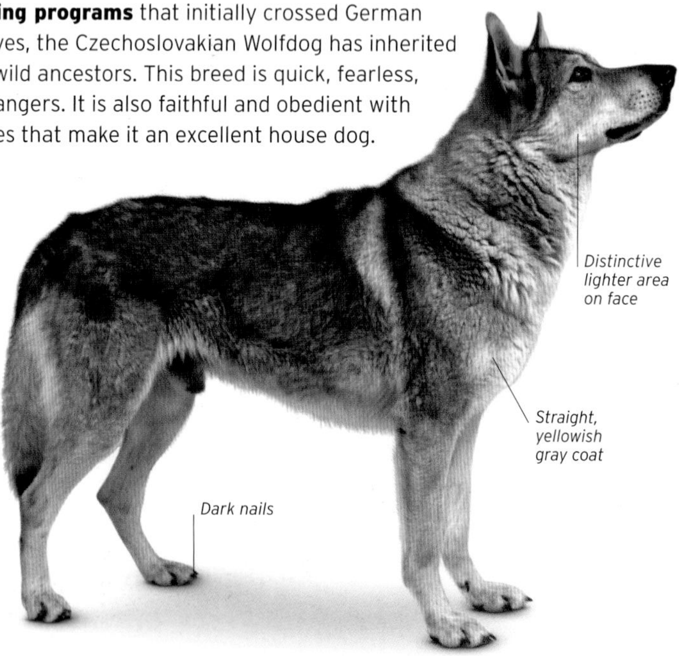

Distinctive lighter area on face

Straight, yellowish gray coat

Dark nails

GERMAN SHEPHERD DOG

THIS INTELLIGENT AND VERSATILE DOG IS ONE OF THE MOST POPULAR BREEDS WORLDWIDE AKC

Height range
23–25in (58–63cm)

Weight range
49–88lb (22–40kg)

Life span Over 10 years

Origin Germany

Other colors

Sable Black

As the name implies, this breed (formerly known as the Alsatian) originally worked as a shepherd dog and a protector of sheep. Highly adaptable and trainable, the German Shepherd Dog has proved valuable as a guard dog, guide dog, and tracker, and is widely used by police and armed forces all over the world. Despite occasional bad publicity for aggressive behavior, German Shepherd Dogs produced by reputable breeders usually have a steady temperament. When trained by a responsible owner and allowed to enjoy an active outdoor lifestyle, this dog can become a trusted and faithful member of the family. Coats range from short-haired to long-haired.

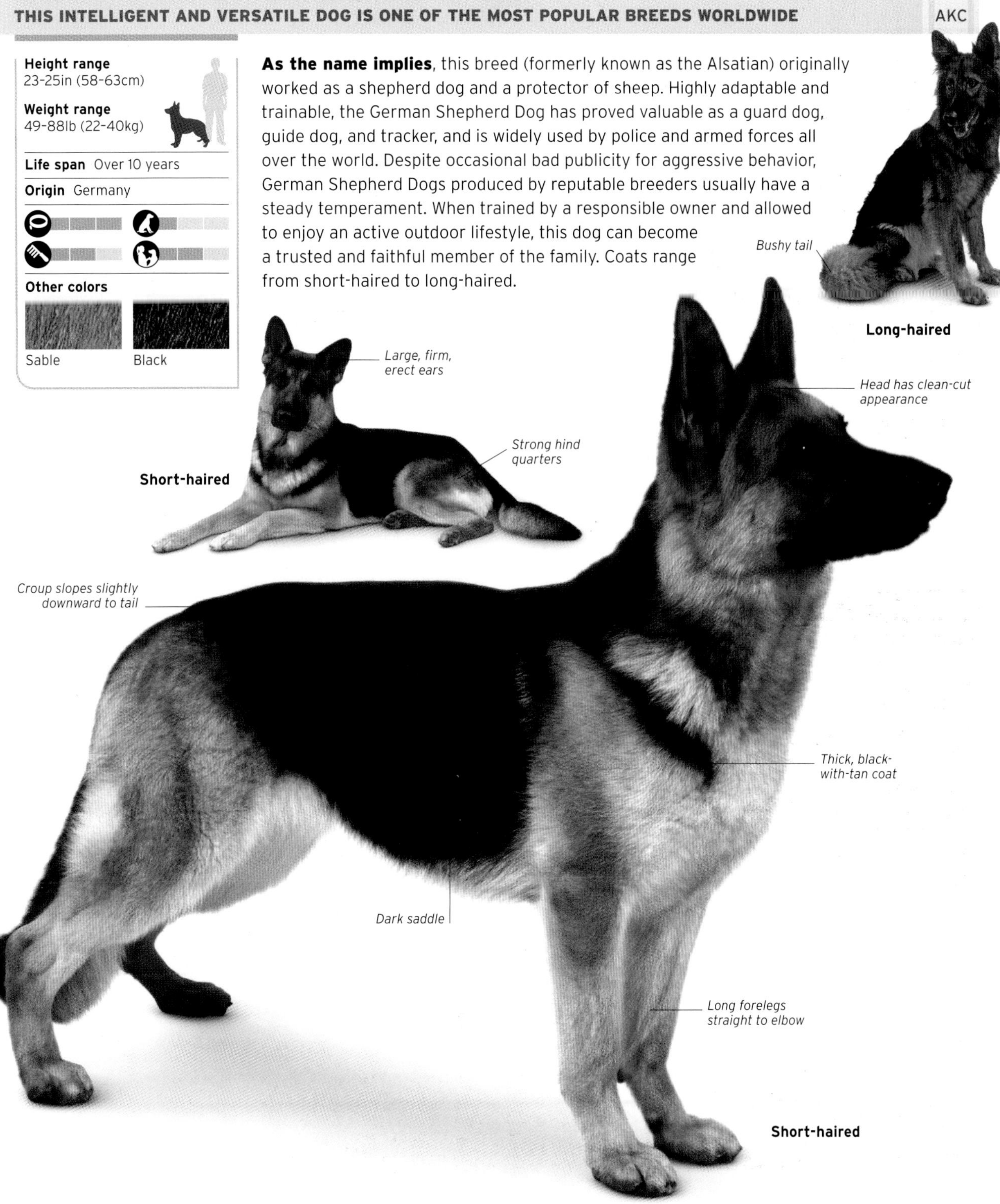
Bushy tail
Long-haired
Large, firm, erect ears
Head has clean-cut appearance
Strong hind quarters
Short-haired
Croup slopes slightly downward to tail
Thick, black-with-tan coat
Dark saddle
Long forelegs straight to elbow
Short-haired

KING SHEPHERD

EASY TO TRAIN, THIS DOG IS RELIABLE WITH CHILDREN AND OTHER PETS

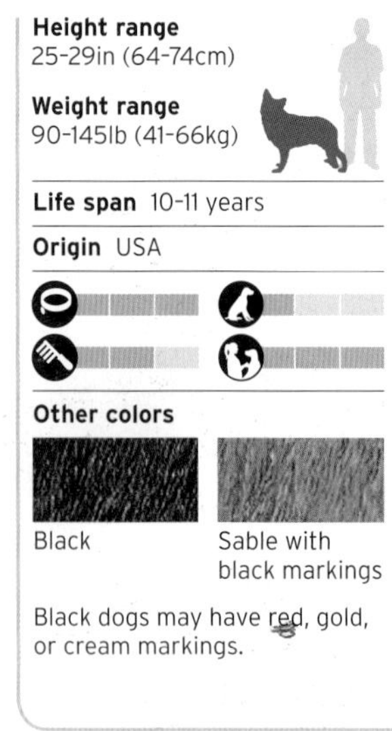

Height range
25–29in (64–74cm)

Weight range
90–145lb (41–66kg)

Life span 10–11 years

Origin USA

Other colors

Black

Sable with black markings

Black dogs may have red, gold, or cream markings.

Developed in the United States and recognized since the late 1990s, this large and handsome dog clearly shows the German Shepherd Dog (see p.35) in its breeding history. King Shepherds love to work as herders or guard dogs, but have a placid and tolerant nature that allows them to fit in well with a family. There are two coat types: smooth and rough.

High-set, erect ears
Long, muscular body with black saddle
Ruff of longer hair around neck
Predominately black muzzle
White markings on chest
Well-plumed tail
Weather-resistant, thick, tan coat

Rough-coated

PICARDY SHEEPDOG

THIS DOG ADORES LONG WALKS AND IS GENTLE WITH CHILDREN, BUT DISLIKES BEING LEFT ALONE FCI

Height range
22–26in (55–65cm)

Weight range
51–71lb (23–32kg)

Life span 13–14 years

Origin France

Other colors

Dark gray

Fawn brindle

May have white markings.

The history of the Picardy Sheepdog is uncertain, but this tough-looking breed may have originated over a century ago in the Picardy region of northeastern France. With quiet and patient training, this dog makes a sociable companion and a good playmate for children. The rugged coat is relatively easy to groom.

Finely shaped head hidden by long hair

High-set, erect ears

Long eyebrows do not obscure eyes

Hair on muzzle forms moustache and beard

Thick, fawn coat, harsh and crisp to touch

Lighter hair on chest

Long tail curves slightly at tip

DUTCH SHEPHERD DOG

USED FOR GUARDING, HERDING, AND AGILITY WORK, THIS DOG CAN ALSO MAKE A GOOD PET

FCI

Height range
22–24in (55–62cm)

Weight range
66–68lb (30–31kg)

Life span 12–14 years

Origin The Netherlands

Not often seen outside the Netherlands, and relatively uncommon even there, in the last 200 years this breed has become far more than an all-purpose farm dog. The Dutch Shepherd Dog has been used for security and police work, as a guide dog, and in obedience trials. Reliable and affectionate, the breed also makes a good family dog, though it has a natural wariness of strangers. There are three varieties of the Dutch Shepherd Dog: long-haired, short-haired, and rough-haired. The rough-haired type needs to have its coat plucked by a professional dog-groomer about twice a year.

Erect ears
Silver-brindle coat
Long-haired
Fawn-brindle coat
Short-haired
Coarse eyebrows
Harsh, wavy, silver-brindle coat
Feathering on underside of tail
Shorter hair below hock on hind legs
Light feathering on back of legs
Rough-haired

LAEKENOIS

THIS RARE BELGIAN SHEPHERD DOG IS DISTINGUISHED BY ITS UNUSUAL COAT KC

Height range 22-26in (56-66cm)

Weight range 55-65lb (25-29kg)

Life span Over 10 years

Origin Belgium

Of the four breeds of Belgian Shepherd Dog, this wiry-coated variety was the first to be developed, in the 1880s. The Laekenois is named after the Château de Laeken, near Antwerp, and was once much favored by the Belgian royal family. Rarely seen, this delightful dog deserves to be more widely appreciated.

Area of darker shading
Shorter hair on muzzle
High-set, erect ears
Head carried high with alert expression
Body powerful but not heavy
Round feet
Wiry, reddish fawn coat

BELGIAN SHEEPDOG

THIS BRIGHT AND ACTIVE DOG LOVES OUTDOOR LIFE AND IS FULL OF CURIOSITY AKC

Height range 22-26in (56-66cm)

Weight range 50-75lb (23-34kg)

Life span Over 10 years

Origin Belgium

From 1893 black-coated Belgian Shepherd Dogs were selectively bred at a kennel in the village of Groenendael, near Brussels. This handsome variety is now extremely popular. Like most dogs formerly used for work, the Belgian Sheepdog needs an owner who understands the importance of early socializing and firm but kindly control.

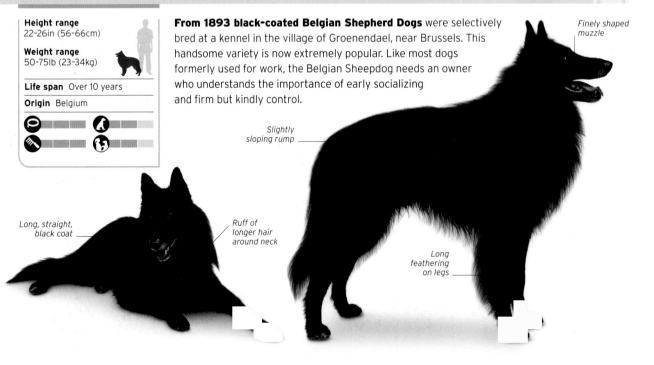

Finely shaped muzzle

Slightly sloping rump

Long, straight, black coat

Ruff of longer hair around neck

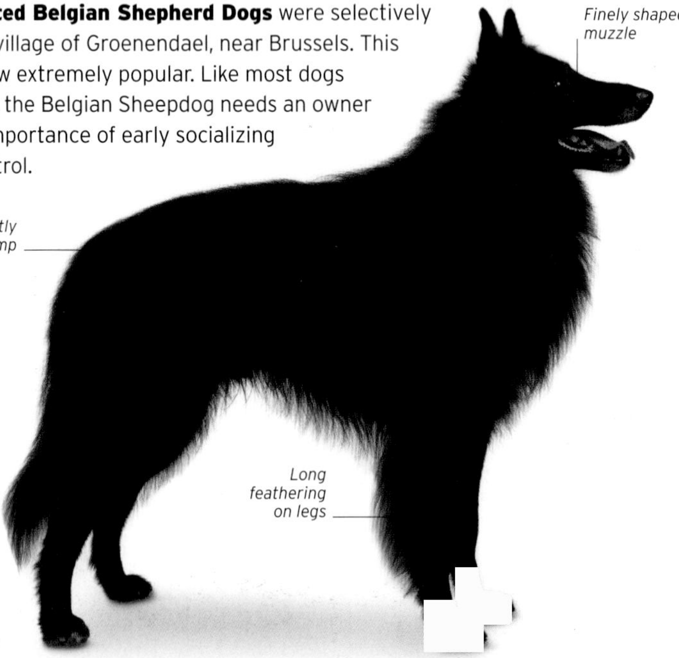

Long feathering on legs

BELGIAN MALINOIS

A VERY HARDY AND ENERGETIC DOG WITH STRONG GUARDING INSTINCTS AKC

Height range 22–26in (56–66cm)

Weight range 60–65lb (27–29kg)

Life span Over 10 years

Origin Belgium

Other colors

Gray

Red

All colors have black overlay.

Believed to have originated in Malines, in Belgium, the Belgian Malinois is a short-haired variety of the Belgian Shepherd Dog. Like its fellow breeds, it is a natural guard dog. Although its behavior may be unpredictable, with responsible training the Belgian Malinois socializes well and makes a loyal companion.

Thicker collar around neck
Triangular ears, mostly black
Distinctive black mask
Almond shaped, brown eyes
Pointed muzzle and medium stop
Short, straight, fawn coat with black tips to the hairs
Darker tip on bushy tail

BELGIAN TERVUREN

THIS DOG HAS A DOMINANT PERSONALITY AND ENJOYS A GOOD RUN, BUT SHOULD BE SUPERVISED AKC

Height range 22–26in (56–66cm)

Weight range 40–65lb (18–29kg)

Life span Over 10 years

Origin Belgium

Other colors

Gray

All colors have black overlay.

The most popular of the Belgian Shepherd Dogs worldwide, this variety was named after the village where it was developed by a local breeder. The Belgian Tervuren has strong protective instincts and is frequently used for guarding and police work. Its beautiful, black-tipped coat sheds regularly and needs plenty of grooming.

Head carried high

Strongly muscled back

Upright, muscular neck

Abundant "breeches" on hind quarters

Black ears and mask

Red coat

Rich, long, fawn coat with black overlay

MUDI

THIS ACTIVE AND PLAYFUL FAMILY DOG ALSO MAKES A FEARLESS GUARD DOG FCI

Height range
15–19in (38–47cm)

Weight range
18–29lb (8–13kg)

Life span 13–14 years

Origin Hungary

Other colors

Fawn

Blue merle, ash

Brown

May have white markings.

Originally used as a working dog by Hungarian sheep- and cattle-herders, this rare breed is tough, bold, and energetic. With its friendly and adaptable nature, the Mudi makes a good house dog. It needs plenty of exercise to stay fit and healthy, and responds well to sympathetic training.

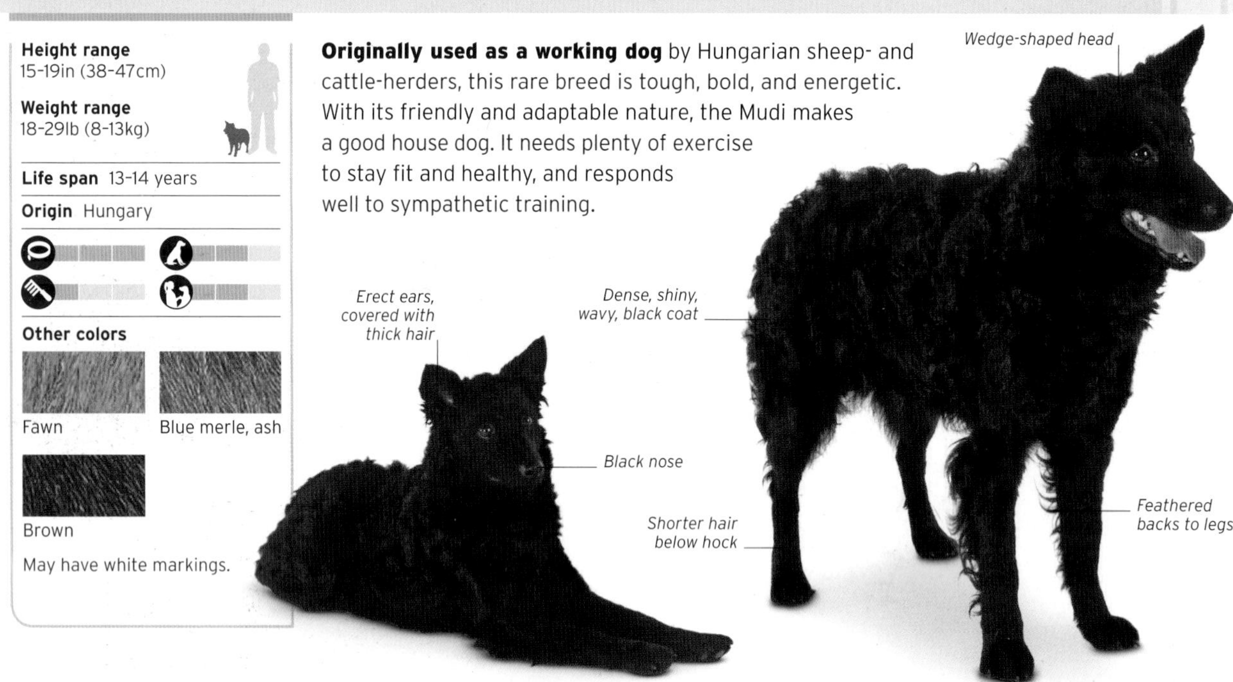
Wedge-shaped head
Erect ears, covered with thick hair
Dense, shiny, wavy, black coat
Black nose
Shorter hair below hock
Feathered backs to legs

STANDARD SCHNAUZER

LIVELY BUT OBEDIENT, THIS DOG IS GOOD-TEMPERED WITH CHILDREN AKC

Height range
17–20in (44–50cm)

Weight range
31–44lb (14–20kg)

Life span Over 10 years

Origin Germany

Other colors

Black

The medium-sized Standard Schnauzer was established as a breed in the 1880s in southern Germany. Alert and agile, the Standard Schnauzer was used primarily as a versatile farm dog with a formidable reputation for rat-hunting. Placid and affectionate, but with a lively sense of fun, the breed is now popular as a family dog.

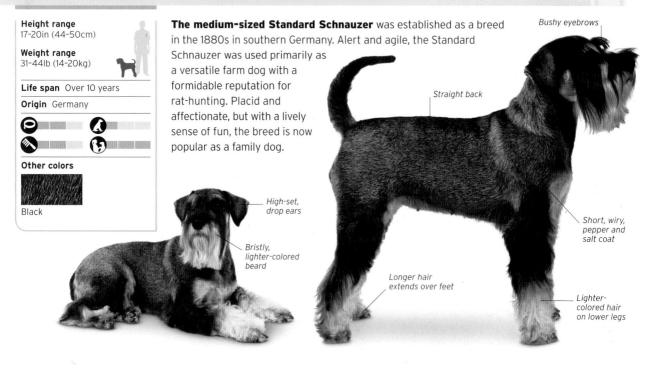

Bushy eyebrows

Straight back

High-set, drop ears

Bristly, lighter-colored beard

Short, wiry, pepper and salt coat

Longer hair extends over feet

Lighter-colored hair on lower legs

GIANT SCHNAUZER

AN EVEN-TEMPERED, INTELLIGENT, AND EASY-TO-TRAIN DOG

AKC

Height range
24-28in (60-70cm)

Weight range
65-90lb (29-41kg)

Life span Over 10 years

Origin Germany

Other colors

Pepper and salt

Robust and powerfully built, the Giant Schnauzer from southern Germany was originally used for farm work and cattle-herding. By the 20th century the breed's intelligence, trainability, and impressive appearance had been recognized as ideal qualities for a guard dog. This breed is now widely used by police and security forces, but an equable temperament also makes it suitable as a home watchdog and pet. Despite its size, the Giant Schnauzer is easily manageable if given plenty of exercise. Its dense, wiry, double-layered coat needs regular maintenance, with daily grooming and an occasional trim.

Dark eyes

Deep chest

Bushy eyebrows overhang eyes

Drop ears with rounded tips

Tail carried high

Dense, wiry, black coat

Bearded muzzle

Strong, graceful neck

Slight feathering on back of legs

BOUVIER DES ARDENNES

A RARE DOG WITH A LONG-ESTABLISHED REPUTATION AS A WILLING WORKER

FCI

Height range
20–24in (52–62cm)

Weight range
49–77lb (22–35kg)

Life span Over 10 years

Origin Belgium

Other colors

Variety of colors

This hardy, active, former cattle-herder from the Belgian Ardennes is now rarely seen, either as a working dog or a house dog. A handful of enthusiasts have kept the breed in existence, and with its adaptable temperament and zest for life the Bouvier des Ardennes has the potential for future popularity.

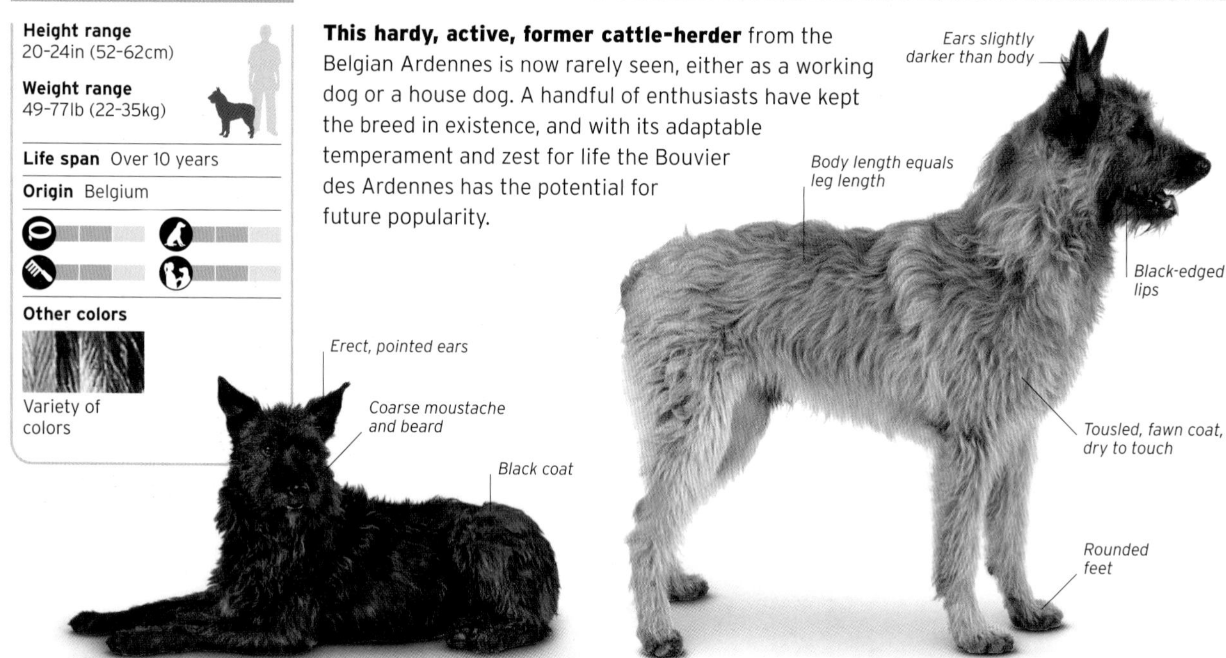
Ears slightly darker than body
Body length equals leg length
Black-edged lips
Erect, pointed ears
Coarse moustache and beard
Black coat
Tousled, fawn coat, dry to touch
Rounded feet

BOUVIER DES FLANDRES

THIS TOWN OR COUNTRY DOG IS HAIRY BUT NOT TOO DIFFICULT TO GROOM

AKC

Height range
23–27in (59–68cm)

Weight range
60–88lb (27–40kg)

Life span Over 10 years

Origin Belgium

Other colors

Variety of colors

May have small, white star on chest.

Of the various types of Bouviers once used in Belgium and France for cattle-herding and guarding, this breed from Flanders is the most commonly encountered. Despite originally being an outdoor dog—with an appropriately weatherproof coat—the Bouvier des Flandres can happily adjust to an urban home.

High-set, drop ears

Heavily feathered tail

Long, coarse beard

Very thick, silver-brindle coat, harsh to touch

Dense coat extends over feet

CROATIAN SHEPHERD DOG

THIS HERDING AND GUARDING DOG IS MORE SUITED TO WORK THAN DOMESTICITY

FCI

Height range
16-20in (40-50cm)

Weight range
29-44lb (13-20kg)

Life span 13-14 years

Origin Croatia

Relatively small and lightly built for a shepherd dog, this breed is active and alert. Easy to train for work, the Croatian Shepherd Dog may be harder to handle as a house dog because of its natural herding and guarding instincts. Its unusually wavy or curly coat is a distinctive feature.

Narrow muzzle
Erect, triangular ears, lined with long hair
Wavy, black coat
Short hair on face
Backs of legs slightly feathered
Shorter hair on lower legs

SARPLANINAC

THIS MAGNIFICENT AND VERY PROTECTIVE WORKING DOG IS HAPPY TO LIVE OUTDOORS

FCI

Height range
Over 23in (over 58cm)

Weight range
66-99lb (30-45kg)

Life span 11-13 years

Origin Macedonia

Other colors

Any solid color

Formerly known as the Illyrian Shepherd Dog, this impressive breed is now named after the Sarplanina Mountains of Macedonia where it originated. The Sarplaninac is very much an outdoor, working dog. Although it has a sociable, though protective, temperament, its size and energy levels make it impractical as a family pet.

Drop ears
Broad, slightly rounded top to head
Longer hair forms ruff around neck
Heavily feathered, bushy tail
Long, dense, dark brown coat
Broad chest
Long feathering on hind quarters
Yellowish gray lower legs

KARST SHEPHERD DOG

THIS RELIABLE AND DEVOTED DOG NEEDS A SPACIOUS HOME AND CORRECT HANDLING

FCI

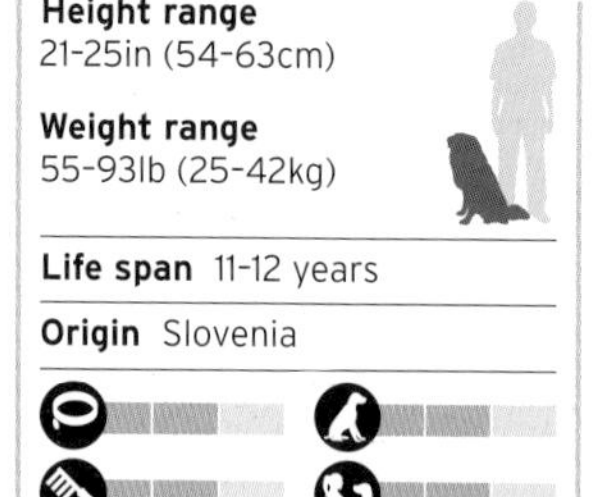

Height range
21-25in (54-63cm)

Weight range
55-93lb (25-42kg)

Life span 11-12 years

Origin Slovenia

Formerly known as the Illyrian Shepherd, this dog was separated from another breed of the same name and renamed the Karst, or Istrian, Shepherd Dog in the 1960s. Used for herding and guarding in the alpine Karst region of Slovenia, this excellent working dog can make a good companion with careful training and early socialization.

Hair on neck forms ruff and mane

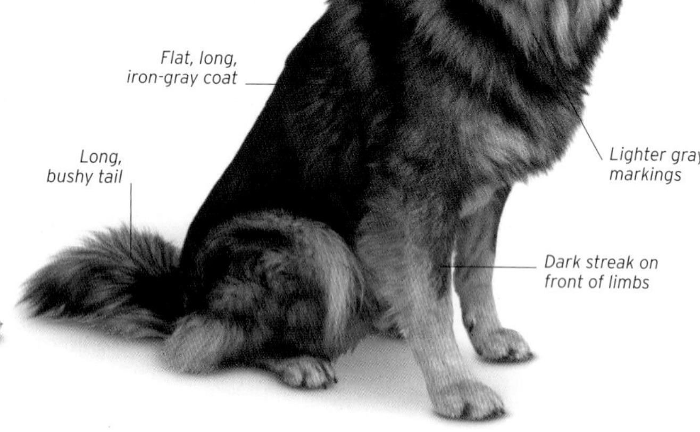
Head as wide as it is long
Flat, long, iron-gray coat
Long, bushy tail
Lighter gray markings
Dark streak on front of limbs

ESTRELA MOUNTAIN DOG

THIS DOG, FOR LARGE HOMES ONLY, CAN LIVE OUTSIDE IF GIVEN SHELTER

KC

Height range
24-28in (62-72cm)

Weight range
77-132lb (35-60kg)

Life span Over 10 years

Origin Portugal

Other colors

Wolf-gray | Black brindle

May have white markings on underside and extremities.

A livestock-guardian from the Estrela Mountains of Portugal, this fearless, rugged dog was bred to protect flocks against predators such as wolves. The Estrela Mountain Dog is a loyal and friendly, but strong-willed, companion that needs consistent and patient obedience training. There are long-coated and short-coated varieties of the breed.

Dark face mask
Black hairs intermingle with fawn hairs

Long head with broad, rounded skull
Thick ruff around neck and chest
Thick, slightly wavy, fawn topcoat

Long-coated

PORTUGUESE WATCHDOG

THIS CALM-NATURED WATCHDOG MAY BE TOO BIG AND STRONG FOR MANY OWNERS FCI

Height range 25–29in (64–74cm)

Weight range 77–132lb (35–60kg)

Life span 12 years

Origin Portugal

Other colors

Wolf-gray | Black

Coat may be brindled and will always have white markings; white coats have patches of one of the colors.

Possibly descended from the powerful mastiffs brought into Europe from Asia by nomadic herders, this breed is also known as the Rafeiro de Alentejo, named after the Alentejo region of Portugal. Traditionally used for guarding, the Portuguese Watchdog is vigilant and suspicious of strangers. Formidable in size and strength, though not aggressive, this dog is unsuitable for novice handlers.

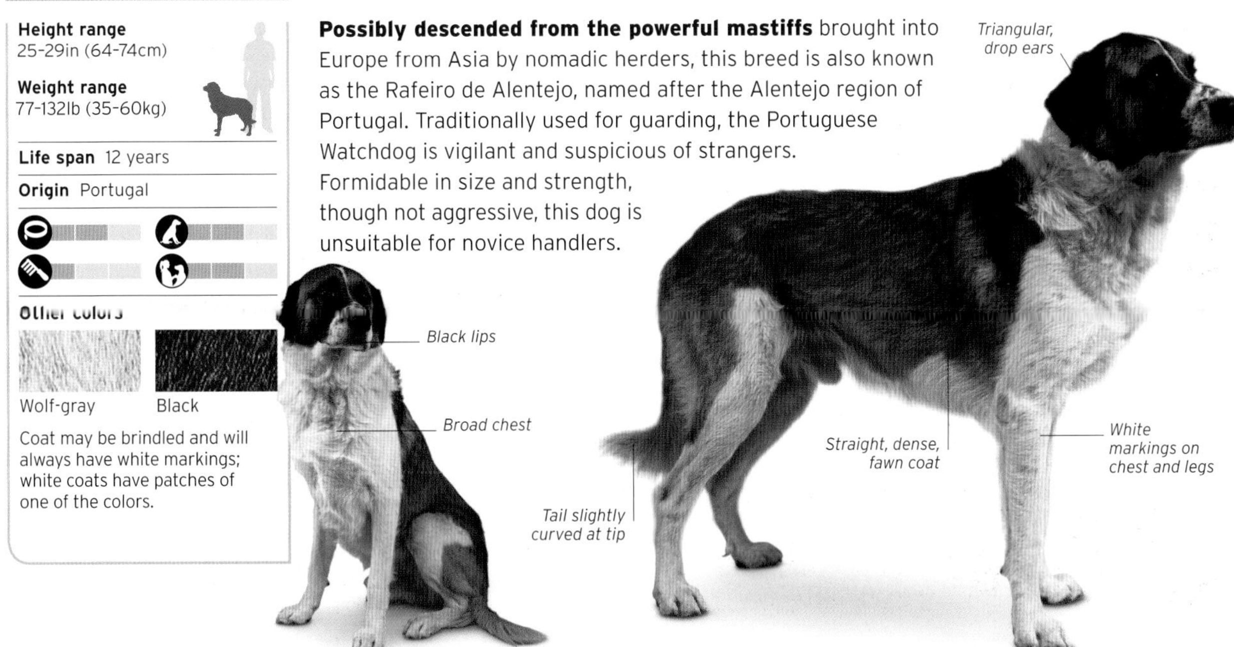
Triangular, drop ears
Black lips
Broad chest
Straight, dense, fawn coat
White markings on chest and legs
Tail slightly curved at tip

CASTRO LABOREIRO DOG

THIS BOLD AND VIGILANT WATCHDOG IS BETTER SUITED TO WORK THAN FAMILY LIFE FCI

Height range 22–25in (55–64cm)

Weight range 55–88lb (25–40kg)

Life span 12–13 years

Origin Portugal

Other colors

Wolf-gray

May have a small, white spot on chest.

Named after its home village in the mountains of northern Portugal, this dog, sometimes known as the Portuguese Cattle Dog, was bred to work as a livestock-guardian. Its distinctive alarm bark starts low and ends high-pitched. This dog develops a strong bond with family members but may be hostile to strangers.

Triangular, drop ears

Almond-shaped eyes

Tail long-haired on underside, usually carried low

Short, very thick, harsh-textured, "mountain" brindle coat

PORTUGUESE SHEEPDOG

THIS HIGHLY INTELLIGENT DOG LIKES TO BE ACTIVE FCI

Height range
17-22in (42-55cm)

Weight range
37-60lb (17-27kg)

Life span 12-13 years

Origin Portugal

Other colors

Variety of colors

May have a small amount of white on chest.

In its native country this shaggy, agile dog is sometimes known as the "monkey dog." The Portuguese Sheepdog loves to be outdoors, herding. Lively and extremely intelligent, the breed has also gained popularity as a companion and sporting dog in Portugal, although it is little known elsewhere.

Large eyebrows do not obscure eyes
Fawn coat
Long beard and moustache
Black, shaggy coat resembles goat hair
Tan markings on lower legs

CATALAN SHEEPDOG

A PLEASANT-NATURED DOG, BUT PROTECTIVE OF HOME AND FAMILY KC

Height range
18-22in (45-55cm)

Weight range
45-60lb (20-27kg)

Life span 12-14 years

Origin Spain

Other colors

Gray

Black and tan

Sable

May have white markings.

Bred in Catalonia as a flock-herder and guard, this hardy dog has an attractive weatherproof coat that allows it to work in almost any conditions. With high intelligence, a quiet temperament, and a readiness to please, the Catalan Sheepdog is relatively easy to train and makes an excellent family companion.

Crest on top of head
Fringed ears hang close to head
Round, dark amber eyes
Rough-textured, fawn coat
Long hair extends over feet

PYRENEAN SHEPHERD

A LIVELY COMPANION, ALMOST IMPOSSIBLE TO TIRE OUT, WITH A STRONG HERDING INSTINCT AKC

Height range
15-19in (38-48cm)

Weight range
15-30lb (7-14kg)

Life span 12-13 years

Origin France

Other colors

Gray | Blue

Black | Black and white

Blue coats may be merle, slate, or brindle. Unmixed colors are preferred.

Small and lightly built for a sheepdog, this breed has long been used for herding flocks in the French Pyrenees. It remained almost unknown beyond its native mountain regions until the beginning of the 20th century. Lithe, energetic, and ready to join in any interesting activity, the Pyrenean Shepherd does well in canine sports such as agility trials. For an active family, the Pyrenean Shepherd is an excellent pet. The breed comes in two coat varieties—long or semi-long—and may have a rough or smooth face.

Fawn coat with black hairs
White markings on chest
Fawn coat with black hairs
Fawn coat woollier on hind quarters
Long, swept-back hair on face and cheeks
Long hair on legs extends over toes

Semi-long, rough-faced

Semi-long, smooth-faced

Long-haired, rough-faced

BEARDED COLLIE

THIS DOG IS CALM BUT ALERT AND ACTIVE, SO BEST SUITED TO A RURAL HOME AKC

Height range
20–22in (51–56cm)

Weight range
45–55lb (20–25kg)

Life span Over 10 years

Origin UK

Other colors

Sandy, Red-brown, Blue, Black

Until the middle of the 20th century the Bearded Collie was familiar only in Scotland and the north of England, where it was valued as a sheepdog. Now widely appreciated for its attractive appearance, compact size, and gentle nature, this breed has great appeal as a pet. However, it is more likely to enjoy the space of a rural home than a compact urban environment.

Arched eyebrows do not cover eyes
Long, slate-gray outer coat
Large nose
Long moustache on muzzle
White collar
Toes hairy between pads

BRIARD

THIS LARGE AND BOISTEROUS DOG NEEDS A FIRM HAND AND PLENTY OF EXERCISE AKC

Height range
23–27in (58–69cm)

Weight range
77lb (35kg)

Life span Over 10 years

Origin France

Other colors

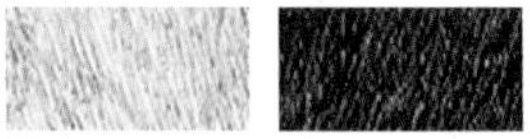

Slate-gray, Black

In its native country this large and lively French breed works as a herder and guarder of sheep. Bold and protective, but not aggressive, the Briard is an excellent family companion if given regular exercise and room to run and play. This is not a low-maintenance dog because the Briard's long, thick coat needs a lot of grooming.

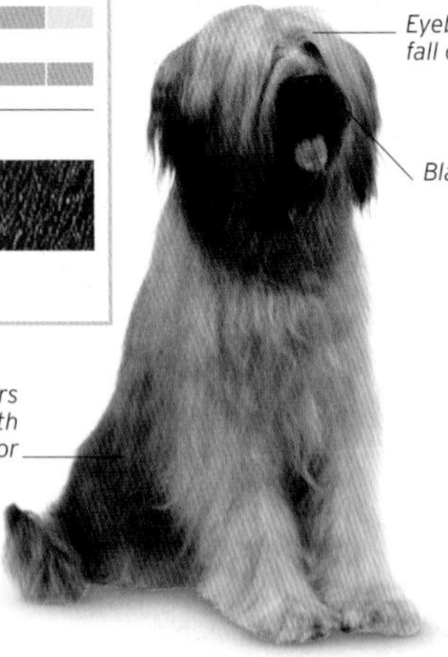

Short, high-set, long-haired ears

Eyebrows fall over eyes

Black nose

Darker hairs blend in with main body color

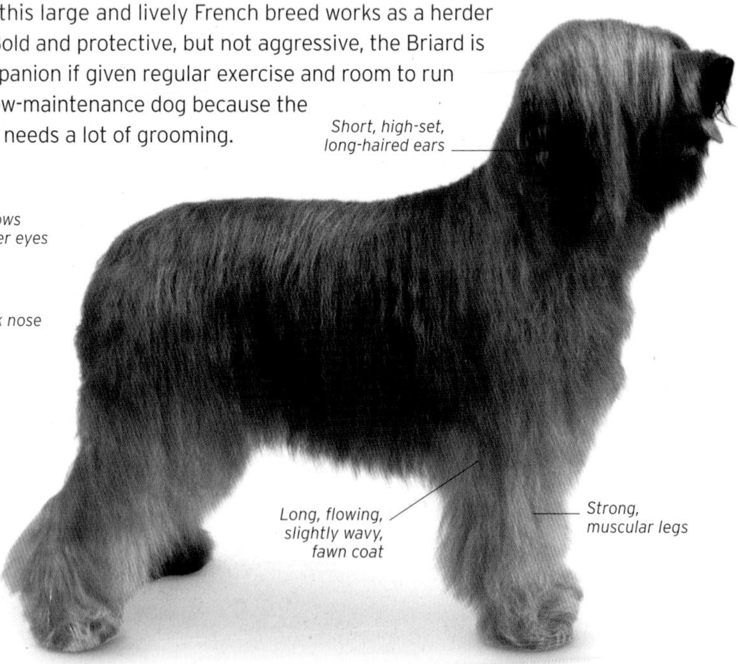

Long, flowing, slightly wavy, fawn coat

Strong, muscular legs

OLD ENGLISH SHEEPDOG

THIS GOOD-TEMPERED AND INTELLIGENT DOG NEEDS FREQUENT GROOMING

AKC

Height range
22-24in (56-61cm)

Weight range
60-90lb (27-41kg)

Life span Over 10 years

Origin UK

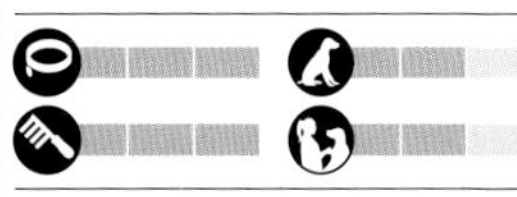

Other colors

Gray

Any shade of gray, grizzle, or blue. Body and hind quarters of solid color, with no white patches.

This breed is considered to be native to the UK, although it may have its earliest origins in various types of continental sheepdog. It was once the custom to completely dock the tails of Old English Sheepdogs, and the alternative name of Bobtail Sheepdog is still sometimes used. This big, strong dog requires a great deal of exercise and preferably wide open spaces to work off its energy. Its owner should be prepared to devote time and care to daily grooming, to prevent the heavy, shaggy coat from becoming tangled and matted.

Eyes obscured by coat

Adult and puppy

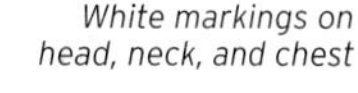

White markings on head, neck, and chest

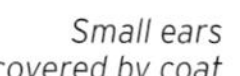

Small ears covered by coat

Deep, relatively short body

Longer coat on hind quarters

Very thick, shaggy, blue coat with white markings

Long, lean, tapering head

Dark eyes with intelligent, inquisitive expression

Semierect ears

Smooth-haired face

Long, very dense, harsh-textured, sable and white coat

Abundant, white mane

Profuse feathering on hind quarters

Smooth hair below hock

Well-feathered tail

COLLIE

THIS PROUD AND BEAUTIFUL, SWEET-TEMPERED DOG MAKES A LOVELY FAMILY COMPANION AKC

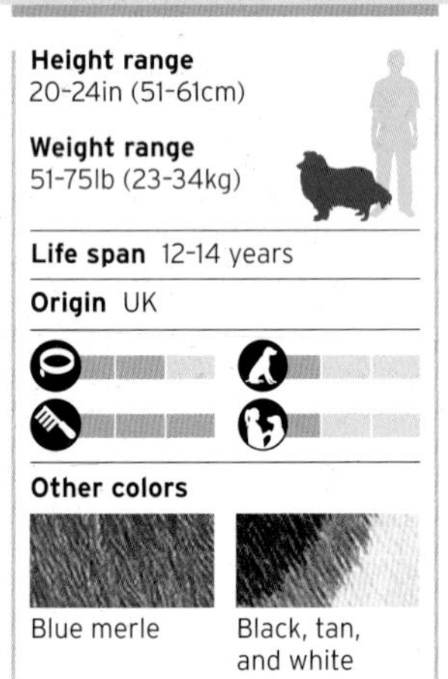
Height range
20–24in (51–61cm)
Weight range
51–75lb (23–34kg)
Life span 12–14 years
Origin UK
Other colors
Blue merle
Black, tan, and white

This rich-coated breed, a descendant of the rather less-refined Scottish working shepherd dogs, is much admired today as a pet and in the show ring. The Collie's history may go back as far as Roman Britain, but dogs recognizably of this type did not attract wide attention until the 19th century. Queen Victoria is credited with popularizing the breed both in Europe and the United States. Later, "Lassie," the highly intelligent star of film and television, confirmed the Collie's status as one of the best-loved dogs of all time.

This breed is mild-tempered and tolerant of other dogs and pets. It is highly responsive to training and makes an affectionate and protective companion. However, the people-loving Collie readily accepts visitors to the home and therefore does not make a good guard dog. An athletic breed, it is eager for fun and will take part with brio in canine sports such as agility trials.

The herding instinct has not been entirely bred out of Collies; their sharp awareness of movement may trigger an impulse to "round up" friends and family. Early socializing can prevent this trait from becoming a nuisance.

Like all breeds originally intended as working dogs, the Collie becomes restless when under-exercised or left alone for long periods, and may start to bark excessively. However, given an energetic daily run, it can be kept in a modestly sized house or large apartment.

This dog's long, thick coat needs regular grooming to prevent tangles and matting. More frequent grooming sessions may be needed when the dense undercoat is being shed, which occurs twice a year.

SMOOTH COLLIE

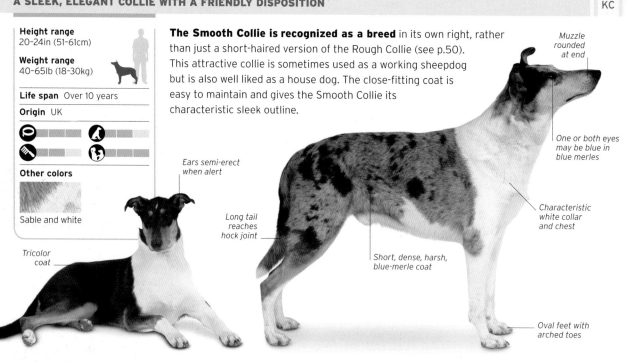

A SLEEK, ELEGANT COLLIE WITH A FRIENDLY DISPOSITION KC

Height range
20–24in (51–61cm)

Weight range
40–65lb (18–30kg)

Life span Over 10 years

Origin UK

Other colors

Sable and white

The Smooth Collie is recognized as a breed in its own right, rather than just a short-haired version of the Rough Collie (see p.50). This attractive collie is sometimes used as a working sheepdog but is also well liked as a house dog. The close-fitting coat is easy to maintain and gives the Smooth Collie its characteristic sleek outline.

Muzzle rounded at end

One or both eyes may be blue in blue merles

Ears semi-erect when alert

Characteristic white collar and chest

Long tail reaches hock joint

Tricolor coat

Short, dense, harsh, blue-merle coat

Oval feet with arched toes

SHETLAND SHEEPDOG

A GENTLE-NATURED, FAMILY-FRIENDLY DOG THAT HAS BOUNDLESS ENERGY AKC

Height range
14–15in (35–38cm)

Weight range
14–37lb (6–17kg)

Life span Over 10 years

Origin UK

Other colors

Sable | Blue merle

Black and tan | Black and white

First bred in the rugged Shetland Islands, beyond the northern coast of mainland Scotland, this miniature collie is hardy and resilient. Bursting with energy but easily trained and affectionate, the Shetland Sheepdog adapts well to family life and is a loyal pet. Regular grooming sessions are necessary to maintain the beautiful coat.

Black rim around eyes
Long, thick, tricolor coat
Close-set ears
Smooth hair on face
Dense mane
Long-haired tail

BORDER COLLIE

THIS SUPER-INTELLIGENT, ACTIVE DOG NEEDS AN EXPERIENCED OWNER

AKC

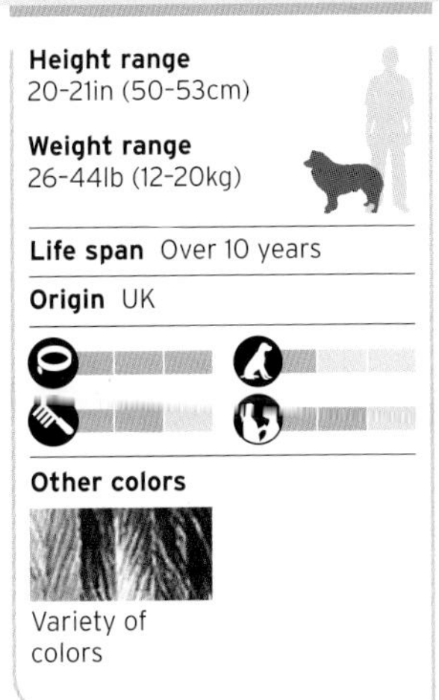

Height range
20–21in (50–53cm)

Weight range
26–44lb (12–20kg)

Life span Over 10 years

Origin UK

Other colors

Variety of colors

The Border Collie's reputation for intelligence reaches far beyond the borderland counties of the UK where it originated. Its excellence as a working sheepdog is legendary, and watching it in action at competitive events has become a popular spectator sport. Tireless energy, low boredom threshold, and an independent spirit make it an unsuitable pet for owners with restricted space or a sedentary lifestyle. However, this dog is highly responsive to experienced handling, and will reward commitment to training by becoming a faithful and obedient companion. The Border Collie has two coat varieties: smooth or moderately long.

Ears set well apart

Distinct stop

Muscular, athletic body

Low-set tail reaches hocks

Dense, black and white coat

Feathering on forelegs

Moderately long coat

POLISH LOWLAND SHEEPDOG

EASY TO TRAIN AS A SHEEPHERDER, GUARD DOG, OR COMPANION

AKC

Height range
17-20in (42-50cm)

Weight range
31-35lb (14-16kg)

Life span 12-15 years

Origin Poland

Other colors

Any color

Bred to work on the plainlands of Northern Europe as a herder and a guard dog, this delightfully shaggy dog is both rugged and agile. The Polish Lowland Sheepdog has brains as well as brawn and takes readily to training for a variety of purposes. Exercise and grooming should be high on its owner's agenda.

Long hair falls over eyes
Blunt muzzle
Heart-shaped drop ears hidden by hair
Thick, long, fluffy, black coat, fades with age
Oval-shaped feet

DUTCH SCHAPENDOES

THIS LITHE AND AGILE DOG WITH A JOYFUL TEMPERAMENT NEEDS TO BE FULLY OCCUPIED

FCI

Height range
16-20in (40-50cm)

Weight range
26-44lb (12-20kg)

Life span 13-14 years

Origin The Netherlands

Other colors

Any color

Swift, tireless, and intelligent, this breed is the perfect natural sheepherder. Moving as if on springs, a working Dutch Schapendoes can run at high speed and bound lightly over almost any obstacle in its path. The breed has the temperament to make a good companion but will not thrive without activity.

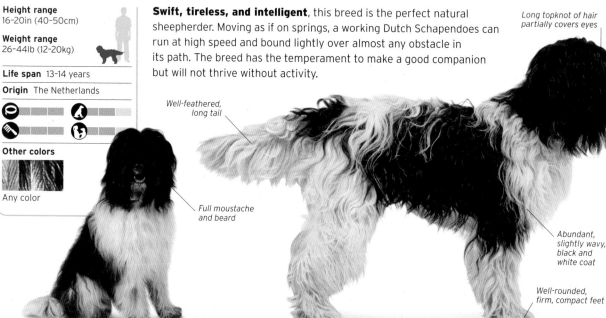

Long topknot of hair partially covers eyes

Well-feathered, long tail

Full moustache and beard

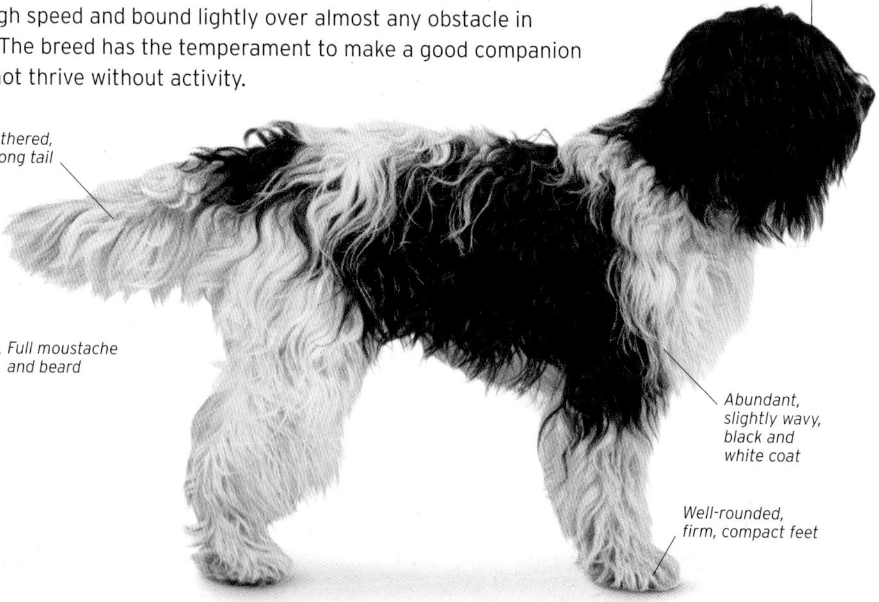

Abundant, slightly wavy, black and white coat

Well-rounded, firm, compact feet

SOUTH RUSSIAN SHEPHERD DOG

SAFE ONLY IN EXPERIENCED HANDS, THIS DOG NEEDS PLENTY OF UNDERSTANDING FCI

Height range
24-26in (62-65cm)

Weight range
106-110lb (48-50kg)

Life span 9-11 years

Origin Russia

Other colors

Ashen-gray

Straw

Yellow and white

This big sheepdog from the Russian steppes was bred not to round up flocks but to guard them against fierce predators. Quick to react, naturally dominant, and highly protective, the South Russian Shepherd Dog, also known as the Ovtcharka ("sheepherder" in Russian), needs an owner who can establish authority early on.

Elongated head with broad forehead
Long, dense, white coat with coarse texture
Smallish, triangular drop ears
Feet covered with long hair

CARDIGAN WELSH CORGI

A SMALL, STURDY, AND ACTIVE DOG WITH A STRONG PERSONALITY AKC

Height range
11-12in (28-31cm)

Weight range
24-37lb (11-17kg)

Life span 12-15 years

Origin UK

Other colors

Any color

White markings, if present, should not dominate.

The two varieties of Welsh Corgi were classified as separate breeds in the 1930s. Less popular as a house dog than its relative, the Pembroke Welsh Corgi (see p.56), the Cardigan Welsh Corgi can be distinguished by its larger round ears and longer body. Full of character, it fits well into a small home.

Large, erect ears, rounded at tips
Harsh-textured, short, brindle coat
Relatively long, low-slung body
Fox-like head
Short, sturdy legs
Long, heavy tail
Large, rounded feet

PEMBROKE WELSH CORGI

A SHARP AND CONFIDENT WATCHDOG WITH A BIG BARK FOR ITS SIZE

AKC

Height range
10-12in (25-30cm)

Weight range
20-26lb (9-12kg)

Life span 12-15 years

Origin UK

Other colors

Fawn and sable

The two breeds of Welsh Corgi have a long history as cattle-herders and guard dogs in Wales. The more widely known of the two breeds, the Pembroke Welsh Corgi, is distinguishable from the Cardigan Welsh Corgi (see p.55) by its slightly smaller ears and shorter tail. This alert and energetic little dog makes an excellent watchdog and enjoys family life. Their tendency to occasionally revert to their herding instincts and nip ankles can be minimized by early training. Pembroke Welsh Corgis tend to put on weight easily, so need a well-regulated regime of diet and exercise.

Red coat with white markings
Erect ears, rounded at tips
Tail carried low
Fox-like head with typical markings
Black and tan coat
Level topline
White markings on chest
Short legs

SWEDISH VALLHUND

THIS UNUSUAL BREED IS ALERT, FRIENDLY, AND WILLING TO PLEASE

AKC

Height range
12–14in (31–35cm)

Weight range
26–35lb (12–16kg)

Life span 12–14 years

Origin Sweden

Other colors

Steel-gray Red

Red and gray coats may be mixed with brown or yellow.

Like the Welsh Corgis (opposite and p.55), which at first glance it closely resembles, the Swedish Vallhund has been used for centuries as a cattle-herding dog. This tough and workmanlike breed continues to make itself useful on Swedish farms. The Swedish Vallhund is uncommon as a house dog but is gradually becoming more widely known and appreciated for its happy personality. It is lively and companionable, always alert, and eager to respond to its owner's demands. Kept active and occupied, the Swedish Vallhund is likely to enjoy robust health and a long lifespan.

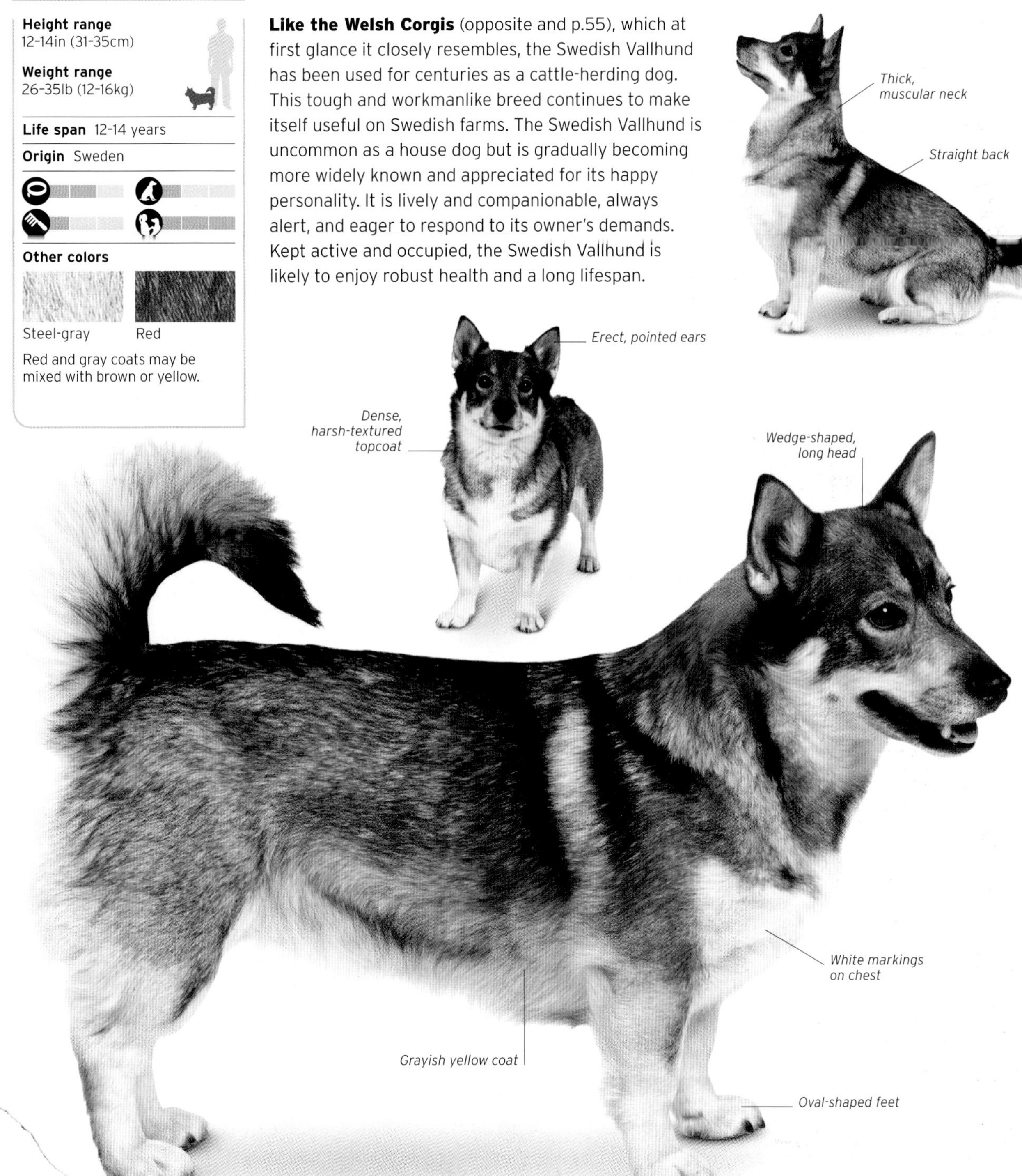
Thick, muscular neck
Straight back
Erect, pointed ears
Dense, harsh-textured topcoat
Wedge-shaped, long head
White markings on chest
Grayish yellow coat
Oval-shaped feet

NEW ZEALAND HUNTAWAY

THIS INTELLIGENT AND FRIENDLY DOG BARKS READILY

Height range
20-24in (50-61cm)

Weight range
40-65lb (18-30kg)

Life span 12-14 years

Origin New Zealand

Other colors

Tricolor

Dark brindle

Currently may still appear in other colors.

The New Zealand Huntaway lacks a breed standard and is not recognized by any kennel club due to its mixed breeding, which may include German Shepherd Dog (see p.35), Rottweiler (see p.81), and Border Collie (see p.53). Developed in New Zealand to be a working sheepdog, it is an excellent worker and is also gaining popularity as a house dog.

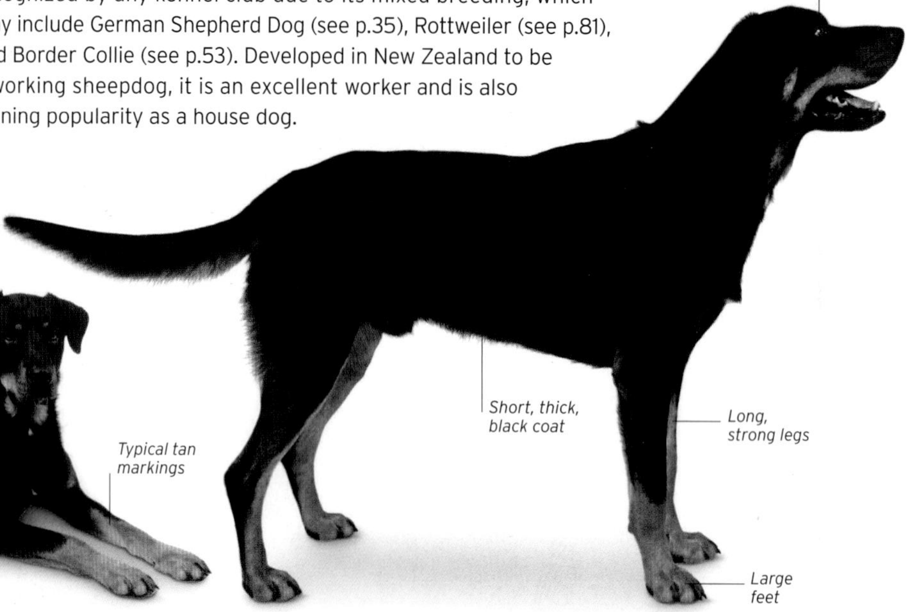

Bright-eyed, alert expression

Short, thick, black coat

Long, strong legs

Typical tan markings

Large feet

AUSTRALIAN KELPIE

A TOUGH, HARDY, AND TIRELESS DOG WITH A STRONG NATURAL HERDING INSTINCT FCI

Height range
17-20in (43-51cm)

Weight range
24-44lb (11-20kg)

Life span 10-14 years

Origin Australia

Other colors

Variety of colors

The Australian Kelpie was developed to work as a sheepdog in the vast open expanses of Australia. Energetic and agile, the breed has seemingly endless reserves of stamina, and a low boredom threshold. An all-action dog, it is best suited to a working life where its herding skills can be put to full use.

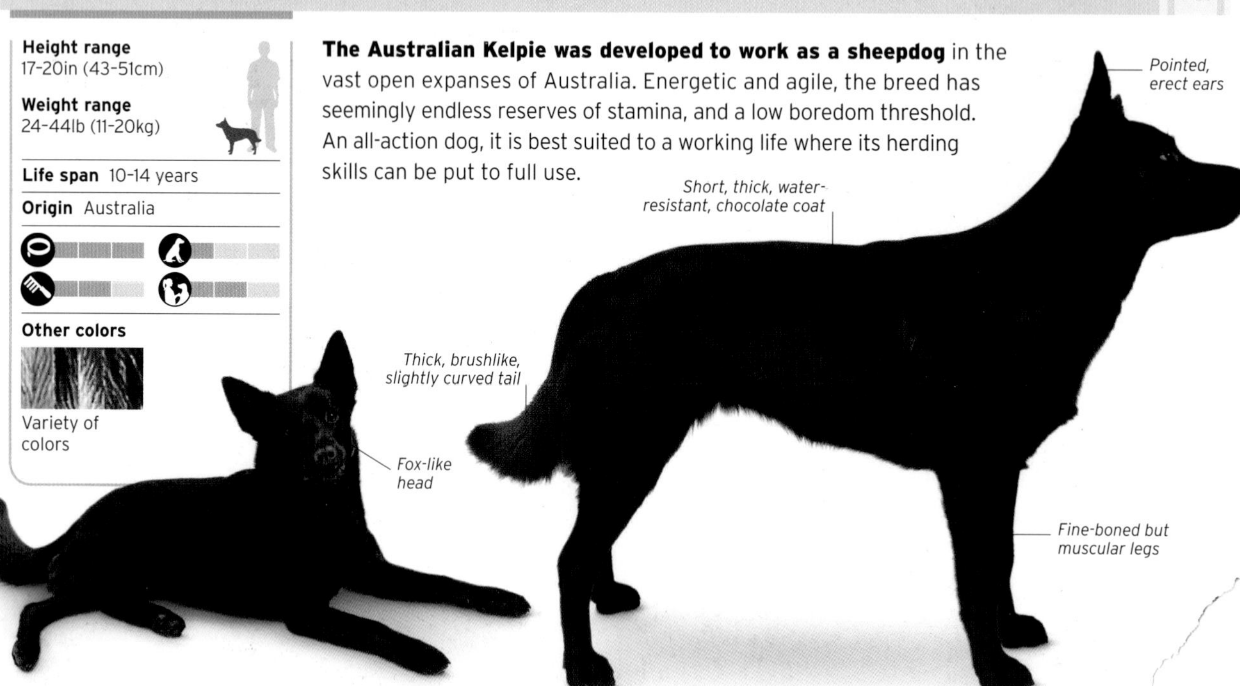
Pointed, erect ears
Short, thick, water-resistant, chocolate coat
Thick, brushlike, slightly curved tail
Fox-like head
Fine-boned but muscular legs

AUSTRALIAN CATTLE DOG

STRONG AND WORKMANLIKE, THIS TRUSTWORTHY DOG IS A LITTLE WARY OF STRANGERS AKC

Height range
17–20in (43–51cm)

Weight range
30–40lb (14–18kg)

Life span Over 10 years

Origin Australia

Once widely used for cattle-droving and guarding, this breed, also called the Australian Heeler, is little known outside its native country. It has many merits as a family dog, being hardy, alert, companionable, and loyal and devoted to its owner. However, an ancestry that includes the dingo (the wild dog of Australia) has made the Australian Cattle Dog naturally suspicious of strangers. Bred to work strenuous days and cover long distances, no exercise is too much for this energetic dog. Training is not difficult, because the dog is highly intelligent and willing to please.

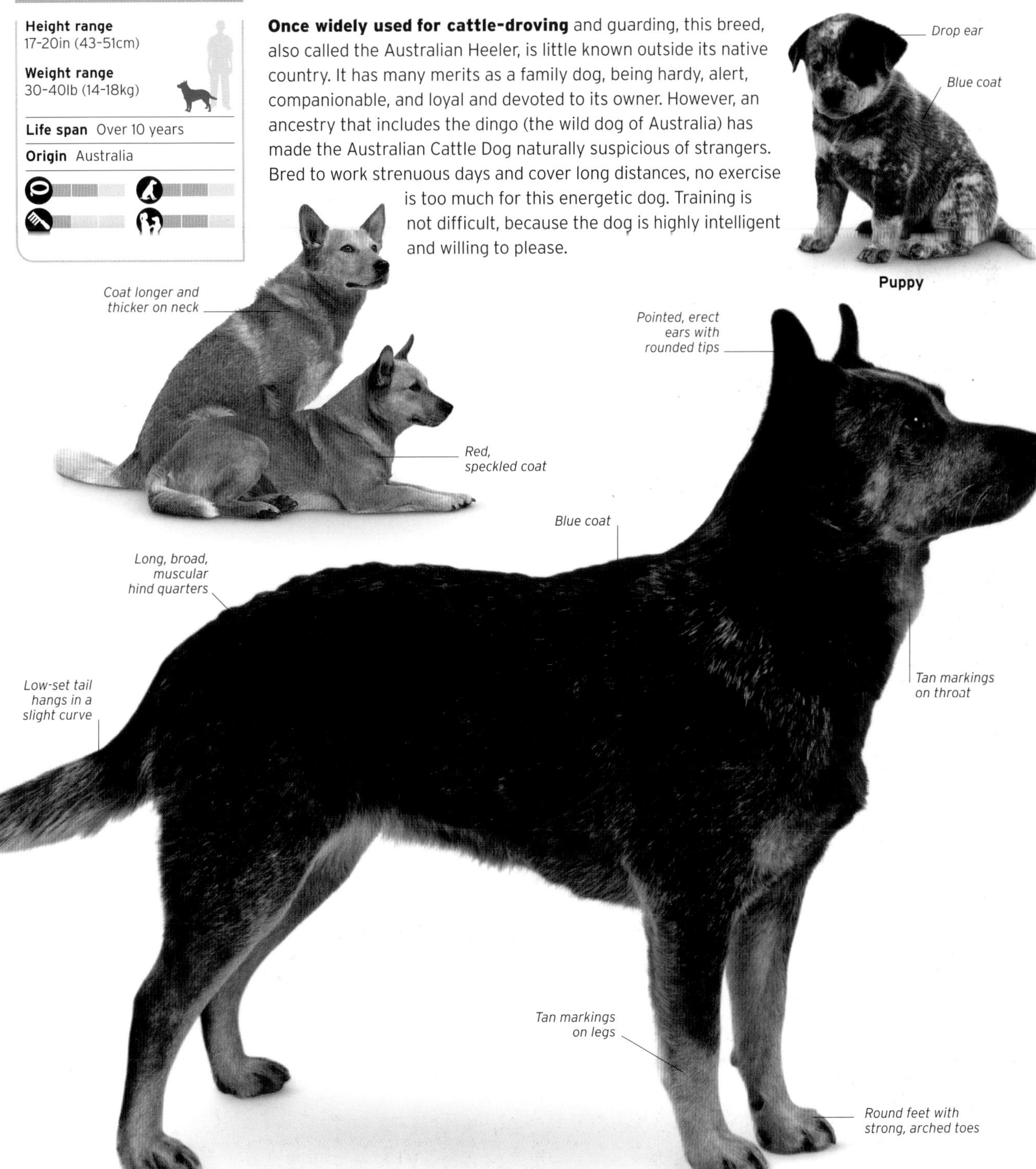
Drop ear
Blue coat
Coat longer and thicker on neck
Pointed, erect ears with rounded tips
Red, speckled coat
Blue coat
Long, broad, muscular hind quarters
Low-set tail hangs in a slight curve
Tan markings on throat
Tan markings on legs
Round feet with strong, arched toes

Puppy

LANCASHIRE HEELER

THIS EXUBERANT DOG LOVES TO PLAY AND RARELY HAS HEALTH PROBLEMS

KC

Height range
10–12in (25–30cm)

Weight range
9–15lb (4–7kg)

Life span 15 years

Origin UK

Other colors

Liver and tan

Intelligent, tough, and workmanlike, the Lancashire Heeler is well suited to its original use as a cattle-herder in the north of England. The breed may have been the result of crosses between the Pembroke Welsh Corgi (see p.56) and the Manchester Terrier (see p.211). Less inclined to be "nippy" than other heelers, this smart-looking little dog is good with families if trained carefully.

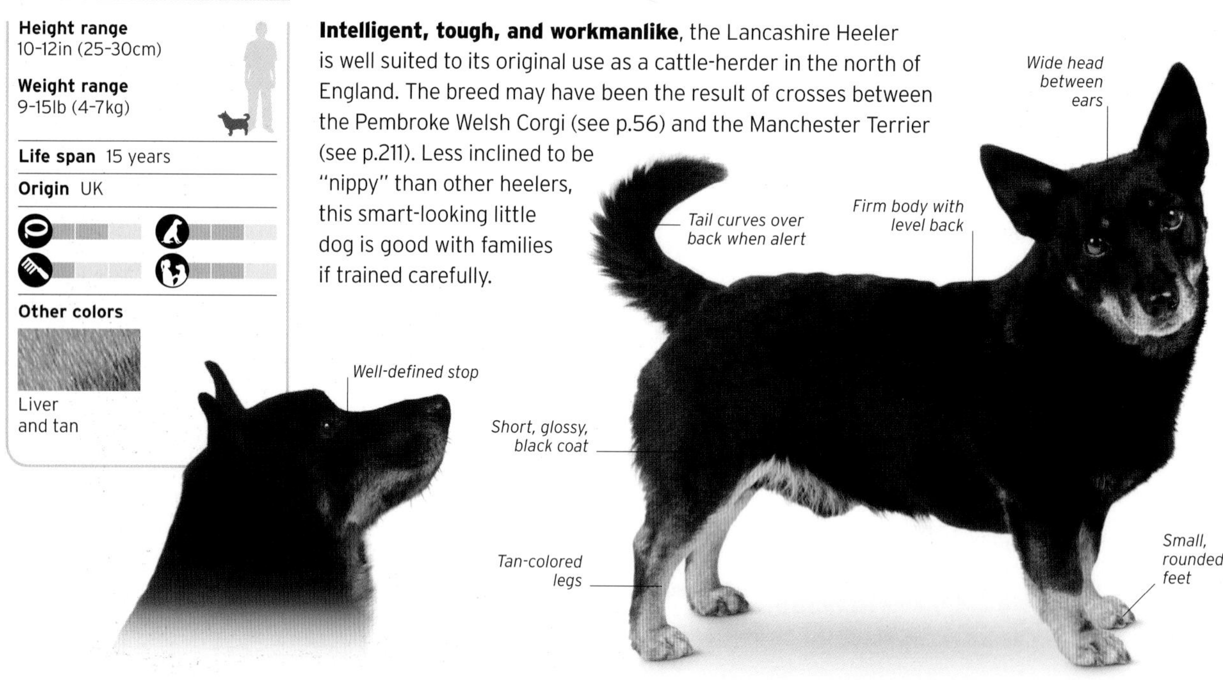
Wide head between ears
Firm body with level back
Tail curves over back when alert
Well-defined stop
Short, glossy, black coat
Tan-colored legs
Small, rounded feet

PUMI

THIS HERDING DOG HAS ADAPTED TO HOME LIFE

FCI

Height range
15–19in (38–47cm)

Weight range
18–33lb (8–15kg)

Life span 12–13 years

Origin Hungary

Other colors

Cream

Gray

Gold

Small, white markings may occur on chest and toes.

The Pumi was developed in Hungary during the 18th century as a cross between the Puli (opposite) and terrier-type dogs from Germany and France. An excellent herder of livestock and a good all-around farm dog, the Pumi has proved to be equally successful as a house dog. Bold and restless, this breed thrives on action.

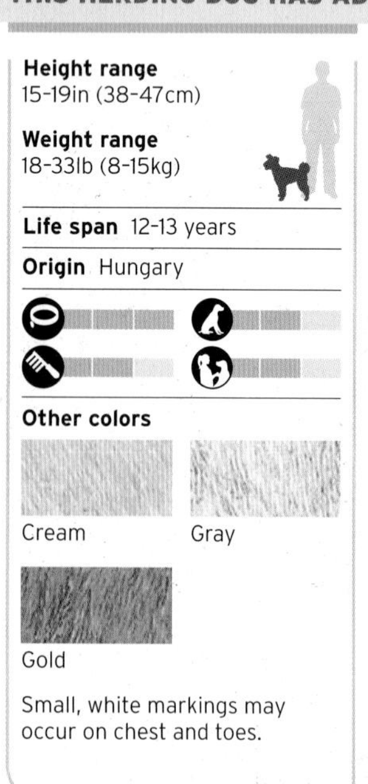
Narrow, terrier-like head
Well-muscled, lean body

Dense, wiry tufts on ears
High-set tail
Thick, curly, black coat

KOMONDOR

NOT FOR NOVICES, THIS DOG NEEDS TACTFUL HANDLING AND SPECIAL GROOMING AKC

Height range
24–31in (60–80cm)

Weight range
79–135lb (36–61kg)

Life span Under 10 years

Origin Hungary

The Komondor was bred to protect livestock, and has strong natural guarding instincts. This characteristic, combined with considerable size and strength, means that ownership should be considered only by those with plenty of dog-handling experience and space. Daily grooming is essential to maintain the Komondor's extraordinary tasselled coat.

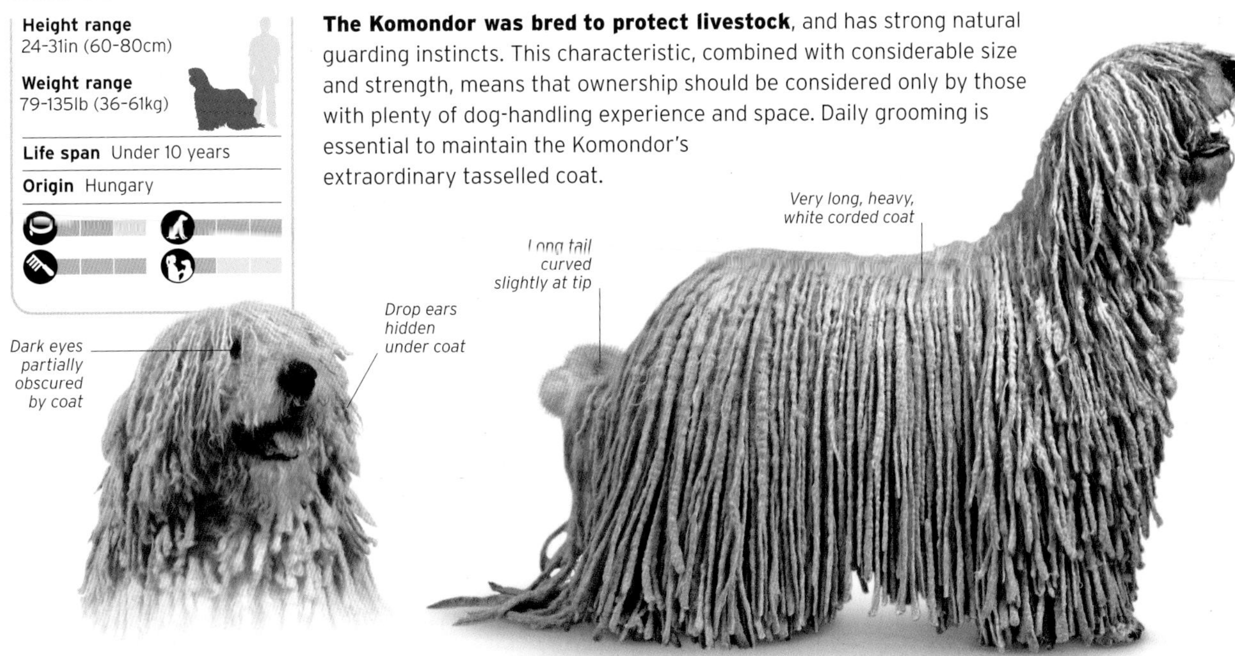
Very long, heavy, white corded coat
Long tail curved slightly at tip
Drop ears hidden under coat
Dark eyes partially obscured by coat

PULI

HIGHLY INTELLIGENT AND EAGER TO PLEASE, THIS DOG NEEDS TIME AND ATTENTION AKC

Height range
14–17in (36–44cm)

Weight range
22–33lb (10–15kg)

Life span Over 12 years

Origin Hungary

Other colors

White

Gray

Fawn

May have small, white marks on chest and feet.

Thought to have been brought into Central Europe by the nomadic Magyar tribes of Asia, the Puli was traditionally used as a herding dog. Affectionate and quick to learn, it makes a good family pet but gets bored easily without fun and company. Its corded coat needs special attention.

Small, black nose

Straight, muscular back

Eyes covered by long-corded, black coat

Profusely coated tail curls over back

Black coat forms long cords

Short, round feet

BERGAMASCO

THIS OUTDOOR DOG NEEDS PLENTY OF SPACE AND GROOMING KC

Height range
21-24in (54-62cm)

Weight range
57-84lb (26-38kg)

Life span Over 10 years

Origin Italy

Other colors

Light fawn (Isabella)

Black

May have white markings.

A sheepdog and guard dog, the powerful Bergamasco was bred for a tough, outdoor life in the northern Italian mountains. Its weatherproof coat is thick, greasy to the touch, and easily becomes matted, but once the coat becomes flocked, grooming time is greatly reduced. The Bergamasco is companionable and loyal but needs firm control.

Broad, straight back
Pronounced stop on skull covered by hair
Tail carried low
Flocked, gray coat

AIDI

PROTECTIVE AND LOVING WITH OWNERS, BUT NOT AN IDEAL HOUSE DOG FCI

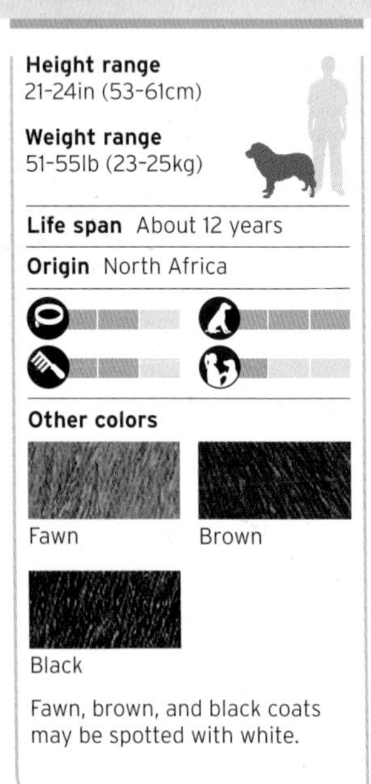

Height range
21-24in (53-61cm)

Weight range
51-55lb (23-25kg)

Life span About 12 years

Origin North Africa

Other colors

Fawn

Brown

Black

Fawn, brown, and black coats may be spotted with white.

Also known as the Atlas Mountain Dog, this type of dog has been used for centuries as a guard dog by the nomadic peoples of Morocco. The Aidi is faithful, fearless, and always on the alert to protect its owners and their possessions. But its strong guarding instincts mean that this dog is not always suited to a domestic lifestyle.

Wide-set, drop ears
Black lips
Black marking
Thick, medium-length, white coat
Long, bushy, low-set tail
Feathering on back of legs

AUSTRALIAN SHEPHERD

THIS EVEN-TEMPERED, INTELLIGENT DOG IS ADAPTABLE TO FAMILY LIFE

AKC

Height range
18-23in (46-58cm)

Weight range
40-64lb (18-29kg)

Life span Over 10 years

Origin USA

Other colors

Red, red merle — Black

All coats may have tan markings.

Not an "Aussie" at all, this shepherd dog was bred in the United States. Its name derives from its ancestors, which were worked by Basque shepherds who emigrated to Australia in the late 19th century and then later moved on to the US. The Australian Shepherd, still useful as a ranch dog and tracker, is becoming increasingly valued as a pet.

Pronounced stop
High-set, drop ears
Tan markings
White hairs extend across neck, chest, and legs
Thick, wavy, blue-merle coat
Bushy tail

MAREMMA SHEEPDOG

POWERFUL, PROTECTIVE, AND VERY MUCH AN OUTDOOR DOG

KC

Height range
24-29in (60-73cm)

Weight range
66-99lb (30-45kg)

Life span Over 10 years

Origin Italy

The sheepherders of the central Italian plains have long used the Maremma Sheepdog to guard their flocks. With an imposing stance and a magnificent, thick, white coat, this handsome dog has obvious attractions but needs expert handling. Like many dogs bred for outdoor work, this sheepdog is not the ideal choice for the home.

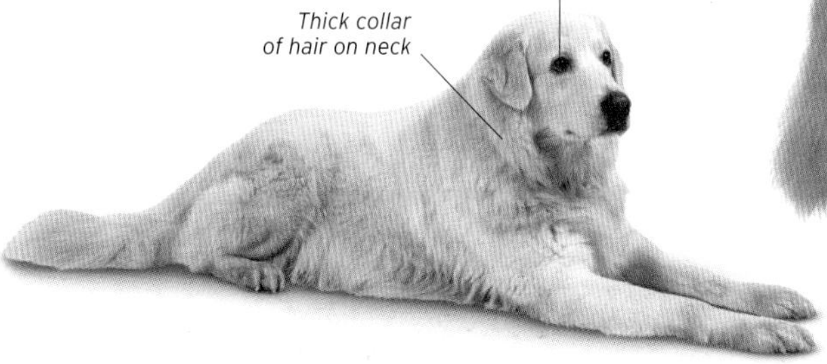

Short hair on face

Small ears hang flat at rest

Thickly haired, low-set tail

Black-rimmed eyes

Thick collar of hair on neck

Heavy, wavy, white coat

HELLENIC SHEPHERD DOG

THIS STRONG-WILLED BREED IS FRIENDLY WITH THOSE IT KNOWS BUT WARY OF STRANGERS

Height range
24–30in (60–75cm)

Weight range
71–110lb (32–50kg)

Life span 12 years

Origin Greece

Other colors

Variety of colors

The ancestors of this breed, which is also known as the Greek Sheepdog, may have been the sheepdogs brought into Greece many centuries ago by Turkish migrants. Tough, brave, and a natural guardian and flock leader, the Hellenic Shepherd Dog has excellent qualities for a working dog, but is too dominant in temperament to make a reliable family companion. There are two coat types: long-haired and short-haired.

Massive, flat-topped head
Dark brown eyes
Triangular, drop ears with darker edges
Abundant hair on tail
Dense, fawn coat with some sabling
Broad chest
White feet and legs

Long-haired

CURSINU

THIS LOYAL AND INTELLIGENT DOG IS ENERGETIC OUTDOORS BUT CALM IN THE HOUSE

Height range
18–23in (46–58cm)

Weight range
Not known

Life span Over 10 years

Origin France

Dogs of this type have existed on the island of Corsica for over a hundred years, although the Cursinu has only been recognized in France since 2003. Energetic, fast-moving, and versatile, it is used for both hunting and herding and although it can adapt to home life, it is probably at its best as a working dog.

High-set, semierect ears
Long tail, carried in curl when active
Short, muscular neck
Flat, wide head
Short to medium-length, fawn-brindle coat
White chest markings
White markings on feet
Long, hare-like feet

ROMANIAN SHEPHERD DOGS

THESE WATCHFUL AND COURAGEOUS DOGS NEED SPACE AND FREEDOM TO RUN

Height range
23–31in (59–78cm)

Weight range
77–154lb (35–70kg)

Life span 12–14 years

Origin Romania

Other colors

White-beige | Black

Bucovina only may appear as white, white-beige, black, or ashen-gray and may have patches of color.

In the mountainous Carpathian region of Romania, shepherds rely on large, robust dogs to guard their flocks in all weathers. Regional breeding has resulted in several distinct types: the Carpatin, the Bucovina, and the Mioritic. All are better suited to outdoor rather than indoor life, and none is widely known as a companion dog. With strong watchdog instincts, Romanian Shepherd Dogs are highly territorial and suspicious of strangers. They need plenty of physical and mental activity, as well as early socialization and firm training.

Coat longer than other Romanian Shepherd Dogs

White coat with light fawn and gray markings

Mioritic

Rough, slightly wavy hair

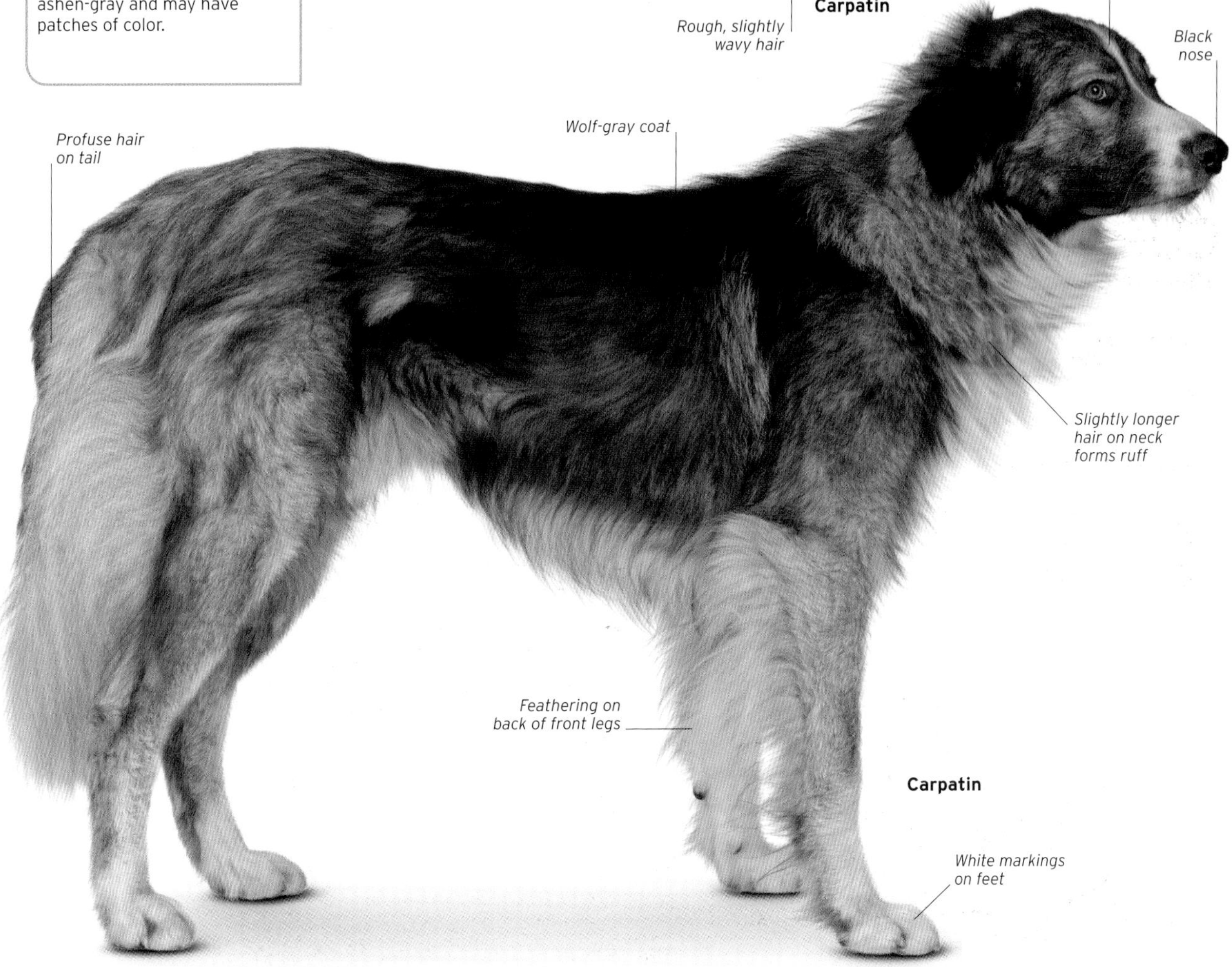

Carpatin

Blaze extends to muzzle

Black nose

Profuse hair on tail

Wolf-gray coat

Slightly longer hair on neck forms ruff

Feathering on back of front legs

Carpatin

White markings on feet

APPENZELL CATTLE DOG

THIS VERSATILE DOG IS WILLING TO WORK BUT ALSO ENJOYS FAMILY LIFE FCI

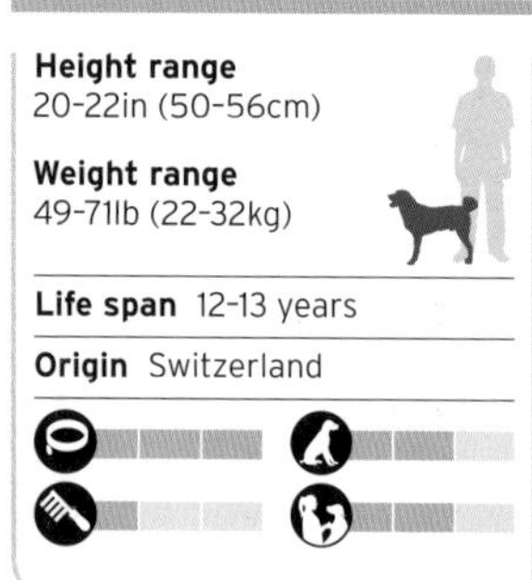

Height range 20–22in (50–56cm)

Weight range 49–71lb (22–32kg)

Life span 12–13 years

Origin Switzerland

Bred for herding and guarding on Alpine farms, the Appenzell Cattle Dog has also taken well to urban life. The breed has a firm following in Switzerland but is not yet widely known elsewhere. Keen, alert, and full of energy, Appenzells are at their best when kept occupied and interested.

White blaze extends to sides of muzzle
Drop ears, raised forward when alert
Tail carried in tight curl
Reddish brown markings on face
White chest
Dense, flat, shiny, tricolor coat

Small, almond-shaped eyes

White feet

ENTLEBUCHER MOUNTAIN DOG

SMART IN APPEARANCE, THIS FAMILY DOG IS FULL OF HIGH SPIRITS AKC

Height range 17–20in (42–50cm)

Weight range 47–62lb (21–28kg)

Life span 11–15 years

Origin Switzerland

The smallest of several long-established Swiss mountain dogs, this cattle-droving breed from the Entlebuch Valley is gaining popularity as a house dog. Bouncing with high spirits, the Entlebucher Mountain Dog is confident and well behaved within the family, but has strong protective instincts and is inclined to be wary around strangers.

High-set, drop ears
Back length longer than leg length
Reddish brown markings above eyes
White chest
Slightly curved, long tail
Short, harsh, glossy, tricolor coat
Reddish brown markings on legs

BERNESE MOUNTAIN DOG

A BEAUTIFULLY MARKED BREED WITH AN ATTRACTIVE PERSONALITY AND KIND NATURE AKC

Height range
23–28in (58–70cm)

Weight range
71–120lb (32–54kg)

Life span Under 10 years

Origin Switzerland

This lovely dog takes its name from the Swiss canton of Berne, where it traditionally worked as a haulage dog for basket-weavers. It is attractive not just in looks but also in temperament, and has become deservedly popular as a family dog. Although large and strong, the Bernese Mountain Dog is highly trainable and has gentle ways that are easy to live with. Generally, the breed is affectionate and reliable with children. The eye-catching tricolor coat needs plenty of grooming to maintain its silky texture and characteristic soft sheen.

Triangular, drop ears
White blaze on head
Broad head with well-defined stop
Long, bushy jet-black tail
Broad, deep chest with white markings
Long, silky, slightly wavy, tricolor coat
Reddish brown markings extend down to feet

GREATER SWISS MOUNTAIN DOG

THIS LARGE, POWERFUL, AND KIND DOG IS GOOD WITH CHILDREN AND OTHER PETS AKC

Height range 24–28in (60–72cm)

Weight range 80–130lb (36–59kg)

Life span 8–11 years

Origin Switzerland

Bred in the Swiss Alps, this huge, strong, striking dog was once used to haul wagons loaded with milk, cheese, and other produce. The Greater Swiss Mountain Dog was also used for cattle-herding and guard duties. The dog had all but disappeared by the beginning of the 20th century, but breeding by enthusiasts saved it from extinction; however, it is still rare. A true working dog, the Greater Swiss Mountain Dog has an agreeable temperament that makes it a sociable family companion for those with room to spare.

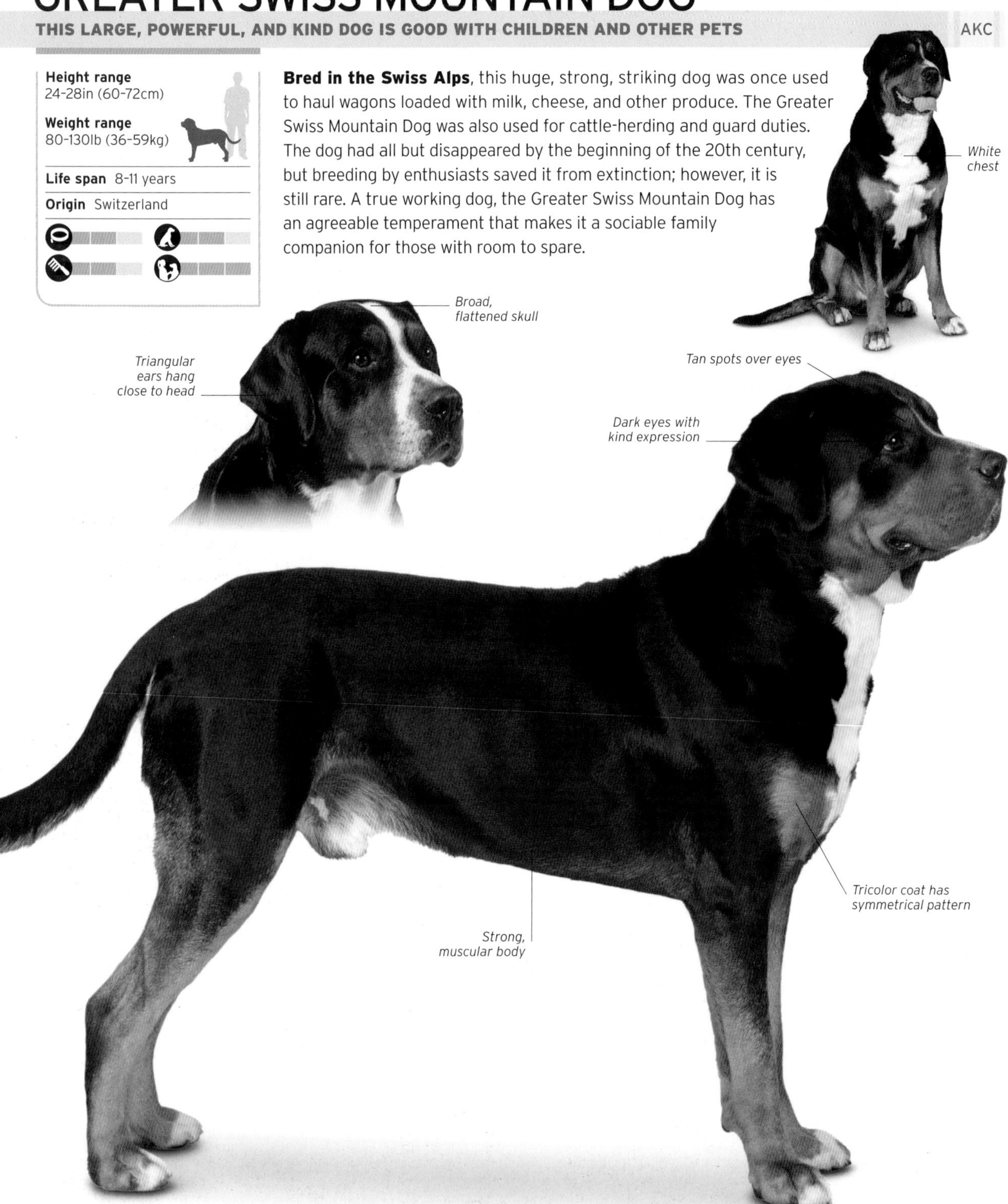
White chest
Broad, flattened skull
Triangular ears hang close to head
Tan spots over eyes
Dark eyes with kind expression
Tricolor coat has symmetrical pattern
Strong, muscular body

WHITE SWISS SHEPHERD DOG

THIS FAMILY-FRIENDLY DOG LIKES CHILDREN BUT CAN BE WARY OF STRANGERS

FCI

Height range
21–26in (53–66cm)

Weight range
55–88lb (25–40kg)

Life span 8–11 years

Origin Switzerland

Pure white shepherd dogs were first brought into Switzerland from North America in the 1970s. Developed over the next two decades, it was recognized in Switzerland as a breed in 1991. Good-tempered and intelligent, it is suitable for both work and companionship. There are two coat types: medium-haired and long-haired.

High-set, erect ears
Arched neck with longer hair
Dark eyes
Bushy tail
White coat
Long-haired

ANATOLIAN SHEPHERD DOG

THIS PROTECTIVE AND LOYAL DOG NEEDS SUPERVISION WITH CHILDREN AND STRANGERS

AKC

Height range
28–32in (71–81cm)

Weight range
90–141lb (41–64kg)

Life span 12–15 years

Origin Turkey

Other colors

Any color

After a long history as a livestock-guardian, this hardy and powerful breed is still used in Turkey as a working dog. Bred for its courage and independence of spirit, the Anatolian Shepherd Dog respects the authority of a firm and loving owner. If kept as a companion dog, training and socializing should begin early.

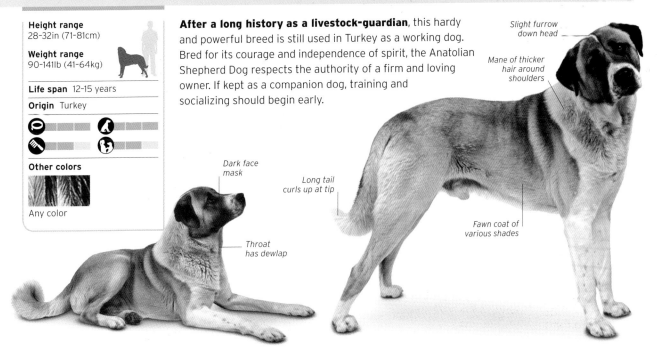

Slight furrow down head

Mane of thicker hair around shoulders

Dark face mask

Long tail curls up at tip

Fawn coat of various shades

Throat has dewlap

AKBASH

THIS HIGHLY PROTECTIVE DOG NEEDS AN EXPERIENCED OWNER

Height range
27–31in (69–79cm)

Weight range
75–130lb (34–59kg)

Life span 10–11 years

Origin Turkey

A powerful Turkish breed developed for guarding flocks, Akbash-type dogs have probably been around for several thousands of years. Used on ranches in North America as a livestock and property guard, the Akbash is best suited to a working life and needs skilled handling to avoid behavior problems. There are two coat types: long-haired and medium-haired.

Triangular, drop ears

Shorter hair on face

Weatherproof, coarse, white coat

Heavily feathered tail

Biscuit-colored shading

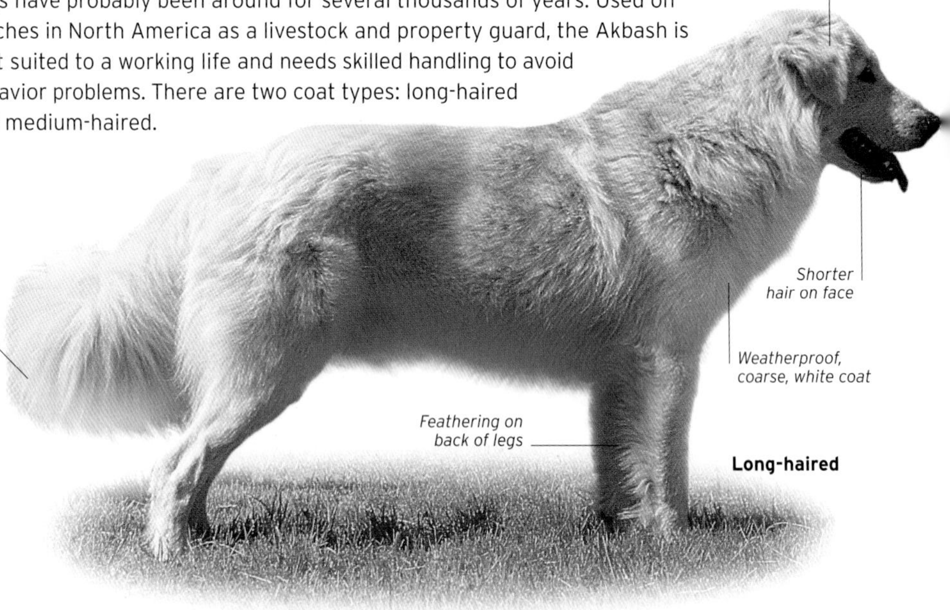

Feathering on back of legs

Long-haired

CENTRAL ASIAN SHEPHERD DOG

NOT AN IDEAL FAMILY DOG, THIS BREED NEEDS A PATIENT AND STRONG-WILLED OWNER FCI

Height range
26–31in (65–78cm)

Weight range
88–174lb (40–79kg)

Life span 12–14 years

Origin Central Asian Republics

Other colors

Variety of colors

The nomadic herdsmen of Central Asia—the regions now known as Kazakhstan, Turkmenistan, Tajikistan, Uzbekistan, and Kyrgyzstan—have used dogs of this type to protect their flocks for hundreds of years. Once bred selectively in the former USSR, this rare breed needs early socialization. There are two coat types: short-haired and long-haired.

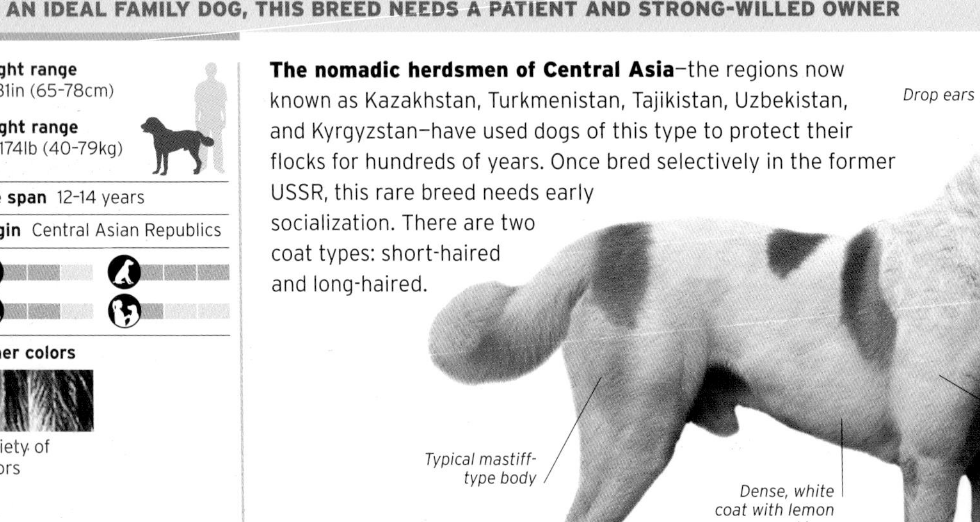

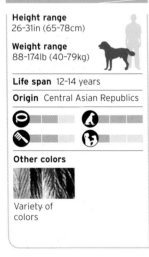

Moderate stop
Drop ears
Powerful shoulders
Typical mastiff-type body
Dense, white coat with lemon markings
Large, rounded feet

Short-haired

CAUCASIAN SHEPHERD DOG

THIS FIERCELY PROTECTIVE DOG DOES NOT MAKE AN IDEAL PET

FCI

Height range
26–30in (67–75cm)

Weight range
99–154lb (45–70kg)

Life span 10–11 years

Origin Russia

Other colors

Variety of colors

Developed from various large dogs, this shepherd dog was once used to guard flocks in the Caucasian regions. In the 1920s selective breeding of this dog began in the former USSR and continued later in Germany. An excellent watchdog, it needs careful handling if it is to be a good companion.

Massive head

Triangular, drop ears with rounded tips

Heavily feathered tail

Deep chest

Dense, coarse, sable coat stands away from body

Feet thickly insulated with white hair

Darker muzzle

Puppy

LEONBERGER

THIS EXCELLENT FAMILY DOG IS GOOD-TEMPERED, CALM, AND FRIENDLY

AKC

Height range
28–31in (72–80cm)

Weight range
99–170lb (45–77kg)

Life span Over 10 years

Origin Germany

Other colors

Sandy

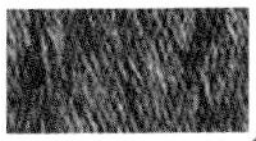

Red

May have white markings.

Named after the Bavarian town of Leonberg, the Leonberger was developed in the mid-19th century as a result of cross-breeding between the Saint Bernard (see p.72) and the Newfoundland (see p.74). After the two World Wars Leonbergers had almost disappeared, but the breed has recovered well and gained wide popularity for its splendid looks and friendly nature.

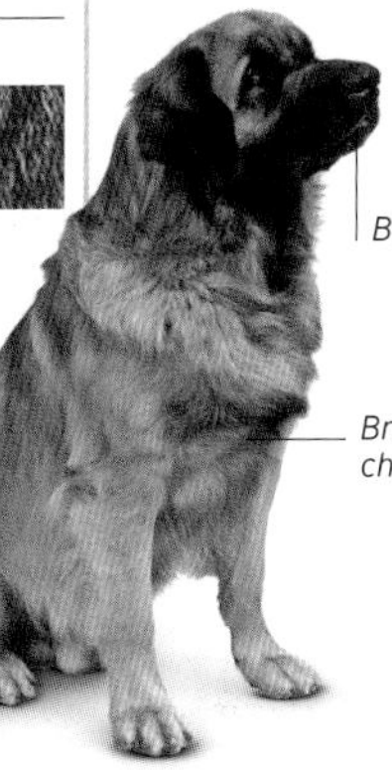

Feathered, high-set ears

Black tips to some hair

Mane on neck and chest

Thick, fairly long, lion-gold coat

Slightly tucked-up belly

Feathered forelegs

Black mask

Broad chest

Feathered tail, lighter on underside

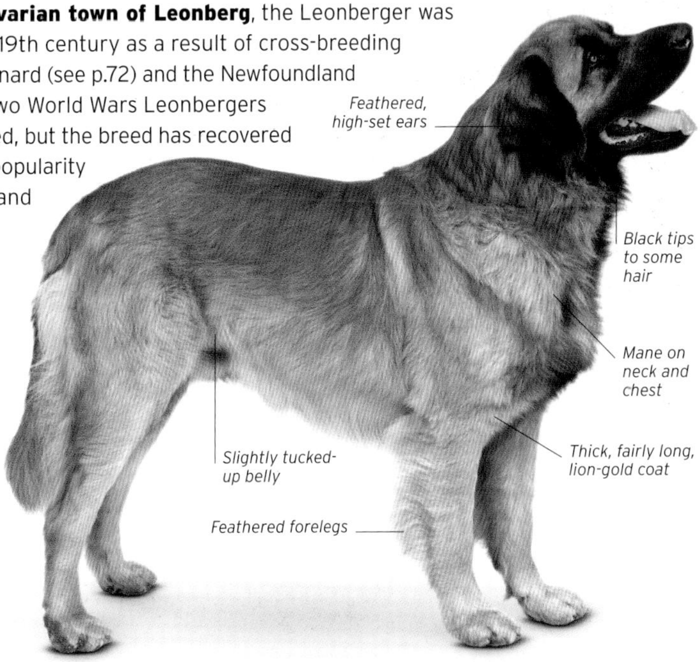

SAINT BERNARD

ALMOST UNRIVALED FOR SIZE, THIS KINDLY GIANT HAS A DELIGHTFUL TEMPERAMENT AKC

Height range
28-30in (70-75cm)

Weight range
130-180lb (59-81kg)

Life span 8-10 years

Origin Switzerland

Other colors

Brindle

Originally crossbred from mastiff-type dogs by the monks of St. Bernard's Hospice in the Swiss Alps, this breed's sometimes exaggerated reputation as a mountain rescue dog extends worldwide. Affectionate and utterly trustworthy, the Saint Bernard has many virtues. It is calm-natured, taking life at a moderate pace. The Saint Bernard is comparatively rare as a house dog due to its colossal size, and the amount of space needed to accommodate its sheer bulk can hardly be over-estimated; food bills are another major consideration. There are two coat types: smooth and rough.

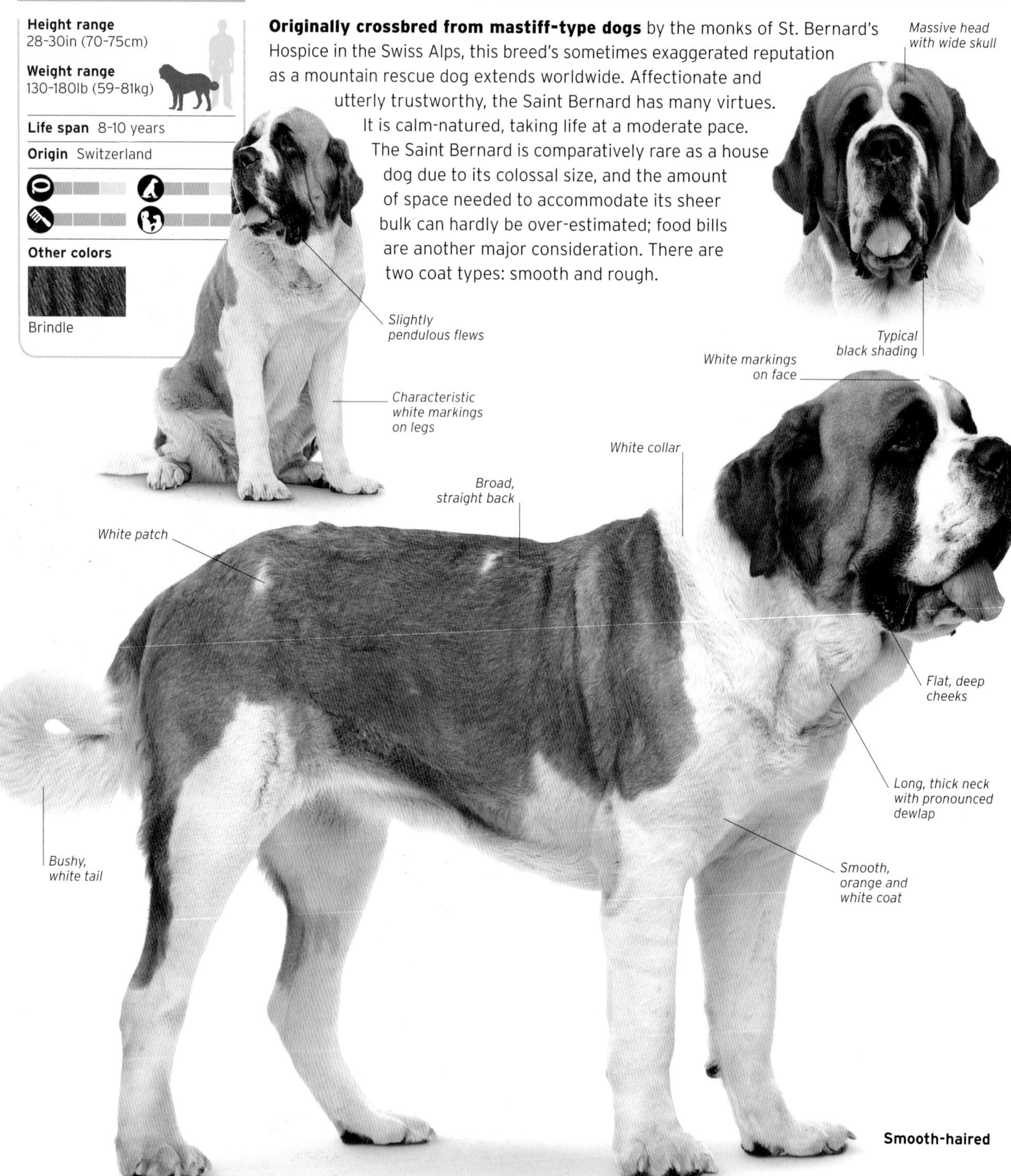
Massive head with wide skull
Typical black shading
Slightly pendulous flews
Characteristic white markings on legs
White markings on face
White collar
Broad, straight back
White patch
Flat, deep cheeks
Long, thick neck with pronounced dewlap
Bushy, white tail
Smooth, orange and white coat

Smooth-haired

TATRA SHEPHERD DOG

ALTHOUGH CALM WITH THE FAMILY, THIS DOG DOES NOT TAKE KINDLY TO STRANGERS

FCI

Height range 24–28in (60–70cm)

Weight range 79–130lb (36–59kg)

Life span 10–12 years

Origin Poland

Still used for protecting and herding flocks in the high Tatra mountains of Poland, this huge and handsome dog takes its duties just as seriously when guarding home and household. Usually gentle and well-mannered with those it knows, the Tatra Shepherd Dog is a force to be reckoned with if it perceives a threat. Firm and fair handling by an experienced owner, and a watchful eye for potential aggression, are essential if this breed is to be kept as a companion. The dog's extremely thick coat sheds heavily and requires frequent grooming.

Massively built body
Triangular drop ears with rounded tips
Black nose with wide nostrils
Long tail reaches hocks
Dense, slightly wavy, white coat
Lips and eyes have dark edges
Deep mane around neck
Hair shorter on lower legs and paws

NEWFOUNDLAND

A COLOSSAL BUT GENTLE AND FRIENDLY DOG WITH A LOVE OF SWIMMING AKC

Height range 26–28in (66–71cm)

Weight range 110–152lb (50–69kg)

Life span 9–11 years

Origin Canada

Other colors

Dark brown

Although the Newfoundland is associated with the Canadian province of the same name, the dog's true origins are uncertain. Historically used by fishermen to retrieve nets, today it is sometimes used for sea rescues. The breed has a protective nature and is renowned for being gentle with children. Its large size rules this dog out as a pet for a small home.

Massive head
Bushy tail
Dense, coarse, slightly oily, black coat
Small, white markings on chest
Feathered forelegs
Large feet

LANDSEER

A BLACK AND WHITE NEWFOUNDLAND MADE FAMOUS BY AN ARTIST FCI

Height range 26–28in (66–71cm)

Weight range 110–152lb (50–69kg)

Life span 9–11 years

Origin Canada

This color variant of the Newfoundland (above) is regarded as a distinct breed in some countries. The Landseer is named after the mid-Victorian British painter Sir Edwin Landseer, who often painted these dogs. Apart from its bicolored coat, this dog shares all the attributes of solid-colored Newfoundlands, being placid, friendly, and dependable.

Distinctive, black saddle

Black head with well-developed stop

Strong neck

Black and white coat

Short hair in front of legs, feathered behind

PYRENEAN MOUNTAIN DOG

THIS GIANT-SIZED DOG IS SATISFIED WITH MODERATE EXERCISE AND LOVES FAMILY LIFE

KC

Height range
26–28in (65–70cm)

Weight range
88–110lb (40–50kg)

Life span 9–11 years

Origin France

Other colors

Pure white

One of the most imposing of all dogs, this breed comes from the French Pyrenees, where its traditional role was as a guarder of flocks. Thoroughly assimilated into modern family life, the Pyrenean Mountain Dog is calm-natured and unaggressive, reliable in the home, and good with children. Despite the dog's huge size and strength, it does not need an excessive amount of exercise and can be quite content with a gentle stroll. However, owners should be prepared to put their energies into grooming to keep the dog's thick coat looking its best.

Tan patches on head
Smallish, triangular ears
Heavy mane around neck and shoulders
Dark amber-colored eyes with black rims
Dense, wavy, white coat
Plumed tail
Tan patch on rump
Double dewclaws on hind legs, hidden by hair

PYRENEAN MASTIFF

A GENERALLY GOOD-NATURED DOG WITH A NOBLE ATTITUDE, BUT SUSPICIOUS OF STRANGERS

KC

Height range 28–32in (72–81cm)

Weight range 120–155lb (54–70kg)

Life span 10 years

Origin Spain

A native of Spain, the Pyrenean Mastiff was originally kept for guarding mountain flocks. Large and courageous enough to take on a bear or a wolf, this breed is now often used as a house guard. Intelligent and calm, with the right training it can also be a good companion dog.

Dense, bristly textured, white coat
Small, almond-shaped eyes
Long, plumed tail
Well-defined face mask
Irregular patch same color as face mask
Double dewlap

TIBETAN KYI APSO

A RARE MOUNTAIN DOG, POSSESSIVE OF HOME AND FAMILY

Height range 22–28in (56–71cm)

Weight range 68–84lb (31–38kg)

Life span 7–10 years

Origin Tibet

Other colors

Any color

Only a handful of Kyi Apsos have appeared outside Tibet and the breed is elusive even in its own country. Traditionally, this dog is a guard of flocks and homes. The Tibetan Kyi Apso has a characteristic springy gait, and is agile and capable of rapid bursts of speed.

Low-set, pendant ears
Tail carried high in a curl
Bearded face
Neck broad relative to body
Strong hind quarters
Dense, wiry, black coat

TIBETAN MASTIFF

ONE OF THE SMALLER MASTIFFS, THIS DOG MAY TAKE TIME TO TRAIN AND SOCIALIZE

AKC

Height range
24–26in (61–66cm)

Weight range
185–309lb (84–140kg)

Life span Over 10 years

Origin Tibet

Other colors

Slate-gray

Gold

Black and gray dogs may have tan markings.

With a history of guarding the livestock of nomadic shepherds in the Himalayas, the Tibetan Mastiff has strong protective instincts. In its native country, it can still be a dog to approach with caution. However, in the West, over a hundred years of selective breeding has greatly reduced the Tibetan Mastiff's tendency to be aggressive. It has become an acceptable house dog and a good companion, although not overtly affectionate. The Tibetan Mastiff takes time to reach full maturity, and needs a patient owner to give it a thorough and steady training.

White star on chest
Tan markings above eyes
Short-haired, drop ears
Bushy tail carried curled over back
Powerful jaws
Coat forms mane around neck and shoulders
Dense, straight, black coat
Feathering between toes

SLOVAKIAN CHUVACH

THIS TOUGH AND FEARLESS DOG MAKES AN EXCELLENT HOUSE DOG GIVEN THE RIGHT TRAINING FCI

Height range 23-28in (59-70cm)

Weight range 68-97lb (31-44kg)

Life span 11-13 years

Origin Slovakia

Originally a shepherd's guard dog from the Slovakian Alps, the Slovakian Chuvach has been developed successfully into a good house dog. This large, powerful breed retains the exceptional alertness and watchfulness that made it a superb defender of farms and livestock. Tactful training is needed to achieve the best results with this breed.

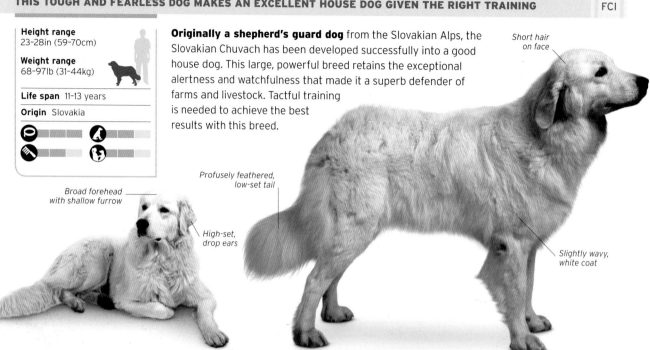

Short hair on face

Profusely feathered, low-set tail

Broad forehead with shallow furrow

High-set, drop ears

Slightly wavy, white coat

KUVASZ

CAN BE AFFECTIONATE, BUT THIS DOG MAY TURN AGGRESSIVE WHEN DEFENDING AKC

Height range 26-30in (66-75cm)

Weight range 70-115lb (32-52kg)

Life span 10-12 years

Origin Hungary

Probably the oldest and best known of Hungary's breeds, the Kuvasz was once used as a shepherd's guard dog. The breed's naturally protective instincts may lead to aggressiveness, and this dog has the potential to become a liability in inexperienced hands. It takes firm training to make the Kuvasz an acceptable house dog.

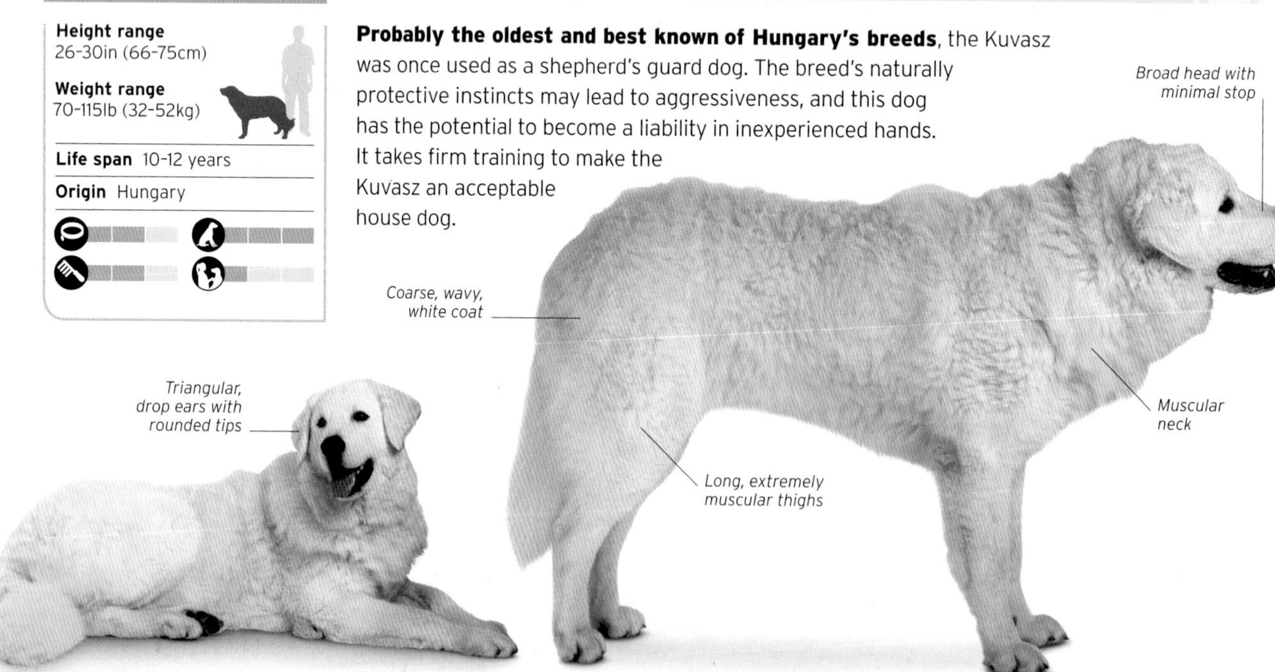
Broad head with minimal stop
Coarse, wavy, white coat
Triangular, drop ears with rounded tips
Muscular neck
Long, extremely muscular thighs

HOVAWART

THIS VERY HARDY, FAITHFUL COMPANION MAY TRY TO DOMINATE OTHER DOGS

KC

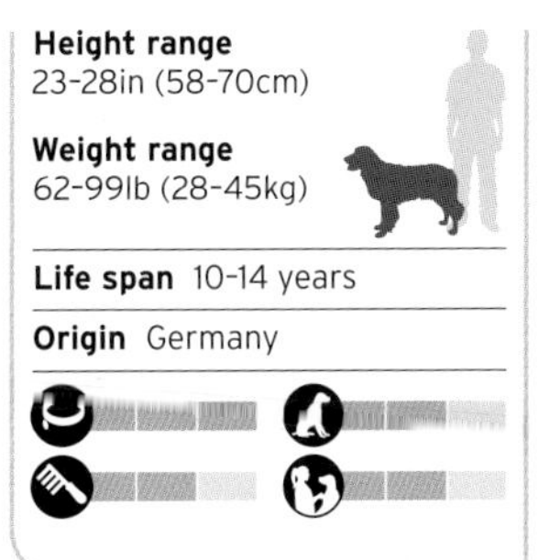

Height range
23–28in (58–70cm)

Weight range
62–99lb (28–45kg)

Life span 10–14 years

Origin Germany

Little known as a companion dog but growing in popularity, the Hovawart has a very long history—its forerunners are thought to have been used as farm dogs in the 13th century. The modern breed was developed in Germany in the first half of the 20th century. The Hovawart is very hardy, ready to go outdoors whatever the weather, and is a friendly and faithful house dog within a family. Although it has a strong-willed personality, the Hovawart is not difficult to train but may need careful handling in the presence of other dogs.

Black and gold coat

Triangular, drop ears

Medium-length, blonde coat

Bushy tail, may show a few white hairs

Skull and muzzle equal in length

Dense, black coat

Feathering on forelegs may be very long

Oval feet with arched toes

BEAUCERON

THIS ACTIVE DOG LOVES WORK BUT NEEDS CAREFUL SOCIALIZATION AKC

Height range
25–28in (63–70cm)

Weight range
65–85lb (29–39kg)

Life span 10–15 years

Origin France

Other colors

Gray, black, and tan

May have a few white chest hairs.

A herding and guard dog from the flatlands of the Beauce region in Central France, the Beauceron is an excellent worker and, in the right situation, a gentle family companion. This big, strong dog can be intolerant of other dogs; early training is needed to minimize potential problems.

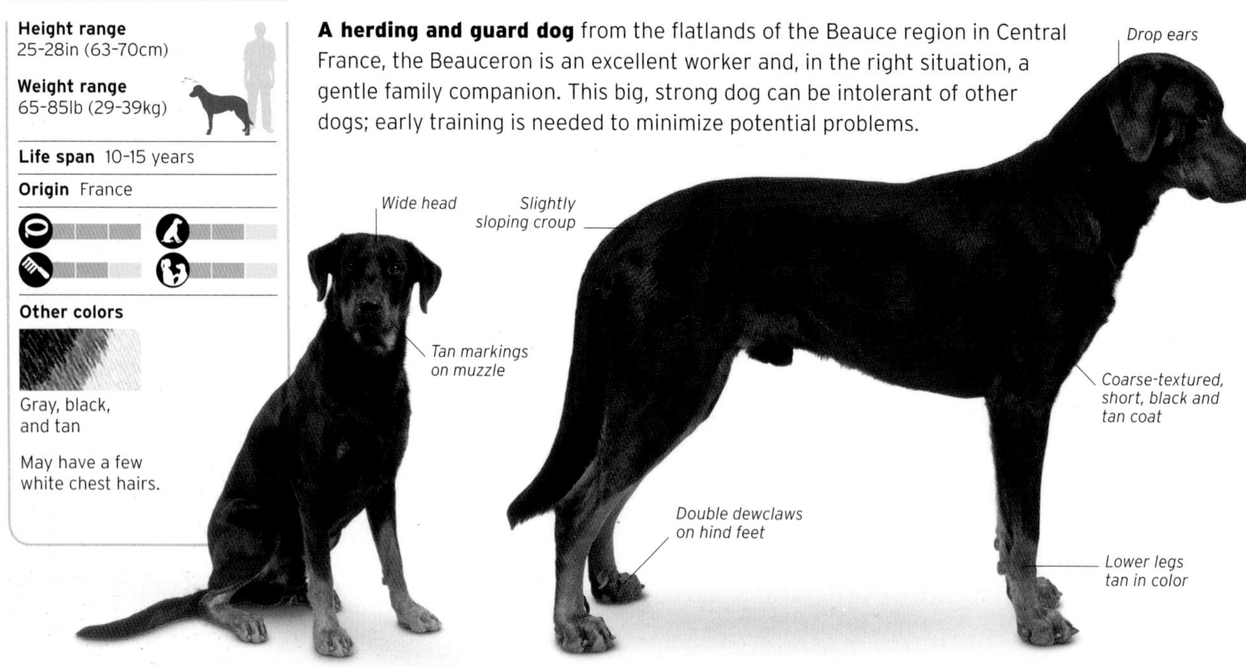

Drop ears
Wide head
Slightly sloping croup
Tan markings on muzzle
Coarse-textured, short, black and tan coat
Double dewclaws on hind feet
Lower legs tan in color

MAJORCA SHEPHERD DOG

MUCH VALUED IN ITS NATIVE COUNTRY, THIS BREED IS LITTLE KNOWN ELSEWHERE FCI

Height range
24–29in (62–73cm)

Weight range
77–88lb (35–40kg)

Life span 11–13 years

Origin Spain

Comparatively rare worldwide, the Majorca Shepherd Dog is regarded with pride in Majorca, where it was once widely used as a shepherd dog, and is now popular as a show dog. Although usually willing to obey, this breed has strong herding instincts and can be defensive with strangers and other dogs.

Small, wide-set eyes

Tapering tail

Short, black coat

Small feet, with arched toes

ROTTWEILER

A BIG AND BURLY DOG SUITED TO FIRM AND RESPONSIBLE OWNERS AKC

Height range 23-27in (58-69cm)

Weight range 84-130lb (38-59kg)

Life span 10-11 years

Origin Germany

Once used in southern Germany as a cattle dog, the Rottweiler has acquired an unfortunate image as a vicious guard dog and an intimidating status symbol. However, despite the breed's great strength, impressive swagger, and easily aroused protective responses, the Rottweiler is not naturally ill-tempered. With thoughtful training from a firm and experienced owner, who is alert to potential triggers of aggression, this dog makes a calm and obedient companion. Rottweilers are more agile than their size and sturdy build might suggest, and appreciate plenty of vigorous exercise.

Tan markings clearly defined on head
Small, drop ears
Broad, deep chest
Broad head with well-defined stop
Deep muzzle with firm flews
Short, smooth, shiny, black and tan coat
Tan chest markings
Tan markings on legs

CHINESE SHAR PEI

A GENERALLY FRIENDLY TEMPERAMENT IS HIDDEN BEHIND THIS DOG'S SCOWLING FACE AKC

Height range 18–20in (46–51cm)

Weight range 40–55lb (18–25kg)

Life span Over 10 years

Origin China

Other colors

Variety of colors

The early uses of this native Chinese breed included herding and guarding livestock, hunting, and fighting. However, the Chinese Shar Pei's amiable nature and relatively compact size make it suitable as a pet for a town or country home. The dog's distinctive appearance has huge popular appeal and, at least for a while, owning one was a fashion statement. Some breeders sought to increase the Chinese Shar Pei's wrinkly looks by producing dogs with excessively loose and folded facial skin. However, this resulted in eye problems, and the practice is now largely discredited.

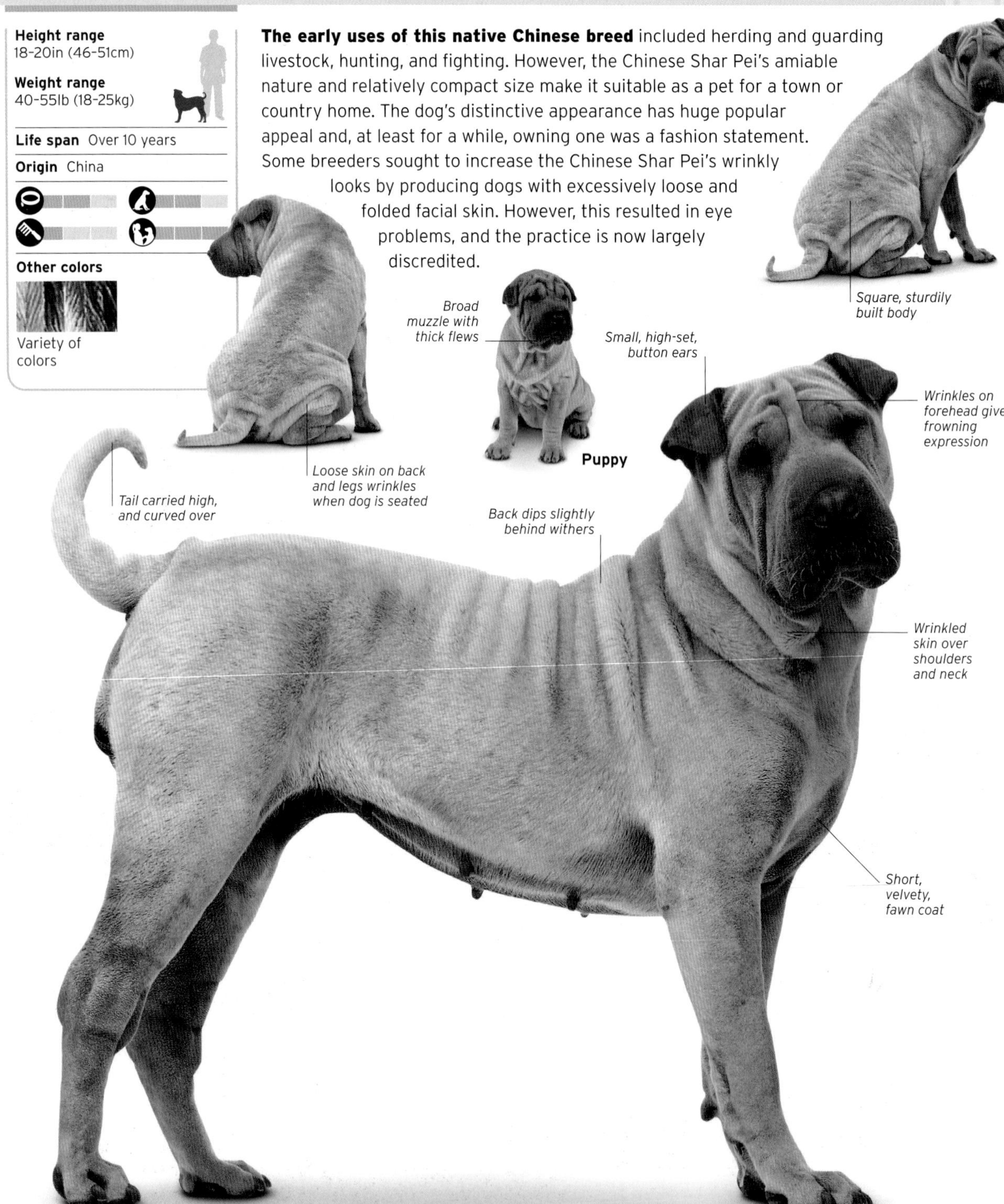
Square, sturdily built body
Broad muzzle with thick flews
Small, high-set, button ears
Wrinkles on forehead give frowning expression
Puppy
Loose skin on back and legs wrinkles when dog is seated
Tail carried high, and curved over
Back dips slightly behind withers
Wrinkled skin over shoulders and neck
Short, velvety, fawn coat

TAIWAN DOG

THIS BREED NEEDS WIDE OPEN SPACES AND IS INCLINED TO CHASE SMALL ANIMALS

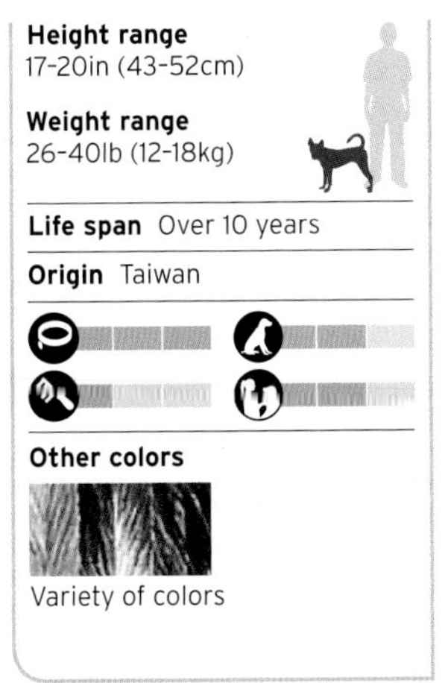

Height range 17–20in (43–52cm)

Weight range 26–40lb (12–18kg)

Life span Over 10 years

Origin Taiwan

Other colors

Variety of colors

The Taiwan Dog, formerly known as the Formosan Mountain Dog, is something of a rarity, even in its native country. It is believed to have descended from the semi-wild dogs once used for hunting in the interior of Taiwan. The breed makes an intelligent family dog, but its hunting instincts need to be kept in check.

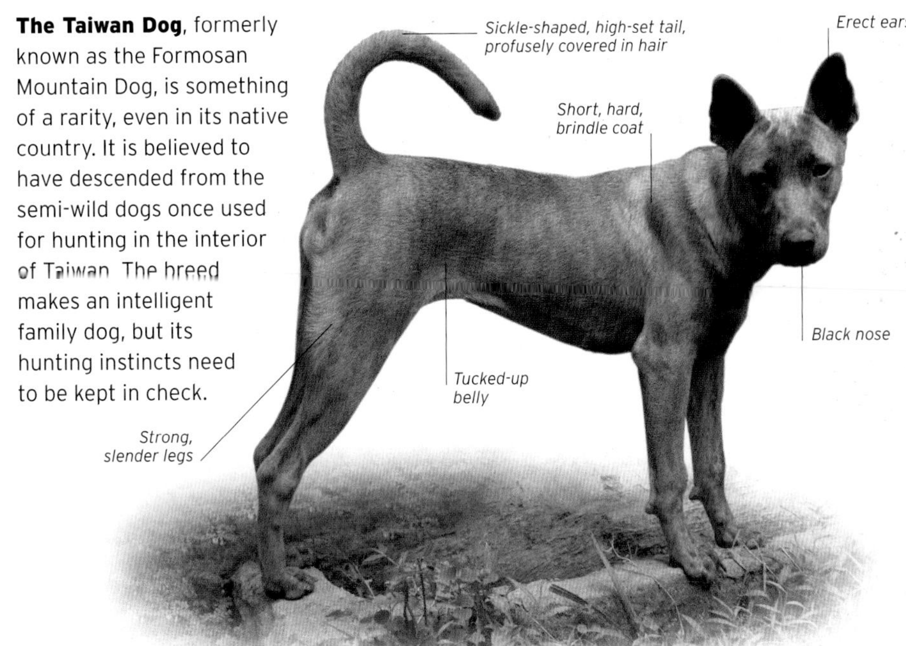
Sickle-shaped, high-set tail, profusely covered in hair
Erect ears
Short, hard, brindle coat
Black nose
Tucked-up belly
Strong, slender legs

MALLORCA MASTIFF

THIS SUPERB WATCHDOG COMBINES COURAGE WITH A CALM TEMPERAMENT FCI

Height range 20–23in (52–58cm)

Weight range 66–84lb (30–38kg)

Life span 10–12 years

Origin Spain

Other colors

Black

The Mallorca Mastiff, also known as the Ca de Bou, has a background that includes fighting and bull-baiting. A powerful breed, it has the typical mastiff-type build and watchful nature. When handled firmly but quietly, this dog socializes well but it is probably better suited to life as a guard dog rather than as a family pet.

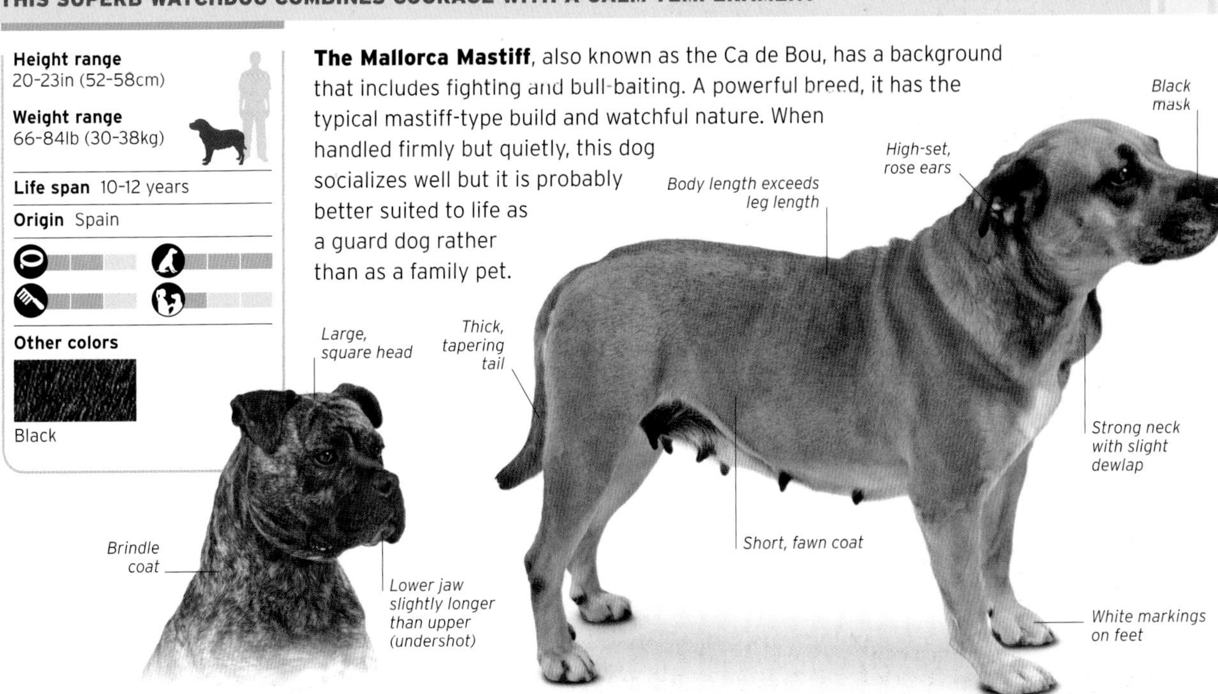
Black mask
High-set, rose ears
Body length exceeds leg length
Large, square head
Thick, tapering tail
Strong neck with slight dewlap
Short, fawn coat
Brindle coat
Lower jaw slightly longer than upper (undershot)
White markings on feet

DOGO CANARIO

LARGE, POWERFUL, AND VERY STRONG-WILLED, THIS DOG IS NOT FOR NOVICE OWNERS FCI

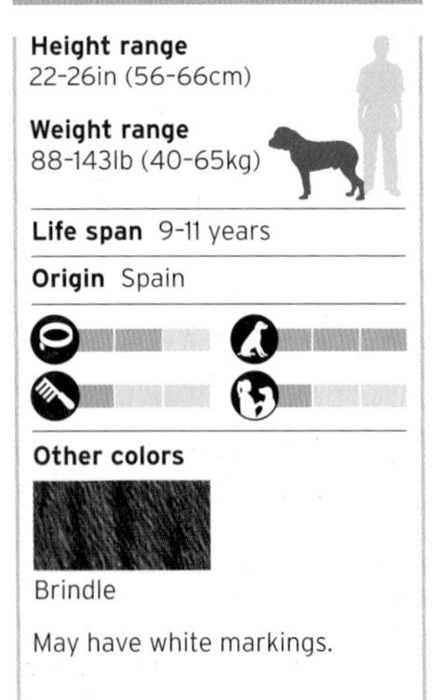

Height range 22–26in (56–66cm)

Weight range 88–143lb (40–65kg)

Life span 9–11 years

Origin Spain

Other colors

Brindle

May have white markings.

Bred in the Canary Islands in the early 19th century as a fighting dog, the Dogo Canario is believed to include the Mastiff (see p.93) in its ancestry. Difficult to train and socialize, a Dogo Canario is manageable if the owner understands and controls the dog's dominant nature. Early socialization is essential.

Square head with powerful jaw
Drop ears
Short, fawn coat
Darker muzzle
Pronounced dewlap
Tail extends to hock
Muscular body
Large, round, cat-like feet

DOGO ARGENTINO

BRED FOR HUNTING, THIS IS A GOOD-NATURED DOG IF SOCIALIZED WELL FCI

Height range 24–27in (60–68cm)

Weight range 79–99lb (36–45kg)

Life span 10–12 years

Origin Argentina

Originating in the 1920s in Cordoba, Argentina, the Dogo Argentino was the creation of a local doctor who wanted a dog for hunting large game. Breeding from old fighting dogs such as mastiffs and the Bulldog (see p.94) produced this new dog. The Dogo Argentino has a kind temperament but can be overprotective.

Characteristic, slightly concave muzzle
Body length exceeds leg length
Long, thick tail
Short, white coat
Strong neck with skin folds at throat
Broad, deep chest
Powerful hind quarters
Round feet

FILA BRASILEIRO

THIS COURAGEOUS AND SELF-CONFIDENT DOG CAN BE WARY OF STRANGERS

FCI

Height range
24–30in (60–75cm)

Weight range
Over 88lb (over 40kg)

Life span 9–11 years

Origin Brazil

Other colors

Any solid color

Bred to guard large estates and livestock, the Fila Brasileiro does not fear intruders of any kind. Huge but beautifully proportioned, this dog exudes confidence and determination. Although the Fila Brasileiro is kind and quiet within a family, the average owner may find the breed's hunting and protective instincts difficult to manage.

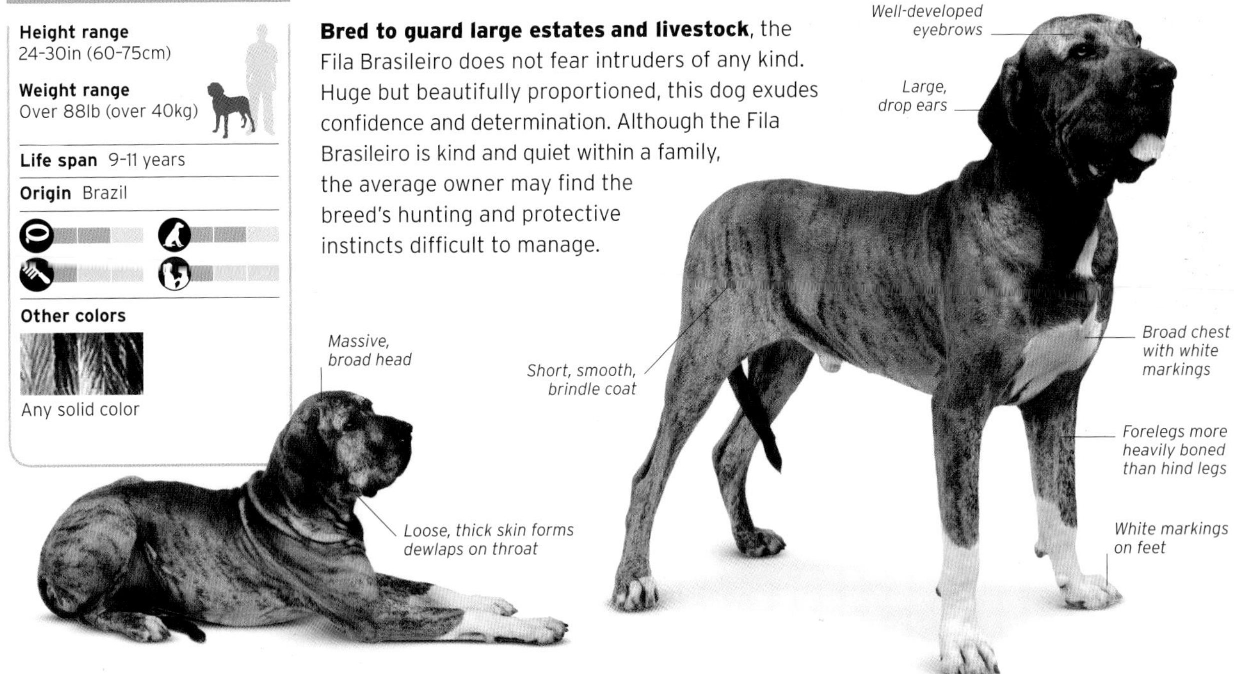
Well-developed eyebrows
Large, drop ears
Massive, broad head
Short, smooth, brindle coat
Broad chest with white markings
Forelegs more heavily boned than hind legs
Loose, thick skin forms dewlaps on throat
White markings on feet

URUGUAYAN CIMARRON

THIS INTELLIGENT AND AGILE DOG NEEDS EARLY SOCIALIZING BUT MAKES A GOOD GUARD DOG

Height range
22–24in (55–61cm)

Weight range
73–99lb (33–45kg)

Life span 10–13 years

Origin Uruguay

Other colors

Fawn

Fawn coats may have black shading.

The ancestors of this breed were brought into Uruguay by Spanish and Portuguese colonists and crossed with local dogs. Bred by farmers in the remote area of Cerro Largo, the Uruguayan Cimarron was used for guarding and herding. Like many working breeds, it needs an experienced owner if kept as a companion.

Triangular ears with rounded tips

Dark muzzle

Muscular, well-defined hind quarters

Strong, powerful jaws

Deep, broad chest

Close-fitting, short-haired, brindle coat

White chest markings

Thick tail reaches hocks

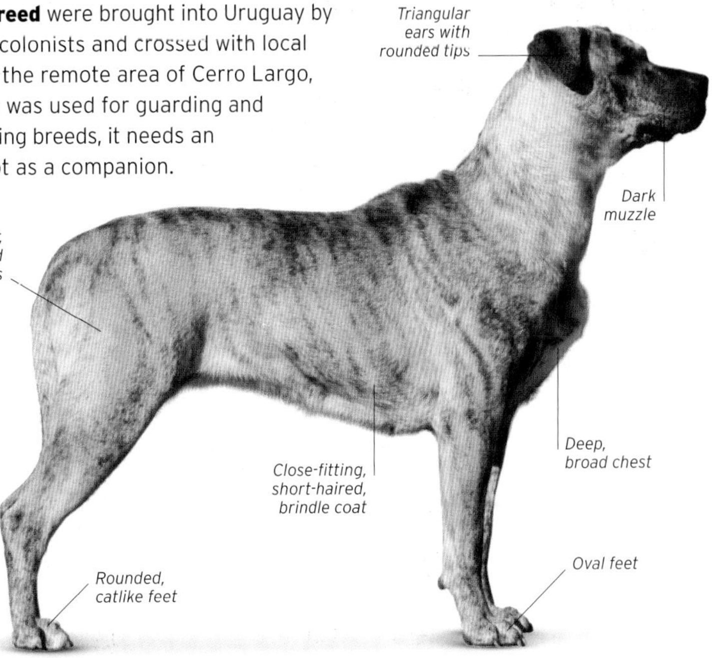

Rounded, catlike feet

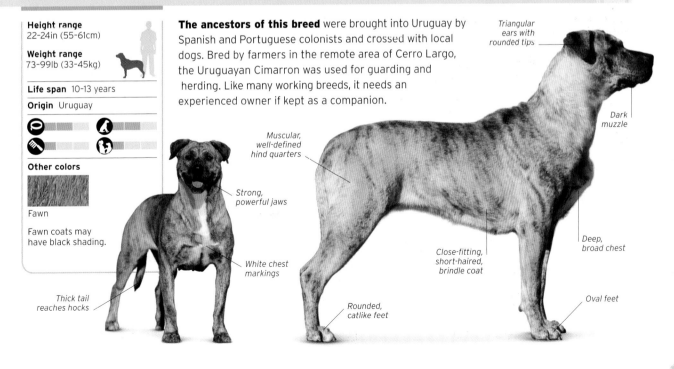

Oval feet

ALAPAHA BLUE BLOOD BULLDOG

IF GIVEN REGULAR EXERCISE, THIS IS A GOOD DOG IN THE HOME BUT NEEDS CAREFUL TRAINING

Height range
18–24in (46–61cm)

Weight range
55–90lb (25–41kg)

Life span 12–15 years

Origin USA

Other colors

White

Dogs may have patches of any color.

Bulldog-type dogs were once commonly used as guards in the plantations of southern Georgia. By the early 19th century such dogs were almost extinct, but dedicated breeding over the next 200 years regenerated the type and produced the Alapaha Blue Blood Bulldog. This dog is still rare and not widely known outside the United States. Muscular and intrepid, an Alapaha Blue Blood Bulldog has strong protective instincts, but it is easy to train to be a well-behaved and affectionate companion. Energetic outdoors, this dog is happiest when given plenty of exercise.

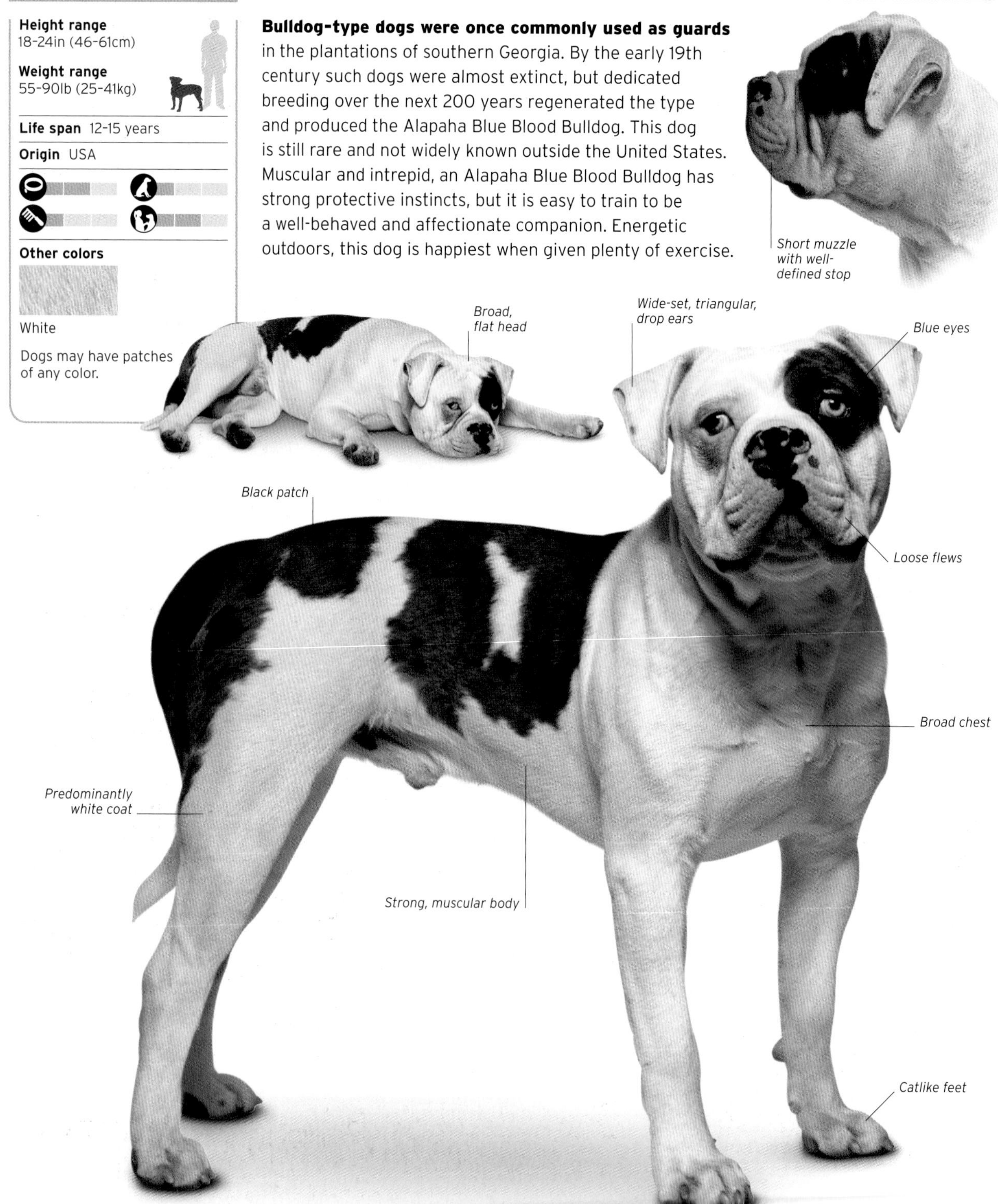
Short muzzle with well-defined stop
Broad, flat head
Wide-set, triangular, drop ears
Blue eyes
Black patch
Loose flews
Broad chest
Predominantly white coat
Strong, muscular body
Catlike feet

BOERBOEL

THIS DOG LOVES FAMILY BUT NOT STRANGERS AND REQUIRES RESPONSIBLE OWNERSHIP

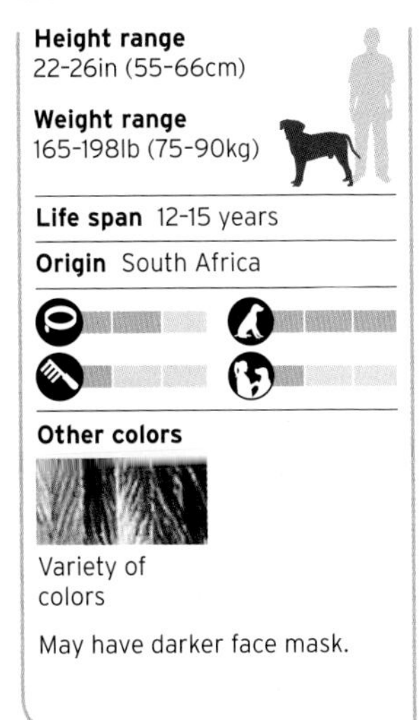

Height range
22–26in (55–66cm)
Weight range
165–198lb (75–90kg)
Life span 12–15 years
Origin South Africa
Other colors
Variety of colors
May have darker face mask.

The Boerboel was developed from the large, mastiff-type dogs brought by settlers to the Cape area of South Africa from the 17th century onward. Affectionate with family and friends, the Boerboel is a formidable guard dog of huge size and strength. An experienced owner and early socialization are very important.

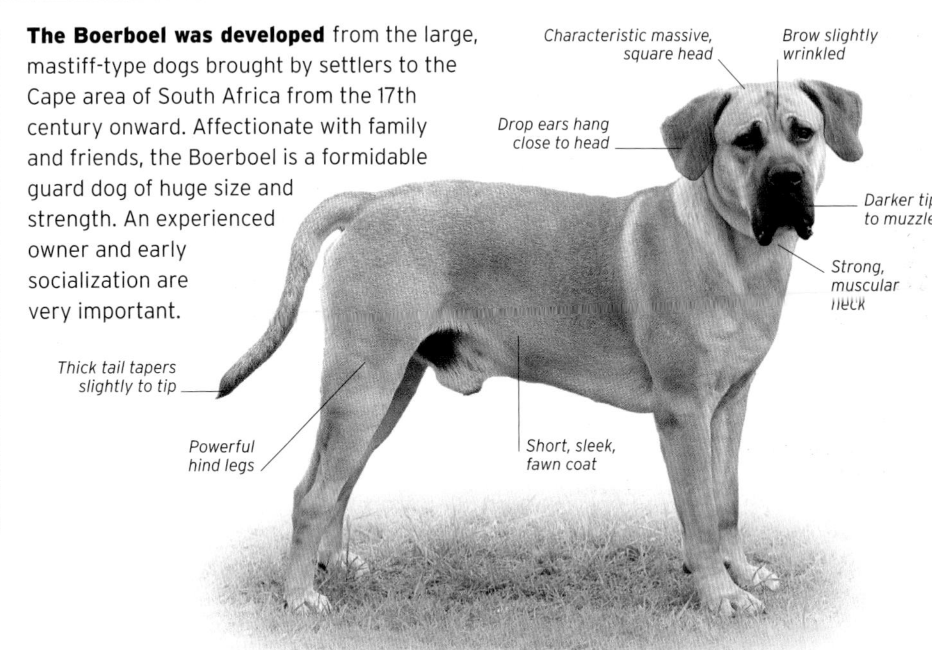

Characteristic massive, square head
Brow slightly wrinkled
Drop ears hang close to head
Darker tip to muzzle
Strong, muscular neck
Thick tail tapers slightly to tip
Powerful hind legs
Short, sleek, fawn coat

SPANISH MASTIFF

A HEAVYWEIGHT DEFENDER OF HOME AND FAMILY, THIS TERRITORIAL MASTIFF NEEDS EXPERT HANDLING FCI

Once used for guarding livestock and homes in Spain, the Spanish Mastiff still carries out its traditional duties. The breed is also popular in its native country as a companion dog. Kind and loyal within the family, this breed can be aggressive with strangers and other dogs.

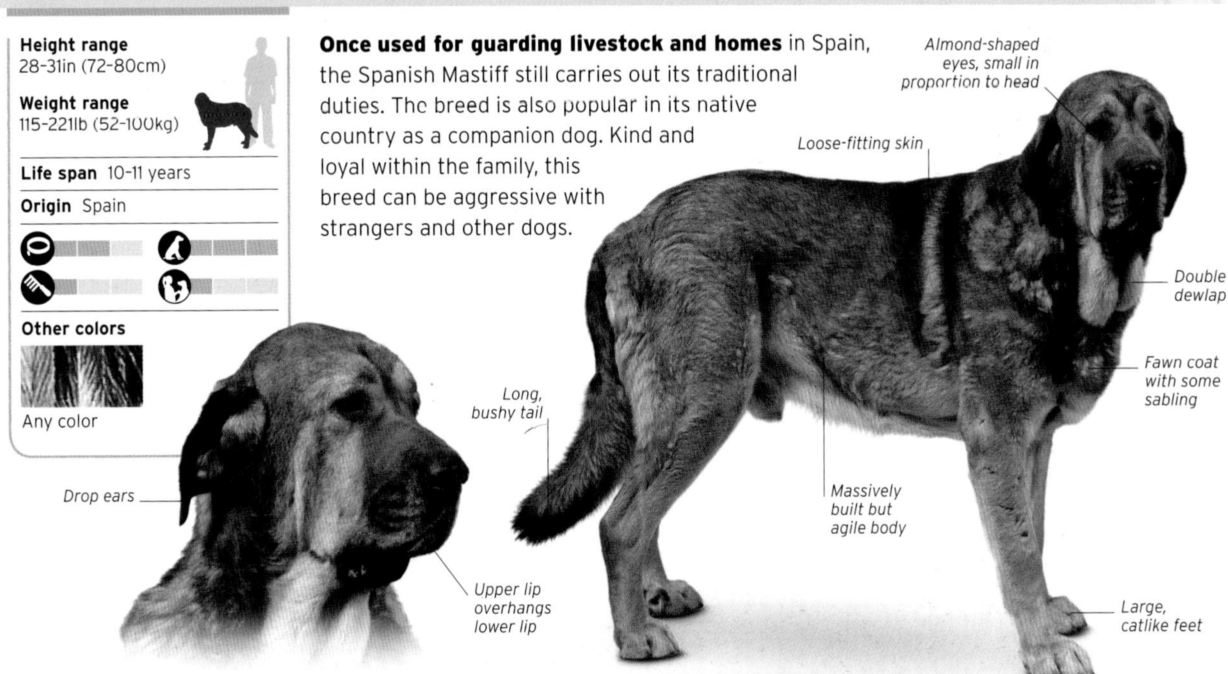

Height range
28–31in (72–80cm)
Weight range
115–221lb (52–100kg)
Life span 10–11 years
Origin Spain
Other colors
Any color
Almond-shaped eyes, small in proportion to head
Loose-fitting skin
Double dewlap
Fawn coat with some sabling
Long, bushy tail
Drop ears
Massively built but agile body
Upper lip overhangs lower lip
Large, catlike feet

High-set tail, held upright
Arched neck
Body square in profile
Distinct stop
High-set ears with rounded tips
Expressive face with dark brown eyes and wrinkled forehead
Lower jaw longer than upper jaw (undershot)
Short, broad muzzle
Muscular hind quarters
White chest
Tucked-up belly
Smooth, fawn coat
White feet and lower legs

BOXER

THIS CLEVER, LOYAL, EXUBERANT, AND FUN-LOVING DOG IS IDEAL FOR AN ENERGETIC OWNER AKC

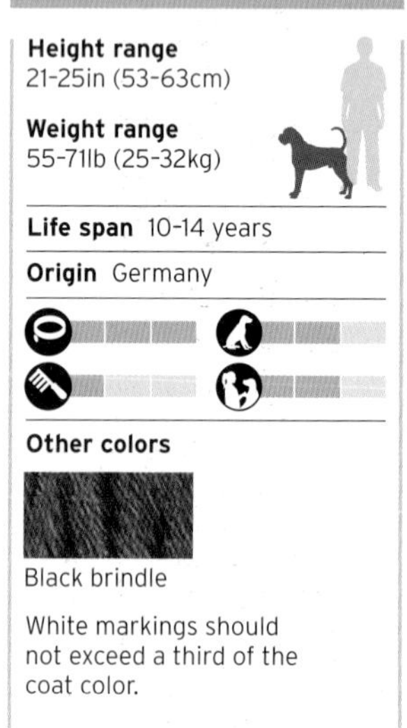

Height range
21–25in (53–63cm)

Weight range
55–71lb (25–32kg)

Life span 10–14 years

Origin Germany

Other colors

Black brindle

White markings should not exceed a third of the coat color.

Once a Boxer-owner, always a Boxer-owner—this German breed is so big on personality that few who live with it ever look at another type of dog. The Boxer in its modern form was developed in the 19th century and its ancestry is thought to include mastiff-type dogs such as the Great Dane (see p.95) and the Bulldog (see p.94). Powerful and athletic, it was bred primarily for fighting and bull-baiting, but was also used for farm work, haulage, and for hunting and holding down large game such as wild boar. Because of its endurance and courage, the breed is used today as a police and military search-and-rescue dog and for guard work.

The Boxer's history, its proud, upstanding attitude, and forward-thrusting jaw give the impression of an intimidating dog, and it can certainly be protective of home and family, but it makes a wonderful companion. It is loyal, affectionate, endearingly attention-seeking, and a boisterous but tolerant friend for children. This energetic breed suits fit, active owners as it retains its high spirits and playfulness into late maturity. Almost any sort of fun keeps a Boxer happy but, ideally, it requires a good two-hour walk every day with plenty of scope for romping around in the open. At home, given its stamina and curiosity, a Boxer enjoys a large yard where it has space to roam and interesting corners to explore.

This highly intelligent dog can be a handful to train but is obedient provided it receives calm and consistent commands and clear leadership. With early socializing, a Boxer is likely to get on well with any other pets in the family, although out on walks its hunting instincts may be aroused if there are birds or small animals to chase.

ST. MIGUEL CATTLE DOG

DEFENSIVE WITH STRANGERS, THIS GUARD DOG NEEDS AN OUTDOOR WORKING LIFE FCI

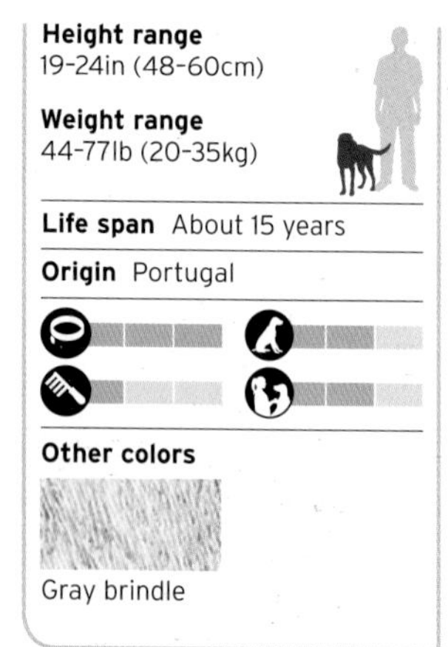

Height range 19-24in (48-60cm)

Weight range 44-77lb (20-35kg)

Life span About 15 years

Origin Portugal

Other colors

Gray brindle

Also known as the Azores Cattle Dog, this robust cattle-herder and guard dog originally came from the Azorean island of São Miguel. The breed is quiet and obedient with a trusted owner but needs careful handling and early socialization where children or strangers are concerned.

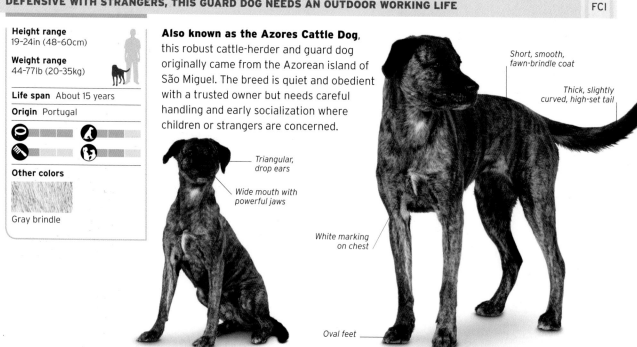

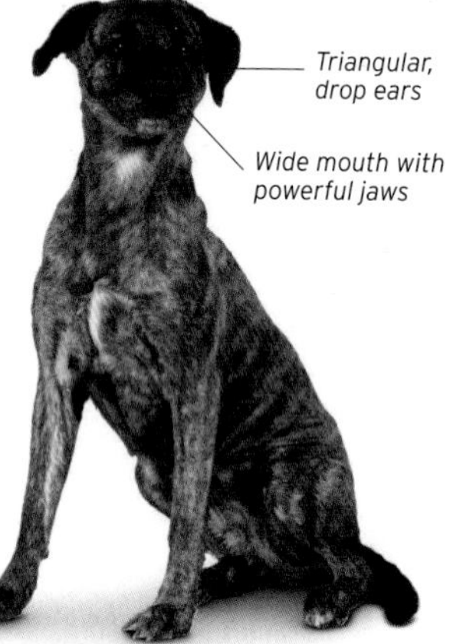
Triangular, drop ears
Wide mouth with powerful jaws

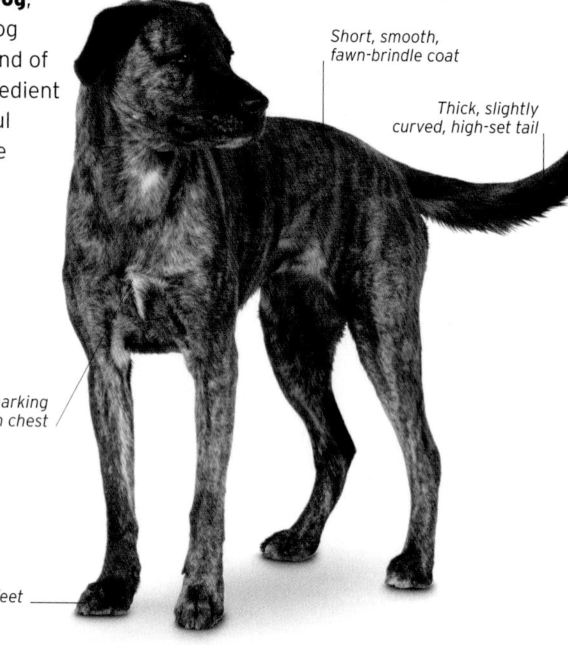
Short, smooth, fawn-brindle coat
Thick, slightly curved, high-set tail
White marking on chest
Oval feet

CANE CORSO

THIS POWERFUL BUT GRACEFUL DOG NEEDS AN EXPERIENCED HANDLER AKC

Height range 24-27in (60-68cm)

Weight range 88-110lb (40-50kg)

Life span 10-11 years

Origin Italy

Other colors

Gray

Stag-red

Brindle

May have white markings.

Descended from Roman fighting dogs, the Cane Corso is now used mainly for guarding and tracking. More graceful in build than many types of mastiff, this is nonetheless an extremely strong and robust breed. It can make a good house dog, but experienced and responsible ownership is essential.

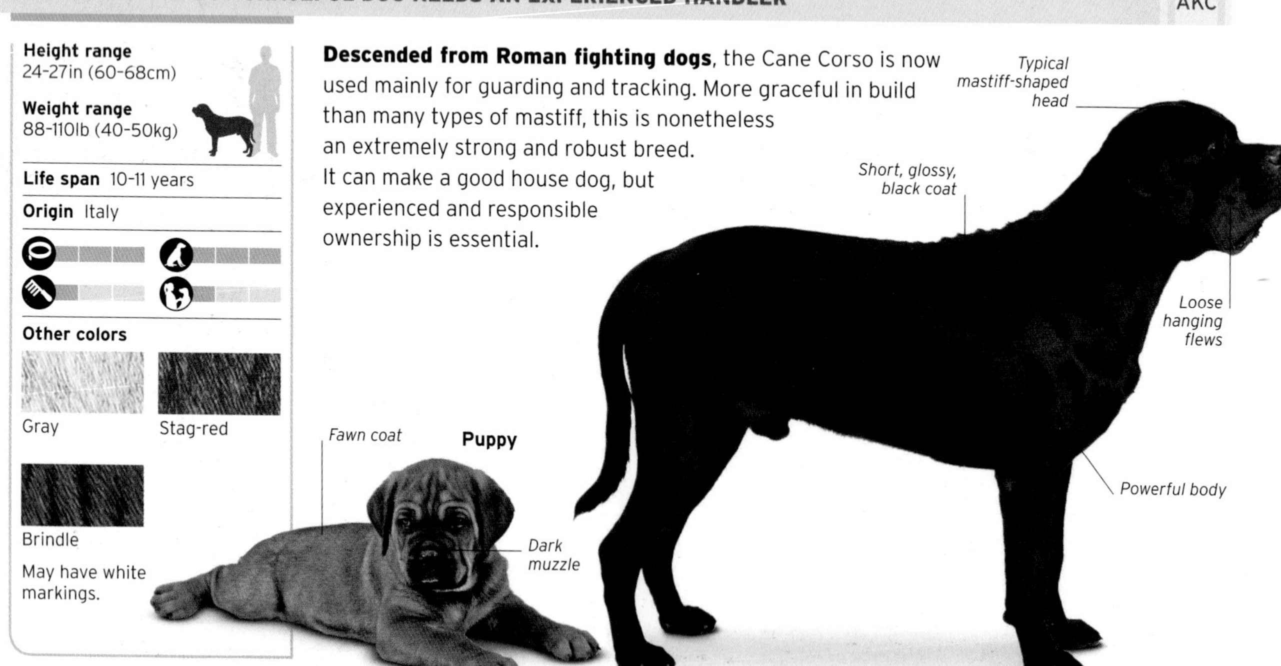
Typical mastiff-shaped head
Short, glossy, black coat
Loose hanging flews
Powerful body
Fawn coat
Puppy
Dark muzzle

NEAPOLITAN MASTIFF

THIS CANINE HEAVYWEIGHT MAKES A LOYAL COMPANION FOR A RESPONSIBLE OWNER AKC

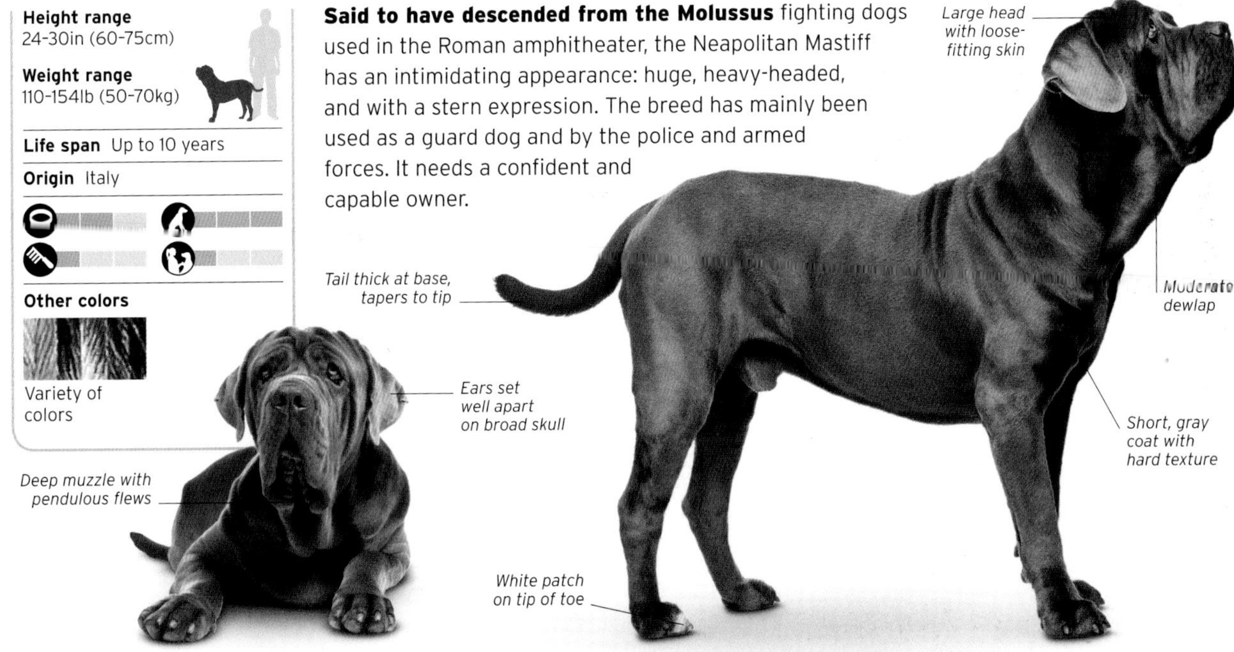
Large head with loose-fitting skin
Moderate dewlap
Short, gray coat with hard texture
Tail thick at base, tapers to tip
Ears set well apart on broad skull
Deep muzzle with pendulous flews
White patch on tip of toe

Height range
24–30in (60–75cm)

Weight range
110–154lb (50–70kg)

Life span Up to 10 years

Origin Italy

Other colors

Variety of colors

Said to have descended from the Molussus fighting dogs used in the Roman amphitheater, the Neapolitan Mastiff has an intimidating appearance: huge, heavy-headed, and with a stern expression. The breed has mainly been used as a guard dog and by the police and armed forces. It needs a confident and capable owner.

DOGUE DE BORDEAUX

THIS NON-AGGRESSIVE GUARD DOG IS MORE AGILE THAN ITS SIZE SUGGESTS AKC

Height range
23–27in (58–68cm)

Weight range
99–110lb (45–50kg)

Life span 10–12 years

Origin France

This old French breed was once used for hunting and fighting. The Dogue de Bordeaux's instincts make it a natural guard dog but, lacking aggression, it is easier to train and socialize than some mastiff types. Experienced handling is still necessary, however, if this powerful and athletic dog is to fit comfortably into a family home.

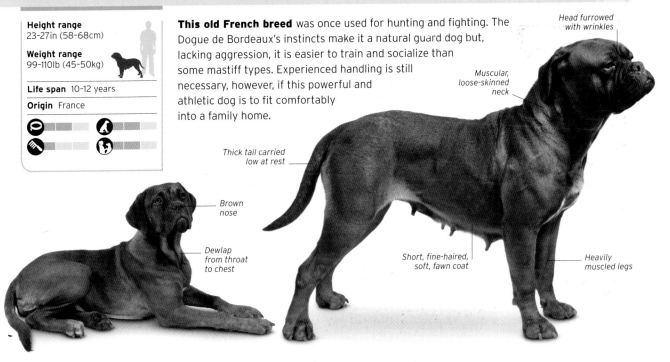

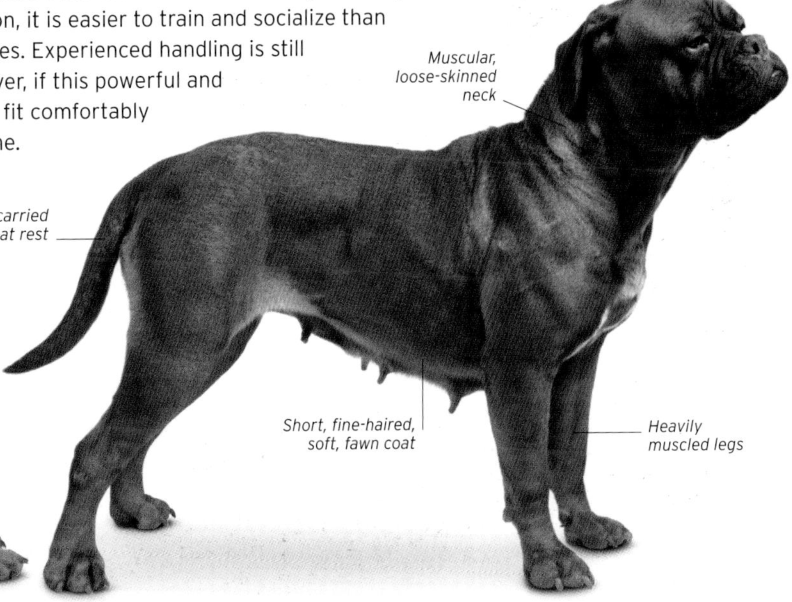

Head furrowed with wrinkles

Muscular, loose-skinned neck

Thick tail carried low at rest

Brown nose

Dewlap from throat to chest

Short, fine-haired, soft, fawn coat

Heavily muscled legs

BROHOLMER

THIS LARGE MOLOSSUS DOG IS BOTH STRONG AND CALM FCI

Height range
28-30in (70-75cm)

Weight range
88-154lb (40-70kg)

Life span 6-11 years

Origin Denmark

Other colors

Black

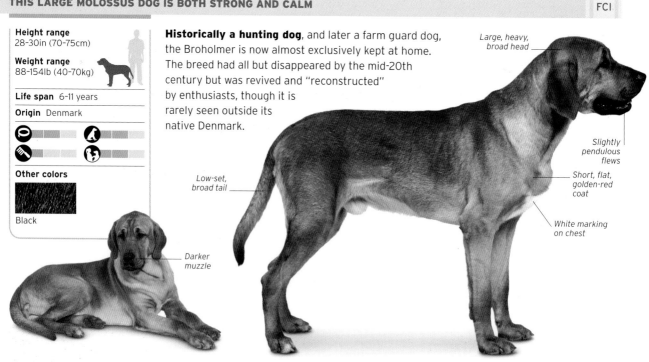

Historically a hunting dog, and later a farm guard dog, the Broholmer is now almost exclusively kept at home. The breed had all but disappeared by the mid-20th century but was revived and "reconstructed" by enthusiasts, though it is rarely seen outside its native Denmark.

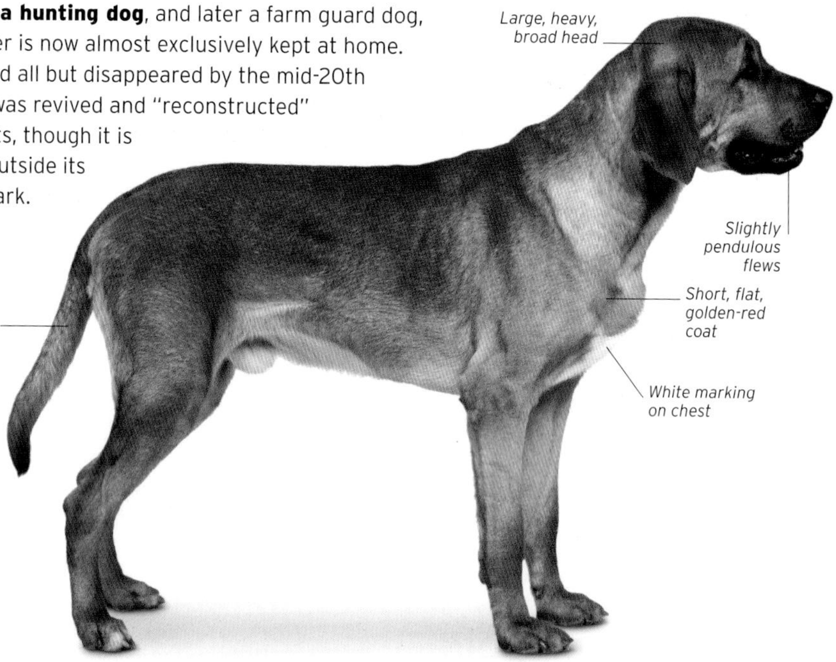

Large, heavy, broad head

Slightly pendulous flews

Short, flat, golden-red coat

White marking on chest

Low-set, broad tail

Darker muzzle

BULLMASTIFF

HIGH SPIRITS AND A CHEERFUL TEMPERAMENT UNDERLIE THIS IMPOSING DOG AKC

Height range
24-27in (61-69cm)

Weight range
90-130lb (41-59kg)

Life span Under 10 years

Origin UK

Other colors

Red

Brindle

A cross between the Old English Mastiff and the Bulldog (see p.94), the Bullmastiff was developed to be a gamekeeper's guard dog. With a more reliable temperament than many other mastiff types, this breed makes an intelligent and faithful house dog. The Bullmastiff's square and solid frame houses a lively spirit and boundless energy.

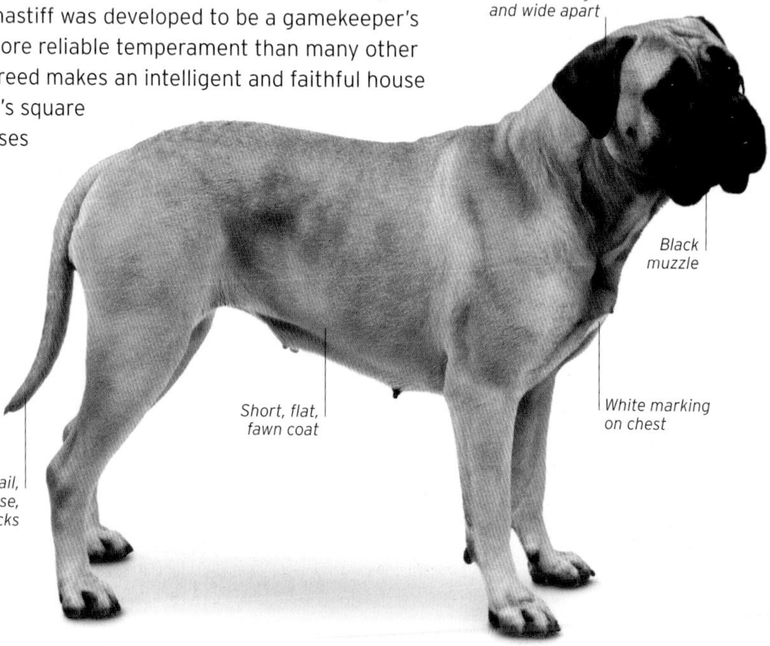

Dark ears set high and wide apart

Black muzzle

White marking on chest

Short, flat, fawn coat

Thick, muscular neck

High-set tail, broad at base, tapers to hocks

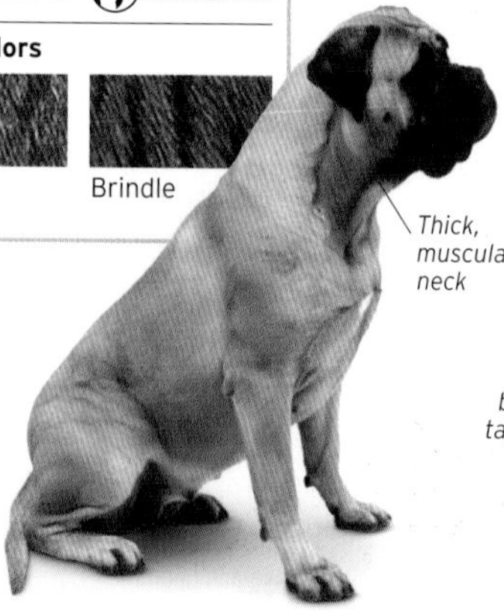

MASTIFF

THIS CALM, AFFECTIONATE DOG NEEDS PLENTY OF HUMAN COMPANY AKC

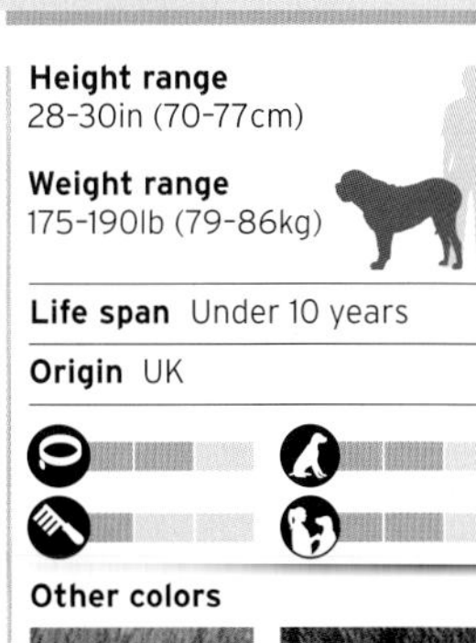

Height range
28–30in (70–77cm)

Weight range
175–190lb (79–86kg)

Life span Under 10 years

Origin UK

Other colors

Apricot | Black brindle

May have areas of white on body, chest, and feet.

With a history of guarding, fighting, and even bear-baiting, the Mastiff is surprisingly even-tempered and easy to get on with. Sheer size is probably the most serious drawback to housing, feeding, and exercising this enormous breed. A Mastiff likes company, preferably human, and is ready to offer loyalty and affection. It is intelligent and trainable but needs an owner with both the experience and physical strength to exert firm control and ensure that its guarding instinct does not get out of hand.

Wide set, small eyes
Forehead wrinkles when alert

Pendulous flews

Small, flat, black ears, set high on head

Black muzzle

Short, fawn coat, thickest over neck and shoulders

Long, broad body

Straight, big-boned legs

BULLDOG

FULL OF CHARACTER, THIS DOG IS A SYMBOL OF COURAGE, DETERMINATION, AND TENACITY AKC

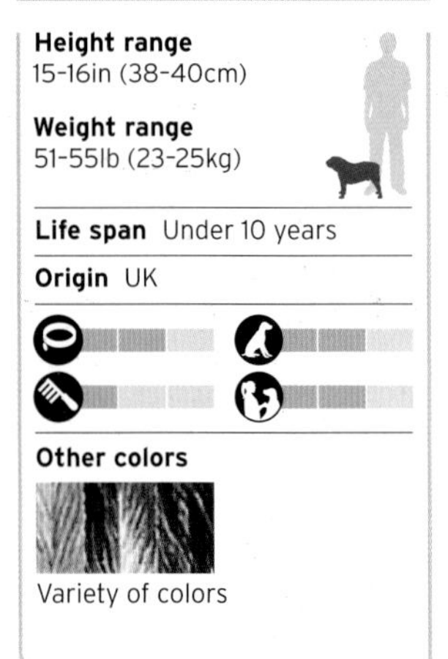
Height range
15-16in (38-40cm)
Weight range
51-55lb (23-25kg)
Life span Under 10 years
Origin UK
Other colors
Variety of colors

Once used for bull-baiting, and legendary for its refusal to let go of an adversary, the Bulldog has acquired a mellower reputation as a good-natured and lovable companion. The dog does have a stubborn streak as well as a protective instinct, and these traits need handling with tact, though they rarely develop into aggression. With a squat and massively muscled body, wrinkled head, and upturned nose, this breed has character rather than beauty. Despite its waddling gait, the Bulldog needs sufficient exercise to avoid it gaining too much weight.

Smooth, fawn coat

Broad, round, deep chest

Thick, short forelegs set wide apart

Lower jaw longer than upper jaw (overshot)

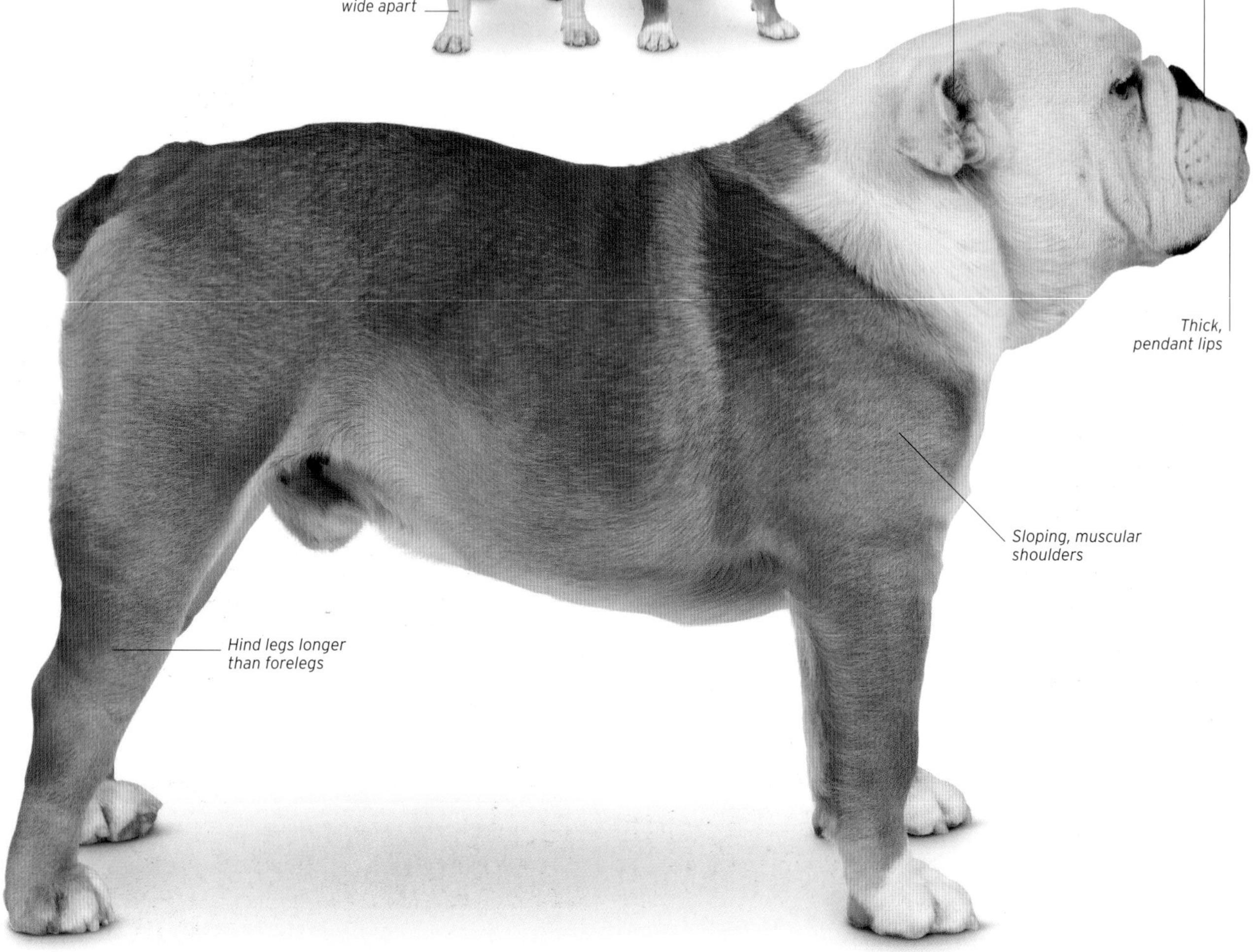

High-set, rose ears

Distinctive upturned nose

Thick, pendant lips

Sloping, muscular shoulders

Hind legs longer than forelegs

GREAT DANE

GENTLE AND EASY TO MAINTAIN, THIS DOG TAKES UP A LOT OF ROOM

AKC

Height range
28-30in (71-76cm)

Weight range
101-119lb (46-54kg)

Life span Under 10 years

Origin Germany

Other colors

Blue

Black

Brindle

Elegance and dignity combined with gigantic size make the Great Dane one of the most impressive of all dogs. Once a hunting dog in Germany, the easy-going Great Dane is content to be a house dog, provided there is enough room for it to flop comfortably. As well as space, the breed needs plenty of exercise.

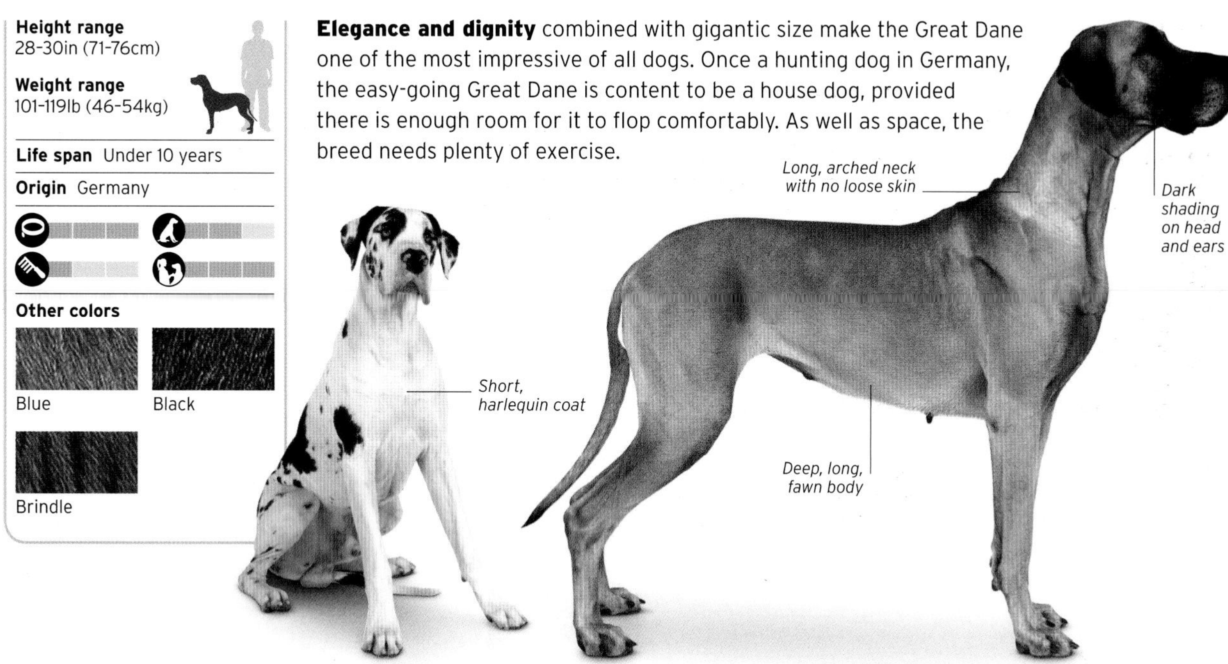
Long, arched neck with no loose skin
Dark shading on head and ears
Short, harlequin coat
Deep, long, fawn body

TOSA

FORMERLY BRED AS A FIGHTING DOG, THIS BREED NEEDS AN EXPERIENCED HANDLER

FCI

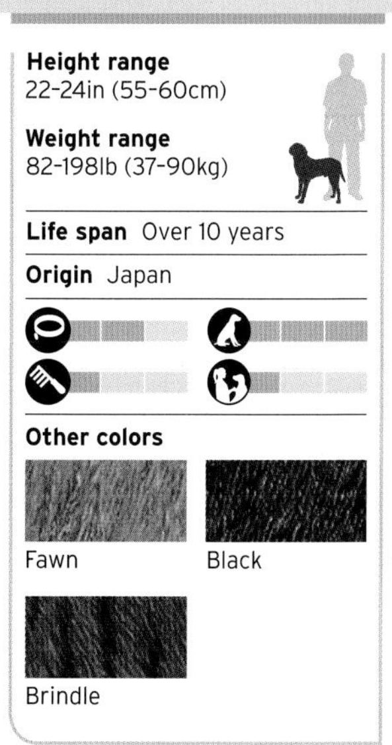

Height range
22-24in (55-60cm)

Weight range
82-198lb (37-90kg)

Life span Over 10 years

Origin Japan

Other colors

Fawn

Black

Brindle

The Tosa was developed from progressive crossbreeding between Japanese fighting dogs and Western breeds such as the Bulldog (opposite), Mastiff (see p.93), and Great Dane (above). Very large, strongly built, and possessing a latent fighting instinct, the Tosa is considered to be a dog that should only be owned by expert handlers.

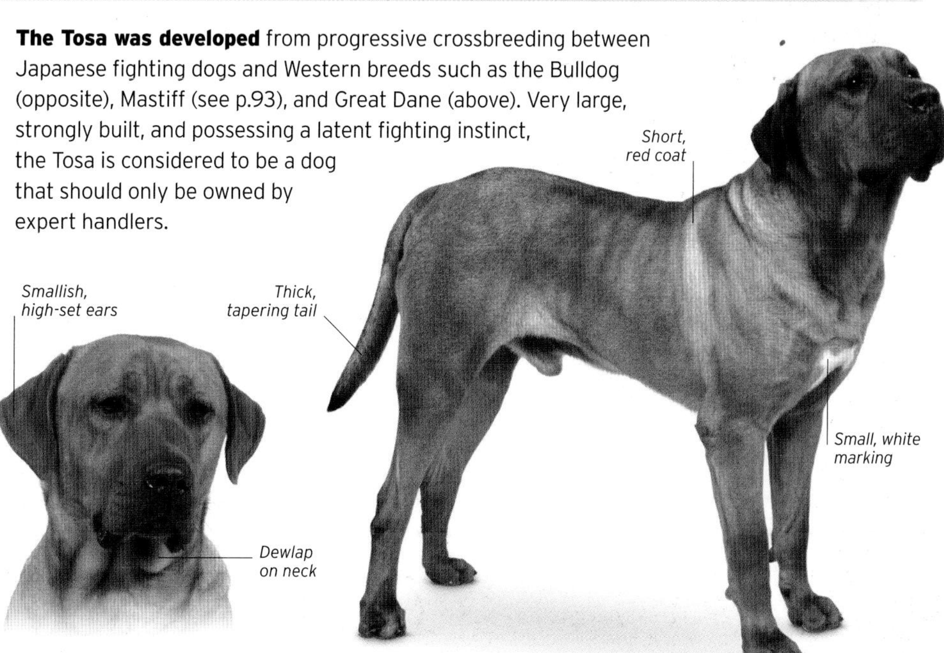
Short, red coat
Smallish, high-set ears
Thick, tapering tail
Small, white marking
Dewlap on neck

PULLING TOGETHER
A team of Siberian Huskies plows effortlessly through deep snow. With an experienced handler, these hardy and tireless dogs work superbly together.

SPITZ-TYPE DOGS

A team of huskies pulling a sled over icy wastelands epitomizes the type of dog known as a Spitz. In fact, this group has diverse uses, including herding, hunting, and guarding; many smaller types are kept solely as pets. Descent from wolves is apparent in most Spitz dogs: the shape of the head, the typical wolf coloring, and an alert expression.

The smiling-faced Samoyed originated in Siberia

Many of the modern Spitz breeds seen today originated centuries ago in Arctic regions, though a number, including the Chow Chow and Akita, come from East Asia. The more ancient history of the Spitz group remains uncertain. One theory currently being explored is that Spitz-type dogs all have their earliest origins in Asia, some migrating alongside tribal movements into Africa and others across the Bering Strait to North America.

Breeds such as the Greenland Dog and Siberian Husky were used most famously for sled-hauling by the polar explorers of the 19th and early 20th centuries. These tough dogs worked in appalling weather conditions, often on a diet of poor food, and not infrequently ended up being eaten themselves when their owners ran out of rations. Such Spitz-type sled dogs were also once widely used by North American hunters and fur-trappers. Today the sled-hauling Spitz breeds are popular for endurance racing and with tourists who want to try their hand at dog-driving. Other Spitz dogs have been bred for hunting large game such as wolf and bear, and for herding reindeer. The Akita, originally from Japan, was developed as a fighter and bear-hunter and now often works as a guard dog. Among the small, nonworking Spitz dogs are the Pomeranian, selectively bred down in size from a larger type of dog, and the newly created Alaskan Klee Kai, a miniature husky.

Spitz dogs, both large and small, have the characteristics of animals bred specifically for living in extremely cold climates. Typically, they have a very thick double coat, which varies in length and density according to the origin of a breed. Other features for preventing heat loss in low temperatures are small, pointed, furry ears, and well-furred feet. An attractive addition to many breeds is the distinctive "spitz" tail that curls upward over the back.

As house dogs, most Spitz breeds are happy with family life, but they are not the easiest of dogs to train. Without sufficient exercise and amusement they can resort to disruptive behavior such as digging holes and barking.

EX-FIGHTER
The burly Akita was once a fighting dog in its native Japan.

SMALLEST SPITZ
The tiny Pomeranian is the smallest of the Spitz-type breeds. Although it was bred as a pet, this dog has a strong character and is full of indomitable Spitz spirit.

CANADIAN ESKIMO DOG

THIS FRIENDLY DOG NEEDS A FIRM HAND BUT IS HAPPY BELONGING TO A HUMAN "PACK" KC

Height range
20–28in (50–70cm)

Weight range
40–88lb (18–40kg)

Life span Over 10 years

Origin Canada

Other colors

Any color

One of the oldest breeds of sled dog in the world, the Canadian Eskimo Dog, or Inuit Dog, is built for survival in the harshest conditions. This breed has a natural instinct for running with a pack and likes company, either canine or human. Training should be firm, ideally with plenty of fun.

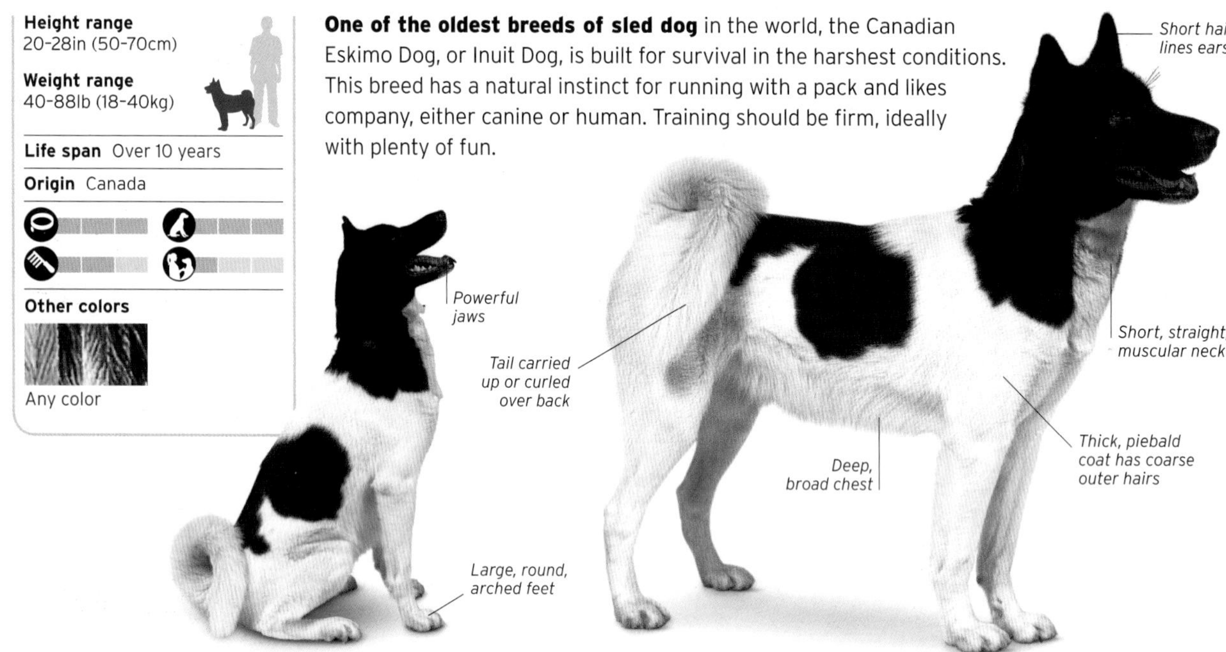
Short hair lines ears
Powerful jaws
Tail carried up or curled over back
Short, straight, muscular neck
Thick, piebald coat has coarse outer hairs
Deep, broad chest
Large, round, arched feet

GREENLAND DOG

THIS DOG HAS GREAT STRENGTH AND ENDURANCE AND LOVES OUTDOOR ACTION KC

Height range
20–27in (51–68cm)

Weight range
60–106lb (27–48kg)

Life span Over 10 years

Origin Greenland

Other colors

Any color

The classic sled dog of polar expeditions, the Greenland Dog was used by Arctic peoples for hunting and transportation long before European and American explorers discovered its worth. Powerful, strong-willed, and stubborn, though generally happy-natured, this dog needs patient training and does best in the hands of an expert.

Small, wide-set ears

Bushy tail curls loosely over back

Hair forms long "breeches" on hind quarters

Thick, weatherproof coat is dark above and light below

Muscular, compact body

Sturdy, heavily boned legs

Large feet with thick hair between toes

SIBERIAN HUSKY

THIS VERSATILE AND SOCIABLE DOG FINDS CHASING SMALL ANIMALS IRRESISTIBLE AKC

Height range
20–24in (51–60cm)

Weight range
35–60lb (16–27kg)

Life span Over 10 years

Origin Siberia

Other colors

Any color

Long used as a sled dog by the indigenous peoples of eastern Siberia, the Siberian Husky has great endurance, an appetite for work, and resistance to extreme cold. The breed is still popular in the Arctic, particularly in sports such as dogsled-racing. Siberian Huskies make peaceable and lovable companions but need vigorous exercise to burn off some of their energy. They have a strong pack instinct, and are unlikely to be happy living in isolation. A Siberian Husky tends to see small animals as natural prey, so caution is needed if other pets are kept.

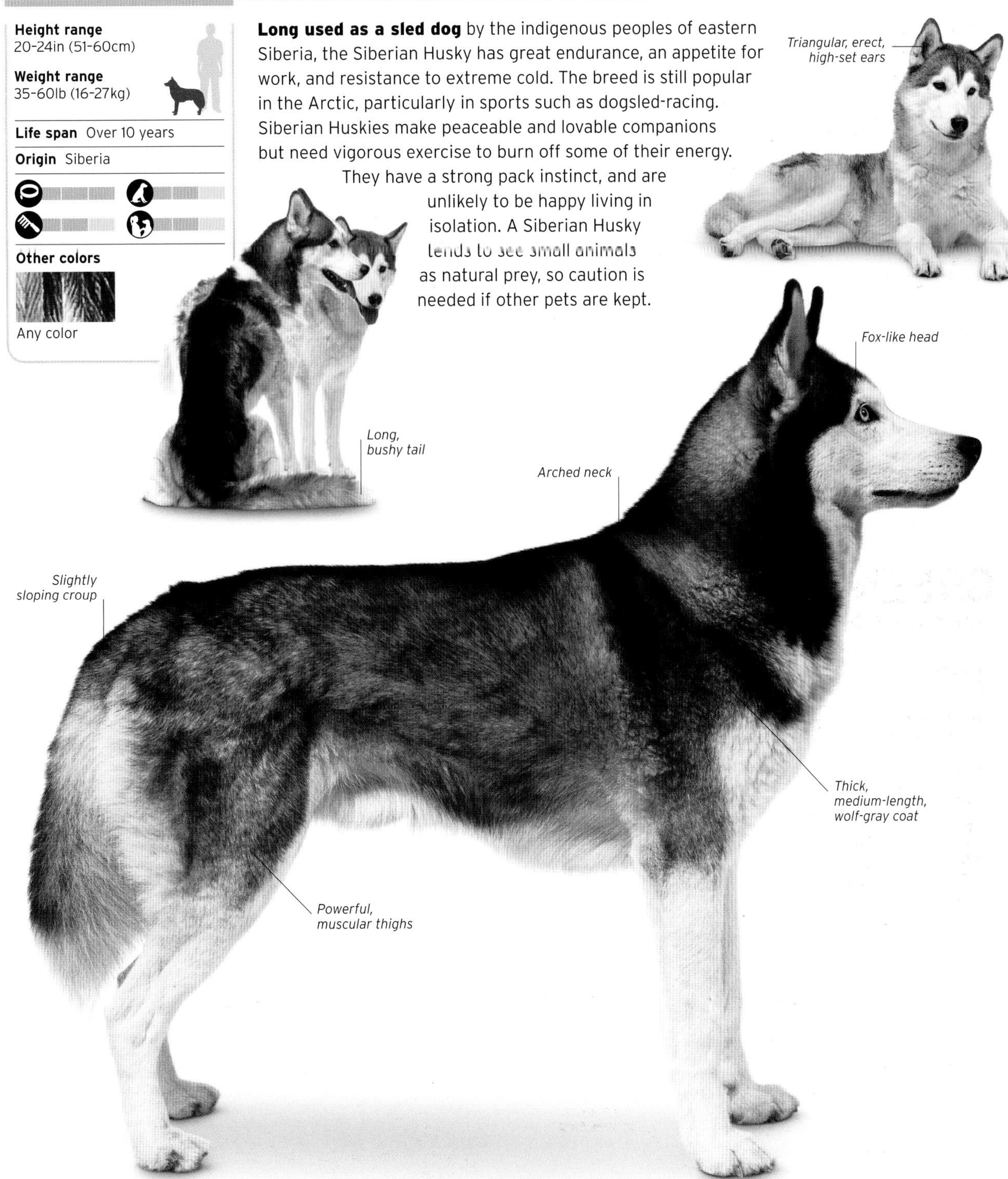
Triangular, erect, high-set ears
Long, bushy tail
Fox-like head
Arched neck
Slightly sloping croup
Thick, medium-length, wolf-gray coat
Powerful, muscular thighs

Erect, triangular ears with rounded tips and furry inner surfaces

Furry tail curls up over back

Thick, coarse, wolf-gray outer coat over oily, woolly, deep undercoat

Slight furrow between eyes

Black nose

Thicker hair around neck

White predominates on underbody

Heavily muscled thighs

ALASKAN MALAMUTE

A LARGE, SLED-PULLING DOG THAT CAN ADAPT WELL TO FAMILY LIFE AKC

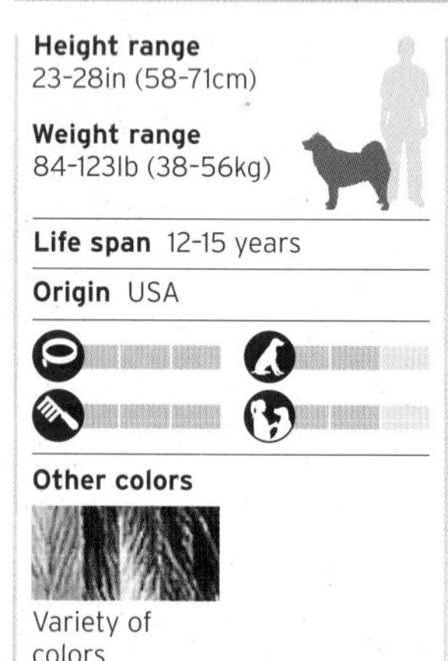

Height range
23–28in (58–71cm)

Weight range
84–123lb (38–56kg)

Life span 12–15 years

Origin USA

Other colors

Variety of colors

All dogs have white underparts.

The wolflike Alaskan Malamute is named after the Native American Mahlemut people, who bred these dogs to pull heavy loads and travel great distances across the snow when sleds were the only mode of transport. Today it is still used to haul freight in remote North American locations, and successfully takes part in sled-racing competitions. Also used on polar expeditions, this breed has staggering amounts of stamina, strength, and tenacity combined with highly tuned senses of direction and smell.

For all its toughness, the Alaskan Malamute is a friendly dog, at least toward people, which means that it cannot be relied on as a guard dog. It likes children but is too big and boisterous to be left alone with a small child. The Alaskan Malamute, especially the male, tends to be intolerant of strange dogs, and without thorough socializing can quickly become aggressive. The breed also has a strong chasing instinct and can disappear far and fast in pursuit of small animals that it sees as prey. Owners should be cautious about where and when to exercise this dog off leash. A quick learner, the Alaskan Malamute has a strong will, so needs firm handling and training in good habits right from the start.

The Alaskan Malamute settles well into domestic life as long as it has at least two hours of exercise each day and outdoor space to roam in. A bored dog, with energy to spare, can be destructive if left at home without supervision. Although its thick coat sheds in spring, there is a risk of overheating if the dog is overexercised in hot weather, and it needs access to shade. The hardy Alaskan Malamute is happy to sleep outdoors, provided it has a companion.

ALASKAN KLEE KAI

THIS ENERGETIC MINI HUSKY IS CONFIDENT WITH OWNERS BUT WARY OF STRANGERS

Height range
Toy:
Up to 13in (Up to 33cm)
Miniature:
13–15in (33–38cm)
Standard:
15–17in (38–44cm)

Weight range
Toy:
Up to 9lb (Up to 4kg)
Miniature:
9–15lb (4–7kg)
Standard:
15–22lb (7–10kg)

Life span Over 10 years

Origin USA

Other colors

Any color

This miniature version of the Alaskan Malamute (see p.100), was developed to be a house dog and is found in three sizes: toy, miniature, and standard. It fits well in a modestly-sized home but, like its larger relative, has a great deal of energy and needs plenty of exercise to stay in good physical and mental health. Typical of husky-type breeds, the Alaskan Klee Kai appreciates company and likes to be treated as a pack member within a family. Reserved with strangers, this dog needs careful training and early socializing.

Eyes are different colors
Standard
Triangular, erect ears
Alert expression
Toy
Distinct stop
Heavy-coated, brushlike tail
Tapering muzzle
Characteristic facial mask
Dense, moderately long, wolf-gray coat
Miniature

CHINOOK

ALWAYS WILLING TO WORK OR PLAY, THIS DOG IS GOOD WITH CHILDREN

Height range
22–26in (55–66cm)

Weight range
55–71lb (25–32kg)

Life span 10–15 years

Origin USA

Developed as a sled dog at the beginning of the 20th century in the US, the Chinook is the result of various crosses between mastiffs, the Greenland Dog (see p.98), and shepherd dogs. Active but gentle-natured, this is a fun-loving breed and makes an excellent all-around family dog.

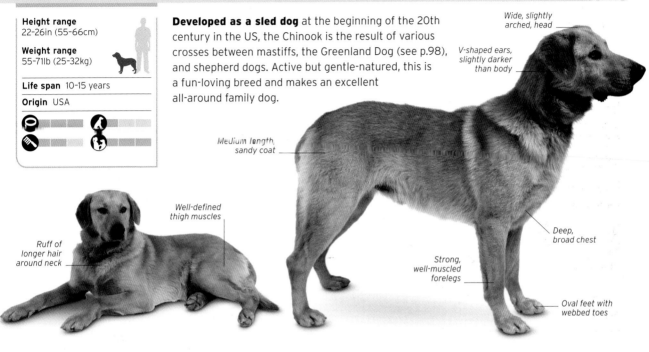

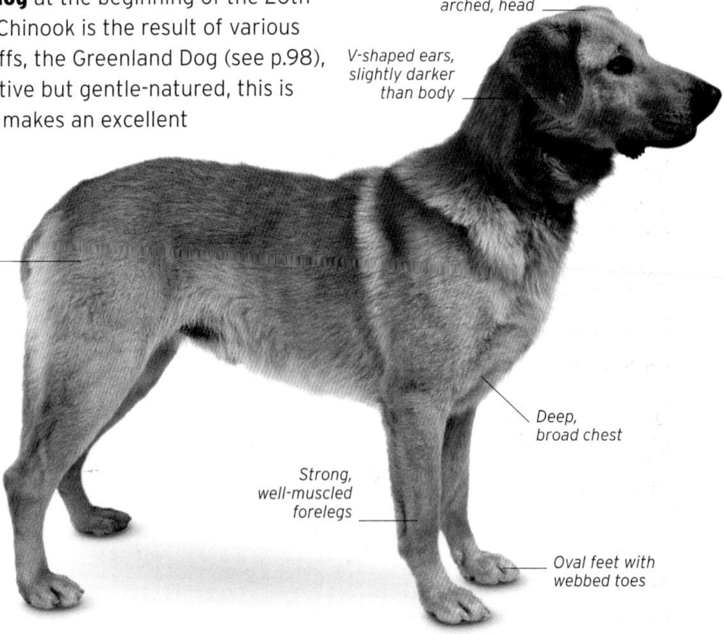

Wide, slightly arched, head

V-shaped ears, slightly darker than body

Medium length, sandy coat

Well-defined thigh muscles

Ruff of longer hair around neck

Deep, broad chest

Strong, well-muscled forelegs

Oval feet with webbed toes

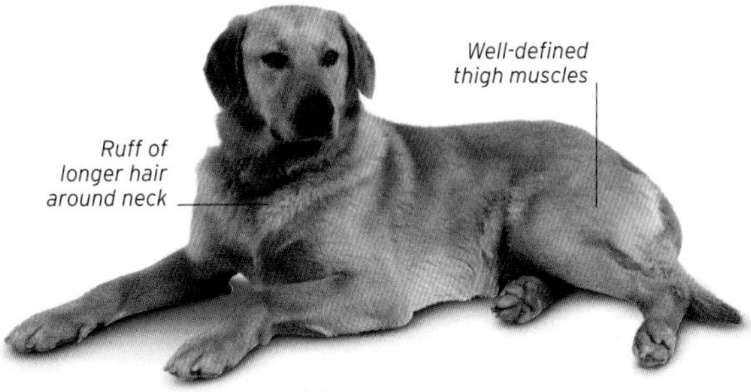

KARELIAN BEAR DOG

THIS BOLD, ASSERTIVE BREED IS NOT AGGRESSIVE WITH PEOPLE BUT MAY RESENT OTHER DOGS FCI

Height range
20–22in (52–57cm)

Weight range
44–51lb (20–23kg)

Life span 10–12 years

Origin Finland

Developed in Finland, this fearless hunting dog was bred to challenge big game, particularly bear and elk. The Karelian Bear Dog has a strong fighting instinct, which does not turn into aggression against people but may cause trouble with other dogs. This breed is unlikely to settle well into domestic life.

High-set tail curled over back
Straight nose bridge
Thicker hair on neck
Straight, harsh-textured, black and white outer coat
Well-defined white markings are common
Slightly tucked-up belly
Strong-boned legs

WEST SIBERIAN LAIKA

AN INTELLIGENT AND ALERT DOG WITH A KEEN NOSE AND STRONG HUNTING INSTINCT

FCI

Height range
20–24in (51–62cm)

Weight range
40–50lb (18–22kg)

Life span 10–12 years

Origin Russia

Other colors

Variety of colors

Bred for hunting in the forests of Siberia, this handsome dog is very popular in its native country. The breed is strong and confident, and eager to follow game, either large or small. Although the West Siberian Laika has a steady temperament, its readiness to hunt makes it unsuitable as a house dog for most families.

High-set ears held erect

Sable coat on neck and shoulders forms longer collar

Tail carried in tight curl over back

Sandy coat

Oval, slightly deep-set eyes

Long, muscular upper forelegs

Feet with hair between toes

EAST SIBERIAN LAIKA

BORN TO HUNT, THIS DOG IS CALM AND EASY-GOING WITH PEOPLE

FCI

Height range
21–25in (53–64cm)

Weight range
40–51lb (18–23kg)

Life span 10–12 years

Origin Russia

Other colors

White

Karamis

Piebald

The popularity of this Russian hunting dog is widespread in its own country and also reaches into Scandinavia. Bred for work, the East Siberian Laika is tough, active, and confident. Although it has a strong instinct for following big game, it is controllable, steady-tempered, and friendly with people.

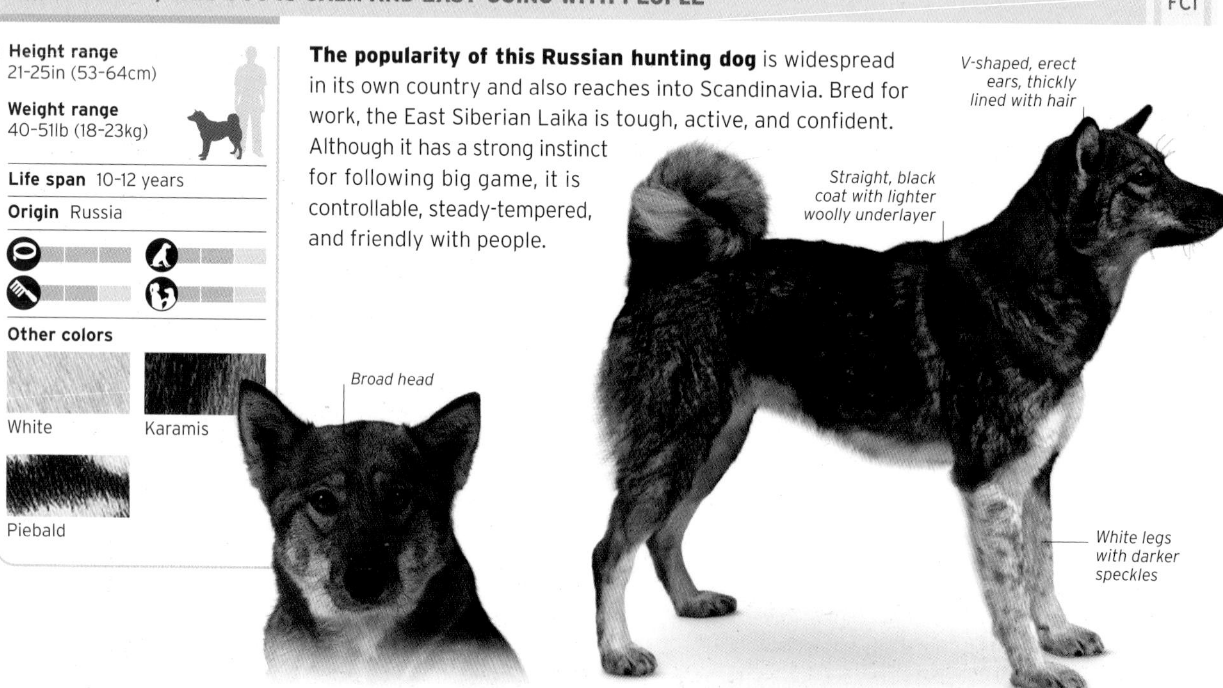
V-shaped, erect ears, thickly lined with hair
Straight, black coat with lighter woolly underlayer
Broad head
White legs with darker speckles

RUSSIAN-EUROPEAN LAIKA

A STRONG AND WORKMANLIKE BREED, NOT SUITED TO FAMILY LIFE FCI

Height range
19-23in (48-58cm)

Weight range
44-51lb (20-23kg)

Life span 10-12 years

Origin Russia

Other colors
White
Black

This Laika was only acknowledged as a distinct breed in the early 1940s. Strong but lean-limbed, the Russian-European Laika has been used mainly for hunting in Russia's northern forests. A steady worker, this dog is excellent when used for its traditional purpose but does not adapt well to a domestic lifestyle.

Tail carried over back
Narrow, triangular head
Black nose
Hair on hind legs forms "breeches"
Harsh-textured, black coat with white markings
Well-muscled, slender legs

FINNISH SPITZ

BRISK AND JAUNTY, THIS DOG ENJOYS FAMILY FUN AND IS USUALLY PATIENT WITH CHILDREN AKC

Height range
15-20in (39-50cm)

Weight range
31-35lb (14-16kg)

Life span 12-15 years

Origin Finland

Finland's national dog was bred for hunting small game and is still used for sport in Scandinavia. With its pert, fox-like appearance, luxuriant coat, and enthusiasm for play, the Finnish Spitz makes an appealing family pet. The breed has a tendency to bark a great deal; this should be discouraged at an early age.

Small, pointed ears
Reddish brown coat with sparsely distributed black hair
Bushy tail
Outer corners of eyes tilt upwards
Lighter-colored underparts
Fox-like head with narrow muzzle
Square, strong body

Long, bushy tail carried over back, falls to one side

Muscular, broad back

Dark eyes rimmed with black

Broad, wedge-shaped head

Typical "smiling" expression

Erect, round-tipped ears, thickly lined with hair

Ruff of longer, denser hair around neck

Thick, soft, white coat with silver-tipped outer hairs

Feathering on back of front legs

SAMOYED

THIS STRIKINGLY ATTRACTIVE DOG MAKES AN EXCELLENT FAMILY PET AKC

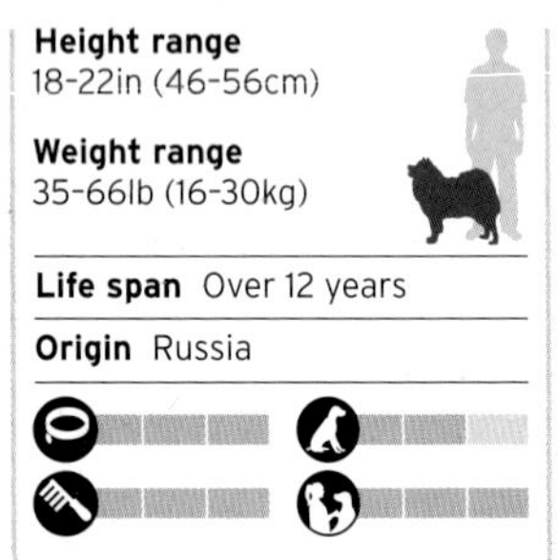

Height range 18-22in (46-56cm)

Weight range 35-66lb (16-30kg)

Life span Over 12 years

Origin Russia

Developed centuries ago by the nomadic Samoyede people of Siberia, this beautiful dog was used for herding and guarding reindeer and for sled-hauling. This tough, outdoor worker was also very much a family dog, taking its place in its owner's tent and enjoying human companionship. These dogs were brought to England in the 1800s and were first seen in the United States around a decade later. Numerous myths and unsubstantiated stories link the Samoyeds to the polar expeditions of the late 19th and early 20th centuries, but it appears likely that this breed was included among sled teams taken to the Antarctic during the heyday of polar exploration.

The modern Samoyed retains the sociable and easy-going temperament that made it so valued as part of a nomadic family. Behind the "smiling" expression characteristic of the breed is an affectionate nature and a desire to be friends with everyone. However, the Samoyed retains the watchdog instincts for which it was bred. Although never aggressive, it will bark at anything that arouses its suspicion. This dog craves company and likes to be kept occupied mentally and physically. Intelligent and spirited, a bored or lonely Samoyed will resort to mischief—whether it is digging holes or finding a way to escape through a fence. The breed responds well to thoughtful handling, but training requires patience and persistence on the part of its owner.

Daily grooming is essential to keep the Samoyed's magnificent, stand-out coat in order and maintain its distinctive silvery sheen. Seasonal shedding of the undercoat can be very heavy but, except in very warm conditions, normally occurs only once a year.

FINNISH LAPPHUND

THIS FRIENDLY AND LOYAL DOG, WITH SOME HERDING INSTINCTS, IS QUICK TO LEARN AKC

Height range 17-19in (44-49cm)

Weight range 33-53lb (15-24kg)

Life span 12-15 years

Origin Finland

Other colors

Any color

Developed from the dogs used as reindeer-herders and guards by the Sami people of Lapland, the Finnish Lapphund is enjoying growing popularity, both in Finland and elsewhere. Affectionate and faithful, this adaptable breed is willing to work, but is equally happy as a family pet and watchdog.

Dark brown eyes

Long, dense, black coat

Erect ears

Profusely long-haired tail

Thick mane, especially in males

White markings on chest

Feathering on back of front legs

Tan markings on legs

Well-arched, oval feet

LAPPONIAN HERDER

BRED FOR HERDING, THIS DOG HAS A DOCILE TEMPERAMENT AND PLENTY OF ENERGY FCI

Height range 18-20in (46-51cm)

Weight range Up to 66lb (up to 30kg)

Life span 11-12 years

Origin Finland

Originally bred from Finnish Lapphunds (above), German Shepherd Dogs (see p.35), and working collies, this dog was recognized as a separate breed in the 1960s. The Lapponian Herder, or Lapinporokoira, is still kept for work by reindeer-hunters, and sometimes as a house dog. This breed has a calm and friendly nature.

Erect ears lined with dense hair
Tail extends below hock length
Tan markings on deep chest
Dense, black coat
Tan markings on face
Fairly wide-set, oval, dark eyes
Oval feet, covered with thick hair
Dark brown coat

SWEDISH LAPPHUND

FRIENDLY BUT NEEDING FIRM CONTROL, THIS DOG CAN BE NOISY AND RESTLESS IF LEFT ALONE KC

Height range
16–20in (40–51cm)

Weight range
42–46lb (19–21kg)

Life span 9–15 years

Origin Sweden

Other colors

Brown

Black and brown

May have white mark on chest, feet, and tip of tail.

Similar to the Finnish Lapphund (opposite) in all but color, the Swedish Lapphund was once used as a reindeer-herder by the nomadic Sami people. This breed is popular in Sweden as a house dog but remains uncommon elsewhere. It enjoys company and tends to bark if left alone for long periods of time.

Wedge-shaped head
Dark brown eyes
Shorter hair on face
Long-haired, bushy tail, curled over back
Erect ears, set well apart
Moderate stop
Dense, black coat stands out from body
Compact, oval feet

SWEDISH ELKHOUND

THIS POWERFUL AND AGILE DOG IS NOT SUITABLE FOR AN URBAN LIFESTYLE FCI

Height range
20–26in (52–65cm)

Weight range
Up to 66lb (up to 30kg)

Life span 12–13 years

Origin Sweden

Developed in Sweden's northern forest regions, this large upstanding dog, also known as the Jämthund, was once kept for hunting elk, bear, and lynx. Popular with Sweden's military forces, this breed is the country's national dog. Although good with families, the Swedish Elkhound needs careful handling when around other dogs or pets.

Wolflike head

Dense, dark gray topcoat

Thickly coated tail, carried in a curl

Strong neck

Longer hair on chest

Brown eyes with keen expression

High-set, erect ears lined with thick hair

Cream undercoat

Belly moderately tucked up

Characteristic lighter markings

Strong, oval feet

NORWEGIAN ELKHOUND

THIS CALM DOG IS GOOD WITH CHILDREN, BUT MAY BARK AT STRANGERS AKC

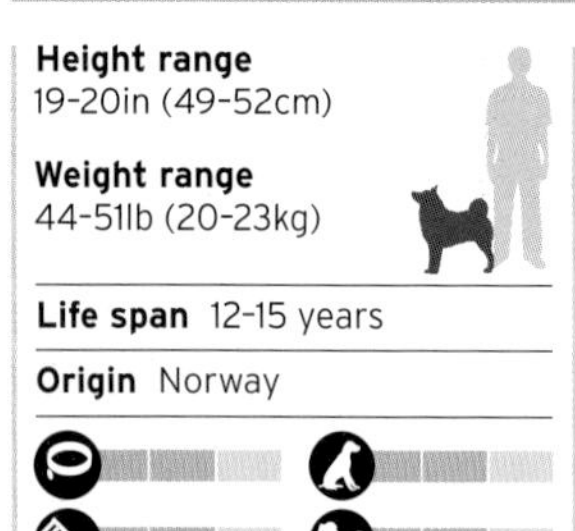

Height range
19-20in (49-52cm)

Weight range
44-51lb (20-23kg)

Life span 12-15 years

Origin Norway

Believed to have existed in Scandinavia for many hundreds of years, the Norwegian Elkhound was once used for tracking game, and is sturdy enough for sled hauling. Impervious to cold and wet weather, this dog likes to be outdoors. The breed has a strong hunting instinct and needs patient training.

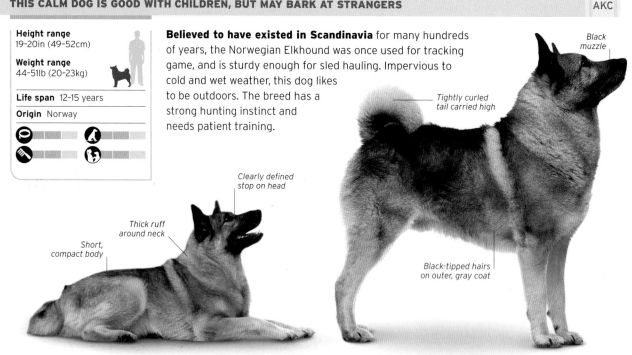

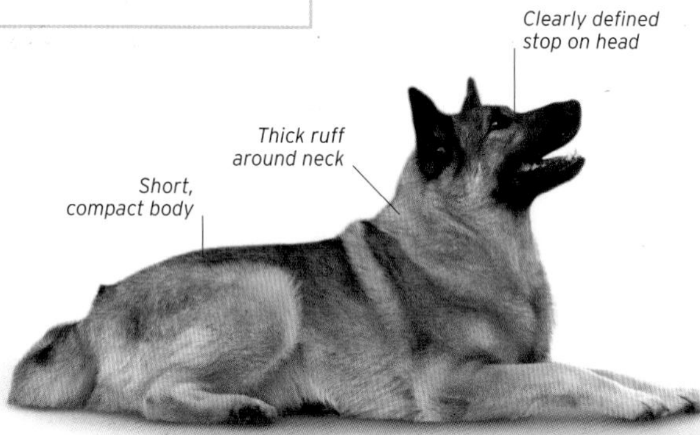
Clearly defined stop on head
Thick ruff around neck
Short, compact body

Black muzzle
Tightly curled tail carried high
Black-tipped hairs on outer, gray coat

BLACK NORWEGIAN ELKHOUND

THIS DOG FORMS STRONG FAMILY BONDS, BUT MAY BE A LITTLE STUBBORN TO TRAIN FCI

Height range
17-19in (43-49cm)

Weight range
40-60lb (18-27kg)

Life span 12-15 years

Origin Norway

This breed is a smaller, rarer version of the gray-coated Norwegian Elkhound (above). Originally bred for tracking game, it is versatile enough to be a sled dog, herder, watchdog, or family companion. It tends to bark readily but can be taught to stop on command.

Broad top of head
Small, white marking on feet

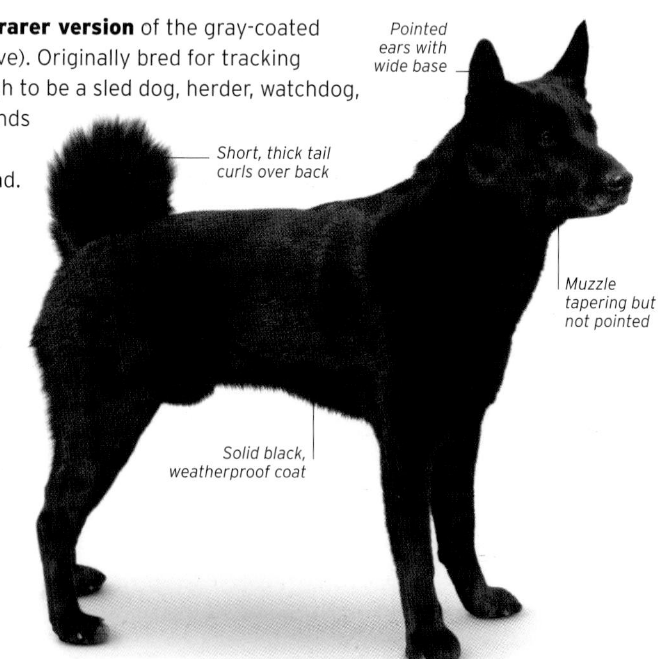
Pointed ears with wide base
Short, thick tail curls over back
Muzzle tapering but not pointed
Solid black, weatherproof coat

HOKKAIDO DOG

FEARLESS YET GENTLE AT HOME, THIS DOG NEEDS SUPERVISION WITH OTHER ANIMALS FCI

Height range 18–20in (46–52cm)

Weight range 44–66lb (20–30kg)

Life span 11–13 years

Origin Japan

Other colors

Variety of colors

Dogs of this type were brought to the Japanese island of Hokkaido by the migrating Ainu people (Ainu Dog is the breed's alternative name). Although medium-sized, the Hokkaido Dog was bold and tough enough to hunt bears. Careful training and socializing can make this dog a good companion and home guardian.

Strong, straight back
Thick tail curled over back
Muscular neck
Smallish, dark, triangular eyes
Harsh, straight, sesame-colored coat

SHIKOKU

THIS BREED RESPONDS READILY TO AFFECTION, BUT SHOULD NOT BE TRUSTED WITH SMALL PETS FCI

Height range 18–20in (46–52cm)

Weight range 35–57lb (16–26kg)

Life span 10–12 years

Origin Japan

Other colors

Sesame and black sesame

Once used as a boar-hunter in remote mountain regions of Japan, the Shikoku remained largely inaccessible for crossbreeding. As a result, this breed is very true to its origins. Resilient, agile, and keen to chase other animals, the Shikoku is challenging to train but forms a close bond with people it loves and trusts.

Firmly erect ears

Typical "spitz" tail

Dark eyes have keen expression

Moderately long, wedge-shaped muzzle

Deep chest

Powerful hind quarters

Red-sesame coat

Muscular, thick neck

AKITA

THIS DOG HAS VARIABLE TEMPERAMENT AND REQUIRES EXPERIENCED HANDLING

AKC

Height range
American:
24–28in (61–71cm)
Japanese:
23–28in (58–70cm)

Weight range
American:
65–115lb (29–52kg)
Japanese:
78–99lb (34–45kg)

Life span 10–12 years

Origin Japan

Other colors

Any color

This breed was first developed in 19th-century Japan as a fighting dog, before breeders in the US took an interest. Sometimes referred to as the American Akita, this substantial and strikingly handsome dog has a quiet dignity but also a tendency to be domineering with other dogs. Without an experienced owner to set the rules at a young age, this breed may become wayward or aggressive. A smaller dog, the Japanese Akita Inu, shares a common early ancestry with its American cousin and in many countries is now regarded as a separate breed.

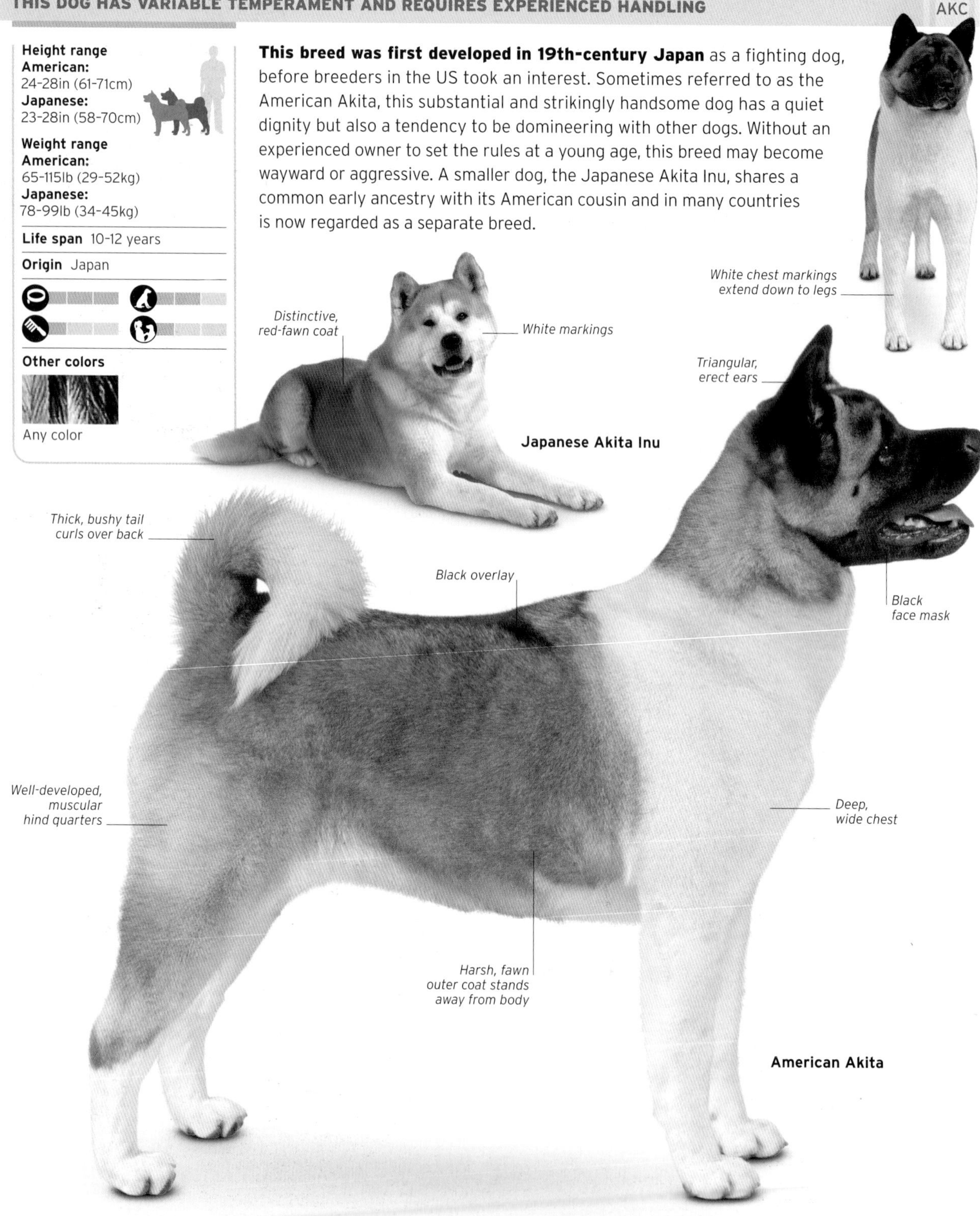
White chest markings extend down to legs
Distinctive, red-fawn coat
White markings
Triangular, erect ears
Thick, bushy tail curls over back
Black overlay
Black face mask
Well-developed, muscular hind quarters
Deep, wide chest
Harsh, fawn outer coat stands away from body

Japanese Akita Inu

American Akita

CHOW CHOW

THIS DOG IS LOYAL TO ITS OWNER BUT STANDOFFISH WITH STRANGERS

AKC

Height range
18-22in (46-56cm)

Weight range
46-71lb (21-32kg)

Life span 8-12 years

Origin China

Other colors

Cream

Gold

Blue

Although not seen in the West until the 19th century, dogs of this type have been known in China for around 2,000 years. The breed's original uses included guarding and hunting, and it may possibly have been a source of meat and fur. No other dog looks quite like this breed, with its stocky build, scowling face, and unique blue-black tongue. The Chow Chow is very independent and may have a stubborn streak, so needs firm training and early socializing. There are two varieties: rough-coated with an immensely thick, standout coat; and smooth-coated with short, dense hair.

Characteristic scowling expression
Unique blue-black tongue
Small, thick, rounded ears
Distinctive stop
Tail carried over back
Profuse, red coat stands out from body
Lighter hair on back of legs
Small, round feet

Rough-coated

KOREAN JINDO

THIS INDEPENDENT DOG HAS A STRONG HUNTING INSTINCT AND NEEDS EARLY SOCIALIZING KC

Height range
18–21in (46–53cm)

Weight range
20–50lb (9–23kg)

Life span 12–15 years

Origin Korea

Other colors

White
Red
Black and tan

Named after the Korean island of Jindo where it originated, the breed is popular in Korea but something of a rarity elsewhere. Used to hunt game, both large and small, the Korean Jindo's keen instinct for chasing other animals may be difficult to curb.

Stiff, fawn hairs stand away from body
Erect, pointed ears, lined with dense hairs
Longer coat on backs of thighs
Thicker hair on neck
Tucked-up belly
Rounded, catlike feet

SHIBA INU

THIS KEEN, PERKY, FAST-MOVING DOG HAS A STRONG URGE TO HUNT AKC

Height range
15–16in (37–40cm)

Weight range
15–24lb (7–11kg)

Life span 12–15 years

Origin Japan

Other colors

White
Black and tan

Red dogs may have a black overlay (red sesame).

Japan's smallest hunting dog, the Shiba Inu is a "national treasure" and has been known in its native country for hundreds of years. Bold and lively, the Shiba Inu makes a happy family dog. However, it can be unreliable with other pets, if not socialized early on, and needs to have its hunting instinct controlled outdoors.

Small, triangular ears incline slightly forward

Longer-haired tail carried in high curl

Dark brown eyes are keen and alert

Coarse-haired, red coat

Whitish under-markings

Rounded, catlike feet

KAI

THIS ONE-MAN DOG IS GOOD AT GUARDING BUT IS BEST KEPT ON A LEASH OUTDOORS FCI

Height range
19–21in (48–53cm)

Weight range
25–55lb (11–25kg)

Life span 12–15 years

Origin Japan

Other colors

Range of red brindles

One of the oldest and purest of Japan's native dog breeds, the Kai was given the status of "national treasure" in 1934. An active and athletic hunter, used to running in packs, this dog may settle reasonably well into being a home companion but is not recommended for a novice owner.

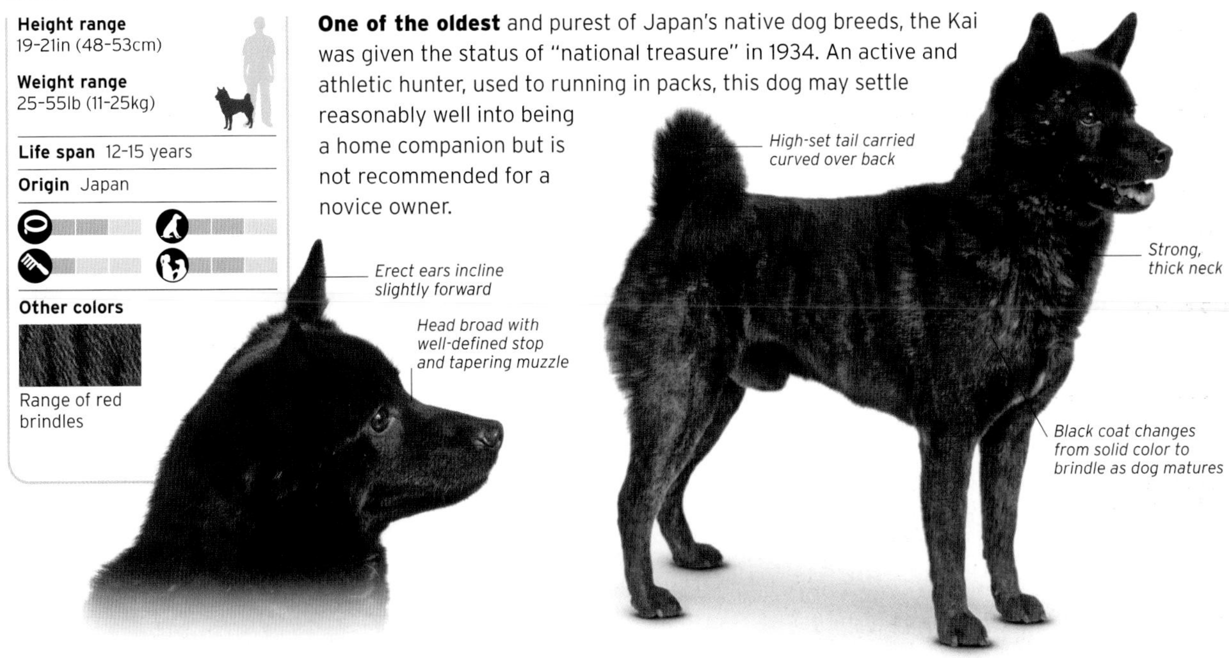
Erect ears incline slightly forward
Head broad with well-defined stop and tapering muzzle
High-set tail carried curved over back
Strong, thick neck
Black coat changes from solid color to brindle as dog matures

KISHU

THIS NATURAL HUNTER IS GOOD WITH OTHER DOGS BUT CAN BE SELF-WILLED FCI

Height range
18–20in (46–52cm)

Weight range
29–60lb (13–27kg)

Life span 11–13 years

Origin Japan

Now rare but much prized, the Kishu was possibly bred hundreds of years ago for hunting large game in Japan's mountainous Kyushu region. A "national treasure," this dog is quiet and faithful but can be a handful as a companion because of its strong instinct to chase.

Erect ears incline forward

Some longer, black hairs

Short, straight, well-muscled back

Thick, fringed tail carried in curl over back

Dark brown eyes

Dense, white coat

Short, straight, coarse, red coat

White markings on feet and lower legs

JAPANESE SPITZ

SUITABLE FOR SMALL HOMES, THIS SOCIABLE AND CONFIDENT SPITZ LOVES EXERCISE KC

Height range 12–15in (30–37cm)

Weight range 11–22lb (5–10kg)

Life span Over 12 years

Origin Japan

Although the Japanese Spitz looks like a miniature version of the Samoyed (see p.106), there is no evidence that the two have a common descent. The breed was developed in Japan, and the popularity of this bright and energetic little dog has spread worldwide. Persistent barking is characteristic but can be controlled with training.

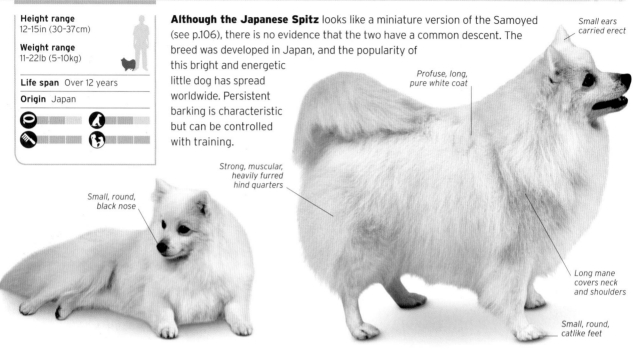

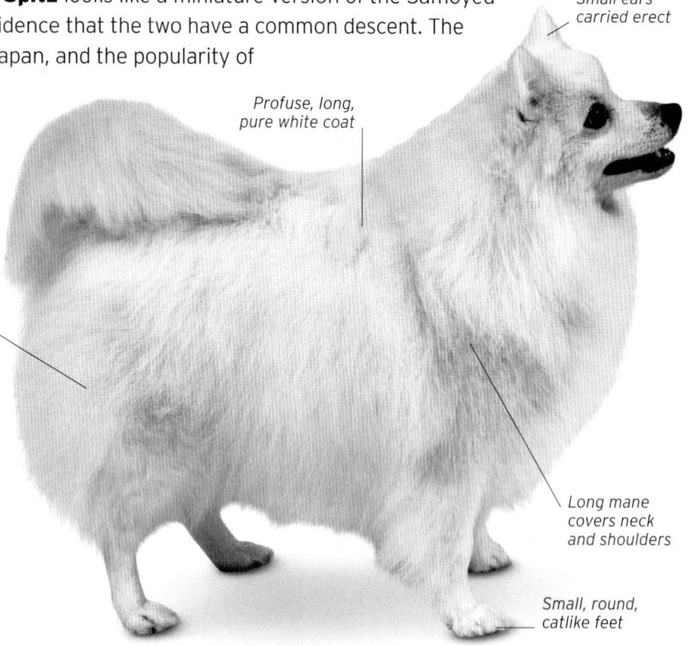

Small ears carried erect

Profuse, long, pure white coat

Strong, muscular, heavily furred hind quarters

Small, round, black nose

Long mane covers neck and shoulders

Small, round, catlike feet

EURASIER

THIS FAMILY-LOVING DOG IS A LITTLE RESERVED WITH STRANGERS BUT NOT EASILY PROVOKED KC

Height range 19–24in (48–60cm)

Weight range 40–71lb (18–32kg)

Life span Over 12 years

Origin Germany

Other colors

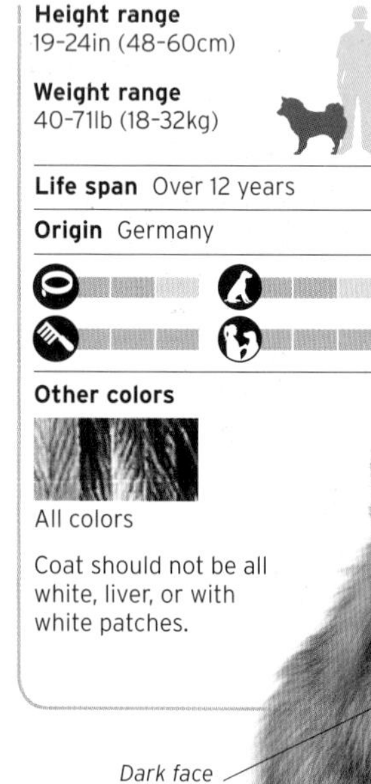

All colors

Coat should not be all white, liver, or with white patches.

A modern and still rare breed, the Eurasier was created in Germany in the 1960s from crossing the Chow Chow (see p.113), German Wolfspitz (see p.118), and Russian Samoyed (see p.106). A good companion dog, it is even-tempered and calm but watchful. It readily forms close family bonds.

Harsh-textured topcoat

Straight, strong back

Triangular, erect ears

Collar of longer hair

Fawn coat with black hairs

Dark face mask

ITALIAN VOLPINO

SMALL BUT INTREPID, THIS ALERT DOG HAS A BRIGHT AND PLAYFUL PERSONALITY FCI

Height range
10-12in (25-30cm)

Weight range
9-11lb (4-5kg)

Life span Up to 16 years

Origin Italy

Other colors

Red

A favorite in Italy for over a century, this appealing little dog was kept by nobility as a pampered pet, and by farmers as a watchdog. Quick to bark at strangers, the Italian Volpino alerted bigger guard dogs to potential trouble. Lively and fun-loving, the breed is suitable for almost any type of home.

Short muzzle
Long-haired tail carried in curl
Well-feathered hind quarters
Thick collar of hair around neck
Long, dense, white coat
Round eyes

SCHIPPERKE

THIS SHARP, INQUISITIVE DOG IS PROTECTIVE DESPITE ITS SMALL SIZE AKC

Height range
10-13in (25-33cm)

Weight range
13-18lb (6-8kg)

Life span Over 12 years

Origin Belgium

Other Colors

Variety of colors

Sometimes called the Belgian Barge Dog, this breed was once used by Flemish river-boatmen to guard their barges and keep down rat populations. In the house, the Schipperke has lost none of its watchful instincts and is wary of strangers. A dog with a lively and likeable personality, it is an entertaining companion.

Small, triangular ears

Wedge-shaped, fox-like head

Dense, black coat

Tail naturally very short

Long "culottes" on back of thighs

Thickset body

Distinctive mane and cape around neck and shoulders

KEESHOND

THIS NON-AGGRESSIVE WATCHDOG IS EASY TO TRAIN, AFFECTIONATE, AND SOCIABLE AKC

Height range
17–18in (43–46cm)

Weight range
33–44lb (15–20kg)

Life span 12–15 years

Origin The Netherlands

The Keeshond was used in the 18th century by the river-boatmen and farmers of Holland as a watchdog. Not aggressive, this intelligent and outgoing breed has an amiable nature that makes it a much-loved companion dog. The Keeshond is willing to learn, and mixes well with people and other pets.

Characteristic "spectacle" markings around eyes
Long, thick ruff around neck
Gray and black coat
High-set tail curls over back
Hair forms dense "breeches" on backs of thighs
Well-defined shoulder markings
Shorter cream-colored hair on lower legs and feet

GERMAN WOLFSPITZ

INTELLIGENT AND QUICK TO LEARN, THIS GOOD WATCHDOG IS EXCELLENT WITH FAMILIES

Height range
17–22in (43–55cm)

Weight range
60–71lb (27–32kg)

Life span 12–15 years

Origin Germany

The German Wolfspitz is one of the oldest-known European dogs. It has given rise to the Keeshond and in some countries the two are not regarded as separate types. Highly trainable, it is eager to be a part of family life. Suspicious of strangers, this dog barks readily but is not aggressive.

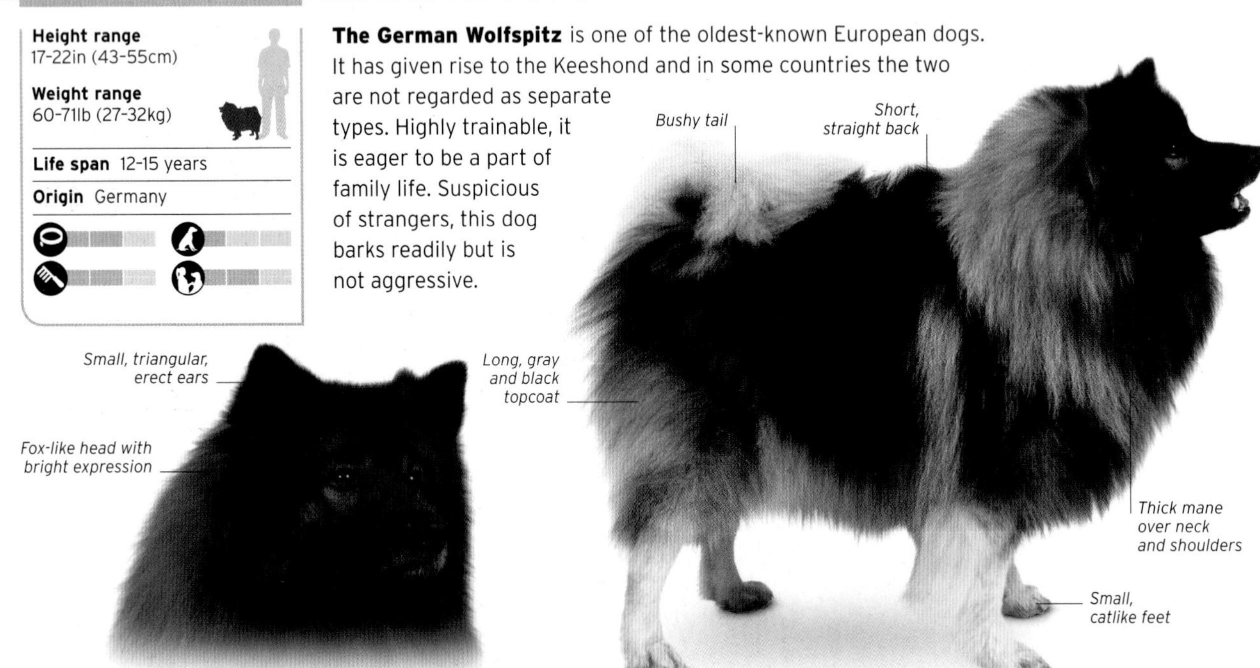
Bushy tail
Short, straight back
Small, triangular, erect ears
Long, gray and black topcoat
Fox-like head with bright expression
Thick mane over neck and shoulders
Small, catlike feet

GERMAN SPITZ

A BUSTLING AND HAPPY DOG, WITH GOOD WATCH INSTINCTS, AND SUITABLE FOR ANY HOME KC

Height range
Klein:
9-11in (23-29cm)
Mittel:
12-15in (30-38cm)
Gross:
17-20in (42-50cm)

Weight range
Klein:
18-22lb (8-10kg)
Mittel:
24-26lb (11-12kg)
Gross:
38-40lb (17-18kg)

Life span 14-15 years

Origin Germany

Other colors

Variety of colors

There are three sizes of the German Spitz—Klein (small) and Mittel (standard) are both recognized by KC, and Gross (giant) is recognized by FCI. They all are descendants of the herding dogs once used by nomadic tribes of the Arctic. German Spitzes need patient training because they have an independent spirit that can turn into wilfulness without firm leadership. Once their place in the family has been established, these cheerful and affectionate dogs are excellent companions for owners of all ages. Thorough and regular grooming sessions are needed to prevent the immensely thick coat from becoming matted.

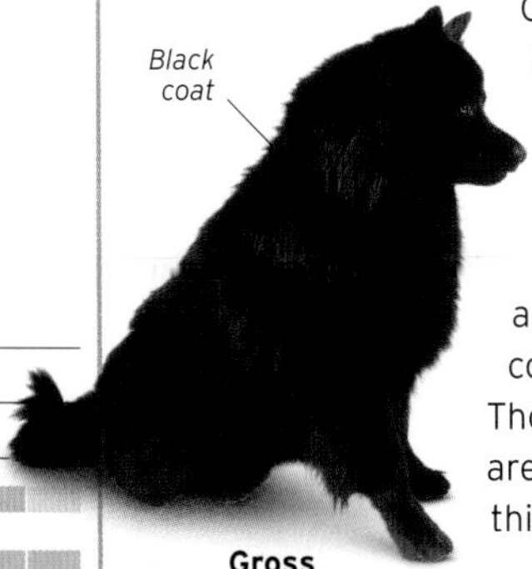

Black coat

Gross

White coat

Wolf-sable coat

Klein

Short hair on face

Moderately broad head

Compact, square body

Tail curls over back

Thick frill around neck and shoulders

Long feathering on backs of legs

Profuse double coat with long, orange-sable outer hair

Mittel

ICELANDIC SHEEPDOG

A SMART, CHEERFUL, VOCAL, AND COMPANIONABLE DOG AKC

Height range 17-18in (42-46cm)

Weight range 20-31lb (9-14kg)

Life span 12-15 years

Origin Iceland

Other colors

Gray

Chocolate brown

Black

Tan and gray dogs may have black masks.

Also called the Friaar Dog, this hardy, muscular breed was brought to Iceland by early settlers. Its agility over rugged terrain and shallow water plus its keen barking make it perfect for herding livestock. As a pet, it requires plenty of exercise. There are two coat types: long-haired and short-haired.

Erect ears slightly rounded at tip
Smallish, rectangular, powerful body
Typical spitz tail curls over back
Black pigmented lips
White markings on face
Thick, waterproof tan coat with white markings

Long-haired

NORWEGIAN LUNDEHUND

THIS ACROBATIC, PROTECTIVE HUNTER HAS AN INDEPENDENT STREAK AKC

Height range 13-15in (32-38cm)

Weight range 13-15lb (6-7kg)

Life span 12 years

Origin Norway

Other colors

White

Gray

Black

Black and gray coats have white markings; white coat has dark markings.

Also called the Norwegian Puffin Dog, this amazingly agile dog can tilt its head back over its shoulder and splay its forelegs out sideways. Once used as a puffin-hunter, these traits, as well as an extra toe on each foot, enabled the dog to reach precarious nests. As a pet, it needs plenty of training and exercise.

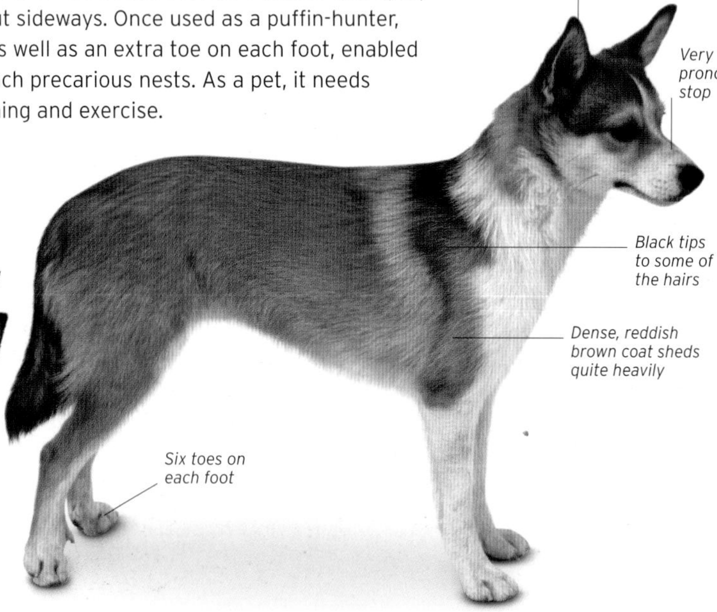

Triangular, erect ears

Very pronounced stop

Black tips to some of the hairs

Wedge-shaped head

Dense, reddish brown coat sheds quite heavily

Six toes on each foot

NORDIC SPITZ

THIS LIVELY, LOVING, LONG-LIVED DOG HAS NO DOG ODOR

FCI

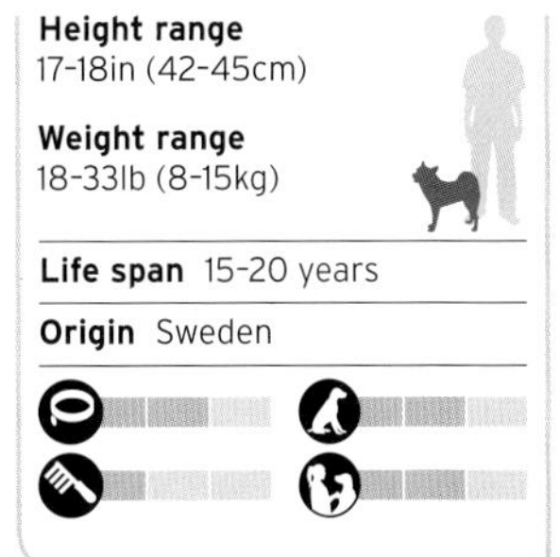

Height range 17–18in (42–45cm)

Weight range 18–33lb (8–15kg)

Life span 15–20 years

Origin Sweden

This small, light spitz is Sweden's national dog, though it is little known outside its native country. Its local name, Norbottenspets, means "spitz from the county of Bothnia." It was once used to hunt squirrels and, more recently, game birds. A bright-eyed, bushy-tailed dog, the Nordic Spitz is not difficult to train as a house pet, but requires regular, energetic exercise.

Erect, black ears

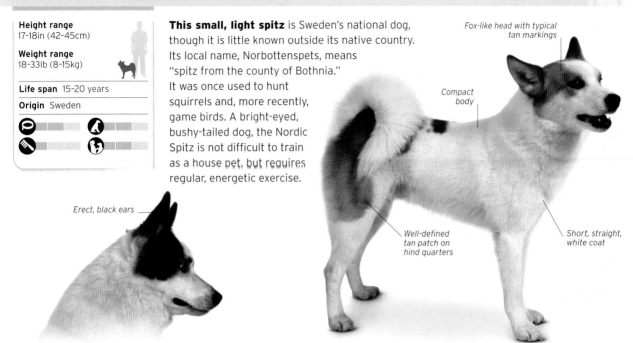

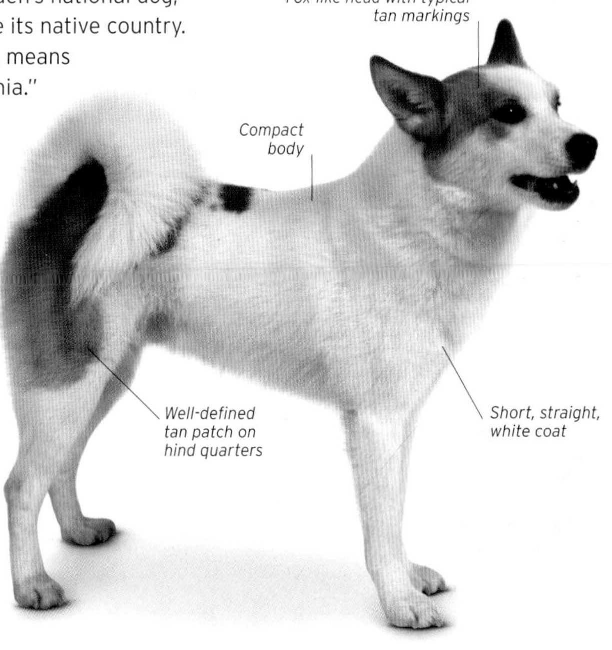
Fox-like head with typical tan markings
Compact body
Well-defined tan patch on hind quarters
Short, straight, white coat

NORWEGIAN BUHUND

THIS WORKING FARM DOG NEEDS AN ENERGETIC, OUTDOOR-LOVING OWNER

AKC

Height range 16–18in (41–46cm)

Weight range 26–40lb (12–18kg)

Life span 12–15 years

Origin Norway

Other colors

Red

Coat may be wolf-sable. Red, wheaten, and wolf-sable coats may have a black mask, ears, and tip to tail.

This medium-sized, agile farm dog was once used to guard against bears and wolves. Today the breed thrives when it has plenty of exercise and constant training. A keen barker that molts heavily twice a year, this may not be the ideal dog for a house-proud owner.

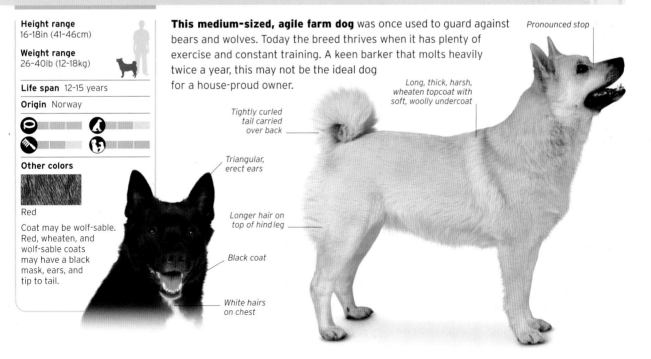

Pronounced stop

Long, thick, harsh, wheaten topcoat with soft, woolly undercoat

Tightly curled tail carried over back

Triangular, erect ears

Longer hair on top of hind leg

Black coat

White hairs on chest

PAPILLON

THIS DAINTY AND DELIGHTFUL DOG IS A LIVELY AND INTELLIGENT COMPANION AKC

Height range
8–11in (20–28cm)

Weight range
4–11lb (2–5kg)

Life span 14 years

Origin France/Belgium

Other colors

Black and white

White

White coats may have any color patches except liver.

Also known as the Continental Toy Spaniel, this little dog makes a charming companion. Often portrayed in European court paintings (the breed was a particular favorite of Marie Antoinette), the Papillon has eye-catching "butterfly-wing" ears and distinctive facial markings. A drop-eared variety is known as the Phalene (French for moth). These dogs love human companionship and enjoy plenty of play and exercise. They require early socializing with other dogs and strangers. The long, fine, silky coat needs daily grooming to prevent mats forming.

Long-fringed, "butterfly-wing" ears
Drop ears
Long, plumed tail falls over back
Full, soft, tricolor coat
Fine, pointed muzzle on rounded head
Elongated hare-like feet

Phalene

POMERANIAN

AN AFFECTIONATE MINIATURE BREED THAT IS BRAVE AND PROTECTIVE DESPITE ITS SMALL SIZE AKC

Height range
9-11in (22-28cm)

Weight range
4-6lb (2-3kg)

Life span 12-15 years

Origin Germany

Other colors

Any solid color

Should be free from black or white shading.

Smallest of the German Spitz-type dogs (see p.119), the Pomeranian was selectively bred down to "toy" size during the 19th century. Intelligent and attention-seeking, the Pomeranian readily returns affection and will become devoted to its owner. Amazingly fast for their size, these dogs should be supervised if running loose. The thick coat is not difficult to groom.

Heavily plumed tail carried over back
Smooth-haired, fox-like face
Longer hair on hind quarters
Soft, fluffy, orange coat
Abundant frill around neck, shoulders, and chest

AMERICAN ESKIMO DOG

ULTRA-BRIGHT, OBEDIENT, AND FUN-LOVING, THIS DOG ENJOYS WORK AND PLAY AKC

Height range
Miniature:
9-12in (23-30cm)
Toy:
12-15in (30-38cm)
Standard:
Over 15-19in (Over 38-48cm)

Weight range
Miniature:
6-11lb (3-5kg)
Toy:
11-20lb (5-9kg)
Standard:
20-40lb (9-18kg)

Life span 12-13 years

Origin USA

Despite its name, this is not a true Eskimo breed, but was developed in Germany and probably brought to the US by German settlers in the 19th century. Once seen performing tricks in traveling circuses, the American Eskimo Dog is a fast learner and eager to please. The breed comes in three sizes: toy, miniature, and standard.

Triangular, erect, slightly blunt-tipped ears
Long, white guard hairs form topcoat
Round eyes, set well apart with black rims
Jet-black lips
Profuse ruff at neck and chest
Toy
Toy

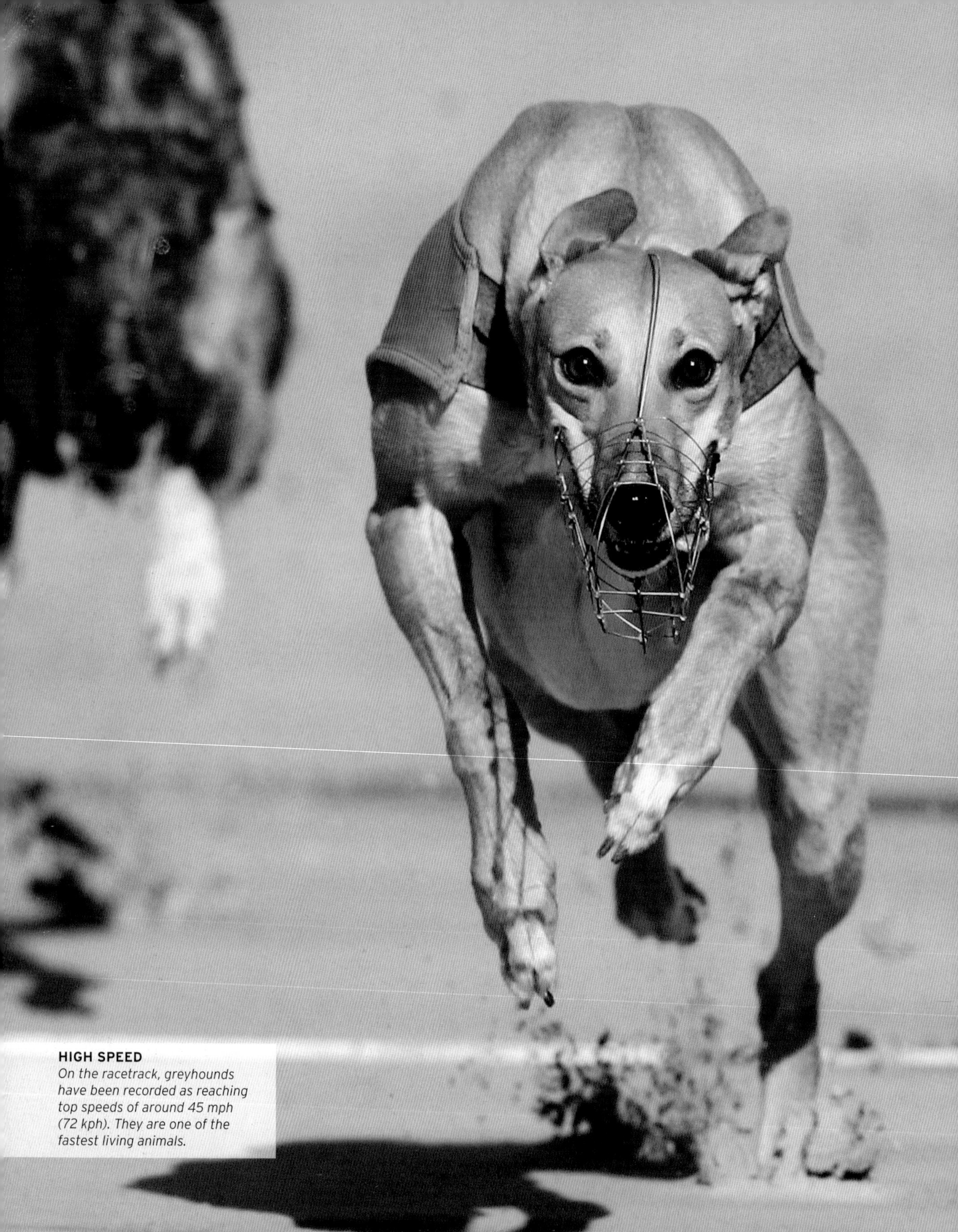

HIGH SPEED
On the racetrack, greyhounds have been recorded as reaching top speeds of around 45 mph (72 kph). They are one of the fastest living animals.

SIGHT HOUNDS

Canine speed-merchants, the sight hounds—or gazehounds as they are sometimes called—are hunting dogs that locate and follow their prey primarily by using their keen eyesight. Streamlined, lightly framed, but powerful, a sight hound in pursuit of quarry moves fast and turns with great flexibility. Many dogs in this group were bred to hunt specific prey.

Irish Wolfhounds were used for hunting in Roman times

As shown by archaeological evidence, lean, leggy dogs have been hunting alongside humans for thousands of years, but the early development of modern sight hounds is not entirely clear. It is likely that many crosses involving a diversity of other breeds, including terriers, went into the creation of classic sight hounds such as the Greyhound and the Whippet.

Most sight hounds are easily recognizable as a type. Selective breeding has developed characteristics designed to promote speed: strong, supple backs and an athletic build enable the body to stretch out at full gallop; long-striding, elastic limbs; and powerful hindquarters to provide impulsion. Another characteristic is a long, narrow head that either lacks a pronounced stop or, as in the case of the Borzoi, has no stop at all. Typically in a sighthound bred to hunt and snap up small prey, the head is carried low when the dog runs at full stretch. Another common feature of sight hounds is a deep chest accommodating a larger than usual heart and allowing for good lung capacity. Short or fine silky coats tend to be the norm among this group of dogs; only the Afghan Hound is very long-haired.

Graceful and aristocratic, sight hounds during their history have been the favored hunting dogs of the wealthy and wellborn. Greyhounds, or at least coursing dogs very similar to the modern breed, were kept by the pharaohs of ancient Egypt. For centuries Salukis were, and occasionally still are, used by sheikhs for hunting gazelle in the desert. In pre-Soviet Russia the spectacular Borzoi was the dog of choice for the nobility and even royalty, specifically bred for running down and killing wolves.

Today sight hounds are used for racing and coursing and are very often kept as pets. Usually nonaggressive, although sometimes a little aloof, sight hounds make attractive family dogs but need handling with caution when outdoors and may be best exercised on a leash. Their instinct to chase small animals can be strong enough to override all obedience training. A sight hound chasing after what it perceives to be prey is almost impossible to stop.

HOME LIFE
Many former racing greyhounds settle down well as family companions. Their desire to chase can be channeled into play.

ARISTOCRAT
The long-nosed Borzoi looks purely decorative, but this dog was once used in Russia for hunting and could bring down a fully grown wolf.

GREYHOUND

THE SWIFTEST OF ALL DOGS, BUT DOCILE AND GENTLE AT HOME AKC

Height range
27-30in (69-76cm)

Weight range
60-66lb (27-30kg)

Life span 11-12 years

Origin UK

Other colors

Any color

Capable of reaching 45mph (72km/h) in short bursts, the sleek and powerful Greyhound is purpose-built for running. Although the modern Greyhound was developed in the UK, the breed's earliest ancestors may have been the similar-looking dogs depicted in Egyptian tombs dating back some 4,000 years BCE. Originally bred to hunt hare, today these dogs are raced for sport. As a pet, the Greyhound needs only moderate daily exercise, and is happy lounging around at home the rest of the time.

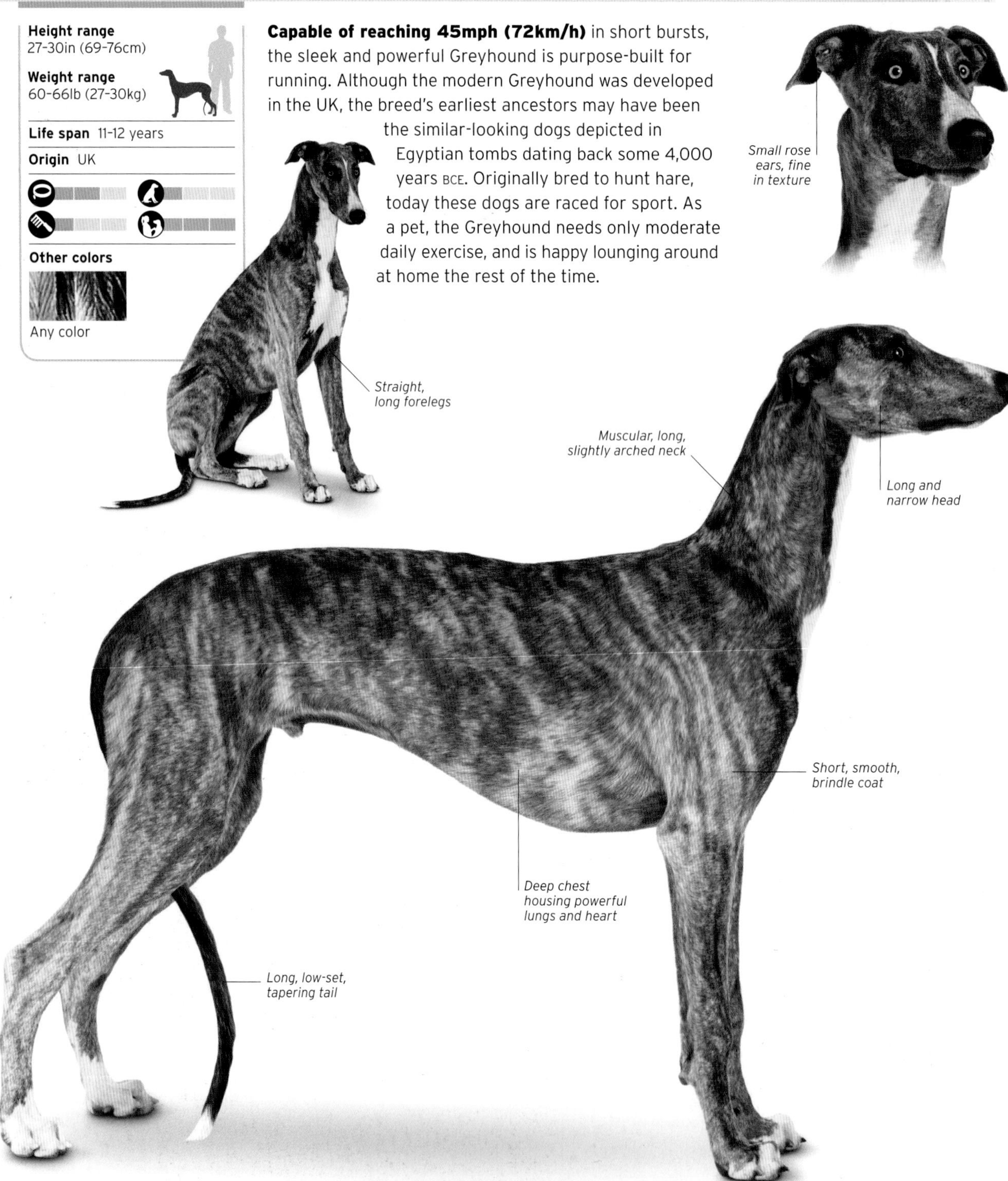
Small rose ears, fine in texture
Straight, long forelegs
Muscular, long, slightly arched neck
Long and narrow head
Short, smooth, brindle coat
Deep chest housing powerful lungs and heart
Long, low-set, tapering tail

ITALIAN GREYHOUND

THIS MINIATURE, SATIN-SKINNED GREYHOUND ENJOYS CREATURE COMFORTS AKC

Height range
13–15in (32–38cm)

Weight range
8–10lb (4–5kg)

Life span 14 years

Origin Italy

Other colors

Variety of colors

Black and blue with tan markings, and brindle not permitted.

This mini-greyhound was a much favored pet in the courts of the Renaissance, and still loves to be pampered. Despite its small size, the Italian Greyhound is fast and can reach 40mph (60km/h) in a sudden chase. The breed's short coat makes it susceptible to the cold, but it does need regular outdoor exercise.

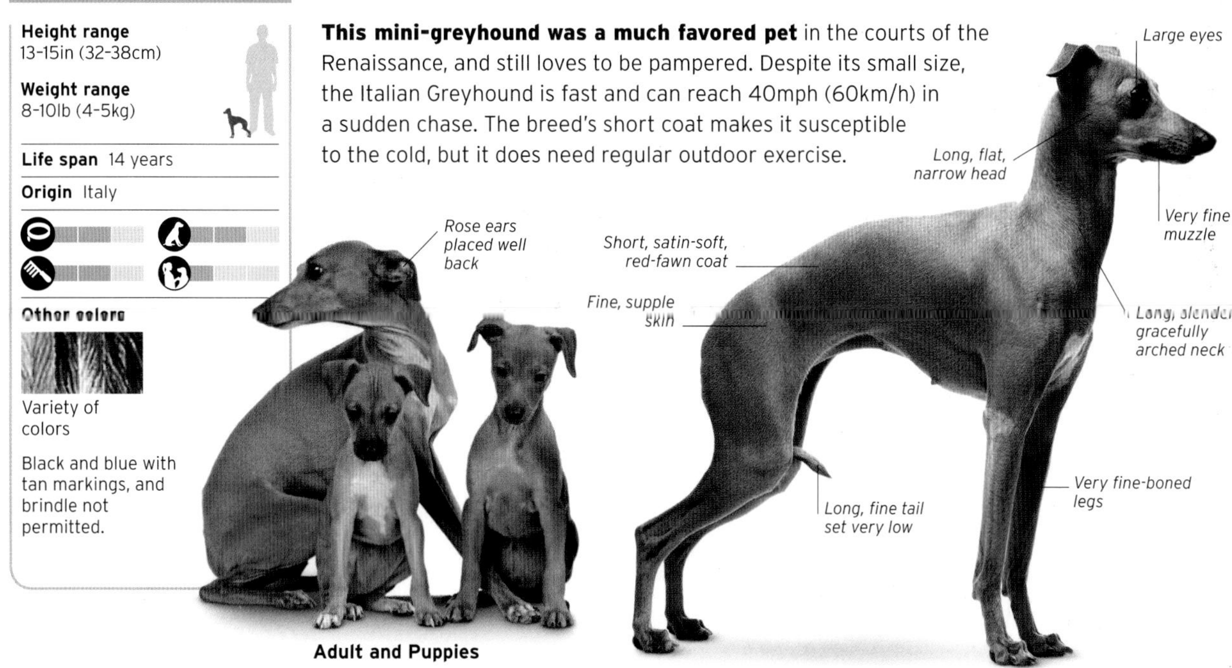

Large eyes
Long, flat, narrow head
Very fine muzzle
Rose ears placed well back
Short, satin-soft, red-fawn coat
Fine, supple skin
Long, slender, gracefully arched neck
Very fine-boned legs
Long, fine tail set very low

Adult and Puppies

HUNGARIAN GREYHOUND

THIS VIGILANT HOUSE DOG IS PACKED WITH SPEED AND STAMINA FCI

Height range
24–28in (62–70cm)

Weight range
55–88lb (25–40kg)

Life span 12–14 years

Origin Hungary

Other colors

Any color

This dog, once used for hunting hare and fox, may have entered Hungary with the Magyars over 1,000 years ago. Not as fast as a Greyhound (opposite) but tougher and tireless, the Hungarian Greyhound (or Magyar Agar) needs a regular run. It makes a faithful and protective companion.

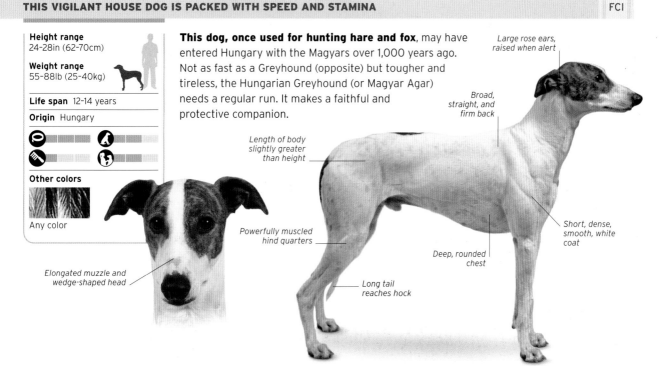

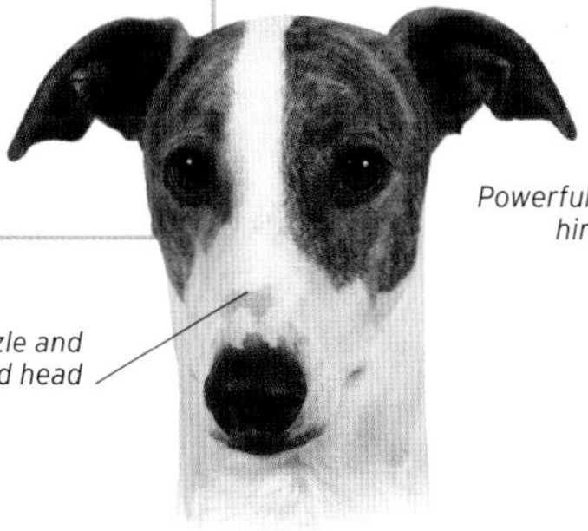

Large rose ears, raised when alert

Broad, straight, and firm back

Length of body slightly greater than height

Short, dense, smooth, white coat

Powerfully muscled hind quarters

Deep, rounded chest

Elongated muzzle and wedge-shaped head

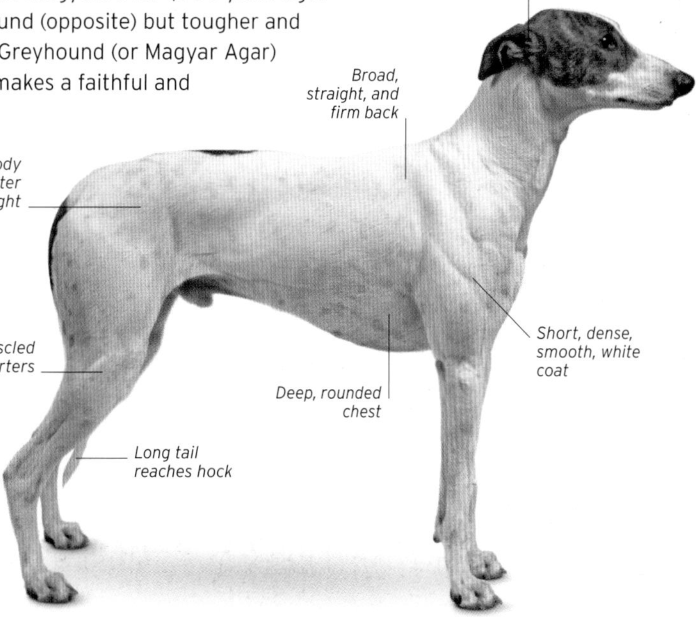

Long tail reaches hock

Expressive, oval eyes

Rose ears

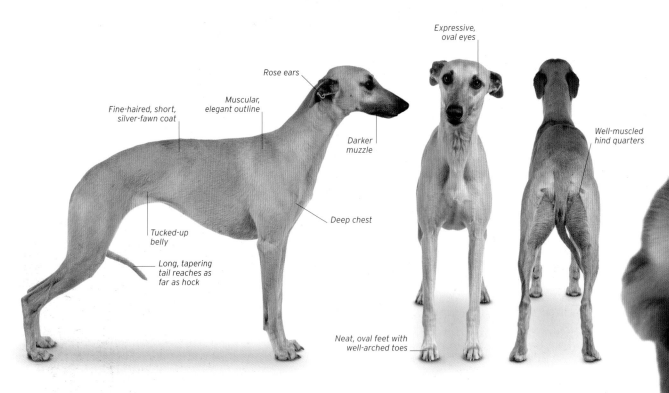

Muscular, elegant outline

Fine-haired, short, silver-fawn coat

Darker muzzle

Well-muscled hind quarters

Deep chest

Tucked-up belly

Long, tapering tail reaches as far as hock

Neat, oval feet with well-arched toes

WHIPPET

THE ULTIMATE SPRINTER, THIS DOG IS CALM, SWEET-NATURED, AND ADORING AT HOME AKC

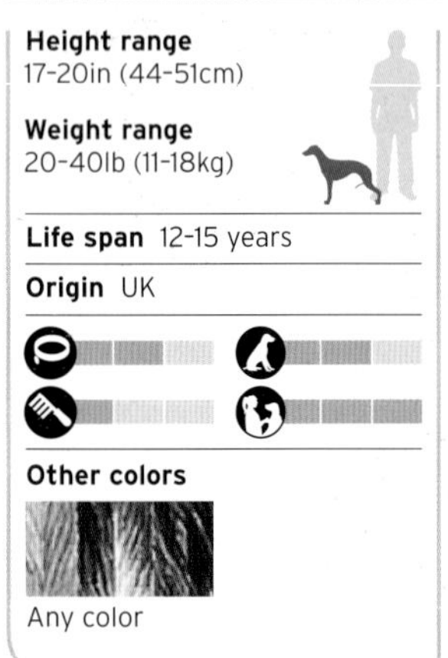
Height range
17–20in (44–51cm)
Weight range
20–40lb (11–18kg)
Life span 12–15 years
Origin UK
Other colors
Any color

The fastest domesticated animal for its weight, the Whippet is capable of speeds of up to 35mph (56kph). It has impressive powers of acceleration and can twist and turn at speed with dexterity. This elegant little dog was developed in the north of England in the late 19th century by crossing the Greyhound (see p.126) with various terriers. Originally bred for hunting hare, rabbit, and other small game, the Whippet soon became popular as an affordable sporting dog. Whippet racing, held wherever there was enough space for dogs to sprint a few hundred feet, became a regular fixture for working men of mill and mining towns. Today it is still used for racing, as well as lure coursing and agility trials, but is mostly kept as a pet.

Quiet, docile, and affectionate, the Whippet behaves well in the house and is gentle with children. A sensitive breed, it needs tactful handling and is easily distressed by rough play or harsh commands. With its delicate skin and short, fine hair, the Whippet needs to wear a coat in cold weather. Its own coat is almost odor-free, without a "doggy" smell even when wet. Puppies with long coats are occasionally born but are not officially recognized.

The Whippet has abundant energy and should be given regular exercise and, in safe areas, plenty of opportunity to run free. It is generally good with other dogs but has a strong hunting instinct and chases cats and small animals if given the chance. A Whippet will tolerate, or at least ignore, a household cat if the two are raised together but it should not be left unsupervised with other family pets such as rabbits or guinea pigs. This breed is wary with strangers, so it makes a reasonable watchdog. Toward its owners, the Whippet shows unswerving loyalty.

BORZOI

THIS NOBLE RUSSIAN HOUND, COMBINES SPEED, ELEGANCE, AND A CERTAIN NONCHALANCE AKC

Height range
27–29in (68–74cm)

Weight range
60–105lb (27–48kg)

Life span 11–13 years

Origin Russia

Other colors

Variety of colors

This large, frilly-haired, almost feline dog is arguably the most aristocratic of sight hounds. Once known as the Russian Wolfhound, it was bred to hunt wolves for tsars and nobles; often over 100 of these dogs would chase wolves through the snowbound tundra. Outside Russia the Borzoi has been bred for many years for companionship. Today the dog is happy in a regular home environment but needs plenty of long walks and runs. It also requires a routine of brushing and bathing to keep its long, wavy coat lustrous.

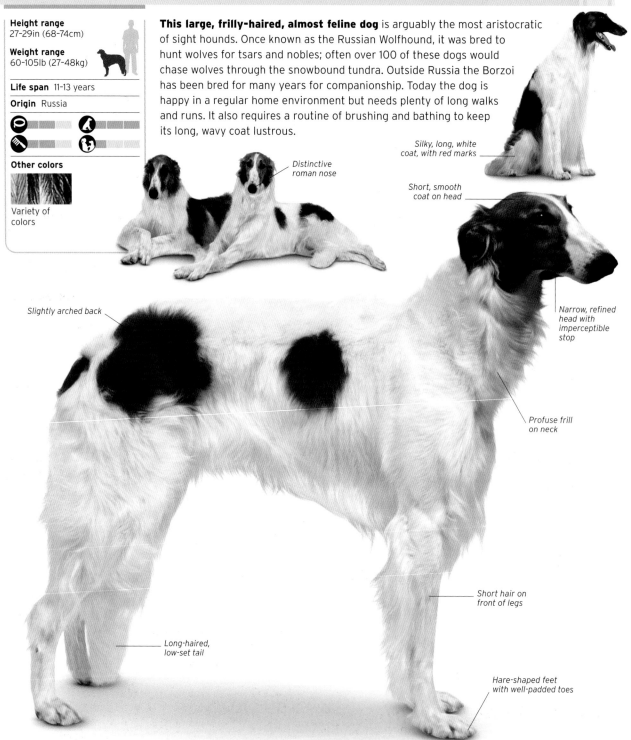

Silky, long, white coat, with red marks

Distinctive roman nose

Short, smooth coat on head

Narrow, refined head with imperceptible stop

Slightly arched back

Profuse frill on neck

Short hair on front of legs

Long-haired, low-set tail

Hare-shaped feet with well-padded toes

SALUKI

THIS SLIM-FRAMED, SLEEK, GAZELLE-HUNTER IS LOYAL AND COURAGEOUS AKC

Height range
23-28in (58-71cm)

Weight range
35-65lb (16-29kg)

Life span 12 years

Origin Persia

Other colors

Variety of colors

Reputed to be one of the few breeds that were mummified with the pharaohs of the Sumerian Empire, the Saluki (named after an ancient city) is esteemed in the Middle East for its swiftness over sand and is used for hunting with falcons. It is not an especially demonstrative or tactile pet and may seem somewhat aloof. There are two coat types: smooth and feathered.

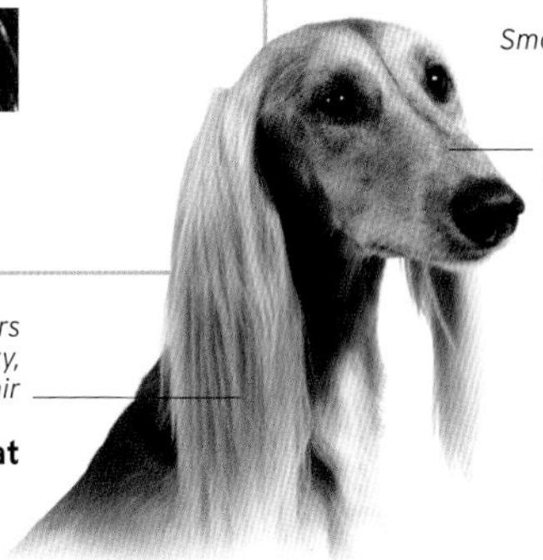

Pendant ears with long, silky, golden hair

Long, narrow head

Feathered coat

Long, slender, supple neck

Smooth, soft, silky coat

Deep, narrow chest

Slight feathering on back of legs

Black coat with tan markings

Feathered coat

POLISH GREYHOUND

THIS POWERFUL CHASER IS A FAST BUT FAMILY-FRIENDLY HOUND FCI

Height range
27-31in (68-80cm)

Weight range
143-187lb (65-85kg)

Life span 12-15 years

Origin Asia

Other colors

All colors

Possibly a mix of the Greyhound (see p.126) and the Borzoi (opposite) in origin, the Polish Greyhound is stronger and sturdier than other sight hounds. It is bred to hunt bustard (a large, crane-like bird) and wolves, and is a popular track racer. The Polish Greyhound requires firm training, plenty of exercise, and regular brushing.

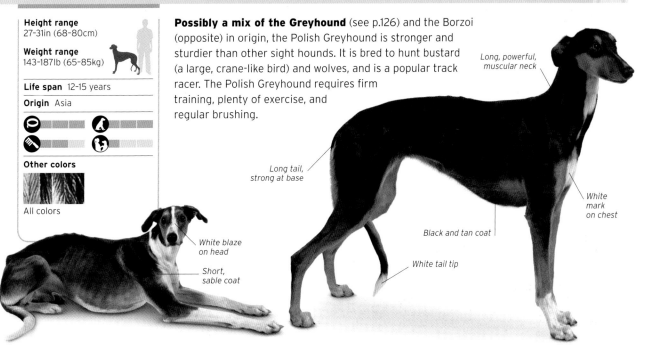

Long, powerful, muscular neck

Long tail, strong at base

White mark on chest

Black and tan coat

White tail tip

White blaze on head

Short, sable coat

IRISH WOLFHOUND

A LOYAL, DIGNIFIED, AND DOCILE HOUND, THIS GENTLE GIANT IS THE WORLD'S TALLEST BREED AKC

Height range
28–34in (71–86cm)

Weight range
105–150lb (48–68kg)

Life span 8–10 years

Origin Ireland

Other colors

Variety of colors

This seriously large and heavy dog can reach well over 6ft (1.8m) tall when standing on its hind legs. Once used to hunt wolves by Irish chieftains and kings, it later served as an army dog and is the Regimental Mascot of the Irish Guards. It makes a gentle companion and guard dog.

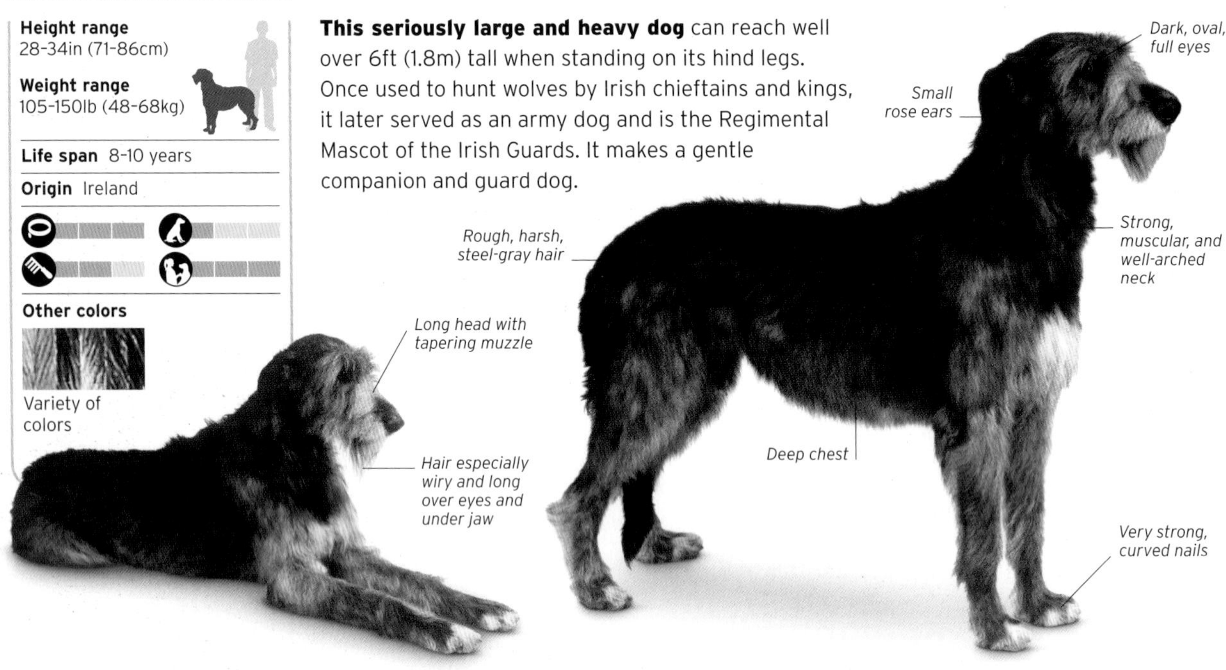
Dark, oval, full eyes
Small rose ears
Strong, muscular, and well-arched neck
Rough, harsh, steel-gray hair
Long head with tapering muzzle
Hair especially wiry and long over eyes and under jaw
Deep chest
Very strong, curved nails

SCOTTISH DEERHOUND

THIS FAST, FEARLESS, FRIENDLY DOG HAS A ROMANTIC SCOTTISH PAST AKC

Height range
28–30in (71–76cm)

Weight range
82–101lb (37–46kg)

Life span 10–11 years

Origin UK

Other colors

Red-fawn or sandy-red

Black brindle

Once the preserve of Scottish stag-hunting nobility, this shaggier version of the Irish Wolfhound (above) is now as much at home in a cosy living room as by a baronial log fire. It is lazy and companionable indoors so long as it has a strenuous walk every day and outdoor space to roam in.

Small rose ears
Pointed muzzle
Long, strong neck
Coat softer on head and chest
Silky haired, lighter-colored moustache and beard
Harsh, thick, wiry, dark blue-gray coat
Long tail, thick at base, carried low
White toes

AFGHAN HOUND

GLAMOROUS, ALOOF, AND HIGH-MAINTENANCE, THIS BREED IS THE SUPERMODEL OF DOGS AKC

Height range 25–29in (63–74cm)

Weight range 50–60lb (21–29kg)

Life span 12–14 years

Origin Afghanistan

Other colors

Any color

The glossiest and most elegant of dogs, the exact origin of the breed is unknown but it is thought to have been brought along trade routes to Afghanistan, where tribal chieftains used it to track deer, wild goats, and snow leopards. The Afghan Hound's long, luxurious coat protected it from the extreme climate of its original mountain home. In the 1930s Marx Brother "Zeppo" brought the breed to the US; and it has since been popular with celebrities. However, this independent and lively companion is also at home in sports and obedience events.

Dark eyes, almost triangular-looking, slanting slightly upward
Long muzzle and skull
Abundant top knot
Pendant ears covered with long, silky hair
Tail is relatively bare, carried in a ring and raised when moving
Long, silky, gold coat has fine texture except along short, close saddle
Feet strong and covered with thick, long hair

RAMPUR GREYHOUND

A SPEEDY, POWERFUL HUNTING DOG THAT IS NOT SUITABLE FOR URBAN LIFE

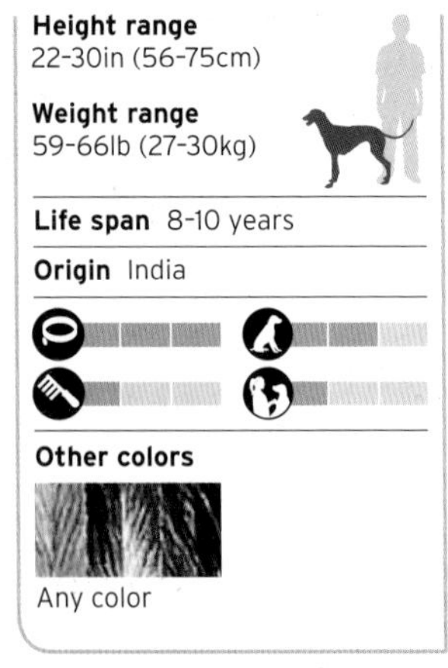

Height range 22-30in (56-75cm)

Weight range 59-66lb (27-30kg)

Life span 8-10 years

Origin India

Other colors

Any color

Now rare, the Rampur Greyhound was once the favorite sporting companion of Indian princes. Used mainly to hunt jackal and deer, this powerful dog was also capable of bringing down wild boar. The breed's origins are uncertain, but may include crosses between the English Greyhound and native Indian breeds chosen for their strength and tenacity.

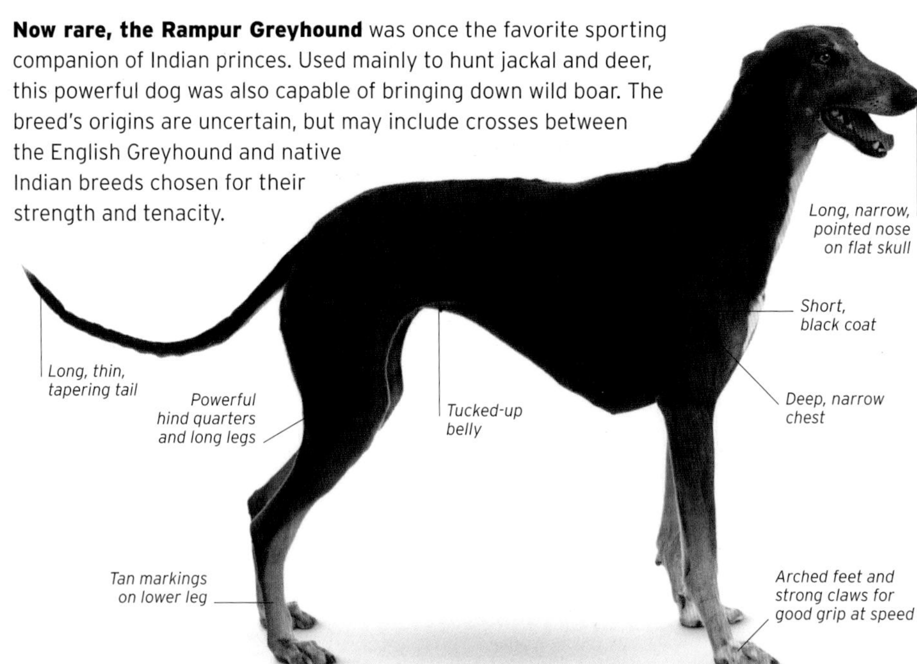
Long, narrow, pointed nose on flat skull
Short, black coat
Deep, narrow chest
Long, thin, tapering tail
Powerful hind quarters and long legs
Tucked-up belly
Tan markings on lower leg
Arched feet and strong claws for good grip at speed

SLOUGHI

THIS ELEGANT AND RACY DOG BONDS WITH FAMILY MEMBERS BUT IS ALOOF WITH STRANGERS KC

Height range 24-28in (61-72cm)

Weight range 44-60lb (20-27kg)

Life span 12 years

Origin North Africa

Long established in North Africa, where it is much prized as a hunting dog, the Sloughi has only recently become known in Europe and the US. This quiet-natured breed is a pleasant companion and likes home life. A Sloughi needs early socializing with other household pets since its urge to chase small animals is strong.

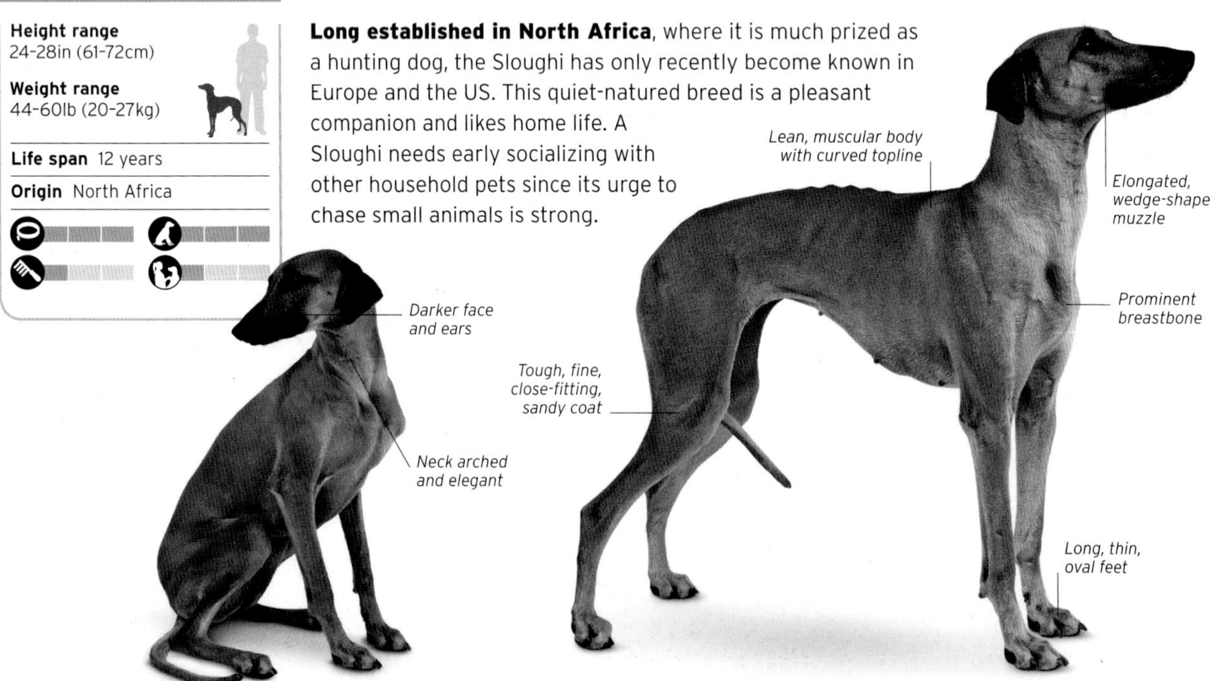
Lean, muscular body with curved topline
Elongated, wedge-shaped muzzle
Darker face and ears
Prominent breastbone
Tough, fine, close-fitting, sandy coat
Neck arched and elegant
Long, thin, oval feet

SPANISH GREYHOUND

BRED TO HUNT, THIS GENTLE BUT UNDEMONSTRATIVE DOG CAN ADAPT TO HOME LIFE KC

Height range 23-28in (58-72cm)

Weight range 44-66lb (20-30kg)

Life span 12 years

Origin Spain

Other colors

Any color

Thought to be a descendant of dogs that came into the Iberian Peninsula with the Celts, around 500 BCE, the Spanish Greyhound is a fast-footed hunter. Once kept only by royalty, the breed became widely popular for coursing and racing. Spanish Greyhounds are not hard to train as house dogs but have high exercise requirements. There are two coat varieties: smooth-haired and wire-haired.

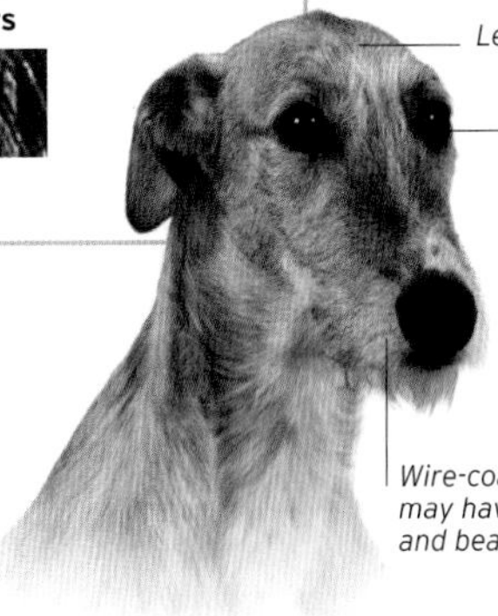

Very shallow stop

Long, straight back

Lean, long head

Almond-shaped eyes

Sandy colored coat

Compact, well-muscled body

Long tail ending in a fine point

Wire-coated variety may have moustache and beard

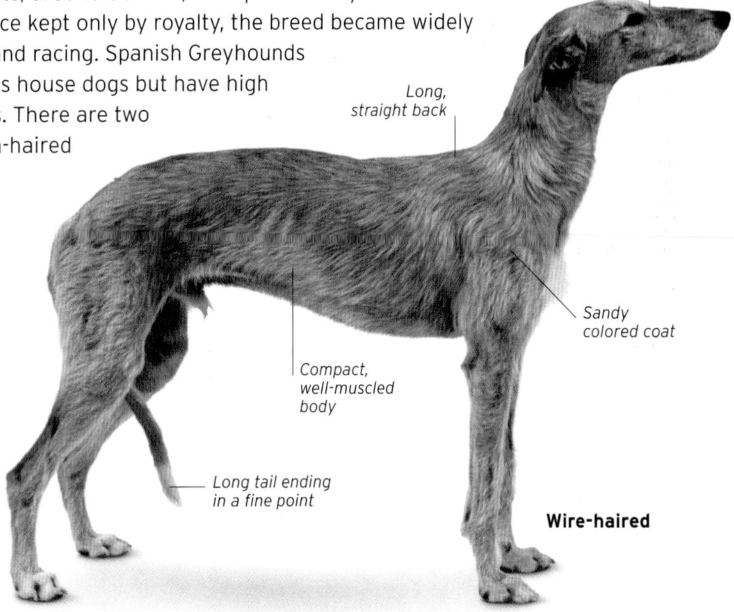

Wire-haired

AZAWAKH

CAPABLE OF ASTONISHING SPEED, THIS SMALL-GAME HUNTER CAN BE KEPT AS A PET KC

Height range 24-29in (60-74cm)

Weight range 33-55lb (15-25kg)

Life span 12-13 years

Origin Mali

This long-legged hound comes from the desert areas of the southern Sahara. The Azawakh is used by nomadic tribes for hunting, guarding, and as a companion dog. It has an exceptionally fine skin, beneath which the muscular, rangy frame is clearly apparent. With kind, firm handling and a daily run, the Azawakh settles well as a house pet.

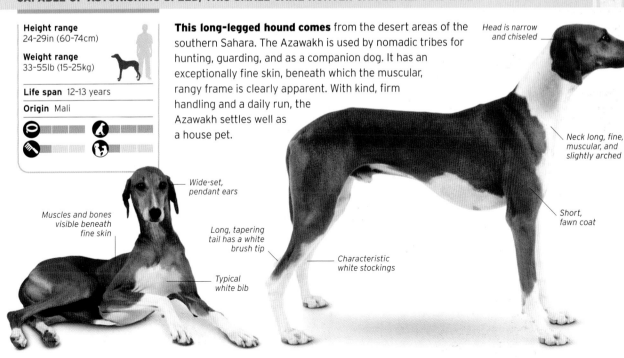

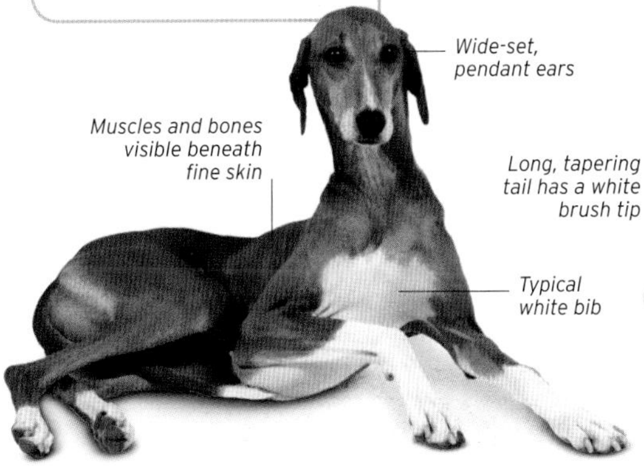

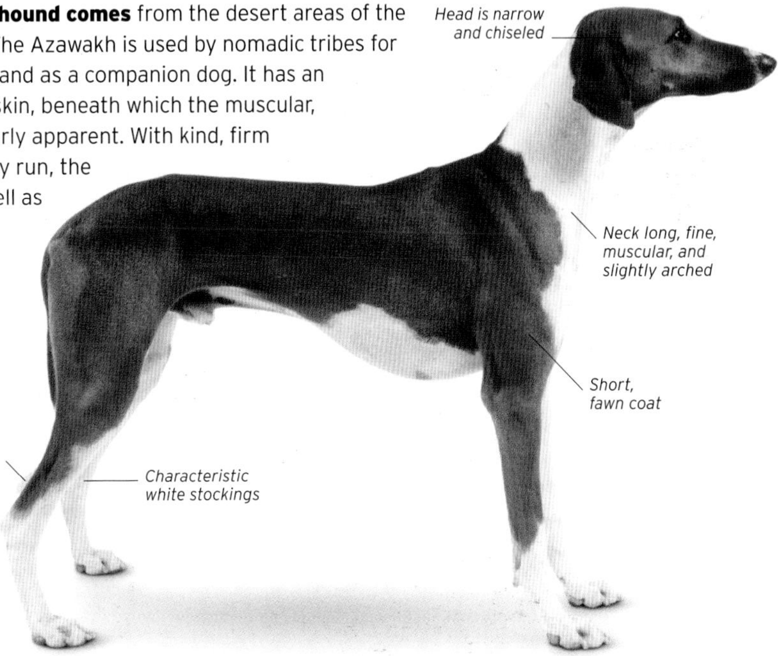

Head is narrow and chiseled

Neck long, fine, muscular, and slightly arched

Wide-set, pendant ears

Muscles and bones visible beneath fine skin

Long, tapering tail has a white brush tip

Short, fawn coat

Characteristic white stockings

Typical white bib

PACK HUNTING
Foxhunting with pack hounds was once a familiar rural sight. The modern alternative is drag-hunting—where hounds follow an artificial scent.

SCENT HOUNDS

A keen sense of smell is an essential part of being a dog. The sharpest noses belong to the scent hounds, which track prey more by following scent than by using their eyes as the sight hounds do (see pp.124-25). These dogs, which once hunted in packs, have a natural ability to pick up a trail, even if it is days old, and will follow it single-mindedly.

The Otterhound is one of the rarest scent hound breeds

It is not known exactly when certain dogs were first recognized for their exceptional ability to hunt by scent. The origins of the modern scent hound possibly date back to the mastiff-type dogs of the ancient world, brought into Europe by traders from the region that is now Syria. By the Middle Ages hunting with packs of scent hounds was a widespread and popular sport, the quarry including fox, hare, deer, and wild boar. Pack hunting arrived in North America in the 17th century with English settlers who brought their own foxhounds with them.

Scent hounds come in all sizes, but typically have substantial muzzles packed with odor-detecting sensors, loose, moist lips that also aid scent detection, and long, pendant ears. Bred for staying power rather than speed, they are strong-bodied, especially in the forequarters. The breeds of scent hound known today were selectively developed not only according to the size of prey that they followed but to the countryside that the hunts covered. The English Foxhound, for example, is comparatively fleet and lightly built for accompanying a mounted hunt over mostly open terrain. Similar in general appearance but much smaller, the Beagle hunted hare, sometimes in thick undergrowth, with followers on foot. Some short-legged dogs were bred to follow or dig out quarry below ground. The best known of these small scent hounds is the Dachshund, an agile little dog, adept at getting in and out of tight spots. The Otterhound, which hunted its quarry in rivers and streams, sometimes swimming for much of the time, has a water-repellent coat and more extensive webbing between its toes than most dogs.

With a widespread ban on hunting with hounds, the future of breeds such as the English Foxhound or Harrier is uncertain. Although usually gregarious and good with other dogs, pack hounds rarely make satisfactory house pets. They need space, are often vocal, and their eagerness to follow any scent trail can make them difficult to train.

EVER POPULAR
Long-eared and low-slung, the Basset Hound was once much admired for its hunting ability and is now loved for its appearance alone.

AMERICAN COONHOUND
This Bluetick Coonhound is a typical example of the large, handsome coonhounds popular in the United States for hunting and trials.

BRUNO JURA HOUND

THIS MOUNTAIN HUNTING DOG IS SWEET-TEMPERED BUT NOT OFTEN SEEN AS A COMPANION

FCI

Height range
18-22in (45-57cm)

Weight range
34-44lb (16-20kg)

Life span 10-11 years

Origin Switzerland

One of two similar breeds of hound developed in the Swiss Jura mountain region, this is one of four laufhunds (see p.176) that probably descended from older, heavier French breeds. Used mainly for hare-hunting, it has a powerful nose and great strength and agility when working on steep terrain. Restless and ever on the go, this breed does not enjoy indoor confinement.

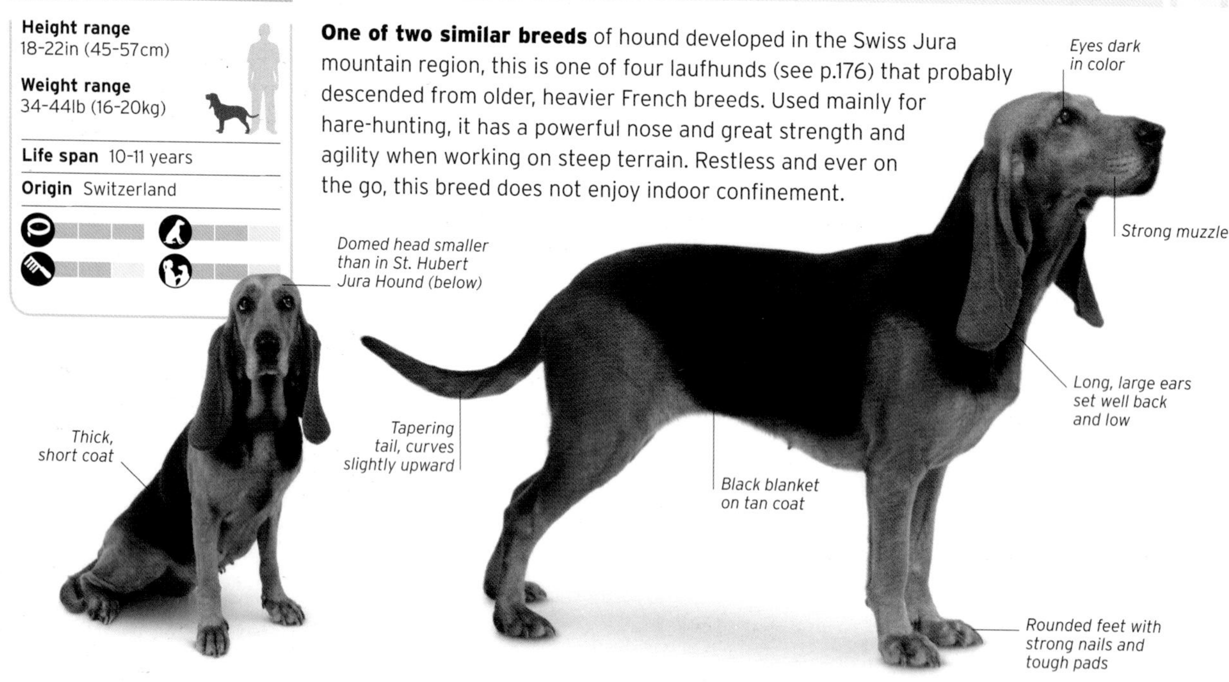
Eyes dark in color
Strong muzzle
Domed head smaller than in St. Hubert Jura Hound (below)
Long, large ears set well back and low
Thick, short coat
Tapering tail, curves slightly upward
Black blanket on tan coat
Rounded feet with strong nails and tough pads

ST. HUBERT JURA HOUND

ROBUST, AGILE, AND SKILLED AT TRACKING, THIS DOG IS BEST KEPT FOR OUTDOOR WORK

FCI

Height range
18-23in (45-58cm)

Weight range
33-44lb (15-20kg)

Life span 10-11 years

Origin Switzerland

Sharing a common history with the Bruno Jura Hound (above) and closely resembling it, the St. Hubert Jura Hound is distinguished by its larger size and smoother coat. A keen tracker, the St. Hubert Jura Hound bays loudly when following a scent. It has great stamina for hunting hare, foxes, or deer.

Massive, domed head
Back straight, broad, and muscular
Loose upper lip covers lower lip
Dark hazel to brown eyes
Large, pendant ears
Smooth, short, tan coat with black blanket
Forelegs straight and strong

BLOODHOUND

GENTLE AND SOCIABLE DESPITE ITS SIZE, THIS DOG HAS A DEEP BELLING VOICE

AKC

Height range
23–27in (58–69cm)

Weight range
79–110lb (36–50kg)

Life span 10–12 years

Origin Belgium

Other colors

Black and tan

Liver and tan

Originally developed in Belgium by the monks of the Abbaye de Saint-Hubert, the Bloodhound (known in Belgium as the St. Hubert Hound) may have been among the dogs brought to England with William the Conqueror in 1066. Massive, wrinkly, and droopy-eared, this is the classic sleuthhound of detective stories. The Bloodhound is renowned for its superlative tracking abilities over varied terrain and can pick up a scent that is several days old. Good-natured and mild-mannered, this dog is also an excellent family companion for those with room to spare.

Very long, pendant ears
Long, thick, tapering tail
Deep-set eyes give solemn expression
Smooth, short, weatherproof, shaded red coat
Heavy, loose upper lip
Pronounced dewlap
Lower ears curl inward

Long, pendant ears fold in on leading edge
Head well-covered with hair
Rough, waterproof, black and tan coat
Hair slightly longer on underside of tail
Deep chest
Large, round feet with well-developed webbing between toes
High-set tail reaches hock

OTTERHOUND

EASY-GOING AND AFFECTIONATE, THIS DOG HAS RETAINED A STRONG HUNTING INSTINCT AKC

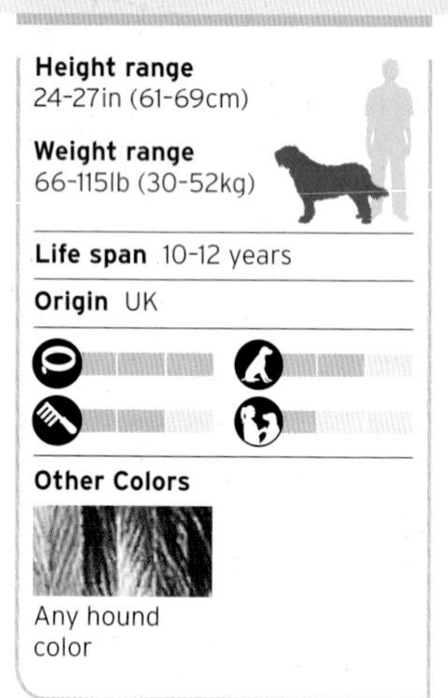
Height range
24–27in (61–69cm)
Weight range
66–115lb (30–52kg)
Life span 10–12 years
Origin UK
Other Colors
Any hound color

As its name suggests, this shaggy-coated hound was once used for hunting otters. Though its exact origins are uncertain, dogs of a similar type, working in packs, were known in England from about the 18th century, and there are records of otter-hunting with pack hounds as far back as the 12th century. When otters became a protected species, and otter-hunting was banned in the UK in 1978, the number of Otterhounds declined sharply. The breed is now considered rare, with fewer than 60 puppies being registered by the Kennel Club each year. Small numbers of Otterhounds are found in other countries, including the USA, Canada, and New Zealand.

The Otterhound is a strong, energetic dog that, given sufficient exercise, readily adapts to life in the home. It is intelligent and good-natured but, as is the case with many former pack hounds, can be difficult to train. Being large and boisterous, the breed is not recommended for small homes or families with elderly members or young children, because there is a risk of them being knocked over. The Otterhound is best suited to owners who enjoy outdoor activities and have a large yard or access to open spaces where the dog can run safely. Bred for hunting in water, this hound loves swimming and will splash around happily in streams for hours if given the opportunity.

The Otterhound's dense, coarse coat is slightly oily, and therefore water-repellent. Regular grooming is usually enough to keep the long topcoat free from tangles; in wet weather mud tends to collect but can be brushed out easily when dry. The dog's longer facial hair may need washing occasionally.

GRIFFON NIVERNAIS

TOUGH AND INDEPENDENT, THIS DOG CAN BE NOISY AND NEEDS A FIRM OWNER FCI

Height range 21-25in (53-63cm)

Weight range 51-55lb (23-25kg)

Life span 12-15 years

Origin France

One of the oldest French sporting dogs, this breed has bloodlines that include the English Foxhound (see p.158) and the Otterhound (see p.140). Used for tracking wild boar, the Griffon Nivernais has great endurance. It may work individually but usually hunts with a pack. The rough, tousled coat provides protection against thick vegetation.

High-set tail
Eyes dark with lively, penetrating gaze
Large, black nose
Dense, rough, shaggy, sandy coat overlaid with black

GRAND GRIFFON VENDEEN

THIS WELL-PROPORTIONED, PASSIONATE HUNTER IS INTELLIGENT AND FAMILY-FRIENDLY FCI

Height range 24-27in (60-68cm)

Weight range 66-77lb (30-35kg)

Life span 12-13 years

Origin France

Other colors

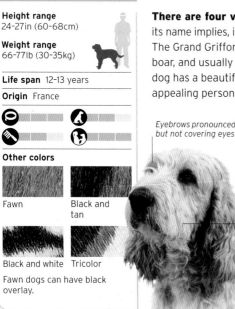

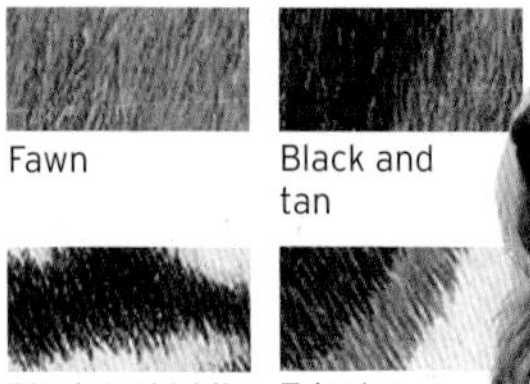

Fawn

Black and tan

Black and white

Tricolor

Fawn dogs can have black overlay.

There are four varieties of Griffon Vendéen and this one, as its name implies, is the largest; it is also the longest established. The Grand Griffon Vendéen is used for hunting deer and wild boar, and usually works as a packhound. This attractive dog has a beautiful musical voice and an appealing personality.

Narrow ears, covered in fine hair, and inward turning

Eyebrows pronounced, but not covering eyes

Long, feathered tail

Front of muzzle has square appearance

Coarse, bushy, white and orange coat

GRAND BASSET GRIFFON VENDEEN

THIS SHORT-LEGGED BREED IS A DEDICATED WORKING HUNTER KC

Height range
15–17in (38–44cm)

Weight range
40–44lb (18–20kg)

Life span 12 years

Origin France

This basset-type Griffon Vendéen hound was originally developed for hunting hare. Today it is used for tracking all types of game from rabbits to wild boar. Brave and tenacious when on the trail, the short-legged Grand Basset Griffon Vendéen is adept at working in difficult countryside such as dense scrub.

Long, pendant ears
Prominent nose with wide nostrils
White coat with orange markings
Flat, hard hair with thick undercoat
White coat with black and orange markings

PETIT BASSET GRIFFON VENDEEN

ENERGETIC AND OUTGOING, THIS FAMILY DOG IS CHEERFUL, CONFIDENT, AND CURIOUS AKC

Height range
13–15in (33–38cm)

Weight range
24–42lb (11–19kg)

Life span 12–14 years

Origin France

Smallest of the Griffon Vendéen breeds, the Petit Basset Griffon Vendéen is an alert, active, and vigorous hound, capable of a long day's hunting. Short legs, a body twice the dog's height, and a thick, rough coat make this breed ideal for work in dense, brambly undergrowth. Full of restless energy, like all hounds, the Petit Basset Griffon Vendéen is a family dog for people who enjoy spending time outdoors.

Pendant ears turned inward

Back straight from withers to croup

Coat rough, thick, and coarse

Long eyebrows, beard, and moustache

White coat with dark markings

BRIQUET GRIFFON VENDEEN

SHAGGY AND COARSE-HAIRED, THIS IS A HAPPY-GO-LUCKY SCENT HOUND FCI

Height range
19–22in (48–55cm)

Weight range
35–53lb (16–24kg)

Life span 12 years

Origin France

Other colors

Fawn with black overlay

Black and tan

Black and white

Black, tan, and white

Briquet means "medium sized"—an apt description for this well-proportioned hound. A handsome and determined chaser of wild boar and roe deer, it is a scaled-down version of the Grand Griffon Vendéen (see p.142), from which it was bred. This hound hunts in a pack but can adapt to urban life if introduced to it early on.

Long, pendant ears set below eye level
Bushy eyebrows noticeable but not covering the eye
Brown nose
Long, white and orange hair

BASSET HOUND

THIS LOW-SLUNG, FLOPPY-EARED DOG IS GENTLE-NATURED AND A SUPERB TRACKER AKC

Height range
13–15in (33–38cm)

Weight range
40–60lb (18–27kg)

Life span 10–13 years

Origin France

Other colors

Variety of colors

Any recognized hound color.

Equally happy by the fireside or in the field, the Basset Hound was bred by French monks to hunt in heavy cover. Unlike its depiction as a buffoon in some cartoons, this consummate sniffer dog is very intelligent and extremely tenacious. As a family pet, the Basset Hound is placid and affectionate.

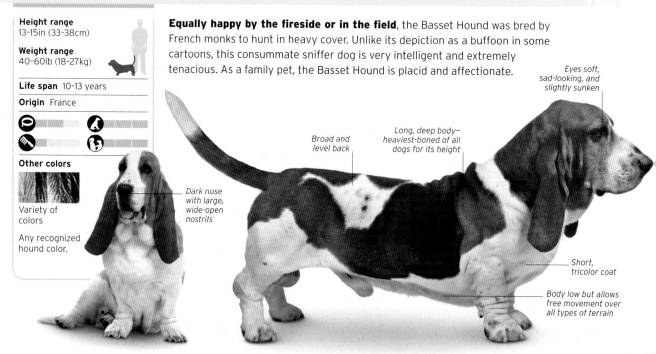

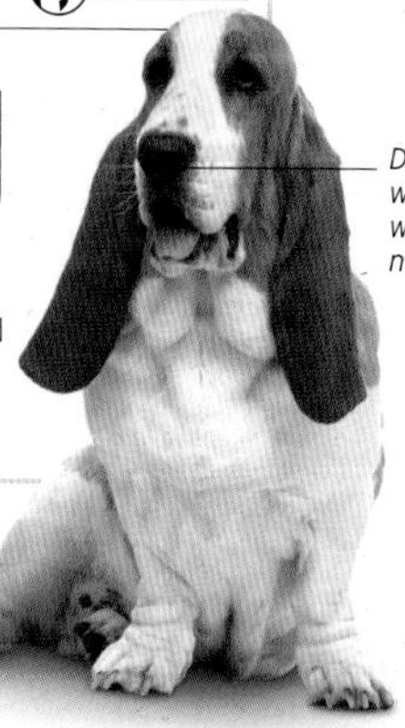

Eyes soft, sad-looking, and slightly sunken

Broad and level back

Long, deep body—heaviest-boned of all dogs for its height

Dark nose with large, wide-open nostrils

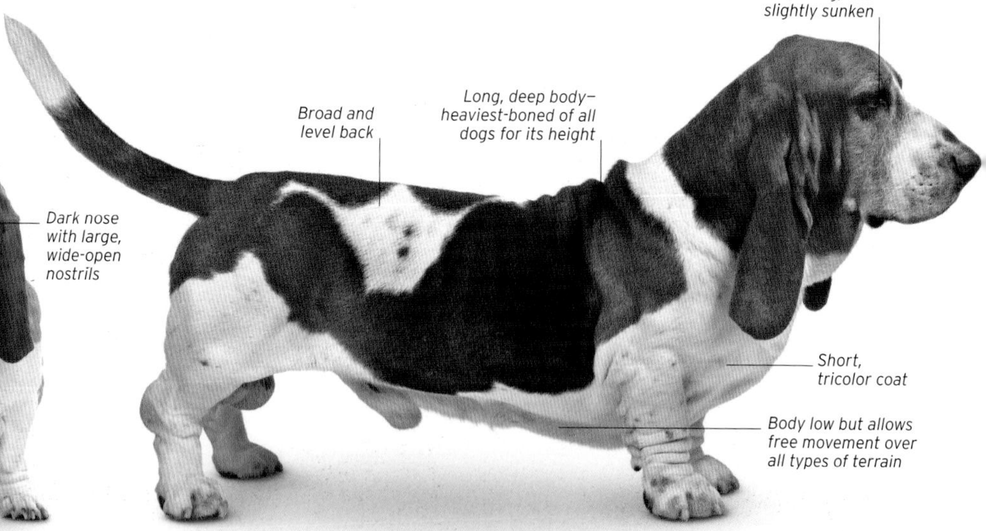

Short, tricolor coat

Body low but allows free movement over all types of terrain

BASSET ARTESIEN NORMAND

THIS SHORT-LEGGED, DETERMINED HUNTING DOG IS A LIVELY, DEVOTED FAMILY PET FCI

Height range 12-14in (30-36cm)

Weight range 33-44lb (15-20kg)

Life span 13-15 years

Origin France

Other colors

Tan and white

This low-slung, long-bodied dog from the Artois and Normandy regions of France, is renowned for searching, tracking, flushing out, and pursuing hare, rabbit, and deer—either individually or in small packs. This elegant hound has a very deep bark, perhaps surprising for its size. Like many hounds, it requires experienced training.

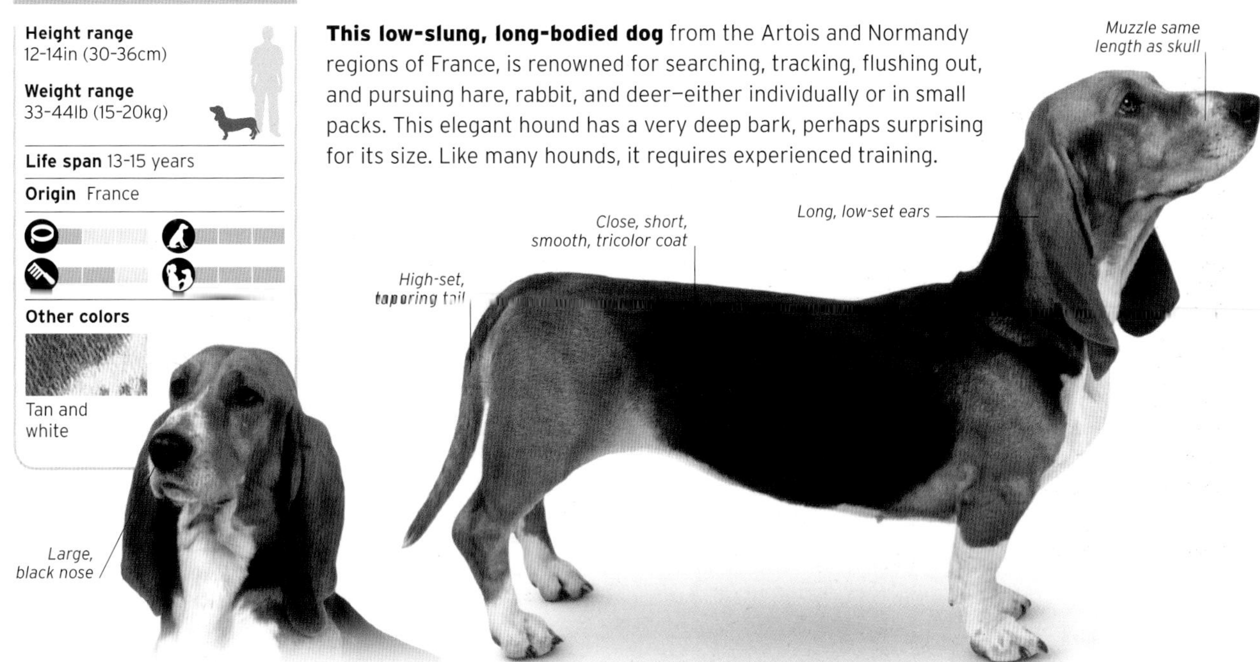
Muzzle same length as skull
Long, low-set ears
Close, short, smooth, tricolor coat
High-set, tapering tail
Large, black nose

BASSET FAUVE DE BRETAGNE

AN AGILE, COMPACT FAMILY DOG WITH AN EASY-GOING, CHEERFUL DISPOSITION KC

Height range 13-15in (32-38cm)

Weight range 35-40lb (16-18kg)

Life span 12-14 years

Origin France

This versatile and nimble hound has the same qualities as the breed from which it is derived: the Griffon Fauve de Bretagne (see p.146). It is courageous and has a well-developed sense of smell, which makes it ideal for tracking and search and rescue. Although wiry, a weekly brush and comb is all that its coat requires.

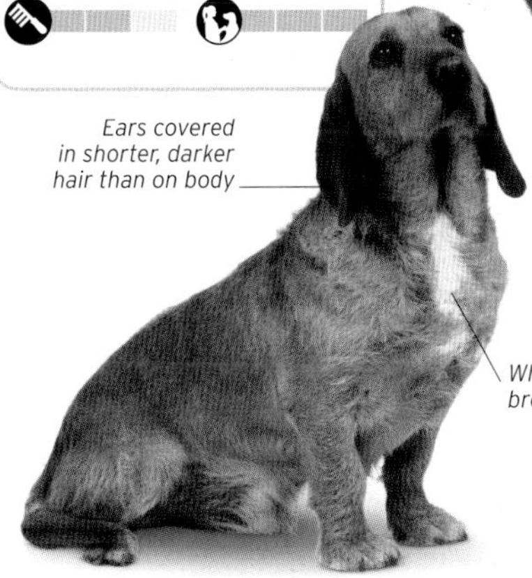

Slightly tapering muzzle with brown nose

Tail medium length and set high

Ears covered in shorter, darker hair than on body

White spot on broad chest

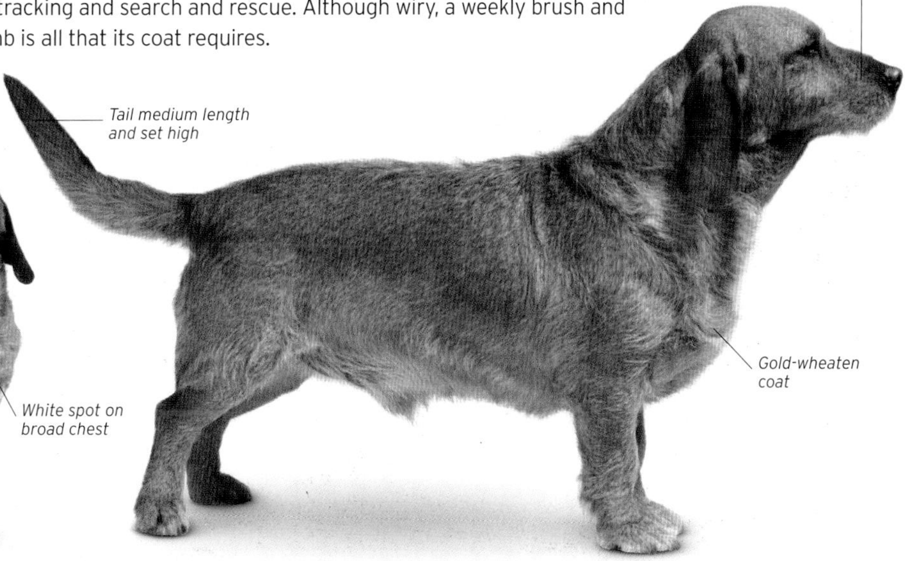

Gold-wheaten coat

GRIFFON FAUVE DE BRETAGNE

THIS HARDY, WIRY RABBIT-CHASER IS AN EASY-GOING FAMILY DOG WHEN OFF DUTY FCI

Height range 19-22in (47-56cm)

Weight range 40-49lb (18-22kg)

Life span 12-13 years

Origin France

One of the oldest French hounds, with ancestors dating back to the 1500s, the Griffon Fauve de Bretagne was bred in Brittany to guard against wolves. Today it is a versatile hunter and lively housedog. Its short-legged cousin is the Basset Fauve de Bretagne (see p.145).

Dark brown eyes
Low-set ears curl in on front edge
Black nose
Tail carried in a sickle shape
Broad chest
Wiry, very rough, red-wheaten coat
Compact feet

ISTRIAN WIRE-HAIRED HOUND

THIS TOUGH BUT GENTLE HOUND IS SUITED TO HUNTING FOX AND HARE IN MOUNTAINOUS TERRAIN FCI

Height range 18-23in (46-58cm)

Weight range 35-53lb (16-24kg)

Life span 12 years

Origin Croatia

With its boundless tenacity and passion for hunting, the Istrian Wire-haired Hound is similar to the smooth-coated variety (opposite). Due to its stubborn nature it can be difficult to train, so is not an ideal pet. It is known as the Istarski Oštrodlaki Gonic in its homeland on the Istrian peninsula of Croatia.

Oval-shaped, dark eyes

Orange speckling on ears

Tail has orange hairs at base

Black nose

Broad, deep chest extends to elbows

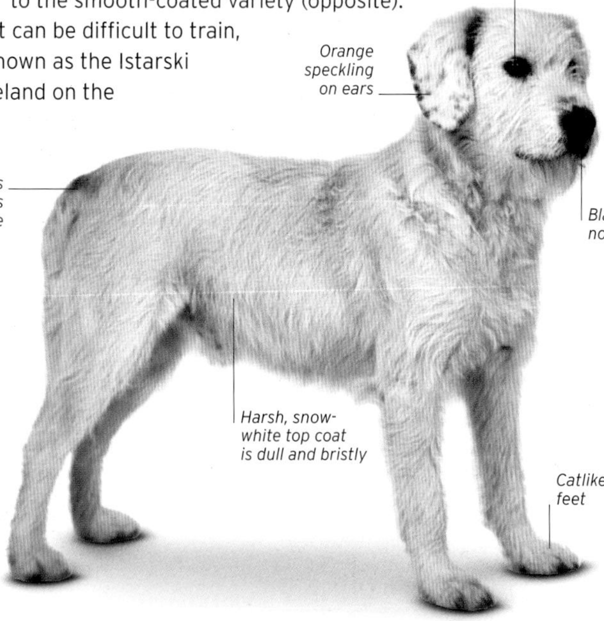

Harsh, snow-white top coat is dull and bristly

Catlike, narrow feet

ISTRIAN SMOOTH-COATED HOUND

RESEMBLING A LONG-LEGGED FOXHOUND, THIS IS THE OLDEST OF THE BALKAN HOUNDS FCI

Height range
17-22in (44-56cm)

Weight range
31-44lb (14-20kg)

Life span 12 years

Origin Croatia

Originally bred for hunting hare and fox in the vast open terrain of Istria, the handsome and well-built Istarski Kratkodlaki Gonic, as it is known in its native land, displays a stunning snow-white coat. It is kept across the Istrian peninsula as a working dog but also makes a contented housedog in a rural household.

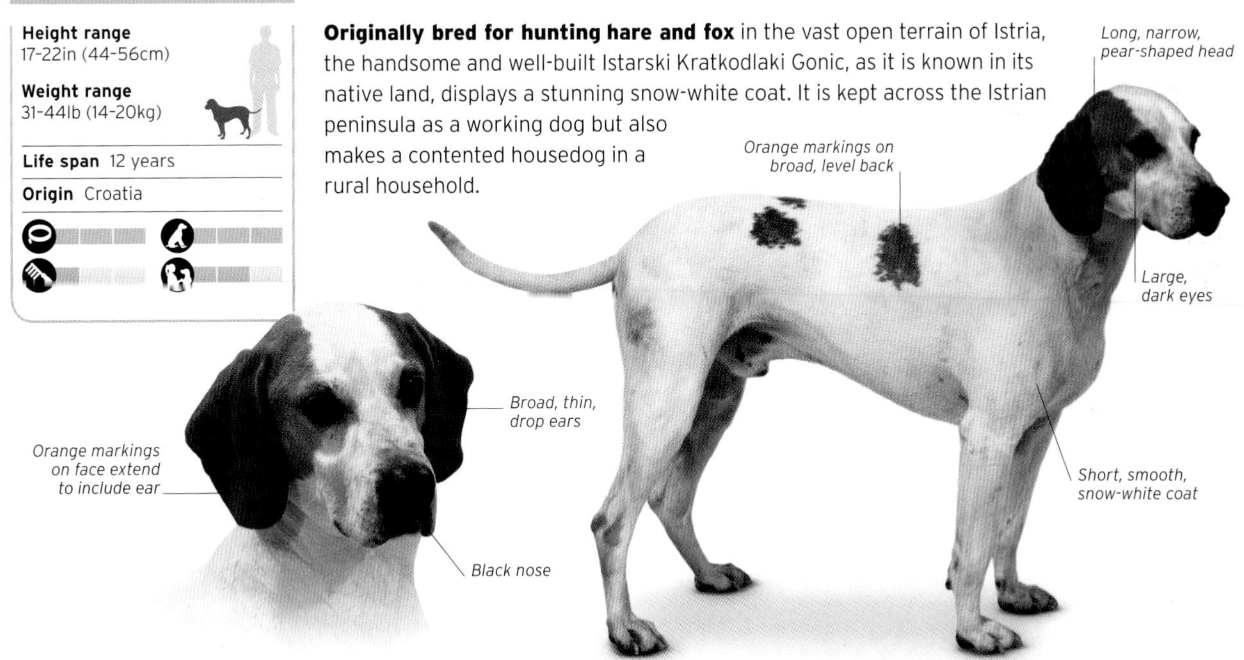
Long, narrow, pear-shaped head
Orange markings on broad, level back
Large, dark eyes
Broad, thin, drop ears
Orange markings on face extend to include ear
Short, smooth, snow-white coat
Black nose

STYRIAN COARSE-HAIRED MOUNTAIN HOUND

THIS RARE WORKING DOG IS IDEAL FOR HIGH ALTITUDE AND HUNTING ON ROUGH TERRAIN FCI

Height range
18-21in (45-53cm)

Weight range
33-40lb (15-18kg)

Life span 12 years

Origin Austria

Other colors

Red

May have white marking on chest.

This medium-sized dog has the agility to twist and turn on difficult, steep terrain, having developed its hunting skills in the mountains of Austria and Slovenia. It can make a calm and good-natured pet. It is also known as the Peintingen Hound after its 18th-century developer, who crossed a Hanoverian Scent Hound (see p.178) with an Istrian Wire-haired Hound (opposite).

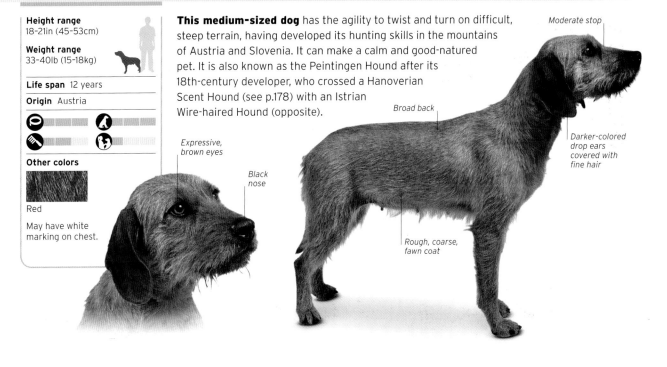

Moderate stop
Broad back
Darker-colored drop ears covered with fine hair
Expressive, brown eyes
Black nose
Rough, coarse, fawn coat

AUSTRIAN BLACK AND TAN HOUND

SUPPLE AND TIRELESS, THIS DOG IS SUITED TO TRACKING PREY ACROSS MOUNTAINOUS TERRAIN FCI

Height range
19-22in (48-56cm)

Weight range
33-51lb (15-23kg)

Life span 12-14 years

Origin Austria

Sometimes known as the Brandlbracke, the Austrian Black and Tan Hound has descended from the Celtic Hound. Popular locally, it was bred to seek out hare and track down wounded animals with its highly tuned senses of smell and direction. It works eagerly and has a calm temperament.

Tan markings above eyes
Body length longer than leg length
Drop ears
Smooth, short, thick, black and tan, close-fitting coat with silky sheen
Tucked-up belly
Long, tapering tail hangs down at rest
Tan markings on lower legs

SPANISH HOUND

A STRONG-WILLED HUNTING DOG OF NOBLE ANCESTRY FCI

Height range
19-22in (48-57cm)

Weight range
44-55lb (20-25kg)

Life span 11-13 years

Origin Spain

The ancestors of the Spanish Hound date back to the Middle Ages. Also known as Sabueso Español, this dog is a specialized, lone hare-hunter that will track its prey all day, following the commands of an experienced owner. There is considerable variation in the height of this breed: males being much larger than females.

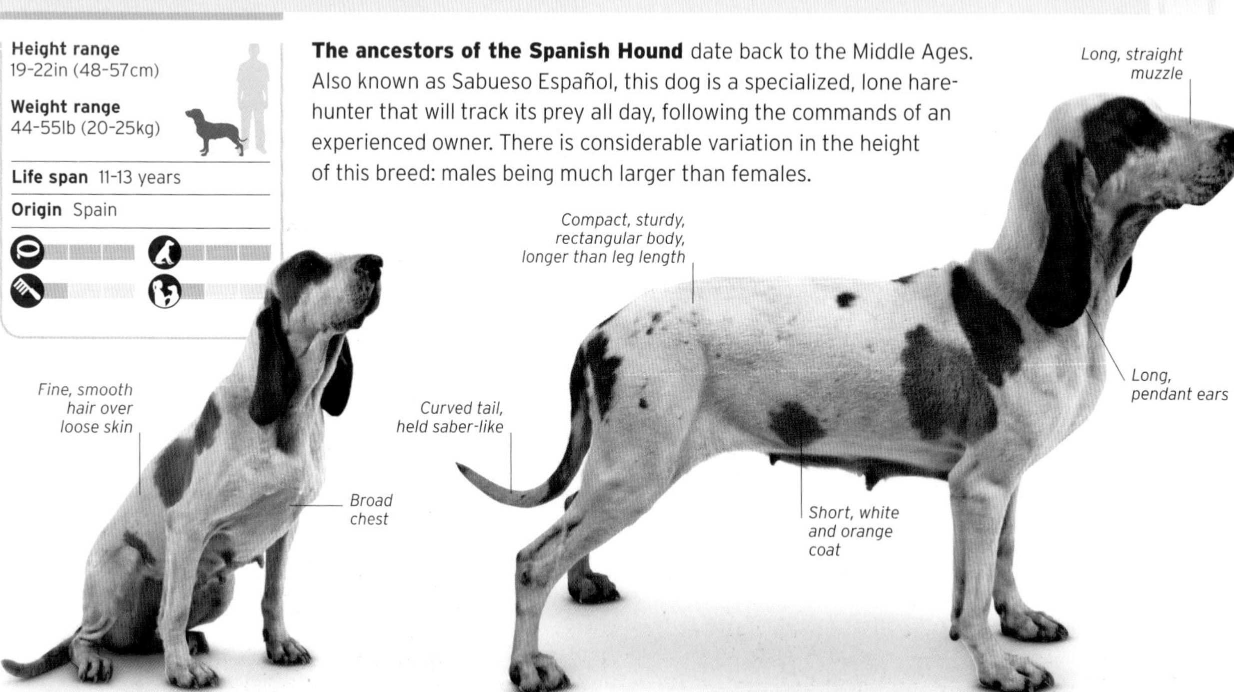
Long, straight muzzle
Compact, sturdy, rectangular body, longer than leg length
Long, pendant ears
Fine, smooth hair over loose skin
Curved tail, held saber-like
Broad chest
Short, white and orange coat

SEGUGIO ITALIANO

THIS INTELLIGENT AND SWEET-NATURED HOUND MAKES A GOOD ACTIVE COMPANION

KC

Height range
19–23in (48–59cm)

Weight range
40–62lb (18–28kg)

Life span 10–14 years

Origin Italy

Other colors

Wheaten

Black and tan

Originally bred as a boar-hunter, this Italian hound is today more often used to track hare and rabbits. It is a fast sprinter and has the stamina for running long distances. Usually calm and quiet, when at work the Segugio Italiano emits an excited and distinctive, high-pitched bark. It is good with children and other dogs provided it is well trained, has access to open spaces, and is exercised regularly. Although usually cautious in temperament, even a well-trained dog is likely to take off if it spots a rabbit. There are two coat varieties: wire-haired and short-haired.

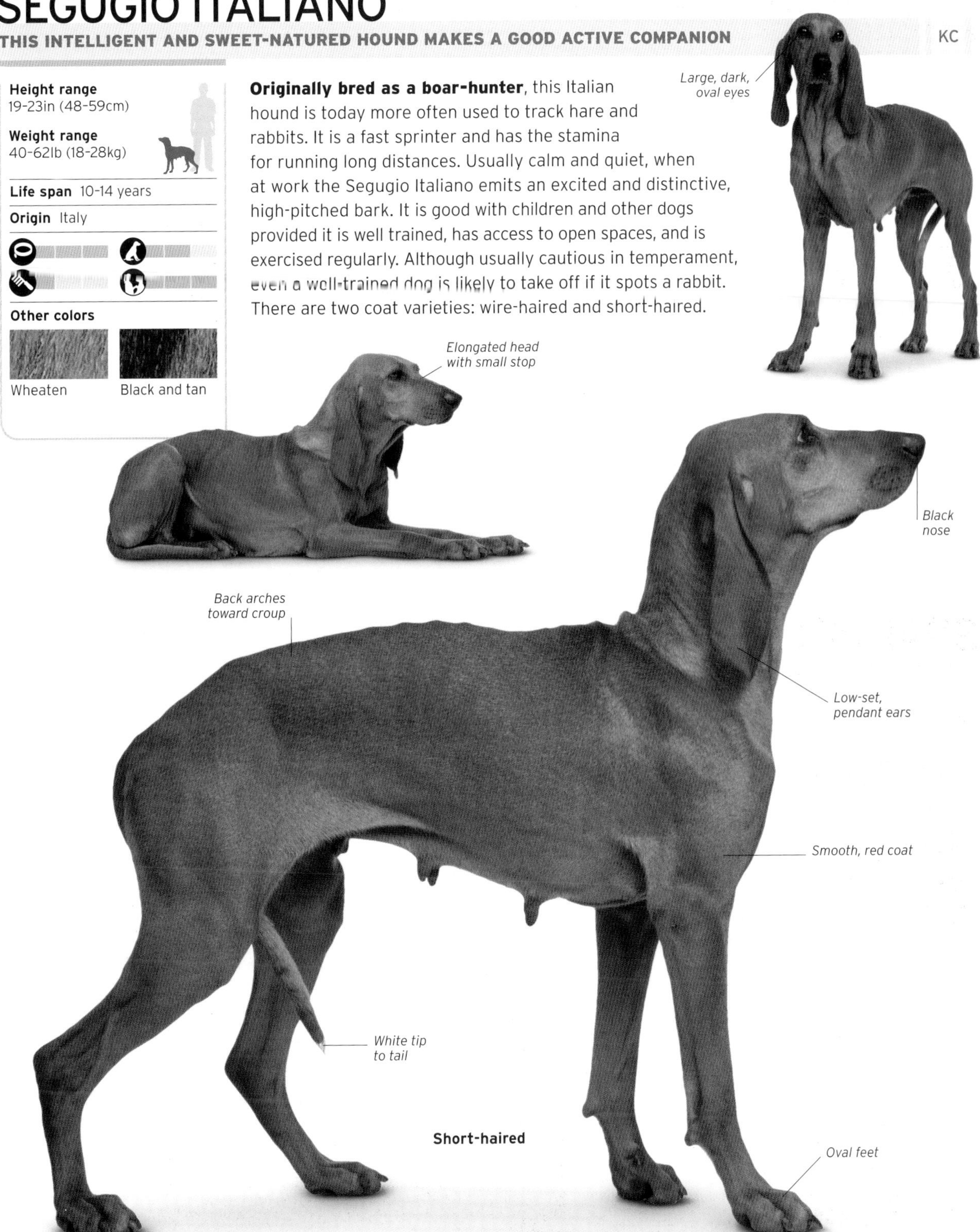
Large, dark, oval eyes
Elongated head with small stop
Black nose
Back arches toward croup
Low-set, pendant ears
Smooth, red coat
White tip to tail
Oval feet

Short-haired

HARRIER

THIS SUPREMELY ACTIVE AND EAGER HOUND IS AN ENTHUSIASTIC EXPLORER AND TRACKER AKC

Height range
19–22in (48–55cm)

Weight range
42–60lb (19–27kg)

Life span 10–12 years

Origin UK

Once popular for pack hunting, this handsome, classically proportioned hound was probably developed as a smaller version of the English Foxhound (see p.158). Originally used to hunt hare with foot followers, Harriers later hunted foxes with mounted followers. Today the dog makes a great outdoor companion and agility competitor.

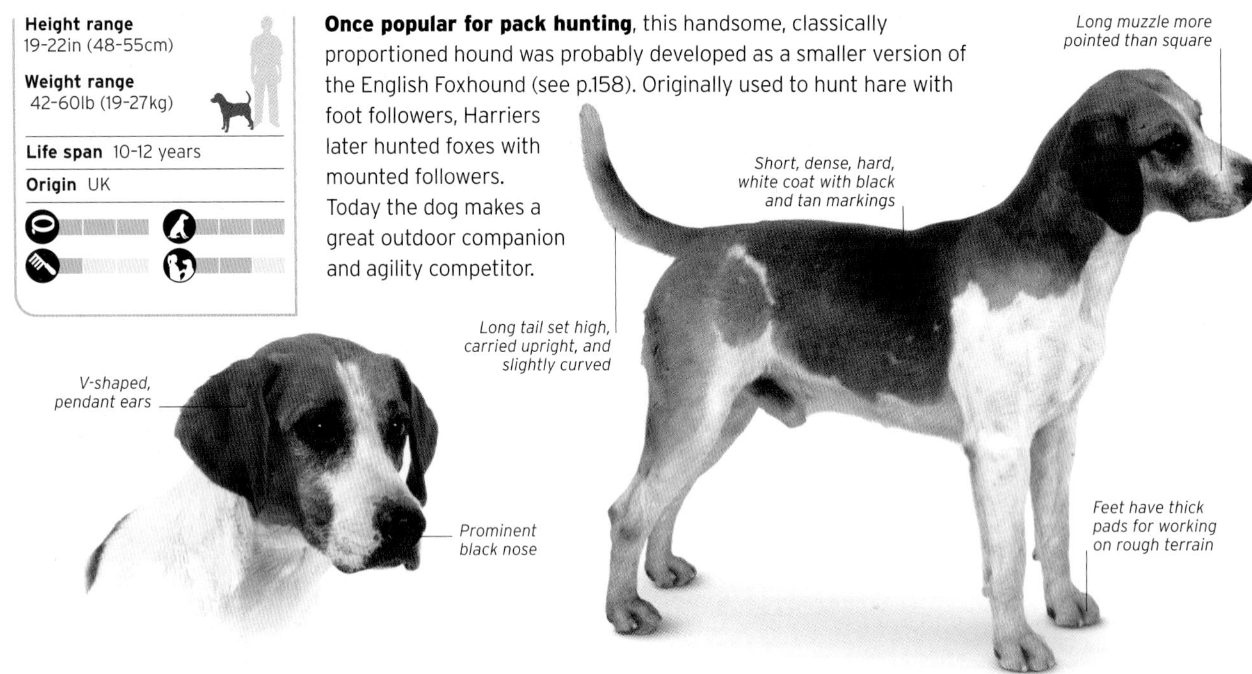
Long muzzle more pointed than square
Short, dense, hard, white coat with black and tan markings
Long tail set high, carried upright, and slightly curved
V-shaped, pendant ears
Prominent black nose
Feet have thick pads for working on rough terrain

BEAGLE HARRIER

A GOOD COMPANION DOG WITH A VERY CALM TEMPERAMENT, BUT KEEN TO FOLLOW SCENT FCI

Height range
18–20in (46–50cm)

Weight range
42–46lb (19–21kg)

Life span 12–13 years

Origin France

Larger than a Beagle (see p.152) but smaller than a Harrier (above), this attractive little hound is thought to have both these breeds in its ancestry, although it may not be the result of a direct cross. Beagle Harriers are not often seen outside France, where they have been used for hunting small game since the late 1800s. This dog has a pleasant temperament and makes a good family pet.

Square, compact body
Eyes have eager and intelligent expression
Narrow muzzle on broad head
Tricolor coat
Deep, broad chest
Rounded, catlike feet

ANGLO-FRANCAIS DE PETITE VENERIE

THIS WORKING PACKHOUND IS NOT SUITED TO AN URBAN LIFESTYLE FCI

Height range
19-22in (48-56cm)

Weight range
35-44lb (16-20kg)

Life span 12-13 years

Origin France

Other colors

Tan and white

Also known as the Petit Anglo-Français, this hound was developed in France and is the result of cross-breeding between English and French scent hounds, a few hundred years ago. The breed is now rare and mostly seen in Continental Europe, where it is still used for small game hunting (to which its name, Petite Vénerie, alludes).

Large, brown eyes
High set, thin tail
Low-set, pendant ears
Short, dense, glossy, tricolor coat

PORCELAINE

THIS INSTINCTIVE HUNTER IS TRAINABLE AS A HOUSE DOG BUT NEEDS AN ACTIVE LIFE FCI

Height range
21-23in (53-58cm)

Weight range
55-62lb (25-28kg)

Life span 12-13 years

Origin France

Possibly the oldest of the French packhounds, with origins in the Franche-Comte on the French-Swiss border, this breed is named for the distinctive glaze-like sheen of its beautiful white coat. It is used primarily for hunting deer and wild boar. If kept as a pet, this hound needs plenty of exercise and tactful training.

Long, lean, finely chiseled head

Well-developed black nose

Highly characteristic orange ticking on ears

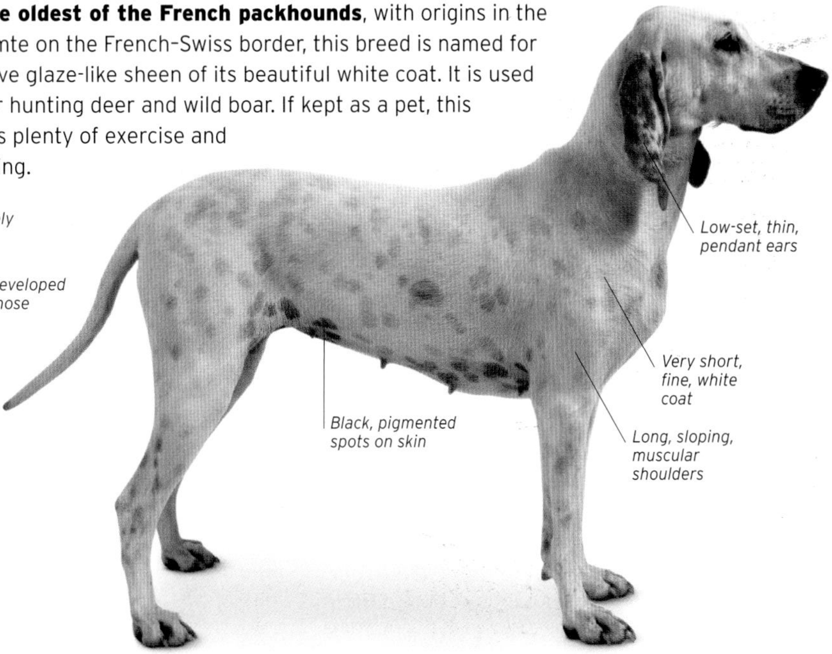

Black, pigmented spots on skin

Low-set, thin, pendant ears

Very short, fine, white coat

Long, sloping, muscular shoulders

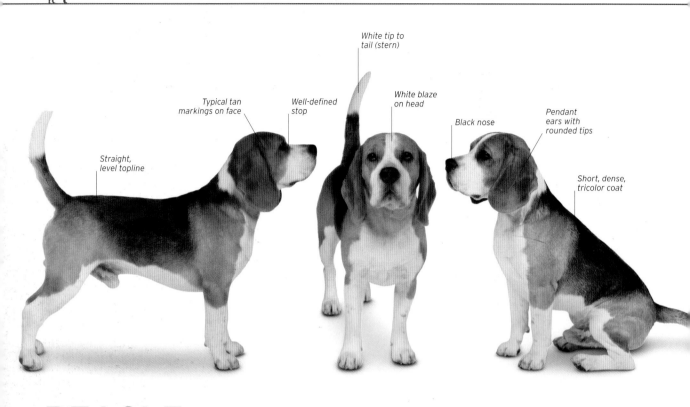

White tip to tail (stern)
Typical tan markings on face
Well-defined stop
White blaze on head
Black nose
Pendant ears with rounded tips
Straight, level topline
Short, dense, tricolor coat

BEAGLE

ONE OF THE MOST POPULAR SCENT HOUNDS, THIS DOG IS ACTIVE, HAPPY-GO-LUCKY, AND AMIABLE AKC

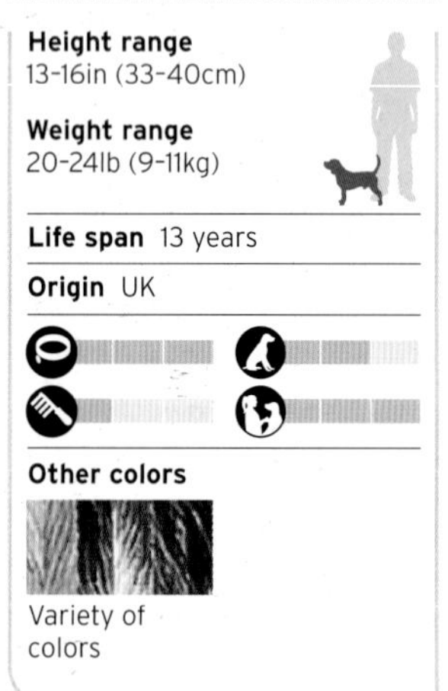
Height range
13-16in (33-40cm)
Weight range
20-24lb (9-11kg)
Life span 13 years
Origin UK
Other colors
Variety of colors

A sturdy, compact dog with a merry disposition, the Beagle looks rather like an English Foxhound (see p.158) in miniature. The Beagle's origins are unclear, but it appears to have a long history, possibly being developed from other English scent hounds such as the Harrier (see p.150). In England, from the 16th century onward, packs of small beagle-type hounds were kept to hunt hare and rabbit, but it was not until the 1870s that a standard for the modern Beagle was recognized. Since then the breed has remained remarkably popular, at first for hunting and now as a companion dog. This versatile hound has also been used by law enforcement agencies to sniff out drugs, explosives, and other illegal items.

The Beagle's friendly and tolerant nature make it an excellent pet, provided it has plenty of company and exercise—it does not easily tolerate long periods of solitude, which may lead to behavioral problems. A typical scent hound, this dog is highly active and has a strong instinct for following a trail. Left alone in an inadequately fenced yard, or allowed to run off leash, a Beagle can disappear swiftly and stay away for hours. The breed has a loud bark and can be noisy, which may irritate neighbors if the barking becomes excessive. Fortunately, Beagles are relatively easy to train, and do best with an owner who combines fondness with firmness and clear leadership. This breed is good with children old enough to understand how to handle a dog, but cannot be considered safe with small family pets.

In the United States two sizes are recognized, based on the height of the dog at the withers: those under 13in (33cm) and those between 13in (33cm) and 15in (38cm).

SCHILLERSTOVARE

THIS RARE, TIRELESS TRACKER HUNTS SOLO AND IS THE SWIFTEST SWEDISH HOUND FCI

Height range 19-24in (49-61cm)

Weight range 33-55lb (15-25kg)

Life span 10-14 years

Origin Sweden

A rare breed, the Schillerstovare is much prized for its hunting speed and stamina, especially over snow. This dog's thick coat insulates it well from its native climate. It tracks alone, rather than in a pack, and emits a deep-throated bay to pinpoint the position of its prey—hare or fox. The breed is named after its breeder, farmer Per Schiller.

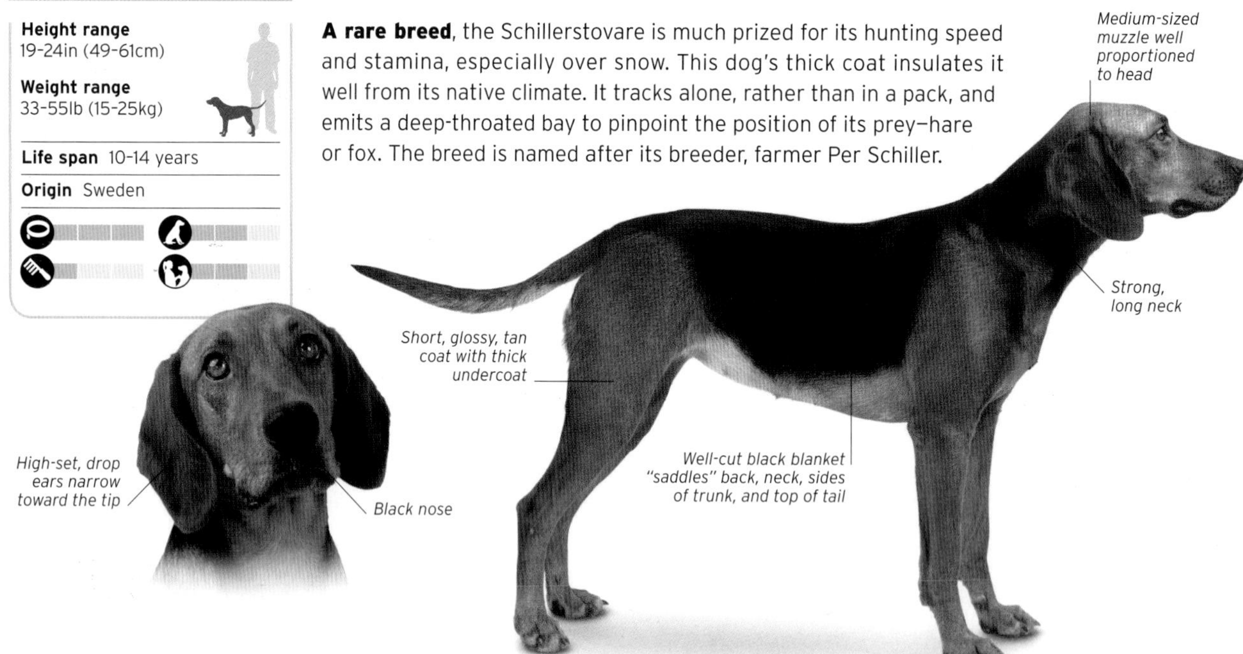
Medium-sized muzzle well proportioned to head
Strong, long neck
Short, glossy, tan coat with thick undercoat
Well-cut black blanket "saddles" back, neck, sides of trunk, and top of tail
High-set, drop ears narrow toward the tip
Black nose

HAMILTONSTOVARE

SWEDEN'S MOST POPULAR FOXHOUND IS VERY LOYAL AND A GOOD COMPANION AND PROTECTOR KC

Height range 18-24in (46-60cm)

Weight range 51-60lb (23-27kg)

Life span 10-13 years

Origin Sweden

Developed by Count Adolf Patrick Hamilton, a founder of the Swedish Kennel Club, this handsome, easy-going hound loves to roam fields and flush out small game. The Hamiltonstovare is a mix of English Foxhound (see p.158) stock (it has also been called the Swedish Foxhound) and Holstein Hound, Hanovarian Haidbrake, and Courlander Hound.

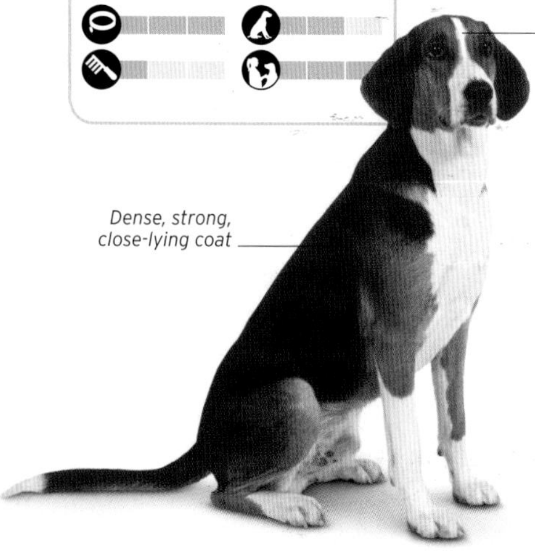

White blaze on face

Dense, strong, close-lying coat

Short, dense, soft undercoat

Tricolor coat with no one color dominating

White "socks" on lower legs and feet

SMALANDSSTOVARE

THIS ROBUST ALL-WEATHER HUNTER AND WORKER FORMS A STRONG BOND WITH ITS OWNER

FCI

Height range
17–21in (42–54cm)

Weight range
33–44lb (15–20kg)

Life span 12 years

Origin Sweden

This Swedish Hound, also known as the Småland Hound, is thought to date back to the 16th century and takes it name from the dense forest of Småland in southern Sweden where it was used to hunt fox and hare. It has a distinctive black coat with tan markings similar to that of a Rottweiler (see p.81).

High-set, medium-length ears with rounded tips
Head shorter and more wedge-shaped than most hounds
Square, well-muscled body
Typical tan marking above eyes
Naturally short tail
Thick, shiny, black and tan coat
Small, white markings on toes

HALDEN HOUND

THIS NORWEGIAN FOXHOUND IS A RELATIVELY RARE HUNTING AND FAMILY DOG

FCI

Height range
20–26in (50–65cm)

Weight range
51–64lb (23–29kg)

Life span 10–12 years

Origin Norway

The largest of the four stovare breeds, this hound loves a speedy chase over snowy open spaces. Like other Norwegian dogs bred as hunting companions, the Halden Hound is not widely known outside its native land. It was developed in Halden in the southeast, by crossing an English Foxhound (see p.158) with a local "beagle."

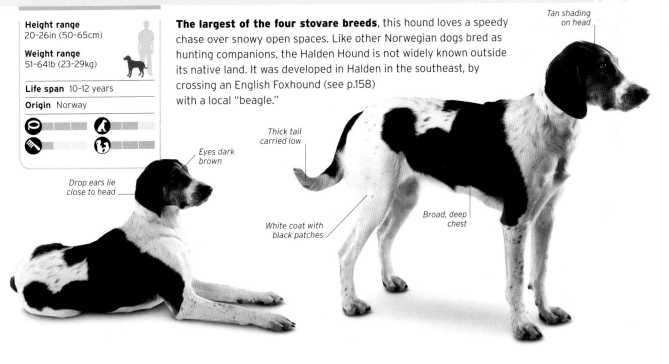

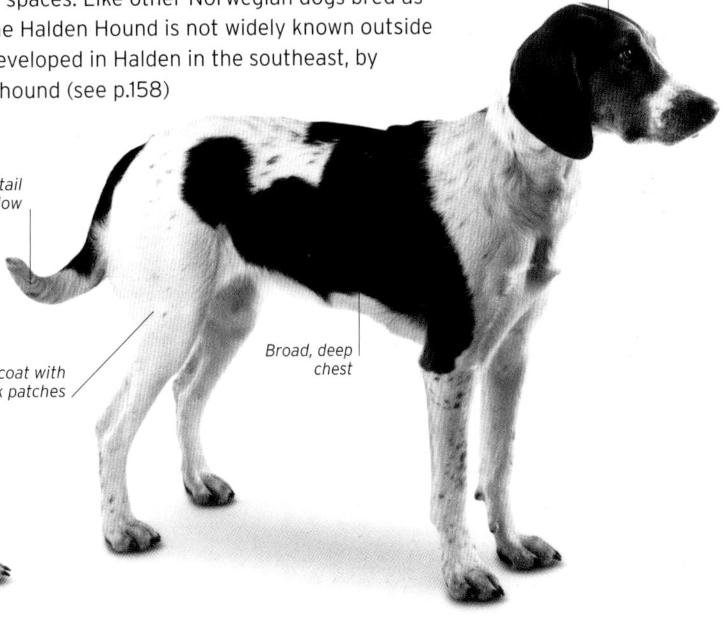

Tan shading on head

Thick tail carried low

Eyes dark brown

Drop ears lie close to head

White coat with black patches

Broad, deep chest

NORWEGIAN HOUND

A BEAUTIFULLY COATED HARE-HUNTER AND FIRST-CLASS FAMILY HOUND FCI

Height range 19-22in (47-55cm)
Weight range 35-51lb (16-23kg)
Life span 11-14 years
Origin Norway
Other colors
Tricolor

Trusting, friendly, and easy to handle when not hunting, the Norwegian Hound, or Dunker, is designed to track hare in snow in temperatures as low as -59°F (-15°C). Originally named after Captain Wilhelm Dunker, this hound was bred from other Norwegian and Russian hare-hounds in the early 1800s.

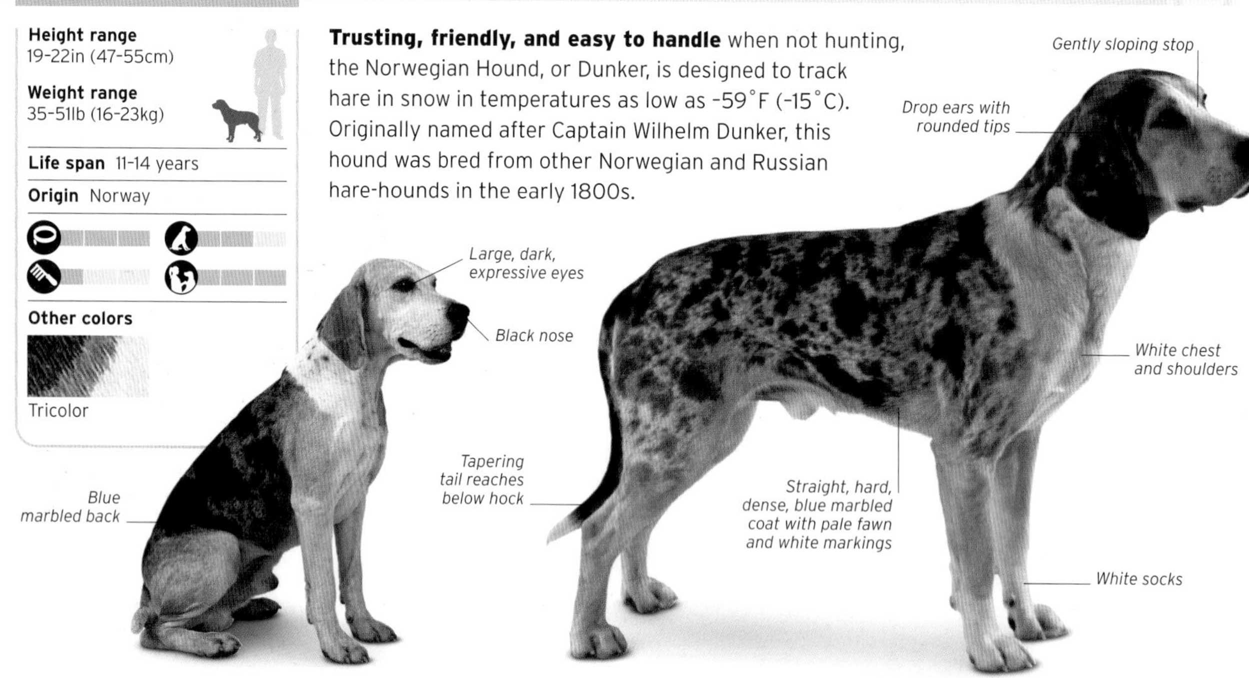
Gently sloping stop
Drop ears with rounded tips
Large, dark, expressive eyes
Black nose
White chest and shoulders
Tapering tail reaches below hock
Straight, hard, dense, blue marbled coat with pale fawn and white markings
Blue marbled back
White socks

FINNISH HOUND

A CALM AND FRIENDLY DOG AT HOME AND AN ENERGETIC AND TIRELESS TRACKER ON THE MOVE FCI

Height range 20-24in (52-61cm)
Weight range 46-55lb (21-25kg)
Life span 12 years
Origin Finland

By far Finland's most popular hunting dog, this hound is bred to drive hare and fox in the country's snowy forests. It hunts with unfailing eagerness, but at home it is an easy-going and manageable pet. Although generally placid, the Finnish Hound can sometimes be shy of strangers.

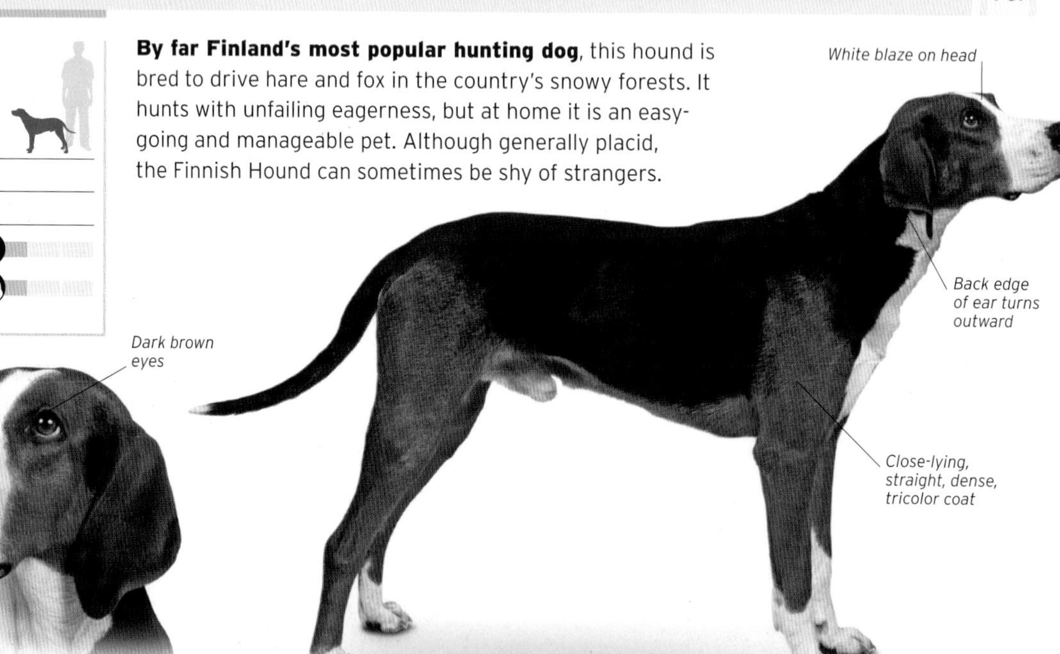
White blaze on head
Back edge of ear turns outward
Dark brown eyes
Well-developed, black nose
Close-lying, straight, dense, tricolor coat

HYGEN HOUND

A BRIGHT HUNTING DOG, LIVELY COMPANION, AND RELIABLE HOUSE WATCHDOG

FCI

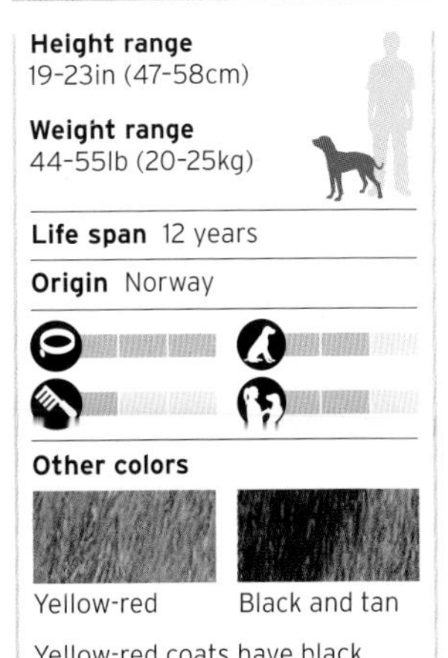

Height range 19-23in (47-58cm)

Weight range 44-55lb (20-25kg)

Life span 12 years

Origin Norway

Other colors

Yellow-red | Black and tan

Yellow-red coats have black shading.

A more lightweight dog than the Norwegian Hound (opposite), this breed from Ringerike and Romerike in eastern Norway is purpose built for the snowy Arctic expanses and has the stamina to bound through them tirelessly. Quite compact like the Smålandsstövare (see p.155), this is a quick-thinking hunter that loves long walks.

Thin, soft, drop ears with rounded tips
White blaze on head
Tail with black shading and white tip
Head and snout shorter and wider than Norwegian Hound (opposite)
Black nose
Dense, shiny, harsh, red-brown coat with white markings

AMERICAN FOXHOUND

BRED FOR SPEED AND DISTANCE, THIS DOG NEEDS AN ENERGETIC OWNER

AKC

Height range 21-25in (53-64cm)

Weight range 40-66lb (18-30kg)

Life span 12-13 years

Origin USA

Other colors

Any color

These dogs have the most august of patrons—the first president of the United States, George Washington. He bred them from French and English hounds to produce a taller and more athletic, stand-alone breed. American Foxhounds love running in packs, hunting singly, or competing in field trials.

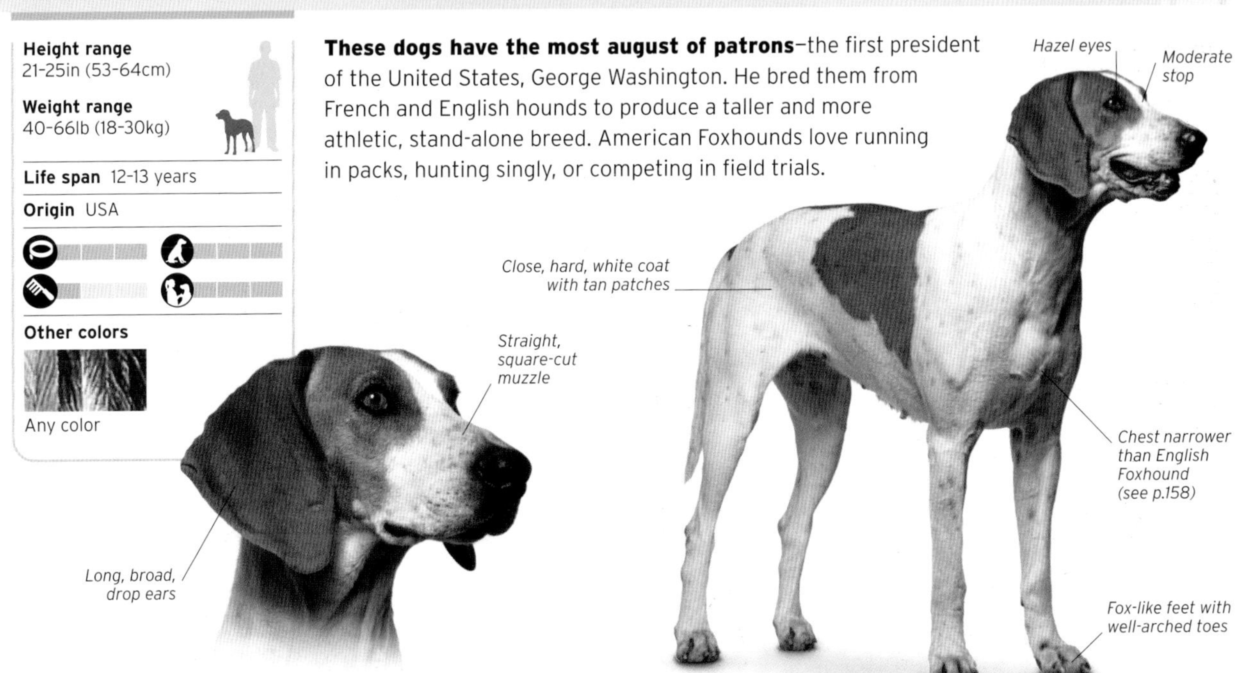
Straight, square-cut muzzle
Long, broad, drop ears
Close, hard, white coat with tan patches
Hazel eyes
Moderate stop
Chest narrower than English Foxhound (see p.158)
Fox-like feet with well-arched toes

ENGLISH FOXHOUND

A GOOD-NATURED, ACTIVE DOG WITH A SUNNY APPROACH TO LIFE

AKC

Height range
23-25in (58-64cm)

Weight range
55-75lb (25-34kg)

Life span 10-11 years

Origin UK

Other colors

Variety of colors

Any recognized hound color.

The ancestry of the English Foxhound goes back centuries. By the 1800s more than 200 packs of foxhounds were kept in England for hunting foxes over a variety of terrain. An active, bold, and passionate hunter, this hound is highly responsive to training but can also be stubborn and self-willed, especially when on the scent. Historically kenneled in packs rather than kept as house dogs, the English Foxhound nevertheless makes a good companion, is very friendly toward people, and is excellent with children. Would-be owners should be aware that these hounds can retain their playfulness, liveliness, and stamina into old age.

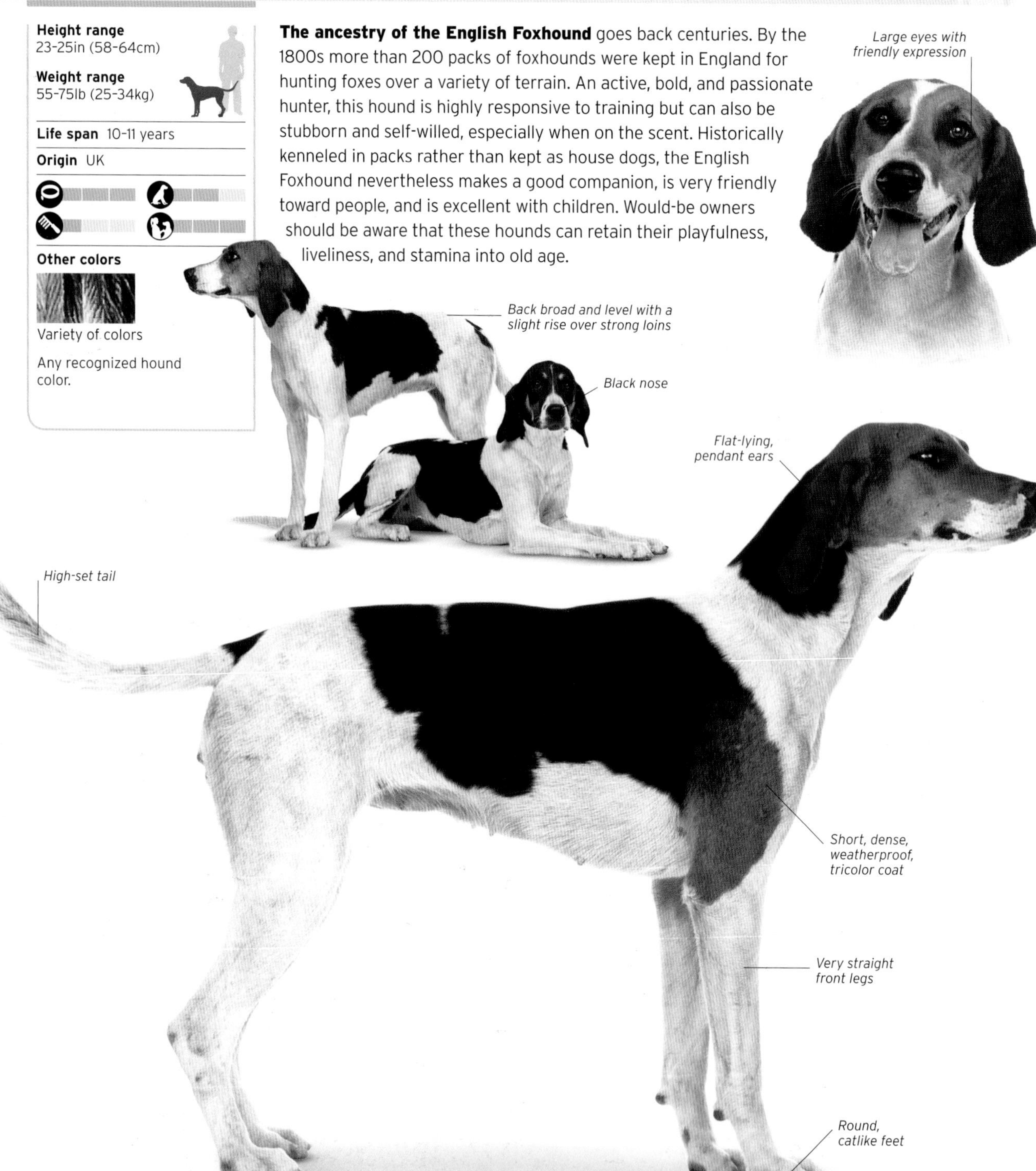
Large eyes with friendly expression
Back broad and level with a slight rise over strong loins
Black nose
Flat-lying, pendant ears
High-set tail
Short, dense, weatherproof, tricolor coat
Very straight front legs
Round, catlike feet

CATAHOULA LEOPARD DOG

THIS SKILLFUL, STRONG-WILLED HUNTER IS SUITED TO AN EXPERIENCED OWNER

Height range
20–26in (51–66cm)

Weight range
50–90lb (23–41kg)

Life span 10–14 years

Origin USA

Other colors

Variety of colors

This striking-looking Louisiana herding dog and hunter of wild boar and raccoon is a mix of Spanish colonial greyhound, mastiff, and native Red Wolf. It can work well in swamps, forests, and more open terrain. Named after a parish in its home state, the Catahoula Leopard Dog is an alert watchdog, wary of strangers, but calm and dedicated to its household.

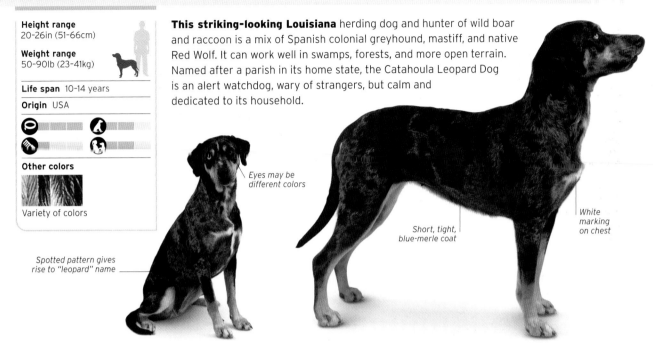

Eyes may be different colors

Spotted pattern gives rise to "leopard" name

Short, tight, blue-merle coat

White marking on chest

PLOTT

RUTHLESS AND DETERMINED WHEN HUNTING, THIS HOUND IS RESPONSIVE AND ALERT AT HOME AKC

Height range
20–25in (51–64cm)

Weight range
40–60lb (18–27kg)

Life span 10–12 years

Origin USA

This powerful, brindled hound is used for hunting raccoon, though it also hunts big cats, bear, coyote, and wild boar. It is one of only a few breeds with acknowledged American origin. The original Plott was bred in the 1750s in the Smokey Mountains by the Plott family, using boar-hunting Hanoverian Hounds brought over from Germany.

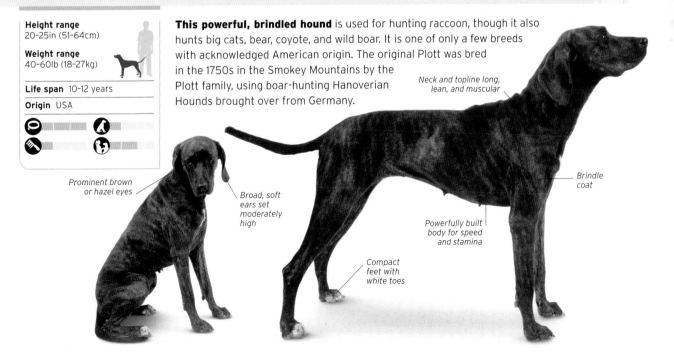

Neck and topline long, lean, and muscular

Prominent brown or hazel eyes

Broad, soft ears set moderately high

Brindle coat

Powerfully built body for speed and stamina

Compact feet with white toes

BLACK AND TAN COONHOUND

MAINLY USED FOR HUNTING, THIS DOG IS CALM AND FRIENDLY IN THE HOME AKC

Height range 23-27in (58-69cm)

Weight range 51-75lb (23-34kg)

Life span 10-12 years

Origin USA

This big hunting dog probably descends from the Bloodhound (see p.139) and a now-extinct old English breed called the Talbot Hound. Tough and powerful, the Black and Tan Coonhound is a superb tracker of raccoon, opossum, and even cougar, baying loudly when it has chased its quarry up a tree.

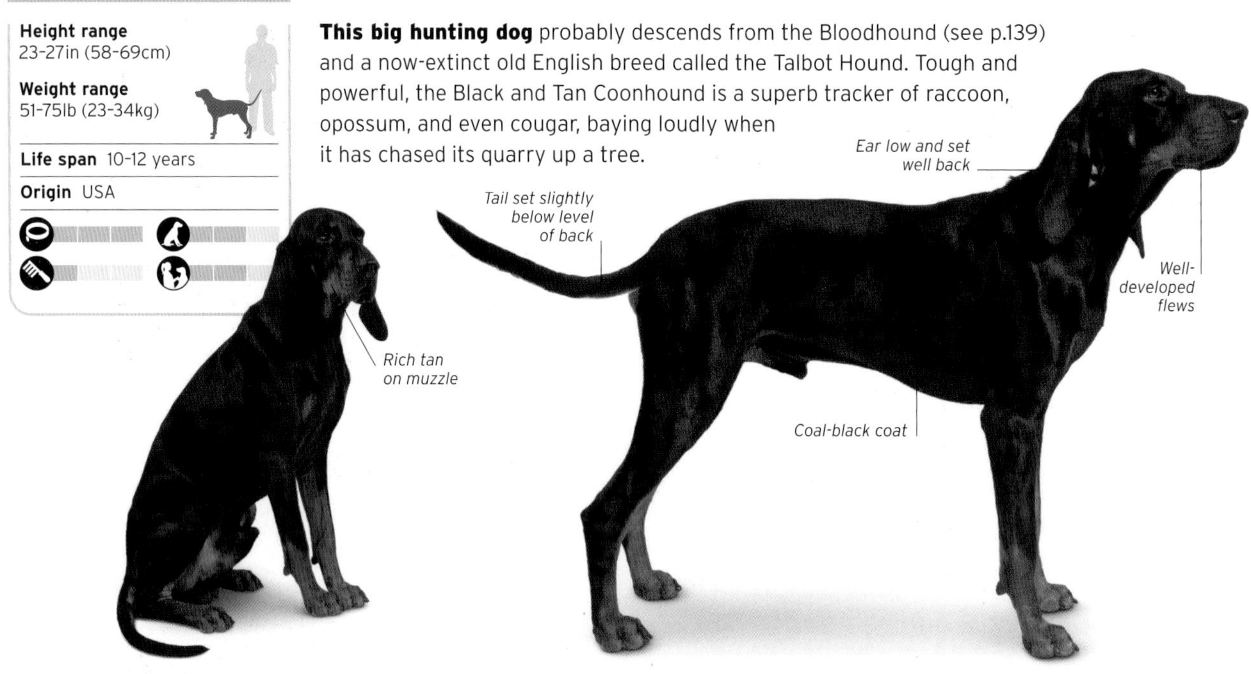
Ear low and set well back
Tail set slightly below level of back
Well-developed flews
Rich tan on muzzle
Coal-black coat

REDBONE COONHOUND

THIS DOG NEEDS A LOT OF EXERCISE AND MAY FIND CHASING IRRESISTIBLE AKC

Height range 21-27in (53-69cm)

Weight range 46-71lb (21-32kg)

Life span 11-12 years

Origin USA

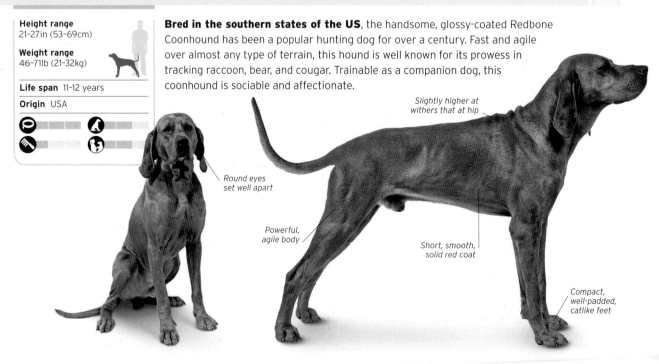

Bred in the southern states of the US, the handsome, glossy-coated Redbone Coonhound has been a popular hunting dog for over a century. Fast and agile over almost any type of terrain, this hound is well known for its prowess in tracking raccoon, bear, and cougar. Trainable as a companion dog, this coonhound is sociable and affectionate.

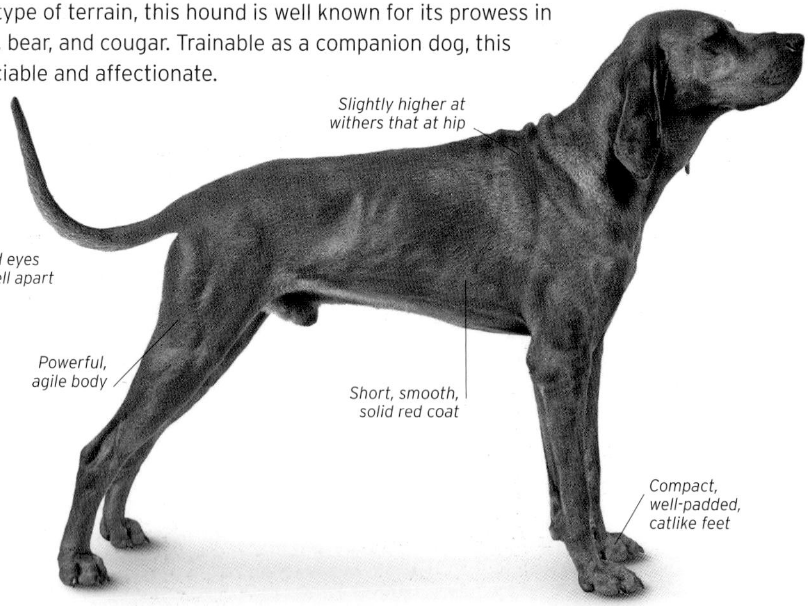

Slightly higher at withers that at hip
Round eyes set well apart
Powerful, agile body
Short, smooth, solid red coat
Compact, well-padded, catlike feet

BLUETICK COONHOUND

THIS ENERGETIC WORKING BREED NEEDS SUPERVISION OUTDOORS AKC

Height range 21–27in (53–69cm)

Weight range 44–79lb (20–36kg)

Life span 11–12 years

Origin USA

A breakaway breed, originally regarded as the English Coonhound, the Bluetick Coonhound has had its devoted followers since the 1940s. Although mainly used to track raccoon and opossum, this hound also hunts deer and bear. Happiest when working, the Bluetick Coonhound has proved to be highly successful at obedience and agility trials.

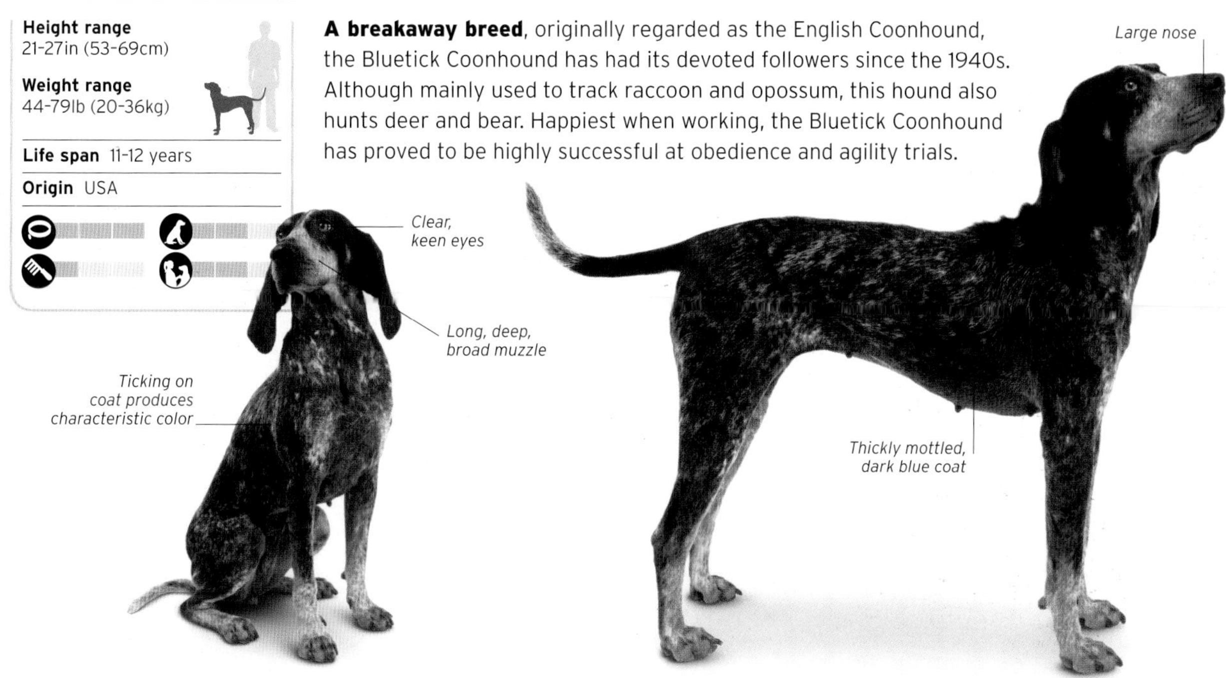
Large nose
Clear, keen eyes
Long, deep, broad muzzle
Ticking on coat produces characteristic color
Thickly mottled, dark blue coat

TREEING WALKER COONHOUND

THIS POPULAR COONHOUND MAKES AN EXCELLENT COMPANION WHEN SOCIALIZED AKC

Height range 20–27in (51–68cm)

Weight range 51–71lb (23–32kg)

Life span 12–13 years

Origin USA

Other Colors

White

White coats have tan or black spots.

This fast and efficient racoon-hunter has been recognized as a distinct breed since the 1940s. In the US this breed is much admired for its outstanding abilities in coonhound competitions. It is a dog that appreciates a friendly home environment and loves people.

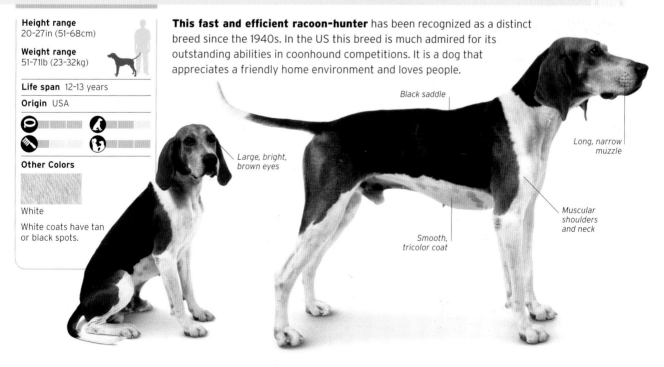

Black saddle

Large, bright, brown eyes

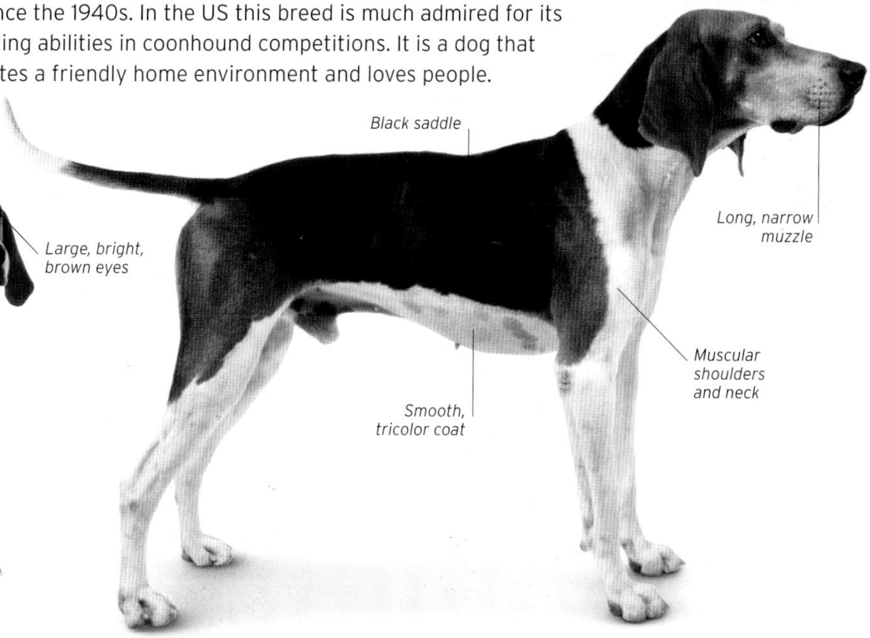

Long, narrow muzzle

Muscular shoulders and neck

Smooth, tricolor coat

AMERICAN ENGLISH COONHOUND

THIS AMERICAN-BRED HUNTER IS FULL OF ATHLETIC POISE AND PACE AKC

Height range
23–26in (58–66cm)

Weight range
46–90lb (21–41kg)

Life span 10–11 years

Origin USA

Other colors

Red and white

White and black

May also have a blue and white ticked coat.

This energetic and intelligent dog evolved from English Foxhounds (see p.158), which were brought to the New World. It was bred to adapt to rougher terrain, hunting fox by day and raccoon by night. It shows an effortless trot and never appears to get tired. Quite similar to the Treeing Walker Coonhound (see p.161), it can adopt both the "cold nose" trail (straddling an old track for hours to locate the animal that left it) or follow a scent fast in pursuit of a fresh, active trail. As a pet, it needs firm handling but in return will be a devoted companion and good guard dog.

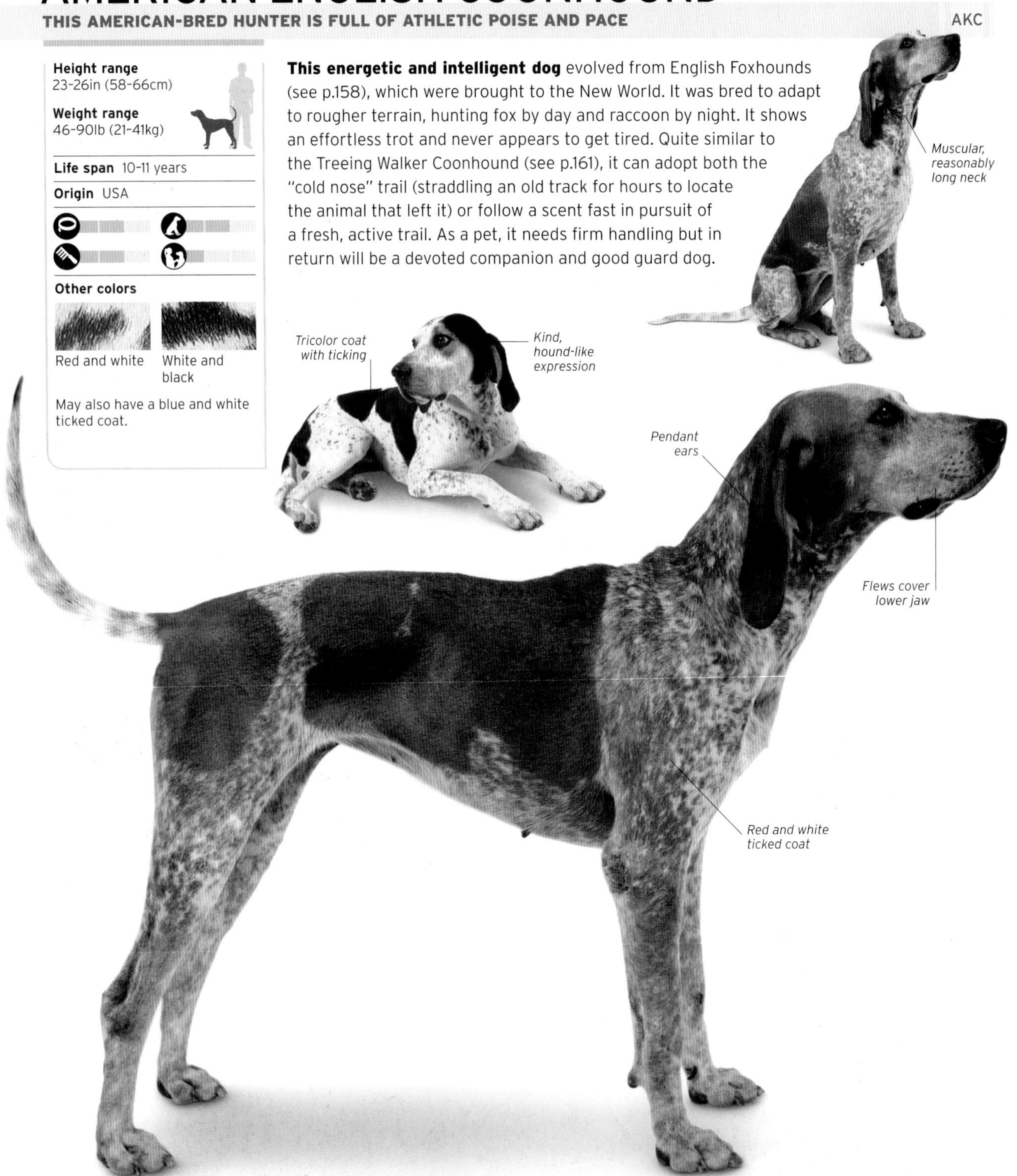
Muscular, reasonably long neck
Tricolor coat with ticking
Kind, hound-like expression
Pendant ears
Flews cover lower jaw
Red and white ticked coat

ARTOIS HOUND

THIS FRIENDLY, LIKEABLE FRENCH HOUND MAKES A WELL-BEHAVED HUNTING COMPANION

FCI

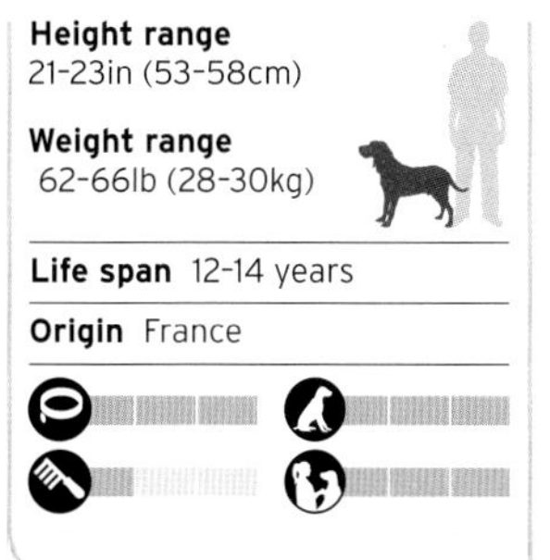
Height range
21–23in (53–58cm)
Weight range
62–66lb (28–30kg)
Life span 12–14 years
Origin France

The sometimes precocious Artois Hound is an excellent hunting companion that needs lots of exercise. It can be distinguished from other French scent hounds by its flat, open, pendant ears. The Artois Hound has a strong directional sense, a very keen nose, precise pointing, speed on the move, and drive. Its ancestry goes back to the Great Artois Hound (and back to the Saint Hubert), while some English blood also modified the breed. In the early 1990s this robust and courageous hunter of hare, deer, and boar was brought back from near extinction, although it is still rare.

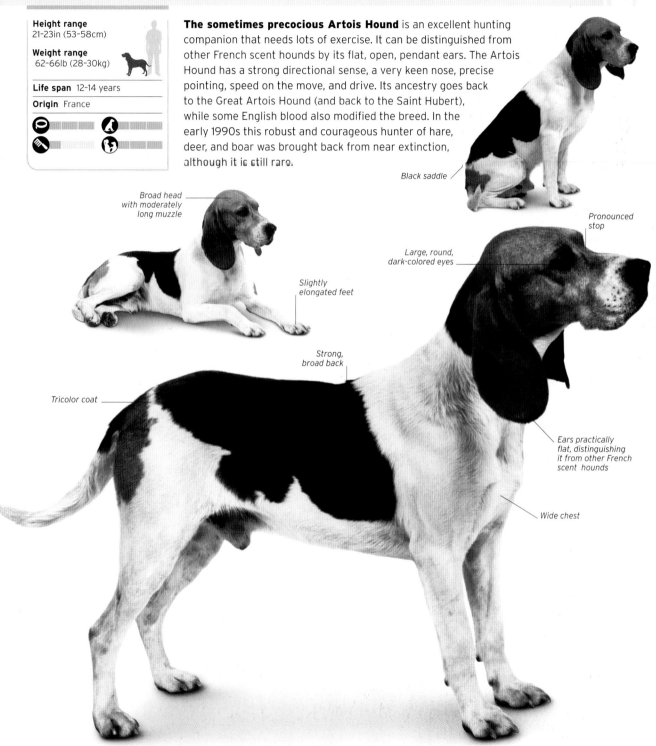

Black saddle

Broad head with moderately long muzzle

Slightly elongated feet

Pronounced stop

Large, round, dark-colored eyes

Strong, broad back

Tricolor coat

Ears practically flat, distinguishing it from other French scent hounds

Wide chest

ARIEGEOIS

AN ELEGANT DOG, THIS IS THE SMALLEST OF THE HOUNDS FROM THE SOUTH OF FRANCE

FCI

Height range
20-23in (50-58cm)

Weight range
55-60lb (25-27kg)

Life span 10-14 years

Origin France

A relative newcomer—France officially recognized it in 1912—this dog is also called the Ariege Hound, after the dry, rocky region it comes from on France's border with Spain. Its forebears include the Grand Bleu de Gascogne (opposite), the Grand Gascon-Saintongeois (opposite), and local medium-sized hounds. The Ariégeois excels as a hare-hunter but is also known for its friendly nature.

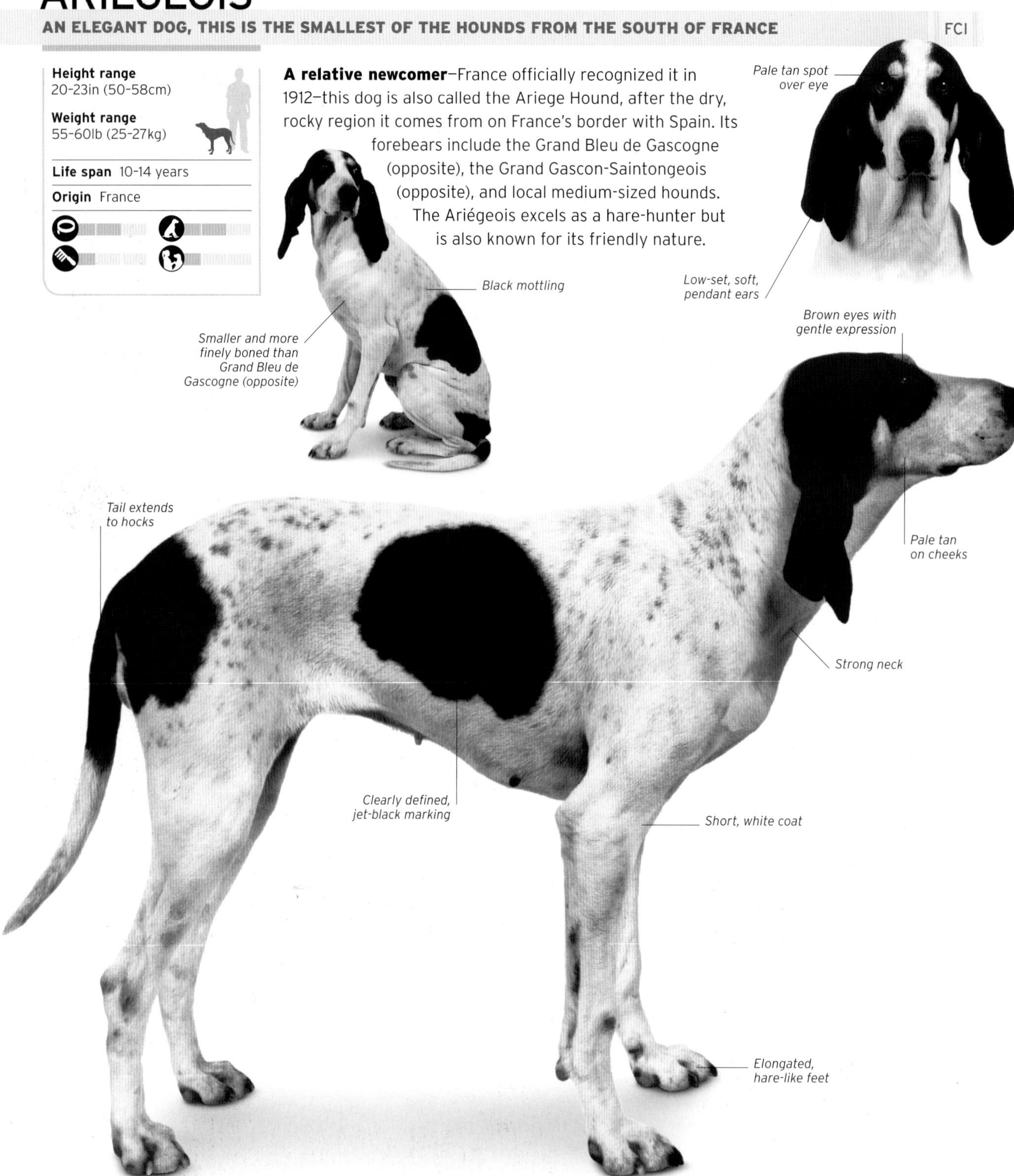
Pale tan spot over eye
Low-set, soft, pendant ears
Black mottling
Smaller and more finely boned than Grand Bleu de Gascogne (opposite)
Brown eyes with gentle expression
Tail extends to hocks
Pale tan on cheeks
Strong neck
Clearly defined, jet-black marking
Short, white coat
Elongated, hare-like feet

GASCON-SAINTONGEOIS

THIS ROE-DEER PACKHOUND HAS AN AMIABLE TEMPERAMENT FCI

Height range
Petit:
21-24in (54-62cm)
Grand:
24-28in (62-72cm)

Weight range
Petit:
53-55lb (24-25kg)
Grand:
66-71lb (30-32kg)

Life span 12-14 years

Origin France

This rare breed, from the Gascony area of France, is also known as the Virelade Hound after the Baron de Virelade who crossed the Saintongeois with the Grand Bleu de Gascogne (below), and the Ariégeois (opposite). It is a high-stamina hunter, with a fine-tuned sense of smell. There are two sizes: Petit and Grand.

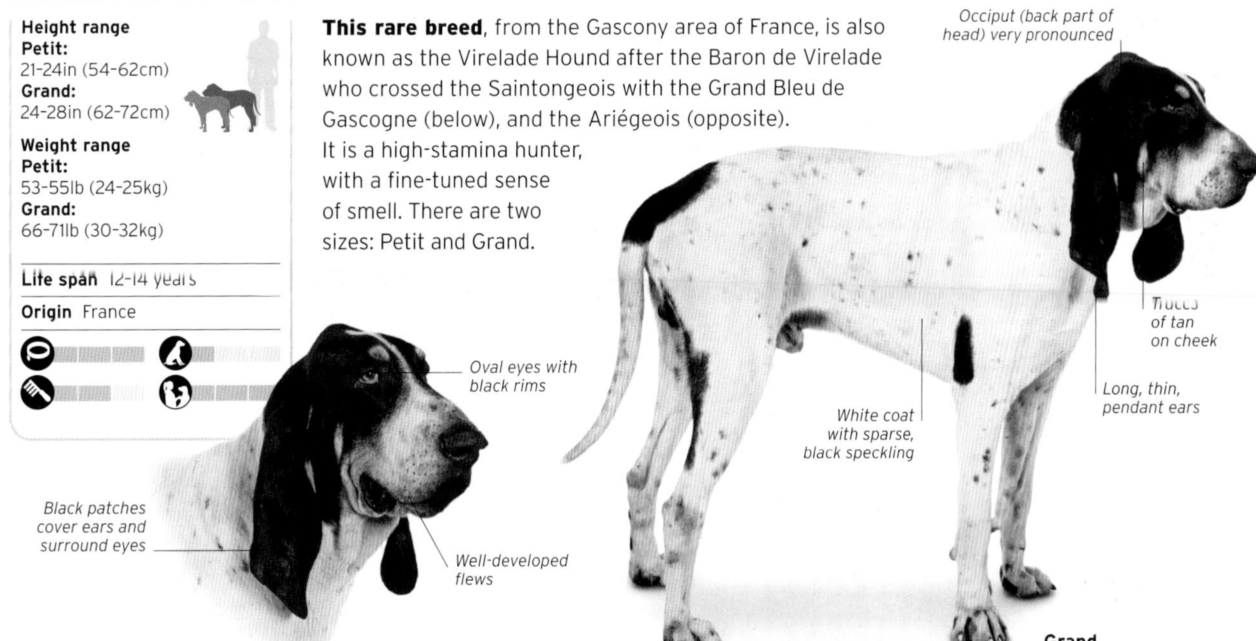
Occiput (back part of head) very pronounced
of tan on cheek
Long, thin, pendant ears
White coat with sparse, black speckling
Oval eyes with black rims
Black patches cover ears and surround eyes
Well-developed flews

Grand

GRAND BLEU DE GASCOGNE

A LARGE WORKING HOUND WITH GREAT STAMINA AND TENACITY KC

Height range
24-28in (60-70cm)

Weight range
80-120lb (36-55kg)

Life span 12-14 years

Origin France

This large trail hound has a powerful voice, is solidly built, and is recognizable by the dark mottling on its white skin—which creates a shimmering blue color. Unsuitable for city living, it needs plenty of exercise. Originally used to hunt wolves, its quarry today is hare. Its scenting skills are highly developed and it is single-minded when on a trail.

Black marks cover ears and surround eyes

Tan markings on face

Well-developed flews

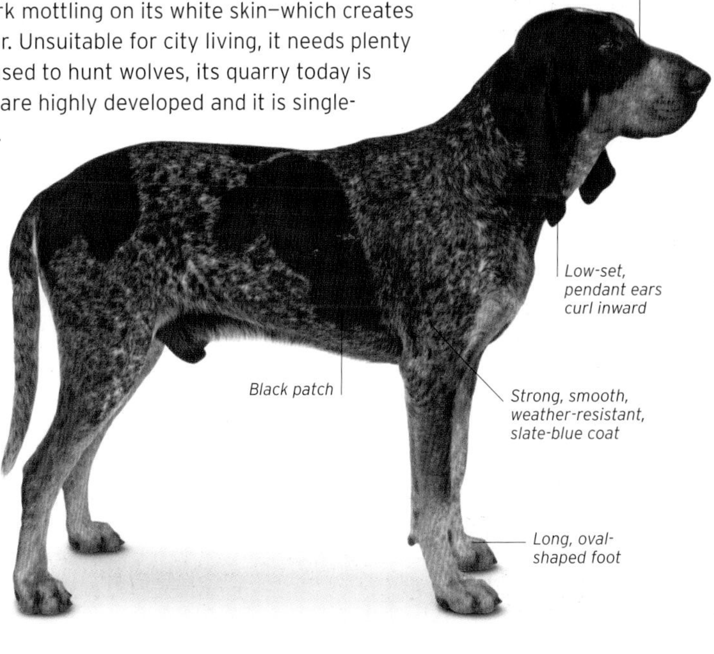

Well-developed stop

Low-set, pendant ears curl inward

Black patch

Strong, smooth, weather-resistant, slate-blue coat

Long, oval-shaped foot

PETIT BLEU DE GASCOGNE

THIS KEEN-NOSED HOUND IS READY TO FOLLOW SCENT BUT IS EASILY BORED FCI

Height range 20-23in (50-58cm)

Weight range 88-106lb (40-48kg)

Life span 12 years

Origin France

Bred down in size from the Grand Bleu de Gascogne (see p.165), the Petit Bleu de Gascogne was developed for hunting hare but is also used to pursue larger game. With a fine nose and a musical voice, this hound works well either as an individual or in a pack. If kept as a companion, it needs a firm hand and a lot of exercise.

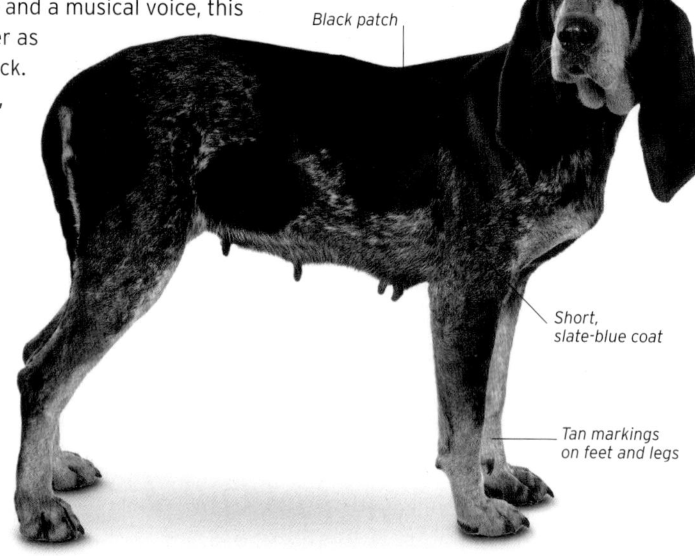
Dark chestnut eyes
Black patch
Pendant, low-set ears
Long, refined muzzle
Short, slate-blue coat
Tan markings on feet and legs
Well-developed dewlap

BLUE GASCONY GRIFFON

THIS ALL-WEATHER HUNTER IS TIRELESS AND FULL OF SPIRIT FCI

Height range 19-22in (48-57cm)

Weight range 36-40lb (17-18kg)

Life span 12-13 years

Origin France

A cross between the Petit Bleu de Gascogne (above) and wire-coated hounds, this dog has a coarse, shaggy coat that allows it to work in harsh conditions. A comparatively rare breed, it was specifically developed to hunt deer, fox, and rabbit. It has stamina rather than great speed and a remarkably efficient nose.

Long, wiry eyebrows
Long, pendant ears
Tan markings on muzzle
Coat denser and longer on shoulders
Long tail tapers to thin point
Harsh, shaggy, slate-blue coat

BASSET BLEU DE GASCOGNE

THIS ELEGANT BASSET HOUND HAS A DELIGHTFUL TEMPERAMENT BUT CAN BE STRONG-WILLED

KC

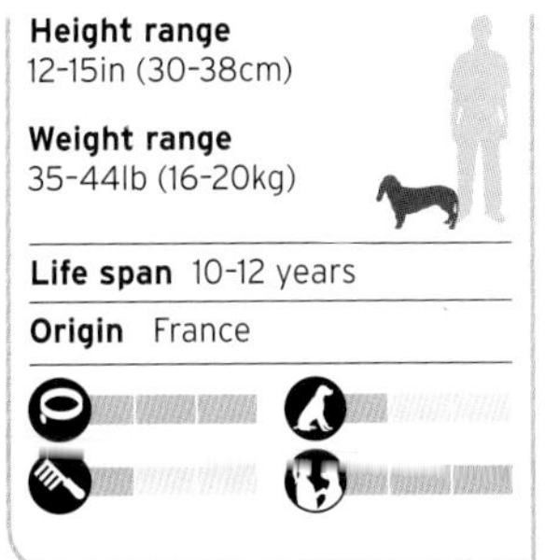

Height range
12-15in (30-38cm)
Weight range
35-44lb (16-20kg)
Life span 10-12 years
Origin France

In 12th-century France blue hounds of this type were used to hunt wolves, deer, and boar. The modern breed of Basset Bleu de Gascogne was established in the 20th century and is not as widely known as some other Gascony hounds. A low-slung dog, it is not fast moving but makes up for lack of speed with great determination, tracking quarry for hours once on the scent. This hound is an enthusiastic outdoor companion as well as a fine household pet but, like many hounds, takes patience to train and socialize.

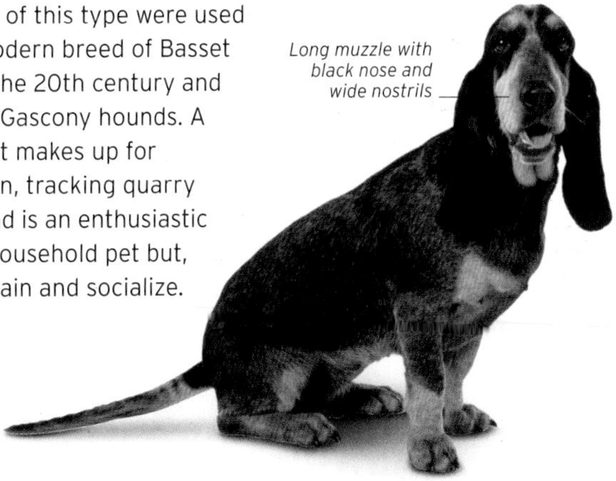

Long muzzle with black nose and wide nostrils

Long, pendant ears

Short, dense coat, with clearly defined, black saddle

Tan spot above each oval eye

Long tail extends below hock

Moderately developed flews

A mix of black and white hairs give coat slate-blue appearance

Strong, oval feet with black nails

POITEVIN

A REAL BOUNDER THROUGH THE THICKETS, THIS HOUND IS BRAVE AND BIG-HEARTED

FCI

Height range
24–28in (62–72cm)

Weight range
132–146lb (60–66kg)

Life span 11–12 years

Origin France

Other colors

White and orange

Wolf-colored hair also often occurs.

This big, courageous hound is adept at fast and furious pack hunting over rough ground, and once hunted the wolves that used to roam the province of Poitou below Vendée and Brittany in western France. Today, after several infusions of "new blood," this powerfully muscled breed shows great prowess and stamina in pursuing wild boar and deer in packs, and can hunt all day. It is a very hard worker that will follow its quarry through water and bays a lot. It is the longest-serving of the French pack hounds.

Saddle of black hair over back

Muzzle narrows toward nose

Large, brown eyes

Long, narrow head

Arched back

Thin, cone-shaped ears

Sleek, shiny, tricolor coat

Well-muscled body with deep, narrow chest

Rounded feet

BILLY

A SUPERB HUNTING DOG AND EASY-GOING FAMILY PET FCI

Height range
21–28in (53–70cm)

Weight range
55–73lb (25–33kg)

Life span 12–13 years

Origin France

A sleek, attractive breed built for speed, the Billy has remained relatively obscure even in its native France. Its forebears are the now extinct Montemboeuf, Ceris, and Larye breeds. Its quirky name comes from Château de Billy in Poitou where Gaston Hublot du Rivault bred this instinctive deer hunter in the late 1800s.

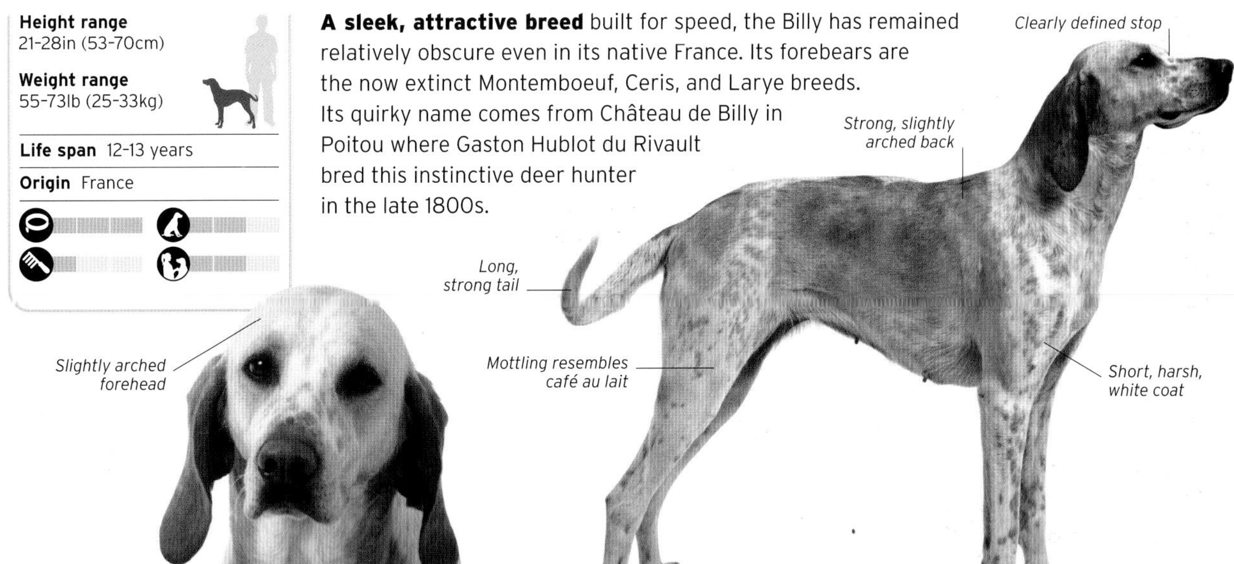
Clearly defined stop
Strong, slightly arched back
Long, strong tail
Slightly arched forehead
Mottling resembles café au lait
Short, harsh, white coat

FRENCH TRICOLOR HOUND

THE YOUNGEST OF THE FRENCH HOUNDS, AND SIMILAR TO THE POITEVIN IN LOOKS AND ABILITY FCI

Height range
24–28in (60–72cm)

Weight range
75–77lb (34–35kg)

Life span 11–12 years

Origin France

Perhaps the most popular hound in France, the French Tricolor Hound was blended from the Poitevin (opposite) and Billy (above) to try to create a home-grown pack hound without English Foxhound (see p.158) blood (though there is a hint of Great Anglo-French Tricolor Hound, see p.170). Today these strong, well-muscled pack dogs hunt game such as deer and wild boar.

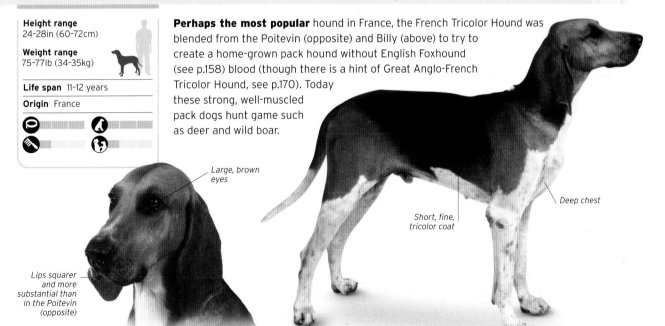

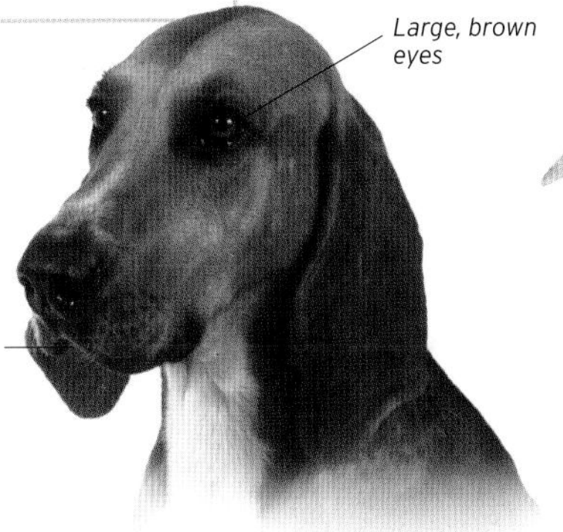

Large, brown eyes

Deep chest

Short, fine, tricolor coat

Lips squarer and more substantial than in the Poitevin (opposite)

GREAT ANGLO-FRENCH TRICOLOR HOUND

THIS HOUND IS HAPPIEST WHEN HUNTING IN A PACK FCI

Height range
24–28in (60–70cm)

Weight range
66–77lb (30–35kg)

Life span 10–12 years

Origin France

Like several French scent hounds, the name says what it is: a tricolored dog with cross-Channel connections—the "Great" refers to the game it hunts, such as red deer, not the dog's size. Its coat and character come from the tricolored Poitevin (see p.168), and the powerful muscles and stamina from the English Foxhound (see p.158).

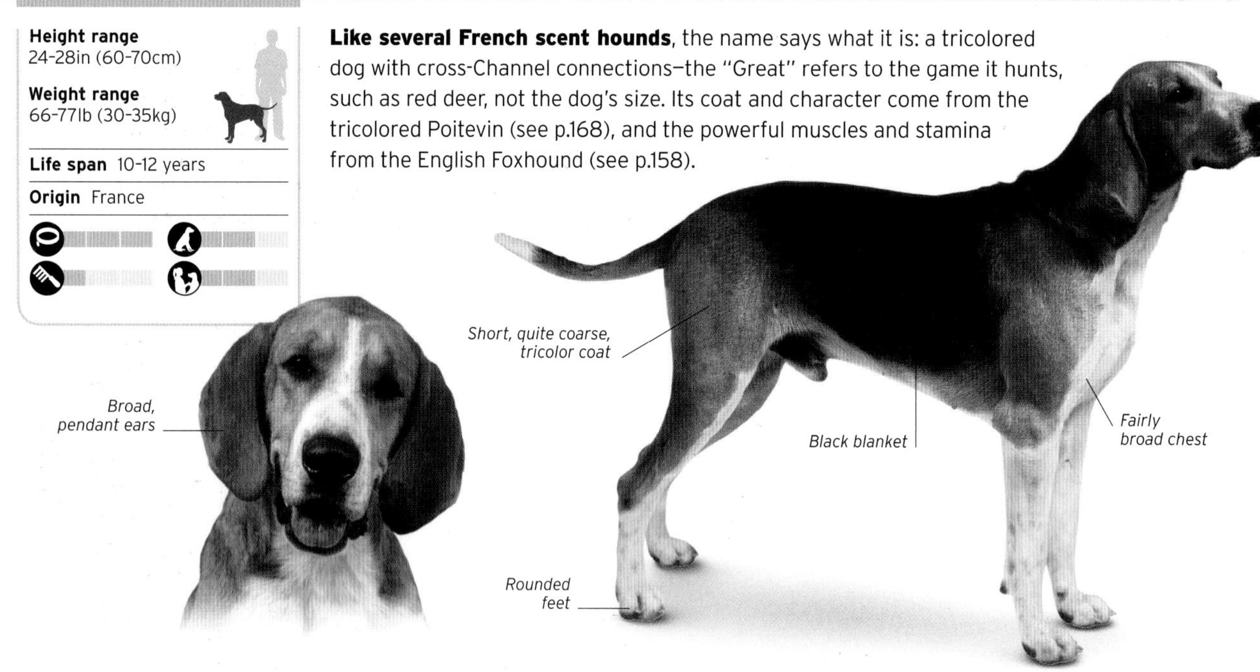
Broad, pendant ears
Short, quite coarse, tricolor coat
Black blanket
Fairly broad chest
Rounded feet

GREAT ANGLO-FRENCH WHITE AND BLACK HOUND

A BIG, ENERGETIC DOG USED FOR LARGE GAME HUNTING FCI

Height range
24–28in (62–72cm)

Weight range
66–77lb (30–35kg)

Life span 10–12 years

Origin France

This Anglo-French scent hound is one of three color-based varieties recognized as separate breeds. It originated in the 1800s from a mix of Bleu de Gascogne and Gasçon Saintongeois hounds crossed with English Foxhound (see p.158). Most live in kennels in France, and are used to hunt deer in packs. Very few of these powerful, sturdy hunters are kept as domestic pets.

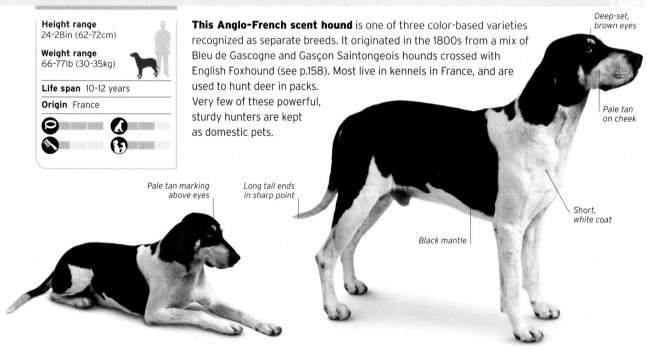

Deep-set, brown eyes

Pale tan on cheek

Pale tan marking above eyes

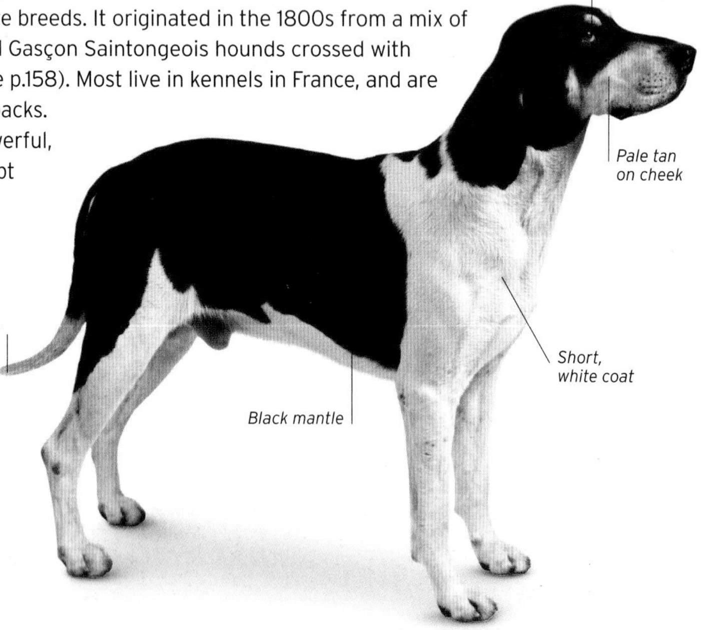

Long tail ends in sharp point

Short, white coat

Black mantle

FRENCH WHITE AND BLACK HOUND

A SWIFT-FOOTED, STAMINA-PACKED HUNTER THAT GIVES ENDLESS CHASE

FCI

Height range
24–28in (62–72cm)

Weight range
57–66lb (26–30kg)

Life span 10–12 years

Origin France

There is a growing population of these big, powerful dogs in France, and it is perhaps not surprising given that this handsome breed is highly regarded for hunting roe deer in packs. It is a friendly dog but more likely to form a close relationship with its master in a kennels than an owner in a modern house. It may have links with the famous Hound of Saintonge, whose own origins are uncertain but which was bred to hunt wolves. The modern French White and Black Hound is a mix of Bleu de Gascogne and Gasçon Saintongeois hounds.

Black mantle
Tan marking above eyes
Long, thin tail
Slightly arched back with dipping croup
Pendant ears
Short, dense, white and black hair
Bluish speckling on legs

GREAT ANGLO-FRENCH WHITE AND ORANGE HOUND

BRED TO LIVE AND WORK IN A PACK, THIS HOUND IS NOT A GOOD CHOICE FOR APARTMENT LIFE

FCI

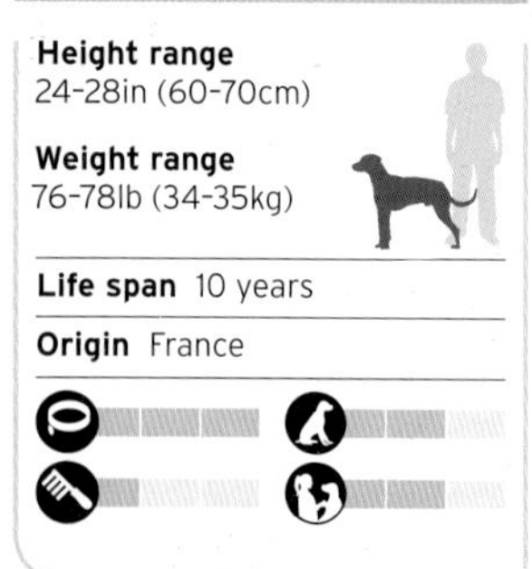
Height range
24-28in (60-70cm)
Weight range
76-78lb (34-35kg)
Life span 10 years
Origin France

One of three breeds of the Great Anglo-French pack-hunting dogs produced in the early 19th century, this hound is the result of crossing the English Foxhound (see p.158) with a large, French scent hound—the Billy (see p.169). Although trainable and kind-natured, this dog lives to hunt and is too energetic to be happy in complete domesticity.

Drop ears with rounded tips
Well-defined stop
Orange patch
Large, dark brown eyes
Deep chest
Sleek, short, relatively thin, white coat

FRENCH WHITE AND ORANGE HOUND

THIS BREED REQUIRES STRENUOUS EXERCISE BUT MAY SETTLE IN A SPACIOUS HOME

FCI

Height range
24-28in (62-70cm)
Weight range
60-71lb (27-32kg)
Life span 12-13 years
Origin France

Rarely seen, the French White and Orange Hound is a relatively new hunting dog—only gaining recognition in the 1970s. Easier to manage than most packhounds, this dog is usually reliable with children and other dogs but must be supervised around small pets. It loves action and should not be kept in a confined space.

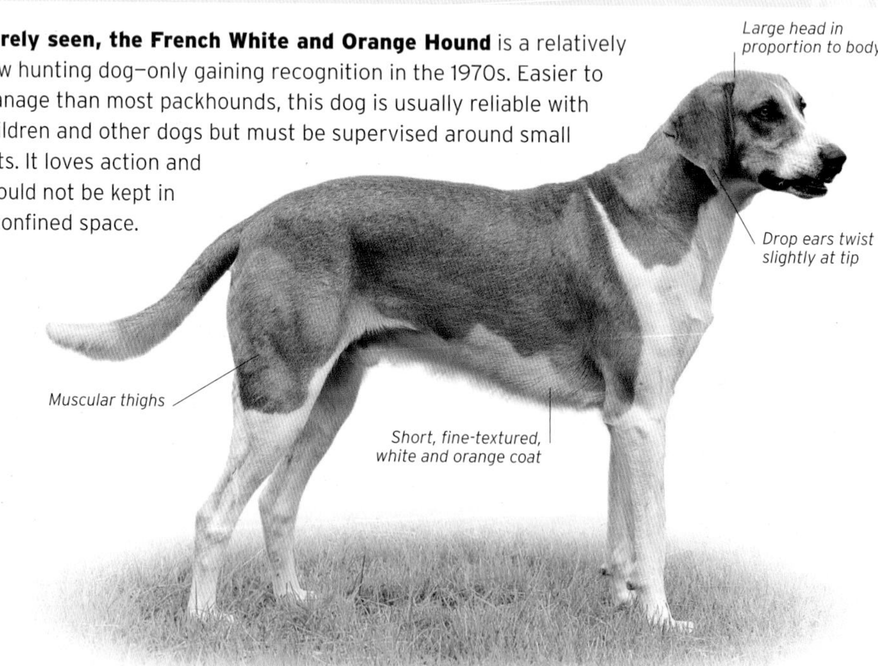
Large head in proportion to body
Drop ears twist slightly at tip
Muscular thighs
Short, fine-textured, white and orange coat

WESTPHALIAN DACHSBRACKE

THIS ENERGETIC DOG HAS AN EVEN TEMPERAMENT BUT NEEDS FIRM TRAINING FCI

Height range
12–15in (30–38cm)

Weight range
33–40lb (15–18kg)

Life span 10–12 years

Origin Germany

A short-legged version of the German Hound (see p.175), this sturdy little dog was bred to hunt small game in areas too thickly overgrown for larger dogs to penetrate. Playful and cheerily good-natured, the Westphalian Dachsbracke makes a delightful companion and is well suited to family life.

Bridge of nose slightly arched
Black mantle
Body length greater than leg length
White tip to tail
White collar and chest
Puppy
Smooth, red coat
White blaze extends down muzzle

ALPINE DACHSBRACKE

THIS FRIENDLY DOG IS HAPPY TO BE OUT ALL DAY IN ALL WEATHERS FCI

Height range
13–17in (34–42cm)

Weight range
27–48lb (12–22kg)

Life span 12 years

Origin Austria

Other colors

Vieräugl (black and tan)

Hunting dogs very similar in appearance to the Alpine Dachsbracke existed hundreds of years ago and may have been the predecessors of this small hound. In the 1930s the modern breed was recognized as one of Austria's top scent hounds. Sturdy and tireless, and bred to hunt, the Alpine Dachsbracke is not an ideal house dog.

Well-defined stop

Dense, dark deer-red coat, interspersed with black hairs

Slightly arched head with definite furrow

Drop ears with well-rounded tips

Prominent chest bone

White markings on chest

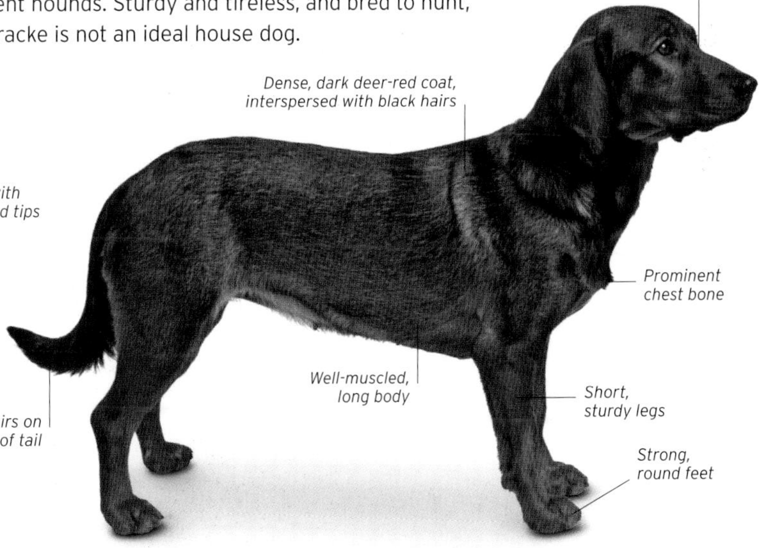

Well-muscled, long body

Short, sturdy legs

Longer hairs on underside of tail

Strong, round feet

DACHSHUND

INQUISITIVE, BRAVE, AND LOYAL, THIS DOG IS POPULAR AS A COMPANION AND WATCHDOG AKC

Height range
Miniature:
5–6in (13–15cm)
Standard:
8–9in (20–23cm)

Weight range
Miniature:
9–11lb (4–5kg)
Standard:
20–26lb (9–12kg)

Life span 12–15 years

Origin Germany

Other colors

Variety of colors

Despite their small size, Dachshunds need plenty of exercise and mental stimulation to maintain their cheerful and loving temperament. Strong-willed, they tend to ignore commands when on the scent of prey. Dachshunds will bark protectively at unexpected visitors but are good with older children. There are three coat types: smooth-haired, long-haired, and wire-haired. The long-haired varieties need daily grooming. Two sizes are recognized by the AKC, miniature and standard; but three sizes, based on chest circumference, are recognized by the FCI.

Black and tan coat, coarse to touch
Forefeet bigger and broader than hind feet
Wire-haired
Shiny, black and tan coat
Smooth, red coat
Smooth-haired
Hair shorter on head
Very shallow stop
Pendant, feathered ears
Body much longer than leg length
Long, silky, shaded red coat
Long-haired

GERMAN HOUND

USUALLY GOOD WITH CHILDREN AND OTHER DOGS, THIS HOUND PREFERS OUTDOOR LIFE FCI

Height range
16–21in (40–53cm)

Weight range
35–40lb (16–18kg)

Life span 10–12 years

Origin Germany

For centuries numerous hunting dogs of the type known as brackes existed in Germany. Today the German Hound, or Deutsche Bracke, is one of the few to survive. This hound, bred by combining several bracke varieties, is still used mainly for hunting. Although good-natured, the German Hound does not adapt well to life indoors.

White blaze on head
Slightly arched back with black blanket
Broad, pendant ears
Short, smooth, tan coat
White chest markings
Distinctive flesh-pink nose, edged with black
White markings on feet

DREVER

THIS SPORTING DOG IS RARELY KEPT SOLELY FOR COMPANIONSHIP FCI

Height range
12–15in (30–38cm)

Weight range
31–35lb (14–16kg)

Life span 12–14 years

Origin Sweden

Other colors

Variety of colors

In the early 20th century a small, short-legged hound from Germany, the Westphalian Dachsbracke, was imported to Sweden. The breed proved popular as a game tracker, and by the 1940s the Swedes had developed their own version, the Drever. Because of its strong hunting instinct, this breed is best kept as a sporting dog.

Drop ears with rounded tips

Large head in proportion to body

White neck hair extends down to chest

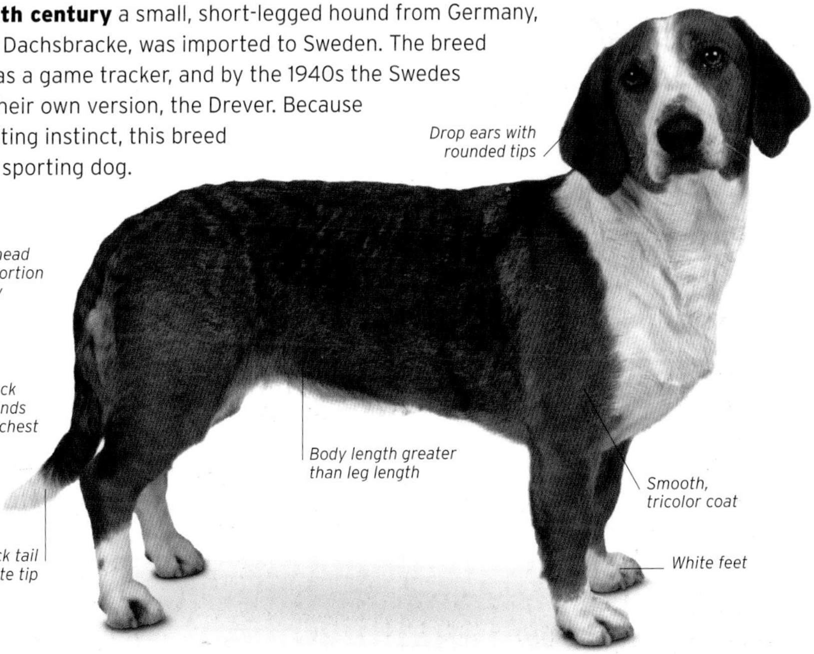

Body length greater than leg length

Smooth, tricolor coat

Long, thick tail with white tip

White feet

LAUFHUND

A NOBLE-HEADED, KEEN, AND LEAN HOUND WITH ROMAN ROOTS FCI

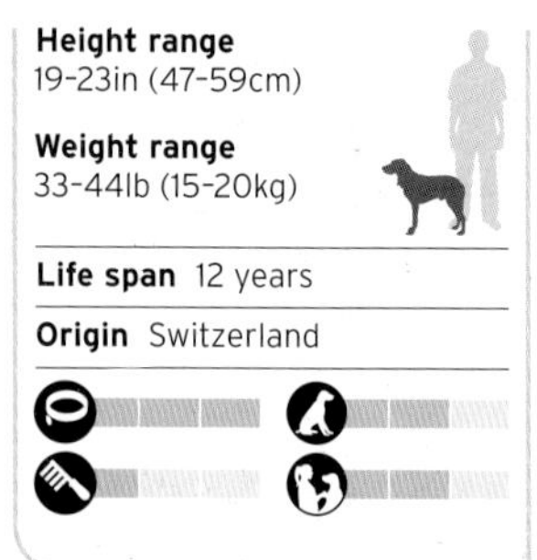

Height range
19-23in (47-59cm)
Weight range
33-44lb (15-20kg)
Life span 12 years
Origin Switzerland

This breed, also known as the Swiss Hound, is a keen-nosed tracker that moves easily across Alpine terrain. It is bred to sniff out the track of hare, fox, and roe deer with its long muzzle. There are four distinct varieties—Bernese, Lucerne, Schwyz Laufhunds, and the Bruno Jura (p.138)—each named after a Swiss canton and identified by its coat colors. (A further variety, the Thurgovia, has died out.) The fine sculpted head and well-proportioned body lends the Laufhund an air of nobility. At home they are relaxed and quite docile.

Forehead lacks any furrow or wrinkle

White coat with orange patches

Schwyz

Blue coat, a result of a combination of white and black hairs

Light to dark tan markings on cheeks

Lucerne

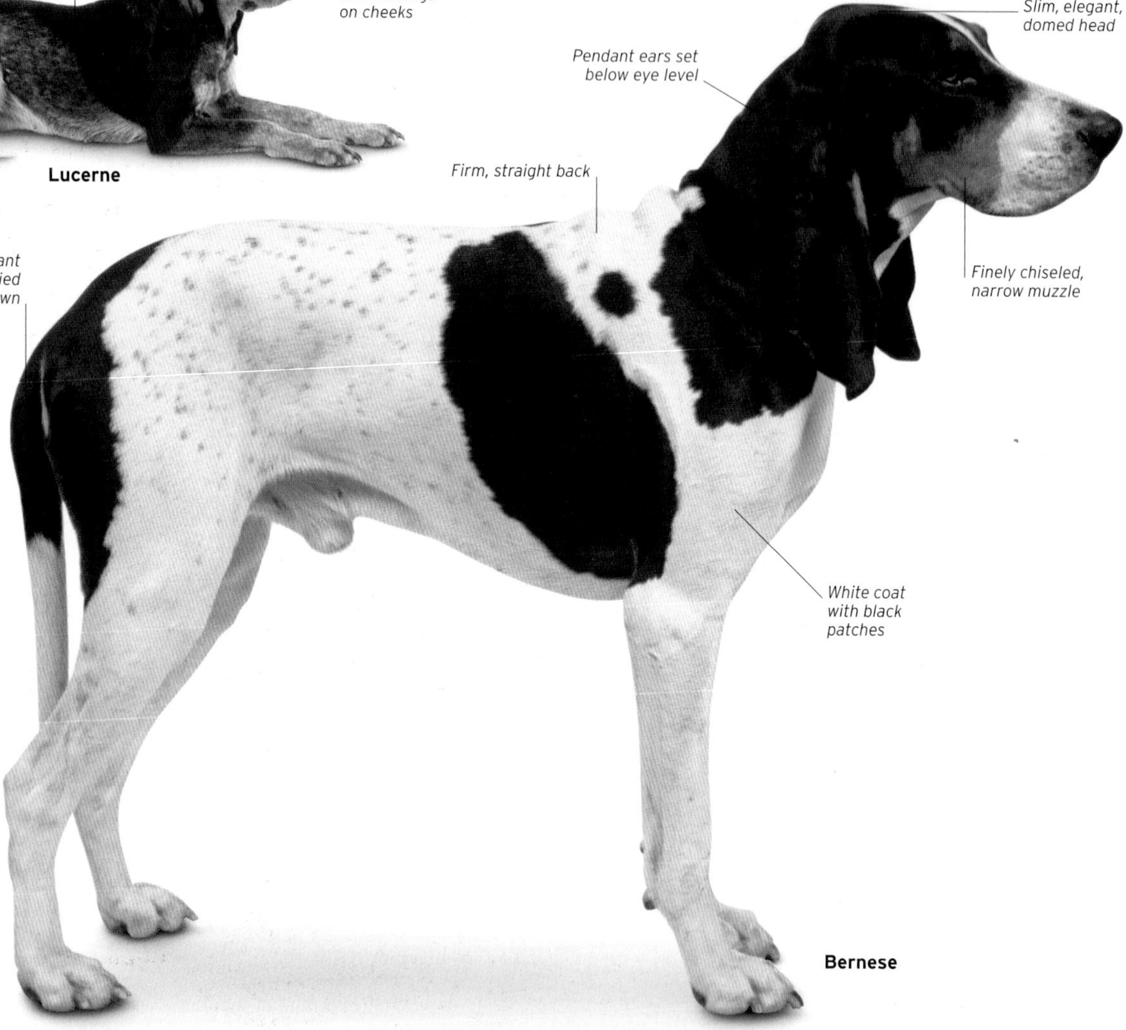

Slim, elegant, domed head

Pendant ears set below eye level

Firm, straight back

Elegant tail carried hanging down

Finely chiseled, narrow muzzle

White coat with black patches

Bernese

NEIDERLAUFHUND

A SMALLER, SHORTER-LEGGED, HIGHLY VOCAL SWISS HOUND

FCI

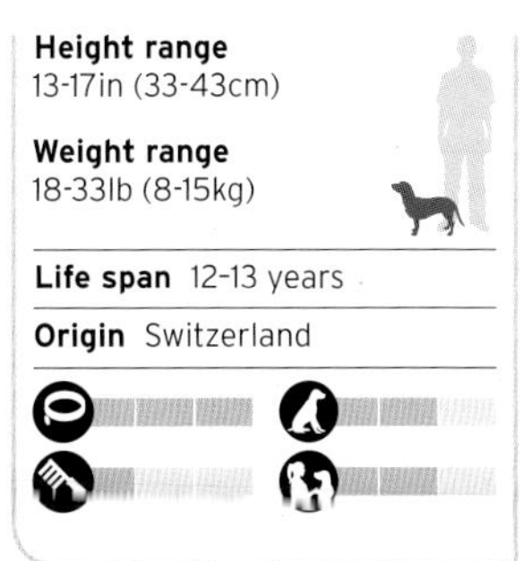

Height range 13-17in (33-43cm)

Weight range 18-33lb (8-15kg)

Life span 12-13 years

Origin Switzerland

This reduced version of the Laufhund (opposite) was bred specifically to make the most of the Swiss cantons' high-mountain game reserves. Being slower than the Laufhund, it can track big game more efficiently than its larger cousin (which is too fleet of foot in an enclosed area). This short-barreled, stocky version has a great nose for game such as wild boar, badger, and bear. The Bernese Neiderlaufhund comes in a smooth-haired and a rarer rough-coated version with a small beard. The other Neiderlaufhunds are the Schwyz, Jura, and Luzerne Niederlaufhund.

Harsh, dense, white coat with black and tan markings

Soft undercoat

Bernese rough-coated

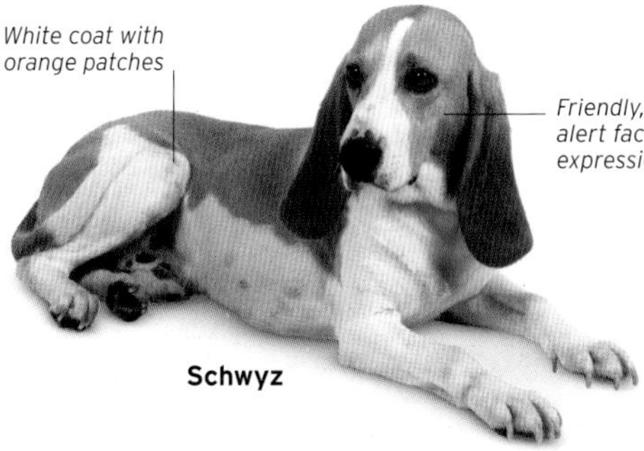

Tan marking over eyes

White coat with orange patches

Friendly, alert facial expression

Schwyz

Lucerne

Long tail carried down when active

Long, pendant ears

White coat with black and tan patches

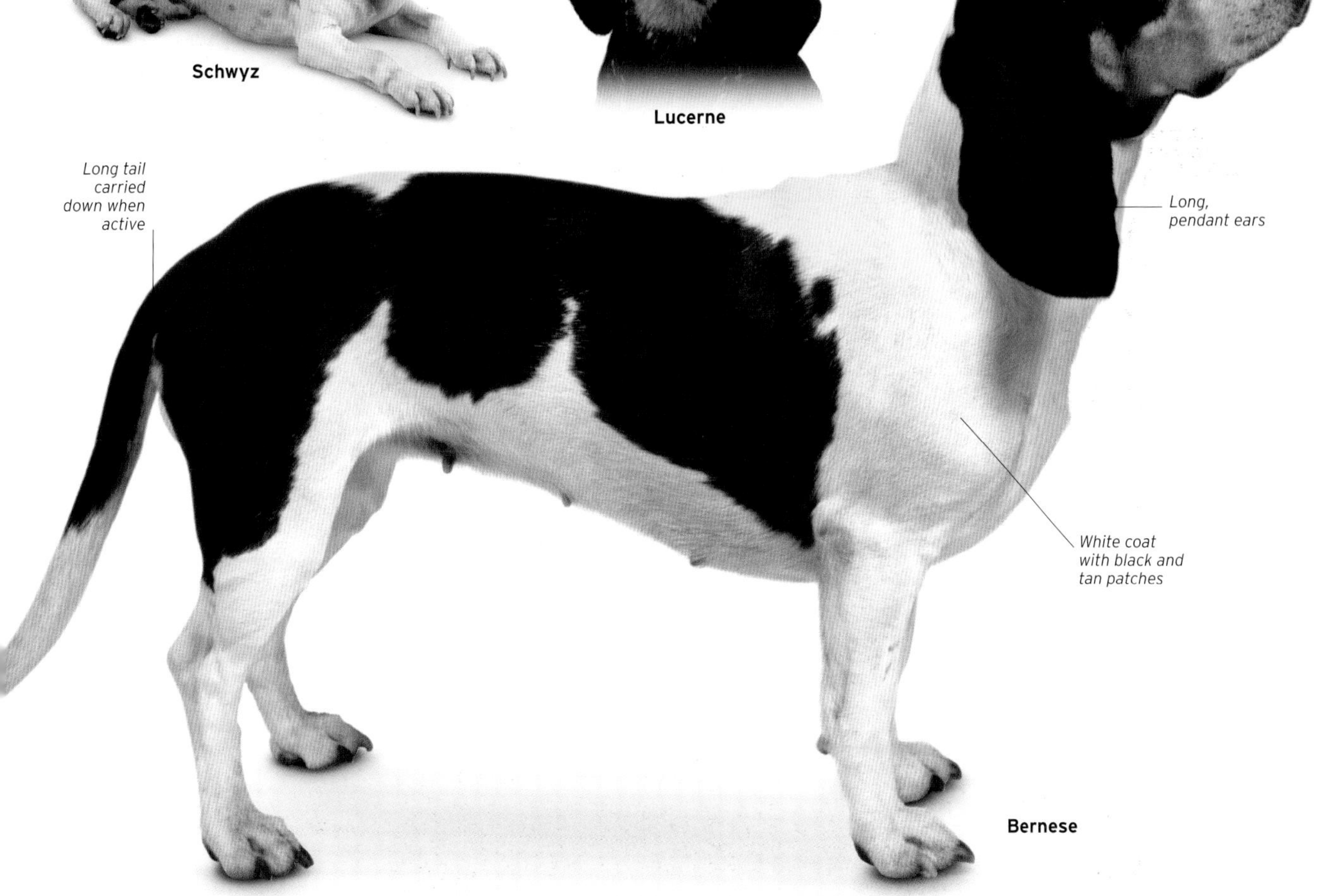

Bernese

BAVARIAN MOUNTAIN HOUND

AMENABLE TO TRAINING, THIS HOUND NEEDS PLENTY OF PHYSICAL AND MENTAL ACTIVITY KC

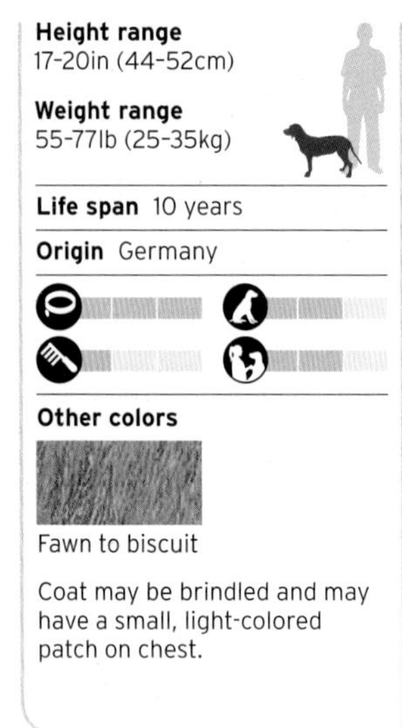

Height range 17-20in (44-52cm)

Weight range 55-77lb (25-35kg)

Life span 10 years

Origin Germany

Other colors

Fawn to biscuit

Coat may be brindled and may have a small, light-colored patch on chest.

This handsome hound, with a relatively light build, was first bred in the 1870s specifically to work in mountainous regions. A peerless tracker, the Bavarian Mountain Hound is used to follow large game, such as wild boar and deer. Steady-natured, though needing a lot of exercise, it makes a good family dog.

Dark, alert eyes
Broad, flat head
Back rises slightly toward hindquarters
Dark mask
Broad, pendant ears
Short, harsh, close-fitting, red coat

HANOVERIAN SCENT HOUND

BRED FOR STRENUOUS WORK, THIS SUPERB TRACKING DOG IS NOT A GOOD HOUSE DOG FCI

Height range 19-22in (48-55cm)

Weight range 55-88lb (25-40kg)

Life span 12 years

Origin Germany

A classic big game tracker, dogs of this type have been well established since the Middle Ages, when they were taken hunting on leashes. The modern breed, little changed in appearance, is still used for tracking wounded game. Intensely loyal to a trusted handler, this dog is cautious with strangers.

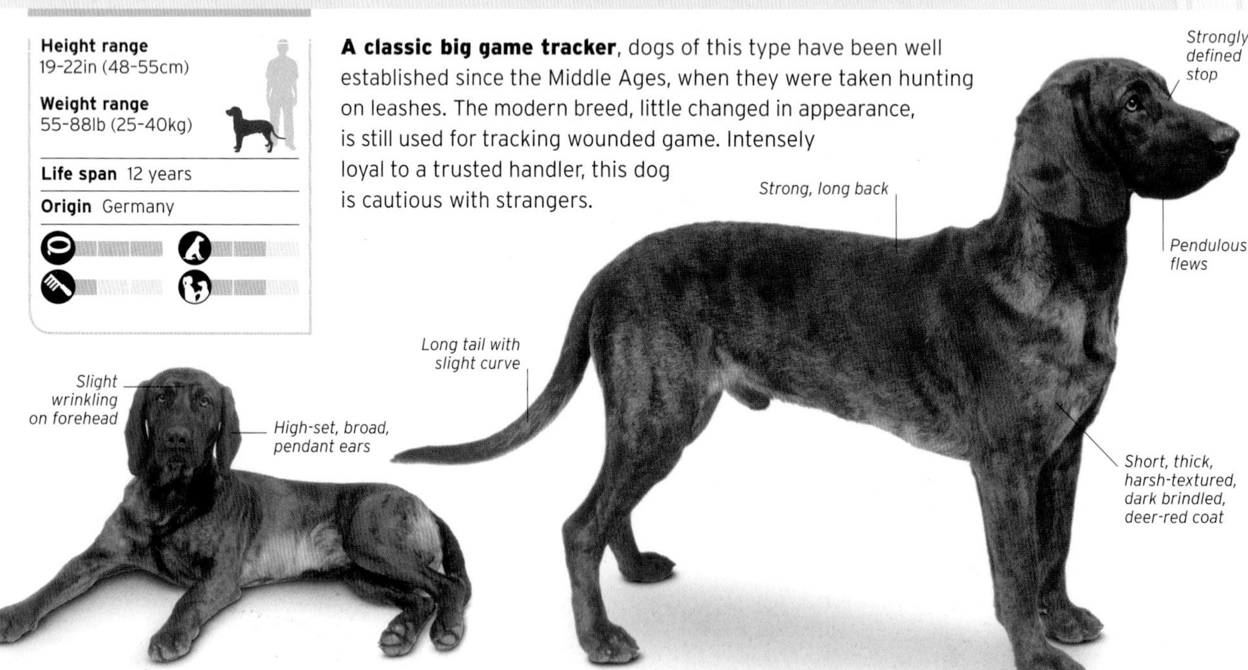
Strongly defined stop
Strong, long back
Pendulous flews
Long tail with slight curve
Slight wrinkling on forehead
High-set, broad, pendant ears
Short, thick, harsh-textured, dark brindled, deer-red coat

DOBERMAN PINSCHER

THIS LOYAL AND OBEDIENT FAMILY DOG COMBINES STRENGTH WITH GRACE

AKC

Height range
26–27in (65–69cm)

Weight range
66–88lb (30–40kg)

Life span 13 years

Origin Germany

Other colors

Fawn (Isabella) Blue

Brown

Reportedly created around 1860 by a German tax official called Louis Dobermann, this dog is the result of a number of crossings thought to include the German Shepherd Dog (see p.35), the Greyhound (see p.126), the Rottweiler (see p.81), and the Weimaraner (see p.246). From these, the Doberman Pinscher inherited a collection of admirable traits, including guarding and tracking abilities, intelligence, endurance, speed, and good looks. Widely used for police and security work, this breed is also popular as a town or country house dog. Dobermans love being part of family life—the more active the better.

Typical rust-red markings
Almond-shaped eyes
Flat-topped, long head
Back slopes gently down toward croup
Smooth, short, black and tan coat
Compact, catlike feet

BLACK FOREST HOUND

A MOUNTAIN HUNTING DOG WITH AN EXCEPTIONAL SENSE OF SMELL AND DIRECTION FCI

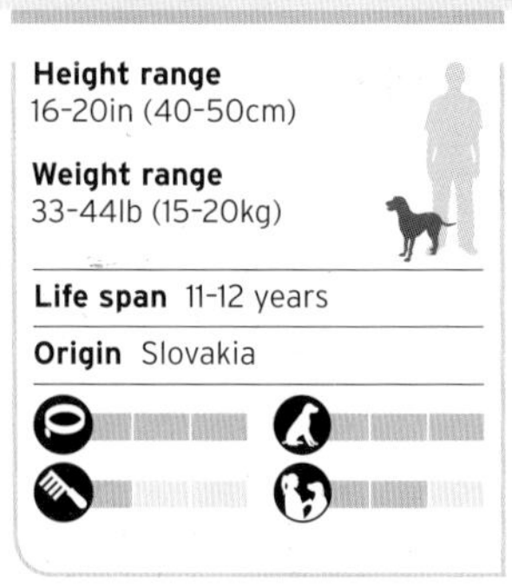

Height range
16–20in (40–50cm)

Weight range
33–44lb (15–20kg)

Life span 11–12 years

Origin Slovakia

The Black Forest Hound, or Slovenský Kopov, originated in the foothills and snowy mountain forests of central Eastern Europe. It is used to hunt boar, deer, and other game in small packs or alone. Local hunters like the breed because it can follow a scent for hours through dense thickets, protected by its coarse coat.

Eyelids always black
Slightly tapered, black nose
Black coat with tan markings
Oval-shaped feet with well-arched toes

Drop ears with rounded tips
Tan spots above eyes
Tan-colored muzzle

POLISH HOUND

THIS LITHE AND PERSISTENT DOG HAS A FRIENDLY CHARACTER FCI

Height range
22–26in (55–65cm)

Weight range
44–71lb (20–32kg)

Life span 11–12 years

Origin Poland

Evolving from a heavier bracke and lighter scent hound, this rare breed emerged as a large game hunter in Poland's thick mountainous forests. The ancestors of this hound hunted in packs for Polish nobility during the Middle Ages. The Polish Hound displays superb tracking abilities regardless of how fast it is running.

Tip of ears twist
Moderately pronounced dewlap
Black saddle
Short, fawn coat

TRANSYLVANIAN HOUND

MEDIUM-SIZED AND SHORT-HAIRED, THIS IS A RARE HUNGARIAN HUNTING DOG FCI

Height range
22-26in (55-65cm)

Weight range
55-77lb (25-35kg)

Life span 10-12 years

Origin Hungary

Also known as the Hungarian Hound, or Erdelyi Kopó, this hardy hunting dog was once the preserve of Hungarian kings and princes. Then, as now, its keen sense of direction, and hardiness in heavy, snowbound Carpathian forests and climate extremes made it the large game hunter of choice. However, it remains an extremely rare breed.

Tan spots above dark brown eyes
Black lips
Coarse, short, black coat
Drop ears widen and then taper to a rounded tip
Clearly defined tan markings

POSAVAZ HOUND

THIS VERY HARDY SCENT HOUND HAS BEEN BRED TO HUNT HARE AND FOX FCI

Height range
18-23in (46-58cm)

Weight range
35-53lb (16-24kg)

Life span 10-12 years

Origin Former Yugoslavia

The Croatian name for the Posavaz Hound, Posavski Gonic, can be translated as "scent hound from the Sava valley," and its robust build makes it ideally suited to the dense underbrush of the Sava river basin. Passionate in the hunt, this hound is quite docile in the home.

Long, narrow head

Straight, dense, reddish wheaten coat

White muzzle

Large, dark eyes

White collar and chest

Flat, thin, drop ears with rounded tips

BOSNIAN ROUGH-COATED HOUND

AN IMPLACABLE HUNTER ON THE TRAIL BUT QUIET AND GENTLE AT HOME

FCI

Height range
18–22in (45–56cm)

Weight range
35–55lb (16–25kg)

Life span 12 years

Origin Bosnia and Herzegovina

Other colors

Tricolor

Formerly known as the Illyrian Hound, this breed has been a huntsman's companion since the 19th century. A hardy, solidly built dog, it has a thick, coarse-haired coat that enables it to work in bitterly cold weather and through thick undergrowth.

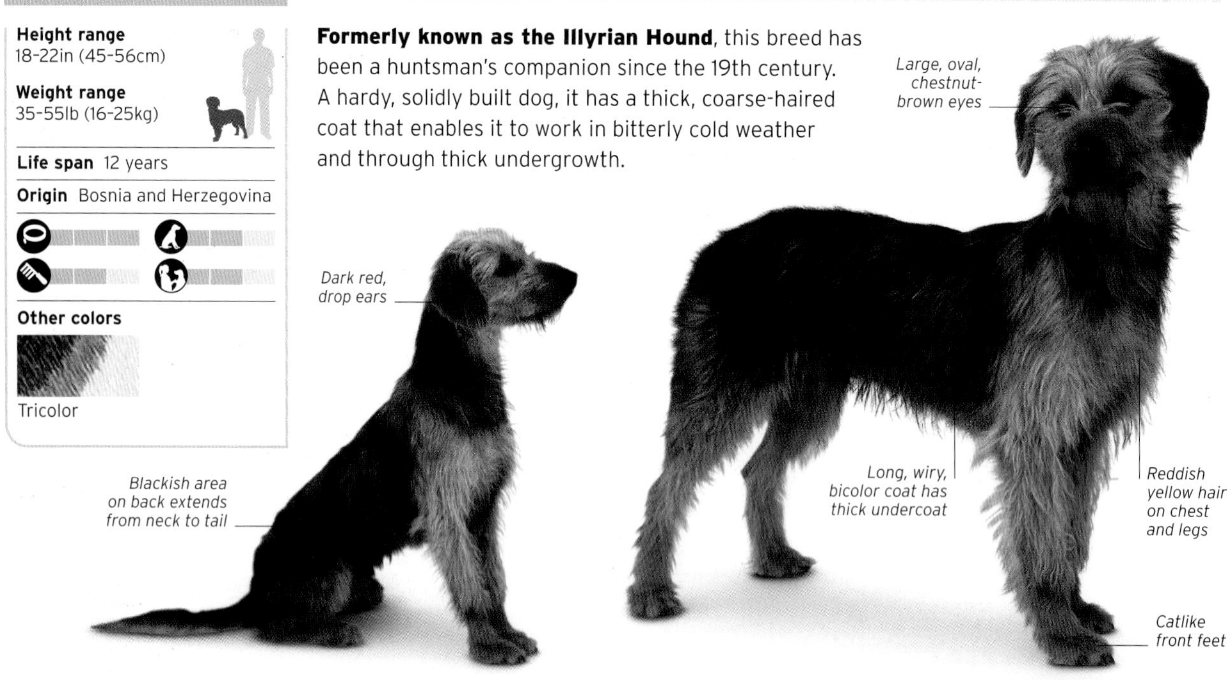
Large, oval, chestnut-brown eyes
Dark red, drop ears
Blackish area on back extends from neck to tail
Long, wiry, bicolor coat has thick undercoat
Reddish yellow hair on chest and legs
Catlike front feet

MONTENEGRIN MOUNTAIN HOUND

THIS CLASSIC BALKAN SCENT HOUND MAKES A GOOD COMPANION DOG

FCI

Height range
17–21in (44–54cm)

Weight range
44–55lb (20–25kg)

Life span 12 years

Origin Serbia

Also known as the Serbian Mountain Hound, this rare dog from the Planina region of Serbia has a calm, gentle nature that is appreciated by nonhunting owners. Nevertheless, it remains a superb hound for hunting fox and hare, or even larger animals such as deer and wild boar.

Tan markings on face

Long, pendant ears

Tail carried saber fashion

Moderately developed flews

Glossy, black and tan coat–rough to the touch

Tan markings on chest

SERBIAN TRICOLORED HOUND

A LOYAL, DEPENDABLE WORKER AND LOVING COMPANION FCI

Height range 17-22in (44-55cm)

Weight range 44-55lb (20-25kg)

Life span 12 years

Origin Serbia

Once regarded as a variety of the Montenegrin Mountain Hound (opposite), this rare breed has striking white markings that distinguish it from its relative. Used to hunt fox and hare, or occasionally larger game, it also makes a gentle and devoted family dog.

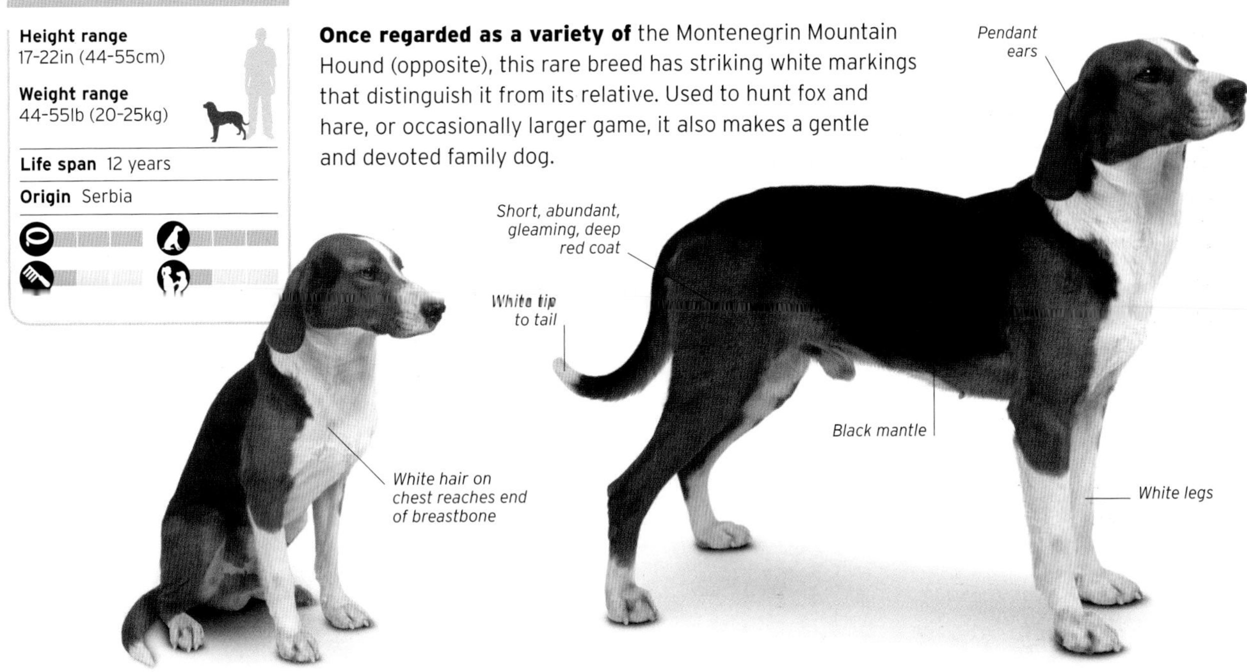
Pendant ears
Short, abundant, gleaming, deep red coat
White tip to tail
Black mantle
White legs
White hair on chest reaches end of breastbone

SERBIAN HOUND

HAPPIEST IN COMPANY, THIS HOUND NEEDS PLENTY OF OUTDOOR ACTION FCI

Height range 17-22in (44-56cm)

Weight range 93-123lb (42-56kg)

Life span 12-14 years

Origin Serbia

This pack-hunting dog with a booming voice tracks game of all sizes from rabbit to elk and boar. Away from the hunt, it is sweet-natured and makes a good companion for an active family, especially if there are other dogs around. The Serbian Hound is also a fine watchdog.

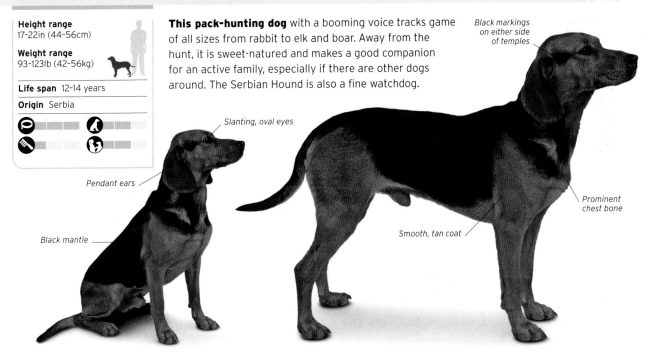

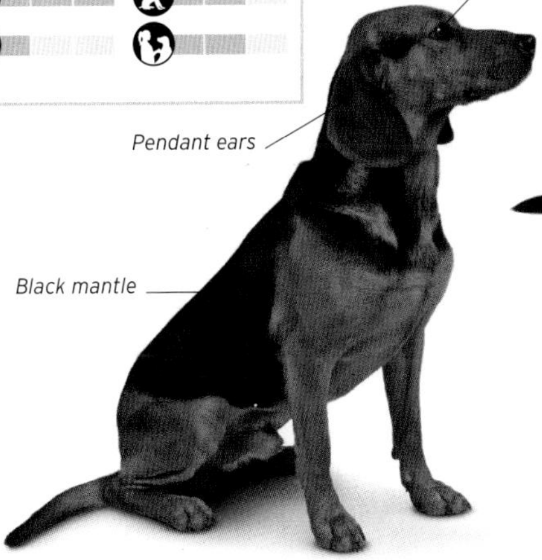

Black markings on either side of temples

Slanting, oval eyes

Pendant ears

Black mantle

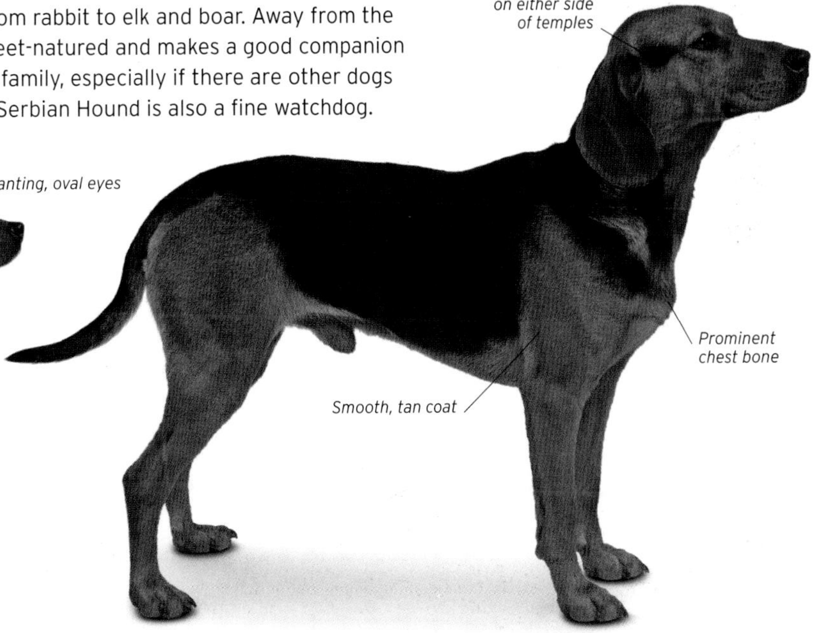

Prominent chest bone

Smooth, tan coat

HELLENIC HOUND

THIS FAST AND POWERFUL HOUND HAS A STRONG CHARACTER AND A GREAT NOSE FOR SCENT FCI

Height range 18-22in (45-55cm)

Weight range 37-44lb (17-20kg)

Life span 11 years

Origin Greece

Descended from the traditional scent hounds of ancient Greece, the Hellenic Hound has a musical hunting voice that carries over long distances. Once used to hunt boar and hare, if trained with care, the breed can be a pleasant companion, but without plenty of space to run in can develop bad behavior.

Shallow stop
Back long in proportion to height
Typical hound-shaped head
Graceful, powerful neck
Drop ears with rounded tips
Tan markings on face
Short, smooth, black and tan coat
Tail tapers to pointed tip

MOUNTAIN CUR

THIS TOUGH AND COURAGEOUS DOG IS A NATURAL HUNTER BUT RESPONDS WELL TO TRAINING

Height range 16-26in (41-66cm)

Weight range 40-60lb (18-27kg)

Life span 12-16 years

Origin USA

Other colors

Variety of colors

Originating in North America when early settlers from Europe crossed their hunting dogs with native dogs, the Mountain Cur was first recognized in the 1950s. It is still used for hunting racoon and larger game such as bears. Mountain Curs are not indoor dogs, but with the right training they make good companions.

Short, dense, red coat
Muscular back
Strong, muscular neck
Broad head
White markings on chest
Drop ears
Large, dark eyes
White tips on toes

RHODESIAN RIDGEBACK

BOISTEROUS AND HIGHLY STRUNG, THIS DOG NEEDS AN ENERGETIC OWNER AKC

Height range
24-27in (61-69cm)

Weight range
64-90lb (29-41kg)

Life span 10-12 years

Origin Zimbabwe

The distinctive ridge of hair along this dog's back, growing in the opposite direction to the rest of the coat, instantly identifies it. Native to Zimbabwe (formerly Rhodesia), the breed may have descended from dogs brought to southern Africa by European settlers. Because the Rhodesian Ridgeback was once used in packs to hunt lions, it is sometimes known as the African Lion Hound. Despite the breed's fierce image, it is kind-natured and affectionate, and is a good family companion for experienced owners. This dog needs to be kept occupied, since it may develop behavioral problems if bored or under-exercised.

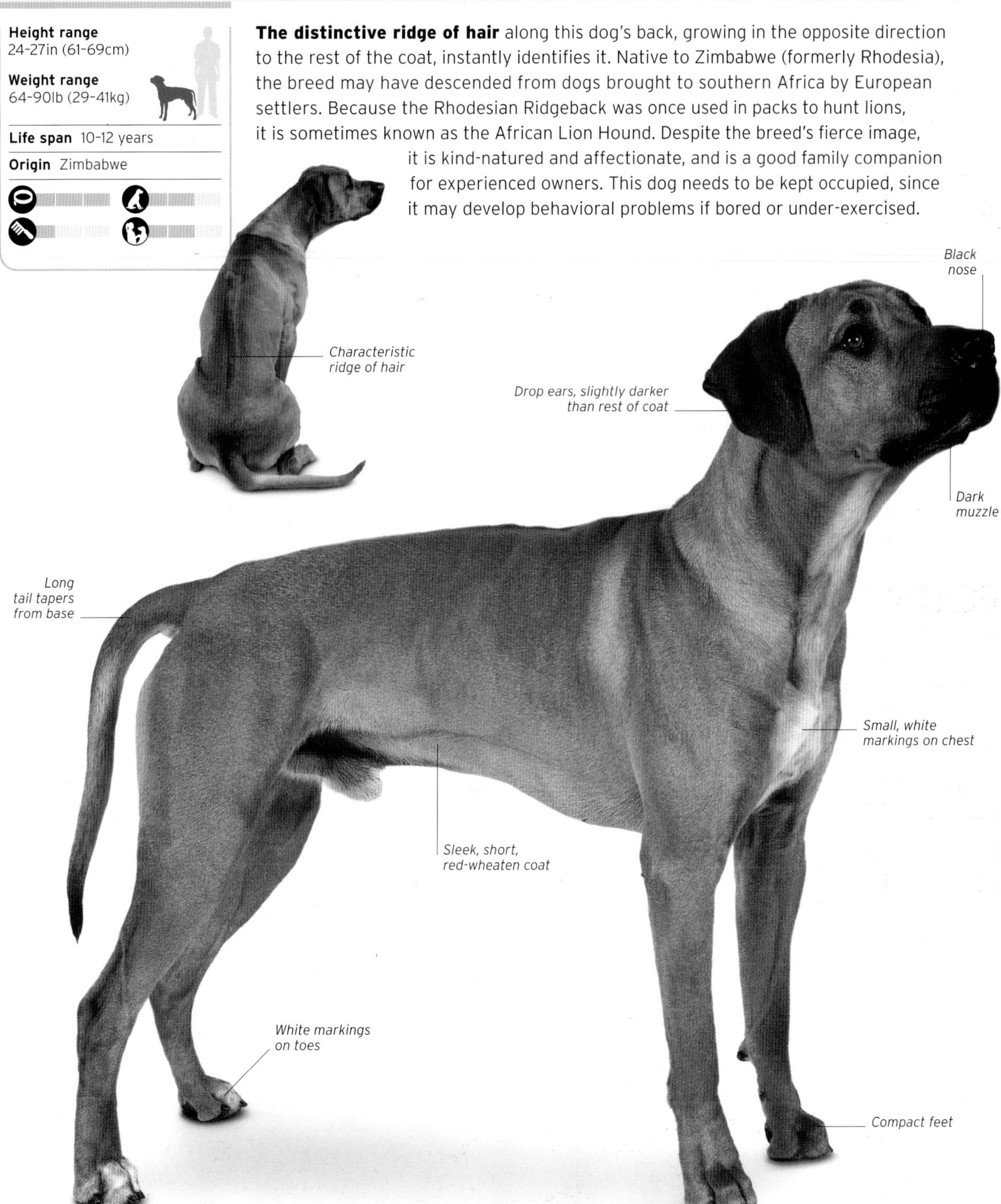
Characteristic ridge of hair
Black nose
Drop ears, slightly darker than rest of coat
Dark muzzle
Long tail tapers from base
Small, white markings on chest
Sleek, short, red-wheaten coat
White markings on toes
Compact feet

DIGGING INSTINCT
Intent on his task, this Airedale Terrier is doing what comes naturally—excavating a hole. Most terriers are inveterate diggers and tunnelers.

TERRIERS

Tough, fearless, self-confident, energetic—a terrier can claim all of these descriptions, and more. The terrier group takes its name from the Latin word *terra* (earth), referring to the original use of various types of small dog as hunters of underground-dwelling vermin, such as rats. However, some modern terriers are large dogs, bred for different purposes.

Once a fighting dog, the Bull Terrier is now a family favorite

Many breeds of terrier originated in the UK, where they were traditionally regarded as hunting dogs for the working man. Some are named after the regions they first came from: Norwich Terrier, Yorkshire Terrier, Lakeland Terrier. Others are known by the types of animal they used to hunt: for example, Fox Terrier and Rat Terrier.

Terriers are by nature quick to react and show great persistence when on the track of quarry. They possess independent, some would say willful, characters and are ready to stand their ground against larger dogs. The dogs developed for hunting below ground, including the much-loved Jack Russell and Cairn Terriers, are small, sturdy, and short-legged. Terriers with longer legs, such as the Irish Terrier and the beautiful Soft Coated Wheaten Terrier, were once used for hunting above ground and also as guard dogs for protecting flocks. The largest terriers of all include the Airedale Terrier, originally bred for hunting badger and otter, and the impressively built Russian Black Terrier, which was specifically developed for military use and guard duties.

In the 19th century a different type of terrier became popular. Crosses between terriers and bulldogs produced such dogs as the Bull Terrier, the Staffordshire Bull Terrier, and the American Pit Bull Terrier, breeds intended for the vicious and now illegal sports of pit-fighting and bull-baiting. With their broad heads and powerful jaws, these dogs suggest a close affinity with mastiffs and are, in fact, likely to be related to that group.

Most types of terrier are today kept as pets. Intelligent and usually friendly and affectionate, they make excellent companions and watchdogs. Because of their inherent traits, terriers need to be trained and socialized early to prevent trouble with other dogs and pets. Hunting-type terriers also love to dig and can wreak havoc in a yard if unsupervised. The modern breeds of those dogs historically used for fighting are now largely free from aggression and, when properly trained by an experienced owner, are usually trustworthy with families.

LIVELY COMPANION
The sparky Jack Russell is among the best known of various small working terrier breeds now enjoying popularity as pets.

MIXED HISTORY
Terriers have highly variable origins. This Miniature Pinscher has Italian Greyhound in its ancestry.

WEST HIGHLAND WHITE TERRIER

A CHEEKY AND CHEERFUL CHARACTER, THIS TERRIER CAN BE BOSSY WITH OTHER DOGS AKC

Height range
10–11in (25–28cm)

Weight range
15–22lb (7–10kg)

Life span 9–15 years

Origin UK

One of the best loved of all small terriers, the "Westie" was developed in Scotland in the 19th century from Cairn Terriers (opposite). This hardy little dog's original role was to hunt fox, badger, and vermin such as rats. Today West Highland White Terriers are suitable town or country pets for all types of home. They have boundless energy and are always ready for walks or to play with children. Early social training is recommended for this breed, as they have large egos for their size and can be overbearing with other dogs.

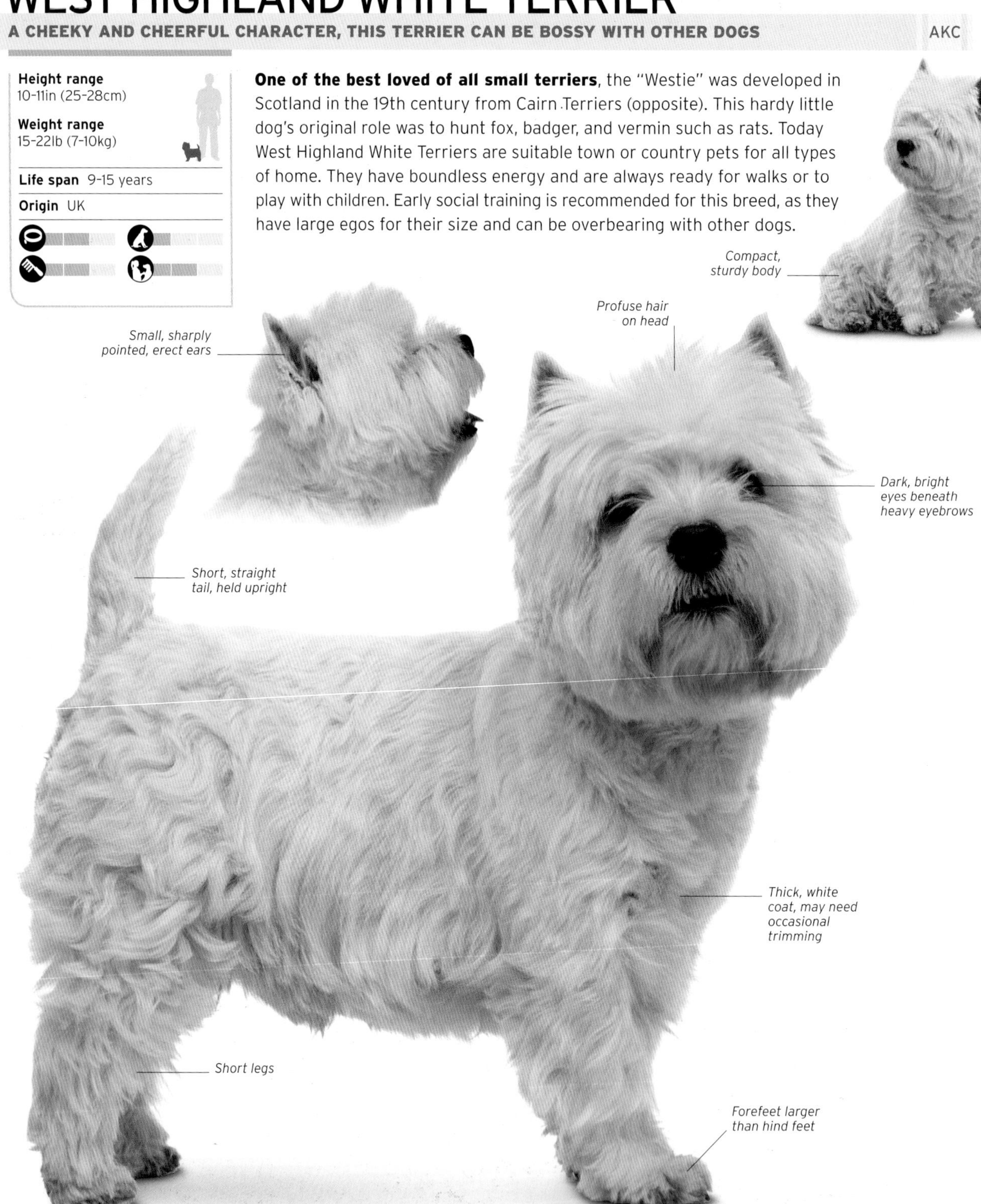
Compact, sturdy body
Profuse hair on head
Small, sharply pointed, erect ears
Dark, bright eyes beneath heavy eyebrows
Short, straight tail, held upright
Thick, white coat, may need occasional trimming
Short legs
Forefeet larger than hind feet

CAIRN TERRIER

THIS LIVELY DOG IS IDEAL WITH CHILDREN BUT MAY CHASE OTHER PETS

AKC

Height range
11-12in (28-31cm)

Weight range
13-18lb (6-8kg)

Life span 9-15 years

Origin UK

Other colors

Nearly black

Coat may be brindled.

Originating in the Western Isles of Scotland, the Cairn Terrier was bred for hunting vermin. Amusing and full of character, this sturdy terrier is small enough for apartment life and energetic enough for romping around a large country home; it fits in anywhere. The Cairn Terrier's urge to chase anything that moves should be discouraged early on.

Dark ears with shorter hair
Harsh, coarse, wheaten coat
Shaggy eyebrows overhang dark, hazel eyes
Gray coat
Cream coat
Forefeet larger than hind feet

SCOTTISH TERRIER

THIS SMALL DOG HAS GREAT DIGNITY AND IS ALERT AND READY TO BE PROTECTIVE

AKC

Height range
10-11in (25-28cm)

Weight range
20-24lb (9-11kg)

Life span 9-15 years

Origin UK

Other colors

Wheaten

Coat may be brindled.

This breed was first named in the late 19th century, but dogs of this type existed in the Scottish Highlands much earlier. Powerful and agile, despite their short stature, "Scotties" were bred as vermin-hunters like the West Highland White Terrier (opposite) and Cairn Terrier (above). Affectionate and watchful, the Scottish Terrier is a good home companion.

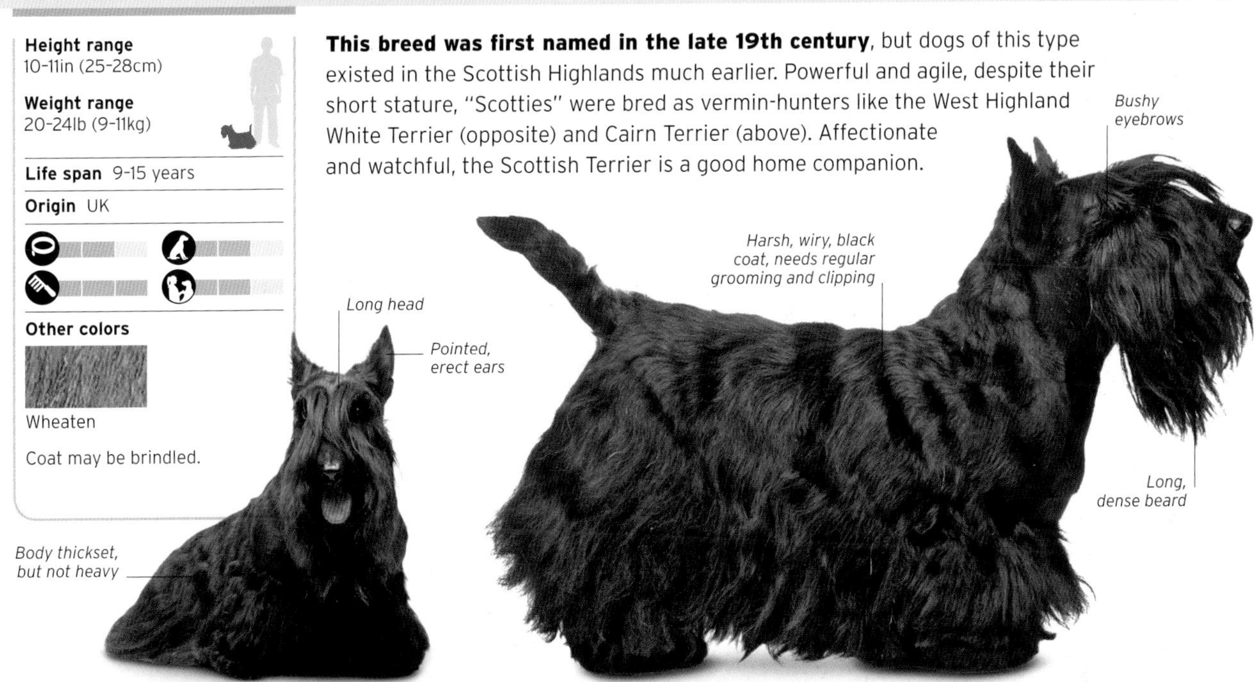
Bushy eyebrows
Harsh, wiry, black coat, needs regular grooming and clipping
Long head
Pointed, erect ears
Long, dense beard
Body thickset, but not heavy

CESKY TERRIER

TOUGH, FEARLESS, AND SOMETIMES WILLFUL, THIS DOG NEEDS PATIENT TRAINING AKC

Height range
10–13in (25–32cm)

Weight range
13–22lb (6–10kg)

Life span 12–14 years

Origin Czech Republic

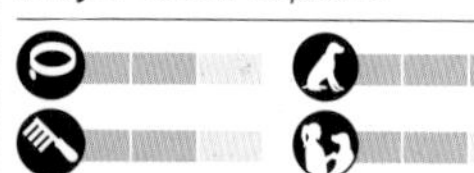

Other colors

Liver

Can have yellow, gray, or white markings on the beard and cheeks, neck, chest, belly, and limbs, sometimes with a white collar or a white tip to the tail.

A 20th-century breed developed for burrowing work, this dog is also known as the Czech or Bohemian Terrier. It is still used as a working dog, and its natural wariness of strangers makes it a useful watchdog. For a terrier, this dog has a relatively relaxed, playful character and it is sometimes simply kept as a companion. However, the breed retains some terrier stubbornness and an inclination to snap, so needs consistent training from an early age. The typical clip of the coat is short on the body, leaving long curtains of hair on the face, legs, and belly.

Triangular, drop ears

Yellow-white color of lower leg and feet matches beard

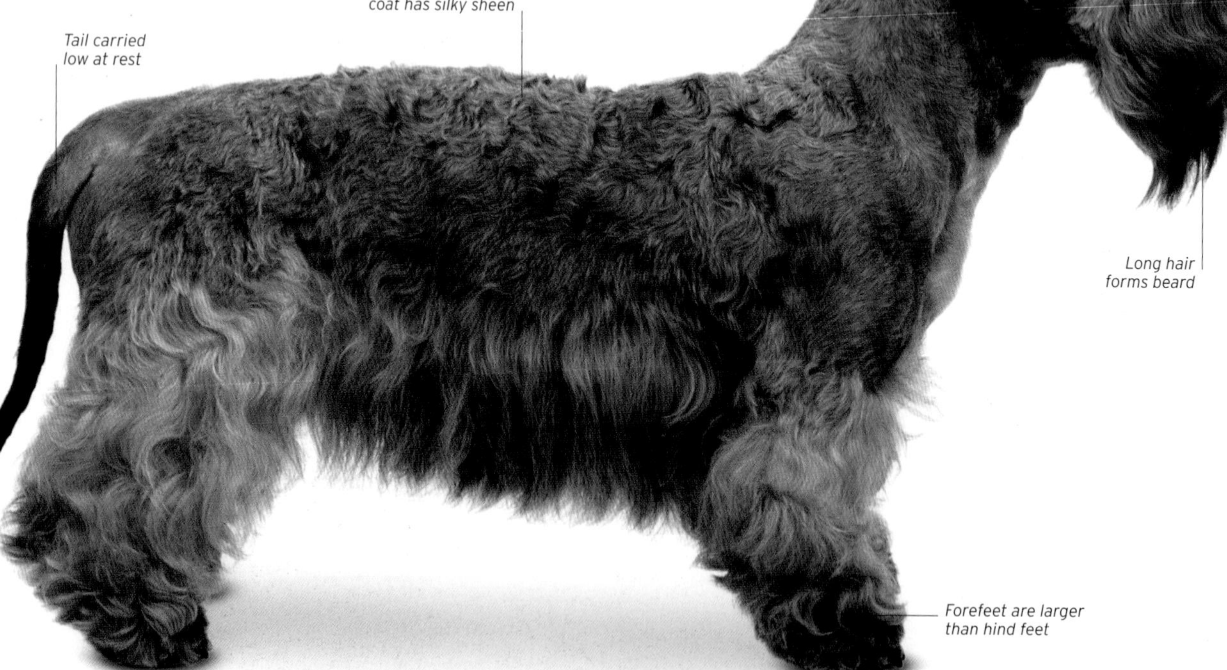

Hair left long on front of head

Slightly wavy, gray-blue coat has silky sheen

Tail carried low at rest

Long hair forms beard

Forefeet are larger than hind feet

SEALYHAM TERRIER

THIS POWERFUL, INTELLIGENT, AND SPIRITED DOG IS AN ATTRACTIVE BUT CHALLENGING BREED AKC

Height range
10-12in (25-30cm)

Weight range
18-20lb (8-9kg)

Life span 14 years

Origin UK

Originally bred in Wales to tackle badgers and otters, this breed has no working role today but is kept as a pet. Their territorial nature makes Sealyham Terriers good watchdogs but they can be aggressive toward other dogs, and an innate stubbornness means that persistence in training is required. The show clip is distinctive, but requires regular maintenance.

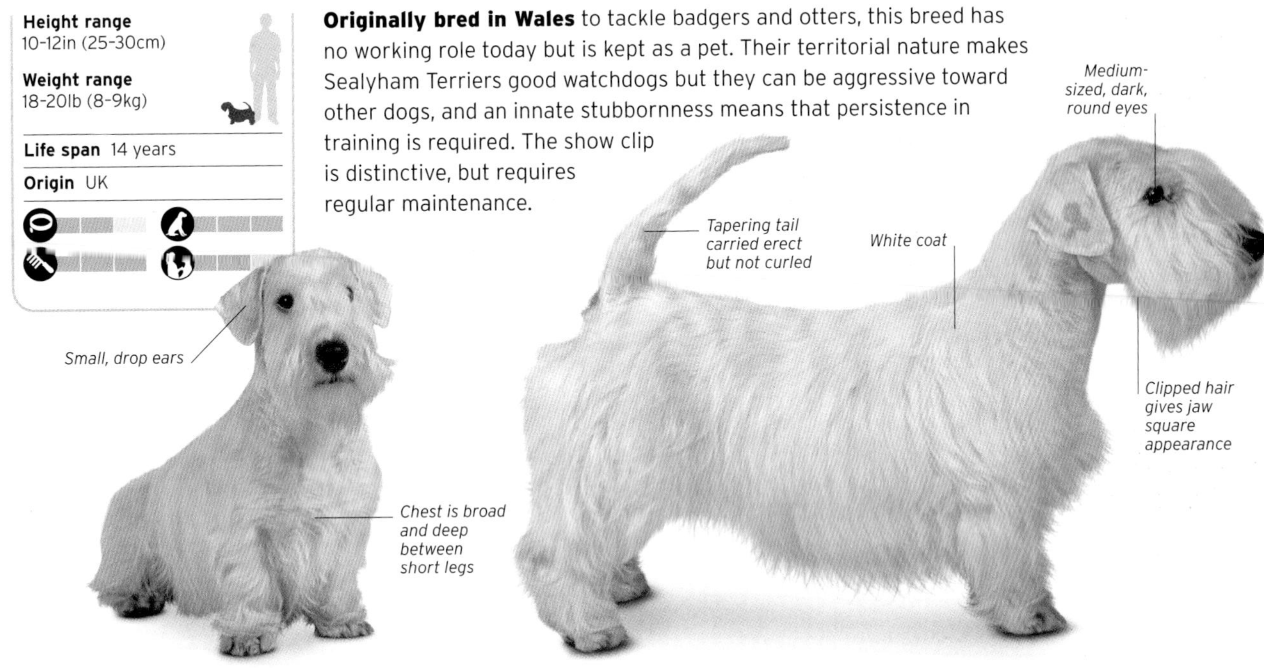
Medium-sized, dark, round eyes
Tapering tail carried erect but not curled
White coat
Small, drop ears
Clipped hair gives jaw square appearance
Chest is broad and deep between short legs

NORFOLK TERRIER

THIS STURDY, CHEERFUL DOG IS HAPPY IN A TOWN OR COUNTRY HOME AKC

Height range
9-10in (22-25cm)

Weight range
11-13lb (5-6kg)

Life span 14-15 years

Origin UK

Other colors

Red

Black and tan

Coat may be grizzled.

This small terrier was bred from various rat-catching dogs, and is an energetic hunter. Because ratters work in packs, this breed is more sociable with other dogs than most terriers, but cannot be trusted with other pets. It makes a good guard dog or companion for families with older children.

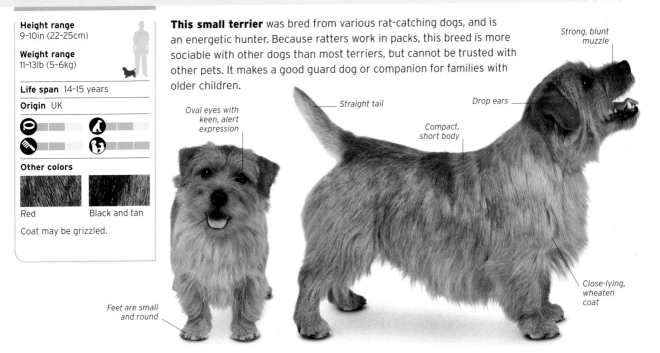

Strong, blunt muzzle

Straight tail

Drop ears

Oval eyes with keen, alert expression

Compact, short body

Close-lying, wheaten coat

Feet are small and round

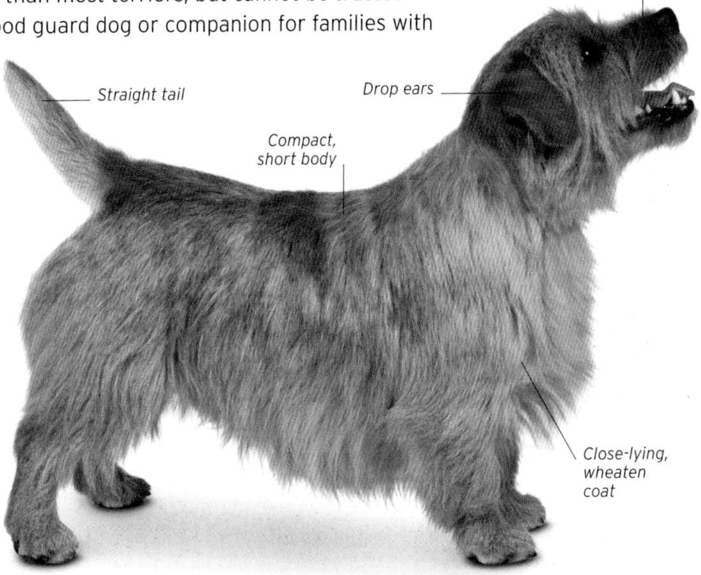

Small, erect, V-shaped ears

Long facial hair (topknot) tied back with ribbon

Dark eyes have intelligent, alert expression

Tail darker than rest of body

Black nose

Fine, silky, dark steel-blue coat

Level back

Long coat parted in center from nose to end of tail for show purposes

Rich, bright tan facial and chest hair

YORKSHIRE TERRIER

THIS DOG'S CUTE LOOKS AND DIMINUTIVE SIZE BELIE A FEISTY TEMPERAMENT AKC

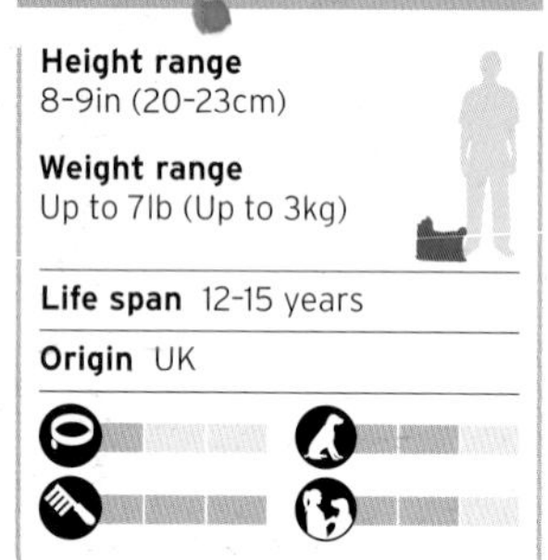

Height range
8–9in (20–23cm)

Weight range
Up to 7lb (Up to 3kg)

Life span 12–15 years

Origin UK

Oblivious to its tiny toy stature, the Yorkshire Terrier has the bravery, energy, and confidence that might be expected of a dog several times its size. An intelligent dog, it responds well to obedience training. However, it is inclined to take advantage of owners who let it get away with behavior that would be unacceptable in a larger dog and can become yappy, snappy, and demanding. With proper handling, this terrier displays its natural character: sweet, affectionate, loyal, and spirited.

The Yorkshire Terrier was developed to catch the rats and mice that infested the woolen mills and mine shafts in the north of England. It was gradually miniaturized through breeding from the smallest individuals, and over time became a fashion accessory that was carried around by its lady owner. However, such pampering is at odds with the Yorkshire Terrier's dynamic nature and it is much happier when allowed to walk for at least half an hour each day. The long, glossy show coat is wrapped around folded papers and secured with elastic bands to protect it outside the show ring. It is very time-consuming to maintain but the dogs generally love the extra attention.

CLIPPED COAT

Owners who do not intend to show their dogs usually clip the coat short every few months.

Puppy

AUSTRALIAN TERRIER

THIS JOYFUL DOG IS GOOD WITH FAMILIES BUT BARKS AT STRANGERS

AKC

Height range Up to 10in (Up to 26cm)

Weight range Up to 15lb (Up to 7kg)

Life span 15 years

Origin Australia

Other colors

Blue with tan

This terrier is likely to have been the result of crosses between various terriers, including the Cairn Terrier (see p.189), the Yorkshire Terrier (see p.192), and the Dandie Dinmont Terrier (see p.217), which were brought to Australia by British settlers in the 19th century. Diminutive yet spirited, the "Aussie" is an excellent house dog but is best exercised on a leash because of a strong instinct to chase.

Hair forms soft topknot on top of head
Distinct stop
Straight back
Shorter hair on muzzle
Erect ears
Shorter hair on lower legs
Slight feathering on forelegs
Harsh, straight, dense, red coat

SILKY TERRIER

THIS AFFECTIONATE AND SOCIABLE BREED NEEDS FIRM LEADERSHIP

AKC

Height range Up to 9in (Up to 23cm)

Weight range Up to 9lb (Up to 4kg)

Life span 12-15 years

Origin Australia

This attractive dog was produced from crosses between the Australian Terrier (above) and the Yorkshire Terrier (see p.192) in the late 19th century. A typical terrier, the Silky Terrier has a fondness for digging holes, and its instinct to chase may put other small pets at risk. Regular grooming is needed to keep this dog's long coat tangle-free.

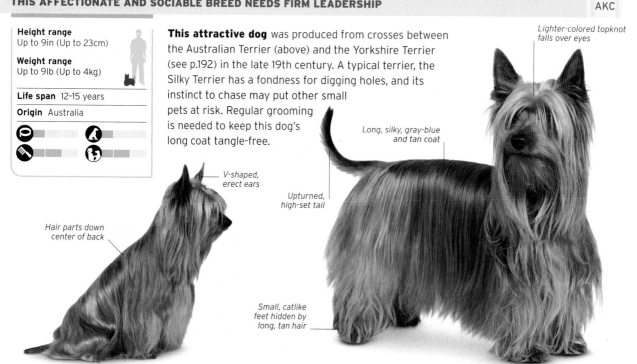

Lighter-colored topknot falls over eyes

Long, silky, gray-blue and tan coat

V-shaped, erect ears

Upturned, high-set tail

Hair parts down center of back

Small, catlike feet hidden by long, tan hair

PARSON RUSSELL TERRIER

THIS ENERGETIC DOG, WITH A STRONG HUNTING INSTINCT, NEEDS FIRM HANDLING AKC

Height range
13–14in (33–36cm)

Weight range
13–18lb (6–8kg)

Life span 15 years

Origin UK

Other colors

White

May have black markings.

Created in England in the early 19th century by a West Country cleric, the Reverend John Russell, this dog was one of two strains originally classified together as the Jack Russell Terrier. Today the longer-legged breed is known as the Parson Russell Terrier, while the shorter-legged dog retains the name of Jack Russell Terrier (see p.196). Intelligent, high-spirited, and restless, the Parson Russell Terrier needs a loving home where fun is a high priority. Behavioral problems, such as excessive barking or snappiness, may occur if this dog is under-exercised or left alone for long periods of time. There are two coat varieties: smooth-haired and rough-haired; both coats have a harsh texture.

Tan markings mostly occur on head
V-shaped, button ears
Eyebrows of longer hairs
High-set, white tail with tan base
Fairly deep-set, dark eyes
Short, rough, white coat
Longer legs than Jack Russell Terrier (see p.196)

Rough-haired

Smooth-haired

Rough-haired

RUSSELL TERRIER

THIS ACTIVE DOG IS A FEISTY BUNDLE OF ENERGY

AKC

Height range
10–12in (25–30cm)

Weight range
11–13lb (5–6kg)

Life span 13–14 years

Origin UK

Other colors

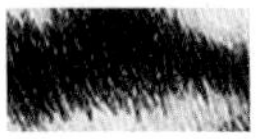

White with black

Bouncy and bold, this working terrier is named after the Reverend John Russell, who bred them in the 1800s to flush out foxes. Today this breed makes an excellent rat-catcher and an affectionate and exuberant companion. It has shorter legs than its more squarely built cousin, the Parson Russell Terrier (see p.195). There are two coat types: smooth-haired and wire-haired.

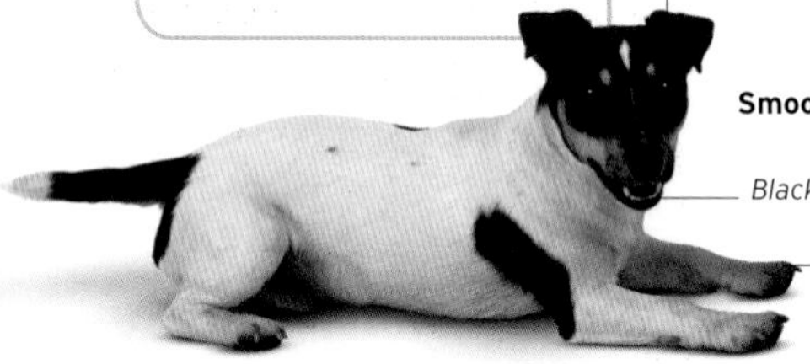

Small, dark, expressive eyes

Black lips

White coat with black and tan markings

Smooth-haired

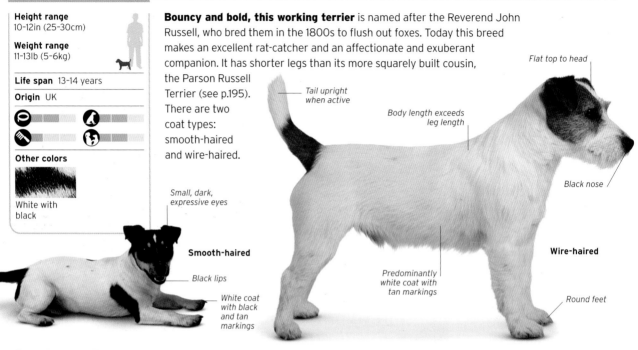

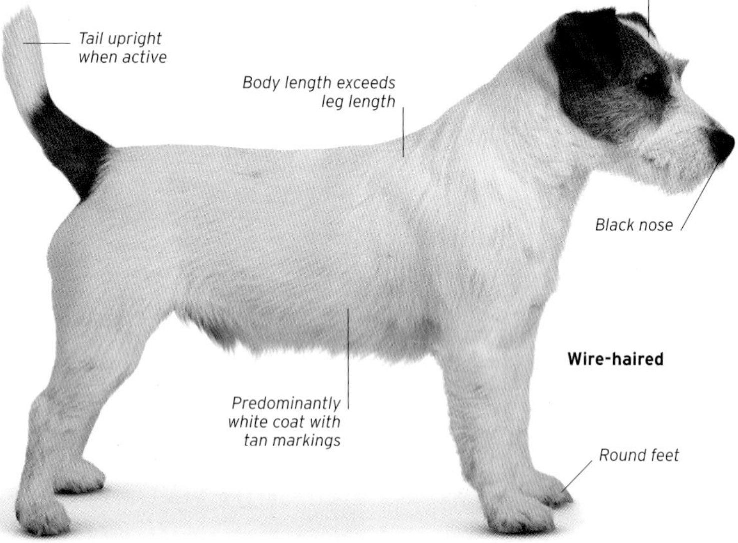

Tail upright when active

Flat top to head

Body length exceeds leg length

Black nose

Predominantly white coat with tan markings

Round feet

Wire-haired

GLEN OF IMAAL TERRIER

A RUTHLESS AND BRAVE HUNTER, THIS TERRIER IS GENTLE AND LOYAL WITH THE FAMILY

AKC

Height range
14in (36cm)

Weight range
35–37lb (16–17kg)

Life span 13–14 years

Origin Ireland

Other colors

Blue

Brindle

This sturdy little dog is more active than its size suggests. It comes from County Wicklow and was used in badger trials until these events were banned in the late 1960s. Now the Glen of Imaal Terrier makes a sensitive, devoted pet as long as it has a calm and firm owner.

Broad, slightly domed head with well-developed stop

Harsh, medium-length, wheaten coat has soft undercoat

Shorter-haired, small, semierect ears

Round, brown eyes

Short legs

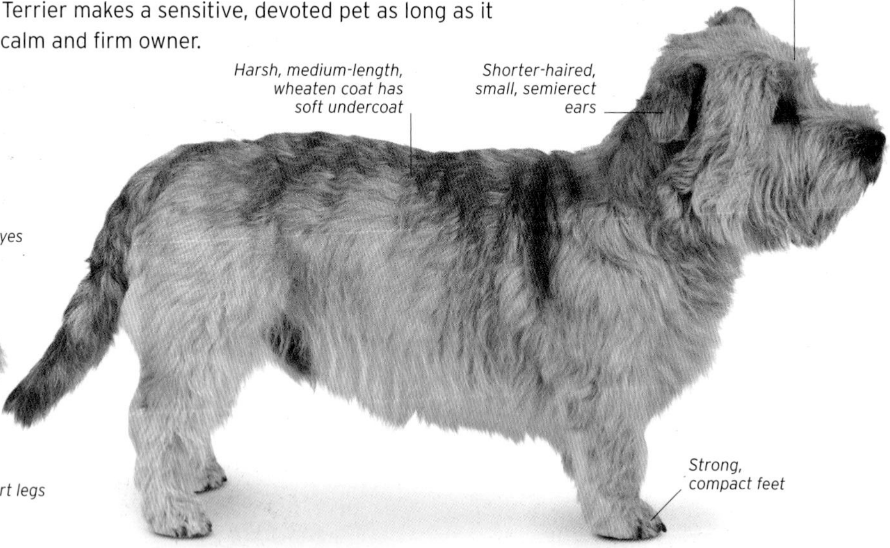

Strong, compact feet

NORWICH TERRIER

A PLUCKY AND FRIENDLY FAMILY PET WITH AN ENDEARING PERSONALITY AKC

Height range
10in (25-26cm)

Weight range
10-12lb (5-6kg)

Life span 12-15 years

Origin UK

Other colors

Wheaten, Red

Red coats may be interspersed with black hairs (grizzled).

One of the smallest working terriers, the Norwich Terrier, like its cousin the Norfolk Terrier (see p.191), strikes a happy balance between courage and gentleness. With its easy-going nature, it is good with children but will bark at strangers. Like all ratting terriers, it is playful and loves to chase.

Erect ears differentiate the Norwich Terrier from the Norfolk Terrier (see p.191)
Short, compact back with black shading
Dark, bright, oval-shaped eyes
Long, coarse hair on neck creates ruff around face
Tan coat
Short, straight, strong forelegs
Rounded, catlike feet

BOSTON TERRIER

A HIGHLY INTELLIGENT, DETERMINED, FRIENDLY, AND ALERT COMPANION DOG AKC

Height range
15-17in (38-43cm)

Weight range
11-24lb (5-11kg)

Life span 13 years

Origin USA

Other colors

Brindle

Brindle coats have white markings.

Dubbed "the American Gentleman" for its quirky yet dapper looks and docile nature, the Boston Terrier makes a good house pet for town or country. This mix of bulldog and several terrier types has lost its ratting instincts and enjoys human company. It has a boisterous streak and needs regular exercise.

Square head with flat top
Erect, pointed ears
Low-set, naturally short tail
Short muzzle with black nose
Wide-set, round, dark eyes
Black coat with white markings
Small, round, compact feet

BULL TERRIER

A FORMIDABLE-LOOKING DOG, BUT KIND AND WELL BEHAVED WITH THE RIGHT OWNER AKC

Height range
21-22in (53-56cm)

Weight range
50-70lb (23-32kg)

Life span 10-12 years

Origin UK

Other colors

Variety of colors

Largely the result of cross-breeding between the Bulldog (see p.94) and terriers of various types, the Bull Terrier was developed for pit-fighting in 19th-century England. A failure at vicious sports, this dog achieved greater success as a pet. The modern breed is normally good-natured and does well with a firm owner.

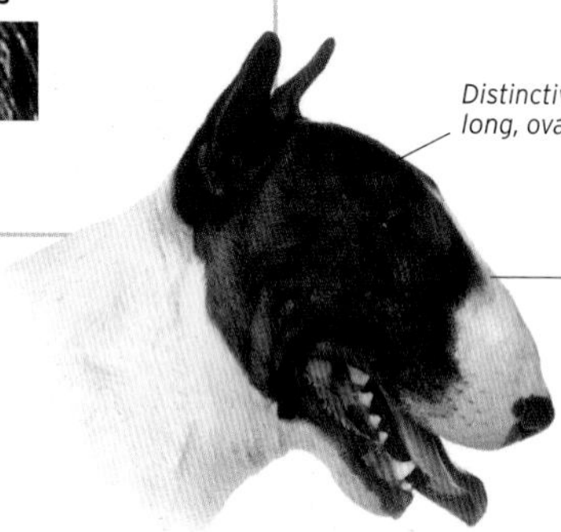

Thin, close-set, erect ears

Narrow, dark eyes

White tip to tail

Distinctive, long, oval head

Wide chest

Convex profile

Hind legs short from hock to foot

Brindle coat with white markings

MINIATURE BULL TERRIER

THIS SMALL AND STRONG DOG LOVES FUN AND BOISTEROUS GAMES AKC

Height range
Up to 14in (Up to 36cm)

Weight range
24-33lb (11-15kg)

Life span 10-12 years

Origin UK

Other colors

Variety of colors

This scaled-down version of the Bull Terrier (above) had almost disappeared by the 1920s. The breed was revived in the following decades, though it is still uncommon. Like its larger relative, the Miniature Bull Terrier needs early training and socializing to ensure it is a good family pet.

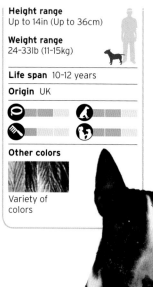

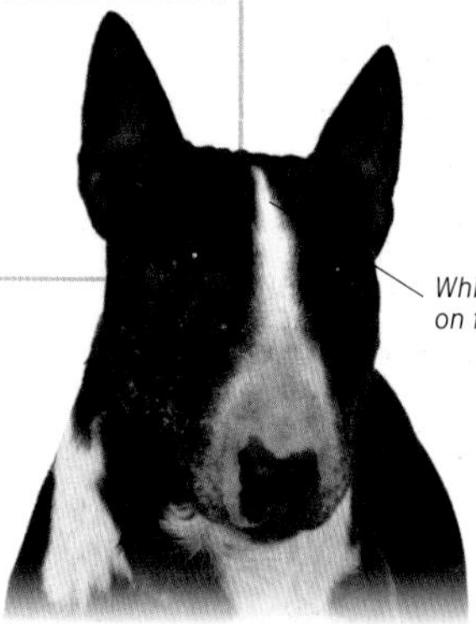

Typical oval head

Incomplete white collar

Short, harsh, glossy, black coat

White blaze on forehead

Round feet

AIREDALE TERRIER

THE LARGEST OF ALL TERRIERS, THIS IS A GOOD FAMILY DOG BUT MAY BE BOISTEROUS AKC

Height range
22–24in (56–61cm)

Weight range
40–64lb (18–29kg)

Life span 10–12 years

Origin UK

Justly known as the "King of Terriers," the Airedale Terrier is big, square, and strong. Originating in the valley of the Aire River in Yorkshire, this breed was first developed around a century ago by local hunters who wanted a robust terrier for catching vermin and larger game such as otters. The breed's subsequent uses have included guarding and military work, but it is also a popular companion. Friendly, intelligent, and full of character, this dog, like many terriers, loves the thrill of the chase and can get up to mischief when bored.

Long, flat head
Drop ears
Wiry, wavy, rich tan coat
Tail carried high when alert
Level back
Bearded muzzle
Dark grizzle saddle

BLACK RUSSIAN TERRIER

THIS BIG, TOUGH, AND VERY PROTECTIVE DOG IS USUALLY FRIENDLY AND MANAGEABLE AKC

Height range
26–30in (66–77cm)

Weight range
83–143lb (38–65kg)

Life span 10–14 years

Origin Russia

First developed in the 1940s, this massively built and hardy terrier was the special creation of the Soviet Army in the former USSR. The breeders' aim was to produce a large dog suitable for military work and able to withstand the severe cold of Russian winters. Among many breeds used in its development were the Rottweiler (see p.81), the Giant Schnauzer (see p.41), and the Airedale Terrier (see p.199). Still relatively uncommon, the Black Russian Terrier is becoming more widely recognized outside its native land. Formidable in size and appearance, the breed is not naturally aggressive and with responsible handling is a friendly and well-adjusted house dog.

Dense beard and whiskers on muzzle

High-set tail, may curve over back

Drop ears with shorter hair

Large, compact feet covered with hair

Wavy, black coat

Long thighs

Square, muscular body

IRISH TERRIER

THIS TERRIER IS WELL-MANNERED IN THE HOUSE BUT NEEDS FIRM CONTROL AROUND OTHER DOGS

AKC

Height range
18–19in (46–48cm)

Weight range
25–27lb (11–12kg)

Life span 12–15 years

Origin Ireland

Other colors

Wheaten

This handsome breed emerged in County Cork in Ireland and is believed to have a long history, though its earliest ancestry is unknown. The Irish Terrier has a delightful temperament and can be trusted with children, but outside the home it is inclined to be belligerent toward other dogs.

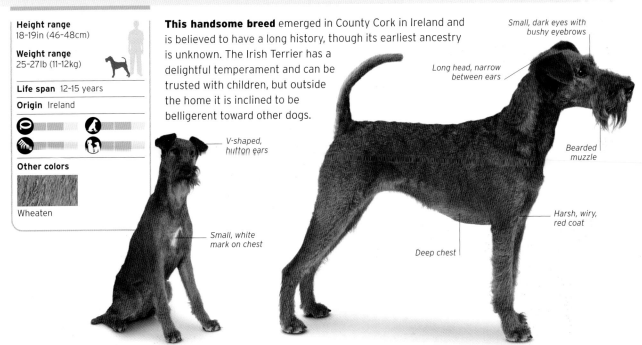

Small, dark eyes with bushy eyebrows

Long head, narrow between ears

V-shaped, button ears

Bearded muzzle

Harsh, wiry, red coat

Small, white mark on chest

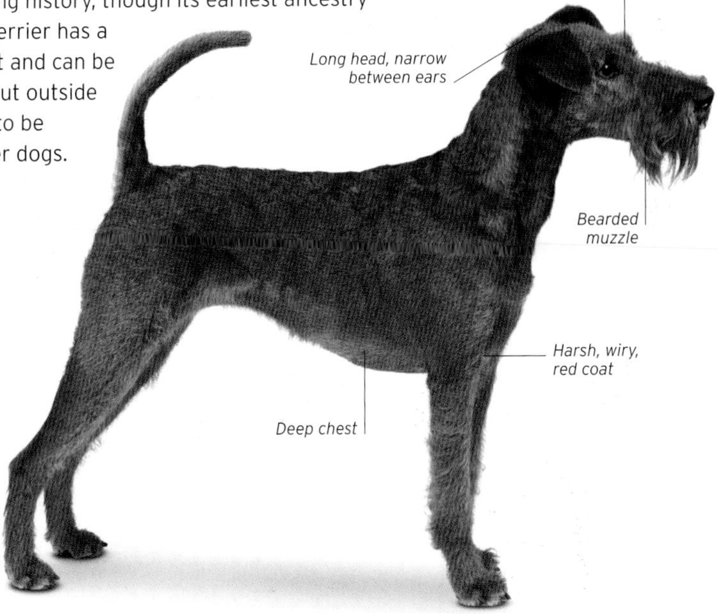

Deep chest

WELSH TERRIER

THIS SMART, NEAT DOG IS HIGH-SPIRITED BUT EASY TO TRAIN

AKC

Height range
Up to 15in (up to 39cm)

Weight range
20–22lb (9–10kg)

Life span 9–15 years

Origin UK

Other colors

Black grizzle and tan

Once used in packs for hunting foxes, badgers, and otters, the Welsh Terrier was recognized as a breed in the 1880s, and this medium-sized terrier has gained attention as a show dog. Although lively and energetic, the Welsh Terrier is easier to manage than many other terriers and is a good house dog.

Small, dark eyes

High-set, small, button ears

Tail held upright

Wiry, black and tan coat

Head flat between ears

Square, compact body

Long thighs

Small, round, catlike feet

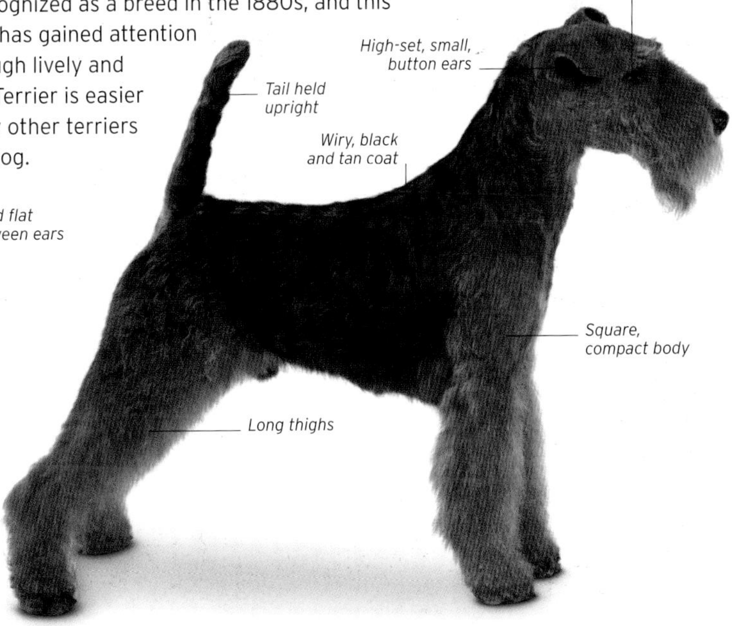

GERMAN HUNTING TERRIER

THIS TIRELESS, FEARLESS, INDEPENDENT DOG ENJOYS A WORKING LIFE

FCI

Height range
13-16in (33-40cm)

Weight range
18-22lb (8-10kg)

Life span 13-15 years

Origin Germany

This classic hunter is the result of Welsh and English terriers being crossed by four Bavarian dog breeders. The German Hunting Terrier is happy to sleep outdoors by night and hunt all day, above or below ground and across all types of terrain, and even water. It needs plenty of exercise and clear leadership. There are two coat types—rough-coated and smooth-coated.

Slight stop
Smooth-coated
Straight, long back
Triangular, button ears
Small, oval, dark eyes
Strong neck
Rough, wiry, black and tan coat
Tan markings on chest
Rough-coated
Forefeet often broader than hind feet

KERRY BLUE TERRIER

A LIVELY, PLAYFUL, AND BOISTEROUS DOG WITH A BIG HEART

AKC

Height range
18-19in (46-48cm)

Weight range
33-37lb (15-17kg)

Life span 14 years

Origin Ireland

The national dog of Ireland is born black, but its coat color gradually changes to blue before the age of two. A versatile farm and guard dog, the Kerry Blue Terrier is intelligent and makes an affectionate and biddable pet as long as it is well trained and handled firmly.

Long, lean head

Dark eyes with keen expression

Beard covers strong jaw and black nose

Blue coat

Neck runs into sloping shoulders

Soft, wavy, luxuriant coat

Deep chest

SOFT COATED WHEATEN TERRIER

THIS HAPPY-GO-LUCKY, AFFECTIONATE DOG MAKES A FAITHFUL FAMILY FRIEND AKC

Height range 18–19in (46–49cm)

Weight range 35–46lb (16–21kg)

Life span 13–14 years

Origin Ireland

Similar to the other Irish terrier breeds, the Soft Coated Wheaten Terrier is probably one of the oldest Irish breeds. It has been used as a ratter and a guard dog, and for herding livestock. The breed has a puppylike temperament even into adulthood, so although good with children, it can be too boisterous with toddlers. A highly intelligent dog, the Soft Coated Wheaten Terrier responds well to training.

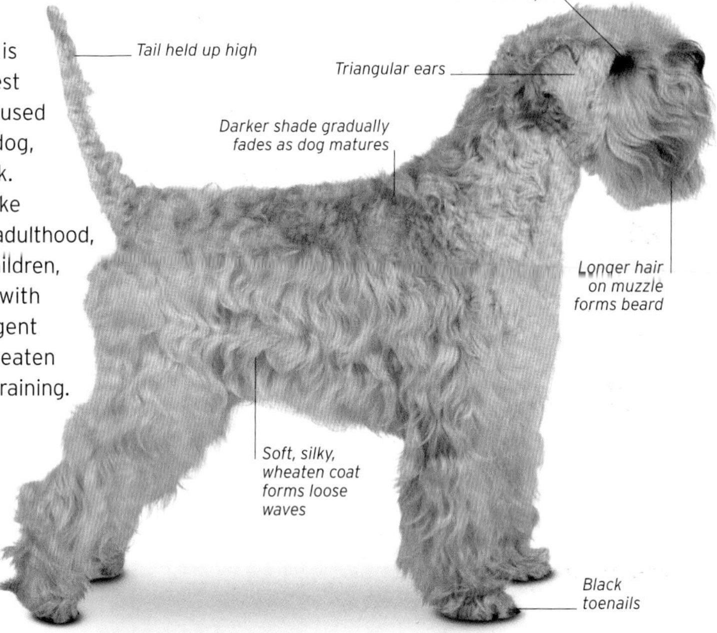

Topknot falls over eyes

Large, black nose

Tail held up high

Dark hazel eyes

Triangular ears

Darker shade gradually fades as dog matures

Longer hair on muzzle forms beard

Soft, silky, wheaten coat forms loose waves

Black toenails

DUTCH SMOUSHOND

AN EASY TO LOOK AFTER, ADAPTABLE, INTELLIGENT, AND COMPANIABLE DOG FCI

Height range 14–17in (35–42cm)

Weight range 20–22lb (9–10kg)

Life span 12–15 years

Origin The Netherlands

This former "coachman's dog" is strong enough to follow a horse and carriage and is also a keen rat-catcher. During the 1970s this breed almost became extinct; it is still rare but is now regaining popularity. This dog makes a good watchdog, gets on well with children, and will even accept the family cat. It needs plenty of exercise.

Forelock falls forward giving a disheveled appearance
Unkempt, coarse, wiry, yellow coat, with weatherproof undercoat
Darker drop ears covered in shorter hair
Thin, black-rimmed lips
Legs slightly less hairy than body
Catlike feet with black nails

BEDLINGTON TERRIER

LOOKS DECEIVE IN THIS KEEN, SWIFT, AND TENACIOUS BREED AKC

Height range
16-17in (40-43cm)

Weight range
18-22lb (8-10kg)

Life span 14-15 years

Origin UK

Other colors

Sandy

Liver

All colors may have tan markings.

The typical terrier spirit lies beneath the sheep-like coat of the Bedlington Terrier. It was bred from the Whippet (see p.128) and other terriers to hunt hare and rabbits above ground. Its sight hound blood has given it not only great speed but a more tolerant temper than some terriers, and it is now kept as a companion. The Bedlington Terrier needs to be sufficiently occupied to avoid behavioral problems developing. If given enough activity, it is an affectionate and dynamic companion. It has a unique show clip.

Show clip leaves tassels on ear tips
Thin, velvety, drop ears
Relatively small eyes
Hair left longer on head
Black nose
Arched, flexible back
Non-shedding, thick, blue coat
Deep chest
Hind legs appear longer than forelegs

BORDER TERRIER

AN ENERGETIC AND CHEERFUL TERRIER WITH A RELAXED PERSONALITY AKC

Short, strong muzzle
High-set, drop ears
Short, thick tail
Dense, grizzled coat has thick undercoat
White mark on chest
Tan hair on legs

Height range 10–11in (25–28cm)

Weight range 11–15lb (5–7kg)

Life span 13–14 years

Origin UK

Other colors

Wheaten

Red

Blue and tan

Originally used for hunting foxes and rats, the Border Terrier still excels in trials but is also a highly popular pet. Its temperament, which is unusually cooperative for a terrier, makes it more tolerant of small children and other dogs. The protective wiry coat is easily stripped in summer.

LAKELAND TERRIER

THIS ROBUST AND CHEERFUL DOG IS BEST SUITED TO AN EXPERIENCED OWNER AKC

Height range 13–15in (33–37cm)

Weight range 15–18lb (7–8cm)

Life span 13–14 years

Origin UK

Other colors

Variety of colors

This determined, agile little terrier was bred to chase foxes over hilly terrain and into their burrows, and it retains the tendency to chase anything that moves—regardless of size—and to be aggressive with other dogs. With training, it makes a fearless guard dog and an enthusiastic companion.

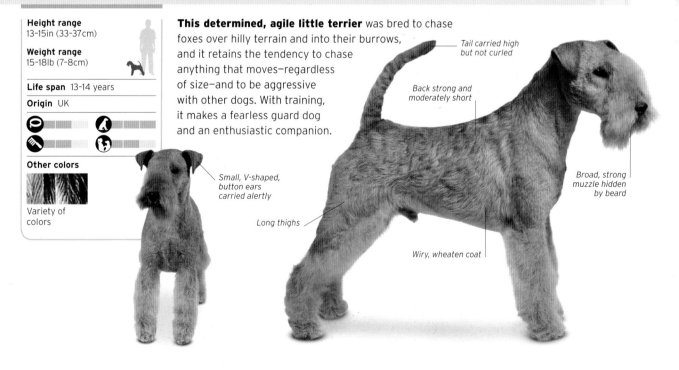

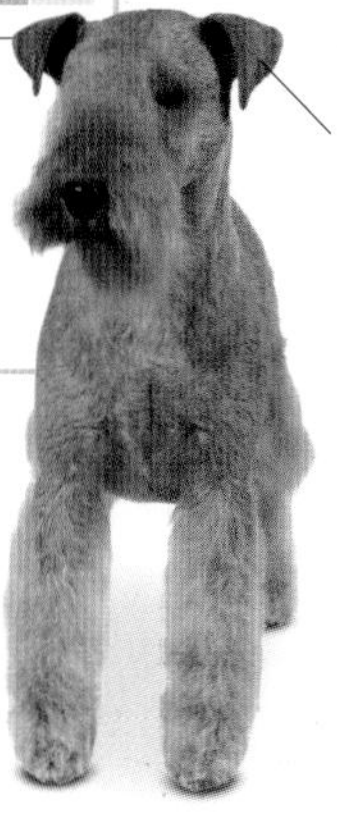

Tail carried high but not curled

Back strong and moderately short

Small, V-shaped, button ears carried alertly

Broad, strong muzzle hidden by beard

Long thighs

Wiry, wheaten coat

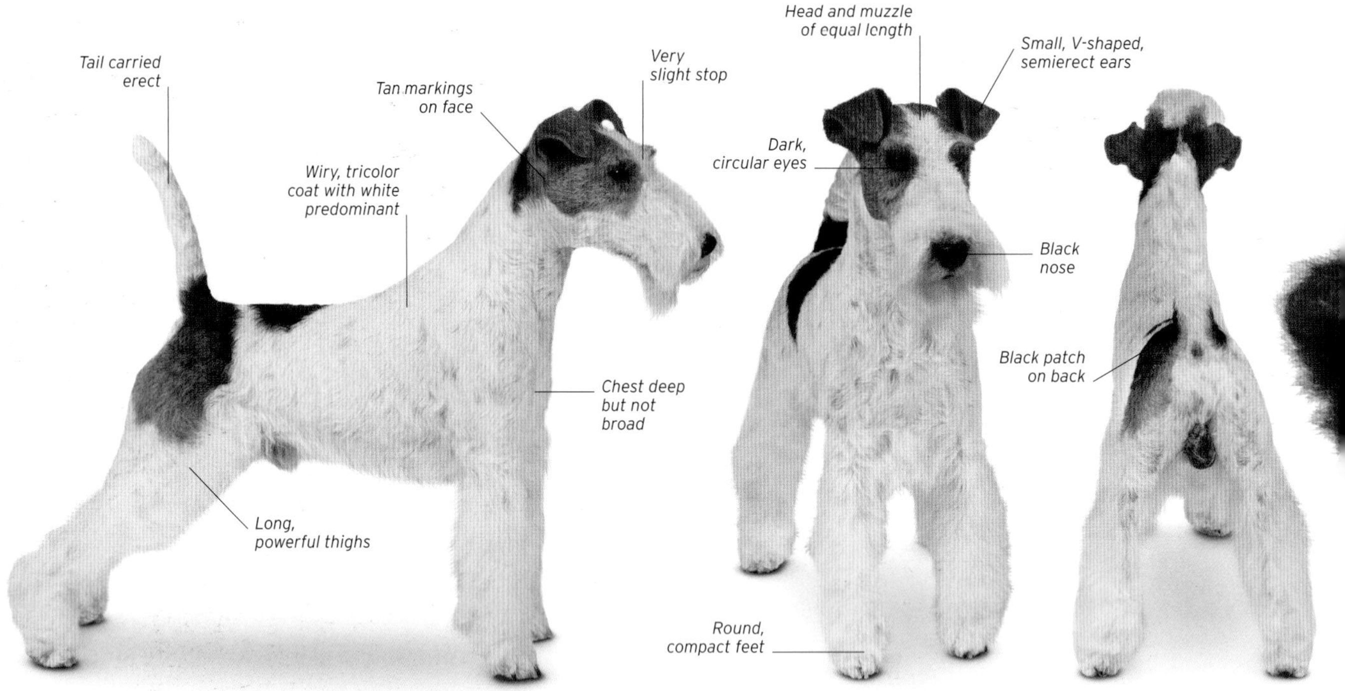

Tail carried erect
Tan markings on face
Wiry, tricolor coat with white predominant
Very slight stop
Head and muzzle of equal length
Small, V-shaped, semierect ears
Dark, circular eyes
Black nose
Black patch on back
Chest deep but not broad
Long, powerful thighs
Round, compact feet

WIRE FOX TERRIER

THIS CHEERFUL, FRIENDLY DOG IS GOOD WITH CHILDREN AND ENJOYS LONG WALKS AKC

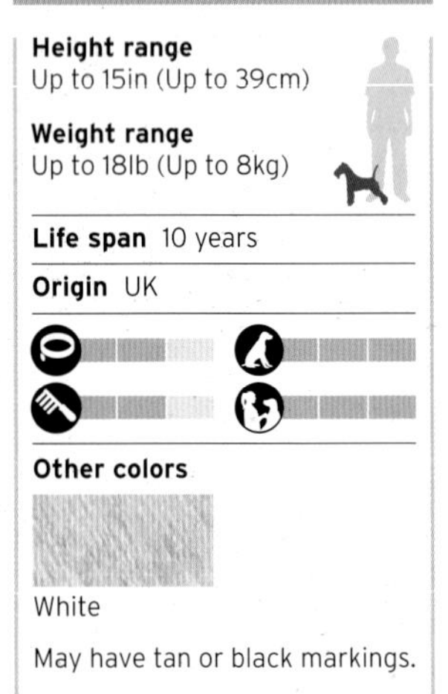

Height range
Up to 15in (Up to 39cm)

Weight range
Up to 18lb (Up to 8kg)

Life span 10 years

Origin UK

Other colors

White

May have tan or black markings.

An energetic and sometimes vocal companion, the Wire Fox Terrier from England was originally kept to kill vermin, hunt rabbit, and tackle foxes that had been run to ground. Its bold and fearless nature and love of digging make early socialization and training essential to prevent snappiness and curb any tendency to dig. If this is done, the Wire Fox Terrier makes a wonderful family pet that loves to play and readily reciprocates any affection it receives.

The Wire Fox Terrier's coat needs regular grooming and "plucking" to remove any shed hair, and more extensive stripping three or four times a year. The coat should never be clipped because this does not remove shed hair and may cause irritation, and also leads to deterioration in coat texture and color. The Wire Fox Terrier is ancestral to several other dog breeds, including the Toy Fox Terrier (see p.208), the Brazilian Terrier (see p.209), the Rat Terrier (see p.211), the Parson Russell Terrier (see p.195), and the Jack Russell Terrier (see p.196).

SMOOTH FOX TERRIER

Much rarer than its wire-haired cousin, the Smooth Fox Terrier's shorter coat requires less grooming. This dog's close-fitting coat clearly shows its very distinctive wedge-shaped head.

JAPANESE TERRIER

AN ELEGANT AND LIVELY LITTLE DOG WITH A SENSITIVE AND PLAYFUL NATURE FCI

Height range
12-13in (30-33cm)

Weight range
4-9lb (2-4kg)

Life span 12-14 years

Origin Japan

Other colors

Black, tan, and white

Also known as the Nippon or Nihon Terrier, this rare breed is strong and athletic for its size. Its ancestors are thought to include the English Toy Terrier (see p.210) and the now extinct Toy Bull Terrier. The Japanese Terrier has been kept as a lapdog, ratter, and retriever, and makes an adaptable family pet as well as a good watchdog.

Pronounced stop
High-set, button ears
Strong, slightly arched back
Short, smooth, glossy, white coat, with black markings
Dark, oval-shaped eyes
Typical black markings on head
Black spots on legs
Small, black nose

TOY FOX TERRIER

THIS SMALL DOG IS FUN-LOVING AND BRAVE, BUT CAN BE BOSSY AKC

Height range
9-12in (23-30cm)

Weight range
4-7lb (2-3kg)

Life span 13-14 years

Origin USA

Other colors

White and tan

White and black

White, chocolate, and tan

Also called the American Toy Terrier, this breed is a cross between the Smooth Fox Terrier (see p.206) and various toy breeds. The result is a dog that is a good ratter but also family-friendly. As with all toy breeds, the Toy Fox Terrier is not recommended as a pet in a home where there are babies and toddlers, but older children will enjoy its zest for life.

Face predominately black with tan markings
Docked tail held upright
Bright, dark, round eyes
Erect, pointed ears
Black patch
Tan markings on cheek
Fine-haired, satin-like, white coat

BRAZILIAN TERRIER

WITH A STRONG TERRIER TEMPERAMENT, THIS FRISKY, SPIRITED DOG IS QUICK TO LEARN

FCI

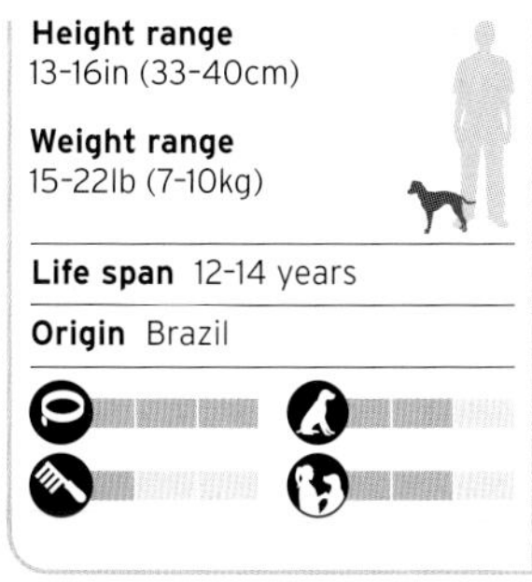
Height range
13–16in (33–40cm)
Weight range
15–22lb (7–10kg)
Life span 12–14 years
Origin Brazil

Bred from European terriers crossed with local Brazilian farm dogs, this breed has marked hunting instincts and is eager to explore and dig as well as track, chase, and kill rodents. Like its smaller cousin, the Jack Russell Terrier (see p.196), the Brazilian Terrier needs to know who is boss. It rewards a firm owner with devotion and obedience and makes a protective—and vocal—watchdog. Ever active, it thrives on a long, daily walk to keep it mentally and physically stimulated, otherwise it becomes restless. When well trained, the Brazilian Terrier makes an excellent family pet.

Alert expression
Typical tan markings on head
Croup slopes to tail
Triangular, drop ears
Short, smooth, predominately white coat
Black marking
Low-set, short tail
Deep chest

ENGLISH TOY TERRIER

A PERKY, FRIENDLY, AND CONFIDENT LITTLE COMPANION DOG KC

Height range
10-12in (25-30cm)

Weight range
7-9lb (3-4kg)

Life span 12-13 years

Origin UK

The oldest British toy breed, the English Toy Terrier used to be called the Miniature Black and Tan Terrier. It differs from its larger cousin, the Manchester Terrier (opposite), only in its size and its erect ears. English Toy Terriers were popular as town pets during Queen Victoria's reign, when toy dogs became fashionable. Before that it was a rat-catcher. Like other terriers, this breed veers from cuddly family pet to voracious rodent-hunter. It bonds with its owner and makes a good watchdog. Because it is small, the English Toy Terrier needs less exercise than the Manchester Terrier and adapts well to city living.

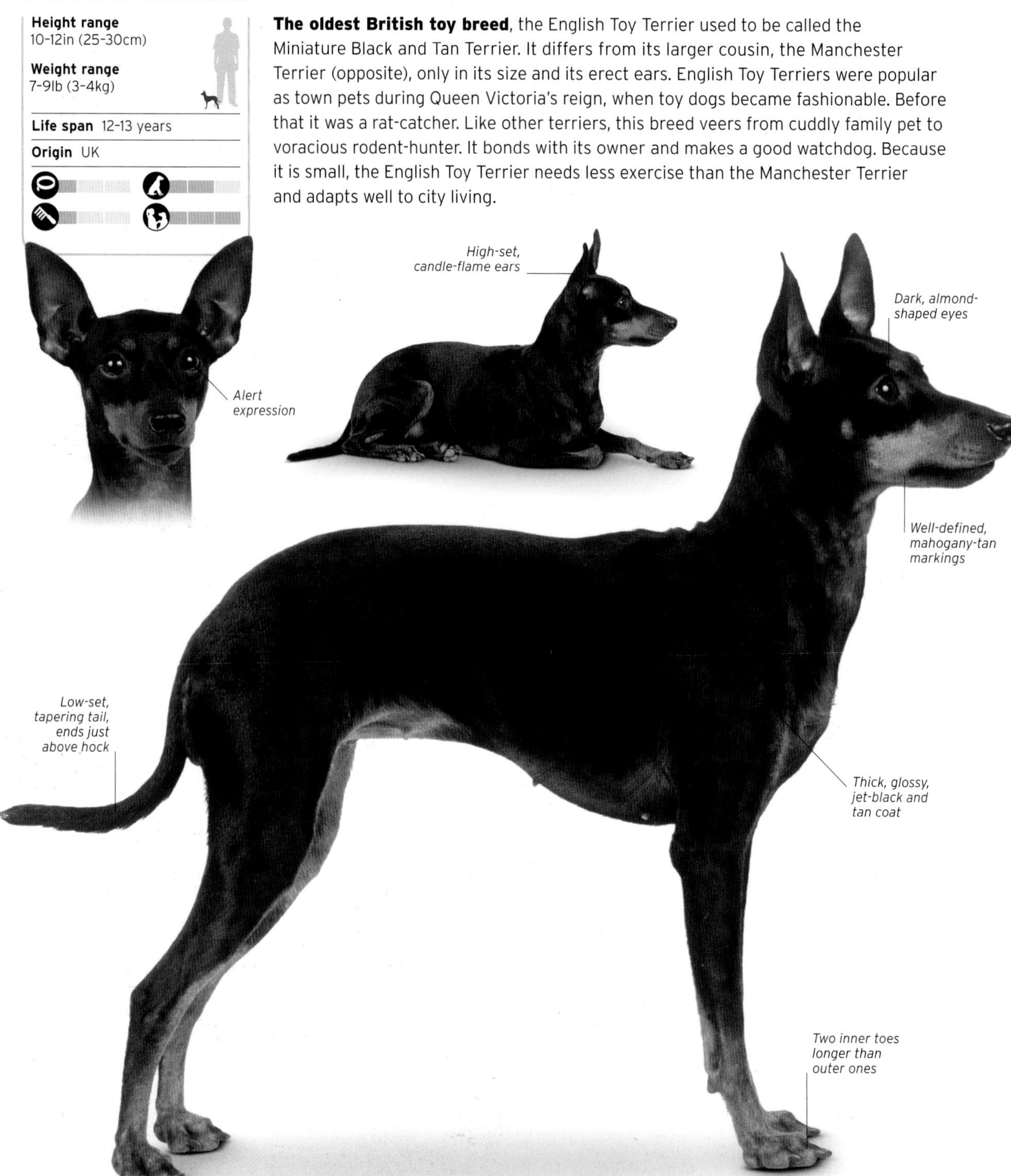
High-set, candle-flame ears
Alert expression
Dark, almond-shaped eyes
Well-defined, mahogany-tan markings
Low-set, tapering tail, ends just above hock
Thick, glossy, jet-black and tan coat
Two inner toes longer than outer ones

MANCHESTER TERRIER

THIS DEVOTED FAMILY PET ADAPTS WELL TO TOWN OR COUNTRY LIFE AKC

Height range 15-16in (38-41cm)

Weight range 11-22lb (5-10kg)

Life span 13-14 years

Origin UK

With its sleek good looks, the Manchester Terrier makes an elegant and lively companion dog, bigger than the related English Toy Terrier (opposite). It takes its name from the weekly rat-killing contests in Manchester that occurred in the 19th century and at which it excelled. Ruthless with vermin, it is gentle with its owners.

Small, V-shaped, button ears
Black nose
Short tail carried low
Slightly rounded back
Smooth, short, glossy, black and tan coat
Tan markings on legs
Well-arched, compact forefeet

RAT TERRIER

AN ENERGY-CHARGED BUNDLE OF FUN FOR HUMANS BUT A TERROR FOR VERMIN

Height range
Miniature:
8-14in (20-36cm)
Standard:
14-22in (36-56cm)

Weight range
Miniature:
7-9lb (3-4kg)
Standard:
11-35lb (5-16kg)

Life span 11-14 years

Origin USA

Other colors

Variety of colors

Tan markings are common.

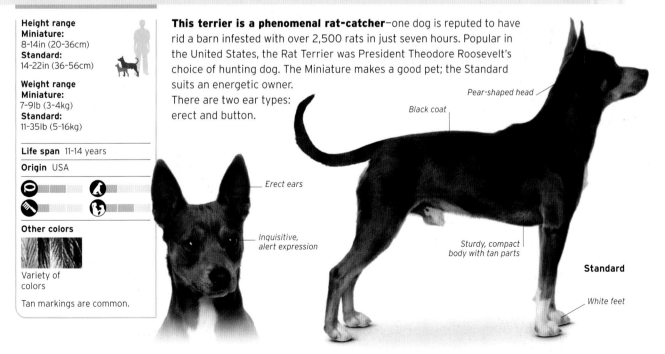

This terrier is a phenomenal rat-catcher—one dog is reputed to have rid a barn infested with over 2,500 rats in just seven hours. Popular in the United States, the Rat Terrier was President Theodore Roosevelt's choice of hunting dog. The Miniature makes a good pet; the Standard suits an energetic owner. There are two ear types: erect and button.

Pear-shaped head

Black coat

Erect ears

Inquisitive, alert expression

Sturdy, compact body with tan parts

Standard

White feet

AMERICAN HAIRLESS TERRIER

THIS DISTINCTIVE-LOOKING DOG, WITH TERRIER TRAITS, IS ALERT AND FRIENDLY

Height range
10–18in (25–46cm)

Weight range
7–13lb (3–6kg)

Life span 12–13 years

Origin USA

Other colors

Any skin color

The first hairless Rat Terriers (see p.211) were the result of a genetic mutation, but were then bred with each other to produce hairless puppies. Apart from its lack of hair, this is a typical, lively terrier. It needs a coat in winter to stay warm and to avoid sunburn in summer. Ears may be erect, semierect, or button.

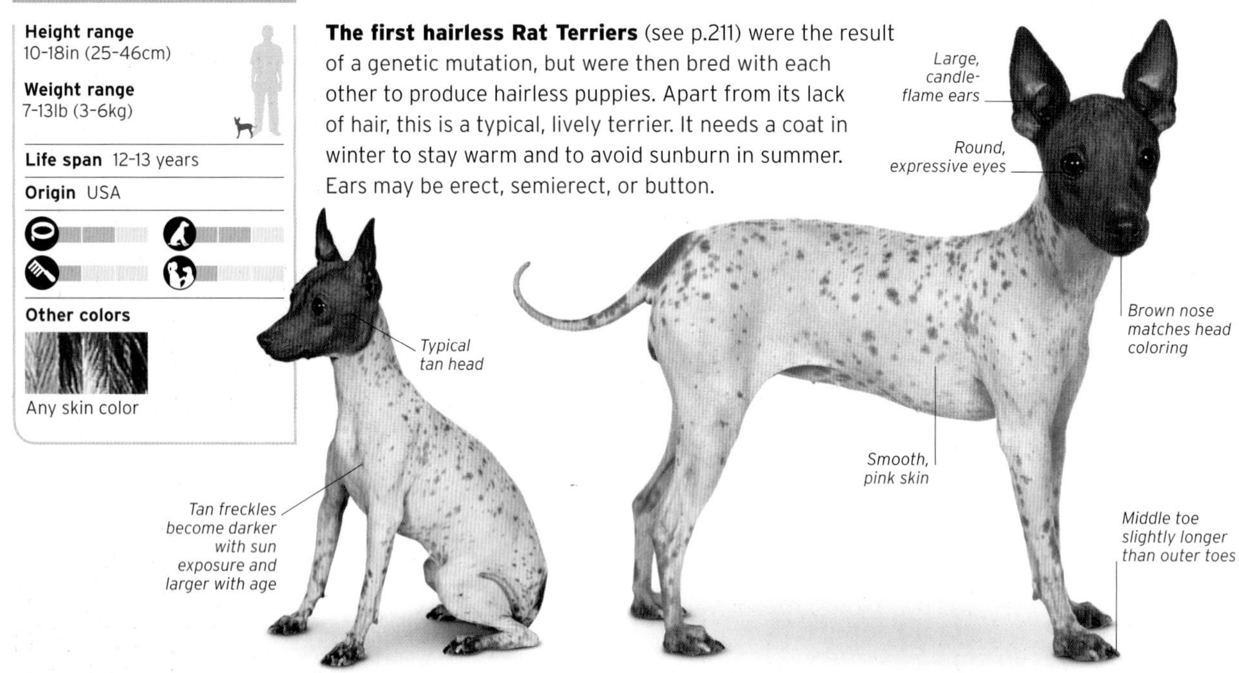
Large, candle-flame ears
Round, expressive eyes
Brown nose matches head coloring
Typical tan head
Smooth, pink skin
Tan freckles become darker with sun exposure and larger with age
Middle toe slightly longer than outer toes

PATTERDALE TERRIER

THIS INDEPENDENT AND TENACIOUS HUNTER-DIGGER NEEDS AN EXPERIENCED OWNER

Height range
10–15in (25–38cm)

Weight range
11–13lb (5–6kg)

Life span 13–14 years

Origin UK

Other colors

Red

Liver or bronze

Black and tan

Coats may be grizzled.

The isolated valleys of the Lake District in England each had their own terrier—this one originates from the village of Patterdale. It remains popular in the UK but has gained favor in the United States too. It makes an excellent hunting companion since it never gives up on its prey. There are two coat types: smooth and broken.

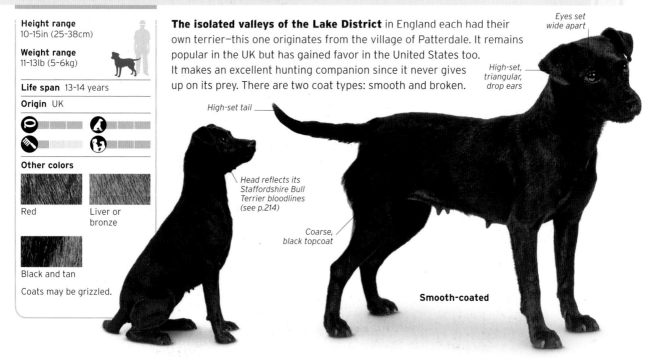

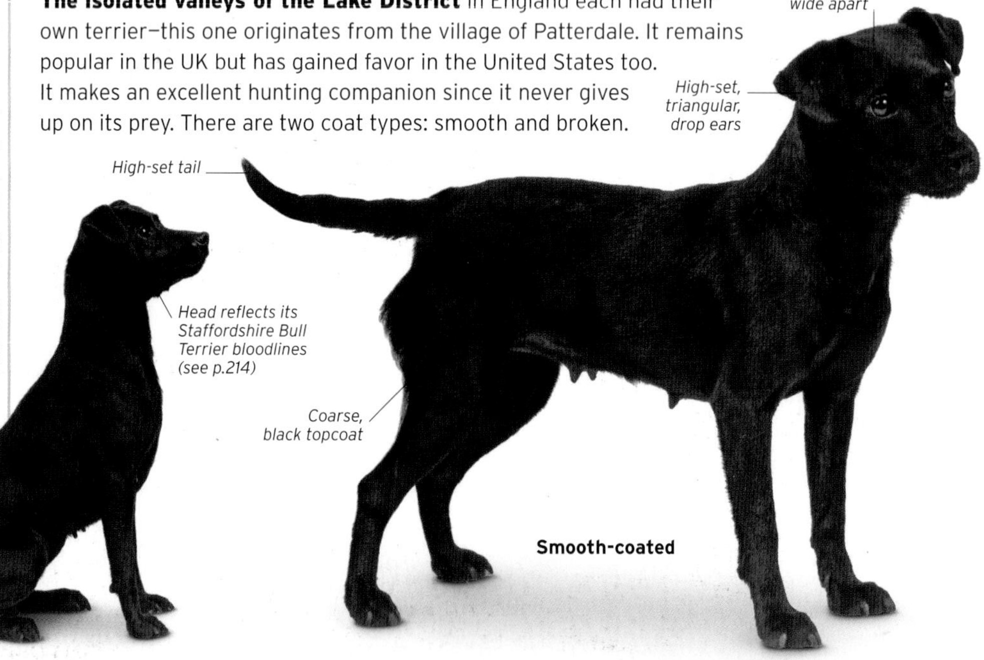

Eyes set wide apart

High-set, triangular, drop ears

High-set tail

Head reflects its Staffordshire Bull Terrier bloodlines (see p.214)

Coarse, black topcoat

Smooth-coated

KROMFOHRLANDER

THIS EVEN-TEMPERED, LOVABLE TERRIER IS GOOD WITH THE ENTIRE FAMILY

FCI

Height range
15–18in (38–46cm)

Weight range
20–35lb (9–16kg)

Life span 13–14 years

Origin Germany

A recent German breed, only recognized since the 1950s, this dog takes its name from its place of origin in Germany. It was bred from a Wire Fox Terrier (see p.206) and a locally owned dog. The result is a kindly, attractive, low-maintenance, eager-to-please dog, which makes a good watchdog and, like other terriers, is a keen ratter. While wary of strangers, it is gentle and playful with familiar people and dogs. There are two coat types: rough-haired and smooth-haired.

Triangular, drop ears
Thick coat lying close to body
Rough-haired
Oval, brown eyes
White blaze with tan speckles
Typical, symmetrical head markings
Gently sloping stop
Irregular-shaped tan markings
White coat
Feathering on upper thighs
Tan speckling on legs
Forefeet and hind feet similar in shape
Smooth-haired

STAFFORDSHIRE BULL TERRIER

THIS FEARLESS DOG LOVES CHILDREN AND CAN ACHIEVE HIGH LEVELS OF OBEDIENCE AKC

Height range
14–16in (36–41cm)

Weight range
24–37lb (11–17kg)

Life span 10–16 years

Origin UK

Other colors

Variety of colors

Originally bred for pit-fighting in the 19th century, the Staffordshire Bull Terrier was developed from crosses between bulldogs and terriers. The modern "Staffie," as it is often affectionately known, has moved on from its historical background to become a people-loving pet, enormously popular in both town and country. This dog is robust, boisterous, and possesses legendary courage. A Staffordshire Bull Terrier is unlikely to back down if challenged by an unfamiliar dog. Firm handling and early obedience training are essential.

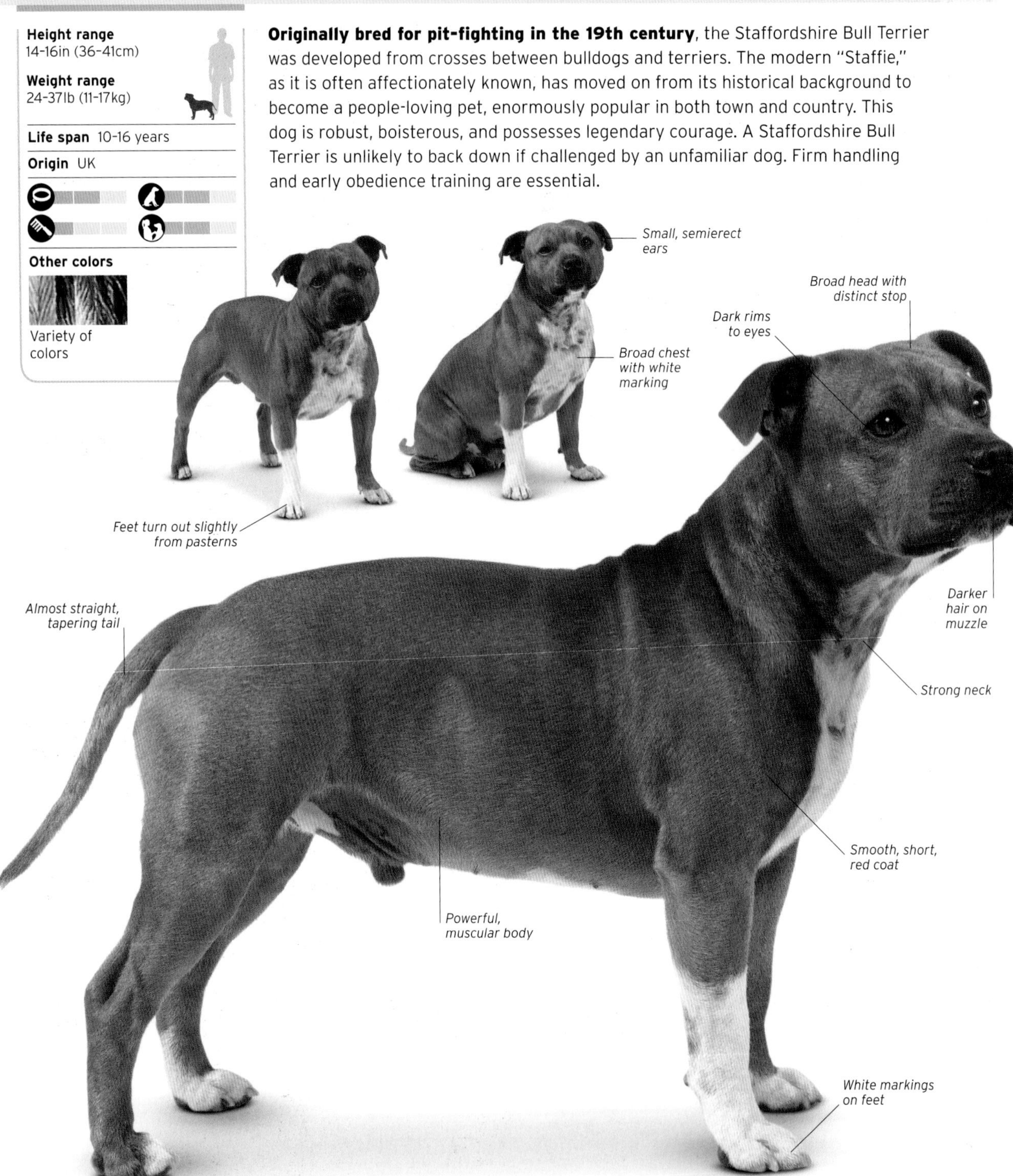

Small, semierect ears
Broad head with distinct stop
Dark rims to eyes
Broad chest with white marking
Feet turn out slightly from pasterns
Almost straight, tapering tail
Darker hair on muzzle
Strong neck
Smooth, short, red coat
Powerful, muscular body
White markings on feet

AMERICAN STAFFORDSHIRE TERRIER

A LARGER VERSION OF THE ENGLISH STAFFIE, THIS IS A COURAGEOUS AND COMPANIONABLE DOG AKC

Height range 17–19in (43–48cm)

Weight range 57–67lb (26–30kg)

Life span 10–16 years

Origin USA

Other colors

Variety of colors

Developed from the Staffordshire Bull Terrier (opposite), this dog was recognized as a separate breed in the United States in the 1930s. Apart from being more heavily built than its English counterpart, the American Staffordshire Terrier shares all the characteristics of the original "Staffie." It is bold and intelligent and makes a loyal family pet.

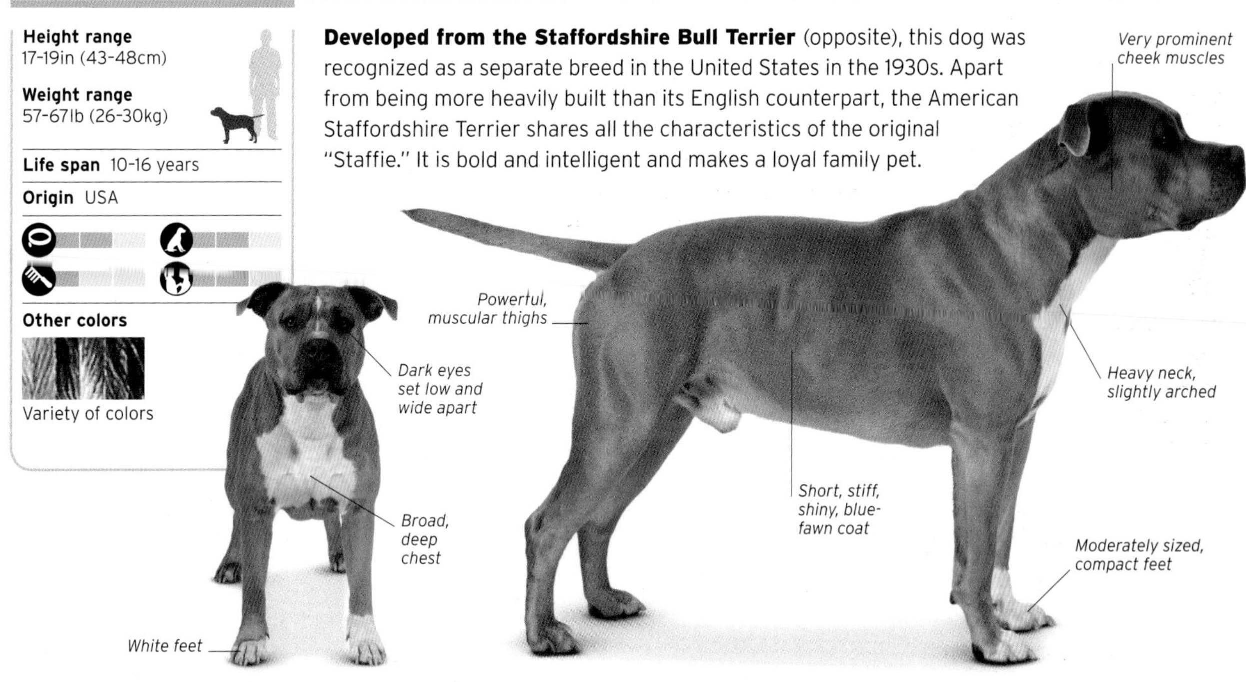
Very prominent cheek muscles
Powerful, muscular thighs
Dark eyes set low and wide apart
Heavy neck, slightly arched
Short, stiff, shiny, blue-fawn coat
Broad, deep chest
Moderately sized, compact feet
White feet

AMERICAN PIT BULL TERRIER

NOT RECOMMENDED FOR MOST OWNERS, THIS DOG NEEDS SKILLED HANDLING

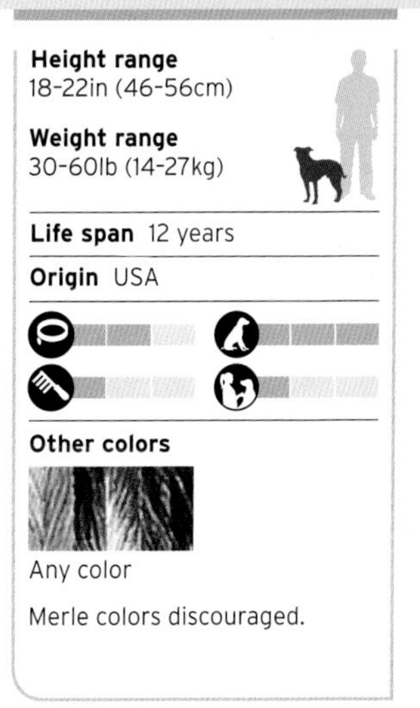

Height range 18–22in (46–56cm)

Weight range 30–60lb (14–27kg)

Life span 12 years

Origin USA

Other colors

Any color

Merle colors discouraged.

The ancestors of the American Pit Bull Terrier were dogs brought to the United States in the 19th century by Irish immigrants. Although bred for fighting, this dog became much loved as a working or family dog. The breed has lately acquired a reputation for aggression, which is vigorously refuted by its supporters.

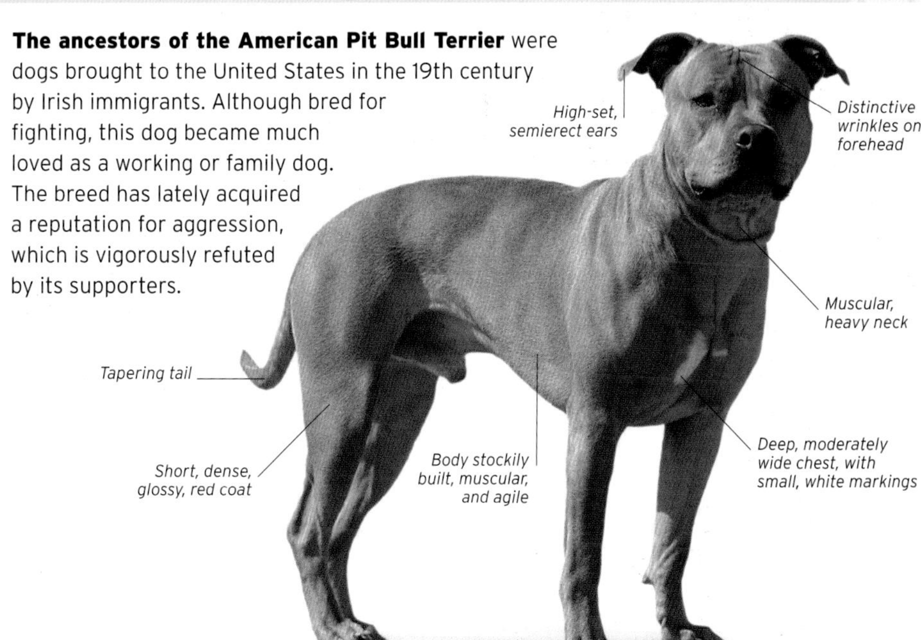
High-set, semierect ears
Distinctive wrinkles on forehead
Muscular, heavy neck
Tapering tail
Short, dense, glossy, red coat
Body stockily built, muscular, and agile
Deep, moderately wide chest, with small, white markings

SKYE TERRIER

FULL OF CHARACTER, THIS DOG OFTEN BECOMES DEVOTED TO ONE PERSON AKC

Height range
Up to 10in (up to 25-26cm)

Weight range
24-40lb (11-18kg)

Life span 12-15 years

Origin UK

Other colors

Cream
Black

May have white spot on chest.

A very old breed from the Western Isles of Scotland, the Skye Terrier was originally used for fox- and badger-hunting. With a long, low-slung body, the Skye Terrier could easily slip into the narrow underground passages used by its quarry. This elegant little dog is active and good-spirited, and makes an excellent pet, becoming devoted to family and home. The long coat that is characteristic of the breed can take several years to grow to its full adult length. To prevent the hair from matting, a Skye Terrier needs a weekly grooming session.

Erect ears, fringed with long, silky hair
Soft, light gay hair covers brown eyes
Hair on ears darker than body hair
Darker hair on face
Black nose
Silky, fawn coat
Body much longer than leg length
Long, straight, gray coat parts down center of back
Lighter patches on coat
Long, feathered tail

Adult and two puppies

DANDIE DINMONT TERRIER

THIS LOVEABLE AND AFFECTIONATE DOG IS GOOD WITH OTHER PETS IF SOCIALIZED EARLY

AKC

Height range
8–11in (20–28cm)

Weight range
18–24lb (8–11kg)

Life span Up to 13 years

Origin UK

Other colors

Mustard

May have white chest hair.

This terrier comes from the border country between England and Scotland, where it was developed to hunt badger and otter. It was named the Dandie Dinmont Terrier after a character who owned a similar-looking dog in a novel by Sir Walter Scott. Game, sensitive, and intelligent, the Dandie Dinmont Terrier thrives on love and attention.

Large, wide-set, dark hazel eyes
Large, domed head covered in soft, silky, light-colored hair
Body length greatly exceeds leg length
Pendant ears set well back
Long, tapering tail with feathering on underside
Lighter-colored lower leg
Pepper coat of dark bluish black hair

MINIATURE PINSCHER

THIS DOG IS HAPPY TO LIVE IN A SMALL SPACE BUT NEEDS REGULAR EXERCISE

AKC

Height range
10–12in (25–30cm)

Weight range
8–10lb (4–5kg)

Life span Up to 15 years

Origin Germany

Other colors

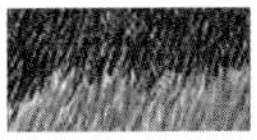

Blue and tan | Brown and tan

Bred in Germany and developed from the much larger German Pinscher (see p.218), this sturdy but graceful dog was once used as a farmyard rat-hunter. The Miniature Pinscher is quick and lively, moving with a characteristic high-stepping, hackney gait. Perfect for a small home, the breed has sharp senses that make it a good watchdog.

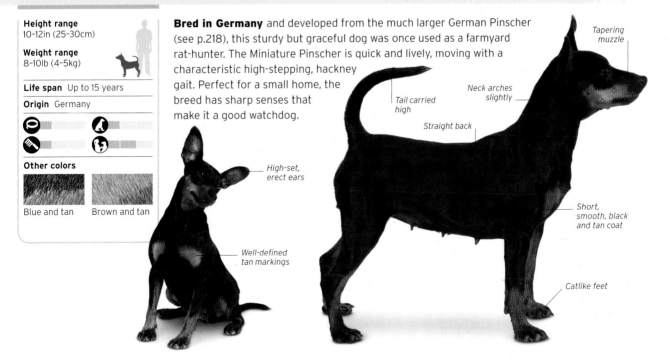

Tapering muzzle
Tail carried high
Neck arches slightly
Straight back
High-set, erect ears
Short, smooth, black and tan coat
Well-defined tan markings
Catlike feet

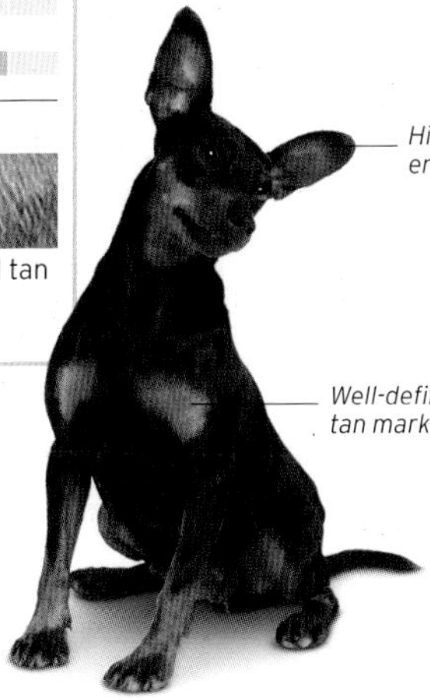

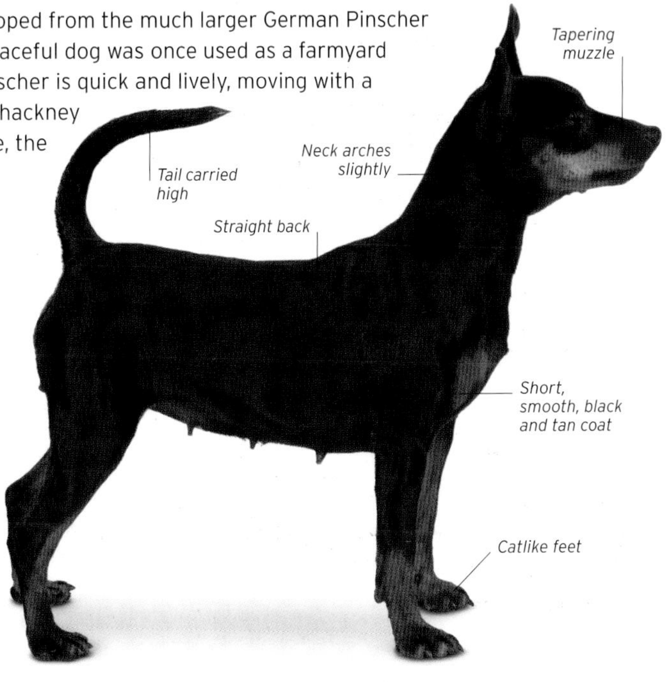

GERMAN PINSCHER

A GREAT COMPANION AND WATCHDOG FOR A FIRM OWNER AKC

Height range
17-19in (43-48cm)

Weight range
24-35lb (11-16kg)

Life span 12-14 years

Origin Germany

Other colors

Isabella

Blue

Also known as the Standard Pinscher, this tall terrier started out as a general-purpose farm dog. It makes a protective guard dog—but needs to be well trained so that it does not become overprotective, bark for too long, or behave aggressively toward other dogs. With the right training it is gentle and responsive.

Dark, oval eyes
Tail sweeps upward
Triangular, drop ears
Short, sleek, thick, stag-red coat
Short, round feet

MINIATURE SCHNAUZER

THIS CHEERFUL, FRIENDLY, FUN-LOVING DOG IS RELIABLE WITH ALL THE FAMILY AKC

Height range
13-14in (33-36cm)

Weight range
13-15lb (6-7kg)

Life span 14 years

Origin Germany

Other colors

White

Black

Black and silver

Popular in North America, as well as in its native Germany, the Miniature Schnauzer is named for its distinctive muzzle (*schnauze* means snout in German). An intelligent little dog, it responds well to obedience training. Despite its small size, it is energetic and needs play off the leash as well as a brisk daily walk to keep it healthy and happy.

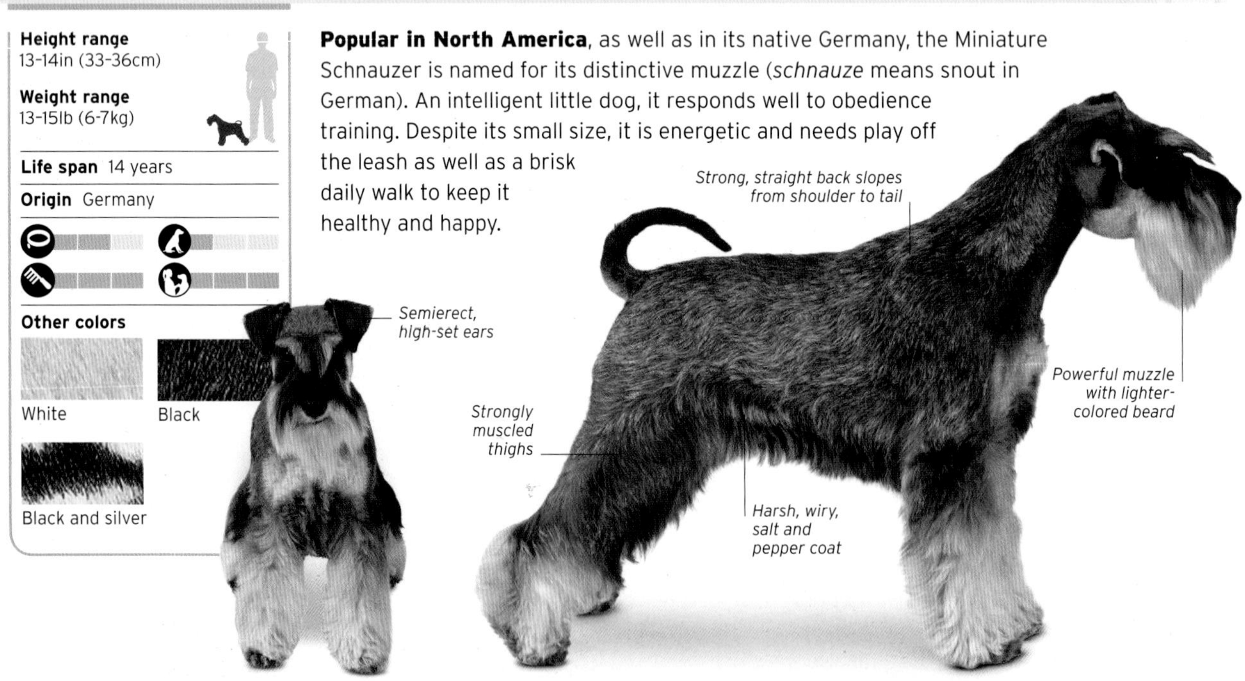
Strong, straight back slopes from shoulder to tail
Semierect, high-set ears
Strongly muscled thighs
Powerful muzzle with lighter-colored beard
Harsh, wiry, salt and pepper coat

AUSTRIAN PINSCHER

THIS ALERT AND FAITHFUL WATCHDOG IS SUITABLE FOR A RURAL OWNER

FCI

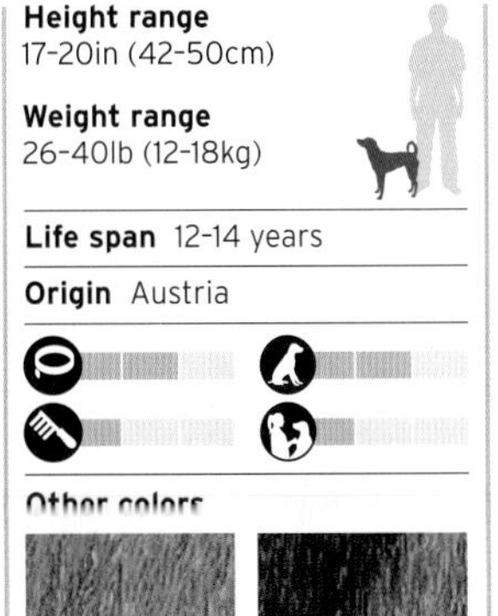

Height range
17–20in (42–50cm)

Weight range
26–40lb (12–18kg)

Life span 12–14 years

Origin Austria

Other colors

Russet gold or brownish yellow

Black and tan

Bred as an all-purpose guard and herding farm dog in its native Austria, this breed rewards a confident owner with complete loyalty and devotion. Barking at anything suspicious, it makes an excellent watchdog for isolated locations, but its protective instincts and fearlessness can lead to aggression.

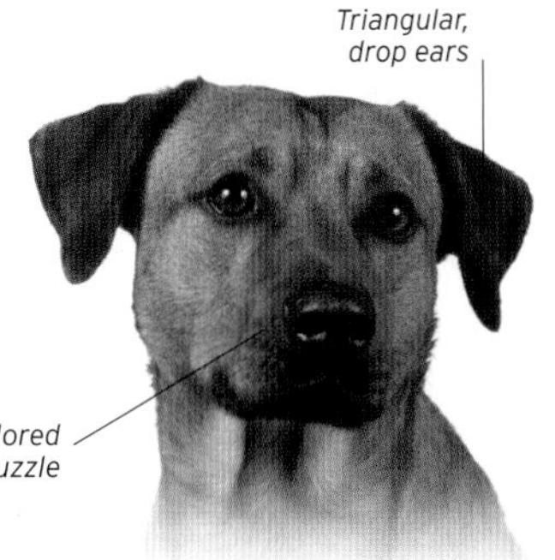

Triangular, drop ears
Darker-colored muzzle

Dense, stag-red coat
White chest markings
Strong, straight legs

AFFENPINSCHER

THIS MISCHIEVOUS, MONKEY-LIKE LITTLE DOG CAPTIVATES WITH ITS AMUSING ANTICS

AKC

Height range
9–11in (24–28cm)

Weight range
7–9lb (3–4kg)

Life span 10–12 years

Origin Germany

Sometimes called the Black Devil, the Affenpinscher is among the oldest of the European toy dogs. It retains its terrier instincts though, and is a brave watchdog and ratter despite its size. With its bright, sometimes stubborn personality, this dog learns easily but needs to know who is boss. It loves to play and gets on well with children who handle it considerately.

Blunt muzzle with wide nostrils
Small, round, dark feet

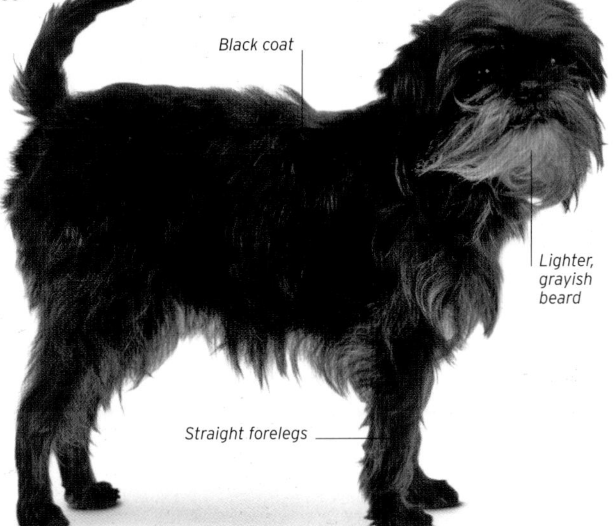

Domed, broad forehead
Black coat
Lighter, grayish beard
Straight forelegs

SOFT MOUTH
Gundogs used for retrieving, like this dual-purpose English Springer Spaniel, are trained to carry game without chewing it.

GUNDOGS

Before the advent of firearms, hunters used dogs to help them locate and chase game. With the introduction of guns, a different type of dog was required. Gundogs were developed to carry out specific tasks and to work more closely with the hunters. The breeds fall into several categories based on the type of work they were bred to perform.

The Lagotto Romagnolo is bred for retrieving from water

The dogs in the gundog group, which all hunt by scent, are classified broadly in three main divisions: the pointers and setters, which locate prey; the spaniels, which flush game out of cover; and the retrievers, which collect fallen prey and bring it back to the hunter. Breeds that combine these functions are known as HPR (hunt/point/retrieve) dogs and include the Weimaraner, German Shorthaired Pointer, and the Vizsla.

Pointers have been used as hunting dogs since the 17th century. They have the extraordinary ability to indicate the location of prey by "pointing"—freezing into position with nose, body, and tail aligned. A pointer remains motionless until the hunter either flushes out the game or instructs the dog to do so. The English Pointer, which features in many old sporting portraits alongside hunting squires and their "bags" of game birds, is a classic example of the type.

Setters also direct attention to game by freezing. Typically used to hunt quail, pheasant, and grouse, these dogs crouch, or "set," when they pick up a scent. Originally, setters were trained to work with hunters who caught game with nets while their dogs prevented the prey from making an escape on the ground.

Spaniels drive out, or flush, game birds, forcing them to take wing into the line of the guns. They watch where a bird falls and are usually sent to retrieve it. This division includes small, silky coated, long-eared dogs such as the Springer Spaniel and Cocker Spaniel, used for finding game on land, and less familiar breeds, such as the Barbet and the Wetterhoun, which specialize in flushing waterbirds.

The retrievers were bred specifically for retrieving waterfowl. In common with some breeds of the spaniel division, these gundogs often have water-resistant coats. They are renowned for their "soft" mouths, and quickly learn to carry game without damaging it.

VERSATILE VIZSLA
The Vizsla is one of various gundog breeds that are skilled at multitasking and combine several functions.

FAMILY RETRIEVER
The water-loving Golden Retriever is a popular bird dog that, because of its gentle, calm, and lovable temperament, has also become a firm family favorite.

COCKER SPANIEL

A SMALL GUNDOG WITH A HAPPY DISPOSITION AKC

Height range
13-15in (34-39cm)

Weight range
15-31lb (7-14kg)

Life span 12-15 years

Origin USA

Other colors

Any color

Known for its sweet, playful nature, the Cocker Spaniel is suited to life as a pet or a working gundog; the breed has speed and stamina and needs plenty of exercise. It also has a tendency toward shyness, so early and regular socialization is important.

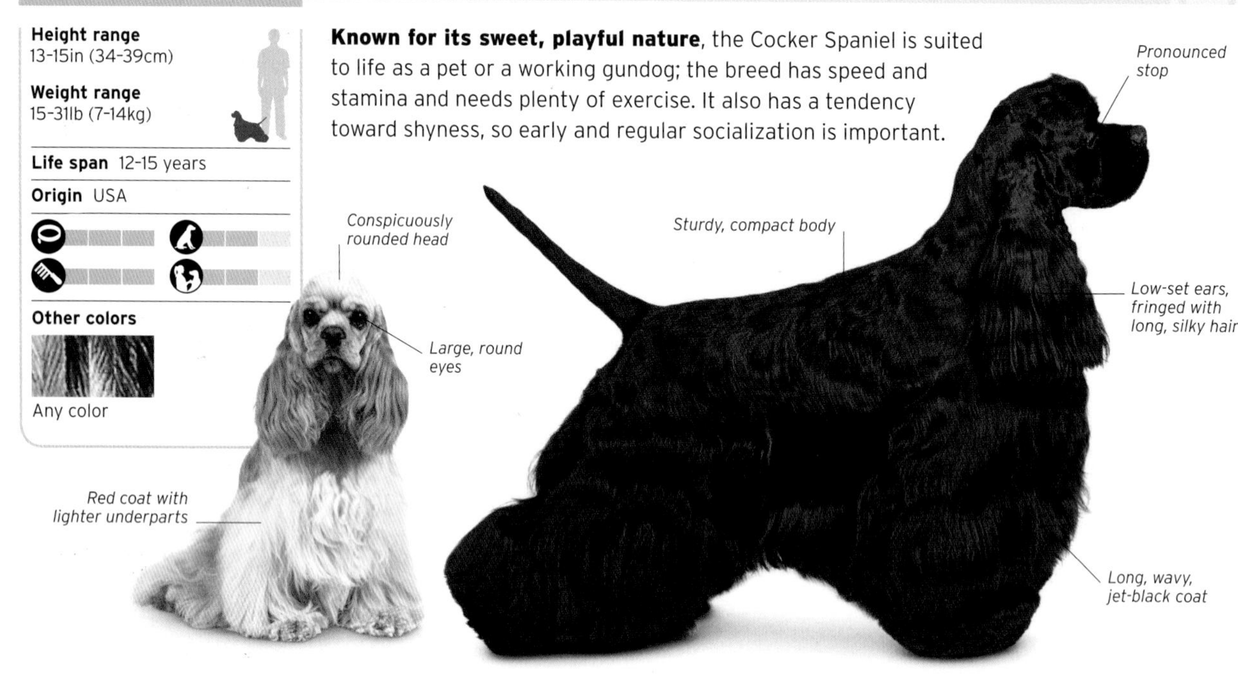
Pronounced stop
Conspicuously rounded head
Sturdy, compact body
Low-set ears, fringed with long, silky hair
Large, round eyes
Red coat with lighter underparts
Long, wavy, jet-black coat

ENGLISH COCKER SPANIEL

THIS GUNDOG IS GENTLE, AFFECTIONATE, AND INTELLIGENT AKC

Height range
15-16in (38-41cm)

Weight range
29-33lb (13-15kg)

Life span 12-15 years

Origin UK

Other colors

Any color

Solid colors should have no white markings.

Originally known as the "cocking spaniel" and used for flushing woodcock and grouse, the English Cocker Spaniel is one of the most popular spaniel breeds. Smaller than the English Springer Spaniel (see p.226), this dog was developed to work in dense undergrowth. Show dogs are sturdier and heavier than working dogs, but both make excellent pets.

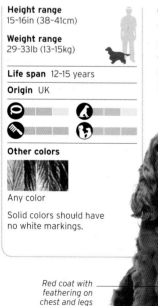

Square muzzle with moderate flews

Black saddle

Ears fringed with long, wavy hair

Feathering on tail

Red coat with feathering on chest and legs

Long, silky, blue-roan coat

GERMAN SPANIEL

THIS GREAT FAMILY DOG IS NOT FOR THE INEXPERIENCED OWNER OR CITY DWELLER FCI

Height range 17–21in (44–54cm)

Weight range 40–55lb (18–25kg)

Life span 12–14 years

Origin Germany

Other colors

Red, Brown, Red roan

An excellent retriever, this dog loves the water. The German Spaniel has masses of stamina and is happiest working, although long, brisk walks will keep it content. This breed will live outdoors, but thrives indoors with a family, and makes a good working gundog and pet.

Brown saddle
Short, fine, brown coat on head
Medium-brown eyes with kind expression
Lightly feathered, drop ears
Dense, wavy, brown-roan coat
Spoon-shaped feet

FIELD SPANIEL

A HIGH-ENERGY WORKING GUNDOG SUITABLE FOR THE COUNTRY DWELLER AKC

Height range 17–18in (44–46cm)

Weight range 40–55lb (18–25kg)

Life span 10–12 years

Origin UK

Other colors

Black, Roan

May have tan markings.

Originally a cross between the Sussex Spaniel (see p.224) and the English Cocker Spaniel (opposite), the Field Spaniel was used for retrieving from water and heavy cover. This docile but high-energy, medium-sized gundog needs to be kept busy and makes the perfect hunting companion for an active family living in the country.

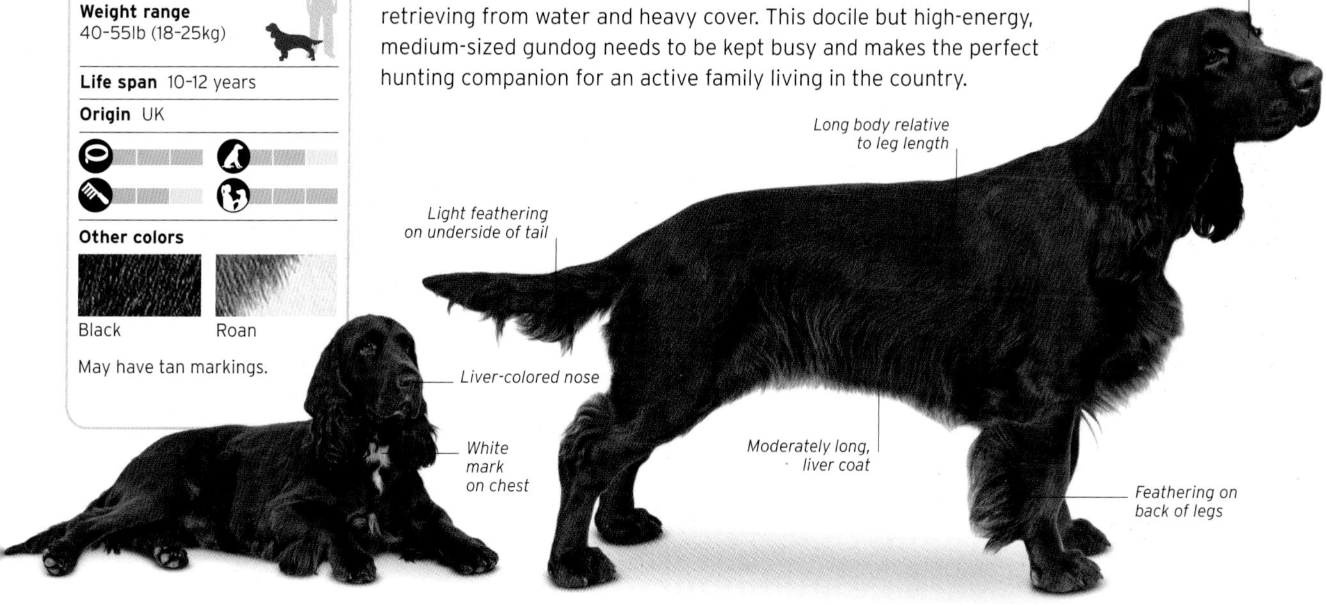

Moderate stop

Long body relative to leg length

Light feathering on underside of tail

Liver-colored nose

White mark on chest

Moderately long, liver coat

Feathering on back of legs

BOYKIN SPANIEL

THIS CHEERFUL, ENERGETIC SPANIEL MAKES A LOYAL AND INTELLIGENT COMPANION AKC

Height range 14–18in (36–46cm)

Weight range 24–40lb (11–18kg)

Life span 14–16 years

Origin USA

Other colors

Liver

May have white hair on chest and toes.

The official state dog of South Carolina, the Boykin Spaniel is a devoted companion and gets on well with other dogs and children. Its easy-going nature and willingness to work make it an ideal gundog or pet for an active family. The Boykin Spaniel's curly coat requires regular grooming.

Shorter hair on face
Traditionally docked tail
Distinctive, oval, brown eyes
Curly, dark chocolate coat
Compact, round feet

SUSSEX SPANIEL

A KINDLY DOG WITH A FROWNING FACE THAT BELIES AN EASY-GOING, ENTHUSIASTIC NATURE AKC

Height range Up to 16in (38–41cm)

Weight range 40–51lb (18–23kg)

Life span 12–15 years

Origin UK

Although active by nature, this English gundog from Sussex will adapt to life in a smaller household providing it is exercised sufficiently. Unlike other gundogs, the Sussex Spaniel will bark, or "give tongue," while working—a trait frowned upon in all other gundog breeds; also distinctive is the rolling action to its gait.

Hazel eyes under wrinkled brow

Long, rich, golden-liver coat

Body length exceeds leg length

Shorter hair on face

Pendant ears covered with long, silky hair

Feathering on chest

Round feet with feathering between toes

CLUMBER SPANIEL

THIS BIG, GOOD-TEMPERED DOG ENJOYS FAMILY LIFE AND A COUNTRY HOME AKC

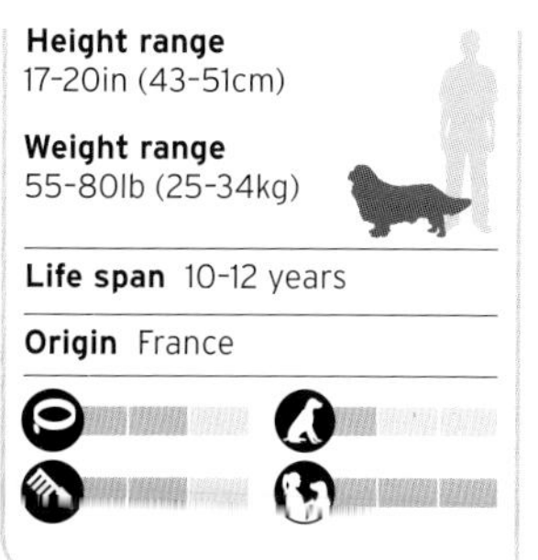
Height range 17–20in (43–51cm)
Weight range 55–80lb (25–34kg)
Life span 10–12 years
Origin France

Although its history has been romanticized, this dog is thought to have originated in 18th-century France, where it was favored by the aristocracy. During the French Revolution Clumber Spaniels may have been brought to England and further developed at Clumber Park in Northumberland, home of the Duke of Newcastle. Muscular and low to the ground, this dog is the most solidly built of all the spaniels. Its calm and steady nature made the breed popular as a gundog but it is now more commonly kept as a pet. Gentle and well behaved, the Clumber Spaniel is easy to train as a companion dog.

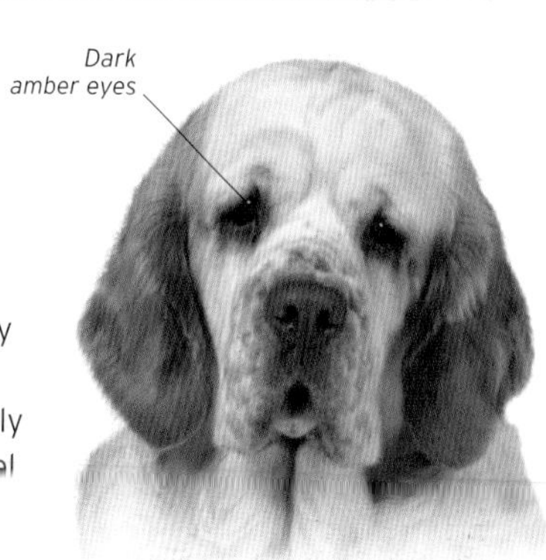
Dark amber eyes

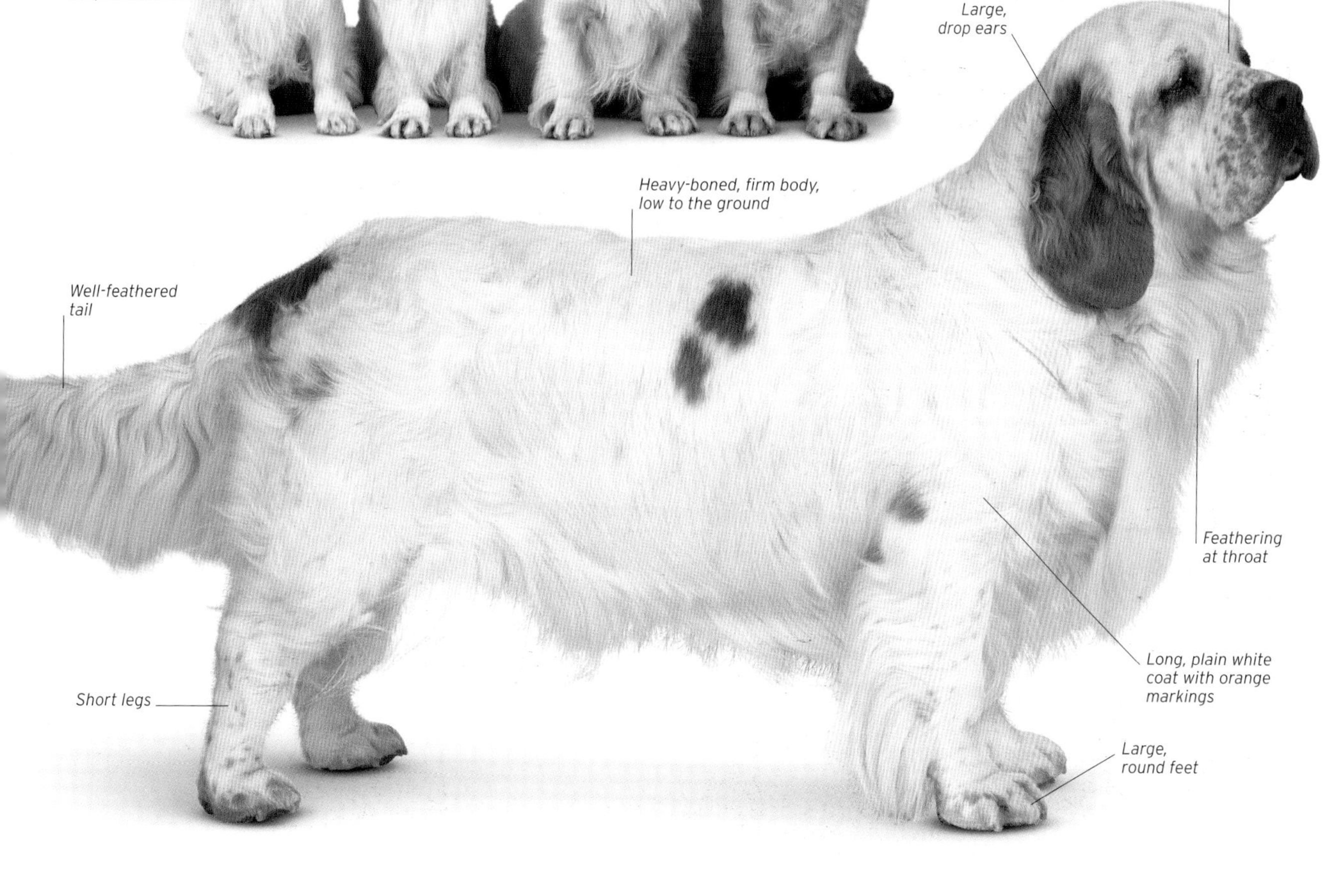

Broad head
Wide, deep chest
Broad, deep muzzle with well-defined stop
Large, drop ears
Heavy-boned, firm body, low to the ground
Well-feathered tail
Feathering at throat
Long, plain white coat with orange markings
Short legs
Large, round feet

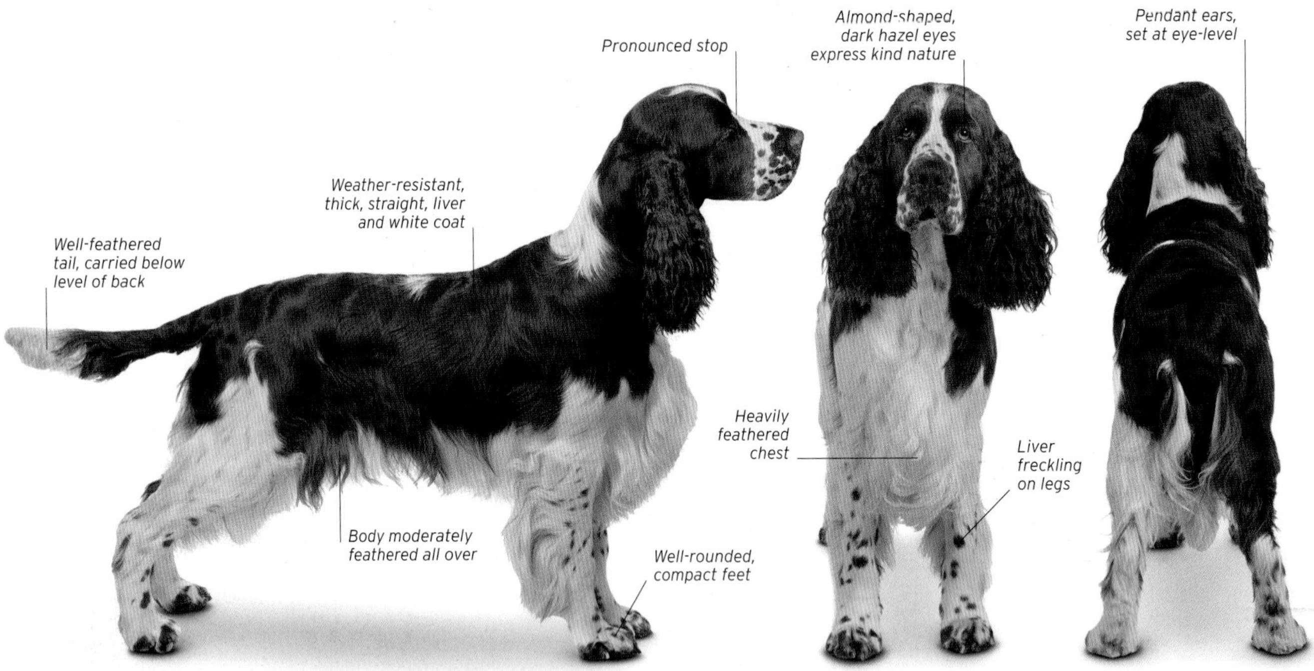

Pronounced stop

Almond-shaped, dark hazel eyes express kind nature

Pendant ears, set at eye-level

Weather-resistant, thick, straight, liver and white coat

Well-feathered tail, carried below level of back

Heavily feathered chest

Liver freckling on legs

Body moderately feathered all over

Well-rounded, compact feet

ENGLISH SPRINGER SPANIEL

FULL OF ENTHUSIASM AND AFFECTION, THIS IS A SOCIABLE WORKING OR COMPANION DOG AKC

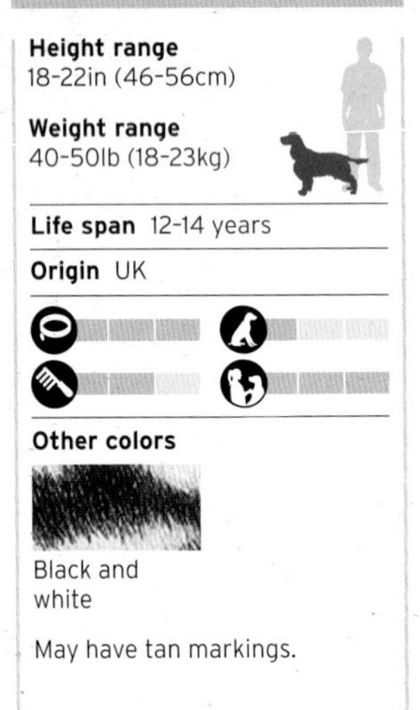
Height range
18–22in (46–56cm)
Weight range
40–50lb (18–23kg)
Life span 12–14 years
Origin UK
Other colors
Black and white
May have tan markings.

This classic gundog is so called because it was originally used to "spring" game—startle birds into the air. Spaniels used as gundogs were once classified according to their size: the larger dogs (called Springers, see pp.226–29) were used for flushing game and the smaller ones (called Cockers, see pp.222–23) for flushing woodcock. Until the beginning of the 20th century the English Springer Spaniel was not recognized as an official breed, although it had developed into a distinct type known as the Norfolk Spaniel.

The English Springer Spaniel will work with hunters in the field all day, undeterred by rough terrain or adverse weather conditions, even jumping into freezing water when necessary. This breed is a popular choice with game shooters but its friendly, biddable disposition makes it an excellent family dog too. It likes company, including children, other dogs, and the household cat. If left alone for too long, it may resort to excessive barking. A nonworking dog needs long, energetic daily walks and will enjoy having a stream to splash in, mud to roll in, or toys thrown for it to retrieve. This breed is bright and willing to learn, and will respond to calm authority. It is highly sensitive, so giving harsh or loud commands is likely to be counterproductive.

The English Springer Spaniel's love of the outdoors means that it needs weekly grooming to prevent its thick coat from becoming matted and dirty and regular trimming, especially of the long feathering on the ears and legs.

There are two types of English Springer Spaniel: working and show. Dogs bred specifically to work in the field tend to have their tails docked and be slightly smaller and of lighter build than dogs produced for showing. Both types make equally good companion dogs.

WELSH SPRINGER SPANIEL

THIS GREAT WORKING DOG LOVES TO BE INCLUDED IN FAMILY ACTIVITIES AKC

Height range
18–19in (46–48cm)

Weight range
35–51lb (16–23kg)

Life span 12–15 years

Origin UK

A close cousin of the English Springer Spaniel (see p.226) and the English Cocker Spaniel (see p.222), this medium-sized Welsh gundog has a jolly disposition and makes a fine family dog and hunting companion. It is inclined to wander, so early and consistent training is imperative.

Finer head than English Springer Spaniel (see p.226)
Low-set, lightly feathered, vine-leaf-shaped ears
Brown nose
Long, muscular neck
Feathering on chest
Feathering above hock
Naturally straight, soft, rich red and white coat
Round, catlike feet

IRISH WATER SPANIEL

THE CLOWN OF THE SPANIEL FAMILY, THIS DOG NEEDS AN ACTIVE LIFE AKC

Height range
20–23in (51–58cm)

Weight range
44–66lb (20–30kg)

Life span 10–12 years

Origin Ireland

This tireless dog is an ideal companion for hikers. Its dark liver coat is virtually waterproof, and the breed's enthusiasm for plunging into ice-cold water earned it the nickname of "Bogdog." Although gentle and faithful, it is slow to mature and can be headstrong, so needs thorough training when young.

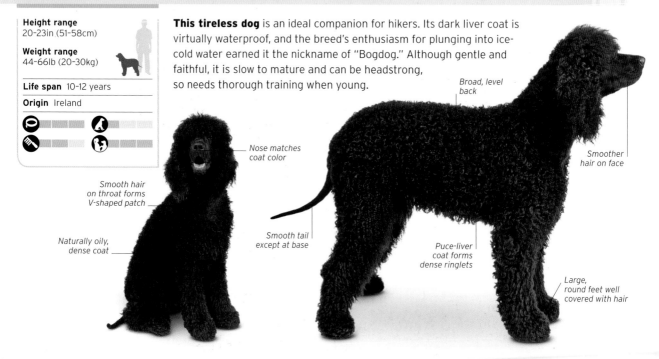

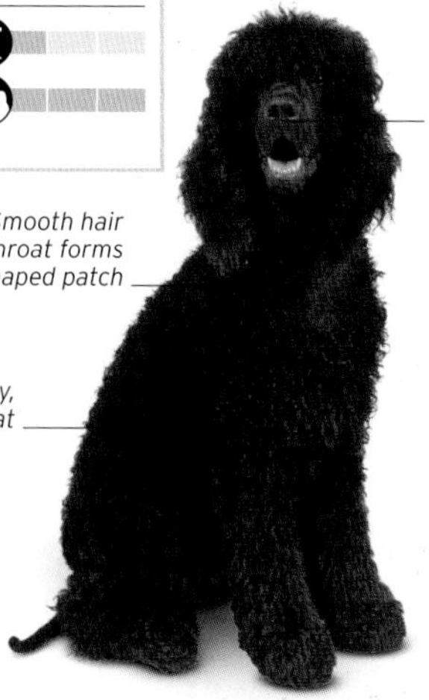

Broad, level back
Nose matches coat color
Smoother hair on face
Smooth hair on throat forms V-shaped patch
Naturally oily, dense coat
Smooth tail except at base
Puce-liver coat forms dense ringlets
Large, round feet well covered with hair

AMERICAN WATER SPANIEL

THIS DOG IS EAGER TO PLEASE AND EASY TO CARE FOR

AKC

Height range
15–18in (38–45cm)

Weight range
26–46lb (12–21kg)

Life span 10–12 years

Origin USA

Other colors

Chocolate

May have a few white hairs on chest and toes.

Originally bred as an all-around hunting and water dog in the Great Lakes region of the United States, the American Water Spaniel's moderate size and lean build allowed it to work from boats as well as on shore. The breed is still used to flush and retrieve waterfowl, but also makes an easy-going companion for an active family. Its dense, curly coat is inherited from ancestors that include the Irish Water Spaniel (opposite) and the Curly Coated Retriever (see p.259). Some dogs have a less tightly curled coat, called the Marcel coat.

Broad head
Ears covered with curly hair
Light brown eyes
Tight, liver curls, oily to touch
Smooth hair on face
Moderate feathering along tail
Moderately feathered legs

Adult and puppy

SPANISH WATER DOG

AN ADAPTABLE WORKING DOG WITH A NO-NONSENSE ATTITUDE KC

Height range
16–20in (40–50cm)

Weight range
31–49lb (14–22kg)

Life span 10–14 years

Origin Spain

Other colors

White

Black

Brown and white

Black and white

This distinctive breed has had many roles and names in its homeland, where it is now called the Perro de Agua. Merchants from North Africa or Turkey may have brought this type of dog to Andalusia, where it is most likely to be found today. The Spanish Water Dog has been used for herding, hunting, and towing boats in ports. It is a biddable, generally level-headed companion but can be impatient with children. Until the 1980s the breed was known only in southern Spain, and it remains rare today.

Brown nose matches color of coat
Light chest markings
Tail barely reaches hocks
Back slopes gently down toward tail
Woolly, brown coat forms cords if left unclipped
Legs slightly shorter than body length
Round feet covered in hair

PORTUGUESE WATER DOG

ACTIVE AND INTELLIGENT, THIS DOG NEEDS AN OWNER TO MATCH AKC

Height range 17–22in (43–57cm)

Weight range 35–55lb (16–25kg)

Life span 10–14 years

Origin Portugal

Other colors

White

Brown

Black and white

Brown and white

Black and brown dogs may have white markings.

Although classed as a gundog, this dog was used to retrieve fishermen's nets as often as hunters' game. The breed's adaptability springs from a lively mind and desire to please, but if not kept busy it can be destructive. There are two coat types: long and wavy or short and curly.

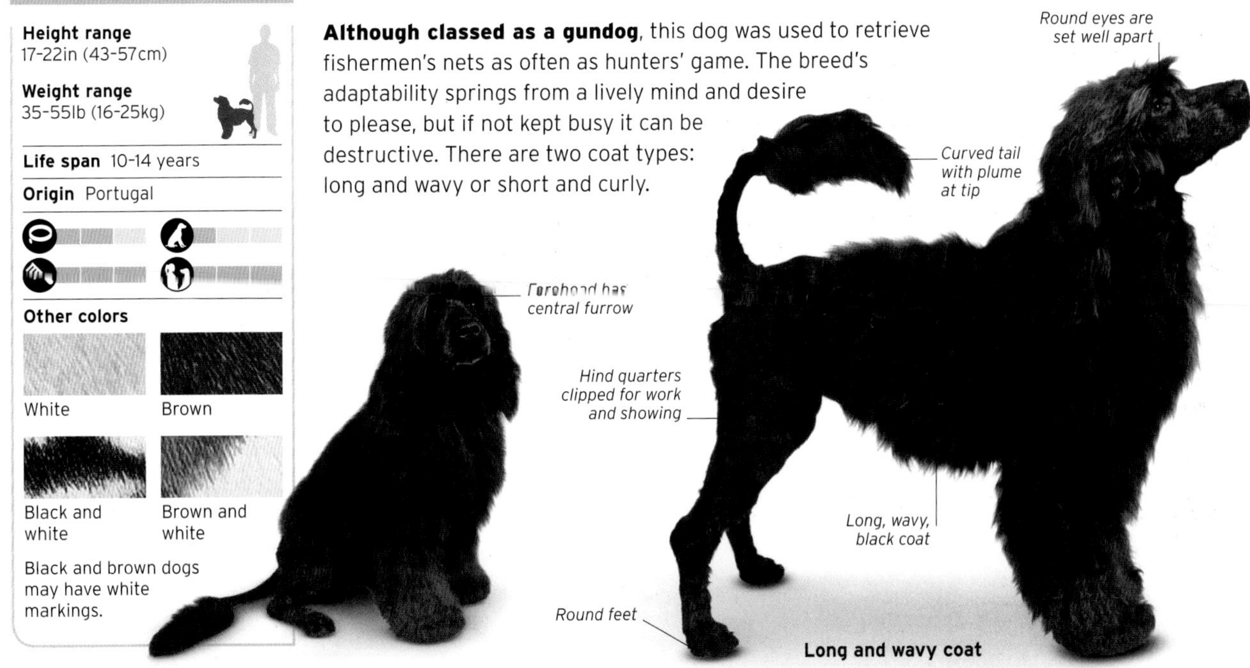
Round eyes are set well apart
Curved tail with plume at tip
Forehead has central furrow
Hind quarters clipped for work and showing
Long, wavy, black coat
Round feet

Long and wavy coat

POODLE (STANDARD)

THIS INTELLIGENT RETRIEVER DOG MAKES AN EASY FAMILY COMPANION AKC

Height range Over 15in (Over 38cm)

Weight range 46–71lb (21–32kg)

Life span 10–13 years

Origin Germany

Other colors

Any solid color

Claimed by France but probably from Germany, this breed was originally a water dog, and the standard size remains closest to those roots. It is popular for crossbreeding because it is robust, clever, and good-tempered. A simple all-over clip is easiest to maintain.

Dark, almond-shaped eyes

Strong, well-chiseled face and jaw

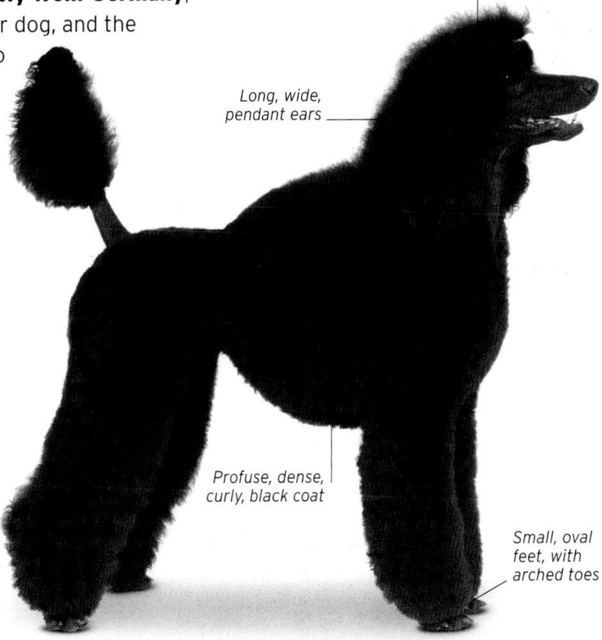

Head carried high

Long, wide, pendant ears

Profuse, dense, curly, black coat

Small, oval feet, with arched toes

FRENCH WATER DOG

THIS RELAXED, AFFECTIONATE DOG NEEDS DAILY GROOMING

FCI

Height range
21-26in (53-65cm)

Weight range
35-60lb (16-27kg)

Life span 12-14 years

Origin France

Other colors

Variety of colors

One of Europe's oldest water dogs, with ancestors dating back to the Middle Ages, the French Water Dog has contributed to many other breeds. Its coat is perfect protection for a working dog but its high maintenance may be one reason why this breed is no longer popular, despite its tolerant, friendly attitude to children and to other dogs.

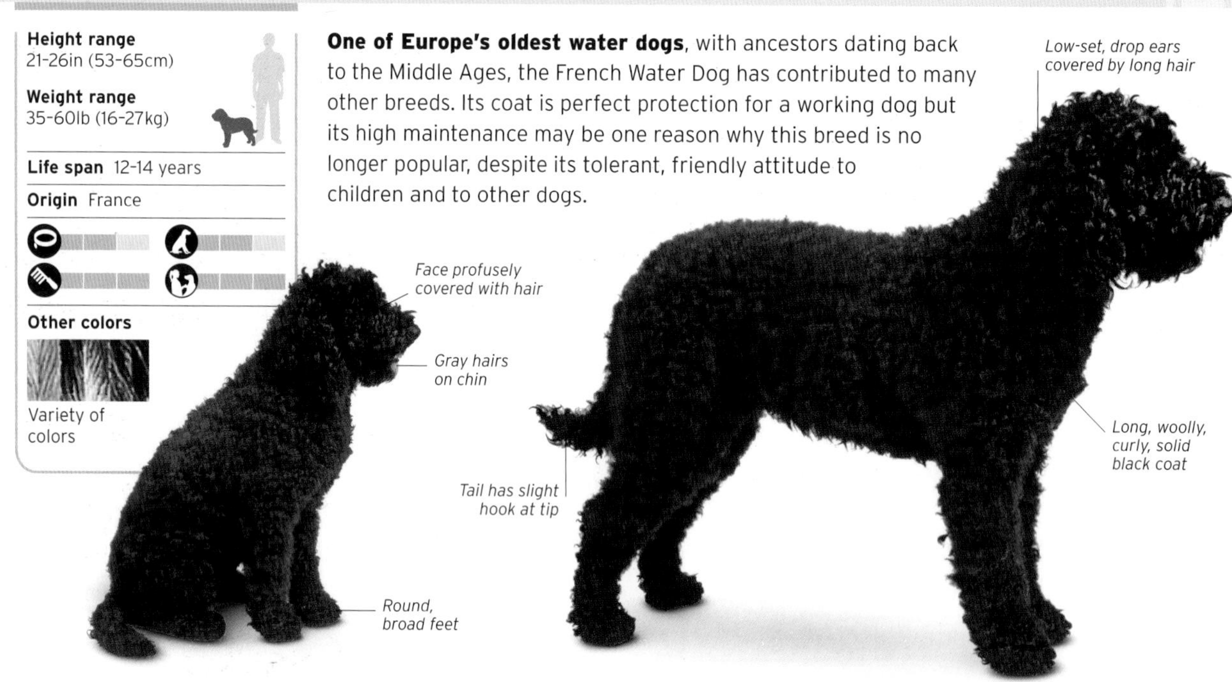

Low-set, drop ears covered by long hair
Face profusely covered with hair
Gray hairs on chin
Long, woolly, curly, solid black coat
Tail has slight hook at tip
Round, broad feet

FRISIAN WATER DOG

THIS CAPABLE, RESERVED BREED DOES BEST WITH A FIRM OWNER

FCI

Height range
22-23in (55-59cm)

Weight range
33-44lb (15-20kg)

Life span 12-13 years

Origin The Netherlands

Other colors

Dark brown

Also known as the Dutch Spaniel or Wetterhoun, this breed was originally used by fishermen to control otters. It is still used for flushing and retrieving, but also as a guard and farm dog. Its independent, slightly suspicious character makes it unsuitable for city living, but it is a reliable and rugged dog for a rural home.

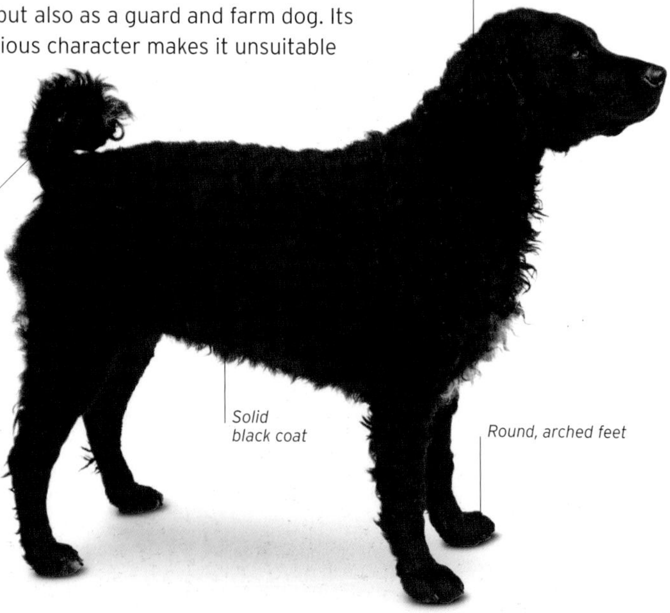

Low-set ears hang flat against head

Rounded top to head

Long tail curled into a ring

White chest markings

Solid black coat

Round, arched feet

CORDED POODLE

SMART AND FRIENDLY, THIS DOG IS WRAPPED IN EASY-CARE DREADLOCKS

Height range
9–24in (24–60cm)

Weight range
45–71lb (21–32kg)

Life span 10–13 years

Origin France

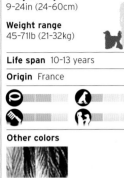

Other colors

Any color

Like other poodles, this is a friendly, intelligent, and level-headed dog that makes a good guard or companion. Corded Poodles have been bred from separate lines of the well-known Standard Poodle (see p.231) for many years but as yet are not recognized as a breed in their own right. Their look was popular in the 19th century but today is rarely seen—even in France. This kind of cording is more often found on herding breeds, offering protection against both weather and predators. Most poodle coats will cord with a little encouragement, and once the cords have formed, are fairly easy to look after.

Muzzle has straight bridge
Black, corded coat
Long, elegant, narrow head
Oblique, almond-shaped eyes
Ears covered with many cords
Level back
Fine, dense, corded, white coat

BRITTANY

THIS ADAPTABLE AND RELIABLE DOG IS IDEAL FOR AN ACTIVE OWNER AKC

Height range
19–20in (47–51cm)

Weight range
31–40lb (14–18kg)

Life span 12–14 years

Origin France

Other colors

Liver and white

Black and white

Black, tan, and white

Colors may be merged and not clearly defined (roan).

Also known as the Brittany Spaniel, and as the Epagneul Breton in its native France, this versatile gundog flushes and retrieves game but is best at simply locating game birds. An old-established breed, the Brittany almost disappeared in the 19th century but today has regained popularity both as a sporting dog and a good-natured family companion.

Muzzle tapered but not pointed
Oval, dark eyes
High-set tail carried just below back level
Orange flecking
Triangular, drop ears
Dense, fairly fine, slightly wavy, orange and white coat
Feathering on forelegs
Compact, round feet

LAGOTTO ROMAGNOLO

THIS AFFECTIONATE AND BOISTEROUS DOG IS BEST SUITED TO A COUNTRY LIFE KC

Height range
16–19in (41–48cm)

Weight range
24–35lb (11–16kg)

Life span 12–14 years

Origin Italy

Other colors

Orange

Brown

Roan

Orange and roan coats may have a brown mask.

This breed originally worked as a retriever in the marshland of northern Italy, then later as a truffle hound. Today it is bred as often for companionship as for work. The Lagotto Romagnolo is good-natured and likes to be kept busy. Its characteristic ringlet coat needs weekly combing and annual clipping.

Moderately large, triangular, drop ears with rounded tips

Liver-colored nose

Deep chest

Woolly, off-white coat forms tight ringlets

Curly, white coat with brown markings

Rounded, compact feet

PONT-AUDEMER SPANIEL

THIS ENGAGING BREED IS ENERGETIC OUTDOORS BUT RELAXED IN THE HOME

FCI

Height range 20–23in (51–58cm)

Weight range 40–53lb (18–24kg)

Life span 12–14 years

Origin France

Other colors

Brown

This French pointer and retriever is a specialist at hunting in water and swampland. The breed is thought to have been developed in the 19th century, and may include the Irish Water Spaniel (see p.228) in its ancestry. The Pont-Audemer Spaniel has never been well known, even in France, and by the 20th century was nearly extinct. It survived in small numbers and is still used for hunting but also makes a gentle house dog. The curly, slightly ruffled-looking coat is not particularly difficult to maintain, though it does need regular care.

Drop ears covered with long, silky hair
Deep, broad chest reaches elbows
Rounded skull with topknot of curly hair
Long, slightly pointed muzzle
Small, dark amber eyes
Tail slightly curved with lighter-colored tip
Curly, disheveled-looking, brown coat with gray and brown mottlings
Round feet with long, curly hair between toes

SMALL MUNSTERLANDER

A LIVELY, INTELLIGENT DOG STILL USED MAINLY FOR HUNTING

KC

Height range 20-21in (52-54cm)

Weight range 40-60lb (18-27kg)

Life span 13-14 years

Origin Germany

One German name for the breed, Heidewachtel or "heath quail dog," describes this dog's first purpose of flushing game birds. Although it is a cheerful and affectionate companion, hunters quickly snap up almost all of the small numbers that are bred each year. Despite its name, this breed is not directly related to the Large Munsterlander (below).

White blaze on head
Medium-length, well-feathered tail
Well-feathered, broad ears
Silky, brown coat
White legs with brown mottling

LARGE MUNSTERLANDER

THIS HUNTING DOG IS HAPPIEST IN THE HOME

KC

Height range 23-26in (58-65cm)

Weight range 64-68lb (29-31kg)

Life span 12-13 years

Origin Germany

The Grosser Munsterlander, as it is called in Germany, is more closely related to the German pointers than the Small Munsterlander (above). It is slow to mature, but makes a calm, highly trainable, and versatile gundog. It positively thrives on close human company and is good with children.

Black mantle
Solid black head
White hairs at tip of snout
Long, dense coat provides insulation
White coat with black flecking
Legs are well feathered

FRISIAN POINTING DOG

THIS ADAPTABLE, ROBUST FARM DOG IS EASY TO LIVE WITH FCI

Height range 20–21in (50–53cm)

Weight range 42–55lb (19–25kg)

Life span 12–14 years

Origin The Netherlands

Other colors

Orange with white markings.

Bred by farmers, this dog, also known as the Stabyhoun, tracks, points, and retrieves alongside hunters. It makes an active and even-tempered family companion, and is excellent with children. This breed, despite efforts to improve its numbers, remains rare even in its native land.

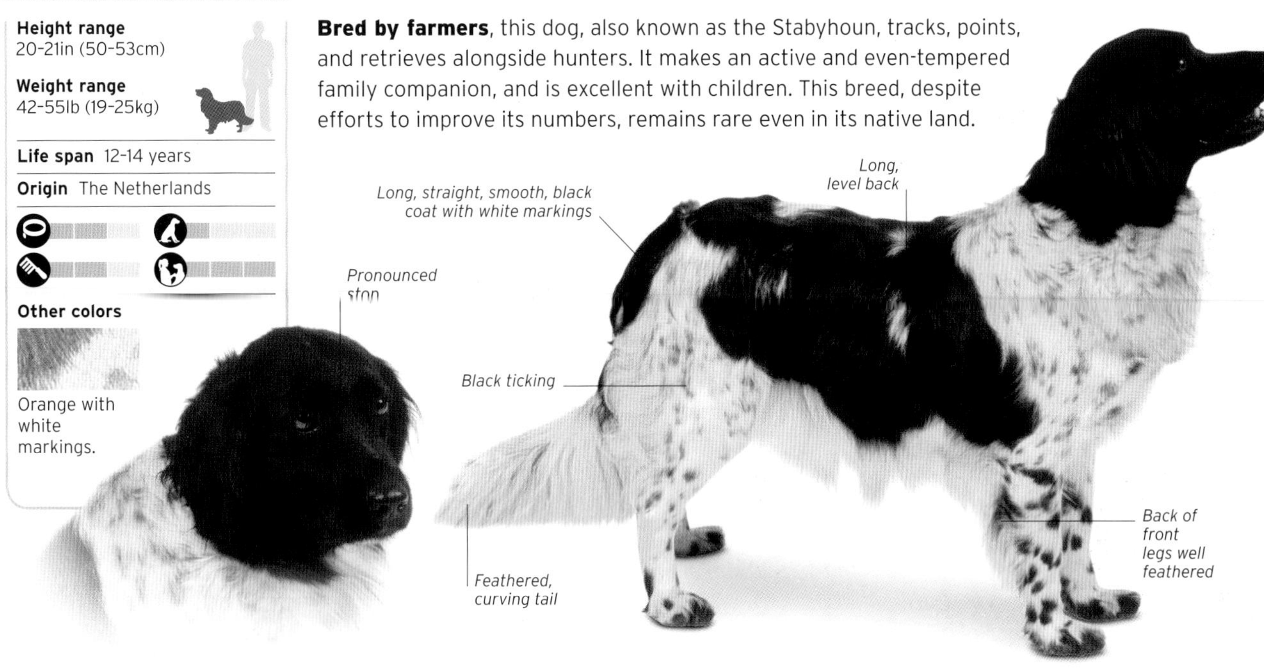
Long, level back
Long, straight, smooth, black coat with white markings
Pronounced stop
Black ticking
Feathered, curving tail
Back of front legs well feathered

DRENTSCHE PARTRIDGE DOG

A DEDICATED HUNTING DOG, BUT CALM ENOUGH FOR CITY LIFE FCI

Height range 22–25in (55–63cm)

Weight range 44–55lb (20–25kg)

Life span 12–13 years

Origin The Netherlands

Somewhere between a pointer and a retriever, the Drentsche Partridge Dog, or Patrijshond, is a typically versatile European hunting dog related to the Small Munsterlander (opposite) and the French Spaniel (see p.240). It makes a reliable and relaxed family companion as long as it has enough activity.

Oval, amber eyes

Brown markings

Well-feathered tail

Wavy, white coat

Brown spots on legs

Drop ears covered with long, silky hair

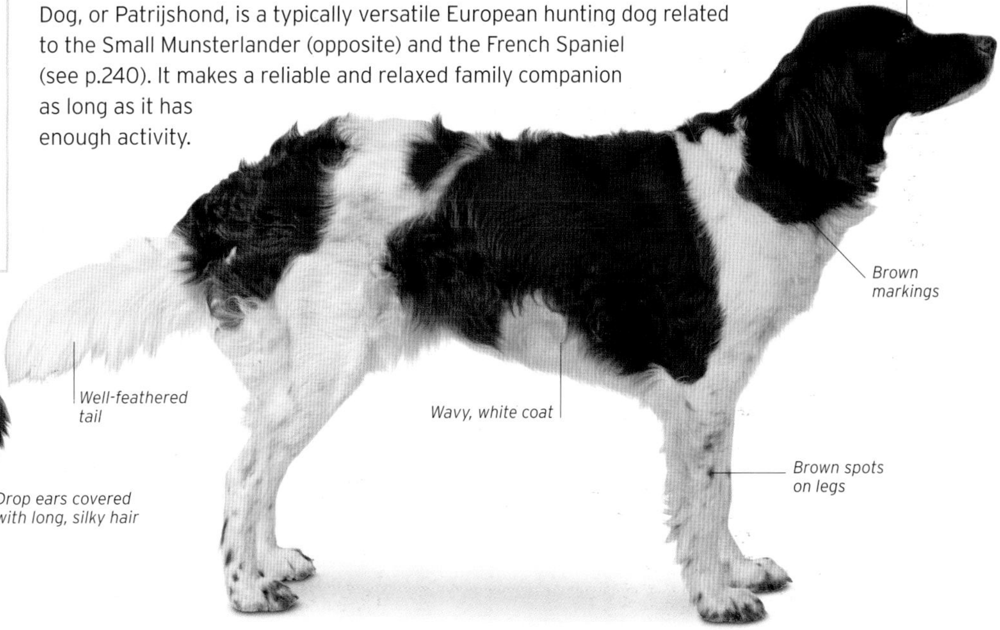

KOOIKERHONDJE

THIS CHEERFUL, ENERGETIC DOG IS NOT SUITED TO CITY LIFE KC

Height range
14–16in (35–40cm)

Weight range
20–24lb (9–11kg)

Life span 12–13 years

Origin The Netherlands

This breed goes by several other names, including Dutch Decoy Spaniel, which describes its original and unusual role. Romping and waving its flag-like tail, never barking, it was used for centuries to lure and drive curious waterfowl into tunnel traps or "kooien" for hunters to catch alive—a task it still performs today for researchers wanting to tag and release birds. It is a rare breed, but its working history makes it a playful, good-natured dog that is dedicated to its owners, although can be aloof with strangers.

White blaze on face
Drop ears covered in long, silky hair
Alert, almond-shaped, deep brown eyes
Sleek, slightly wavy, white coat with orange-red patches
Shorter hair on face
Well-feathered tail
Long hair on neck forms ruff
Feathering on back of front legs
Small, hare-like feet

PICARDY SPANIEL

THIS DOG LOVES OPEN SPACES BUT MAKES A CALM COMPANION AT HOME FCI

Height range 22-24in (55-60cm)

Weight range 44-55lb (20-25kg)

Life span 12-14 years

Origin France

One of the oldest spaniel breeds, the Picardy Spaniel is still used in France to flush birds in woodland and wetland areas. An enthusiastic swimmer, it makes a placid, reliable, and affectionate family dog, which will even adapt to city life if given a reasonable amount of exercise.

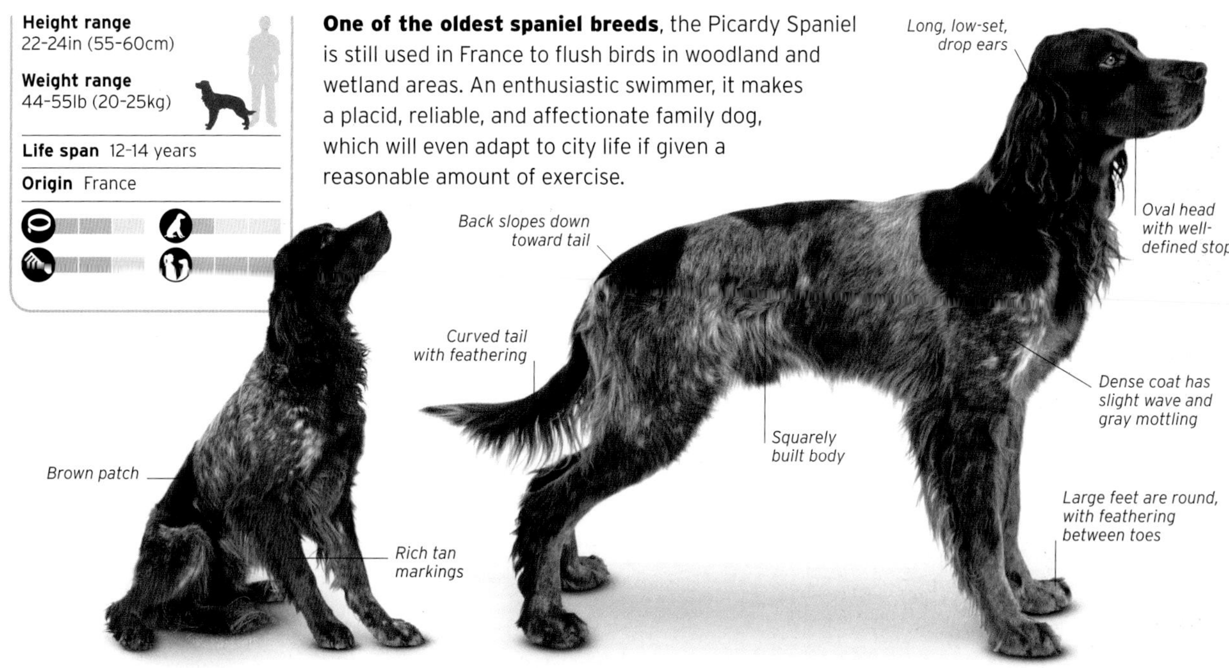
Long, low-set, drop ears
Oval head with well-defined stop
Back slopes down toward tail
Curved tail with feathering
Dense coat has slight wave and gray mottling
Squarely built body
Brown patch
Large feet are round, with feathering between toes
Rich tan markings

BLUE PICARDY SPANIEL

THIS PLAYFUL, GENTLE SPANIEL LOVES PLENTY OF ATTENTION AND EXERCISE FCI

Height range 23-24in (57-60cm)

Weight range 44-46lb (20-21kg)

Life span 11-13 years

Origin France

Mainly used as a water dog for pointing and retrieving snipe in marshland, this quiet and easy-going breed is a fun-loving companion and good with children. However, the Blue Picardy Spaniel's friendly temperament means that it is of little use for guarding.

Well-defined stop
Slightly wavy coat with black patches
Lighter-colored blaze
Pendulous flews
Tail about hock length
Long, drop ears are covered with wavy hair
Gray-black speckling gives bluish shade to coat
Tight, round feet have plenty of hair between toes

FRENCH SPANIEL

THIS FRIENDLY, ELEGANT GUNDOG IS HAPPY ON CITY STREETS OR IN WIDE OPEN SPACES FCI

Height range
22-24in (55-61cm)

Weight range
44-55lb (20-25kg)

Life span 12-14 years

Origin France

In its native land the French Spaniel is claimed to be the original of all hunting spaniels. It is still used for hunting at home and abroad, but because it is level-headed and not inclined to bark, it also makes a good city dog, as long as it is given enough exercise and affection.

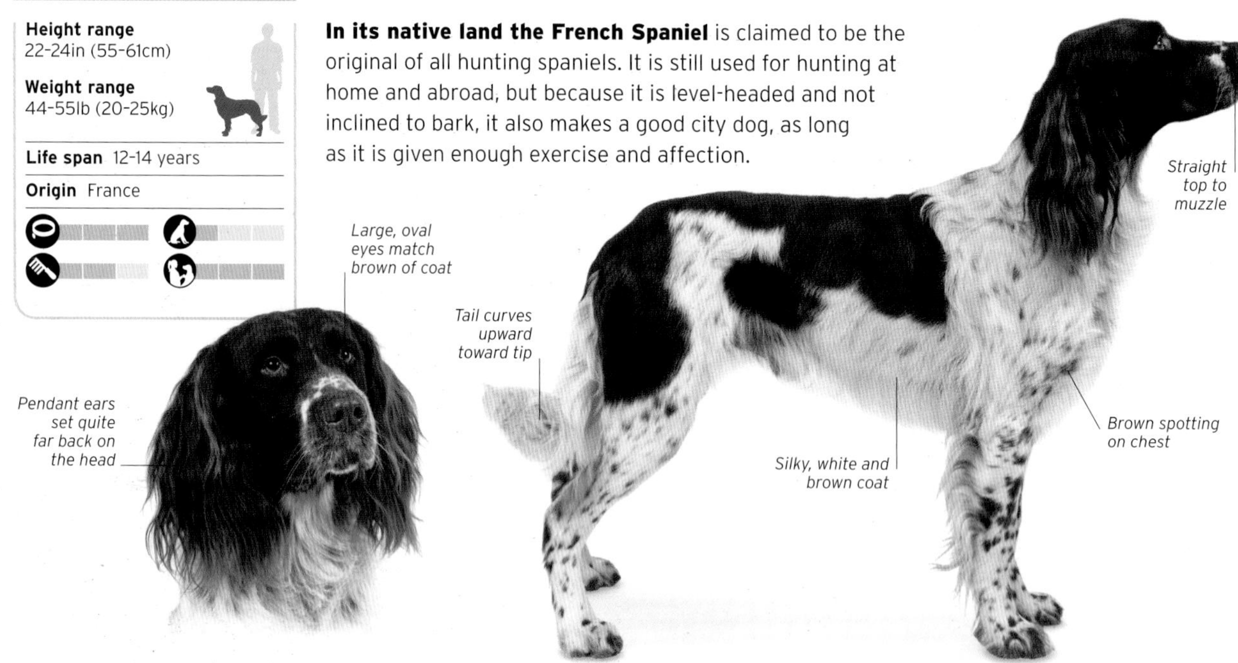

Large, oval eyes match brown of coat
Pendant ears set quite far back on the head
Tail curves upward toward tip
Silky, white and brown coat
Brown spotting on chest
Straight top to muzzle

ENGLISH SETTER

THE PERFECT COUNTRY-HOUSE DOG IN BOTH LOOKS AND CHARACTER AKC

Height range
24-25in (61-64cm)

Weight range
55-65lb (25-30kg)

Life span 12-13 years

Origin UK

Other colors

Orange or lemon belton

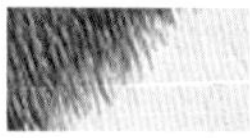

Liver belton

Liver beltons may have tan markings.

Developed to track, set, and retrieve birds, this breed is still worked today, although different bloodlines are used for hunting or home life. Elegant in appearance, the English Setter is a cheerful and tireless companion that needs a good deal of space and activity, but has a calm and reliable temperament.

Light tan marks on face

Square muzzle with slightly pendulous flews

Well-feathered tail

Blue belton coat

Low-set, pendant ears

IRISH SETTER

AN EXUBERANT, ENTHUSIASTIC BREED FOR A PATIENT AND ACTIVE OWNER

AKC

Height range
25-27in (64-69cm)

Weight range
60-71lb (27-32kg)

Life span 12-13 years

Origin Ireland

The red dog, or Modder Rhu, of Ireland started out as a hunting dog and is still an effective worker, but today is more commonly kept as a striking and spirited companion. Slow to mature, it needs firm training from an early age. The breed's devil-may-care attitude and tendency to get into scrapes when young can try an owner's patience, but its sociable nature and zest for life make it worth the extra effort. It does not simply tolerate other dogs and children, but actively seeks them out to play with.

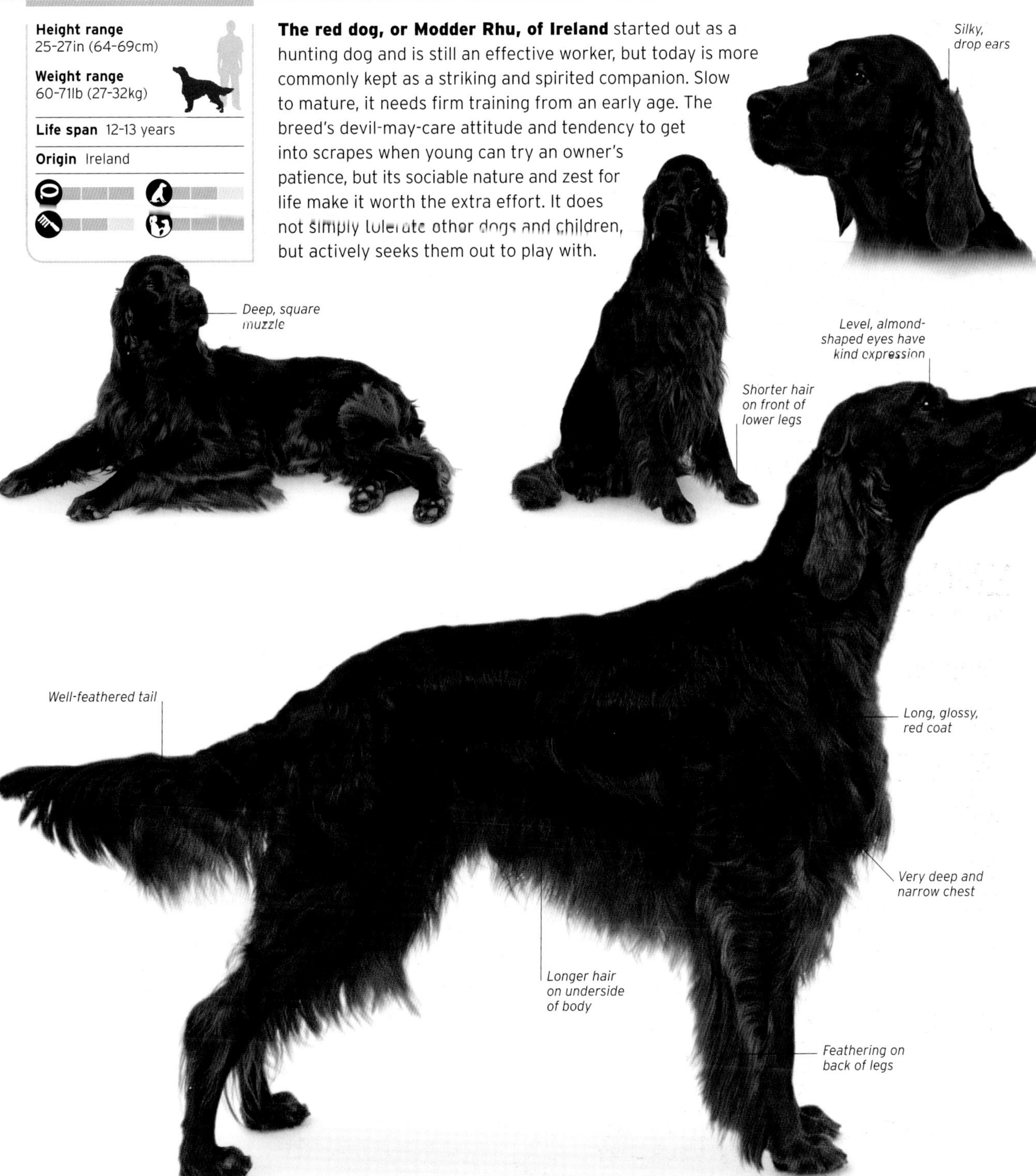
Silky, drop ears
Deep, square muzzle
Level, almond-shaped eyes have kind expression
Shorter hair on front of lower legs
Well-feathered tail
Long, glossy, red coat
Very deep and narrow chest
Longer hair on underside of body
Feathering on back of legs

IRISH RED AND WHITE SETTER

THIS PLAYFUL DOG IS SLOW TO MATURE, BUT IT IS WORTH THE WAIT

AKC

Height range
25-27in (64-69cm)

Weight range
55-75lb (25-34kg)

Life span 12-13 years

Origin Ireland

This setter has the red and white coloring that is typical of many hunting dogs, but today it is more often kept for company. Long overshadowed by the related Irish Setter (see p.241), this intelligent if impulsive breed is slowly gaining the popularity it deserves. Cheerful and energetic, it thrives on attention and firm guidance.

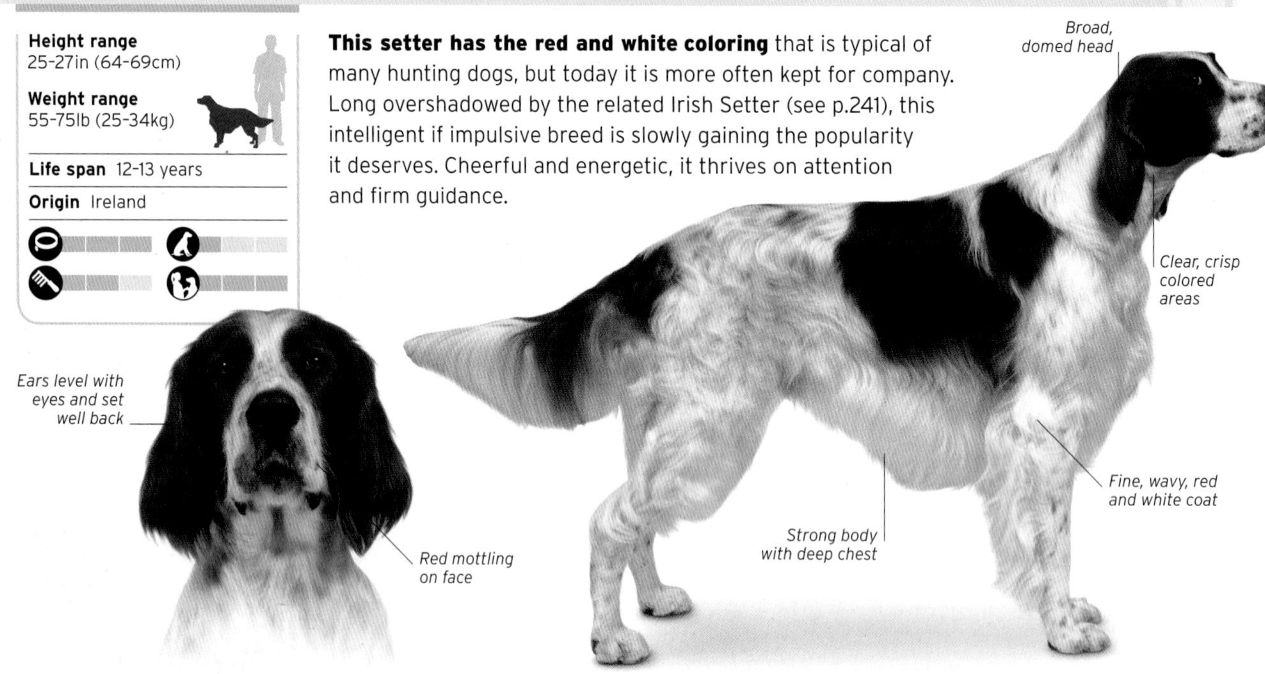
Broad, domed head
Clear, crisp colored areas
Ears level with eyes and set well back
Fine, wavy, red and white coat
Strong body with deep chest
Red mottling on face

GORDON SETTER

AN OUTGOING BUT OBEDIENT CHARACTER BRED FOR WIDE OPEN SPACES

AKC

Height range
24-26in (62-66cm)

Weight range
57-66lb (26-30kg)

Life span 12-13 years

Origin UK

Originally employed in Scotland to track game birds and then freeze once it had located them, changes in hunting fashions have seen this breed move from field to fireside. It brings with it a level-headed and loyal nature, but also a need for daily, vigorous exercise and a good deal of space.

Lean, long neck

Deep head with slightly rounded skull

Shiny, coal-black coat

Fringe on belly may extend to throat

Full feathering on long, muscular thighs

Typical chestnut-red marking on feet and lower legs

NOVA SCOTIA DUCK TOLLING RETRIEVER

THIS GUNDOG HAS ADAPTED WELL TO THE FAMILY ENVIRONMENT

AKC

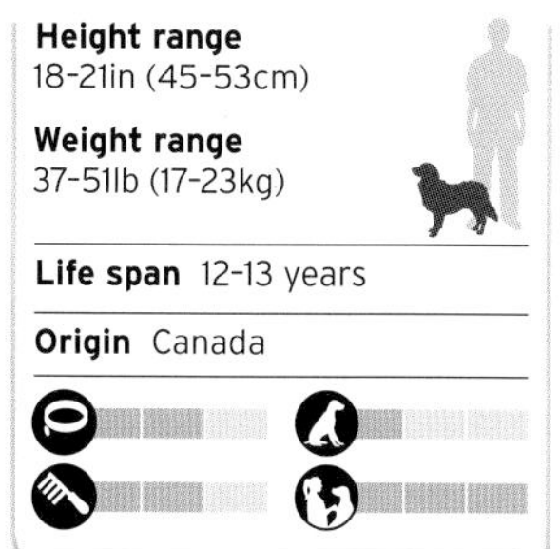

Height range
18–21in (45–53cm)

Weight range
37–51lb (17–23kg)

Life span 12–13 years

Origin Canada

This breed takes its name from its role in an unusual form of duck and goose hunting. The dog used to retrieve sticks—thrown by hunters in a hide—with a great show of activity but no barking, and this would lure in, or "toll," inquisitive birds. Once the birds were in range, the hunters could shoot them and the dog would retrieve them. The ideal dog for this role, its playful, quiet, and obedient qualities make it an excellent companion breed. It is also tireless, so needs plenty of exercise.

Almond-shaped eyes have alert expression

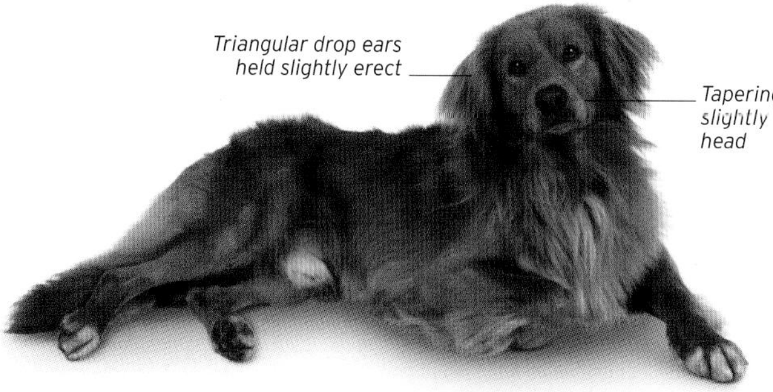

Triangular drop ears held slightly erect

Tapering muzzle with slightly wedge-shaped head

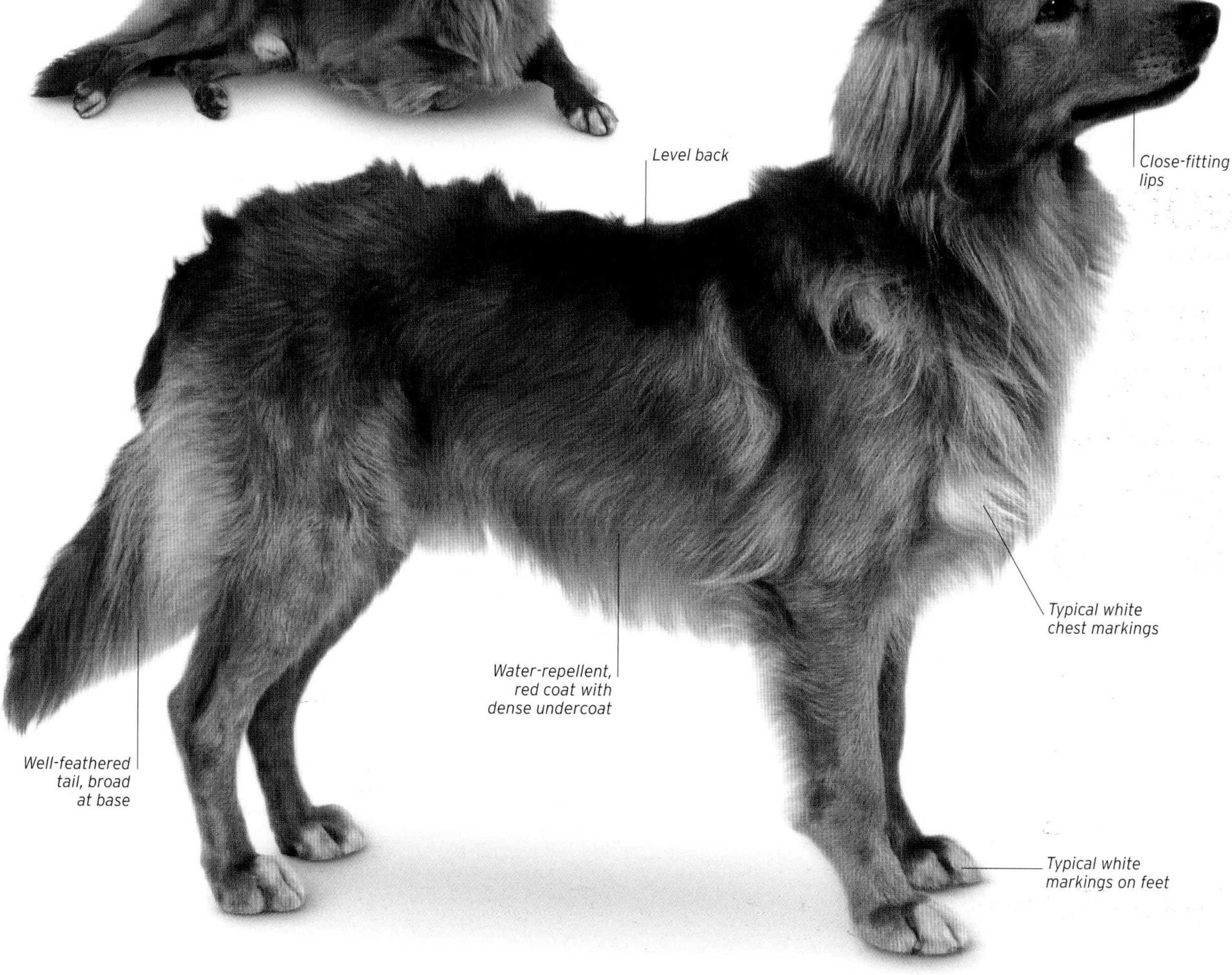

Level back

Close-fitting lips

Typical white chest markings

Water-repellent, red coat with dense undercoat

Well-feathered tail, broad at base

Typical white markings on feet

GERMAN SHORTHAIRED POINTER

THIS INTELLIGENT BREED IS GENIAL AND GENTLE IF KEPT BUSY

AKC

Height range
21–25in (53–64cm)

Weight range
44–71lb (20–32kg)

Life span 10–14 years

Origin Germany

Other colors

Liver

Brown

Black

A superlative hunting dog, which tracks, points, and retrieves over any terrain from heathland to marshland, the German Shorthaired Pointer or Deutsch Kurzhaar is a loyal, obedient breed. In its homeland it has always been kept for the home as well as the hunt, and the breed is generally level-headed and reliable. This is an energetic dog, and individuals can become hyperactive and destructive if they are not given enough exercise. There are three coat types: wire-haired, long-haired, and short-haired. By far the best known is the German Shorthaired Pointer, called GSP by hunters in the UK.

Brown nose
Short-haired
Broad, drop ears, rounded at tips
Wirehaired
Well-defined stop
Medium-sized, brown eyes
Liver patch
Tapering tail with white tip, carried low
Tucked-up belly
Liver coat with white ticking, coarse to touch
Spoon-shaped, compact feet
Shorthaired

CESKY FOUSEK

THIS RURAL BREED IS INTELLIGENT AND ROBUST BUT MAY BE HEADSTRONG FCI

Height range
23-26in (58-66cm)

Weight range
49-75lb (22-34kg)

Life span 12-13 years

Origin Czech Republic

Other colors

Brown

Brown coats may have ticked markings on chest and lower limbs.

This breed, variously claimed to be of Czech, Slovakian, or Bohemian descent, is still a popular hunting dog in these areas but is rare elsewhere. It is loyal and trainable, and usually gentle around people, but is a natural hunter and so may be unreliable with other pets.

Distinctive, bushy eyebrows
Large, drop ears
Tail traditionally docked to two-fifths of length
Beard of soft hair
Deep-set, amber eyes with kind expression
Hard, protective, dark roan coat with brown patches
Brown nose
Compact, spoon-shaped feet

WIREHAIRED POINTING GRIFFON

THIS RUGGED AND RELIABLE BREED IS A FRIENDLY TOWN OR COUNTRY COMPANION AKC

Height range
20-24in (50-60cm)

Weight range
50-60lb (23-27kg)

Life span 12-13 years

Origin The Netherlands

Other colors

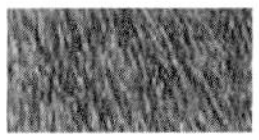

Liver

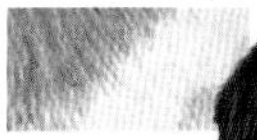

White and orange

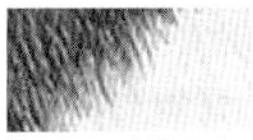

Roan, white, and brown

Related to the German Shorthaired Pointer (opposite), bred by Dutchman Edward Korthals, and adopted by French hunters, this is a versatile and easy-going breed. It is not the fastest gundog but is popular for hunting where obedient, close-working dogs are needed—qualities that also make it a valuable companion.

Body length exceeds leg length

Hairy eyebrows

Shorter, liver hair on ears

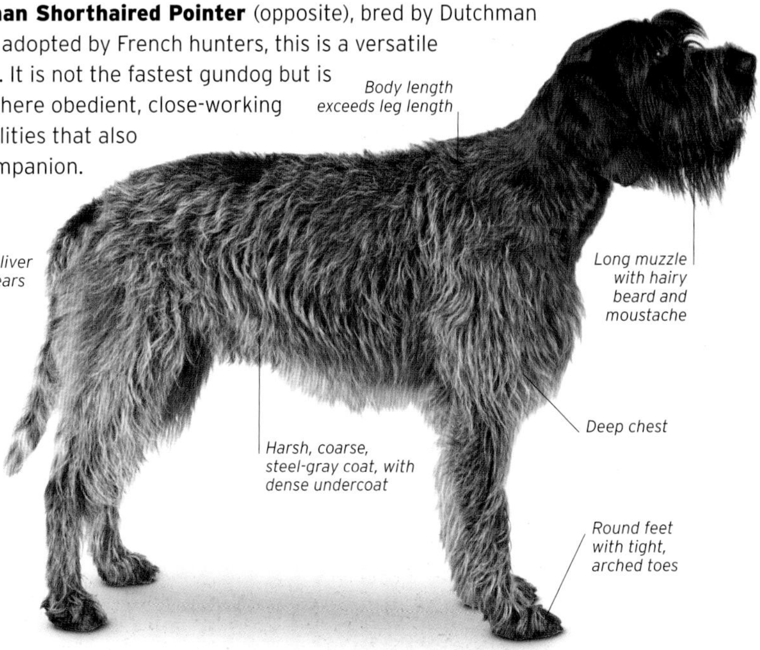

Long muzzle with hairy beard and moustache

Deep chest

Harsh, coarse, steel-gray coat, with dense undercoat

Round feet with tight, arched toes

WEIMARANER

THIS BEAUTIFUL, INTELLIGENT DOG NEEDS PLENTY OF SPACE AKC

Height range
22–27in (56–69cm)

Weight range
55–90lb (25–41kg)

Life span 12–13 years

Origin Germany

Created as an all-purpose hunting, pointing, and retrieving gundog, this 19th-century breed, nicknamed the "Gray Ghost," is a careful, almost stealthy dog in the field. While the Weimaraner may be reserved with strangers, it is a bouncy family companion and can be too boisterous for small children. Elegant lines, striking color, and grace in movement have contributed to this breed's popularity both as a pet and working dog, but it can stay active for hours, and needs an owner with similar stamina. There are two coat types: long-haired and short-haired.

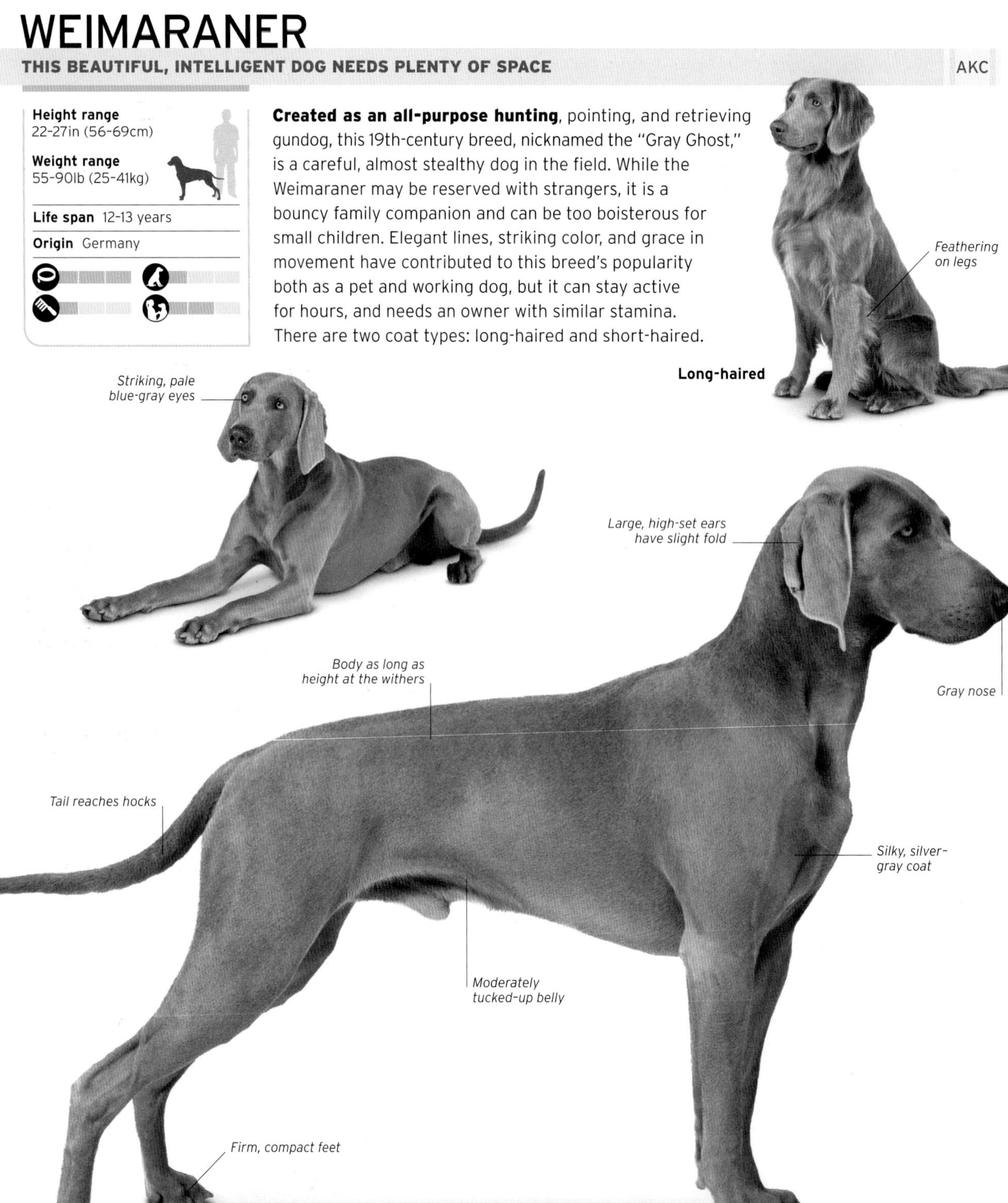
Feathering on legs
Striking, pale blue-gray eyes
Large, high-set ears have slight fold
Body as long as height at the withers
Gray nose
Tail reaches hocks
Silky, silver-gray coat
Moderately tucked-up belly
Firm, compact feet

Long-haired

Short-haired

VIZSLA

THIS LOYAL AND GENTLE DOG IS HIGH-ENERGY BUT LOW MAINTENANCE AKC

Height range
21–25in (53–64cm)

Weight range
44–66lb (20–30kg)

Life span 13–14 years

Origin Hungary

A typical European all-purpose hunting dog thought to date back to the 16th century, the short-haired version of the Vizsla is also known as the Hungarian Short-haired Pointer. It almost died out in World War II, but has since risen in popularity both with hunters and as a family companion. Extremely affectionate, the Vizsla is intelligent and responds well to training. It has almost boundless energy and will seek and retrieve sticks as readily as it will game—all day if allowed. The wire-haired variety, which was developed in the 1930s, has a stronger build than the smooth-haired Vizsla.

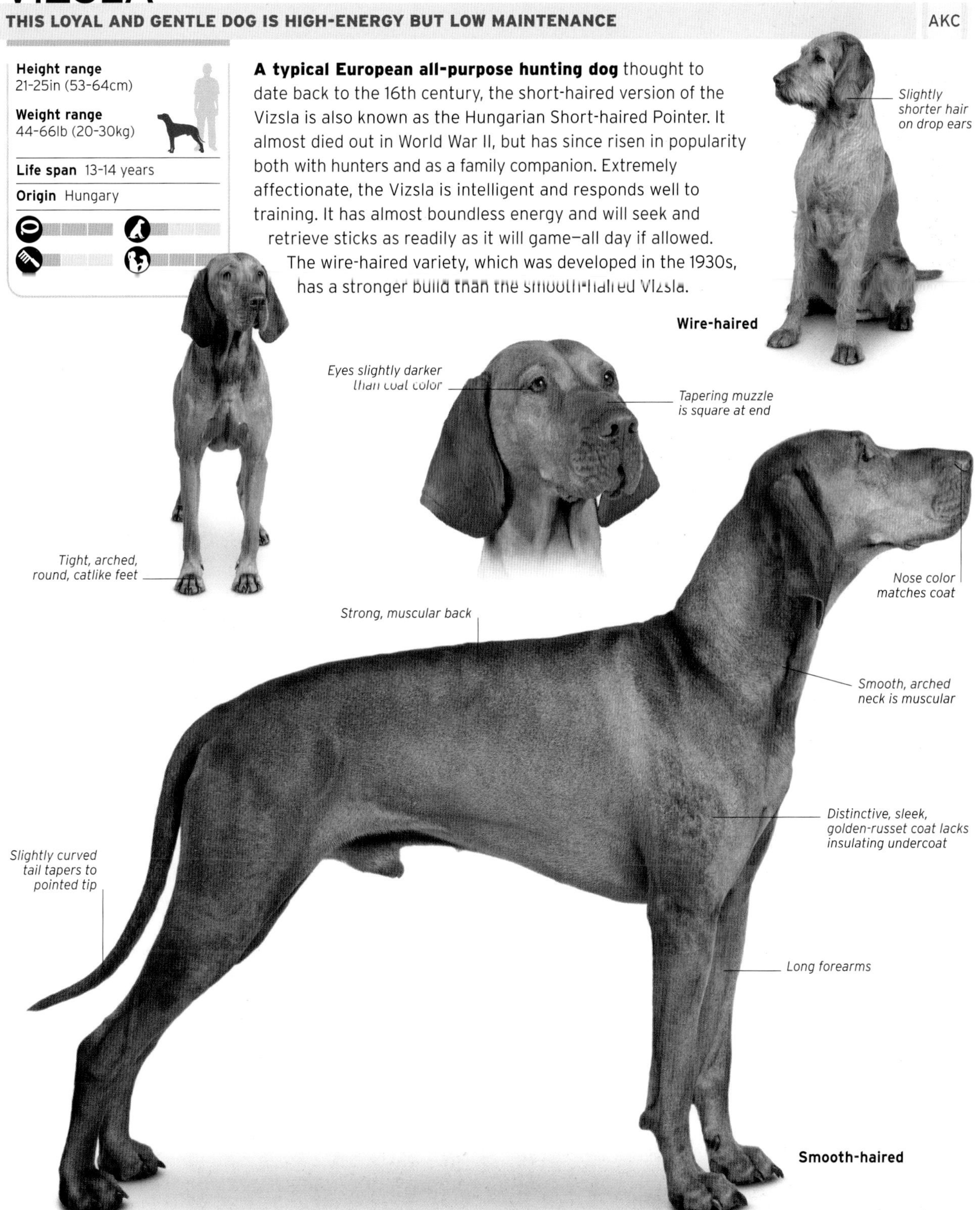
Slightly shorter hair on drop ears
Wire-haired
Eyes slightly darker than coat color
Tapering muzzle is square at end
Tight, arched, round, catlike feet
Nose color matches coat
Strong, muscular back
Smooth, arched neck is muscular
Distinctive, sleek, golden-russet coat lacks insulating undercoat
Slightly curved tail tapers to pointed tip
Long forearms
Smooth-haired

PORTUGUESE POINTING DOG

THIS TIRELESS AND ADAPTABLE HUNTING DOG IS BEST SUITED TO A WORKING LIFE FCI

Height range 20-22in (52-56cm)

Weight range 35-60lb (16-27kg)

Life span 12-14 years

Origin Portugal

Locally known as the Perdigueiro Português, which literally means the Portuguese partridge dog, this breed was used as a pointer for hunters with falcons or nets. Still worked today, the Portuguese Pointing Dog is level-headed and biddable and so also makes an amenable companion. However, this tenacious hunter needs considerable mental and physical activity every day.

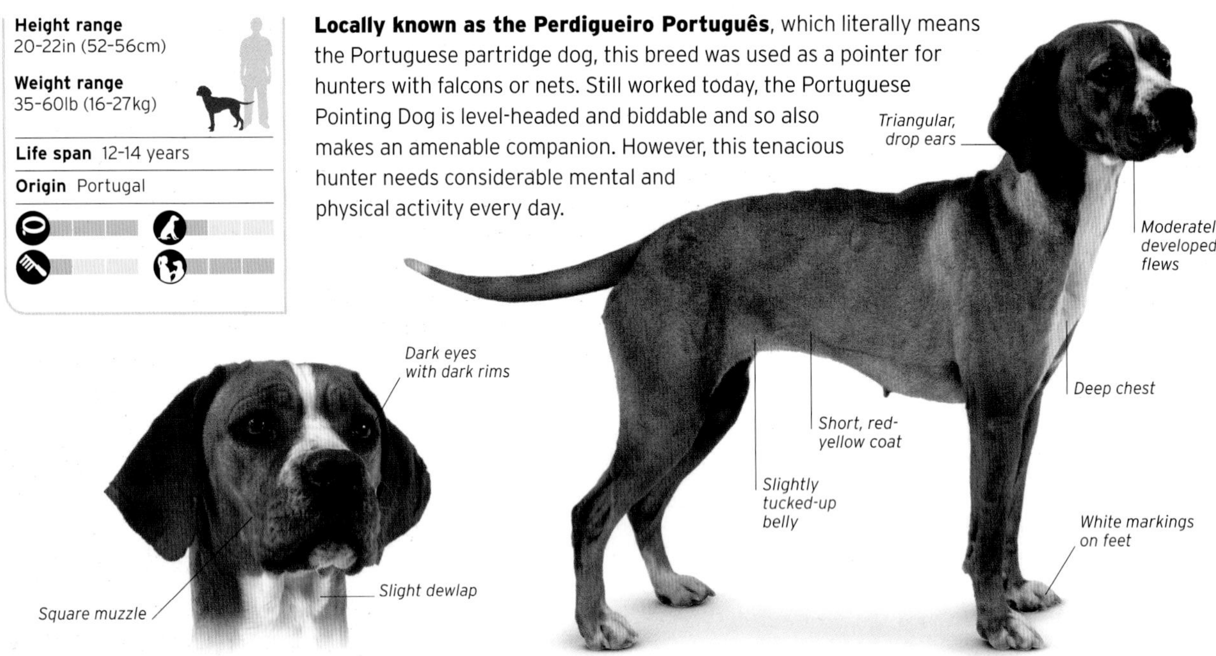
Triangular, drop ears
Moderately developed flews
Deep chest
Short, red-yellow coat
Slightly tucked-up belly
White markings on feet
Dark eyes with dark rims
Slight dewlap
Square muzzle

BRACCO ITALIANO

THIS RARE BREED IS ATHLETIC AND GOOD WITH CHILDREN KC

Height range 22-26in (55-67cm)

Weight range 55-88lb (25-40kg)

Life span 12-13 years

Origin Italy

Other colors

White

White and gold or chestnut

Dogs similar to the Bracco Italiano, or Italian Pointer, can be seen in paintings from the 14th century, when they were used to drive game birds into nets. Still used as a working dog today, this breed also makes a level-headed and gentle companion, though it can be stubborn at times.

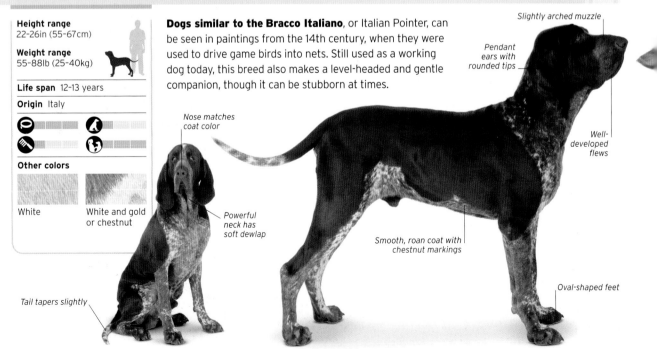

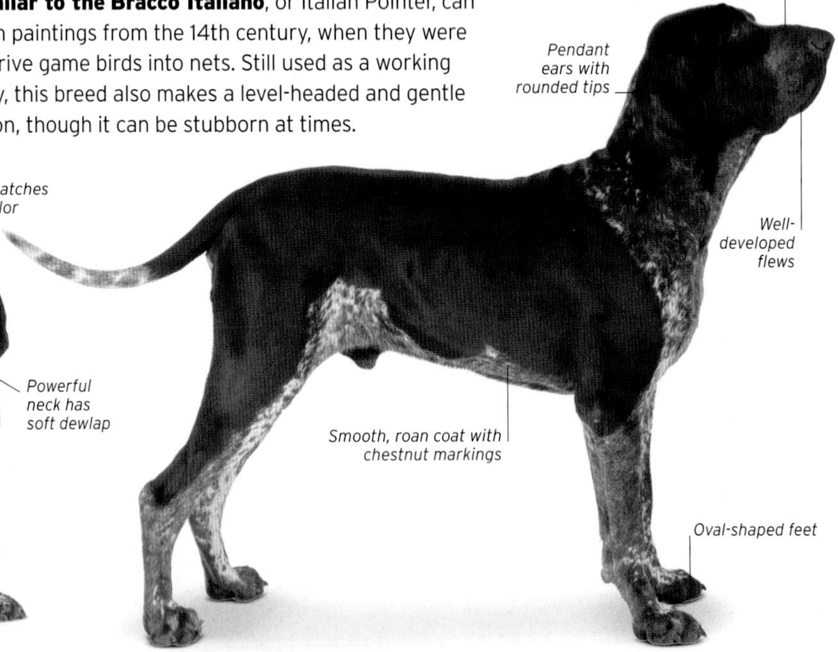

Slightly arched muzzle

Pendant ears with rounded tips

Well-developed flews

Nose matches coat color

Powerful neck has soft dewlap

Smooth, roan coat with chestnut markings

Oval-shaped feet

Tail tapers slightly

SPINONE ITALIANO

THIS EASY-GOING AND RELAXED COMPANION IS NOT IDEAL FOR HOUSE-PROUD OWNERS

AKC

Height range
23-28in (58-70cm)

Weight range
64-86lb (29-39kg)

Life span 12-13 years

Origin Italy

Other colors

White

Orange roan

White and brown or brown roan

This versatile tracker and retriever from northern Italy was the region's most popular hunting breed until the 20th century, and is still worked—its shaggy coat is useful protection in heavy undergrowth. More recently it has become a popular companion breed, prized for its gentle temperament and loyalty. An inclination to move at a slightly slower pace than many gundogs makes the Spinone Italiano a comfortable walking companion. This breed is for those who love the "doggy" nature of dogs: the coarse coat may not be high maintenance but does retain smells, and the breed has a tendency to drool.

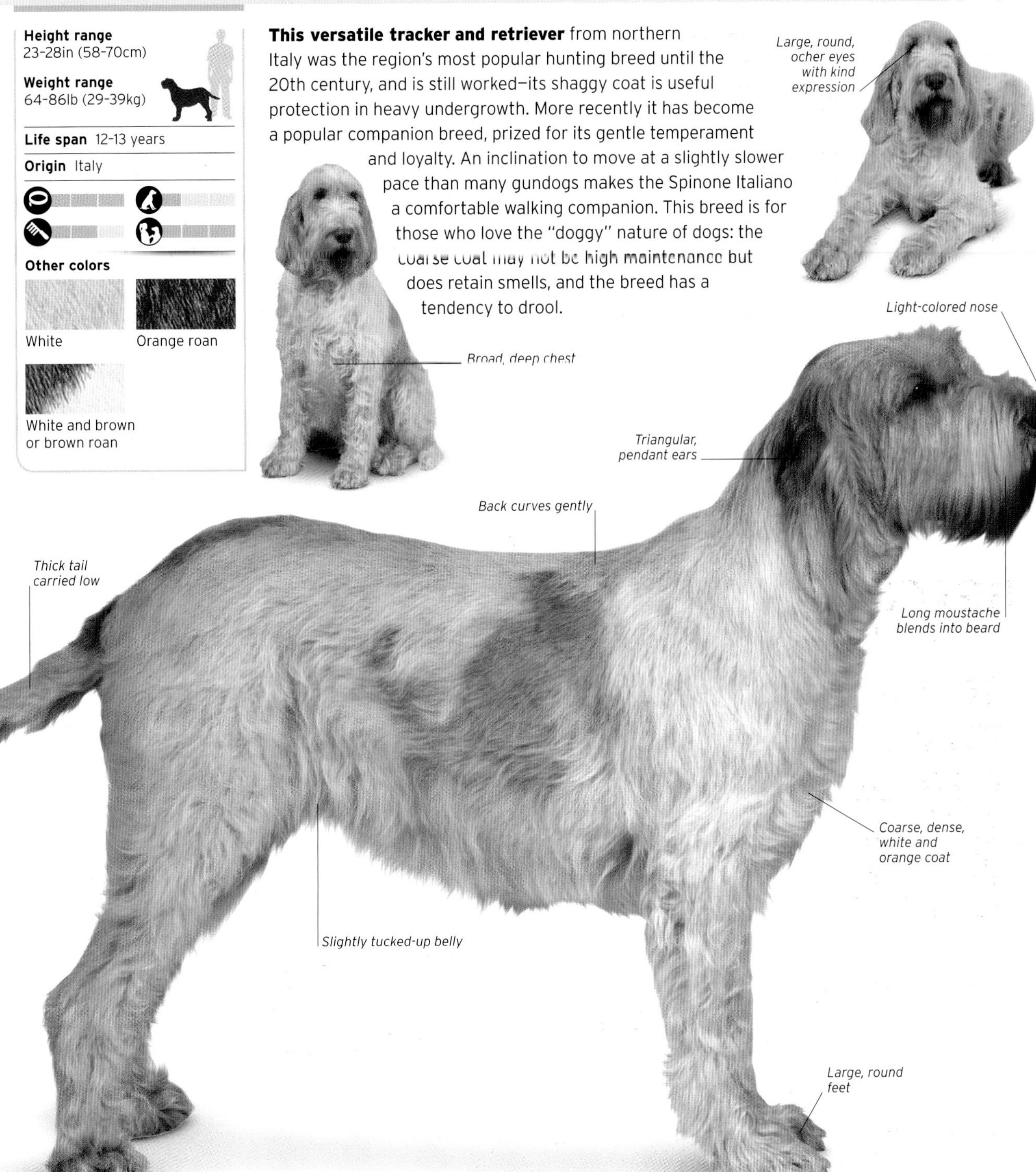
Large, round, ocher eyes with kind expression
Broad, deep chest
Light-colored nose
Triangular, pendant ears
Back curves gently
Thick tail carried low
Long moustache blends into beard
Coarse, dense, white and orange coat
Slightly tucked-up belly
Large, round feet

FRENCH PYRENEAN POINTER

A GRACEFUL DOG SUITED TO OUTDOOR-LOVING OWNERS FCI

Height range
19-23in (47-58cm)

Weight range
40-53lb (18-24kg)

Life span 12-14 years

Origin France

Other colors

Chestnut-brown

Chestnut-brown dogs may have tan markings.

The most popular of the French pointers, the French Pyrenean Pointer is still rare and mostly used for hunting. A swift and tireless breed, it was created in southwest France to work in mountain terrain. It is gentle and affectionate at home, and makes an ideal companion for the more active owner.

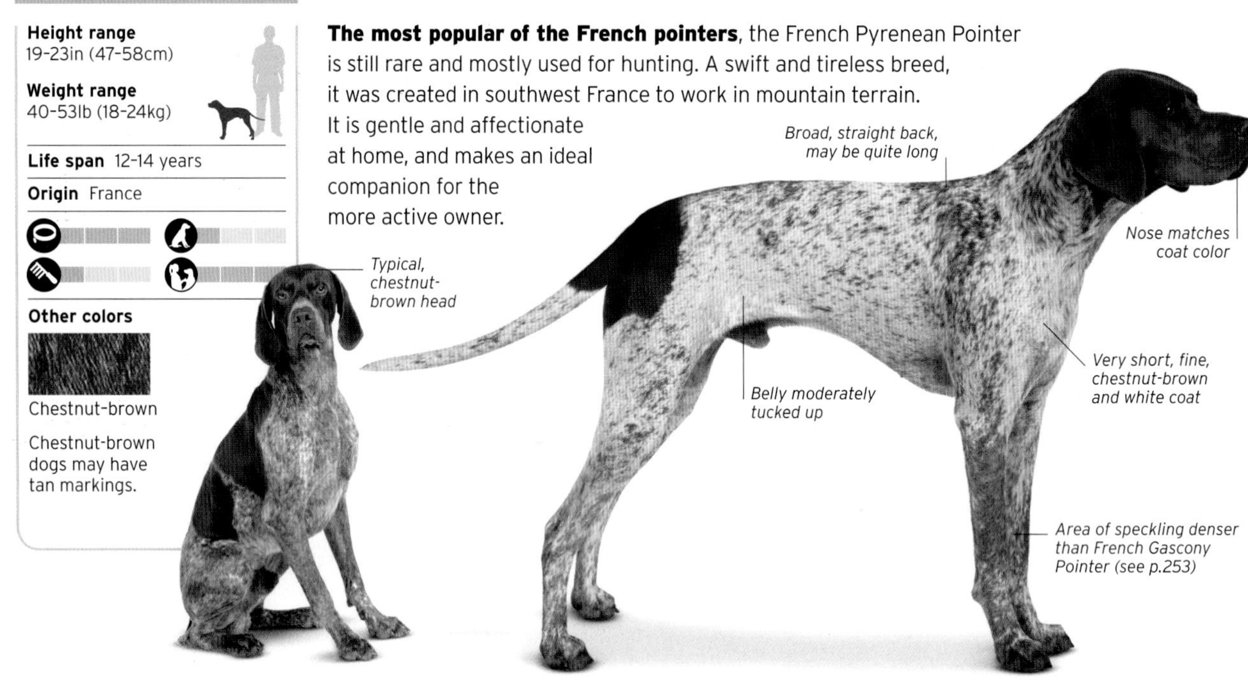
Typical, chestnut-brown head
Broad, straight back, may be quite long
Nose matches coat color
Very short, fine, chestnut-brown and white coat
Belly moderately tucked up
Area of speckling denser than French Gascony Pointer (see p.253)

SAINT GERMAIN POINTER

AFFECTIONATE WITH FAMILY, BUT RESERVED WITH STRANGERS, THIS DOG IS KEEN IN THE FIELD FCI

Height range
21-24in (54-62cm)

Weight range
40-57lb (18-26kg)

Life span 12-14 years

Origin France

Also known as the Braque Saint-Germain, this is a fleet-footed pointer and retriever of birds in field, woodland, and marshland. However, its coat is not sufficiently insulated to make it an all-weather dog. The Saint Germain Pointer is affectionate but sensitive, needing firm yet gentle handling, and adapts surprisingly well to urban family life.

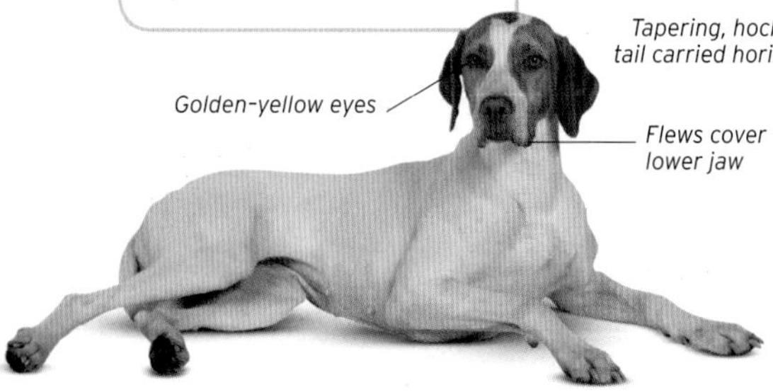

Pink nose

Tapering, hock-length tail carried horizontally

Golden-yellow eyes

Flews cover lower jaw

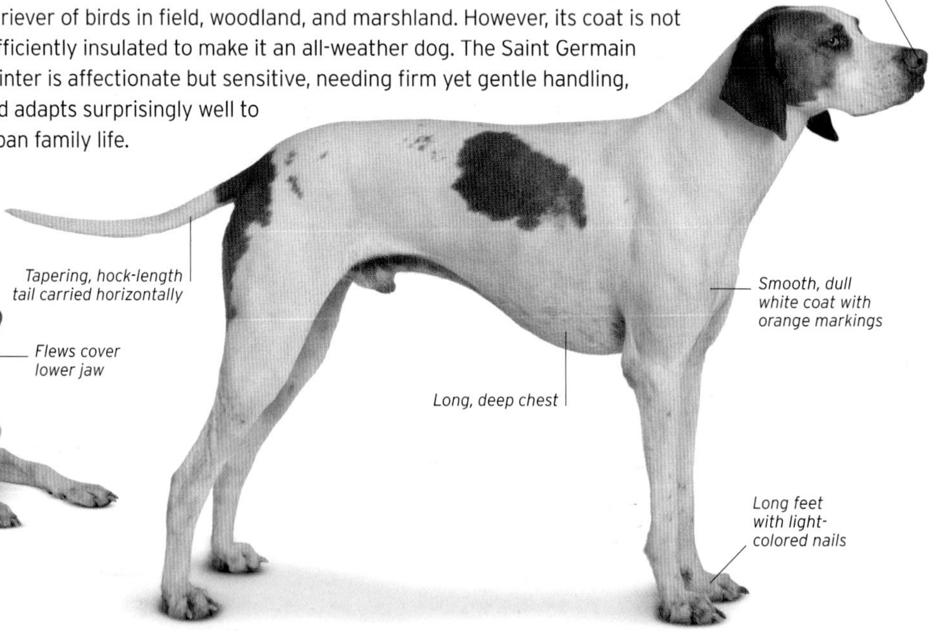

Smooth, dull white coat with orange markings

Long, deep chest

Long feet with light-colored nails

BOURBONNAIS POINTING DOG

THIS TOLERANT AND LEVEL-HEADED BREED IS A GOOD ALL-AROUND GUNDOG FCI

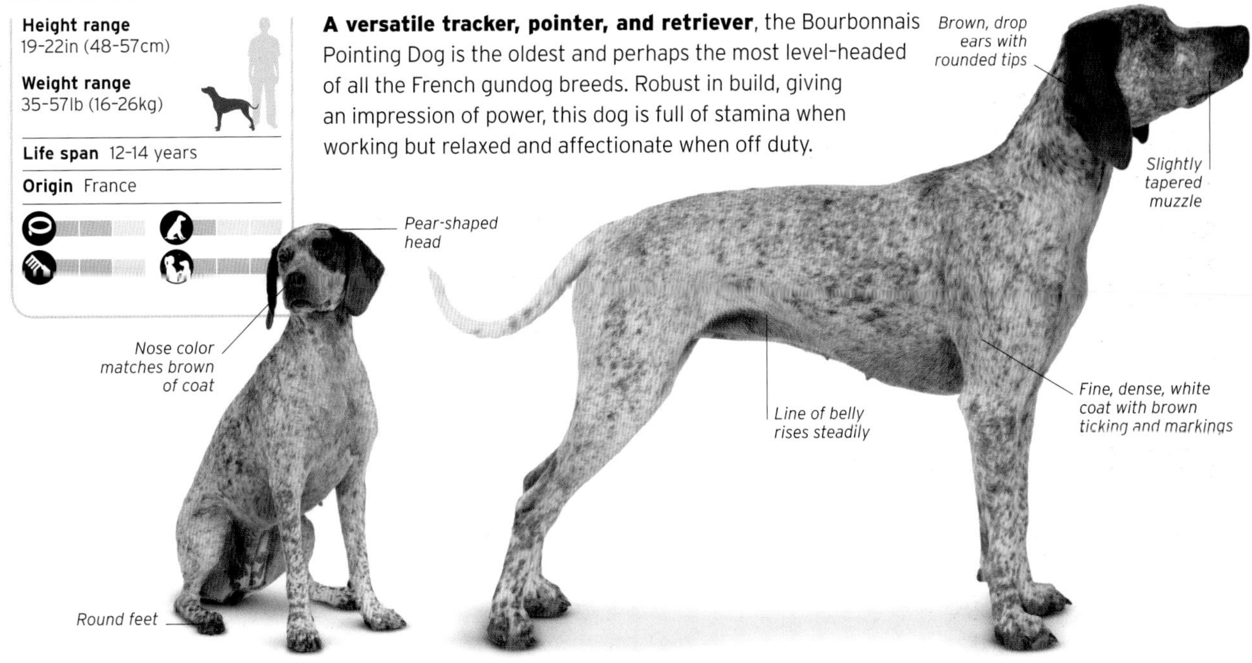
Pear-shaped head
Nose color matches brown of coat
Round feet
Brown, drop ears with rounded tips
Slightly tapered muzzle
Line of belly rises steadily
Fine, dense, white coat with brown ticking and markings

Height range 19-22in (48-57cm)

Weight range 35-57lb (16-26kg)

Life span 12-14 years

Origin France

A versatile tracker, pointer, and retriever, the Bourbonnais Pointing Dog is the oldest and perhaps the most level-headed of all the French gundog breeds. Robust in build, giving an impression of power, this dog is full of stamina when working but relaxed and affectionate when off duty.

PUDELPOINTER

THIS WELL-BALANCED AND ROBUST BREED IS A DOG WORTH SEEKING OUT FCI

Height range 22-27in (55-68cm)

Weight range 44-66lb (20-30kg)

Life span 12-14 years

Origin Germany

Other colors

Dead leaf

Black

Developed for both the field and home, this cross of poodle and pointer aims to be the best of both: intelligent, hardy, and sociable, with excellent all-around working abilities. Most popular with hunters, the Pudelpointer is an amenable and cheerful rural companion.

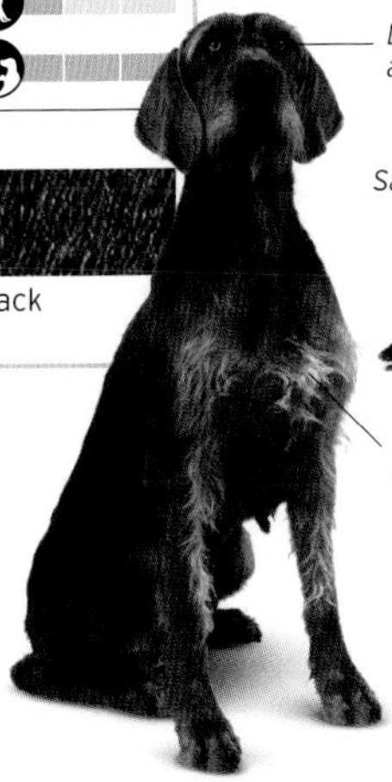

Large, dark, amber eyes

Saber-like tail

White markings on chest

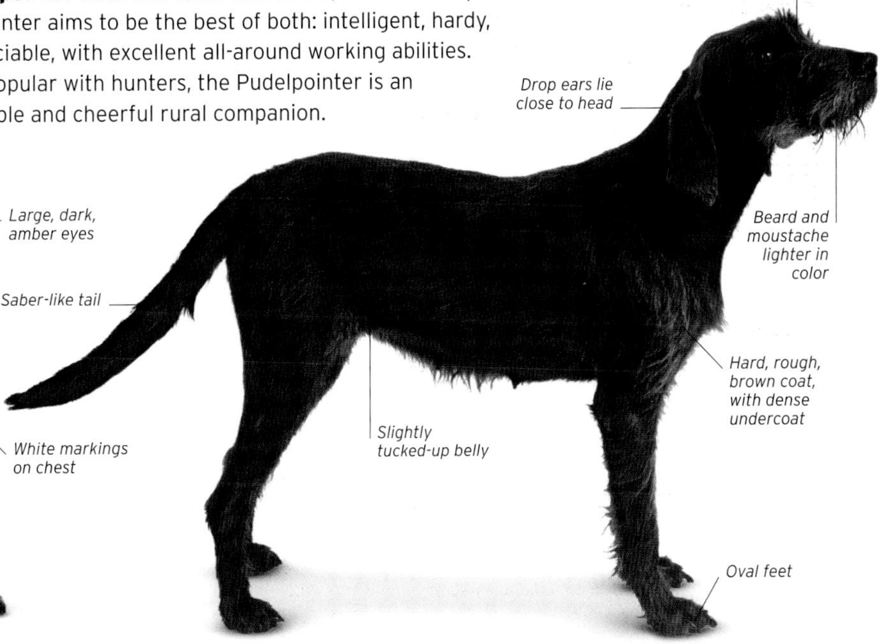

Curling forelock

Drop ears lie close to head

Beard and moustache lighter in color

Slightly tucked-up belly

Hard, rough, brown coat, with dense undercoat

Oval feet

AUVERGNE POINTER

A GOOD-NATURED, OBEDIENT DOG WITH LOTS OF STAMINA FCI

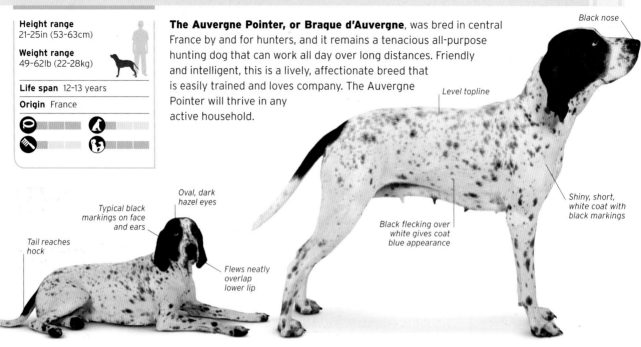

Height range 21–25in (53–63cm)

Weight range 49–62lb (22–28kg)

Life span 12–13 years

Origin France

The Auvergne Pointer, or Braque d'Auvergne, was bred in central France by and for hunters, and it remains a tenacious all-purpose hunting dog that can work all day over long distances. Friendly and intelligent, this is a lively, affectionate breed that is easily trained and loves company. The Auvergne Pointer will thrive in any active household.

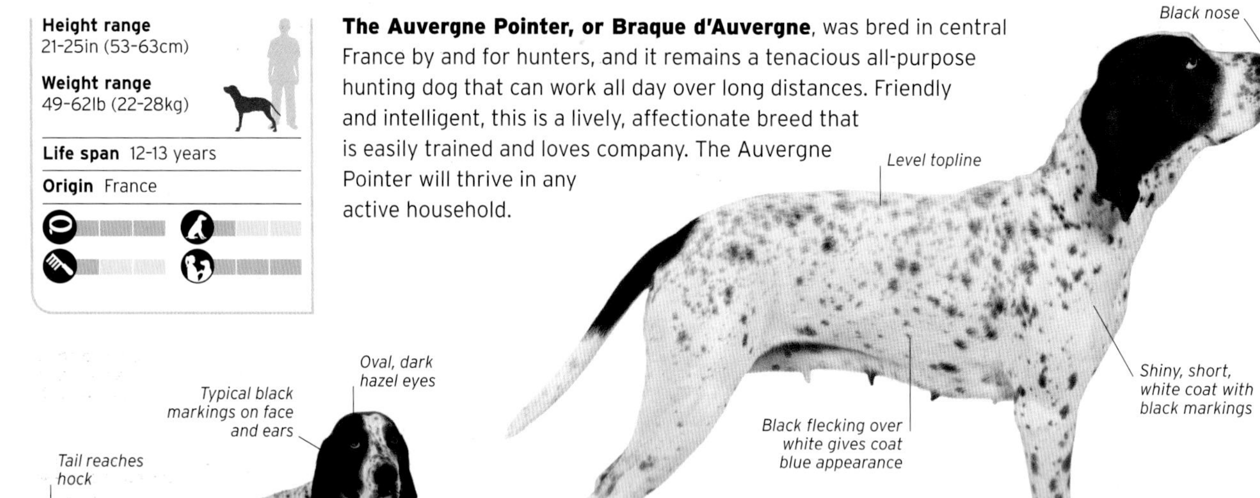
Black nose
Level topline
Shiny, short, white coat with black markings
Black flecking over white gives coat blue appearance
Oval, dark hazel eyes
Typical black markings on face and ears
Tail reaches hock
Flews neatly overlap lower lip

ARIEGE POINTING DOG

AN ELEGANT BREED BEST SUITED TO A HIGHLY ACTIVE, DISCIPLINED LIFE FCI

Height range 22–26in (56–67cm)

Weight range 55–66lb (25–30kg)

Life span 12–14 years

Origin France

Rare even in its homeland in southwest France, the Ariege Pointing Dog, or Braque de l'Ariège, is used for pointing and retrieving, and has some tracking ability. It is almost exclusively owned by hunters, and needs patient training to settle an enthusiastic nature that can spill over into wildness, and plenty to do if it is not to become destructive.

Oval eyes have gentle expression
Flesh-colored nose
Fine, folded, tan ears
Short, glossy, white coat with fawn ticking
Tapering tail
Compact feet with well-arched toes
Long, straight muzzle

FRENCH GASCONY POINTER

THIS DOG IS GENTLE AND INTELLIGENT AT HOME BUT AN AVID HUNTER OUTDOORS FCI

Height range
22–27in (56–69cm)

Weight range
55–70lb (25–32kg)

Life span 12–14 years

Origin France

Other colors

Chestnut-brown

Chestnut-brown dogs may have tan markings.

One of the oldest pointer breeds, the French Gascony Pointer, from southwest France, is still kept as a hunter's dog as well as a household companion. Loyal and affectionate, it has a sensitive nature that responds best to gentle, consistent training. It is a determined and enthusiastic tracker in the field.

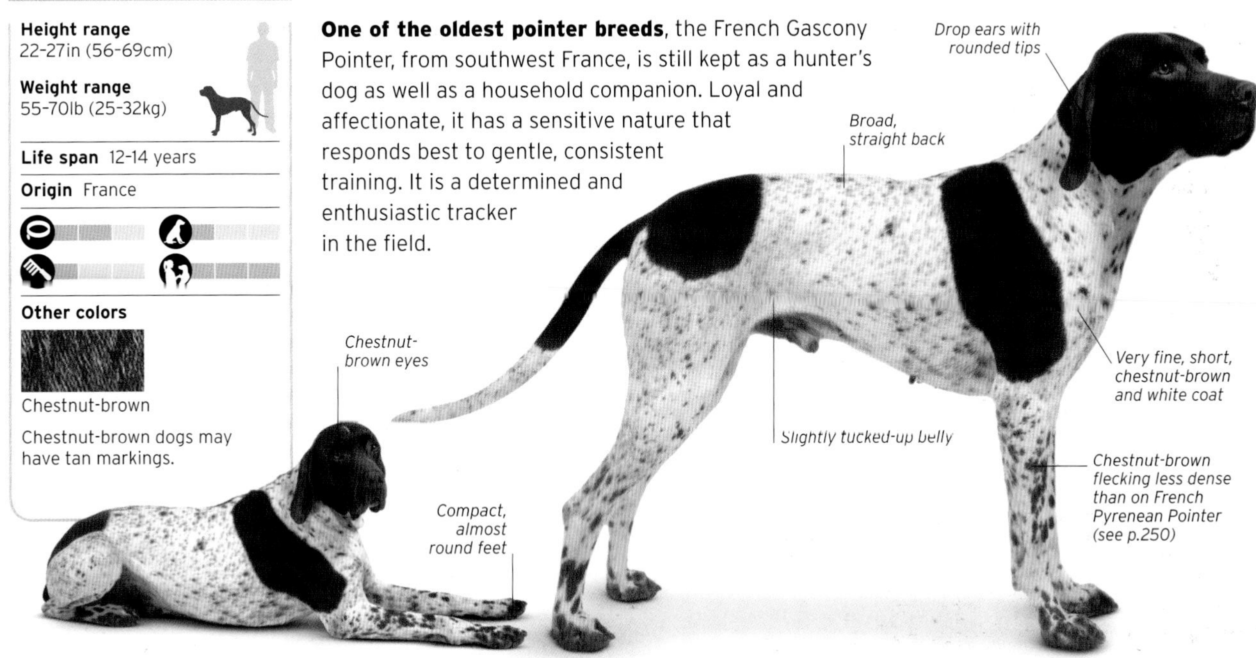
Drop ears with rounded tips
Broad, straight back
Chestnut-brown eyes
Very fine, short, chestnut-brown and white coat
Slightly tucked-up belly
Chestnut-brown flecking less dense than on French Pyrenean Pointer (see p.250)
Compact, almost round feet

SLOVAKIAN ROUGH-HAIRED POINTER

THIS LOYAL, OBEDIENT, AND LEVEL-HEADED BREED LOVES TO WORK KC

Height range
22–27in (57–68cm)

Weight range
55–77lb (25–35kg)

Life span 12–14 years

Origin Slovakia

This breed is found under a variety of names, from Slovensky Pointer to Wire-haired Slovakian Pointer, and Slovenský Hrubosrstý Stavač in its homeland. It is probably descended from German hunting dogs, and shows their typical intelligence, good humor, and energy. Not a breed to leave alone at home, it thrives on company and activity.

Long, lean head

Straight, solid back slopes slightly down toward tail

Longer, softer, lighter-colored hair on muzzle

Drop ears with short, soft hair

Almond-shaped, amber eyes

White markings on chest

Harsh, flat, gray (brown-shaded sable) coat

Rounded feet with well-arched toes

ENGLISH POINTER

THIS ATHLETIC DOG NEEDS PLENTY OF EXERCISE IF KEPT AS A PET

AKC

Height range 24–27in (61–69cm)

Weight range 45–75lb (20–34kg)

Life span 12–13 years

Origin UK

Other colors

Variety of colors

Simply known as the Pointer in the UK and US, this breed is swift and keen when tracking and pointing, tasks for which it has long been used; however, it does not retrieve particularly well. In character, English Pointers are gentle, loyal, and obedient. They are good-natured family companions and reliable with children but can be too boisterous with toddlers. They retain their hunting stamina and need plenty of outdoor space.

White blaze on head
Well-developed, soft flews
Very well-defined stop
Bright, hazel eyes
Liver and white coat
Back slopes gently toward tail
Drop ears
Medium-length tail carried level with back
Fine, hard, short, orange and white coat
Oval feet with well-arched toes

SPANISH POINTER

GENTLE AND INTELLIGENT, THIS BREED IS NIMBLER THAN IT LOOKS

FCI

Height range
23–26in (59–67cm)

Weight range
55–66lb (25–30kg)

Life span 12–14 years

Origin Spain

Also known as the Perdiguero de Burgos, this dog was bred to track deer, but is now mostly used for smaller game. It is a reliable, easy-going breed that fits well into family life. Nonetheless, it is a keen hunter—halfway between a scent hound and a pointer—and thrives on work.

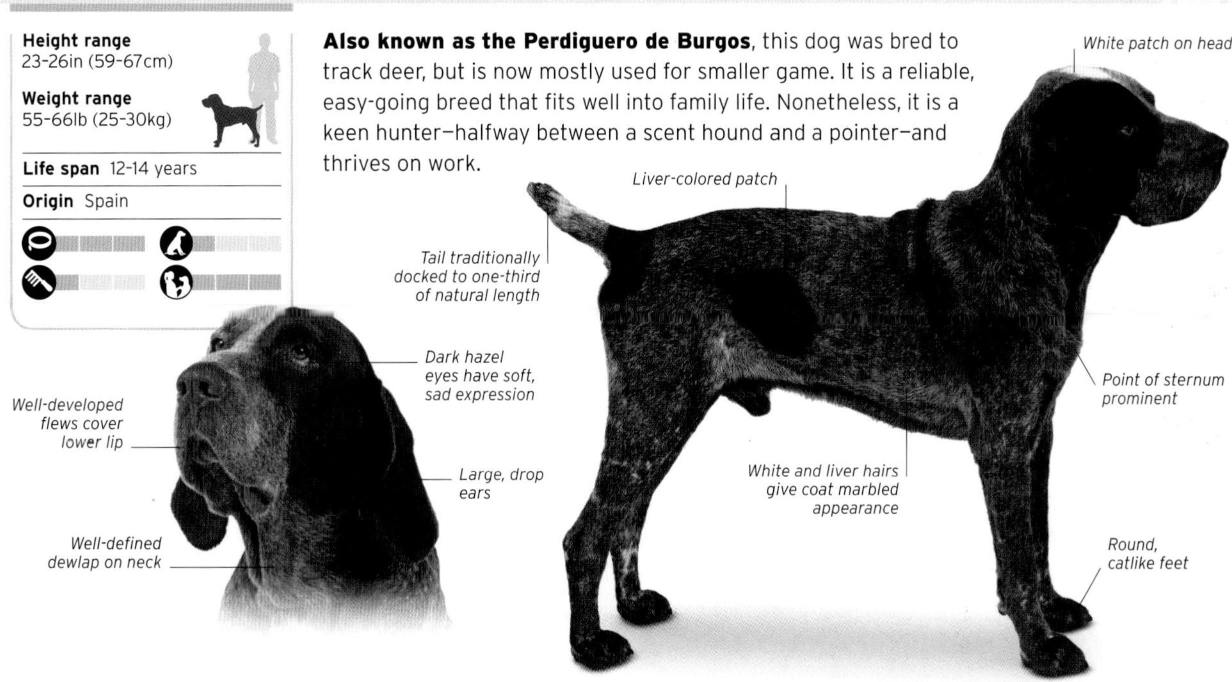
White patch on head
Liver-colored patch
Tail traditionally docked to one-third of natural length
Dark hazel eyes have soft, sad expression
Well-developed flews cover lower lip
Large, drop ears
Well-defined dewlap on neck
Point of sternum prominent
White and liver hairs give coat marbled appearance
Round, catlike feet

OLD DANISH POINTER

THIS ADAPTABLE AND ROBUST DOG MAKES A GENTLE, PATIENT COMPANION

FCI

Height range
20–24in (50–60cm)

Weight range
57–77lb (26–35kg)

Life span 12–13 years

Origin Denmark

Its local name, Gammel Dansk Hønsehund, also translates as Old Danish Chicken Dog or Bird Dog. This breed is still used as a determined tracker, pointer, and retriever, and even as a sniffer dog, but it also makes an even-tempered family dog for those willing to give it plenty to do.

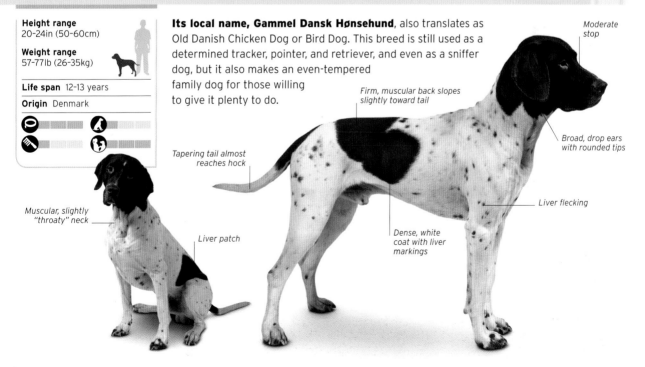

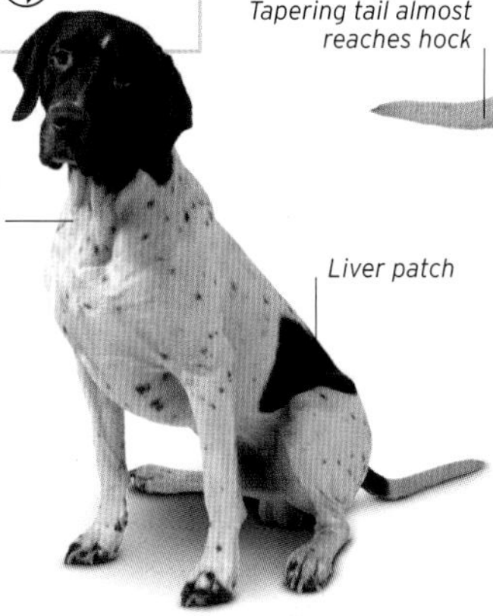

Moderate stop

Firm, muscular back slopes slightly toward tail

Broad, drop ears with rounded tips

Tapering tail almost reaches hock

Liver flecking

Muscular, slightly "throaty" neck

Liver patch

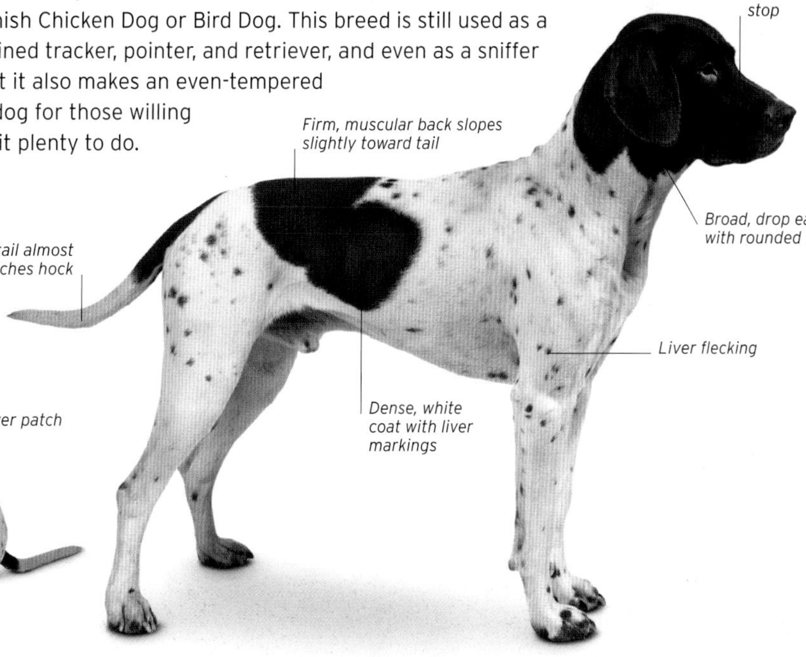

Dense, white coat with liver markings

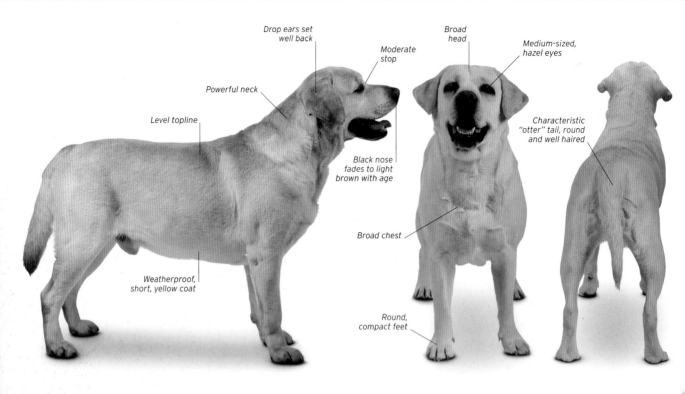

Drop ears set well back
Broad head
Moderate stop
Medium-sized, hazel eyes
Powerful neck
Level topline
Characteristic "otter" tail, round and well haired
Black nose fades to light brown with age
Broad chest
Weatherproof, short, yellow coat
Round, compact feet

LABRADOR RETRIEVER

THIS KIND AND INTELLIGENT FAMILY FAVORITE LOVES SPORTS AND SWIMMING AKC

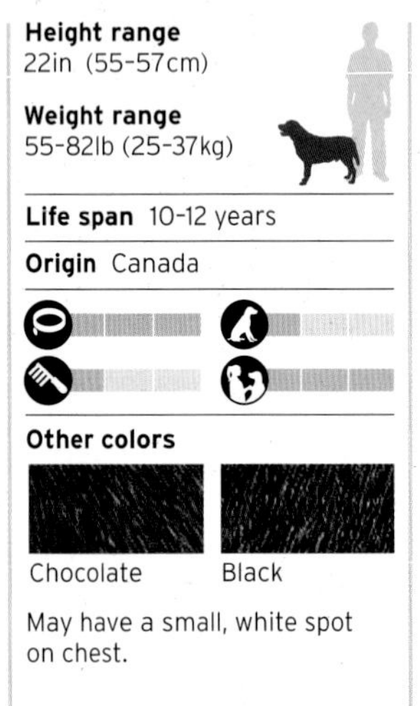

Height range
22in (55–57cm)

Weight range
55–82lb (25–37kg)

Life span 10–12 years

Origin Canada

Other colors

Chocolate Black

May have a small, white spot on chest.

One of the most familiar dogs, the Labrador Retriever has been topping "popular dog" lists for at least two decades. The dogs from which the present-day Labrador Retriever descended were not from Labrador, as is commonly supposed, but from Newfoundland. Here, from the 18th century onward, black dogs with waterproof coats were bred by local fishermen and used to help tow in catches and retrieve escaping fish. Dogs of this early type no longer exist, but a few were brought to England in the 19th century and these led to the development of the modern Labrador Retriever. By the early 20th century the breed was officially recognized and continued to be much admired by field sportsmen for its excellent retrieving skills.

Today the Labrador Retriever is still widely used as a gundog and has proved efficient at other types of work, such as tracking for police forces. In particular, its steady character makes it a superb guide dog for the blind. However, it is as a family dog that this breed has gained great popularity. The Labrador Retriever is loving and lovable, easy to train, anxious to please, and reliable with children and household pets—but it has too amiable a character to make a good guard dog.

This breed has energy to burn and needs to be kept mentally as well as physically active. Long daily walks are essential, preferably with the chance to have a swim along the way. If this dog sees water, it will plunge straight in. Under-exercised and left to its own devices, a Labrador Retriever may be given to excessive barking or become destructive. It tends to gain weight quickly, and lack of exercise combined with its insatiable appetite can lead to weight problems.

GOLDEN RETRIEVER

THIS EXUBERANT, EASY-GOING GUNDOG HAS BECOME A FAMILY FAVORITE AKC

Height range
20-24in (51-61cm)

Weight range
55-75lb (25-34kg)

Life span 12-13 years

Origin UK

Other colors
Cream

Bred as a powerful retriever for long-distance work, the Golden Retriever is used by hunters and in field trials. It is also used as a guide dog and kept as a gregarious pet. Responsive and even-tempered, this dog's main aim in life is to please. Its friendly nature means it does not make a good guard dog.

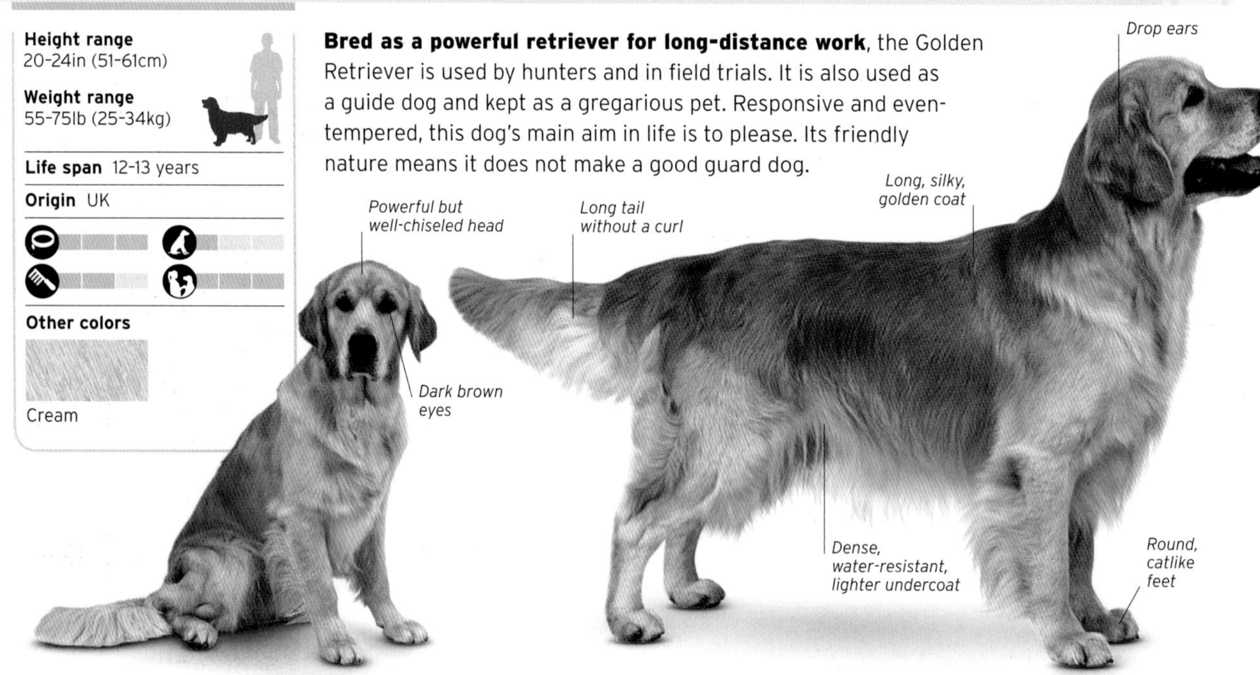
Drop ears
Long, silky, golden coat
Powerful but well-chiseled head
Long tail without a curl
Dark brown eyes
Dense, water-resistant, lighter undercoat
Round, catlike feet

FLAT COATED RETRIEVER

A GOOD-NATURED GREGARIOUS DOG WITH A CORE OF COMMON SENSE AKC

Height range
22-24in (56-61cm)

Weight range
55-80lb (25-36kg)

Life span 11-13 years

Origin UK

Other colors
Liver

One of the earliest retriever breeds, this was once a favorite among gamekeepers. Today it is still worked but is more often found as a good-natured and handsome pet. Lively and brimming with enthusiasm, the Flat Coated Retriever is also level-headed and obedient. It has a deep bark so can make a good guard dog.

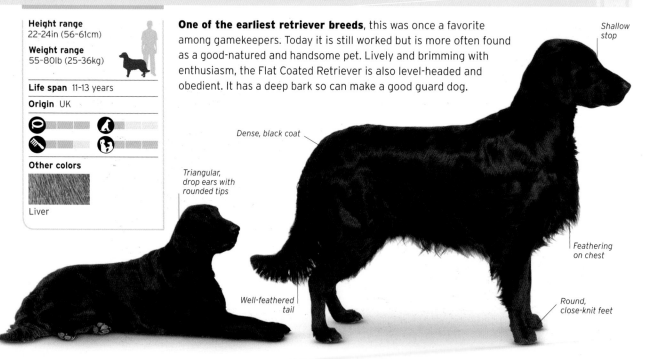

Shallow stop

Dense, black coat

Triangular, drop ears with rounded tips

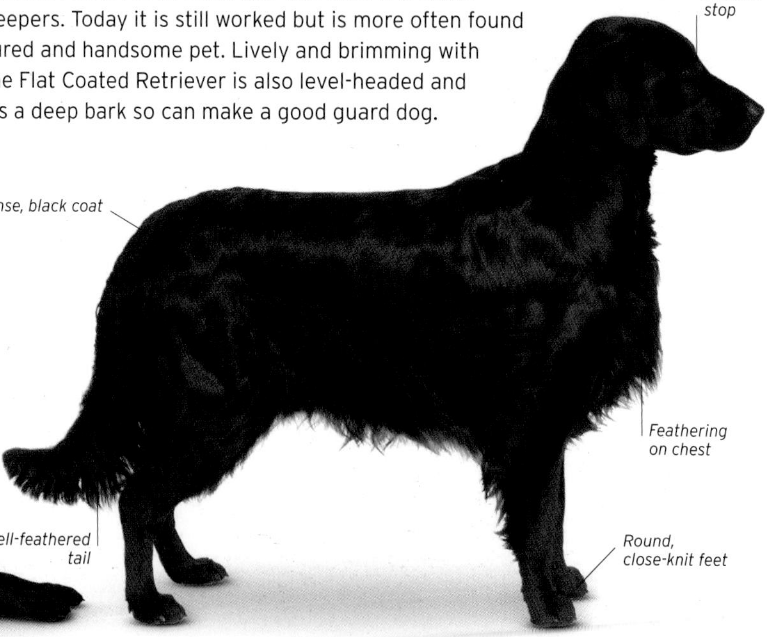

Feathering on chest

Well-feathered tail

Round, close-knit feet

CHESAPEAKE BAY RETRIEVER

THIS EVEN-TEMPERED DOG IS SUITED TO COUNTRY LIFE AKC

Height range 21–26in (53–66cm)

Weight range 55–80lb (25–36kg)

Life span 12–13 years

Origin USA

Other colors

Straw bracken, Red-gold

May have small, white markings.

This retriever originated in the northeastern United States and has much in common with the Curly Coated Retriever (below). A superb water dog, the Chesapeake Bay Retriever has typical retriever gentleness but an alert and determined personality. For those who can provide enough activity, this is an intelligent and biddable companion.

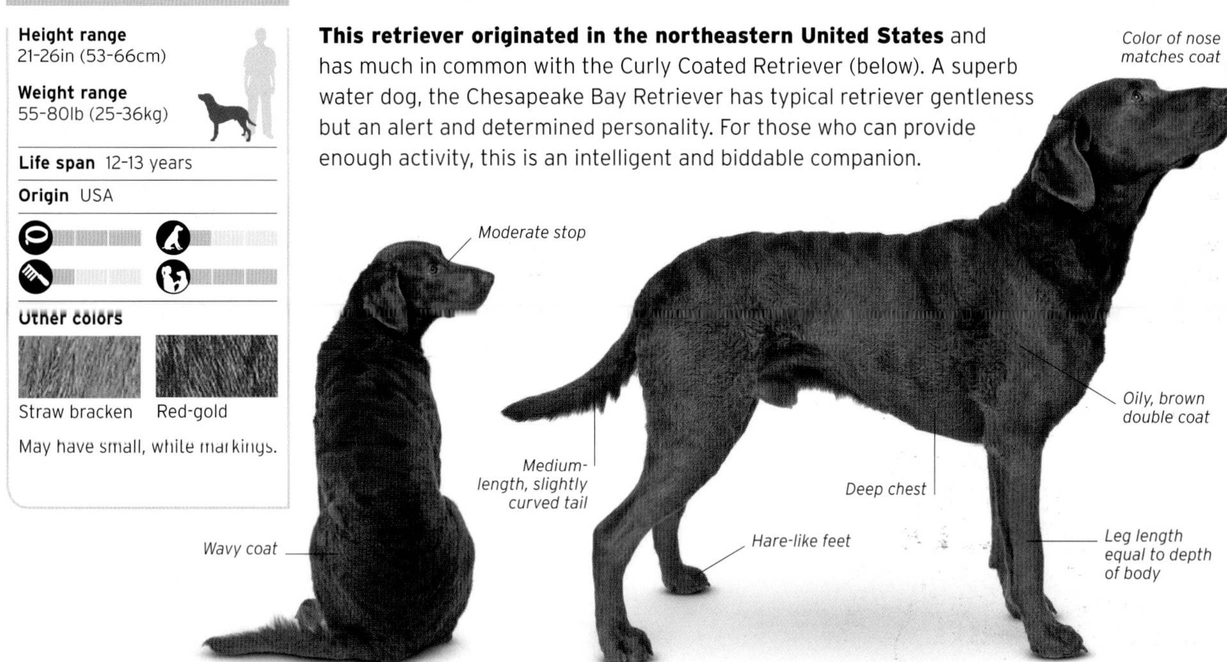
Color of nose matches coat
Moderate stop
Oily, brown double coat
Medium-length, slightly curved tail
Deep chest
Wavy coat
Hare-like feet
Leg length equal to depth of body

CURLY COATED RETRIEVER

THIS ROBUST, ENERGETIC WORKING DOG DOES NOT LIKE TO BE LEFT ALONE AKC

Height range 25–27in (64–69cm)

Weight range 60–70lb (27–32kg)

Life span 12–13 years

Origin UK

Other colors

Liver

Bred for hunting waterfowl, this rare retriever is worked and used as an assistance dog, as well as kept as an affectionate and level-headed companion. High energy levels and a need for company make this dog more suited to a rural life than to an urban home.

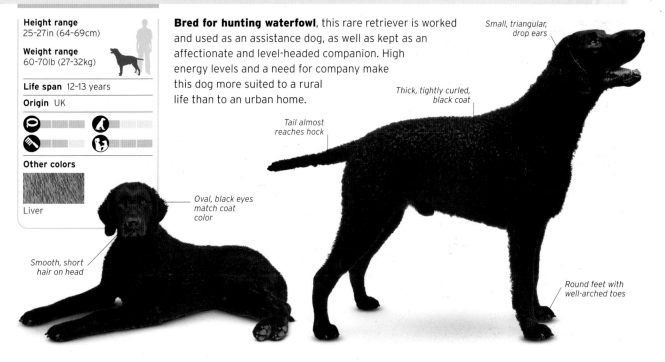

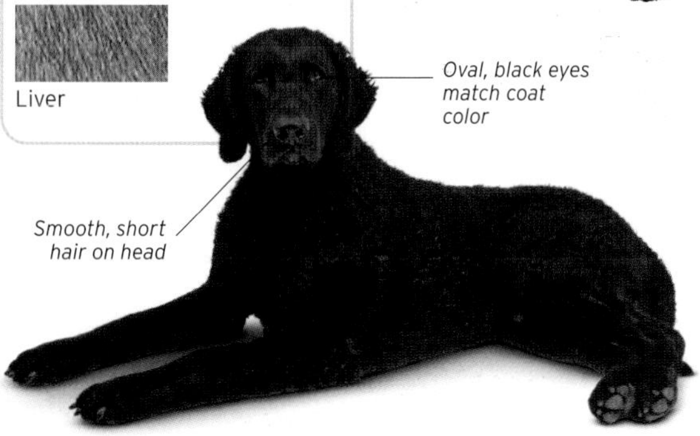

Small, triangular, drop ears

Thick, tightly curled, black coat

Tail almost reaches hock

Oval, black eyes match coat color

Smooth, short hair on head

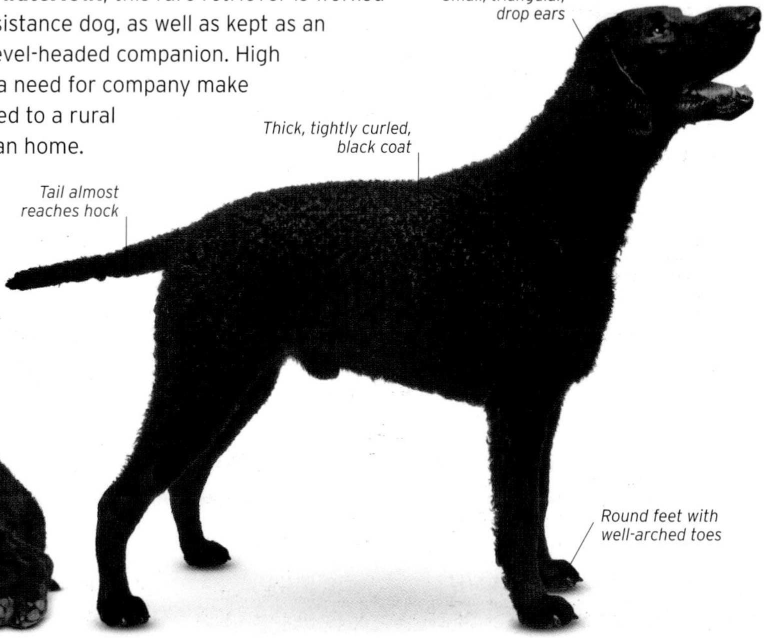

Round feet with well-arched toes

MEXICAN PET
A Chihuahua may fit into a handbag but it is not a fashion accessory. This little breed from Mexico needs exercise as much as any larger dog.

COMPANION DOGS

Almost any dog can provide companionship. Many dogs once used for outside duties, such as herding, have moved indoors with the family. Usually, these breeds have been developed for specific tasks and so are traditionally grouped according to their primary function. With a few exceptions, the companion dogs included here are bred solely as pets.

The Pug's flat face and round eyes are designed to appeal

Most companion dogs are small breeds, created primarily to sit on laps, look decorative, and entertain their owners without taking up much room. Some of them are toy versions of larger working breeds. The Poodle, for example, once used for herding or for retrieving waterfowl, was bred down in size to a toy dog that could no longer perform any practical function. Other, larger, dogs sometimes grouped with companion breeds include the Dalmatian, whose career included a short-lived spell as a carriage escort, as much for prestige as guard duty. Now that this job no longer exists, Dalmatians are rarely used for any working purpose.

Companion dogs have a long history. A number of them originated thousands of years ago in China, where small dogs were kept in the imperial courts as ornaments and a source of comfort. Until the late 19th century companion dogs everywhere were almost exclusively the pampered pets of the wealthy. As such, they often featured in portraits, depicted sitting prettily in the drawing room or with children as a nursery plaything. Some, such as the King Charles Spaniel, owe their enduring popularity to the former patronage of royalty.

Appearance has always mattered in the breeding of companion dogs. Over the centuries selective breeding has produced characteristics, some bizarre, that serve no useful function but are designed to appeal—for example, the humanlike flat faces and large, round eyes of the Pekingese and the Pug. Some have extravagantly long coats, curly tails, or—in the case of the Chinese Crested—no hair at all apart from a few strategically placed tufts on the head or legs.

In modern times companion dogs are no longer a symbol of class. They find a place with owners of all ages and circumstances, in small apartments as well as large country homes. Although still chosen for their looks, these dogs are also sought after as friends that give and demand affection and adapt happily to family activities.

LIVELY COMPANION
Although Dalmatians have great energy and stamina, they are nearly always kept as pets rather than for practical uses.

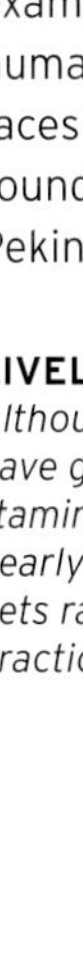

SMALLEST DOG
Few, if any, companion breeds come smaller than the diminutive and delightful Russian Toy.

BRUSSELS GRIFFON

A LIVELY, ALERT, WELL-BALANCED DOG WITH A TERRIER-LIKE DISPOSITION AKC

Height range
9-11in (23-28cm)

Weight range
7-11lb (3-5kg)

Life span Over 12 years

Origin Belgium

Other colors

Black and tan

This stocky little dog originated in Belgium, where it was kept as a stable dog and rode in hansom cabs. With traces of the Affenpinscher (see p.219) in its ancestry, there is a smooth-haired variety (known as the Petit Brabançon) and a rough-haired variety with a distinctive beard. In some countries the rough-haired type is also differentiated by color—black-coated dogs are known as Belgian Griffons, all other colorings as Brussels Griffon. Totally fearless, but very adaptable and affectionate, the breed enjoys a good walk and being pampered. It is not recommended for households with very young children.

Large, dark eyes
Smooth, red coat
Semierect, high-set ears with shorter hair
Wiry, red coat
Round head with upturned nose
High-set tail curves over back when active
Distinctive, bearded chin
Coarse, wiry, black coat
Compact, square body
Rounded, catlike feet

Smooth-haired (Petit Brabançon)

Rough-haired (Brussels Griffon)

Rough-haired (Belgian Griffon)

AMERICAN BULLDOG

THIS LOYAL, RELIABLE, AND BRAVE DOG HAS STRONG PROTECTIVE INSTINCTS

Height range
20–27in (51–69cm)

Weight range
60–125lb (27–57kg)

Life span Up to 16 years

Origin USA

Other colors

Variety of colors

Early English settlers brought the Bulldog (see p.94) with them to America. Two breeders, John D. Johnson and Alan Scott, used the English variety to develop the American Bulldog, which is taller, more active, and more versatile than its English counterpart. Male dogs are significantly heavier than females.

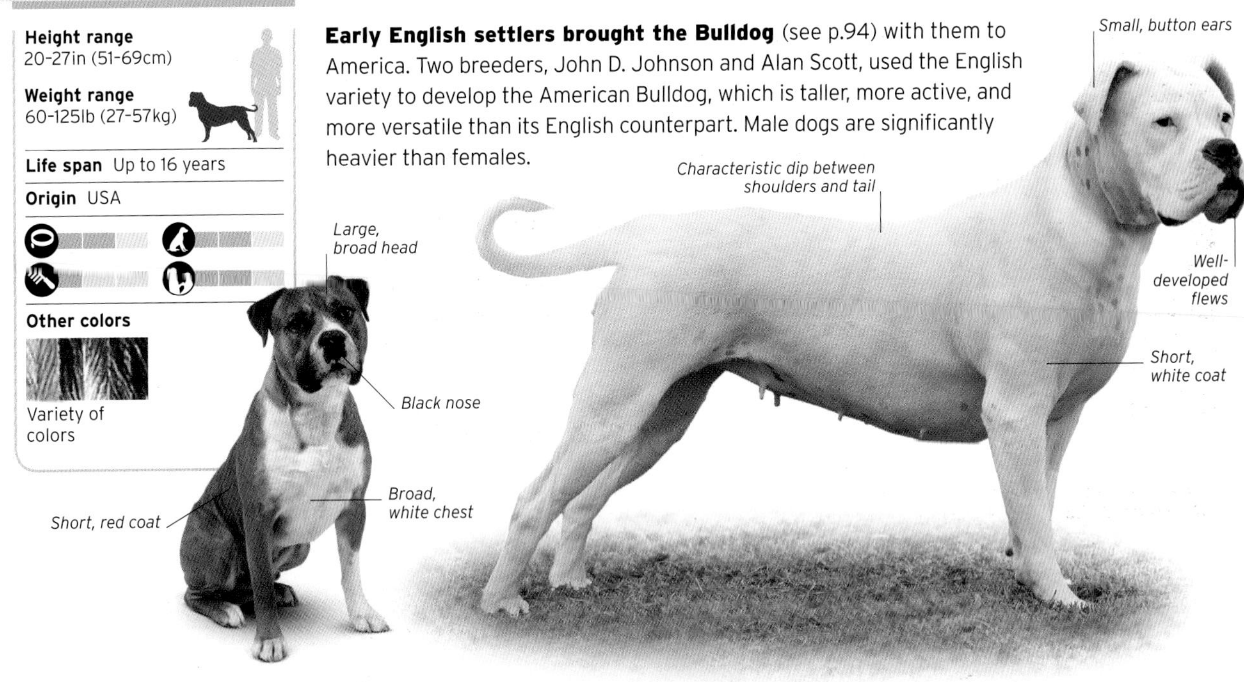
Small, button ears
Characteristic dip between shoulders and tail
Large, broad head
Well-developed flews
Short, white coat
Black nose
Broad, white chest
Short, red coat

OLDE ENGLISH BULLDOGGE

AN EXTREMELY STRONG BUT FRIENDLY AND LOVING COMPANION DOG

Height range
16–20in (41–51cm)

Weight range
50–80lb (23–36kg)

Life span 9–14 years

Origin USA

Other colors

Variety of colors

This muscular dog is a recreation of the original 19th-century Bulldog. It was developed in the United States during the 1970s by David Leavitt to eliminate some of the health problems that are now seen in the modern Bulldog (see p.94). Confident and courageous, these intelligent dogs are excellent family companions. However, they benefit from early socialization and training.

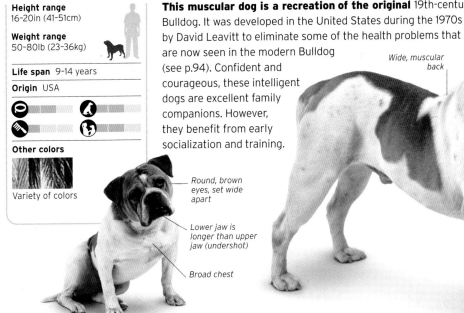

Very pronounced stop

Wide, muscular back

Button ears

Round, brown eyes, set wide apart

Lower jaw is longer than upper jaw (undershot)

Broad chest

Short, glossy, white and tan coat

Rounded, catlike feet

FRENCH BULLDOG

THIS AFFECTIONATE AND INTELLIGENT CLOWN-LIKE DOG THRIVES ON HUMAN COMPANY AKC

Height range
11–13in (28–33cm)

Weight range
24–29lb (11–13kg)

Life span Over 10 years

Origin France

Other colors

Black brindle

A sturdy, compact little dog, the French Bulldog makes an excellent companion, but has few boundaries and will want to share its owner's favorite chair. Always ready for fun, kind but firm direction may be needed. This breed is a descendent of the British Toy Bulldog taken to France in the 19th century.

Wide-set, dark eyes

Distinctive, erect "bat" ears, wide at base, rounded at top

Short, pied coat with white predominant

Strong, thickset neck

Fawn coat

PEKINGESE

DIGNIFIED AND COURAGEOUS YET SENSITIVE, THIS GOOD-NATURED DOG HAS A MIND OF ITS OWN AKC

Height range
6–9in (15–23cm)

Weight range
up to 12lb (up to 5kg)

Life span Over 12 years

Origin China

Other colors

Variety of colors

An aristocrat, whose ancestors can be traced back to the Tang Dynasty (618–907 CE), the Pekingese was considered sacred in China and could only be owned by royalty. The perfect dog for an apartment, it loves exercise but not long walks. Intelligent and fearless, it makes a loyal companion but can be hard to train.

Coarse, straight, long gold topcoat

Very short muzzle

Lionlike mane around face

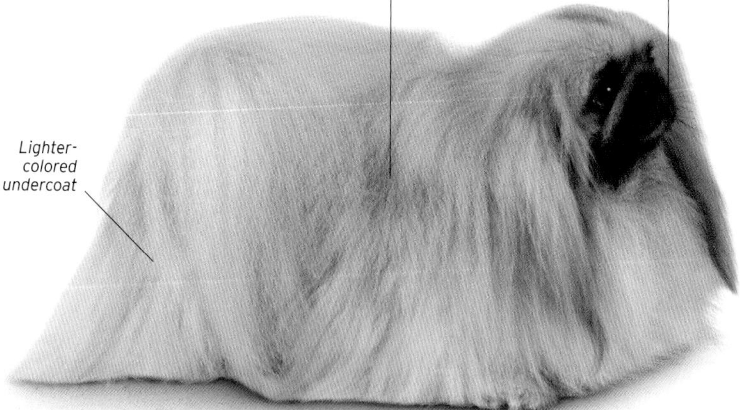

Lighter-colored undercoat

PUG

THIS PLAYFUL AND INTELLIGENT DOG LOVES PEOPLE BUT IS SOMETIMES WILLFUL AKC

Height range
10–11in (25–28cm)

Weight range
13–18lb (6–8kg)

Life span Over 10 years

Origin China

Other colors

Silver

Apricot

Black

This breed, with a long history, originated in China and its ancestors were brought to Europe in the 16th century by the East India Company traders. In Europe it became popular with royalty and aristocracy. The Pug is a small, sturdy, square dog whose stern appearance belies its cheerful personality and great character. It is highly intelligent, outgoing, has a loving disposition, and makes a loyal companion. The Pug is suitable for a novice dog owner and is good with children as well as other pets. This breed needs regular exercise but not a lot of space—so is ideal for apartment life.

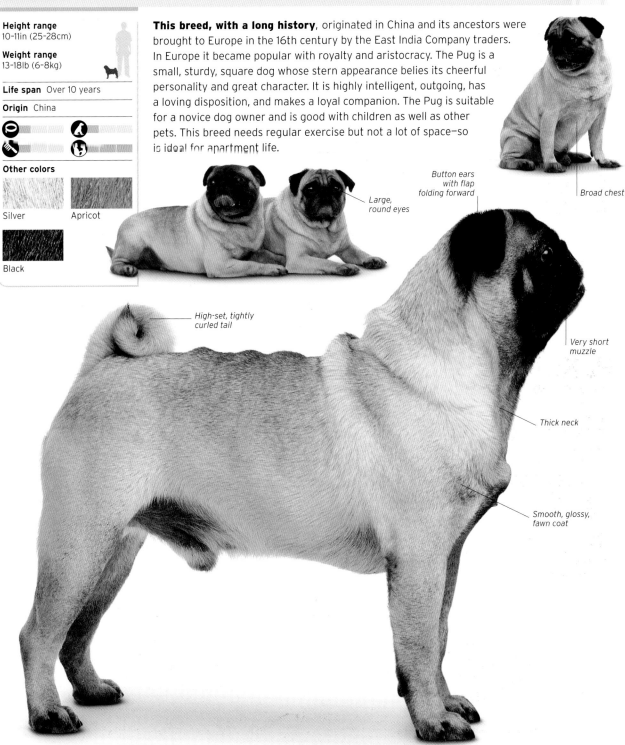

Button ears with flap folding forward

Broad chest

Large, round eyes

High-set, tightly curled tail

Very short muzzle

Thick neck

Smooth, glossy, fawn coat

LHASA APSO

HARDY, INDEPENDENT, AND FRIENDLY, THIS DOG IS NATURALLY SUSPICIOUS OF STRANGERS AKC

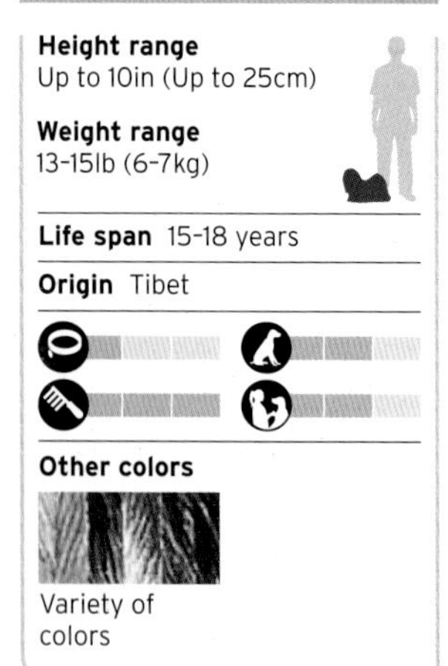

Height range
Up to 10in (Up to 25cm)

Weight range
13-15lb (6-7kg)

Life span 15-18 years

Origin Tibet

Other colors

Variety of colors

First bred in Tibet as a watchdog for temples and monasteries, the Lhasa Apso was brought to Europe via India in the 1920s. It is a small, hardy dog that will happily walk for miles. Its long, flowing coat is not difficult to care for. Very affectionate, it can also be quite stubborn.

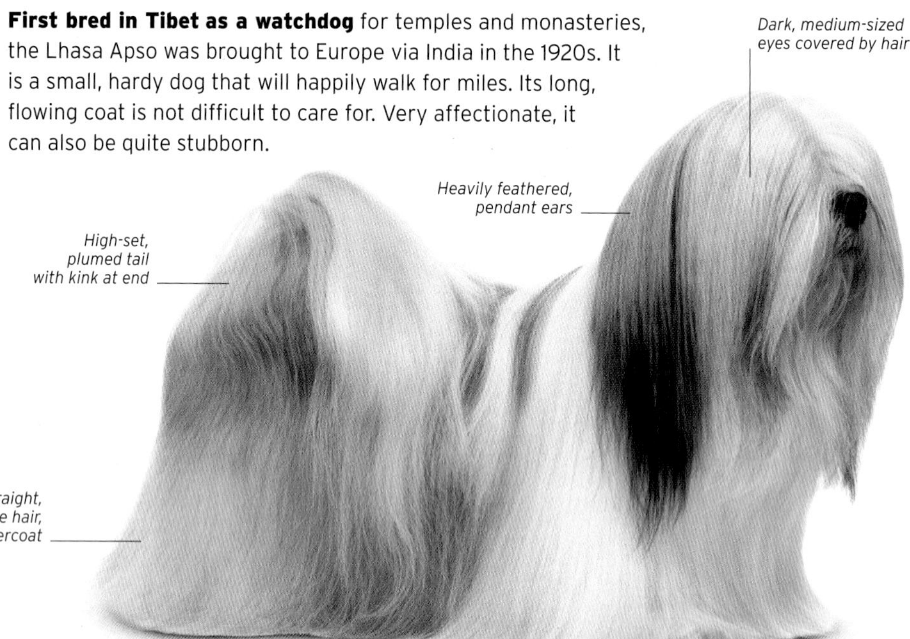

Dark, medium-sized eyes covered by hair
Heavily feathered, pendant ears
High-set, plumed tail with kink at end
Cloak of heavy, straight, wheaten and white hair, with thick undercoat

SHIH TZU

THIS INTELLIGENT, BOUNCY, AND OUTGOING DOG LOVES BEING PART OF THE FAMILY AKC

Height range
Up to 11in (Up to 27cm)

Weight range
11-18lb (5-8kg)

Life span Over 10 years

Origin Tibet/China

Other colors

Variety of colors

This sturdy breed is thought to be a cross between the Lhasa Apso (above) and the Pekingese (see p.264). Abundantly but not excessively coated, it sheds little or no hair, making it a good companion for allergy sufferers. Despite its distinctly arrogant carriage, the Shih Tzu makes an affectionate and friendly pet.

Hair grows upward around the muzzle
Heavily plumed tail with white tip
White blaze on forehead
Short, muscular legs hidden by long coat
Long, dense, black and white topcoat

BICHON FRISE

A GENTLE, INTELLIGENT, AND EXTROVERT DOG WITH A NON-SHEDDING COAT AKC

Height range
9-11in (23-28cm)

Weight range
10-16lb (5-7kg)

Life span Over 12 years

Origin Mediterranean

Sometimes known as the Tenerife dog, the Bichon Frise—a descendant of the French Water Dog (see p.232) and the Poodle (see p.271)—was allegedly taken from Tenerife to France. This is a happy little dog that loves to be the center of attention, and does not like being left alone. It can be slow to house train.

Round, black eyes
White topcoat is coarser than soft, dense undercoat
Pendant ears
Round foot, exaggerated by cut of coat

COTON DE TULEAR

A LOYAL, BRIGHT, AND HIGHLY SOCIABLE DOG WITH A SOFT, COTTON-TEXTURED COAT KC

Height range
10-13in (25-32cm)

Weight range
9-13lb (4-6kg)

Life span Over 12 years

Origin Madagascar

This small, long-haired dog is known for its happy temperament. The Coton de Tulear enjoys the company of humans as well as other dogs and does not like to be left alone. It is sometimes called the Royal Dog of Madagascar, where the dog existed for several hundred years before being introduced to France.

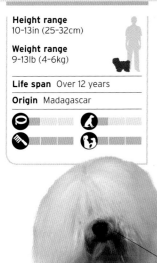

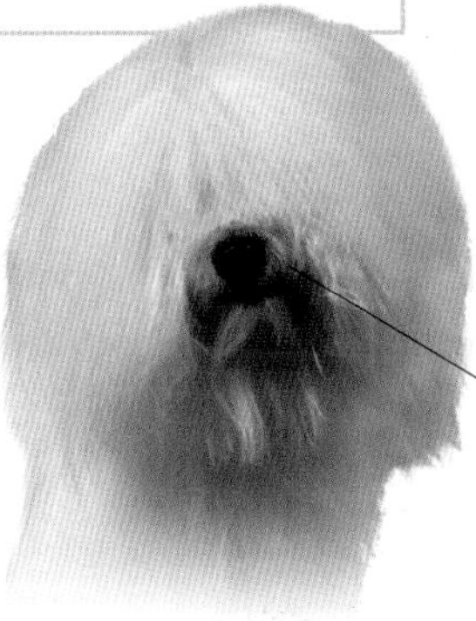

Well-feathered tail

Non-shedding, soft, white coat

Strong, powerful muzzle

Long hair should not reach the ground

LÖWCHEN

AFFECTIONATE, LIVELY, AND OUTGOING, THIS FAMILY-LOVING COMPANION HAS A STYLISH MANE AKC

Height range
10–13in (25–33cm)

Weight range
8–18lb (4–8kg)

Life span 12–14 years

Origin France/Germany

Other colors
Any color

The Löwchen, with origins in France and Germany, has existed as a companion dog for at least 400 years. The name Löwchen is German for little lion, hence its other name, the Little Lion Dog. It is a compact little dog with a bright expression and a reputation for agility and quickness. The Löwchen's intelligent, outgoing attitude makes it a pleasure to live with. It is highly recommended as a family pet and its size and non-shedding coat make it an ideal family dog.

Brown coat with lighter underparts and head

Pendant ears with long fringes

Tail carried high over back

Coat often clipped at back, and long at front

Long, wavy, black coat with silver brindling

Small, round feet covered in hair

BOLOGNESE

THIS HIGHLY INTELLIGENT, LOW-ENERGY DOG ENJOYS INDOOR AND OUTDOOR GAMES KC

Height range
10–12in (26–31cm)

Weight range
7–9lb (3–4kg)

Life span Over 12 years

Origin Italy

Slightly more reserved and shy than its relative the Bichon Frise (see p.267), the Bolognese loves people and will form a close relationship with its owner. Like the Bichon Frise, it has a non-shedding coat. The breed originates from northern Italy. Similar dogs were known as far back as Roman times and are represented in many 16th-century Italian paintings.

High-set, drop ears
Body length same as height to withers
Round, black-rimmed eyes
Distinctive, non-shedding, flocked, white coat

MALTESE

A BRAVE, ENERGETIC, AND FEARLESS DOG, BUT ALSO GENTLE MANNERED AND AMIABLE AKC

Height range
Up to 10in (Up to 25cm)

Weight range
4–7lb (2–3kg)

Life span Over 12 years

Origin Malta

An ancient dog from the Mediterranean, Maltese-like dogs are mentioned in writings as far back as 300 BCE. This is a lively, fun-loving, little dog that belies its picturesque appearance. The long, silky coat is a major commitment—it does not shed but requires daily grooming to prevent matting.

Long facial hair tied back with ribbon
Silky, long, white coat
Tail carried over back with hair to one side
Dark brown, oval-shaped eyes with black rims
Well-feathered, long ears hang close to head
Short, cobby—or square—body

HAVANESE

THIS INTELLIGENT, EASY-TO-TRAIN, AND AFFECTIONATE DOG IS THE PERFECT FAMILY PET AKC

Height range
9–11in (23–28cm)

Weight range
7–13lb (3–6kg)

Life span Over 12 years

Origin Cuba

Other colors
Any color

The Havanese is the national dog of Cuba, where it is known as the Habanero. A relative of the Bichon Frise (see p.267), it was probably brought to Cuba by Italian or Spanish traders. The Havanese loves to be at the center of its family, plays endlessly with children, and is also a good watchdog.

High-set tail carried over back
Pointed, drop ears, set just above eyes
Soft, silky, wavy, wheaten topcoat
Small, hare-like feet hidden by long hair

RUSSIAN TOY

SMALL BUT NOT DELICATE, THIS LOVABLE DOG NEEDS PLENTY OF EXERCISE

FCI

Height range
8–11in (20–28cm)

Weight range
Up to 7lb (Up to 3kg)

Life span Over 12 years

Origin Russia

Other colors

Red

Black and tan

Blue and tan

Also known as the Russkiy Toy, this miniature dog, one of the smallest breeds in the world, is descended from the English Toy Terrier (see p.210). The breed became popular in Russia in the second half of the 20th century but is still something of a rarity outside its native country. Despite its tiny size and fragile appearance, the Russian Toy is active, energetic, and usually has robust health. There are two coat types: smooth-haired and long-haired. The long-haired variety is the more recent development.

Round, prominent eyes
Short, close, brown and tan coat
Smooth-haired
Ears fringed with long, silky hair
Black overlay
Long-haired
Pronounced stop
Small, round head
Well-feathered tail extends to hocks
Long, slightly wavy, fawn coat
Slight feathering on back of legs
Long-haired
Small, oval feet

POODLE (MINIATURE AND TOY)

A HIGHLY INTELLIGENT, EXTROVERT DOG WITH A NATURAL TALENT TO AMUSE

AKC

Height range
Toy:
Up to 11in (Up to 28cm)
Miniature:
11-15in (28-38cm)
Medium:
15-18in (38-45cm)

Weight range
Toy:
7-9lb (3-4kg)
Miniature:
15-18lb (7-8kg)
Medium:
46-77lb (21-35kg)

Life span Over 12 years

Origin France

Other colors

All solid colors

Bred down from the Poodle (Standard) (see p.231) are three other sizes of Poodle: toy and miniature—recognized by the AKC—and medium—recognized by the FCI. The smaller varieties have always been companion dogs, and were popular in the French court between the reign of Louis XIV and Louis XVI. An elegant dog, the Poodle is energetic, playful, affectionate, and eager to please. It is also very adaptable, equally at home in the city or the countryside. The dog's non-shedding coat makes it popular with allergy sufferers, although it does need regular brushing and clipping.

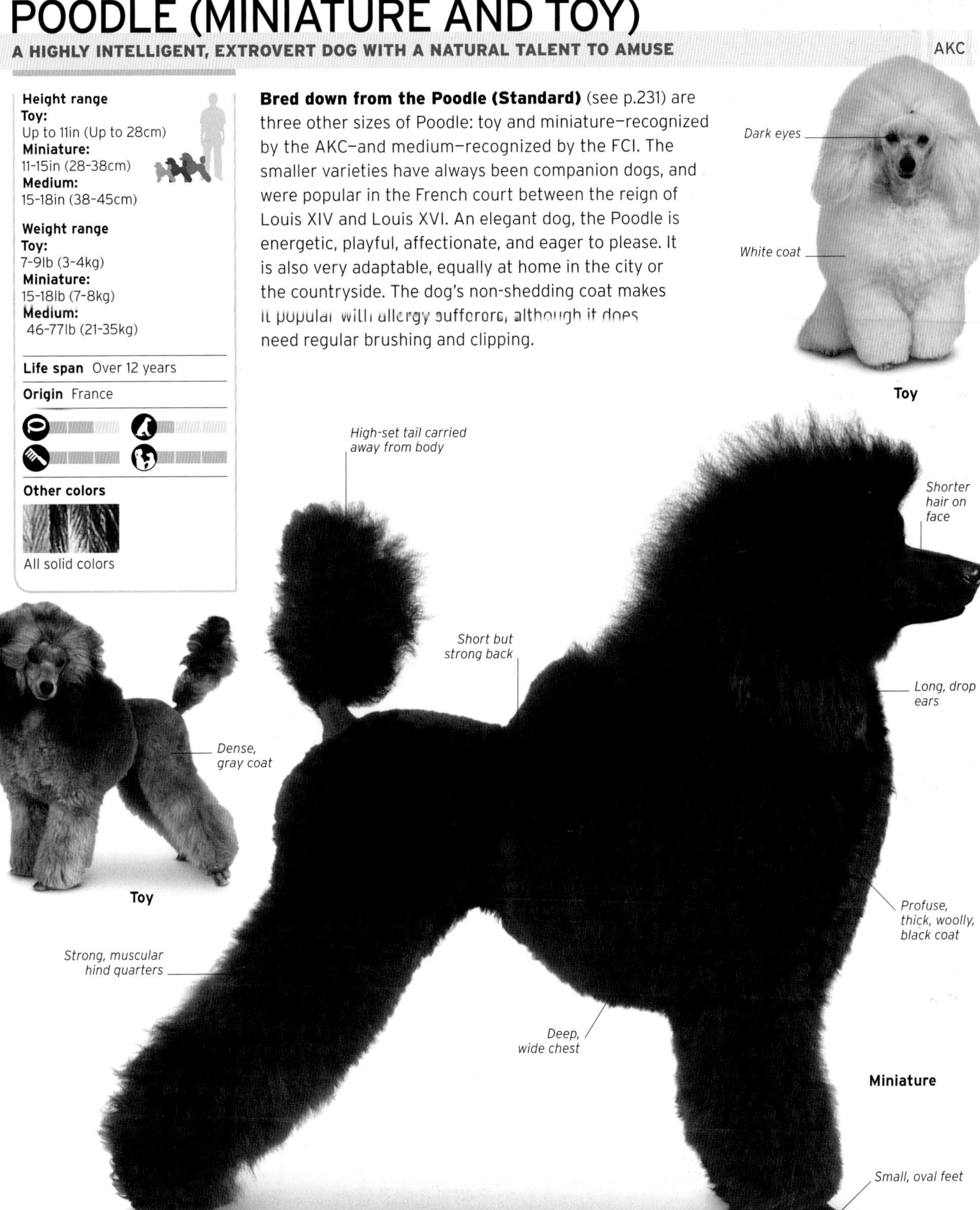
Dark eyes
White coat
High-set tail carried away from body
Shorter hair on face
Short but strong back
Long, drop ears
Dense, gray coat
Profuse, thick, woolly, black coat
Strong, muscular hind quarters
Deep, wide chest
Small, oval feet

Toy

Toy

Miniature

KYI LEO

THIS ATTRACTIVE, RELAXED, COMPACT BREED NEEDS PLENTY OF ACTIVITY

Height range
9-11in (23-28cm)

Weight range
9-13lb (4-6kg)

Life span 13-15 years

Origin USA

Other colors

Variety of colors

May have tan markings.

A playful, affectionate breed that is gaining popularity, the Kyi Leo is named after its parents: Kyi, Tibetan for dog, after its Lhasa Apso parent from Tibet; and Leo, Latin for lion, after its Maltese parent, which was once called the Lion Dog. Suited to indoor life, this alert dog makes a good watchdog.

Long hairs cover head

Tail curls over back when alert

Body length exceeds leg length

Long, thick, silky, black and white coat

Heavily feathered, drop ears

Short muzzle with beard

Rounded feet, with hair between toes

CAVALIER KING CHARLES SPANIEL

OUTGOING, SPORTING, AND ABSOLUTELY FEARLESS, THIS DOG IS EAGER TO PLEASE AKC

Height range
12-13in (30-33cm)

Weight range
11-18lb (5-8kg)

Life span Over 12 years

Origin UK

Other colors

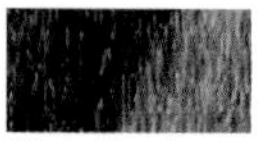

King Charles

Prince Charles

A relative of the King Charles Spaniel (opposite), this breed dates back centuries. With large, dark eyes, a melting expression, and an ever-wagging tail, the Cavalier King Charles Spaniel is game, easy to train, and loves children—making it the perfect family pet. Its silky coat requires regular grooming.

Short muzzle

White lozenge mark on head

High-set, pendant ears

Long, silky, well-feathered, Blenheim-colored coat with slight wave

Well-defined stop

Feathering on back of legs

Ruby-colored coat

ENGLISH TOY SPANIEL

NATURALLY WELL BEHAVED, THIS DOG MAKES A GENTLE AND AFFECTIONATE COMPANION AKC

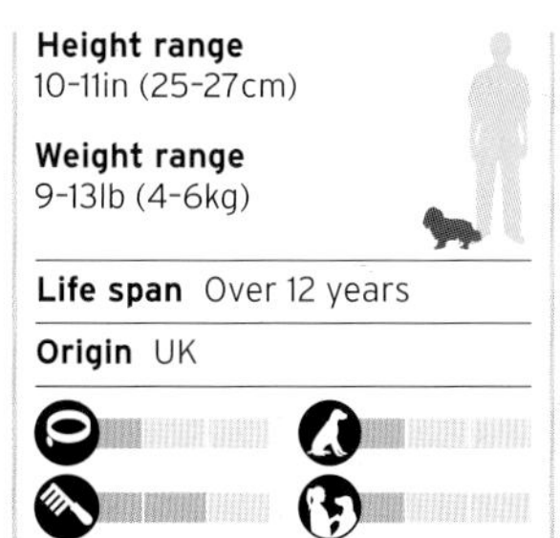

Height range
10–11in (25–27cm)

Weight range
9–13lb (4–6kg)

Life span Over 12 years

Origin UK

Other colors

Ruby King Charles

A very popular, compact little dog, this breed is also known as the King Charles Spaniel. It is related to the Cavalier King Charles Spaniel (opposite), and found in the same color variations, but it is a separate breed. Its ancestors were a favorite of King Charles II of England (1630-85), and often accompanied him on state occasions. A long, silky coat gives this spaniel an aristocratic look. Happy living in an apartment or house, it loves company and makes an excellent family pet, but does not like being left alone for long periods.

Very pronounced stop

Pendant ears

Characteristic domed head

Short, upturned muzzle with large, wide nostrils

Slightly undershot jaw (lower jaw longer than upper)

Blenheim-colored coat

Large, wide-set eyes

Prince Charles-colored, long, silky coat

Tan markings on legs

Well-padded feet

Large, erect ears

Long, flowing crest extends from stop to neck

Fine-grained, smooth, blue skin

Sock of white hair encircles long, narrow feet

Plume of hair on lower section of tail

CHINESE CRESTED

THIS ELEGANT, INTELLIGENT DOG ALWAYS ATTRACTS ATTENTION AKC

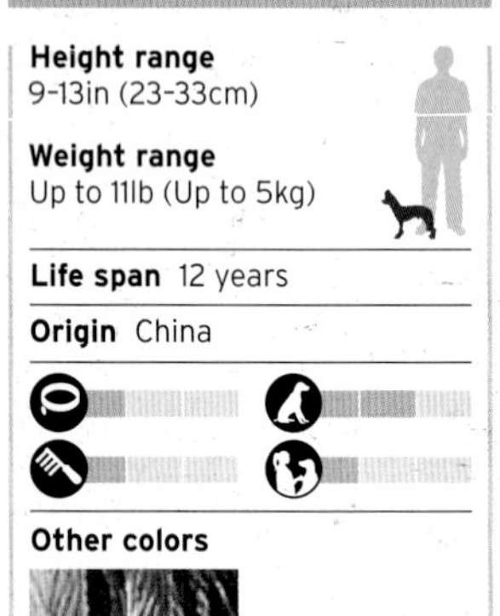

Height range
9–13in (23–33cm)
Weight range
Up to 11lb (Up to 5kg)
Life span 12 years
Origin China
Other colors 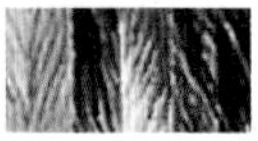
Any color

Hairlessness is a feature of several dog breeds around the world. It is the result of a genetic mutation that was initially considered a curiosity but then became desirable as the breed did not harbor fleas, shed hair, or have body odor. Although the Chinese Crested requires little grooming, its bare skin is sensitive: in winter it needs a coat to keep it warm, and in summer requires protection from the intense heat of the sun, which can burn and dry out its skin. This delicate skin, combined with the fact that the Chinese Crested needs little exercise and activity, makes it unsuitable for families that spend a lot of time outdoors. However, it is an ideal companion dog for older people due to its happy and friendly nature and playful personality.

Some Chinese Crested dogs are more lightly built than others. These fine-boned individuals are referred to as the deer type, while Chinese Crested dogs that have a heavier build are known as the cobby type.

POWDERPUFF VARIETY

Unlike the hairless variety, the Powderpuff Chinese Crested has a long, soft coat, which needs regular grooming to prevent matting. Both coat varieties can occur in the same litter.

CHIHUAHUA

A COMPANIONABLE, CLEVER, TINY DOG WITH A LARGE-DOG PERSONALITY AKC

Height range
6-9in (15-23cm)

Weight range
4-6lb (2-3kg)

Life span Over 12 years

Origin Mexico

Other colors

Any color

Always a single color—never dappled or merle.

The smallest dog breed in the world, the Chihuahua is a highly intelligent, easily trained dog that makes a delightful companion. The breed is thought to have originated in China, but it is named after the Mexican state of Chihuahua, where it first came to prominence in the 1890s. The Chihuahua's size means it can be taken anywhere, making it the perfect lap dog. Possessive by nature, the Chihuahua is also an excellent watchdog and is ready to stand up for itself even if the opposition is far bigger. It is not suitable for a family with young children.

Large, triangular, bat-like ears
Large, round eyes
Distinctive apple-shaped head
Fawn coat with lighter underparts
Short-haired
Medium-length tail carried high over back
Smooth, glossy, red topcoat
Long-haired
Small, dainty feet

TIBETAN SPANIEL

THIS FUN-LOVING, INTELLIGENT, PLAYFUL DOG THRIVES ON HUMAN COMPANY AKC

Height range
10in (25cm)

Weight range
9–15lb (4–7kg)

Life span Over 12 years

Origin Tibet

Other colors

Any color

This small dog has a delightful, easy-going temperament. Bred and owned by the monks of Tibet, the Tibetan Spaniel has a long history and was first brought to the UK around 1900 by returning medical missionaries. In spite of its slightly haughty expression, this dog is only too happy to run around outside and play.

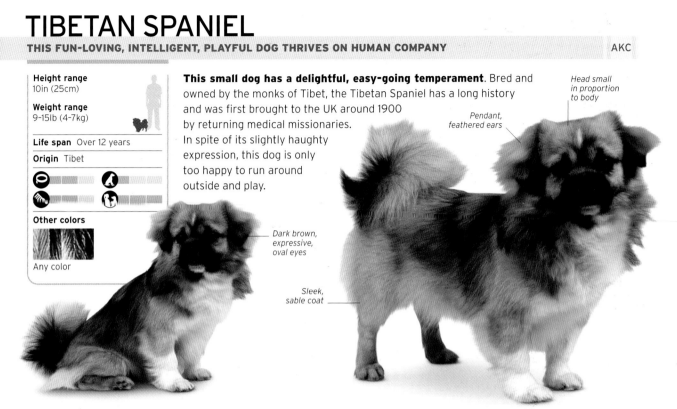

Head small in proportion to body

Pendant, feathered ears

Dark brown, expressive, oval eyes

Sleek, sable coat

TIBETAN TERRIER

AN ATHLETIC, BRIGHT, SURE-FOOTED DOG PACKED WITH ENERGY AND ENTHUSIASM AKC

Height range
14–16in (36–41cm)

Weight range
18–31lb (8–14kg)

Life span Over 10 years

Origin Tibet

Other colors

Variety of colors

Resembling a miniature Old English Sheepdog (see p.49), the Tibetan Terrier was originally bred for herding and was also used as a guard dog for traders journeying to and from China. This medium-sized dog requires a firm hand, but the reward is a loyal, devoted companion. The long coat needs daily grooming to prevent matting.

Silky, caramel and white topcoat

Feathered tail curls over back

Long hair falls over eyes

Feathering covers round, snowshoe-like feet

JAPANESE CHIN

THIS EXTROVERT, STYLISH, LIVELY DOG IS DAINTY BUT DEFINITELY NOT DELICATE AKC

Height range
8-11in (20-28cm)

Weight range
4-7lb (2-3kg)

Life span Over 10 years

Origin Japan

Other colors

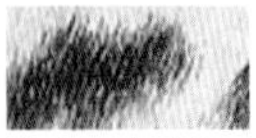

Red and white

Ancestors of the Japanese Chin are thought to have been a royal gift from China to the Emperor of Japan. This dog was bred especially to warm the laps and hands of the ladies of Japan's Imperial Palace. Happy living in a small space, it makes an ideal apartment dog but its profuse coat sheds heavily.

Short, wide muzzle with upturned nose

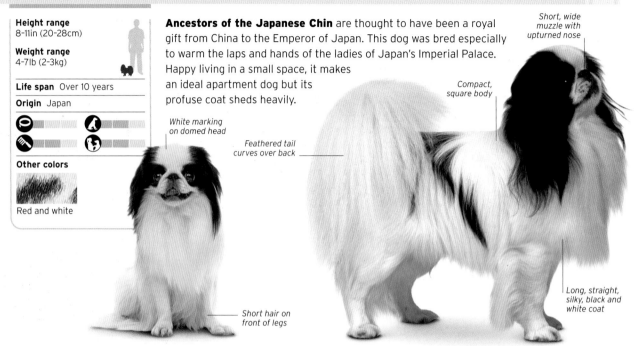

Compact, square body

White marking on domed head

Feathered tail curves over back

Long, straight, silky, black and white coat

Short hair on front of legs

DANISH-SWEDISH FARMDOG

ALERT, ATTENTIVE, AND FRIENDLY, THIS DOG NEEDS A LOT OF EXERCISE

Height range
13-15in (32-37cm)

Weight range
15-26lb (7-12kg)

Life span 10-15 years

Origin Denmark/Sweden

This working dog has been historically used on farms in Denmark and Sweden as a herder, watchdog, and ratter, as well as a companion. Always eager to play, the Danish-Swedish Farmdog is good with children, so can make a great family dog, but it does have a tendency to chase small animals.

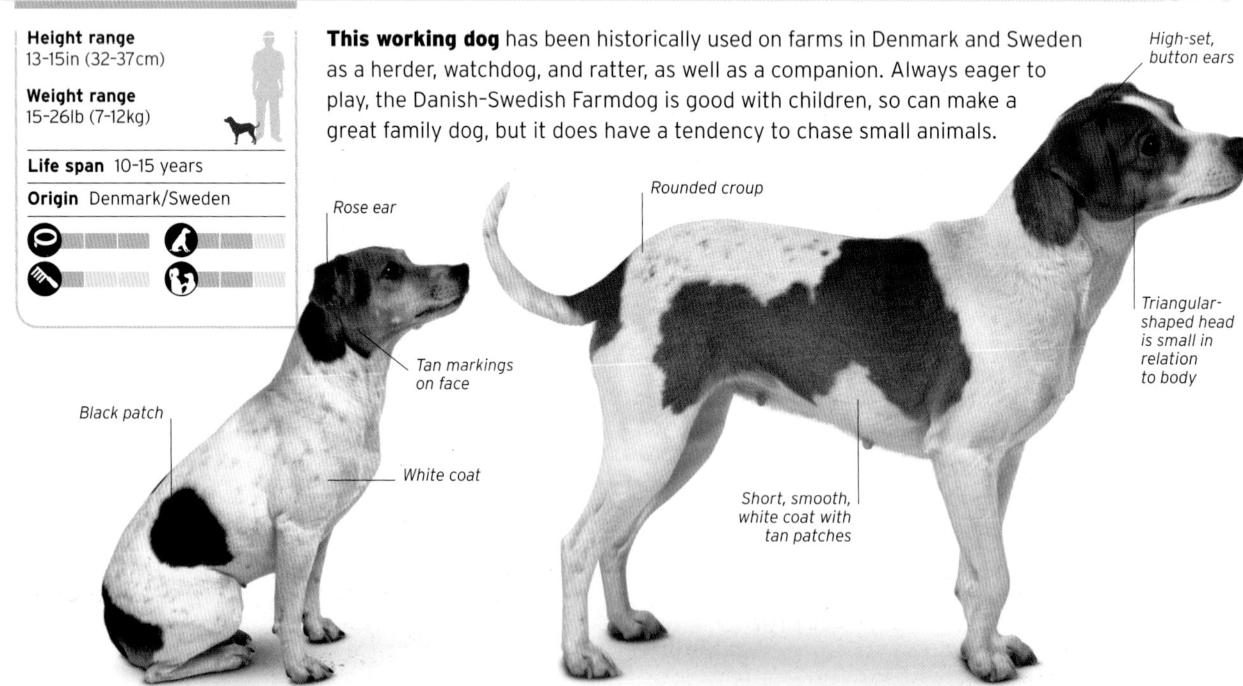
High-set, button ears
Rounded croup
Rose ear
Tan markings on face
Triangular-shaped head is small in relation to body
Black patch
White coat
Short, smooth, white coat with tan patches

DALMATIAN

THIS PLAYFUL AND EASY-GOING DOG NEEDS PLENTY OF EXERCISE AND PERSISTENT TRAINING AKC

Height range
22-24in (56-61cm)

Weight range
40-60lb (18-27kg)

Life span Over 10 years

Origin Unknown

Particularly popular in Britain during the early 19th century, the Dalmatian was known as the "carriage dog," because it was trained to run under or beside horse-drawn carriages and fire engines, often traveling very long distances. The only spotted dog breed, the Dalmatian is intelligent, friendly, and outgoing, and makes an excellent companion. However, it does have a lot of energy and can be stubborn and aggressive with other dogs, so an owner needs to dedicate time to training. The puppies are born pure white, making it difficult to predict whether the spots will be black or liver once mature; this dog's white coat sheds a great deal.

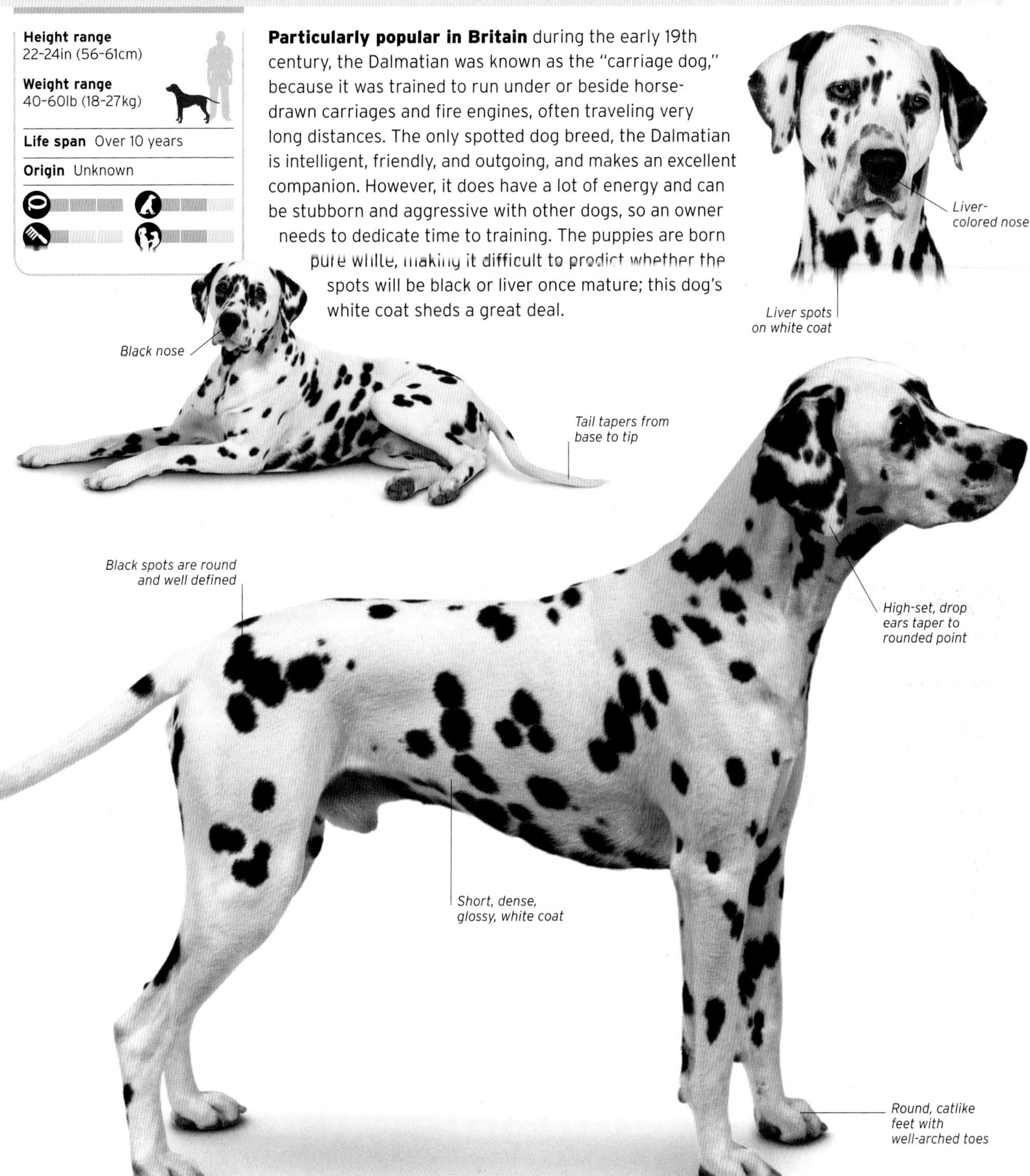
Liver-colored nose
Liver spots on white coat
Black nose
Tail tapers from base to tip
Black spots are round and well defined
High-set, drop ears taper to rounded point
Short, dense, glossy, white coat
Round, catlike feet with well-arched toes

NORTH AMERICAN SHEPHERD

THIS LOYAL LITTLE DOG RETAINS THE HERDING INSTINCT OF ITS ANCESTORS

Height range
13–18in (33–46cm)

Weight range
15–30lb (7–14kg)

Life span 12–13 years

Origin USA

Other colors

Red merle  | Blue merle

Downsized from the Australian Shepherd (see p.63) by American breeders, this dog is sometimes called the Miniature Australian Shepherd. It is highly intelligent, easy to train, and very good with children. The North American Shepherd is eager to please, but can be nervous and quite destructive if left on its own for long periods of time.

Drop ears

Well-feathered tail

Brown eyes

Black coat with tan and white markings

HIMALAYAN SHEEPDOG

THIS DOG IS RESERVED BY NATURE SO CAN MAKE AN EXCELLENT WATCHDOG

Height range
20–25in (51–63cm)

Weight range
50–60lb (3–27kg)

Life span 10–11 years

Origin Nepal

Other colors

Gold | Black

Also known as the Bhotia, this rare dog from the foothills of the Himalayas is related to the larger Tibetan Mastiff (see p.77), but its exact origins and former uses are obscure. This is a powerful dog with a strong herding instinct. Kept as a family pet, it is a good companion and an efficient guard dog.

Thick, bushy tail, loosely turned over back
Drop ears lie close to head
Long, harsh, creamy white topcoat
Black and tan coat
White markings
Catlike feet

THAI RIDGEBACK

THIS TOUGH, INDEPENDENT-MINDED DOG IS VERY ATHLETIC

FCI

Height range
Up to 9in (Up to 20-24cm)

Weight range
50-75lb (23-34kg)

Life span 10-12 years

Origin Thailand

Other colors

Fawn (Isabella) Red

Blue

An old breed and unknown outside Thailand until the mid-1970s, the Thai Ridgeback has since gained recognition in other countries. It was used for hunting, to follow carts, and as a guard dog. Its earlier geographic isolation has resulted in most of its original natural instincts and drives remaining, because there were few chances for it to breed with other dogs. Today it is primarily kept as a companion dog, and is naturally protective of its home and family. It can make a loyal, loving pet, but is often suspicious of other dogs, and can be aggressive or shy if not properly socialized.

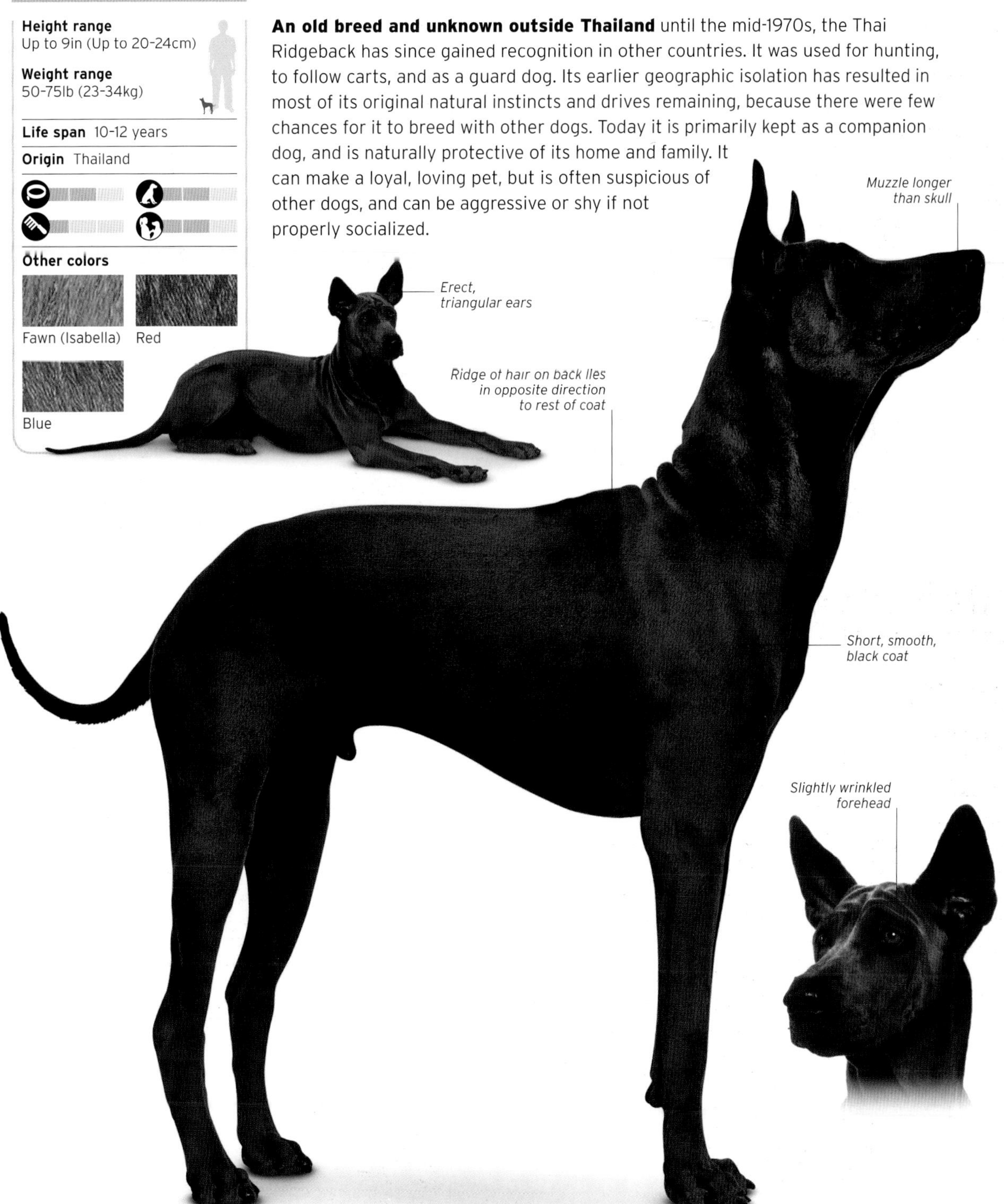
Muzzle longer than skull
Erect, triangular ears
Ridge of hair on back lies in opposite direction to rest of coat
Short, smooth, black coat
Slightly wrinkled forehead

GOLDENDOODLE
This attractive dog is a cross between a Poodle and a Golden Retriever. The characteristics of the Poodle parent are clearly dominant.

CROSSBREEDS

Dogs of mixed breeding vary from the so-called designer dogs, with purebred parents of two different recognized breeds, to the bit-of-everything type, the result of accidental, random crosses (see p.288). Some designer hybrids are now extremely fashionable. They are mostly given whimsical combination names, such as Cockerpoo (a Cocker Spaniel-Poodle cross).

No pedigree, parents unknown–but an excellent companion

One of the reasons for creating modern hybrid dogs was to mix the desired characteristics from one breed with the non-shedding, hypoallergenic coat of another. A cross of this type currently enjoying great popularity is the Labradoodle, a mixture of Labrador Retriever and Poodle. However, even when the parents are readily recognized breeds such as these, it may be impossible to predict which side of the family the puppies will favor. Labradoodles, for example, show little consistency from litter to litter, some puppies inheriting the curly Poodle coat while others are more obviously influenced by the Labrador parent. Such lack of standardization is common in designer crosses, although occasionally it has proved possible to produce a standard and breed dogs to type. An example of this is the Lucas Terrier, the result of crossing the Sealyham Terrier and the Norfolk Terrier. Currently, it is rare for such crosses to achieve breed recognition.

Deliberate mixing of two specific breeds to produce particular characteristics has proliferated since the end of the 20th century, but is by no means a modern trend. One of the best known crossbreeds, the Lurcher, has been around for several hundred years. This dog combines the qualities of speedy sight hounds, such as the Greyhound and Whippet with desirable traits found in other breeds, such as the collie's enthusiasm for work, and the tenacity of the terrier.

Prospective owners of a hybrid designer dog should take into account the personalities and temperaments of both breeds involved in the mix. These may be very different and either one might predominate. It is also important to consider both parent dogs' requirements for general care and exercise.

All crossbred dogs are commonly believed to be more intelligent than pedigree dogs, but there is no sound evidence for this. Random breeds are often said to be healthier than purebreds, and it is true that they are at much lower risk of the inherited diseases prevalent in some breeds.

HEALTHY DOG
Random bred dogs like this terrier cross are usually robust, and are largely free from inherited disorders.

GUNDOG CROSS
The Labradinger is a cross between two popular gundogs–the Labrador Retriever and the English Springer Spaniel.

LURCHER

FLEET-FOOTED OUTDOORS, AT HOME THIS DOG IS LAID-BACK AND RELAXED

Height range
22-28in (55-71cm)

Weight range
60-71lb (27-32kg)

Life span 13-14 years

Origin UK

Other colors

Any color

Famed as a poacher's dog, and used to hunt rabbit and hare, traditionally Lurchers were first-generation crosses of a sight hound with a terrier or a herding dog. Today they are also bred with each other and ideally are greyhound size. In the home Lurchers are peaceful and tolerant, and make fine family companions.

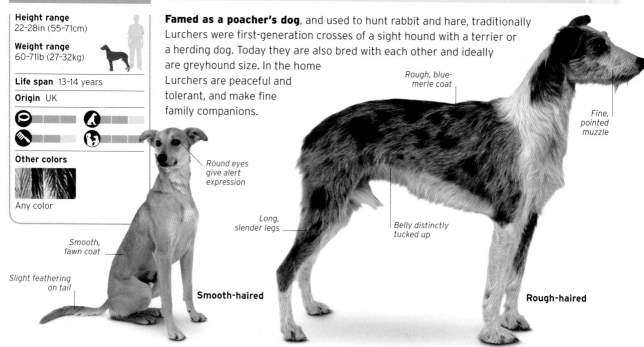

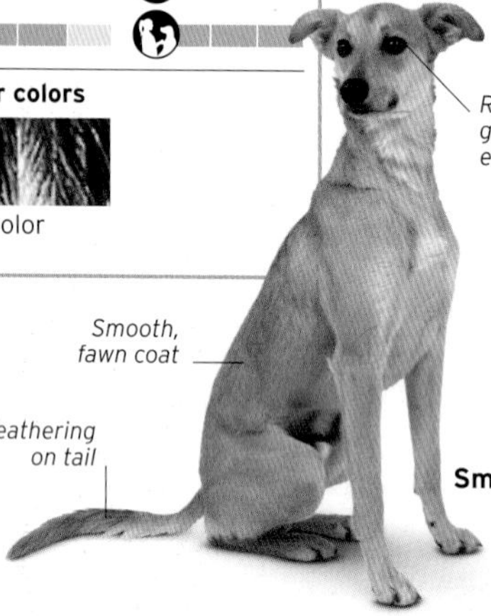

Round eyes give alert expression

Smooth, fawn coat

Slight feathering on tail

Smooth-haired

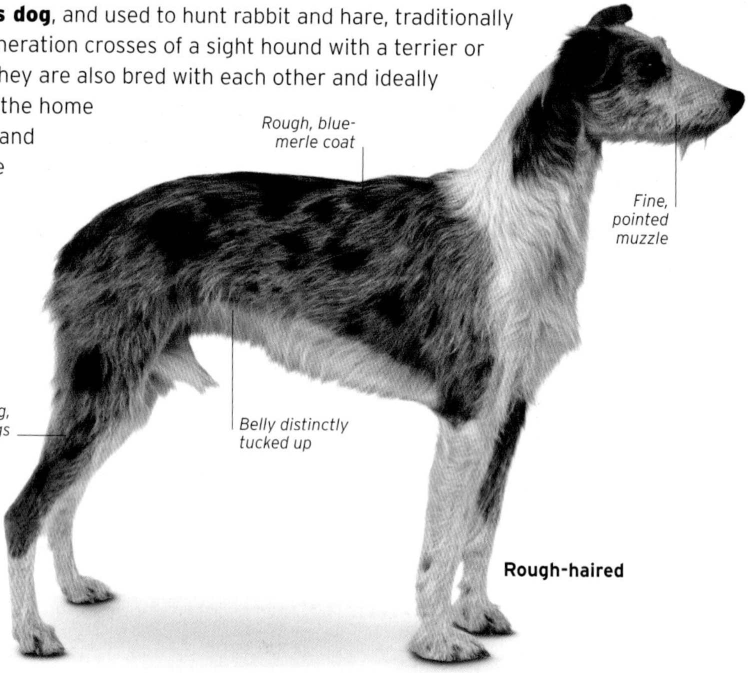

Rough, blue-merle coat

Fine, pointed muzzle

Long, slender legs

Belly distinctly tucked up

Rough-haired

COCKERPOO

THIS INTELLIGENT, GREGARIOUS, AND RELAXED DOG MAKES AN EASY COUNTRY OR CITY COMPANION

Height range
Toy:
Up to 10in (up to 25cm)
Miniature:
11-14in (28-35cm)
Standard:
Over 15in (over 38cm)

Weight range
Toy:
Up to 11lb (up to 5kg)
Miniature:
12-20lb (6-9kg)
Standard:
Over 22lb (over 10kg)

Life span 14-15 years

Origin Mostly USA

Other colors

Any color

Most Cockerpoos are first-generation crosses of a Toy or Miniature Poodle (see p.271) with an Cocker Spaniel or sometimes English Cocker Spaniel (see p.222). They are particularly valued for their tractable and affectionate characters. Their appearance is a variable mix of the parent breeds, but always with a wavy coat that sheds very little.

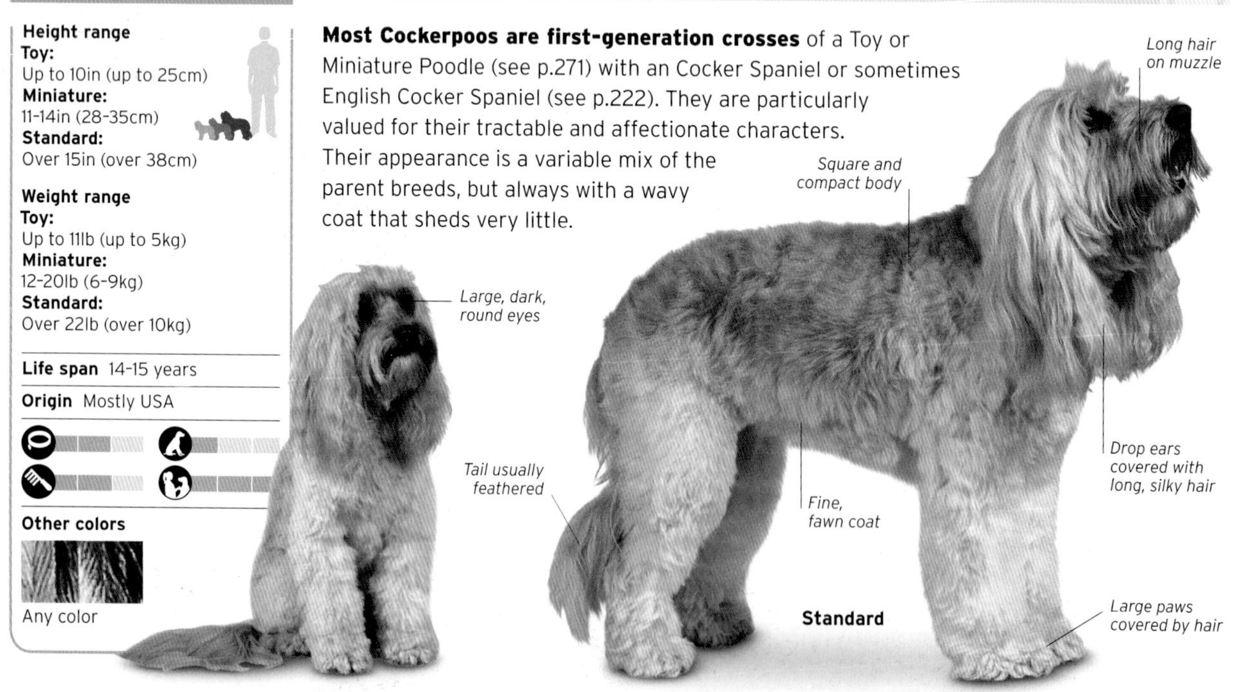
Long hair on muzzle
Square and compact body
Large, dark, round eyes
Tail usually feathered
Fine, fawn coat
Drop ears covered with long, silky hair
Large paws covered by hair
Standard

LABRADOODLE

INCREASINGLY POPULAR, THIS DOG IS RELIABLY PLAYFUL, AFFECTIONATE, AND INTELLIGENT

Height range
Miniature:
14-16in (36-41cm)
Medium:
17-20in (43-51cm)
Standard:
21-24in (53-61cm)

Weight range
Miniature:
15-25lb (7-11kg)
Medium:
30-45lb (14-20kg)
Standard:
50-65lb (23-29kg)

Life span 14-15 years

Origin Australia

Other colors

Any color

The original Labrador-Poodle cross was intended as an assistance dog suitable for allergy sufferers, but the Labradoodle has rapidly gained popularity as a family dog. In its original homeland it is on its way to being a pedigree breed, with a written standard. Elsewhere, this remains a crossbreed, with no official status but in huge demand. First-generation crosses vary in appearance; later Labradoodle-only breedings are more predictable. The dog's personality attracts owners as much as its appearance. It is consistently level-headed and biddable without becoming serious or reserved.

Drop, apricot-colored ears
Large, dark, rounded eyes
Body slightly heavier than a Poodle (see p.271)
Long, curved tail
Tucked-up belly
Curly, cream coat has little dander
Medium-sized, round feet

Standard

BICHON YORKIE

THIS PLAYFUL, SMALL COMPANION DOG IS IDEALLY SUITED TO URBAN LIFE

Height range
9-12in (23-31cm)

Weight range
7-13lb (3-6kg)

Life span 13-15 years

Origin UK

Other colors

Variety of colors

Some crossbreeds are created deliberately, but the first Bichon Frise (see p.267) and Yorkshire Terrier (see p.192) mix was a happy accident that breeders have chosen to repeat. The result is the Bichon Yorkie—a dog that is usually larger than the diminutive Yorkshire Terrier, with the feisty spirit of its terrier parent tempered by the more compliant nature of the Bichon Frise.

Dark nose
Dark, round eyes
High-set ears
Darker, plumed tail carried high when moving
Double-layered, silky, curly, white and orange coat
Round, tight feet

BULL BOXER

THIS FRIENDLY AND BOISTEROUS DOG IS EASIER TO TRAIN THAN OTHER MASTIFF-TYPES

Height range
16-21in (41-53cm)

Weight range
37-53lb (17-24kg)

Life span 12-13 years

Origin UK

Other colors

Any color

The Bull Boxer is a cross between the laid-back Boxer (see p.88) and bull-baiting dogs such as the Staffordshire Bull Terrier (see p.214), which is highly popular but may be difficult with other pets. The Bull Boxer occupies the middle ground in size and character. This dog needs commitment, but rewards its owner well.

Rounded eyes have alert expression

Strong, blunt muzzle with overhanging lip

Broad, deep chest

Long, tapering, curved tail

Small, semierect, drop ears

Powerful build inherited from both parents

Smooth, shiny, short, dense, black coat

White markings on feet

Legs longer than Staffordshire Bull Terrier's

LUCAS TERRIER

THIS FRIENDLY, NON-YAPPY TERRIER GETS ON WELL WITH CHILDREN AND OTHER PETS

Height range
9-12in (23-30cm)

Weight range
11-20lb (5-9kg)

Life span 14-15 years

Origin UK

Other colors

White

Tan coats may have a black or badger-gray saddle. White coats may be marked with black, badger-gray, and/or tan.

This rare working terrier was produced in the 1940s by crossing Norfolk Terriers with Sealyham Terriers (see p.191). The Lucas Terrier is named after its first breeder, Sir Jocelyn Lucas, a British politician and sportsman who wanted to develop a small, nimble dog that was more efficient than the Sealyham Terrier at following game to ground. Smart and eager to please, the Lucas Terrier is easy to train and quietly behaved in the house, provided it has a good daily walk. It has typical terrier traits, such as enjoying play and loving to dig, but is less inclined to bark than many other terrier breeds.

Small, V-shaped ears
Longer hair forms moustache and beard
Black nose
Almond-shaped, dark eyes
Thick-rooted, well-furred tail
Body length exceeds leg length
Medium-length, coarse, light tan coat

GOLDENDOODLE

A DELIGHTFUL NEW CROSSBREED, THIS DOG IS SOCIABLE AND EASY TO LIVE WITH

Height range
Up to 24in (up to 61cm)

Weight range
51-90lb (23-41kg)

Life span 10-15 years

Origin USA

Other colors

Any color

One of the newest "designer dogs," this mixture of the Poodle (see p.271) and the Golden Retriever (see p.258) was first bred in the US in the 1990s. Since then the Goldendoodle's growing popularity has encouraged breeders elsewhere to continue its development. Most of these dogs are first-generation crosses and vary considerably in appearance—some have curly coats while others are wavy or straight. The crossbreed's size depends on whether the Poodle parent is a medium, miniature, or toy variety. Although lively and energetic, Goldendoodles have gentle temperaments and are usually easy to train. They get on well with children and other pets.

Brown nose
Drop ears, slightly darker than rest of coat
Well-defined stop
Dark eyes with kind expression
Darker saddle of hair
Slightly tucked-up belly
Thick, curly, apricot coat
Heavily feathered tail
Front feet larger than back feet

LABRADINGER

THIS ATTRACTIVE ALL-ROUNDER IS SUITABLE AS A FAMILY DOG AND AS A GUNDOG

Height range
18–22in (46–56cm)

Weight range
55–90lb (25–41kg)

Life span 10–14 years

Origin USA

Other colors

Yellow

Liver

Chocolate

A cross between the Labrador Retriever (see pp.256–57) and the English Springer Spaniel (see pp.226–27), this dog is also sometimes known as the Springador. Unplanned breeding of hybrid dogs is likely to have occurred for centuries on traditional country estates where such gundogs were kept. Benefiting from recent interest in fashionable crossbreeds such as the Labradoodle (see p.285), the Labradinger has now acquired both popularity and a name. It is an excellent gundog that can be trained both to retrieve and to flush game, as the spaniel does, and is proving very successful as a family dog.

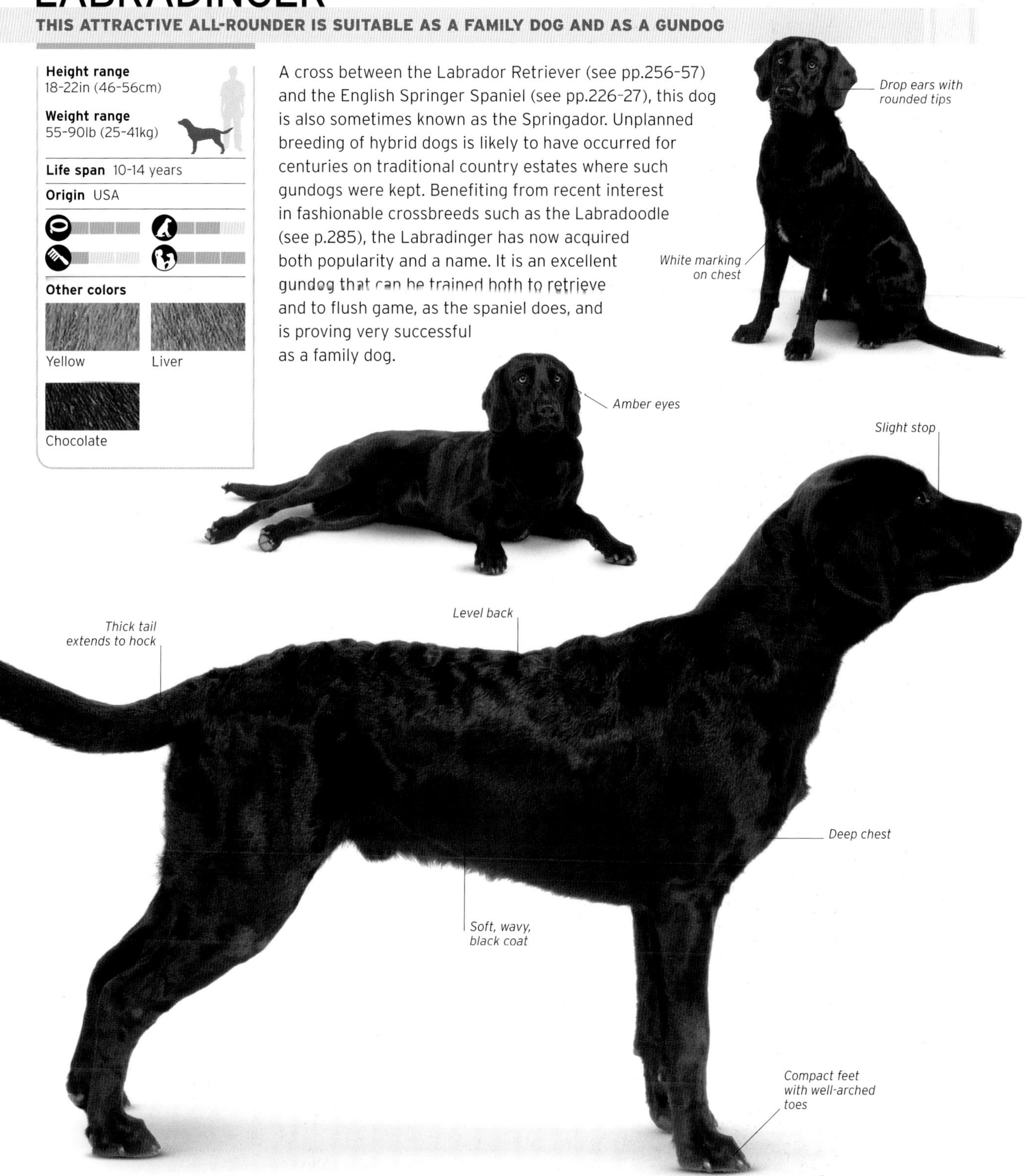
Drop ears with rounded tips
White marking on chest
Amber eyes
Slight stop
Level back
Thick tail extends to hock
Deep chest
Soft, wavy, black coat
Compact feet with well-arched toes

RANDOM-BRED DOGS

THESE DOGS MAY LACK A PEDIGREE BUT THEY CAN PROVIDE LOVE, COMPANIONSHIP, AND FUN

Dogs with random breeding are usually of unknown ancestry, with the parents themselves likely to be the result of accidental mixings that may go back several generations. Choosing a random-bred puppy is something of a lottery for prospective owners because it is difficult to predict what the dog will look like at maturity. Many of the dogs available for adoption in rescue centers are random crossbreds; in the majority of cases they make excellent pets.

Long hairs cover feet

LONG AND SHAGGY
Puppies with soft, fluffy coats often grow up to have long, coarse coats, like this dog's, that require regular grooming to prevent matting.

SOFT AND SILKY
Many random-bred dogs resemble sheepdogs with soft coats and feathering on the chest, legs, and tail. This dog has sheepdog markings too.

LARGE DOG
Random-bred dogs can grow to any size or shape. This large dog may be the same size as one or other of its parents or somewhere inbetween the two.

Expressive, brown eyes

Black, triangular, drop ears

SHORT AND SMOOTH
The short coat and drop ears of this dog suggest a hound-like ancestor, but its merle coloring is less easy to explain.

MEDIUM-SIZED DOG
Many mixed-breed dogs are intermediate in size and sandy in color, like this one.

Well-feathered tail

SMALL DOG
This small dog has some distinctly terrier-like features, including semierect ears and a broad head.

UNIQUE APPEARANCE
Unlike pedigree dogs, no two random-bred dogs are alike. This dog may resemble a terrier superficially but its offspring may look very different.

CARE AND TRAINING

PREPARING FOR ARRIVAL

Forward thinking and early preparation will help to make your puppy's introduction to his new home as stress free as possible. Before the newest member of the family arrives, check that the home environment, both indoors and outdoors, is safe for a young, inquisitive dog. Ensure too that you have all the basic equipment needed for his daily care and development, including his collar, bed, and toys.

A puppy is life-changing

Puppy-proofing your home

Start your safety checks by walking around your home and yard and trying to see everything as your puppy would see it. What looks like a tempting object to chew? Is that table in a prime position to be knocked over? Is there a small gap in the fence that he could squeeze through if he tried? Take preventive action now to avoid trouble later.

Safety indoors

Making your home safe for a dog is similar to making it safe for children. Remember that dogs investigate a new object by chewing it, so place anything potentially hazardous well out of a puppy's reach. Toxic household chemicals are an obvious danger but your puppy could be poisoned by many other things, such as certain pot plants and some human foods, including chocolate. Remind children not to leave small toys lying around for your puppy to pick up and choke on. Watch out for electrical wires, remote controls, and anything else near the floor and small enough for a puppy to gnaw. Objects that you may think are out of reach may just be accidents waiting to happen; for example, a laundry basket is easy to knock over and its contents can create hours of fun for a destructive puppy. You may have to keep some doors in your home closed or perhaps use a stair gate to limit the areas that your new dog can access.

Safety outdoors

Look for gaps in fences and underneath gates, even if you plan to supervise your dog outside. Puppies can rapidly disappear through the smallest holes and thickest hedges if they think there is something interesting on the other side. Keep yard chemicals out of the way. Slug pellets and other garden pesticides look like a tasty treat to dogs; while some are safe for pets, others are harmful if eaten. Do not let your puppy chew garden plants, since a great many common varieties are poisonous. Take care not to leave wheelbarrows or gardening tools leaning against fences where they could be knocked over by a boisterous puppy and cause injury.

HAZARDS FOR YOUR DOG TO AVOID

TOXIC PLANTS | HARMFUL CHEMICALS | UNSTABLE OBJECTS | GAPS UNDER GATE | SLUG PELLETS

TOP TIPS

- **Remember to make a vet** appointment to complete your puppy's vaccinations soon after you bring him home.
- **A good pet insurance policy** provides you with vital peace of mind and reassurance in an emergency.
- **Ask your breeder** if you can take home a towel or blanket that smells familiar to your puppy. It will help to reassure him during the first few nights.

Collars and leashes

To begin with, you will need to buy a small, light puppy collar and replace it as your dog grows. The style of collar depends on what your dog finds most comfortable. For example, long-haired breeds will find a smooth, rolled leather collar more comfortable because it does not pull on their coat as much as a nylon collar. Greyhound-type breeds are happier with a wide, flat collar that is less likely to damage their sensitive necks. Whatever type of dog you have, make sure that the width of his collar exceeds the width of one of his neck vertebrae. When choosing a leash, simply handle a few to see which one feels most comfortable for you.

Harnesses and halters

A typical harness fits around the body with the leash attaching on the dog's back. This can be beneficial for some dogs, since it removes tension from around the neck, but harnesses can be tricky to take on and off, especially with an exuberant or over-excited dog. The harness straps should be well fitted at all points, leaving enough room for you to slip two fingers easily between the harness and the dog's body. Contrary to popular belief, harnesses do not stop a dog from pulling on the leash; only training can do that. If you have a dog that is a determined puller, you may find a halter with a fixed noseband helps to restrain him.

Name tag

Address holder

NAME.................
TEL...................

THE RIGHT COLLAR
Choose a collar for comfort, not fashionable appearance. Avoid any types of collar that tighten when the dog pulls, such as chain collars.

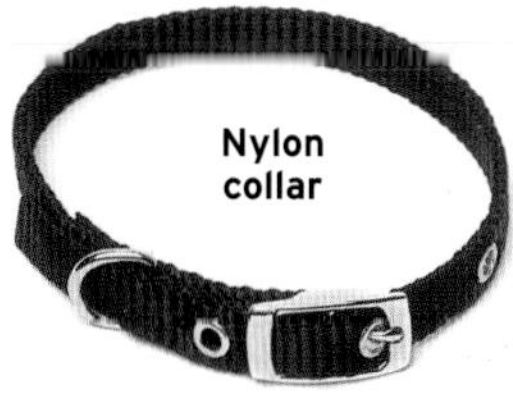
Nylon collar

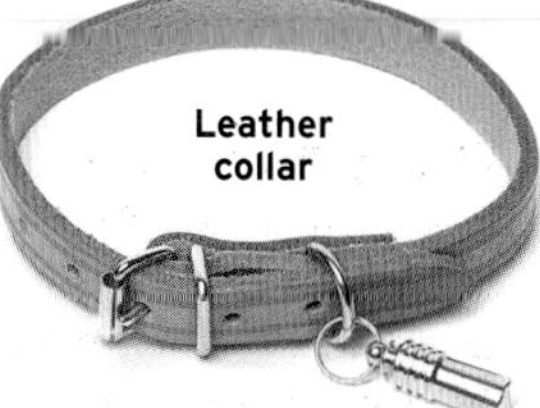
Leather collar

ID TAGS
Include your name and emergency contact details so that people can get in touch with you easily if your dog is lost.

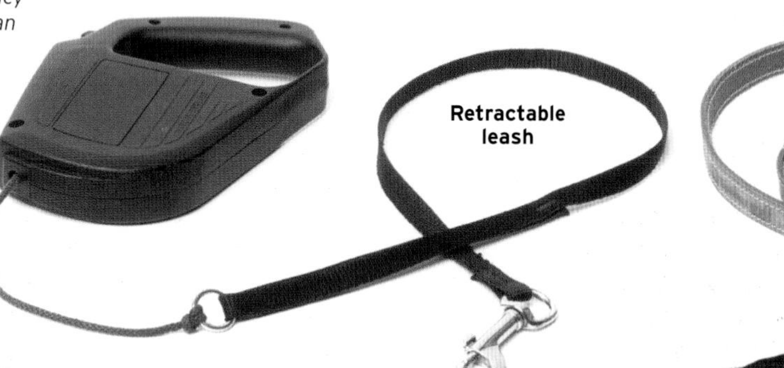
Retractable leash

Short leash

TYPES OF LEASH
Short leashes are ideal for close control—for example, when training. Retractable leashes allow your dog more freedom to run.

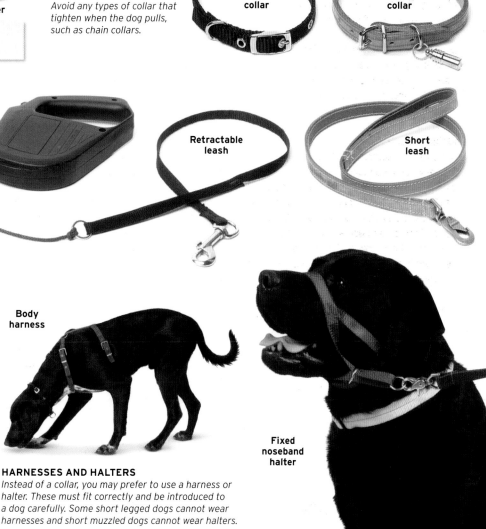

FITTING A COLLAR

A collar should fit securely around a dog's neck without being too tight. As a guide, you should be able to fit two fingers between the collar and the dog's neck. Check the fit regularly as your puppy grows and alter it as necessary. Replace the collar as soon as your puppy grows out of it.

Body harness

Fixed noseband halter

HARNESSES AND HALTERS
Instead of a collar, you may prefer to use a harness or halter. These must fit correctly and be introduced to a dog carefully. Some short legged dogs cannot wear harnesses and short muzzled dogs cannot wear halters.

Types of bed

Dog beds vary widely in price, and until your puppy is settled and fully house-trained it is not worth investing in anything expensive. A new dog may chew or soil his bed, so look for a cheap and washable option.

There are two main types of bed: hard and soft. Hard beds, made from molded plastic, are easy to keep clean. They are also relatively difficult for a young puppy to chew, although a dog who has his adult teeth may inflict some damage. You can use disposable items such as old towels to make a plastic bed comfortable for your dog, safe in the knowledge that you can wash or discard bedding that gets chewed or soiled. These beds are also a good choice for an older dog who suffers from incontinence. Soft, foam-filled beds are more comfortable to sleep on, especially for an older dog who is beginning to experience stiffness in his joints. Although the cover may be washable, these beds are not suitable for young puppies because they like nothing better than pulling the bed's foam filling out, leaving you with the expense of a replacement bed.

STAIR GATE
Use a stair gate to keep your young dog safe in one room without making him feel trapped.

Crates and playpens

Until your new puppy is house-trained, use a crate or a playpen as his personal space. Never confine your dog as a punishment. A crate or playpen should be a place that your dog enjoys—you may even feed him there. A playpen also gives you peace of mind, safely containing your puppy away from trouble while you are in another room. If you introduce your puppy to a crate when he is young, he will be happy to use it for the rest of his life. A puppy soon learns to see his crate as a sort of den, a safe haven where he can go if he feels overwhelmed, anxious, or tired and simply wants to sleep.

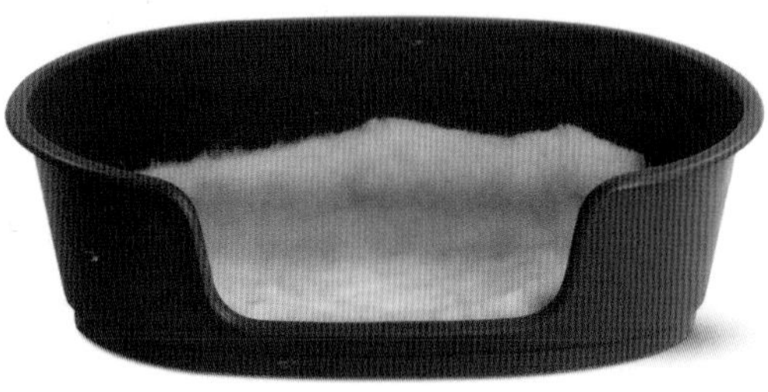

Molded plastic bed

Foam-filled bed

DOG BEDS
Plastic beds are hygienic and hard-wearing. Pad them with soft bedding to make your dog comfortable. Foam-filled beds and beanbags are cosy and attractive but are not suitable for young puppies until they are house-trained and have stopped chewing. Soft beds usually have washable covers that can be removed.

Keep the gate open unless you leave the room

Crate

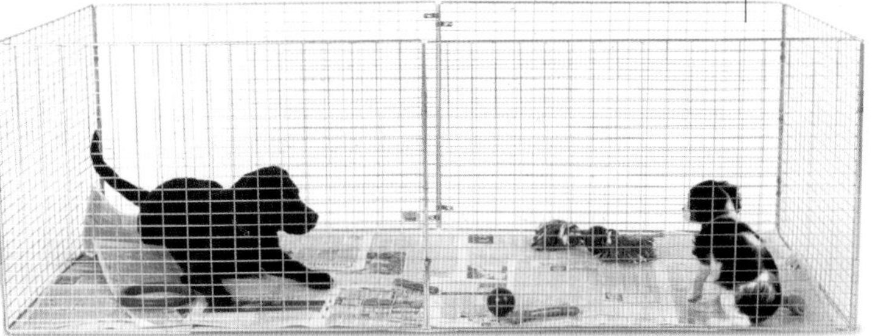

Playpens have open tops

Playpen

USING A CRATE
A crate or playpen allows you to leave your puppy unsupervised when you are busy. He will probably sleep some of the time, but give him plenty of toys to keep him amused. Do not leave him confined alone for long periods at a time.

TOYS FOR YOUNG PUPPIES
Soft toys are best for young puppies who have not yet grown a set of adult teeth. A puppy is likely to go through several toys, so don't buy expensive ones.

Soft toys

Rope tugger

Puppy with chewable rubber ring

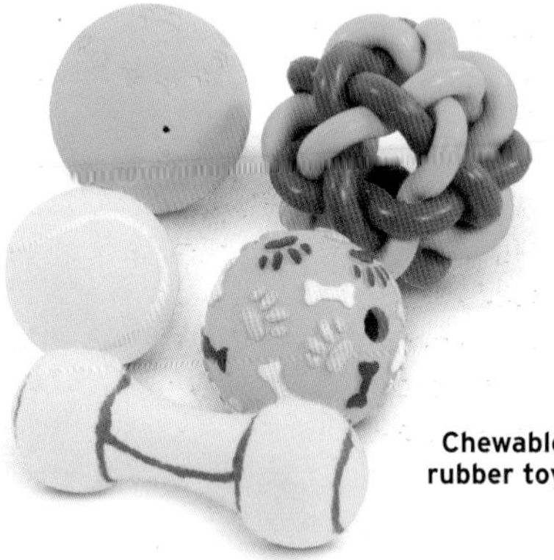

Chewable rubber toys

TOYS FOR OLDER PUPPIES
As puppies get older, they will chew vigorously and need more durable toys. Thick rope tuggers, or toys with a combination of rope and chewable rubber, are a good choice and last a long time.

TOYS FOR ADULT DOGS
Adult dogs also love toys and appreciate those with a variety of textures and materials. Harder toys are best, because they will withstand chewing by a mature dog's full set of teeth.

Rubber and rope bone

Buying toys

Toys provide a dog with mental stimulation and something permissible to chew on. Used for games or during training sessions, they are great for encouraging a dog to interact with his owner. When buying toys, choose only those that are specially designed for dogs. Children's toys are a dangerous substitute since they may have small pieces that a dog can chew off and swallow. Never leave your dog alone with his toys for long periods; even playthings that are meant to be chewed, such as rawhide bones, can be a choking hazard.

Soft toys are best for young puppies while they still have their baby teeth. As puppies get older and begin teething, they are more likely to chew and at this stage stronger toys such as rope tuggers are the best choice. Once your dog is an adult, choose toys with a variety of textures and shapes. Toys that can be thrown or tugged are good as long as you are able to play with your dog, otherwise choose a toy that he can chew on. Some chewable toys have tasty flavors and there are also food-dispensing toys that release treats when played with. These can keep a dog entertained for a long time, and are useful if you are too busy to play. Dogs that are dedicated chewers can often be kept out of mischief with rubber toys, which are very durable, or the ranges of rubber toys that are designed to be stuffed with food. Most dogs have favorite toys, and you will soon get to know which ones your dog likes best.

TOP TIPS

- **Playing with a tug toy** is a great way to train a puppy not to mouth at your hand. Offer to play with him but end the game as soon as his teeth meet your hand.
- **Use food-dispensing toys** to keep your dog entertained if you have to leave him alone for short periods.
- **Keep a favorite toy** hidden out of your dog's reach and use it only as a prized reward during training sessions.

FOOD AND FEEDING

A puppy's dietary needs change as he matures

Keeping a dog healthy is largely a question of feeding him the right food in the right quantities. There are several options: complete, pre-prepared dried or wet foods; raw, uncooked foods; or a diet created from combination of these. Whatever you decide on, aim for a good nutritional balance and tailor the quantities to suit the size and age of your dog.

A balanced diet

Ready-prepared dog food is the choice of many owners since it is both quick and convenient. Reading the labels on processed foods will tell you what type of dog they are suitable for. Make sure you use a type that is appropriate for your dog's age. Some foods are available in puppy, junior, adult, and senior varieties, and buying the right formula is important. When in doubt about what quantities to feed, ask your vet for advice. If you decide to feed your dog a mixture of wet and dried food, be careful to halve the quantity of each so you are not overfeeding him.

A balanced diet consists of the right quantities of nutrients: proteins, carbohydrates, fat, vitamins, and minerals. Using processed foods ensures that you get the balance right; if you feed your dog fresh food, his diet needs a little more thought. A dog's nutritional requirements change as he ages. Puppies need high levels of protein and calcium to aid growth and development. Geriatric dogs, on the other hand, require particularly high-quality protein as well as increased levels of certain vitamins as their kidney function slows down. Reduced kidney function can lead to dehydration, due to too much water being excreted, so you may decide to feed an older dog a wet diet rather than dried food, to increase his water intake. The sort of food your dog eats will also affect the care of his teeth. A dog that is fed exclusively on wet food is more likely to need to have his teeth cleaned regularly.

Your dog needs two bowls: one for food and one for water. Put the food bowl down only at mealtimes and remove it as soon as your dog has finished eating. The water bowl should be left in an accessible place at all times and should always be kept filled with fresh water. Of the various types of bowl available, the best are stainless steel, since they can be thoroughly cleaned after each use and, unlike plastic bowls, cannot be chewed. Bowls with sloping edges are a good choice because they are difficult for your dog to tip over.

WHICH DOG BOWL?
It is best to invest in a sturdy stainless steel bowl with sloping edges rather than a plastic bowl. Pick a size that your new dog can reach into easily.

Stainless steel bowl

Plastic bowl

TYPES OF FOOD
Dry food provides your dog with a complete, age-appropriate diet. Wet food alone may lead to dental problems. Raw food, such as meat and vegetables, takes a little longer to prepare.

Dry food for puppies

Senior food

Canned food

Meat from a pouch

Raw food

FOOD OPTIONS AND AMOUNTS PER DAY

DOG WEIGHT	DRIED FOOD	CANNED FOOD 14OZ (400G)	MEAT FROM A POUCH	RAW FOOD
Pekingese 11lb (5kg)	3oz (75g)	1 can	11oz (300g)	5oz (150g)
Beagle 22lb (10kg)	7oz (200g)	2 cans	1lb 5oz (600g)	11oz (300g)
Border Collie 44lb (20kg)	14oz (400g)	3 cans	2lb 3oz (1kg)	1lb 5oz (600g)
Dobermann 66lb (30kg)	1lb (500g)	4 cans	2lb 10oz (1.2kg)	2lb (900g)
Irish Wolfhound 88lb (40kg)	1lb 5oz (600g)	5 cans	4lb (1.8kg)	2lb 10oz (1.2kg)

TOP TIPS

- **Opened pouches** or cans of wet food will need to be sealed and refrigerated between uses. Dried dog food should also be kept in a sealed container, to keep it fresh and free from contamination.
- **Puppies need** three or four small meals a day, but by the time they are mature will only require feeding morning and evening. Feeding your dog smaller meals twice a day as opposed to one big meal is preferable, as it puts less strain on their digestive systems.
- **Introduce new foods** gradually over several days to avoid stomach upsets.

Treats and chews

If you use a lot of edible treats to reward your dog during training, you may risk overfeeding him. Consider the treats part of your dog's overall diet and slightly reduce the amount of food you give him at mealtimes. Alternatively, you can take part of your dog's main rations to give as treats throughout the day, especially if you use dried food.

Either buy dog treats from a pet shop or make your own at home by chopping up foods such as cheese, chicken, or hot dogs. Dogs are particularly fond of treats that have a strong smell and taste.

Chews are a great way to keep your dog occupied for a while and provide something to take a puppy's mind off chewing your household possessions. They are also very effective at keeping a dog's teeth clean. Be careful what type of chew you give your dog. Canine teeth are extremely strong and can tear apart chews with ease; swallowing the loose parts can lead to choking or a blockage. Never leave a puppy or young dog alone while he has a chew.

PRACTICAL CHOICE
Hide chews not only keep your puppy entertained but also help to clean his teeth. Always supervise him when he is chewing and remove any small pieces he tears off in exchange for a treat.

TREAT VARIETIES
Using a variety of treats keeps your dog motivated during training and allows you to create a hierarchy of rewards. Knowing which treats appeal most to your dog will make training an easier and more enjoyable task.

Cubes of cheese

Bite-sized training treats

Meaty strips

Cooked sausage

FIRST DAYS

Your puppy's first days in his new home are important to the rest of his development. Start as you intend to go on and set the rules right from the beginning. Do not be tempted to be lenient while your dog settles in. He will feel at home much more quickly and easily if you set clear boundaries. The sooner you establish a routine the sooner you will succeed in training your dog.

It's never too early for a puppy to learn

Choosing a name

Family discussions about choosing a name that suits your new puppy are likely to be long and difficult. The name should be something that you feel comfortable calling out in public. It must also be clearly distinguishable from any commands you are likely to want to teach your dog. For example, a dog called "Kit" will find learning the command to "sit" very difficult. Overly long names make training problematic, so pick something with just one or two syllables. Remember that dogs do not understand language, only sounds. Giving your dog a long name that you shorten in some situations will only confuse him. Also to keep it simple for your dog, make sure that all members of your family use the same name to address him.

TRAINING | TEACHING YOUR DOG HIS NAME

1 When your puppy is nearby, crouch down and clearly call his name in a cheery, enthusiastic voice. Use your hands to guide his attention toward you.

2 As your puppy approaches, praise him in an excited tone of voice. Stroke and make a fuss of him when he reaches you.

3 Make sure you show your puppy how pleased you are to see him by giving him lots of warm attention. Never use your puppy's name to scold him.

TRIP OUTSIDE
Your puppy must learn that outside is the place to go to the toilet. Take your puppy into the yard first thing in the morning and last thing at night as well as whenever he wakes from a nap. Also, go outside with him after each feed or after playing with him.

House-training

Some dogs learn to be clean indoors sooner than others, but with all of them the most important factor in house-training is vigilance. Supervision is the key to success in the first few weeks. Your puppy may need to relieve himself at any time, so learn to spot the signs, such as sniffing the ground and circling. You can also try to predict the times when he is most likely to need the toilet. Even in the absence of any signs, take your puppy into the yard at regular intervals, no matter what the weather is like, and wait patiently. Stay with your puppy to make sure that he does not get distracted. When he does go to the toilet, give a command such as "hurry up" and praise him enthusiastically when he has finished.

The occasional house-training accident is inevitable and unless you catch your puppy in the act there is nothing you can do except clean up the mess. Never punish or scold a puppy for having an accident but if you are nearby and spot him squatting, interrupt him with a sharp noise such as clapping your hands. Your aim is to stop him in mid-flow, not to scare him. When he stops, encourage him into the yard and wait for him to perform, giving the command "hurry up" followed by praise as described above.

Continue to take your puppy on regular toilet trips to the yard even when he has stopped having accidents. You may be able to lengthen intervals between trips, but beware the common mistake of stopping house-training as soon as your puppy appears to be clean. It may be simply that you have become better at predicting your puppy's toilet habits and not that he has learned to control himself indoors.

What to do at night

Inevitably, your new puppy will cry or whine at nighttime. This is a natural response to being separated from his mother and litter mates and is unlikely to last for more than a few nights. Ignore him, unless he is being very noisy, in which case he may need to go to the toilet. If you can take him outside to relieve himself in the middle of the night, he will learn to be clean indoors much more quickly. Tiring your puppy out during the day is the best way of getting a peaceful night. Spending time playing with him and feeding him a warm evening meal will make him feel sleepy. Always give your puppy the opportunity to go to the toilet just before you settle him down in his bed.

SECURE PLACE
A crate is the ideal way to keep your puppy safe at night and ensures that any accidents are contained. Spread newspaper on the floor and place a blanket across half the space. A cardboard box is a cheap, disposable alternative.

HANDLING YOUR DOG

Accustom your puppy to regular handling

Getting your dog used to being handled early on will make his day-to-day care much more pleasurable. Teach him to accept being held without protest so that you can perform routine health checks or administer occasional treatments such as ear drops. A dog that is happy to be handled is a joy to groom, and tasks such as nail clipping and tooth brushing will not be a chore or turn into a struggle.

How to handle your dog

Make handling an opportunity for your dog to receive lots of attention, treats, and praise. Handling sessions should be frequent and fun, but keep them short so your dog does not feel smothered. Begin by calling your dog to you and give him some gentle fuss and lots of praise when he approaches. Then practice handling him by examining his ears, eyes, mouth, paws, and tail. After each examination, reward your dog with a treat. When you have finished, spend some more time fussing over him. In the early stages, handling sessions should be no more taxing than that. If your dog appears reluctant for any part of his body to be handled, do not force him.

PETTING
Pet your dog by crouching down to his level and talking to him in a gentle tone. Never lean into his space. If he is willing, slowly put your hand out and stroke his chest; avoid placing your hand directly over his head.

GOOD PRACTICE | EXAMINING YOUR DOG

LIFTING THE EARS
Get your dog used to having the inside of his ear handled. Check that the ear is its usual, dull, pink color with no unpleasant odor or excessive wax.

EXAMINING THE EYES
Handle the area around your dog's eyes with great care. If the eyes need cleaning, wipe them lightly using cotton pads moistened with warm water.

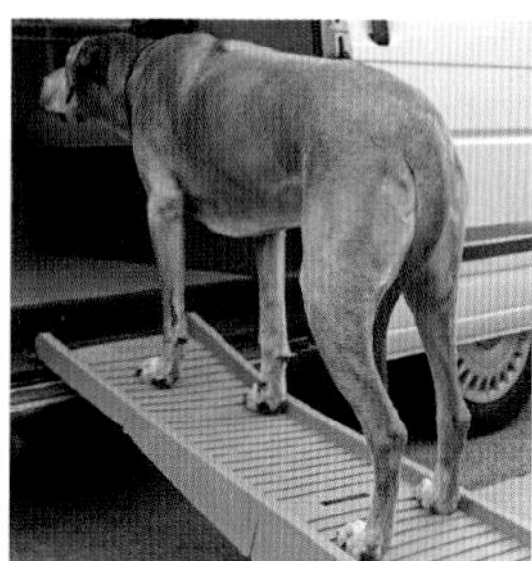

PLENTY OF SUPPORT
When lifting both large and small dogs, support them front and back and hold them close to your body.

You may notice that he suddenly stiffens when you lift up his tail, for example, or growls when you try to pick up his paw. If this is the case, and on checking there is no sign he is hurt, use treats to gradually build up the amount of handling your dog will tolerate. Stiffening and growling are signs of aggression and, if they go unheeded, may result in a bite. Always get advice from a professional behavior counselor to help a reluctant dog accept being handled.

Lifting your dog

A dog that is not used to being lifted may panic and react aggressively if you pick him up, so it is worthwhile practicing lifting your dog. To begin with, simply place your hands to support his front and back, praise your dog, and hold him without lifting him. Reward him with a treat for standing still. Gradually increase the length of time you hold him, before gently lifting him just off the ground. Immediately put him down and reward him with a treat.

Small breeds and puppies are relatively easy for one person to pick up. Larger breeds, however, should not be lifted by one person alone. Any dog over 33lb (15kg) requires two people to lift it, one at the front and one at the back. Dogs can move suddenly, causing strain to the person lifting them; they also risk being dropped, undoing hours of patient training and causing problems for the future. When you lift, bend from the knees to avoid back injury, and check that there are no obstacles on the path to your destination.

GENTLE SLOPE
If lifting your dog is impractical, a ramp is a good alternative, particularly to help older dogs to get into a car.

INSPECTING THE TEETH
Gently lift your dog's lips to check that the gums are pink and there are no signs of soreness. His teeth should be white and lack excessive tartar deposits.

TOUCHING THE PAWS
Check the pads for sore or broken skin, and look in between the toes for injuries or swelling. Examine the nails and get them trimmed or clip them yourself if necessary.

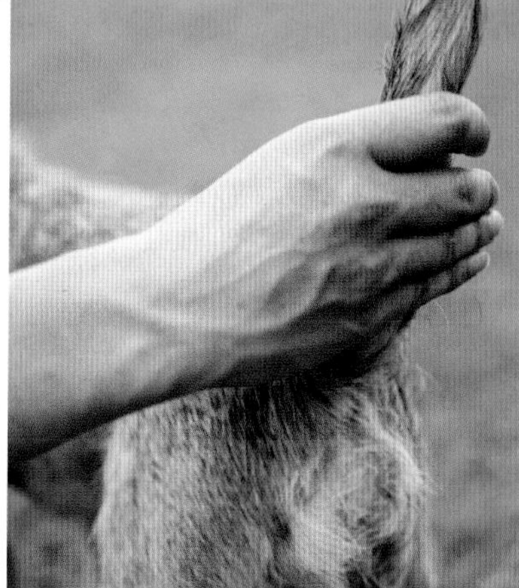

LIFTING THE TAIL
Lift your dog's tail while you tickle his stomach with your other hand. Ensure that the area below the tail is clean and that there are no signs of redness or swelling.

GROOMING

Both dog and owner alike should find grooming an enjoyable experience. The contact encourages a strong bond to develop and is beneficial to your dog. Not only do dogs find being groomed relaxing, but it is also good for their skin and coat. You can check your dog for lumps and bumps, parasites, and minor injuries too, while you brush him.

A dog's coat needs regular grooming—more frequently if it is a show dog

Learning to be groomed

Grooming is really an extended period of handling. It should not be difficult if you have taken the time to teach your dog to accept being restrained. Approach grooming as a training session. Place a towel on the floor and encourage your dog to stand still on it in return for a treat. Calmly stroke and praise him but do not allow him to become overexcited. Introduce your dog to each piece of grooming equipment that you will be using regularly. Let him sniff each brush but do not allow him to chew it. Restrain him gently and move the brush through the coat on his back without pressing too hard. After a few strokes of the brush, stop and reward him with praise and a treat.

No matter what type of coat your dog has, spend time each day practicing grooming and getting him used to the sensation. With a new dog, make grooming sessions very short and always reward him for standing still. Speak to him in a calm, reassuring tone and avoid tugging on tangles or knots, which may hurt him. Gradually increase the length of time you require him to stand still. Be firm from the start. If he tries to bite the brush, do not let him turn the session into a game. Instead, gently turn his head away from the brush. He should remain standing, unless you ask him to sit or lie down so that you can reach another part of his coat. Once he is used to standing still on the towel for an extended time, you can start a proper grooming routine.

DETANGLING
Some coat types, such as the silky coat of the Yorkshire Terrier, are particularly prone to tangles. Silky coats need regular grooming to manage any small knots so that they do not form uncomfortable mats.

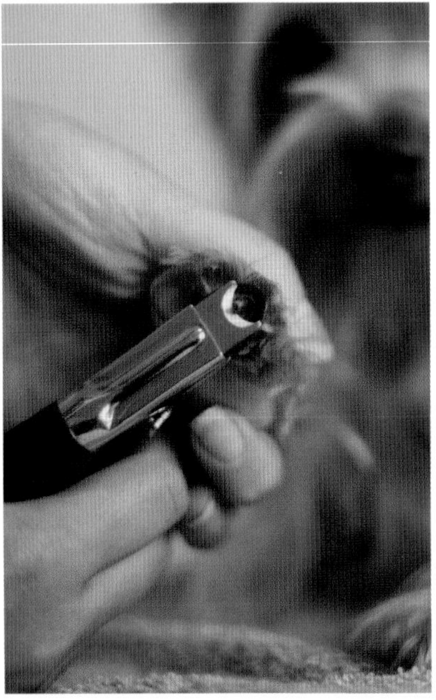

CLIPPING NAILS
Dogs that do not regularly walk on hard surfaces, or that have long hair around their paws, need their nails clipped regularly. Remove the pointed tip of the nail only and be careful to avoid cutting the quick.

GROOMING TOOLS
A rubber brush or glove removes shedding undercoat in smooth-coated breeds. For all other breeds, a slicker brush is the best general tool, although a bristle brush may be preferable for long coats. Use a comb on all coat types as a finishing tool.

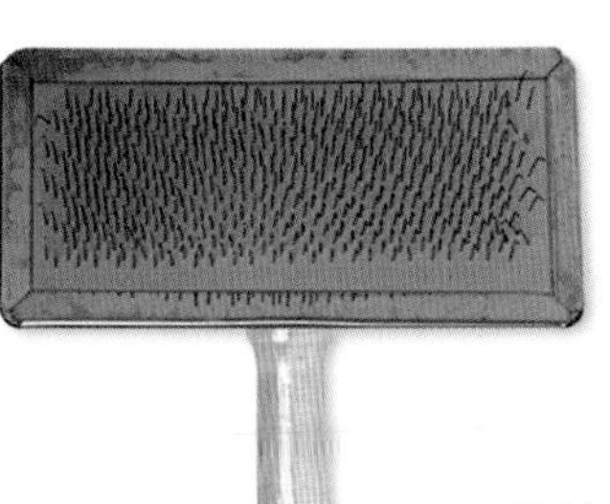

Slicker brush

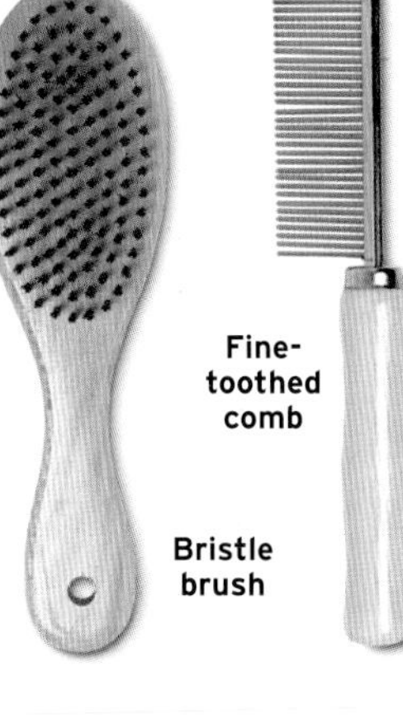

Fine-toothed comb

Bristle brush

Rubber grooming glove

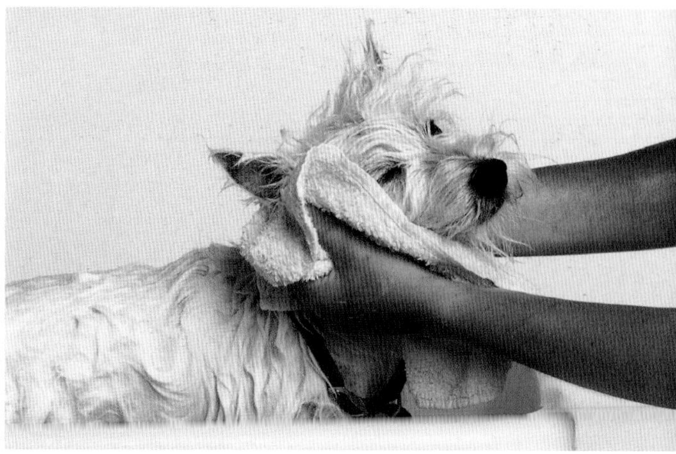

HAVING A BATH
Brush any knots out of your dog's coat then wet him all over—avoid getting water into his eyes and ears. Massage dog shampoo into his coat; never use human shampoo as it can cause painful skin problems. Rinse the shampoo out completely before drying him thoroughly, and finish off with a good brush.

Work your way round

Stick to a routine when you brush your dog to ensure that no areas are missed. Start at the foot of one of his hind legs and use an appropriate tool (see above) to brush from the bottom of the coat outward. Keep tension on the skin with your other hand to prevent the coat from pulling painfully as you brush. Whatever tool you use, make sure you work it right through the coat but be careful not to scrape it painfully on the skin. Work your way up the leg and along your dog's side, then down the front leg to the foot and across the chest. Repeat this process on the other side, then finally brush the tail and around your dog's head.

Mats can form in a dog's long coat when loose underhairs wrap together or when the coat tangles. Matting that occurs in movement spots, such as the armpits, can be very painful. To deal with mats you need a de-matting comb to break up the clumps so that they can be removed with a brush. As well as being time consuming, de-matting can be a very uncomfortable experience for your dog and may make him resent grooming. It is far better to prevent the mats from forming in the first place by brushing your dog at least every other day.

COAT CLIPPING
Clipping the coat is the usual practice for many breeds. Find a professional dog groomer who can do this for you. A good groomer will not rush a new dog and will spend time getting him used to the sound and feel of the clippers, using treats to help him feel comfortable.

TEETH CLEANING

- **Never use human toothpaste**, buy special dog toothpaste instead.
- **Clean one tooth** per day to get your dog used to the sensation.
- **Some dog chews** are designed to help clean your dog's teeth.

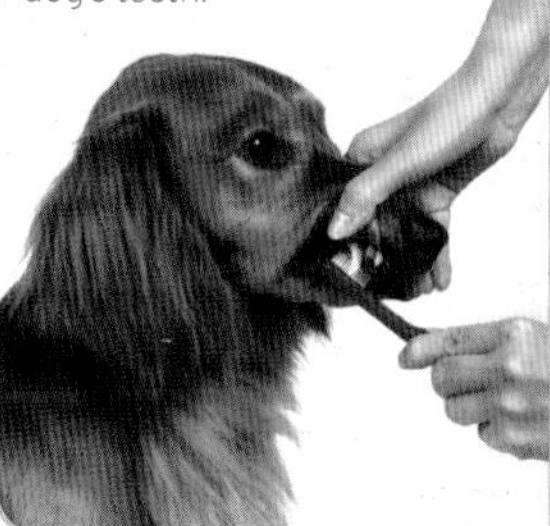

GOOD BEHAVIOR

A well-mannered dog is not only a pleasure to live with but is also happier. If your dog understands the house rules, he will stay out of trouble and can take part in family activities and greet visitors. Preventing bad habits from forming is much easier than trying to undo them later on, so start teaching your new dog how to behave as soon as he arrives in your home.

QUIET CORNER
To encourage your dog to go to his bed, give him a treat or chew to take with him. When he goes to his bed, offer gentle praise and encouragement.

Where to rest

Although it is tempting to allow a new puppy on to the furniture and into your bed when he is very small, you may not want this to happen when he is much bigger, hairier, and dirtier. Changing the rules as your puppy grows up is unfair, so it is best to decide at the start which rooms he can go in and whether he can sit on the sofa. Make sure that the whole family agrees and treats the puppy consistently.

It is very important to give your dog a private corner to relax in on his own, but he may need encouragement to use it. At the times in the day when your dog normally goes to sleep, coax him on to his bed with a gentle cue such as "go to bed." Spend some time there with him, gently stroking him and quietly praising him as he falls asleep. Should he take himself to his bed of his own accord, praise him quietly or toss a treat so that it lands just in front of his nose.

TRAINING | GETTING OFF THE FURNITURE

1 A light, long leash makes it easier to teach your dog to get off the furniture. Use this in the early stages of training when he does not yet understand the appropriate voice cue. If he sits on a forbidden chair or sofa, pick up the long leash and ask him to get off.

2 If encouragement and putting gentle pressure on the long leash fail to make him get down, do not use the leash to drag your dog off the furniture. If he does not jump off immediately, use a toy or a treat to encourage him further.

3 When your dog jumps off the furniture, clearly give the command "off" and praise him. Guide him to his bed and settle him there with praise and treats.

TRAINING | NO JUMPING UP

1 If your dog jumps up, remove all attention by turning your back and folding your arms. Avoid eye contact and do not speak to him until he stops.

2 When your dog has all four feet on the ground, reward him with lots of fuss in the form of praise, treats, and play. If he gets too excited and jumps up again, turn away immediately. He will quickly learn that keeping all four paws on the ground is the key to getting attention.

Good manners

Puppies often receive the most attention from people when they are jumping up or barking, so understandably they often continue to use the same technique as they get older, when such behavior is less appealing. It is not wise to allow even the smallest dog to jump up at anyone, because a boisterous dog can scare people, especially young children, or even cause injuries.

For a dog to learn good manners, he must not receive any attention at all when he is jumping up or barking. This does not just mean withholding praise—to some dogs, being shouted at or pushed away counts as satisfactory attention. Ignore your dog completely to teach him that when he is sitting quietly, people come to him and lavish him with praise, and treats.

GREETING VISITORS
Dogs can get overexcited when visitors call. Control your dog with a long lead to make sure that he is behaving politely before you let visitors say hello.

PLAY-BITING

If your puppy is a persistent play-biter, keep a soft toy nearby to grab quickly whenever you spend time playing with him. Use a big toy so that you can hold on to it without needing to put your hands too close to your dog's teeth.

Teething troubles

Dogs investigate the world with their mouths. Young dogs in particular want to chew everything they come across to find out more about it. This habit often becomes more pronounced at around four months of age, when puppies begin to lose their first teeth. It is natural for puppies to play-bite their litter mates but they must learn never to use their teeth on humans in the same way. This lesson is an important part of teaching a young dog good manners. When your puppy play-bites at your hand, form a fist to make it harder for him to chew and offer him a soft toy instead. Engage him with the toy and have a good game with him, but stop if his teeth touch your hand. Either get up immediately and walk away to indicate the game has ended or keep your hand still and let out a yelp as another puppy would do.

TRAINING | TAKING FOOD GENTLY

1 Hold a tasty treat firmly in your fist and show it to your dog. Keep your fist still as he tries to get the treat, but do not open it if he is touching your hand or chewing or pawing it.

2 When your puppy moves away from your hand, even for a moment, open your fist and allow him to take the treat. This will teach him not to snatch food but to wait for it calmly.

TRAINING | GIVING UP CHEWS

1 When your dog has been enjoying a chew for a while, approach calmly with a really smelly treat. Get close enough for him to smell it and use it to lure him away from his chew.

2 As he moves away from his chew, give him the smelly treat and at the same time calmly pick up the chew with your other hand. Use the treat to keep him distracted.

3 Once he has eaten the treat, immediately give him back the chew. Repeat the lesson at intervals. It won't be long before your dog learns to give up his chews happily.

Preventing food aggression

Dogs can be very possessive about their food and many will guard it against anyone who approaches. Although perfectly normal canine behavior, it is not tolerable in a pet dog and must be discouraged at a very early stage. Training a dog not to be aggressive about food is easy. Simply teach your puppy to expect that anyone who approaches him while he is eating will have something even tastier to offer. When you give your puppy his food, crouch down beside him and gently stroke and talk to him as he eats. Offer him some really tasty treats, such as cooked chicken or cheese, and allow him to take them from you. If he is comfortable with this, progress by putting your hand into his food bowl and letting him take the treat from there. Repeat this once or twice before leaving him to finish his meal. If you approach and your puppy looks up expectantly, lift up his bowl and place some tasty treats in it before returning it to him straight away. Once his response is absolutely predictable, get a variety of different people, including children, to repeat the procedure. As the puppy grows up, repeat this training less frequently but do not stop completely until your dog is fully mature. A dog that has already developed aggression around food poses a genuine risk and will bite anyone who gets too close. Do not attempt to treat this problem without the advice of a professional behavior counselor.

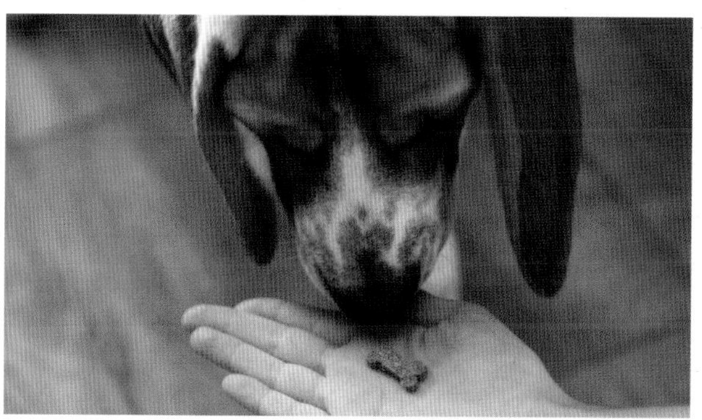

HANDOUT
Offering your dog a treat on the flat of your hand prevents him from accidentally catching you with his teeth. Make sure that friends and children offering him treats are taught this rule.

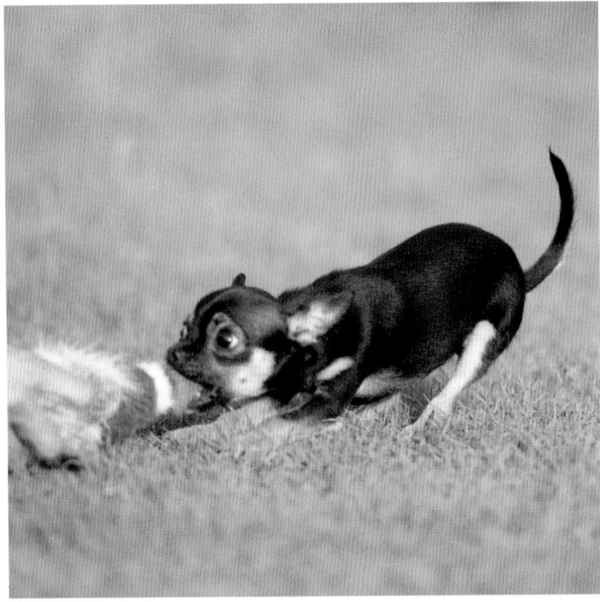

TUG-OF-WAR
Tug games are a great way to interact with your dog as long as you can control when the game begins and when it ends.

Playtime

As highly social animals dogs need interaction with both other dogs and people as much as they need physical and mental exercise. Play can offer this interaction and helps dogs to mature properly, so it is essential that they have as much of it as they need. However, it is during playtime that your dog is most likely to become overexcited and start misbehaving. Teach your puppy the rules of play both with you and with other dogs. He must also learn to stop playing when you tell him to.

Use toys to help your dog learn that play with people is different from play-fighting with other dogs. Playtime should begin and end with a display of good manners, such as a sit. If your puppy gets overexcited, call a halt to the fun until he calms down. Don't restrain him with your hands during play because he will probably try to mouth you or jump up. It may be useful to keep a puppy on a light, long leash during playtime. This allows you to calm him down without offering the temptation of your hands. If this does not work, walk away from your puppy, making it clear that the game is over.

THRILL OF THE CHASE
Many dogs love chasing toys that fly through the air. Keep your puppy on a long leash until he understands the rules.

TOP TIPS

■ **Your dog should be taught** from an early age not to be possessive of his toys. It is understandable that any dog would want to guard a prized possession from human hands, but this can lead to snapping and biting. Spend time trading toys for treats until your dog learns that allowing people to pick up his toys leads to a tasty reward. Teach children that snatching something quickly away from a dog may startle him and possibly arouse aggression.

GOOD PRACTICE | PLAYING

RESPONDING TO A NEW TOY
Allow your puppy to nibble a new toy to find out whether it tastes nice and to check whether it will bite back.

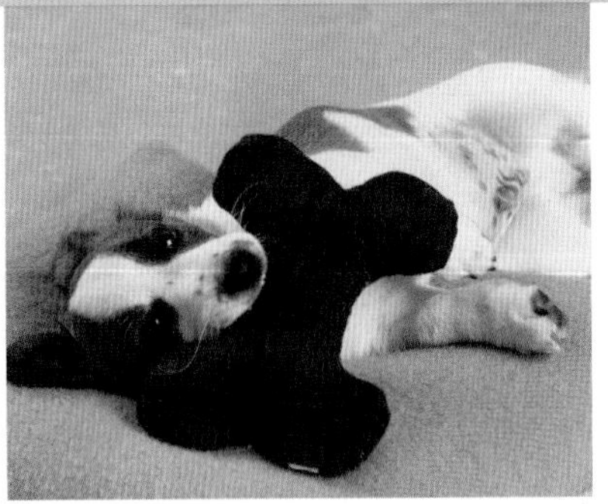

PLAYFULNESS
Do not be alarmed if your puppy growls—he is simply treating the toy like another puppy. This is normal playfulness, not aggression.

GIVING UP A TOY
Occasionally take the toy away from your puppy and praise him before returning it. If he is reluctant to give it up, swap it for a treat.

Barking

Often puppies will "find their voice" at around six months of age. Puppy yapping can be amusing and although it is tempting to encourage this new behavior it is not advisable. As your puppy matures, both you and your neighbors will become weary of persistent barking. If your puppy is prone to barking at certain moments of high excitement—for example, during a game—then use a leash to control his behavior. Give him what he wants only when he is quiet. If your puppy tends to bark excitedly when you are about to do something such as prepare his dinner or get ready for a walk, stop what you are doing until he is quiet. If necessary, sit down calmly on the sofa until he has stopped barking completely. It is worth spending a few extra minutes getting your puppy calm before going out of the door for a walk. Your puppy will realize quickly that barking is completely counterproductive when it comes to getting what he wants, whereas waiting quietly is always rewarded.

OVEREXCITEMENT
If your puppy barks when you are about to go for a walk, ignore it and he will learn that staying quiet is a quicker way to get what he wants.

ON GUARD
Your dog may use barking as an alert signal when the mail arrives. He should not be scolded for this, but do not let alarm barking continue for long.

ATTENTION SEEKING
Barking to gain attention should not be rewarded. Ignore your dog until he is silent or walk away from him, returning with lavish praise when he is quiet.

SOCIALIZATION

Whatever your young puppy experiences will affect the way he responds to the world as an adult dog. At an early age, introduce him to everything he is likely to encounter, from different people and other dogs, to cars and vacuum cleaners. This process, called socialization, is the single most important task you can undertake to ensure that your puppy grows into a friendly family pet.

Everyone's friend

Understanding your dog

Socialization must begin with an understanding of how dogs interact with their surroundings. A puppy views the world very differently from humans. Whereas we rely on our eyes to get information about the world, dogs place much more reliance on their sense of smell. A new puppy learns about things more quickly by smelling and chewing them than by looking at them. In fact, dogs cannot see the same amount of detail as humans or distinguish red from green, but their night vision is far superior to ours. Dogs have a much more acute sense of hearing than humans. This means a noise that is seemingly inconsequential to us may sound loud and scary to a dog.

Puppies go through a series of developmental stages as they mature. These stages are windows of opportunity for socialization, and positive experiences during such times will help to shape your puppy into a happy and balanced adult dog. In his first weeks your puppy is still inquisitive, full of

PAT ON THE HEAD
A well-intentioned pat on the head can be frightening for your puppy. Crouch down and stroke his chest instead.

DOG'S EYE VIEW
People appear huge to a young dog with little experience of the human world. Try not to overwhelm your puppy by looming above him.

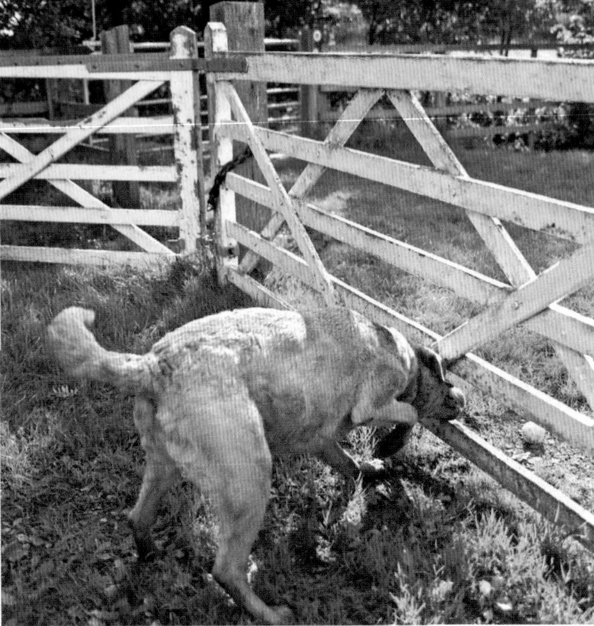

BEHIND THE GATE
Your dog will need help to figure out how things work in a human world. His thought processes are different from ours, and to begin with he may not understand things like gates.

play, eager to please, and also less inclined to be wary of new and unusual things than he will be later on. Some socialization may have happened while your puppy was with the breeder. This is important since the period at which socialization becomes most critical is, broadly speaking, between 8–12 weeks of age, and you may not pick your puppy up until he is about that age. Once you have brought your puppy home, socialization must continue. Anything that he does not come across during his formative period and make a positive association with, will be looked upon with distrust or fear if he meets it as an adult. It is important not to miss this deadline, so introduce your puppy to your friends and their children. Having contact with toddlers and older people is particularly important. Once fully vaccinated, take him out to meet other animals, go for a bus ride, and visit the park to look at the ducks. Socialize your puppy early and socialize him well; you will find it a rewarding and joyful experience.

Getting used to other dogs

Dogs need to learn how to interact with other dogs at the earliest opportunity. A puppy that is not socialized correctly will grow up becoming more and more fearful of other dogs, and this usually leads to aggression. Puppies learn best about getting on with other dogs by playing with puppies of their own age. During play, dogs discover how to read each other's body language and how to respond appropriately. They also learn how to display friendliness as well as how to judge whether another dog is friendly.

MAKING NEW FRIENDS
Meeting a variety of other animals, both large and small, will give your puppy confidence.

Adult dogs can also be very good at teaching puppies how to behave. Make sure that all the adult dogs your puppy meets are friendly and well socialized themselves. It can be difficult to stick to this rule if you take your puppy into public spaces, so stay vigilant and move away quickly from potential trouble. A negative experience at this tender age could be enough to make your puppy wary of other dogs for life. A good puppy class should include interactions with "safe" adult dogs. By taking care that all your puppy's experiences with other dogs are positive, you ensure that he has no reason to be afraid in later life.

HIGHLY PERCEPTIVE
Dogs do not have our acute vision but they are good at detecting movement, however slight. This allows them to predict our movements, sometimes before we are conscious of them ourselves.

PUPPY CLASS
A well-organized puppy class will be of great benefit to your puppy. Look for classes that use only reward-based methods and have only a few puppies playing together at any one time.

Meeting the family

If your puppy is to become a polite, confident dog, you must introduce him to a variety of different people. Puppies soon make friends with all the members of their family but some of them are shy with strangers. Invite visitors of all ages, male and female, to your home, to meet your puppy. Show your visitors how to interact with your puppy but do not let them overwhelm him. Instead, ask them to wait for the puppy to make the first approach before greeting him. When the puppy does come to them, make sure that your visitors give him plenty of treats and gentle attention.

Give your puppy plenty of experiences with children early on so that he becomes used to them, and teach your children how to behave around dogs. Interactions between your dog and children should always be supervised, because children's sudden movements and noises can sometimes startle young puppies. However, do not shy away from such encounters–taking a new puppy to the school entrance when you drop off and pick up your children is a great way to socialize him with children of all ages. Using lots of praise and tasty treats on these visits will guarantee that your puppy remembers the experiences fondly.

Take the time to meet and greet all kinds of different people when you are outside the house with your puppy. Ask joggers and cyclists to stop and say hello to your puppy if he seems to be alarmed by their fast movement. If people are willing and able, get them to crouch down with a treat and wait for him to approach for his reward.

YOUNG PLAYMATE
Children and dogs can become the best of friends, but they need time to get used to one another.

NEW ARRIVAL
Introduce babies and dogs gradually and never leave them alone together. Begin by getting your dog used to the smell of your baby's clothes.

FELINE INTRODUCTION
Introduce a cat by holding your dog to prevent him from chasing it. The cat must be free to escape if it feels threatened.

STRANGE SOUNDS
Introduce noisy objects like vacuum cleaners slowly and with lots of treats. Get your dog used to the movement of the vacuum before turning it on.

New sights and sounds

In addition to other dogs and people, puppies need to get used to the many strange objects they will encounter during their lifetime. Washing machines, coffee grinders, lawn mowers, vacuum cleaners, tumble driers, and cars are all examples of objects that are big, loud, and scary to a young puppy. It is important to take the time to actively seek out these things and allow your puppy to get accustomed to them at his own pace. Do not force him to investigate them—instead, set up situations where he can observe the object from a distance and allow him to approach when he feels more confident. Take treats with you wherever you go and make each new experience fun by playing games with your puppy and rewarding him generously. Watch your puppy closely. If certain objects or experiences disturb him, don't avoid them but gradually familiarize him with them so that he learns not to react negatively. During these more stressful situations distract him with a toy and talk to him until he forgets his nerves. Once he relaxes, you can encourage him to move closer.

ONCOMING VEHICLE
Allow your puppy to get used to cars at his own pace, using treats to reinforce calm behavior. He will lose fear once he accepts they are background objects.

GAME OF CHASE
If your puppy chases vehicles or livestock he may get injured, so discourage this behavior from the start and get professional guidance if needed.

TROUBLE AHEAD
When you see a cyclist or jogger approaching, encourage your puppy to sit quietly. Once they have passed reward him with treats.

Car travel

For a young dog, car travel is a very strange experience at first and he needs time to get used to it. Puppies are usually wary of car rides because the first two trips they go on are when they are taken away from their mother and their first visit to the vet. Neither are very pleasant occasions and can leave many dogs with negative feelings about cars. Spending time rebalancing the way your puppy views the car will prevent traveling problems in the future.

Encourage your dog to investigate the car when the engine is turned off. Get him used to the sound of car doors opening and closing and to the feeling of being in a car. Spend time simply sitting in the car with your dog, or leave him there to sleep, so that he begins to see it as a great place to be. Put him in the place where he will be traveling in the future. For example, if you plan to travel with your dog in a car crate, that is where he should be placed from the start.

When you take your dog on a car journey, make sure he relieves himself before you set off. To begin with, go on lots of short trips that end with something enjoyable like a walk in the woods. By associating car journeys with positive endings, your puppy will soon forget the earlier trips that caused such distress. Over time, gradually increase the length of the journeys as your dog becomes happier and more relaxed in the car.

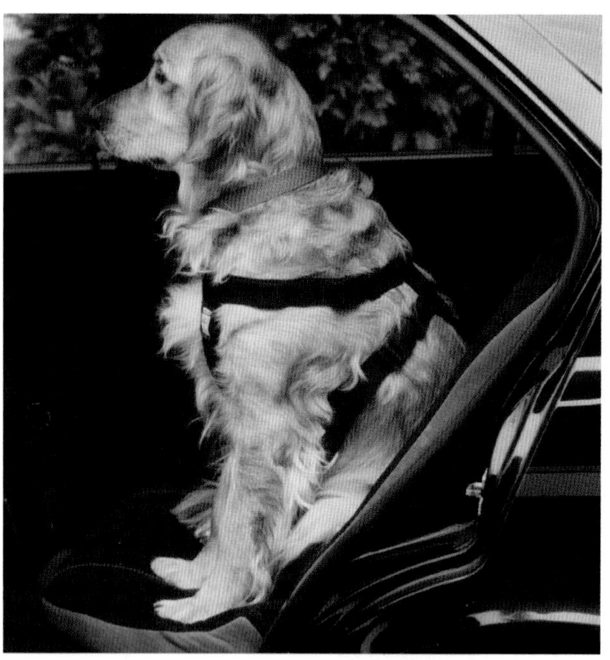

STRAPPED IN
Restraining your dog while he is in the car is essential. It stops him from interfering with the driver or other passengers and prevents him from being thrown around in the car during the journey.

TRAINING | SUCCESSFUL JOURNEYS

1 Before your dog does any traveling, he should learn that cars are fun. Take time to play with him in and around the car and even feed him his dinner in the car.

2 Until your dog is big enough to jump into the car without hurting himself, lift him in and be ready to prevent him from trying to jump out again. Settle him in the car by staying with him, praising him, and giving him lots of treats.

3 A traveling crate is a good way of keeping your dog contained and feeling secure. Dogs that are already used to sleeping in a cage or crate will find this particularly reassuring.

Travel sickness

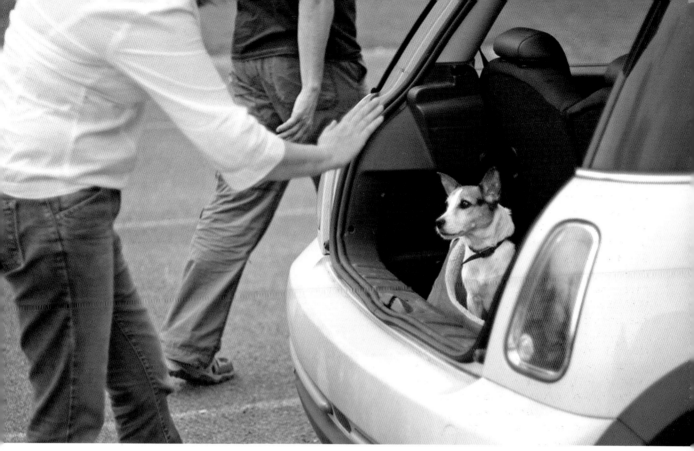

Many dogs suffer from travel sickness because they find it difficult to adjust to the unnatural movement of a car journey. In fact, many problems experienced while traveling with a dog, such as excessive barking or panting, are due to underlying travel sickness making the dog restless. It is possible for many dogs to get over this with time. However, there may also be a psychological element involved, so think about whether your dog has good or bad feelings about the car. If you have a rescue dog, his previous experiences with cars may be unknown so stopping him being sick may be more difficult. Treat a dog that is habitually travel sick in the same way you would a dog who has never traveled before.

TOP TIPS

- **Help prevent car sickness** by making sure your dog has a nonslip surface if he stands up in the car. Take corners slowly and accelerate smoothly.
- **Even on a cool day**, dogs can quickly overheat in a car, so never leave your dog alone in the car for very long.

SAFETY FIRST

Insist that your dog waits until he is asked to get out of the car. He should never jump out as soon as the door opens, since one day he may jump into the road. Restrain him if necessary and praise him for waiting calmly. Teach him to wait for just a few moments at first, gradually extending the length of time.

Spend time with him, making a positive association with the car. Keep the engine off and play games around the car and use lots of treats. When your dog is relaxed in the car, turn the engine on briefly and then play with him. For your first journey with your dog, just go to the end of the road before stopping for more games and treats. In extreme cases, consult your vet.

THIRSTY PASSENGER

The car is one of the few places where your dog may not have free access to water. Be sure to stop regularly to offer him a drink and to relieve himself; he may be more thirsty than usual due to the heat inside the car.

CONTENTED DOG
Take your dog for a walk before leaving him. If he is tired and content, he is likely to accept being left alone and will curl up and go to sleep.

Learning to be left alone

Everyone wants to spend a great deal of time with a new puppy in the first few weeks after his arrival. The general fuss and attention, combined with socialization, usually mean that the puppy is never alone for more than a few of his waking moments. As he gets older and stops receiving such constant attention, he may become anxious at being left alone. Part of his socialization should include teaching him to accept being on his own.

Choose a time when your puppy is ready for sleep. Take him outside to relieve himself before guiding him to his bed and calmly leaving the room. Shut the door behind you and ignore whining and barking until he gives up and falls asleep. This exercise should be repeated until the puppy has learned to settle quietly on his own for a few hours.

Puppies should be discouraged from following their owners around everywhere they go. Make a point of shutting doors behind you as you move around the house so that your puppy cannot always come with you. At first, go back to him quickly and reassure him, so that he knows he has not been abandoned and that you never stay away for long. He will soon learn that there is no need to become worried or nervous at being left alone.

Never scold your dog for something that has happened in your absence. If you leave your puppy for half an hour and return to find he has chewed his blanket, do not punish him. Dogs associate events that occur very close together: scolding your puppy will teach him to be afraid of you coming home, not that chewing a blanket is wrong.

SEPARATION ANXIETY
When dogs are really worried they can work out their anxiety by chewing whatever is nearby, including furniture and other possessions. This is a sign that your dog is not coping with being left alone for long periods.

TOP TIPS

■ **Early on in your puppy's** training, get him comfortable with being alone. Set aside periods during the day where you leave him for a short time. He will rapidly gain confidence.

GRADUAL SEPARATION
Use a stair gate to help an anxious dog build up to full separation. He will be reassured by seeing and hearing you, even if he cannot follow.

Anxiety in the older dog

A mature dog that has never been acclimatized to being left alone may become extremely anxious on his own. Scratching at doorways, panting and pacing, howling, and lapses in toilet training are all signs of a dog that is struggling to cope with being left alone. The damage caused by an anxious dog can be expensive to repair, and there is also a danger that the dog may injure himself.

Deep-rooted separation anxiety can be tricky to overcome. Some dogs are so anxious that they panic at the mere sight of their owner picking up the keys. Long-standing cases may require assistance from a professional behavior counselor and, in the short term, possibly medication to calm the dog down enough to concentrate on learning new lessons. Socialization consists of patiently going back to basics and, to begin with, getting your dog used to being left alone for a few seconds at a time. You can then gradually build up to longer periods of separation.

TRAINING YOUR DOG

To enjoy spending time with your dog, both in the house and outdoors, you need to train him to be well behaved. Training strengthens the bond between the two of you and provides your dog with some of the mental stimulation he craves. If you learn how to communicate with your dog and read his body language, it will make teaching him much easier and more satisfying.

INVITING GESTURE
Facing your dog and crouching down with open arms is a positive signal. Any time you face your dog directly, you are inviting interaction.

Communicating with your dog

Dogs and people have very different ways of communicating with each other. Although dogs become quite good at interpreting what people mean, successful training depends on people learning to "talk dog."

A dog does not understand language; he merely responds to different sounds. "Lie" and "down" may mean the same thing to humans but they sound quite different to dogs. So you should choose a simple verbal cue for each command and stick to it. Tone of voice also matters; puppies learn quickly that a low, growly voice means they are doing something wrong and that treats and attention usually follow a cheery tone. Most important of all is body language. Eye contact is a vital part of communicating with your dog, but remember that a prolonged stare can be seen as a threat. Dogs do not immediately understand hand movements, such as pointing; they have to learn to make an association between what your hand does and what they must do to earn a reward.

HAND SIGNALS
Your dog will probably recognize your hand signals before he learns what the voice cue means. It is important to be as consistent with your hand signals as with your voice cues.

VOICE CUES
With repetition, your dog learns that certain words mean he should perform certain behaviors. A good test to see if your dog has learned the voice cue properly is to see if he will respond to your voice even if you turn your back to him.

Reading a dog's body language

Being able to interpret your dog's body language means you will have a clearer idea of what he is feeling. You cannot train a dog effectively until you have learned to read the signs that tell you when he is happy or when he is scared. When dogs are stressed, it is impossible for them to concentrate on learning. If your dog is not responding well to training, it is important to stop the session straight away and try to analyze what is going wrong.

A relaxed dog shows no signs of tension and will hold his tail roughly level with his back and gently swinging. The ears will most likely be forward and the expression calm. A frightened or anxious dog tucks his tail in between his back legs and pulls his ears back. You may also notice that the dog is tensing his body or cowering. Other signs of fear or anxiety include excessive panting, pacing, or a sudden disinterest in food. A scared dog needs help to work through his worries and should never be punished, as this will only increase his anxiety.

You can also learn a lot about canine body language by observing what happens when your dog meets another. If your dog raises his hackles along his back and carries his tail straight up in the air, it means that he is worried and is trying to make himself appear as large as possible. This body language normally changes as the dogs exchange greetings and, if the other dog is friendly, the initial tension passes. However, raised hackles may also be the prelude to trouble if both dogs decide they do not like one another.

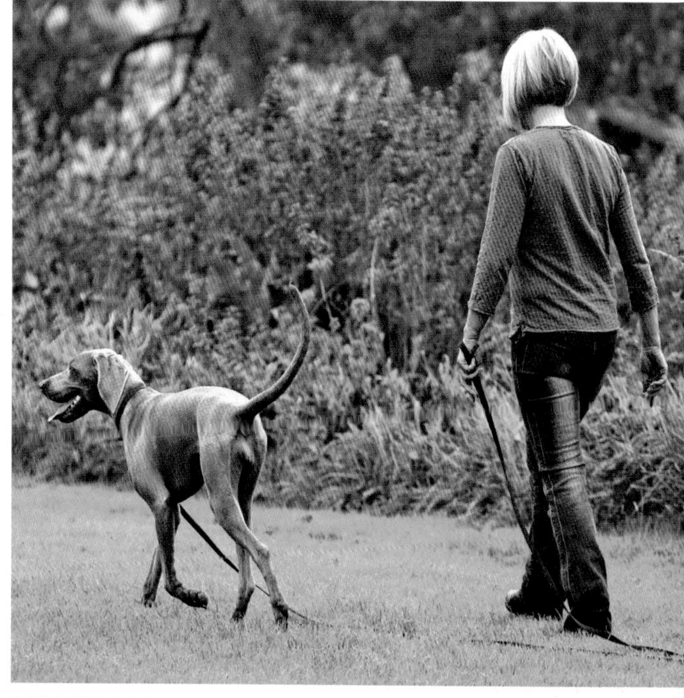

RELAXED DOG
A happy, confident dog will move in a relaxed manner. Any sign of tension, evident in a stiffening of the body, is a warning that he feels uncomfortable. Pay attention to his tail carriage. A tail held erect may suggest overexcitement or aggression, while a tucked-under tail suggests fear and anxiety.

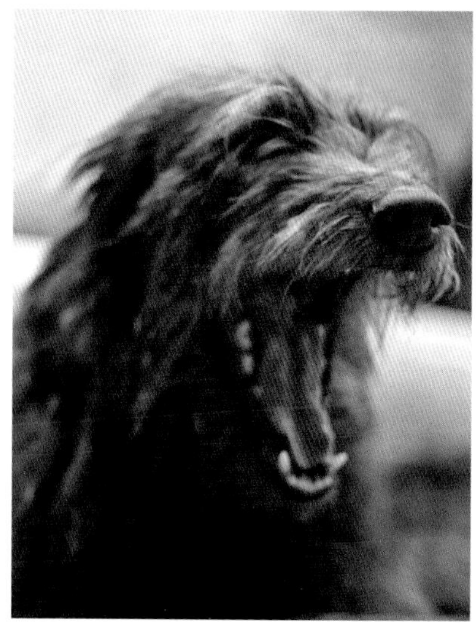

YAWNING
Dogs have many subtle ways of showing that they are feeling anxious or afraid. Signs include yawning or acting sleepy when the dog has no reason to be tired.

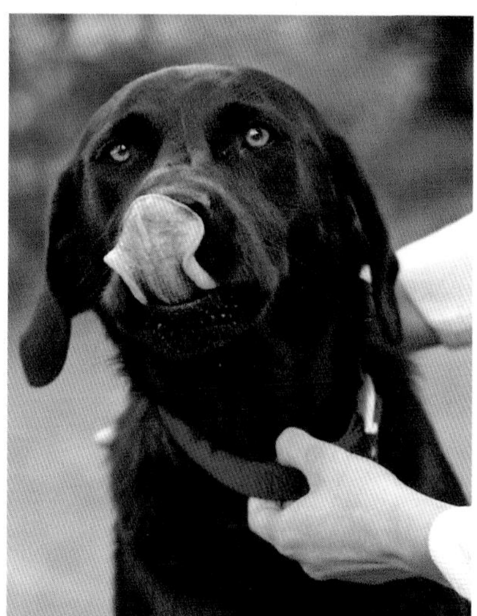

LICKING NOSE
A dog that repeatedly licks his nose or lips, even though there is no tempting food nearby, may be trying to communicate fear, anxiety, or stress.

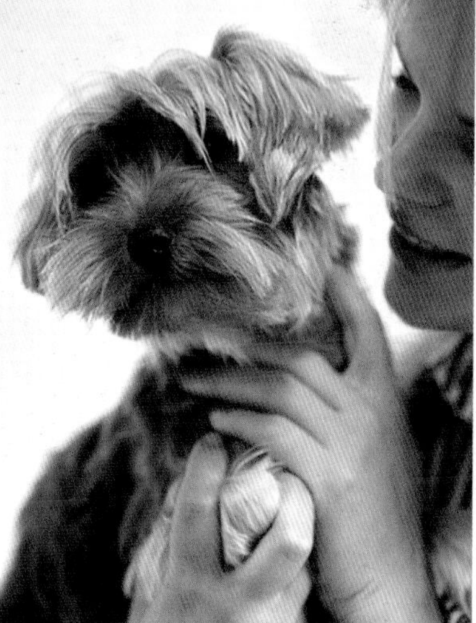

TURNING HEAD AWAY
Dogs sometimes indicate unease by turning their head or whole body away, to break eye contact and distance themselves from what they perceive as a threat.

Rewards-based training

There has been a great deal of research into the best methods for training dogs. The results show that resorting to harsh punishments for disobedience, such as using a choke chain, shouting and hitting a dog, or pinning him down, is simply not effective. Such treatment is likely to cause more problem behaviors, including aggression and anxiety. The most successful way to train a dog is to find out what motivates him and use that to reward him for behaving in the way you want.

To do this, you need to find out what works with your own dog. All dogs are individuals and react differently to rewards, but there are some common motivators that can be used as training aids for the majority of dogs. Simple praise is a very effective reward for a young puppy. Dogs are sociable animals and find positive contact with people in their family unit deeply rewarding. Most dogs will happily do what you ask of them in return for praise.

However, for some dogs the situation in which they find themselves can be so distracting that the desire to please may temporarily be taken over by more impelling urges. For instance, your dog may choose to ignore your calls when he is running after a rabbit. This is not because he no longer loves or respects you; it is simply that for a few thrilling moments he finds the unusual excitement of the chase more rewarding than your praise, which is always on offer. To overcome such distractions during training, you must find other things that are particularly rewarding to your dog. The most powerful motivators used in dog training are toys and food. Use something that your dog really loves and will therefore be strongly motivated to receive.

FAVORITE TOY
Many dogs are motivated by toys. If your dog loves to play, keep his favorite toy aside and bring it out only as a reward during training.

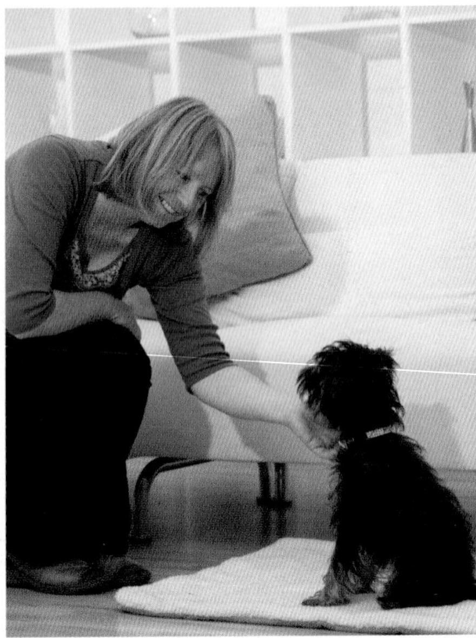

USING PRAISE
One of the best forms of reward is praise. This requires no training aids—you simply have to make a big fuss of your dog. Talk to him in a friendly tone and stroke him.

MOTIVATING FOOD
All dogs find food motivating. Treats used for training should be small, bite-sized pieces of a food that is particularly tasty to your dog. Go for healthy choices such as cooked chicken or cheese.

TIMING REWARDS
Giving rewards too slowly may make your dog learn the wrong thing. If his attention is distracted, by the time he receives the reward, he may not make the connection between it and adopting the desired "sit" position (see above). Be prepared to give your dog his reward as soon as he follows your command (see right) and he will learn very quickly.

The importance of timing

Probably the most important skill for you to master as a dog trainer is good timing. Dogs learn exclusively by association. This means that if they do something and immediately receive a reward, they are more likely to repeat that behavior. Of course, this also causes some behavior problems. For example, if a dog that wants attention jumps up and gets pushed off or shouted at, he has received the attention he wants. Effectively, he has been rewarded for jumping up and is therefore more likely to jump up again. If this is repeated, jumping up becomes a learned behavior—one that is repeated frequently.

Nevertheless, the way that dogs make associations is also extremely useful in teaching them how they should behave. If every time your dog sits he receives a food treat immediately afterward, he will start sitting more frequently. An association has been made between the behavior of sitting and a reward. It is then fairly simple to insert a voice cue as he folds into a sit, creating a learned behavior that your dog will produce on command. However, if you keep your food treats in your pocket and take a few moments to get them out, your dog will have sat, got bored, and jumped up at you by the time he gets the treat. Again, he learns that jumping up is a rewarding behavior and will therefore repeat it more often.

SLEEP TIME
Your puppy will learn better if he sleeps between lessons. A young puppy tires easily, so keep training sessions short with frequent breaks.

Basic commands

Sitting is a behavior that comes quite naturally to puppies and is therefore a good place to start formal training. It is a very easy command for a puppy to learn and gives him a guaranteed way of earning a reward. Because of this, most puppies will offer a sit as the first option when there is a reward available. As your dog gets older and a sit becomes less exceptional, the behavior is less likely to be rewarded, so he will try other methods to get noticed, such as jumping up or barking. Keep rewarding your dog whenever he offers a sit, to reinforce the calm behavior you want from him.

Teaching a puppy to lie down can be more difficult than getting him to sit, but this is probably the most useful of all the basic positions for your dog to learn. Lying down is a more stable position than sitting, meaning that a dog is less likely to move again immediately afterward. Having a reliable "down" command can be vital in emergencies when you need to stop your dog on the spot—for example, if he is running toward a road. Lying down also reinforces a relaxed state of mind and can help to calm a puppy in an exciting situation. Make it one of your puppy's earliest lessons, because the "down" command comes in handy if he becomes distracted during a training session and stops paying attention.

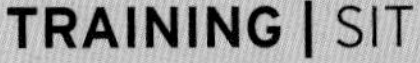

AT THE ROADSIDE

Put the sit command into practice whenever you need control over your dog. For example, asking a puppy to sit at every roadside will teach him not to walk straight into traffic (it is not always possible to shorten a leash in time to prevent mishap). Remember to practice sitting at every roadside you come to—not just at main roads. Your puppy cannot tell what type of road he is approaching.

Start teaching your puppy to lie down when he is highly motivated. For example, if you carry out a training session just before a meal, when he is hungry, he will be more receptive to what you ask because he will be eager for food treats. Encourage him by starting on a soft surface, such as carpet or grass, before moving on to harder, less comfortable surfaces. As with all your commands, be very precise about the meaning of each word. If your command to lie down is "down" then do not use the word "down" to ask your puppy to get off your furniture.

TRAINING | SIT

1 With your dog standing in front of you, hold a treat right in front of his nose and slowly move your hand up and backward, close over his head. Do not let go of the treat immediately.

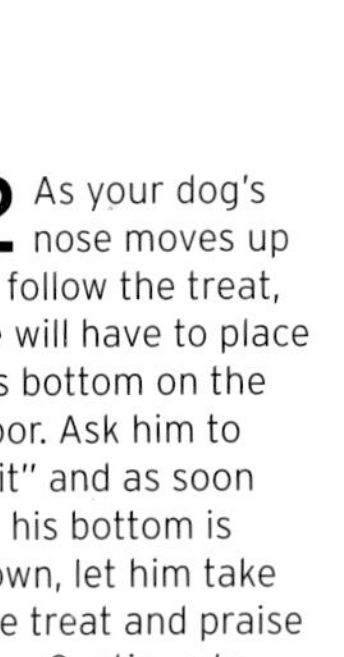

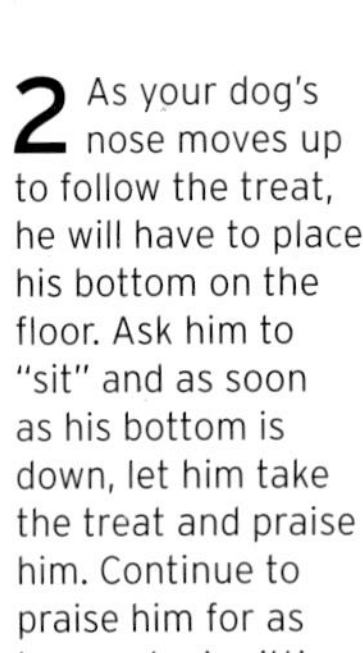

2 As your dog's nose moves up to follow the treat, he will have to place his bottom on the floor. Ask him to "sit" and as soon as his bottom is down, let him take the treat and praise him. Continue to praise him for as long as he is sitting.

3 Once your puppy is reliably performing a sit every time food is lured over his head, move on to giving a clear hand signal while asking him to "sit." Then bend down and lure him into position as before.

TRAINING | DOWN

1 In a distraction-free environment, such as your backyard, attract your dog's attention by showing him that you have a tasty treat. Use the treat to lure your dog into a sitting position but do not let him take it from you.

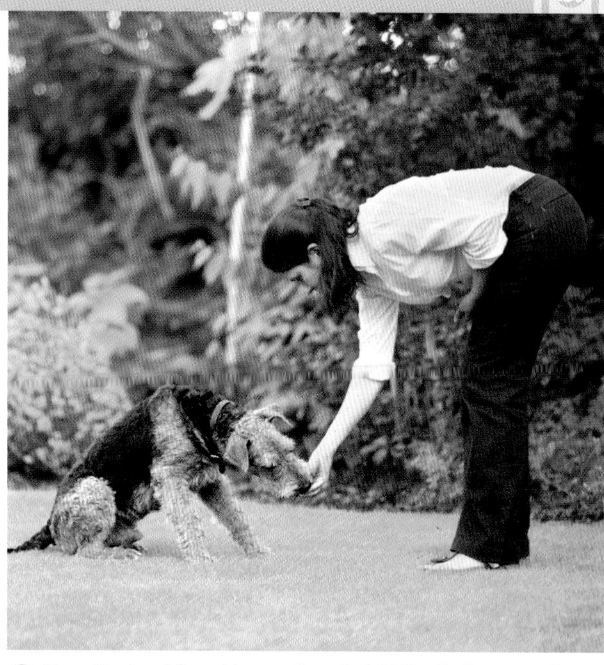

2 Move the treat from his nose in a straight line to the ground. Do this slowly so that your dog's nose follows your hand, but still hold on to the treat. Let him nibble at the treat so that he does not lose interest.

3 As your dog follows the treat, he will gradually fold into a lying position. Once he is fully down, let go of the treat and praise him. Give the command "down" as his elbows touch the ground.

Alternative If your puppy is reluctant to lie down, another method can be used. Make a bridge with your legs and lure him underneath. Use lots of treats and keep your legs positioned over him until he is lying down.

More advanced commands

Teaching your dog a command that means "stay there and wait for me to come back to you" is useful in any number of situations. This command works well for everyday use, both in the house and on walks, but it can also be helpful in other more difficult situations. For example, if your dog escapes and runs across a road, you will want him to wait where he is rather than recrossing the road and putting himself in danger again. Your dog's natural instinct is to follow you, so when you want him to stay in a particular position it will make training easier if you turn sideways to him and avoid eye contact. By doing this he doesn't think you are communicating with him and will therefore be less likely to move toward you.

All dogs need to learn to walk on a leash and must do so without pulling if going for walks is to be an enjoyable experience and not a constant battle. Puppies do not instantly understand what a leash is for and it is natural for them to pull in an attempt to reach an exciting destination sooner. If they learn from the start that pulling on the leash is never successful, they will soon stop trying. Make sure that whenever your puppy pulls, you either stop and wait until he stops or call him back to the correct heel position.

RESISTING TEMPTATION
The "stay" command can be used to teach your dog to ignore food and other temptations. Reward your dog for staying away from human food by giving him a more suitable treat.

TRAINING | WALK ON A LEAD

1 Start your session in an area where there are few distractions. Keeping your dog on a long leash, lure him into the correct position next to your left leg by offering a food treat. Praise him when he is in the correct position by letting him take the treat.

2 Before your dog starts to lose interest and attempts to wander off, show him that you have another treat but hold it out of his reach. Use his name to keep his attention and do not allow the leash to tighten as you get ready to move.

3 Take a step forward and give your dog the command "heel." Immediately bend down and give him a treat. Repeat this exercise, taking single steps, stopping, and quickly pulling out another treat so that your dog does not get distracted.

TRAINING | STAY

1 Ask your dog to "sit". Stand up straight then immediately bend down to reward him with a food treat. Next time, stand up straight and count to two before rewarding him. Gradually extend the amount of time between the sit and the reward.

2 When your dog will stay in front of you for some time, take a step away from him before rewarding him. Repeat, gradually extending the time before the reward. Once he is confident with you one pace away, increase the distance.

4 As your dog becomes more confident and attentive, begin increasing the number of steps before he receives a treat. Do this very gradually, praising him all the time. As soon as the leash tightens, stop and lure him back into position before starting off again.

WALKING TO HEEL

It may not be necessary for your dog to walk precisely to heel at all times, as long as he does not pull on his leash. However, sometimes it is useful to keep your dog close—for example, when walking past people on the sidewalk. Use a similar method to that used to teach long-leash walking (left), keeping your dog in position by using a treat. Once your dog is reliably walking close to you, gradually phase out the treat.

Returning on cue

All dogs love being able to go to the park or out into the country where they can run free, really stretching their legs and playing with toys or other dogs. However, until your dog has learned to return when you call, it is not safe to let him off his leash. You may come across someone who is nervous around dogs or perhaps encounter another dog that is not friendly. Your dog may catch sight of a rabbit or squirrel and run after it toward a road. No matter what the distraction, part of responsible dog ownership is keeping your dog under control—even when he is off-leash. Teaching your dog to come when he is called is imperative.

Puppies are born with a natural instinct to follow, and they never want to be far from you. This makes it easy to get your puppy used to the meaning of the word "come" at an early age. When your puppy is a short distance away from you, crouch down and throw your arms wide, calling his name. As he hurtles toward you, tell him he is a good boy and insert your cue "come." Always reward him with an extra special treat for coming when he is called, so that he knows it is worthwhile. As he gets older and more independent he will be less keen to run straight to you and more likely to continue investigating whatever else has caught his attention. On your first walks with your dog, teach him on a leash to come when called until you are confident he will respond every time.

TOP TIPS

- **Always praise your dog** for coming when called, no matter how long it has taken him. Resist the urge to scold him for taking his time; it will only make him reluctant to return in the future.
- **Using a whistle** as your recall command can be useful as it is a very clear noise that travels a long way.

When he responds well on the leash, switch to an extending leash and practice the command before letting him off completely. Find a safe place to experiment with this stage.

Teaching your dog to fetch a toy is a great way to reinforce the command "come" through play. When your dog has reached a toy you have thrown, he will want to bring it back to you so that you can throw it for him again. Asking him to "come" as he naturally returns to you helps him learn this command. Teaching your dog to fetch properly will also prevent him from developing problem behaviors, such as stealing items and running off.

TRAINING | COME WHEN CALLED

1 Show your dog that you have a really tasty treat in your hand before moving a short distance away. If your dog will not wait, ask someone else to gently hold on to the end of his leash.

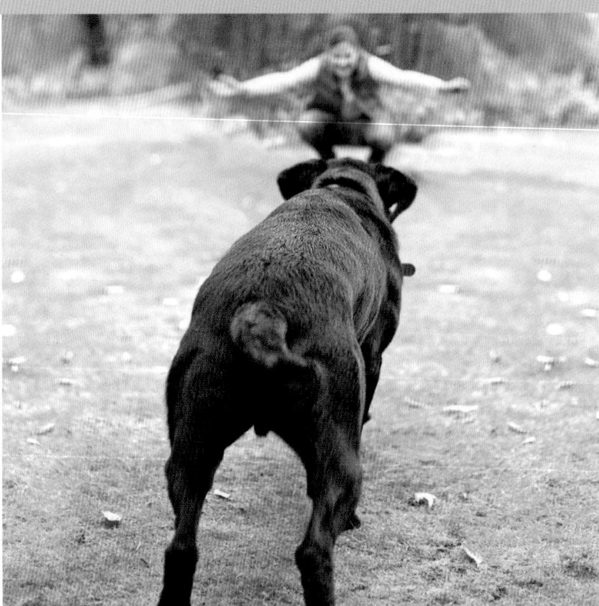

2 Turn and face your dog, crouch down, and spread your arms wide. In a loud, cheery voice call your dog's name and ask him to "come." Keep calling until he responds.

TRAINING | FETCH

1 Get your dog excited by playing with him and his favorite toy. When he is fully focused on the toy, throw it a short distance away.

2 As he heads to his toy, ask him to "fetch." When he reaches it, praise him before immediately calling him in a cheery tone.

3 As soon as your dog moves toward you, encourage him by crouching down and praising him. Exchange his toy for a treat and repeat the process.

4 If your dog drops the toy, run over to it with him and move it to catch his interest. As he grabs it, walk backward a few paces before taking the toy from him.

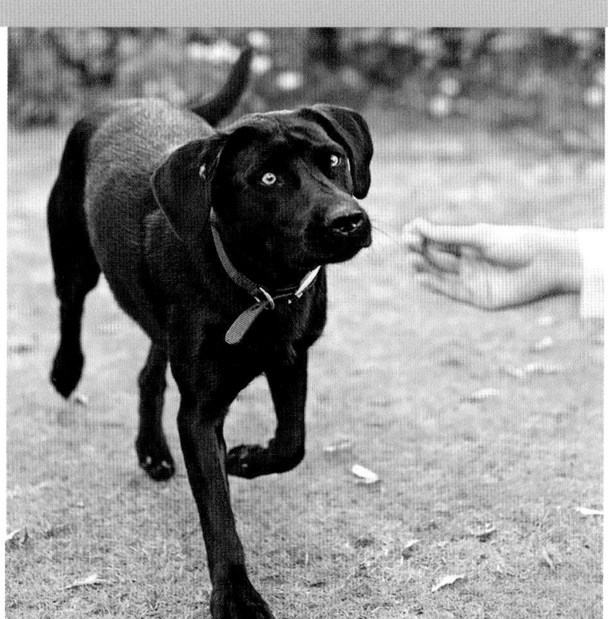

3 As soon as your dog moves toward you, praise him lavishly and keep praising him as he returns. Show him the treat and use it to lure him close to you.

4 When he is right next to you, prevent him from immediately running off again by gently taking hold of his collar before giving him the treat and lots of praise.

HEALTH

It is your responsibility to keep your dog as fit and healthy as possible throughout his life. You should learn the basic facts about health care and how to recognize when a trip to the vet is necessary. Make sure that your puppy is happy and relaxed at the vet's office from an early age—this is important preparation for stress-free visits later on.

If your puppy scratches, check him for fleas

Meeting the vet

Even before you bring a new puppy home you should check in with a local veterinary office. Visit several offices to ask questions and make comparisons, and ask other dog owners, who are likely to be a good source of recommendations. Once you have your new puppy, it is advisable to take him to the vet as soon as possible for a full health check and vaccinations. This is also a good opportunity to seek advice on such matters as feeding and local puppy classes.

Although veterinary offices are strange places, full of unusual smells and noises, puppies are not born fearful of vets. If your puppy's first few visits to the vet's office are largely pleasant experiences, full of treats and cuddles, he is less likely to object to the occasional injection and won't become stressed when later visits are necessary. The vet may allow you to make a social visit with your puppy even if you don't have an appointment. Ask a nurse or receptionist to give your puppy some treats so that he makes a positive association with both the building and the people in it.

On your first official visit to the vet, arrive early having given given your puppy the chance to relieve himself before leaving home. When you enter the office, be aware of other animals, and do not assume that all dogs will be pleased to see a puppy. However, there will be

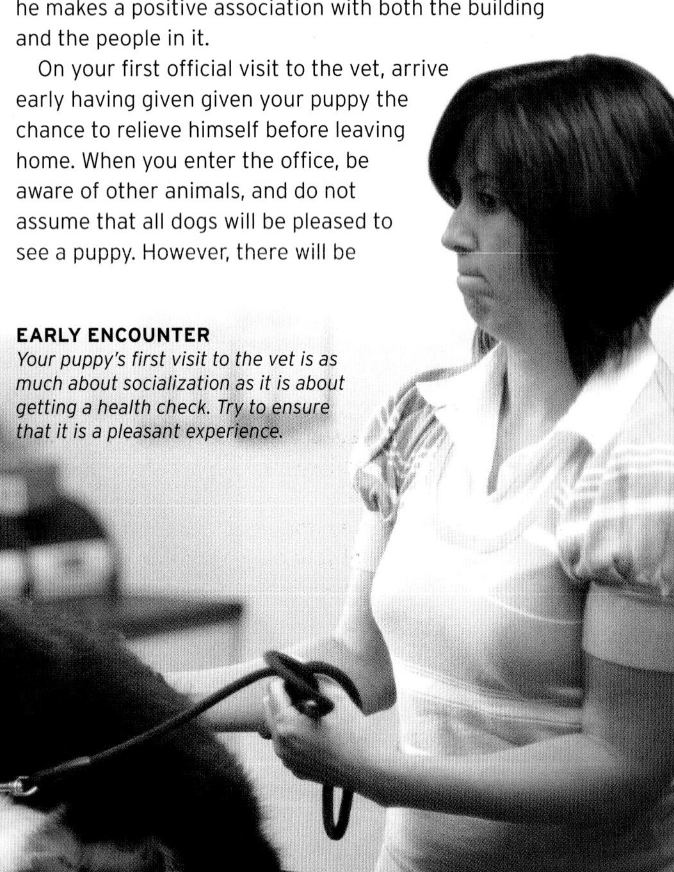

EARLY ENCOUNTER
Your puppy's first visit to the vet is as much about socialization as it is about getting a health check. Try to ensure that it is a pleasant experience.

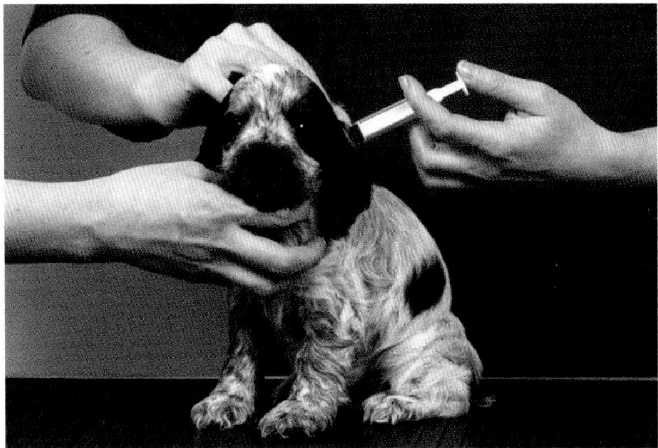

VACCINATIONS
Typically, puppies have their first vaccinations with the breeder and will need a second vaccination shortly after moving to a new home. Routine vaccinations protect against a number of potentially lethal diseases such as distemper, hepatitis, and parainfluenza.

NEUTERED DOGS
Most owners have their pet dogs neutered to prevent accidental matings and unwanted puppies. Your vet can advise you on the best time to get this done.

many people keen to take an interest in your puppy so ask them to make a fuss of him, but don't put him down on the floor unless he has been fully vaccinated.

During the consultation, your vet will want to examine your puppy all over and give him an injection. Take the process slowly, speak reassuringly to your puppy, and provide him with lots of treats throughout the examination, both from your hand and the vet's.

Preventative measures

If your puppy has not already been microchipped by the breeder, ask your vet to do this for you. Although your puppy should wear a collar and tag at all times, having a microchip means he is identifiable even if he loses his collar. Get your vet to check the microchip's location every year when your dog gets his booster vaccinations.

In between routine visits to your vet you need to take steps to protect your dog against common parasites. There are a variety of highly effective worming and flea treatments available; your vet will advise which are best for your puppy.

Unless you intend to breed from your dog you may want to discuss neutering on one of your early visits. Female dogs are usually neutered after their first season; one of the benefits, apart from unwanted pregnancy, is a reduced risk of mammary cancer. Neutered males are less likely to be aggressive and to go wandering. The operation is not usually performed until a dog is physically mature. Your vet will fully explain the advantages and disadvantages of the procedure and recommend when to have it done if you decide to go ahead. Neutering is carried out under anesthetic, so ask about post-operative care of your dog (see p.333).

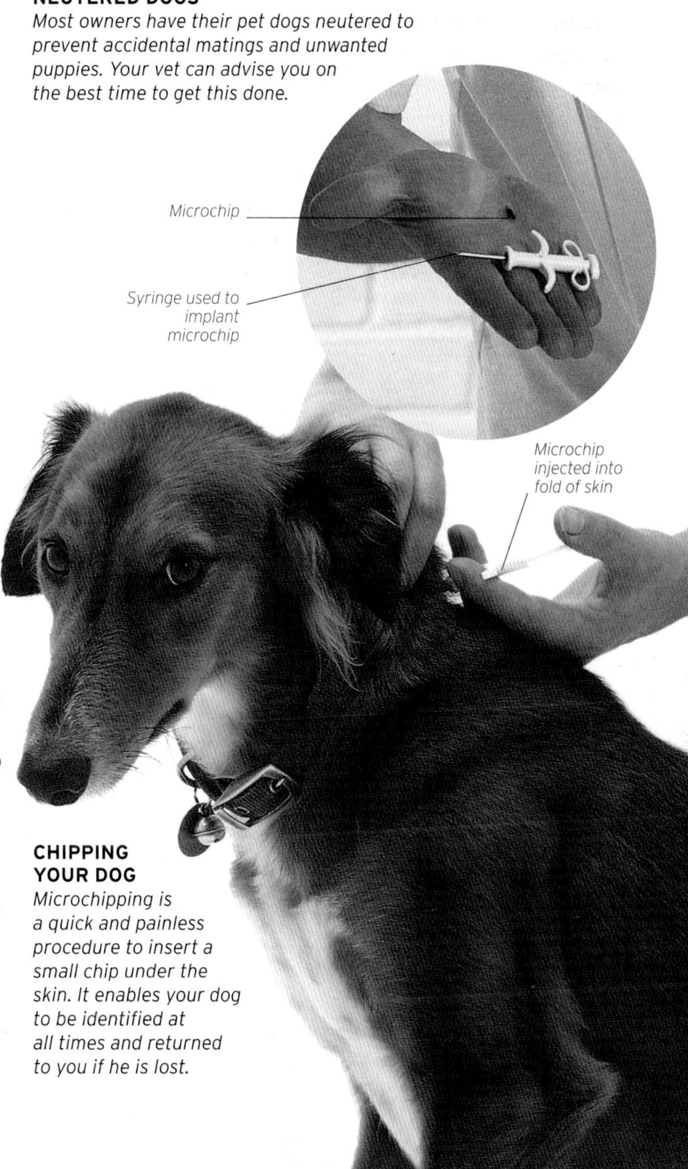
Microchip
Syringe used to implant microchip
Microchip injected into fold of skin

CHIPPING YOUR DOG
Microchipping is a quick and painless procedure to insert a small chip under the skin. It enables your dog to be identified at all times and returned to you if he is lost.

Identifying when your dog is ill

Different dogs react to illness in different ways. As an owner, you know how your dog behaves day to day and are in the best position to recognize any changes away from this norm as soon as they occur. If health problems are recognized and diagnosed early, treatment can start without delay and is more likely to have a successful outcome.

If your dog is in pain, he will probably make this immediately obvious by limping, or yelping when he moves or is handled. Other physical signs of ill health include breathing difficulties such as coughing or heavy panting for no apparent reason. Unusual discharges from the eyes or nose are also signs to be noted, as are excessive scratching, hair loss other than normal shedding, an unwillingness to exercise, or a sudden change in eating or drinking habits. However, not all indicators of ill health are physical signs. Changes in temperament or behavior can also mean that your dog is not well. For example, if your dog becomes unusually aggressive, this may be a protective mechanism because he is uncomfortable or in pain.

It is also wise to keep track of your dog's toilet habits so that you learn what is normal for him. Any sudden change in amount, appearance, or frequency of production of urine or feces can indicate a health problem. Similarly, vomiting may be a sign of ill health. Remember, however, that as natural scavengers, dogs have a very active vomit reflex to protect them from anything toxic they may have eaten.

EMERGENCY EAR BANDAGE
To protect an ear wound and prevent your dog from scratching it, bandage the ear flap flat against the top of the head. A pair of old tights can make a suitable bandage that goes around the neck and is not too constricting.

SECURITY BLANKET
A warm blanket can be beneficial in treating many conditions, including shock or hypothermia. It also comforts your dog if you need to leave him at your veterinary surgery. The scent of the blanket will remind him of home and help to reassure him until you return.

Minor injuries and first aid

Your first response when dealing with any injury should be to take your dog to the vet. However, in some situations you may be able to administer first aid before having to move the dog. In the case of severe injury, call for veterinary help and then put your dog in the recovery position. Lay him on his right side and straighten his head and neck to keep the airway free. Pull his tongue forward and to one side of the mouth so that the airway is open. Monitor his breathing and pulse until help arrives.

If there is extensive bleeding from a wound, this must be controlled until a vet can take over. Apply a piece of clean, absorbent material such as gauze to the site of the injury

TOP TIPS

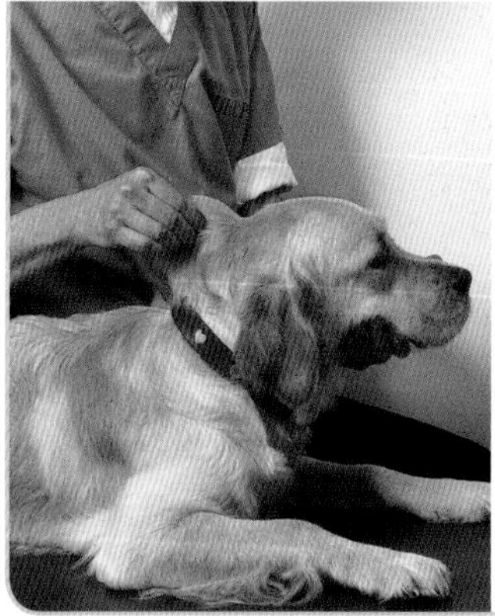

■ **Check for dehydration** Gently pinch the loose skin on your dog's back, lift it slightly then let go. In a well-hydrated dog the skin springs back quickly into position. A dehydrated dog's skin returns more slowly.

■ **Check gum color** Pale gums can indicate shock or internal bleeding and very red gums can be caused by heat stroke or fever. Blue gums suggest a shortage of oxygen in body tissues.

and cover this with bandaging to hold it in place. Take care not to apply too much pressure if you suspect that there is debris in the wound, since you may push it in deeper and cause more damage. Do not attempt to pull any large foreign body, such as broken glass or metal, out of a wound since you could cause severe bleeding.

ELIZABETHAN COLLAR
This protective plastic collar prevents a dog from licking or biting a wound. Dogs wearing the collar need supervision to ensure they can eat, drink, and move around easily.

Home care after surgery

A dog that has had surgery needs plenty of affection and care when he comes home from the vet. He may be very lethargic if he is still recovering from the anaesthetic. On the other hand, he may act as if he is perfectly fine and try to behave as normal, to the detriment of his recovery. Jumping up may pull out stitches or displace broken bones, so encourage your convalescent dog to remain calm by settling him on a blanket in a quiet area of the house, perhaps with a toy to chew, if his vet allows. Make sure children in the household understand that their playmate cannot romp energetically or be allowed to exercise off-leash until he is fully recovered.

After surgery, a dog will almost certainly be given some sort of medication and probably have bandages or stitches. He may have to wear a special collar, called an Elizabethan collar, to prevent him from touching the wound. If your dog was well handled as a puppy, you are unlikely to have difficulty in giving him any prescribed treatment. There is a good chance that he will just enjoy the extra attention.

CONCEALED PILL
The easiest way to give your dog a pill is to hide it in his food. Watch your dog while he eats, and check the bowl afterward to make sure the "hidden" pill has been eaten.

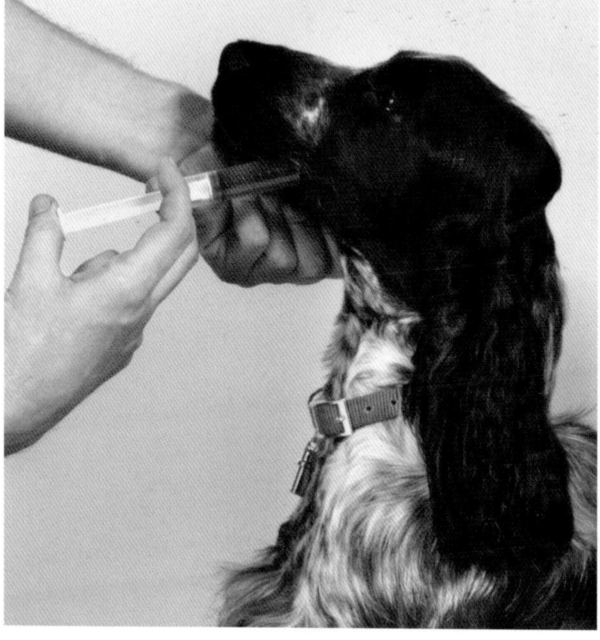

GIVING YOUR DOG MEDICINE
Liquid medicines are best given using a syringe. Gently holding your dog's mouth shut with one hand, insert the syringe under the side of his lip and slowly squirt the medicine into his mouth.

Breed-specific problems

Since humans first started breeding dogs, they have been tailoring them for different purposes. As a result, there is huge diversity among dogs, each breed having its own special qualities and traits. However, in some breeds particular characteristics have been greatly exaggerated, and you will need to take these into consideration if they apply to your chosen pet, because they can cause health problems. For example, dogs that have been bred to have excess, wrinkly skin are very prone to skin infections and require their wrinkles to be cleaned regularly. Similarly, dogs with very thick coats designed to cope with extremes of cold can develop uncomfortable skin conditions when placed in a relatively temperate climate. Hairless breeds feel the cold but are also at risk of sunburn and need to have their skin protected before they go outside. Long-backed dogs may be very good at disappearing down holes after small mammals, but have problems when faced with going up and down stairs and jumping on to sofas. Dogs bred to have a short, flat face are prone to breathing disorders and also heatstroke, because although they pant, the short, muzzle does not give them the means to keep cool effectively.

Weight issues

Dogs are scavengers and tend to eat whatever is placed in front of them because they do not know when they might next find food. For pet dogs with regular access to plentiful food, this natural trait has led to a high incidence of excess weight gain. Overweight dogs, like overweight humans, are at increased risk of serious health problems. Changes in your dog's waistline are hard to spot from day to day, so it's advisable to weigh him regularly as a routine health check. Owners of very large dogs may need to visit the veterinary office to use their scales. If you find your dog is becoming too heavy, aim to reduce his weight gradually by increasing his exercise levels and cutting down his food intake. For a dog that is obese, a vet may recommend a low-fat diet.

OVERWEIGHT
There are many health problems associated with excess weight gain in dogs. Recent studies have shown that the stress placed on a dog's body can shorten his life span by as much as two years.

SKIN PROBLEMS
Deep wrinkles like those of the Chinese Shar Pei provide a breeding ground for bacteria and need regular cleaning to prevent infections.

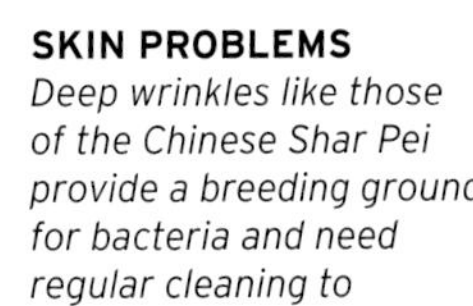

UNDERSHOT JAW
Dogs with undershot jaws, such as the Bulldog, also tend to have short muzzles. In warm environments, air passing through these shorter nasal passages does not have time to cool down properly and as a result these dogs tend to warm up quickly. They must pant to cool down and need to do so for longer than other dogs.

CHECKING YOUR DOG
As your dog gets older, it becomes more important to make regular checks for any new lumps or bumps that may appear. Signs of pain or discomfort should be reported promptly to your vet.

EXTRA REST
Older dogs need increasing amounts of rest and tend to sleep more deeply. Allow them to lie undisturbed whenever possible and to wake up in their own time.

Elderly dogs

Senior dogs often do very well for many years but, as with humans, old age brings the need for changes. If your aging dog loses a few teeth and finds it difficult to eat, ensure that he gets the correct level of nutrients for his age by switching to a specific senior diet, usually softer food that is easier to chew. Senior foods also contain nutrients aimed at easing joint pain, which is common in older dogs. Keep brushing your dog's teeth because plaque build-up tends to increase in older dogs.

An elderly dog will not require the same amount of exercise as before, but a daily walk improves his circulation and provides much-needed stimulation from sights and smells. As your dog spends more time lying down, he may be at risk of developing pressure sores, so pay extra attention to vulnerable areas like elbows. If you own a long-coated breed, check that his coat is not becoming matted.

Keep an eye on your dog's general comfort and make sure that he can still access everything he needs. For example, he may begin to find stairs more challenging or find it difficult to reach down to a water bowl to drink adequately.

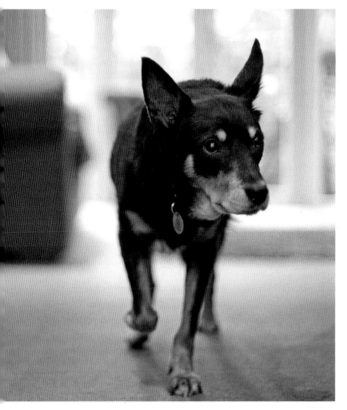

FAILING SIGHT
Many elderly dogs begin to lose their sight and rely on previous knowledge of their surroundings to get around the house. Think before you start moving furniture and confuse your dog with unexpected new obstacles.

Inherited diseases

An inherited disease or disorder is one that is passed from one generation to the next. Such a disease can mean that an individual is born with a medical condition or is genetically predisposed to developing one in later life. In the case of dogs, there are conditions common to each breed that are known to be inherited. These include joint disorders, blindness, and deafness. Responsible breeders do all they can to make sure that dogs affected by these disorders are neutered to prevent them passing on their genes to the next generation. Nevertheless, the nature of inheritance means that these conditions can never be eliminated completely as some dogs are carriers (see box below).

Many inherited disorders can be traced through a pedigree and therefore breeders can take steps to reduce the chances of breeding an affected puppy by choosing their bloodlines for breeding carefully. Good breeders will be able to go back through several generations to tell you whether any of the dogs in their breeding lines have had medical problems. They will also know what, if any, conditions remain a potential source of concern in the puppy of your choice.

For many conditions, especially those with a simple recessive inheritance pattern (see box below), screening tests can be carried out. Ask your breeder to show you the results of any tests that are relevant to your puppy or his parents. If one of the parents is a carrier, then their puppies may be too, so it would be unwise to breed from your dog without screening it first. If both parents are carriers, your puppy is at risk of being affected by the condition. Before you visit a breeder, learn all you can about the screening tests that apply to your chosen dog and his likely conditions, and make sure you know what results to look out for.

GENETICS AND INHERITED DISEASE

A common way for hereditary disorders to be passed on to the offspring is through recessive inheritance. In the example of congenital blindness, dogs may be born blind; be free from the gene that causes blindness; or be a carrier who is not affected by the condition but who carries the gene for blindness and is capable of passing it on.

This diagram shows how a dog can inherit blindness from two perfectly sighted parents. At stage 1, two unaffected dogs are mated, but one carries the recessive gene for blindness (r). All the puppies will be sighted but, on average, half the puppies will carry the recessive gene. If one of these carriers is then mated to another that carries the same recessive gene (stage 2), there is a chance that a quarter of the puppies will be born blind as they have inherited the recessive gene from both parents. The other three-quarters are sighted puppies because they have inherited at least one gene for normal sight.

Key
R = Dominant gene for normal sight
r = Recessive gene for blindness

STAGE 1

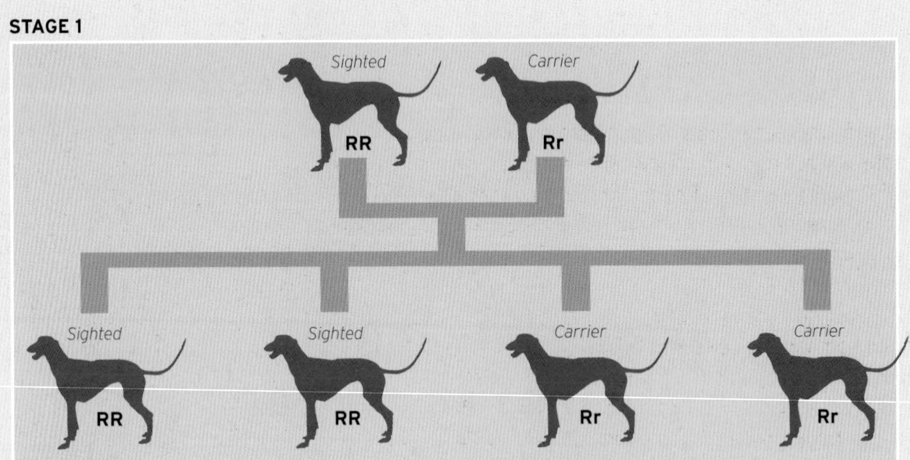
Sighted
RR
Carrier
Rr
Sighted
RR
Sighted
RR
Carrier
Rr
Carrier
Rr

STAGE 2

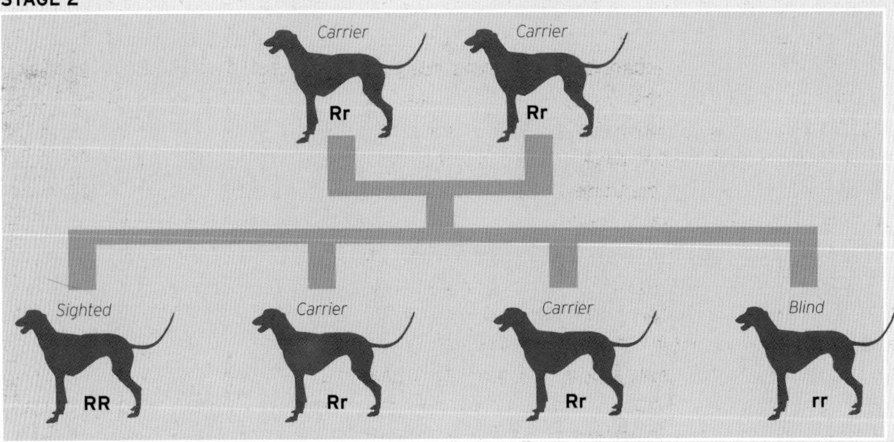
Carrier
Rr
Carrier
Rr
Sighted
RR
Carrier
Rr
Carrier
Rr
Blind
rr

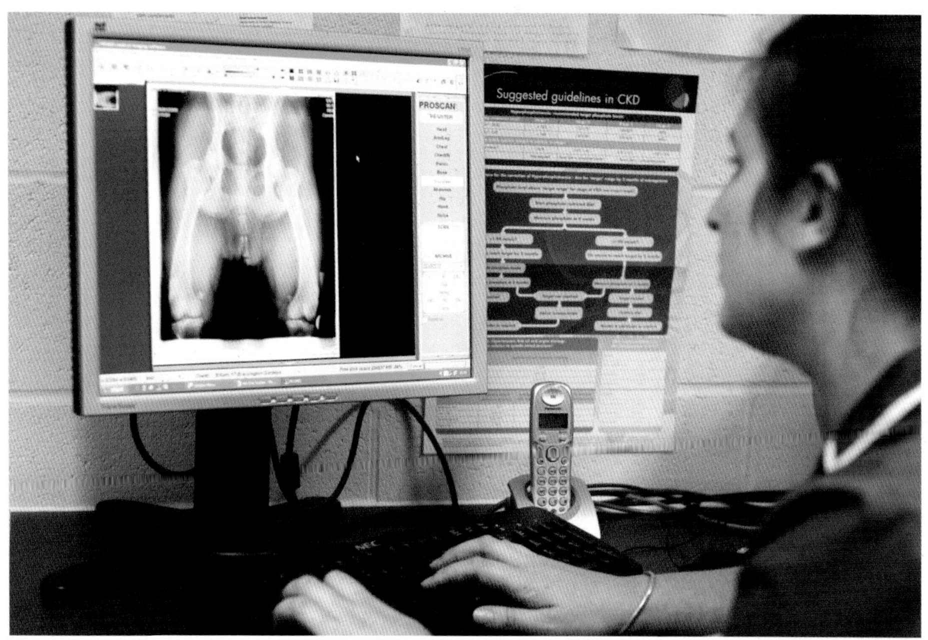
Suggested guidelines in CKD
PROSCAN

SCREENING
The likelihood of breeding puppies that develop the joint disorder hip dysplasia can be reduced by checking whether the parents are affected. This is done by assessing an X-ray of their hip joints and giving each a score that is compared to the average for the breed.

CONGENITAL DEAFNESS
Some breeds can inherit deafness, either complete or partial. There is a link between pigmentation and inherited deafness, and breeds with white variation, such as the Dalmatian, are often more at risk. Deafness should be tested for in all susceptible litters and any affected dogs neutered.

Even an ideal screening result is no guarantee that your puppy will not develop a chronic disorder. If you do have a problem, contact your vet but also be sure to report back to your breeder, who may choose not to repeat the mating that led to your puppy in future.

Think about the future

When you have decided what type of dog you are going to have, it is important to research which hereditary disorders are common problems within that particular breed. Read about each condition and be aware of the implications of taking on a puppy with a problem. Some disorders can be managed relatively easily and do not significantly affect the dog's general well-being and natural lifespan, although some adaptations may have to be made. A deaf dog, for example, needs to be trained using sign language and will not be able to run safely off-leash the majority of the time. Other disorders are potentially life-threatening and may require dedicated day-to-day, long-term management.

Consider also the increased cost of caring for a dog with a chronic condition. You could be faced with many years of vet's bills, regular medication, and special diets—and the expenses will soon add up. Work out what you can realistically cope with before going to visit a litter of puppies. It is all too easy to be persuaded to take on a cute puppy, but you may not have the skills, experience, time, or money to care for him adequately.

INHERITED DISORDERS

DISEASE	DESCRIPTION	CAN IT BE SCREENED FOR?	MANAGING THE DISEASE	TYPES OF DOG AFFECTED
Intervertebral disk disease	Similar to a prolapsed ("slipped") disk in humans; can cause intense pain and even paralysis.	No. The genetics of the condition are not fully understood.	Can be managed with rest and anti-inflammatory drugs; surgery may be necessary in severe cases.	Achondroplastic (dwarf) breeds that originated from a genetic mutation for short limbs.
Hip dysplasia	A condition in which the hip joint develops incorrectly.	Yes. An X-ray can be analyzed and then measured against the breed average.	Careful management and pain relief is normally sufficient; surgery is available but relatively uncommon.	Heavy-bodied breeds, such as the mastiffs.
Elbow dysplasia	Abnormal development of the elbow joint.	Yes. X-rays of each elbow are analyzed and given a numeric score. The overall grade is the higher of the two figures.	Affected dogs often benefit from exercise management and pain relief.	Large breeds. More prevalent in males than females. Rapid growth and weight gain exacerbate the symptoms.
Luxating patella	A congenital condition in which the patella (kneecap) slips out of its groove.	No. Affected dogs should not be used for breeding.	Controlled exercise and diet are the main treatments, with pain relief if necessary; surgery is indicated only in younger dogs or those with extreme mobility difficulties.	Most prevalent in toy breeds.
Aortic stenosis	A congenital disorder in which narrowing of the aortic valve reduces blood flow from the heart. Symptoms include breathlessness.	No. Affected dogs should not be used for breeding.	Exercise management may help dogs that become breathless on exertion.	Most prevalent in large breeds.
Von Willebrand's disease	The most common inherited bleeding disorder in dogs. Varies in severity but can be lethal.	Yes. By blood and DNA tests.	Lifestyle adjustments and the use of blood-clotting drugs.	Not breed or group specific.
Progressive retinal atrophy (PRA)	Deterioration of the retina, leading to blindness.	Yes. A simple test categorizes dogs as affected, carriers, or unaffected.	Lifestyle management.	Occurs in most breeds but inheritance of the condition differs. Genes may be dominant or recessive. Symptoms usually apparent by three years of age.
Cataracts	Clouding of the lens of the eye, causing impaired vision.	Yes. For some breeds there is a DNA test. Affected dogs should not be used for breeding.	Cataracts are removed surgically; the operation is relatively simple.	Not breed or group specific and may occur at any age.
Entropion	Inward turning of the eyelids, causing damage to the surface of the eyeball.	No. Affected dogs should not be used for breeding.	Can be corrected surgically.	Common in brachycephalic breeds (flat-faced with short muzzle) and breeds with heavy, folded skin on the head.
Ectropion	Outward turning of the lower eyelid; may lead to dry eyes and infection.	No. Affected dogs should not be used for breeding.	Can be corrected surgically.	Most prevalent in breeds with loose facial skin, as seen in spaniels and some breeds of hound.

DISEASE	DESCRIPTION	CAN IT BE SCREENED FOR?	MANAGING THE DISEASE	TYPES OF DOG AFFECTED
Distichiasis	Abnormal growth of the eyelashes. May cause pain and discomfort.	No. Affected dogs should not be used for breeding.	A vet may remove the abnormal hairs by plucking.	May occur in any breed but is more common in those with moderate to heavy skin folds on the head.
Deafness	Complete or partial loss of hearing; can occur from birth or over the course of the dog's life.	Yes. A noninvasive, painless test can be carried out by a specialist vet.	A dog completely deaf from birth is not recommended for a pet. Partially deaf dogs often have normal lives.	Most common in dogs with white, spotted, dappled, or merle coats. Some dogs also have blue eyes.
Abnormal dentition	In most breeds, the teeth normally meet in a scissor bite. Deviation from this can result in an overshot or undershot jaw.	No. Affected dogs should not be used for breeding.	Most dogs experience no problems. Occasionally, surgical intervention is called for if the dog has trouble eating or drinking.	An undershot jaw is acceptable in some brachycephalic breeds. In others, it is considered a fault.
Elongated palate	A condition in which the soft palate at the back of the mouth abnormally overlaps the airway, obstructing breathing.	No. Affected dogs should not be used for breeding.	Serious cases can be corrected with surgery to remove excess tissue on the palate.	Most prevalent in brachycephalic breeds.
Hypothyroidism	A deficiency in thyroid hormone that causes slow metabolism.	Yes. A blood test is available. Affected dogs should not be used for breeding.	Typical symptoms such as weight gain, lethargy, and hair loss can be controlled with medication.	Occurs in medium- and large-sized dogs. Symptoms tend to appear when dogs reach middle age.
Diabetes mellitus	A condition in which the dog's ability to metabolize blood sugar is impaired.	Yes. A DNA test is possible but not routinely carried out. Affected dogs should not be used for breeding.	Dogs who eat or drink unusually large amounts may be suffering from diabetes; the condition can be controlled with medication.	Not breed or group specific. More common in females. Symptoms tend to appear when dogs reach middle age.
Cleft palate	The roof of the mouth does not join correctly in the middle, preventing puppies from suckling properly.	No. Any dog that has produced puppies with cleft palates should not be used for further breeding.	Most vets recommend euthanizing affected puppies. Occasionally, it may be possible to hand rear a puppy until it is old enough to undergo corrective surgery.	May occur in any breed or cross-bred dog but most common in brachycephalic breeds.
Megaesophagus	An enlarged esophagus that lacks muscle tone and cannot convey swallowed food down to the stomach. An affected dog constantly regurgitates.	No. Any dog that has produced puppies with megaesophagus should not be used for further breeding.	Depending on the severity of the condition, changes such as feeding small amounts from a raised bowl can have a positive impact.	Not breed or group specific. If condition is congenital, symptoms appear in the first few weeks or months of life.
Epilepsy	A neurological disorder causing characteristic fits or seizures.	Yes. DNA test. Affected dogs should not be used for breeding.	Epilepsy is not curable, but drug therapy can greatly reduce the likelihood of seizures.	Not breed or group specific. If congenital, symptoms appear between six months and five years of age.

GLOSSARY

Achondroplasia–A form of dwarfism that affects the long bones of the limbs, causing them to bow outward. It is a genetic mutation that has been selectively bred for, resulting in short-legged breeds such as the Dachshund.

Almond-shaped eyes–Oval eyes with slightly flattened corners that are present in breeds such as the Kooikerhondje and the English Springer Spaniel.

Beard–Thick, sometimes coarse and bushy hair around the lower facial area. Often seen in wire-haired breeds.

Belton–A coat pattern that is a mix of white and colored hairs (roan) that may have a flecked or ticked appearance.

Bicolor–Any color combined with white patches.

Black and tan–A coat color with clearly defined areas of black and tan. The black color is usually found on the body and the tan color on the underparts, muzzle, and perhaps as spots above the eyes. This pattern also occurs in liver and tan and blue and tan coats.

Blanket, blanket markings–Large areas of color over the back and sides of the body; commonly used to describe hound markings.

Blaze–Broad, white marking running from near the top of the head to the muzzle.

Brachycephalic head–A head that is almost as wide as it is long due to shortening of the muzzle. The Bulldog and Boston Terrier are examples of breeds with this head shape.

Bracke–A term used for continental hounds that specialize in running down small game such as rabbit or fox.

Breeches–Fringing of longer hair on the thighs, which is also known as culottes or trousers.

Breed–Domestic dogs that have been selectively bred to have the same distinctive appearance. They conform to a breed standard drawn up by a breed club and approved by an internationally recognized body, such as the Kennel Club, FCI, or American Kennel Club.

Breed Standard–The detailed description of a breed that specifies exactly how the dog should look, the acceptable colors and markings, and the range of height and/or weight measurements.

Brindle–A color mix in which dark hairs form a striped pattern on lighter background of tan, gold, gray, or brown.

Brisket–The breastbone.

Button ears–Semierect ears in which the top part folds down toward the eye covering the ear opening. They are seen on breeds such as the Fox Terrier.

Candleflame ears–Long, narrow, erect ears that are shaped like a candleflame. They are seen on breeds such as the English Toy Terrier.

Cape–Thick hair covering the shoulders.

Carnassial teeth–Cheek teeth (upper fourth premolar and lower first molar) that are used, rather like a pair of scissors, to slice through meat, hide, and bone.

Catlike feet–Round, compact feet with the toes grouped closely together.

Conformation–The general apearance of a dog that is determined by the development of individual features and their relationship to one another.

Croup–An area of the back just above the base of the tail.

Cropped ears–Ears that are erect and pointed due to surgical removal of part of the ear cartilage. The procedure, which is illegal in many countries, including the UK, is normally carried out when puppies are about 10–16 weeks old.

Dander–Small scales of dead skin shed from the body.

Dapple–A spotted coat of darker markings on a lighter background. Usually used as a description for short-haired breeds only; merle is used to describe the same coloring in long-haired dogs.

Dewclaw–A non-weight-bearing toe on the inner side of the foot. Some breeds, such as the Norwegian Lundehund, have double dewclaws.

Dewlap–Loose, hanging skin that falls in folds on the chin, throat, and neck of some breeds: for example, the Bloodhound.

Docked tail–A tail cut to a specific length in accordance with the breed standard. The procedure is normaly carried out when puppies are only a few days old. The practice is now illegal in the UK and parts of Europe except for the tails of working dogs such as the German Shorthaired Pointer.

Dolichocephalic head–A long, narrow head with an imperceptible stop, as seen in the Borzoi, for example.

Double coat–Coat consisting of a thick, warm underlayer and a weatherproof top layer.

Drop ears–Ears that hang down from their base. Pendant ears are a more extreme form of drop ears, being longer and heavier.

Erect ears–Upright or pricked ears with pointed or rounded tips. Candleflame ears are an extreme type of erect ears.

Estrus–A period of about three weeks in the reproductive cycle during which a female dog can be mated. Primitive breeds tend to come into estrus once a year (as do wolves); in other breeds it is usually twice a year.

Feathers, feathering–Fringes of hair that may be found on the ear margins, belly, backs of legs, and the underside of the tail.

Flews–The lips of a dog. Most commonly used to describe the fleshy, hanging upper lips in dogs of the mastiff type.

Forelock–Lock of hair on the forehead that falls forward between the ears.

Furrow–A shallow groove, visible in some breeds, that runs from the top of the head down to the stop.

Gait–Movement or action.

Griffon–(Fr.) Referring to a coarse or wire coat.

Grizzle–Usually a mixture of black and white hairs, which gives a blue-gray or iron-gray shading to the coat. It is seen in some breeds of terrier.

Group–Dog breeds are classified into various groups by the Kennel Club, FCI, and American Kennel Club. The groups are loosely based on function but no two systems agree. The number and names of the groups differ, as do the breeds that are recognized and included in them.

Hackney gait–Dogs with this type of action, such as the Miniature Pinscher, raise the lower part of the leg particularly high as they walk.

Harlequin–A color pattern comprising irregular-sized patches of black on white; seen only in the Great Dane.

Hock–Joint on the hind leg; equivalent to the human heel; in dogs this is elevated because they walk on their toes.

Isabella–A fawn color found in some breeds, including the Bergamasco and Dobermann.

Mask–Dark coloration on the face, usually around the muzzle and eyes.

Merle–A marbled coat with darker patches or spots. Blue merle (black on a bluish-gray background) is the most common variation.

Mesaticephalic head–Head shape in which the base and width are of medium proportions. The Labrador Retriever and Border Collie are examples of breeds with this type of head shape.

Neutering–A surgical procedure that prevents dogs from breeding. Male dogs are castrated at about six months and female dogs spayed about three months after their first estrus.

Otter tail–A thickly furred, rounded tail that has a broad base and tapers to the tip; the hair on the underside is parted.

Pack– Usually used to describe a group of scent or sight hounds that hunt together.

Pastern–Lower part of the leg, below the carpals (wrist bones) of the foreleg or the hock on the hind leg.

Pendant ears–Ears that hang down from their base; an extreme form of drop ears.

Pendulous lips–Full, loosely hanging upper or lower lips.

Rose ears–Small, drop ears that fold outward and backward so that part of the ear canal is exposed. This type of ear is seen in Whippets.

Ruff–A long, thick collar of stand-out hair around the neck.

Sable–A coat color in which hairs tipped with black overlay a lighter background color.

Saddle–A darker colored area that extends over the back.

Scissors bite–The normal bite of dogs with mesaticephalic and dolichocephalic heads. The upper incisors (front teeth) are slightly in front of but in contact with the lower incisors when the mouth is closed. The other teeth interlock with no gaps and form the cutting edge of the "scissors."

Semierect ears–Erect ears in which only the tip is inclined forward, as seen in breeds such as the Rough Collie (right).

Sesame–A coat color comprising an equal mixture of black and white hairs. In black sesame, there are more black hairs than white; red sesame is a mixture of red and black hairs.

Sickle tail–Tail that is carried in a half circle over the back.

Spoon-like feet–Similar to catlike feet but more oval in shape because the middle toes are longer than the outer toes.

Stop–The indentation between the muzzle and the top of the head, in between the eyes. The stop is almost absent in dolichocephalic breeds, such as the Borzoi, and very pronounced in brachycephalic and dome-headed breeds, such as the Cocker Spaniel and the Chihuahua.

Temperament–The character of a dog.

Topcoat–Outer coat of guard hairs.

Topknot–Long tuft of hair on the top of the head.

Topline–The outline of the dog's upper body from ears to tail.

Tricolor–A coat of three colors in well-defined patches, usually black, tan, and white.

Tucked up–Referring to the belly, an upward curve to the abdomen toward the hindquarters, typically seen in breeds such as the Greyhound and the Whippet.

Undercoat–Underlayer of hair, usually short, thick, and sometimes woolly, that provides insulation between the topcoat and the skin.

Undershot–Facial conformation in which the lower jaw protrudes beyond the upper jaw, seen in breeds such as the Bulldog.

Undershot bite–The normal bite of brachycephalic breeds such as the Bulldog. Because the lower jaw is longer than the upper jaw, the incisor teeth do not meet and the lower incisors are in front of the upper ones.

Withers–The highest point of the shoulder, where the neck meets the back. A dog's height is measured vertically from the ground to the withers.

INDEX

The dog breeds listed in this index may be followed by any combination of the initials AKC (American Kennel Club), FCI (Federation Cynologique Internationale–the World Canine Organization), and KC (Kennel Club). The initials indicate which of these three international organizations recognize the breed. Occasionally the AKC, FCI, and KC recognize the same breed but use a different name to the one used in this book. This alternative name is also listed along with the initials of the organization that uses it. Some breeds have been granted provisional acceptance by the FCI and these are indicated here as FCI*. Other breeds have no initials following their name but may be recognized by other kennel clubs in their country of origin, and be in the approval process of one of the organizations listed here.

A

B

C

INDEX *continued*

D

E

INDEX *continued*

L

M

N

O

P

INDEX *continued*

R

S

INDEX *continued*

T

UV

W

XYZ

ACKNOWLEDGMENTS

Dorling Kindersley would like to thank the following for their kind permission to reproduce their photographs:
(Key: a-above; b-below/bottom; c-center; f-far; l-left; r-right; t-top)
6-7 Fotolia: lunamarina. **8 Dorling Kindersley:** Jerry Young (br). **20-21 Alamy Images:** Juniors Bildarchiv. **22 Corbis:** Cheryl Ertelt / Visuals Unlimited (c). **23 Alamy Images:** FLPA (bl). **32 Getty Images:** AFP (c). **70 Animal Photography:** Eva-Maria Kramer (b, tr). **83 Flickr.com:** Yugan Talovich (tr). **84 Animal Photography:** Eva-Maria Kramer (t). **85 Courtesy of Jessica Snäcka:** Sanna Södergren (b). **87 Animal Photography:** Eva-Maria Kramer (t). **96 Getty Images:** Zero Creatives (c). **108 Alamy Images:** imagebroker (br). Photoshot: imagebroker (bl). **115 Getty Images:** Mitsuaki Iwago (bl). NHPA / Photoshot: Biosphoto / J.-L. Klein & M (br). **124 Getty Images:** (c). **136 Getty Images:** Jupiterimages (c). **148 Alamy Images:** imagebroker (t). **172 Animal Photography:** Eva-Maria Kramer (b). Photoshot: NHPA (t). **173 Animal Photography:** Eva-Maria Kramer (tr, cl). **175 Animal Photography:** Sally Anne Thompson (tr, cl). **186 Alamy Images:** Juniors Bildarchiv (c). **215 Getty Images:** Mark Raycroft (br). **220 Getty Images:** David Tipling (c). **224 Pamela O. Kadlec:** (t). **260 Alamy Images:** RJT Photography (c). **263 Alamy Images:** Farlap (tr). **282 Getty Images:** Steve Dueck (c). **292-293 Corbis:** Ben Welsh / Design Pics

All other images © Dorling Kindersley
For further information see:
www.dkimages.com

Jacket image: front: Corbis

The publisher would like to thank the following people for their assistance with book:
Lez Graham for text; Johnny Pau for design assistance; Monica Saigal, Gaurav Joshi, Suparna Sengupta, and Sreshtha Bhattacharya for editorial assistance; Caroline Hunt for proofreading; Margaret McCormack for the index; The Kennel Club; Jean-Baptiste for help with the Saint Germain Pointers at the Paris Dog Show; John Wilesmith and Stewart Comely from the Three Counties Showground, Malvern; Project Manager Afa Yahiaoui for her help at the World Dog Show, Paris; All committee members and show organizers of the International Dog Show, Genk, Belgium with special thanks to Chairman Willem Vervloet and Deputy Secretary Patricia Claes; Special thanks to the dog handlers and photographer's assistants Hilary Wilkinson, Stella Carpenter, Stephanie Carpenter, and Kim Davies, and photographer Tracy Morgan

The publisher would like to thank the following owners for letting us photograph their dogs:
Breed name (owner's name/dog's name)
Airedale Terrier (Graulus Francois/Hurbie Van'tasbroek); Akita (D. and J. Killilea and A Clure/Ch Redwitch What Goes Around); Alaskan Malamute (Sian and David Luker/Anubis); American Cocker Spaniel (Wilma Weymans/Chicomy's Midnight Special); American Staffordshire Terrier (Kim Hahn/Beauty Power Pride Justify); American Water Spaniel (Sanna Kytöjoki and Tiina Närhi-Jääskeläinen/Afire's Chocolate Robber "Aapo"); Appenzell Cattle Dog (Claas Wentzler/C-Mexx vom Markgrund); Australian Shepherd (Jens Goessens/Leading Angels Diamond Shock Factor); Australian Silky Terrier (I. Leino, shown by Mr. and Mrs. De Bondt/Bombix Moren par Noster); Australian Terrier (Iris Coppée/Ch Cidan von den Grauen Anfurten); Auvergne Pointer (Peteris Zvaigzne/Khyannes Fata Morgana); Beagle (M Cherevko/Valsi Imagemaker for Bravo Vista Maxim; Peter Lakatos/Black Magic of Celestina's Garden); Belgian Griffon (Mr. Nikulins and Patricia Blacky/Harpersband Aleksandra); Blue Picardy Spaniel (Nichael Chayentien/Defi de la Ferme de la Conduene; Richard Floquet/Fangio); Boston Terrier (R Lutz/Macho Tex Mex); Bourbonnais Pointing Dog (Irma Širmeniene/Canine Dawenasti); Bouvier des Flandres (Peter Aerts/Hero von Gewdraa Oel; Nadine and Johan [illegible]

Springer Spaniel (C. Woodbridge and T. Dunsdon/Seaspring Shipwrecked "Eddie"); Entlebucher Mountain Dog (Dog's Name: Kazanova iz Blagorodnogo Domh); Field Spaniel (C.H. and J. Holgate/Ewtor McEwan at Nadavin); Flat Coated Retriever (Steve Hammersley/Stranfaer Doctor Foster); Fox Terrier–Smooth-haired (Mr. and Mrs. Pitel/Clara); Fox Terrier–Wire-haired (Veronique Gehan/Legend of Crudy Zapphir); French Bulldog (Jack Meerten/Usm u.d Mestreechteneerkes); French Pyrenean Pointer (Mr. and Mrs. Jacques Brain/Elfy de Bois le Bon; Maria Fernelius/Farin de la Balingue); German Hunting Terrier (W.F.D (Fred) Amiabel/Faita vom Eichblatt); German Pointer–Short-haired (Shelley Fisher/Will I Am Of Ankherwood JW); German Pointer–Wire-haired (Karel Brusten/Hans); Giant Schnauzer (Marie-France Seewald/Gloris Gaia); Glen of Imaal Terrier (Marc Vande Wiele/Fiddlers Green Bel-Ami); Goldendoodle (James Harrison/Elsie); Great Swiss Mountain Dog (Astrid and Oliver Thomas/Aljosha vom Muckenbruch); Greyhound (Uwe and Cordelia Schmidt/Artefakt Demigodat Resch Wind); Griffon Fauve de Bretagne (Michel Imbert and Daniel Carrat/Carlos); Hungarian Kuvasz (Jeanette De Jong/Grada-Merieno A Gázdaság Rol); Hungarian Vizsla–Smooth-haired (Jessie Claire Van Brederode/INT LUX NL CH Bink V D Achtoevenslag; Irma Sirmeniene/Malomkozi); Hungarian Vizsla–

Connoisseur); Parson Russell Terrier–Wire-haired (Katinka Stotyn/Jenny and Coldy); Pembroke Welsh Corgi (J. Whitehead/Wharrytons Golden Legacy; L. A. Weedall/CH Bronabay Cherish The Moment JW; L. A. Weedall and N. A. Bogue/Bronabay Troopin The Colour; M, Fairall, handled by Emma/Bertley Harvester); Petit Brabançon (Olga Gordienko and Patricia Blacky/Zerkalo Dushi Eminem); Pont-Audemer Spaniel (Mr. and Mrs. Stalter/Divora des Marais de la Risle); Poodle–Miniature (A. Corish and J. Rowland/Dechine It's A Secret At Tinkersdale); Poodle–Toy (S. É. Martin/Philora Silver Thomas and Philora Vanilla Ice); Pyrenean Sheepdog (Per Toie Romstad/Quidam); Romanian Shepherd Dog–Carpatin (Marian Crisan/Cronos and Dog's Name: Gorun de Ovican); Romanian Shepherd Dog–Mioritic (Anne Lasti/Agada and Boss Nordic Delight); Rottweiler (Yvonne Bekkers/Munanis Enjoy); Rough Collie (J. Margetts/Libby); Russian Black Terrier (Kristiane van den Driesch and Elena Graf/Christo Russkaya 12 Chigasovo); Russian Toy–Long-haired (Anna Bogdanova/Stempfort Beatrix); Russian Toy–Short-haired (Dog's Name: Malenkaya Makiya Detomasopantera); Saint Germain Pointer (Brigitte Turmel/Diwan de Rosa Bonheur; Corinne Mercier/Divine de la Noue des Aulnes); Samoyed (Chris Brookes/Kyia); Sealyham Terrier (owned by A. Klimeshova bred by Olga Ivanova/Olbori Missis Marpl); Shipperke (Mrs. Lefort/Buffy; Mrs. Oreal/Frambois); Slovakian Pointer–Rough-haired (L. A. H. and A. J. H. van Heynsbergen/1X [illegible]ka Van De Merlin Hoeve); Smooth [illegible]llie (Jane Evans/Southcombe [illegible]rman); Soft Coated Wheaten [illegible]rier (Ammette Buscher and Alima [illegible]nmering/Duke-Camillo Vombelker-[illegible]); Spanish Water Dog (Dawn [illegible]braith/Valentisimo Neuschocoa); [illegible]ndard Poodle (L. Woods and J. [illegible]n/Afterglow Tough Luck); St. [illegible]el Cattle Dog (Noelle Lecoeur/[illegible]e Querida da Casa da Praia); [illegible]ex Spaniel (Mr. and Mrs. J C [illegible]nkland/Jubilwell Mars At Nyrrela); [illegible]dish Vallhund (A. W. M. Muys/[illegible]rikas Ivriga IDA); Vizsla (Gillian [illegible]Finch); Weimaraner–Short-[illegible]ed (C. Mutlow/Risinglark Hawk [illegible] JW); Weimaraner–Long-haired [illegible]iberley Harman/Lassemista [illegible]o); Welsh Springer Spaniel [illegible]olien Kemerlincke/Precious; [illegible]l Jada and Marian Smolenaers/[illegible]ermind From Kind Of Magic); [illegible]h Terrier (PMJ Krautscheid/[illegible]ant From Michel); Whippet [illegible] Walker/Shoalingam Silver [illegible]w); White Swiss Shepherd [illegible](Andre Maryse/C'Keops and [illegible]no); Yorkshire Terrier (S. T. [illegible]uthers/Champion Frasermera [illegible]pting Kisses JW; Margaret [illegible]rie-Bryant/Roxanne)